MANAGEMENT SECRETS

of the

NEW ENGLAND PATRIOTS

MANAGEMENT
SECRETS
of the
NEW ENGLAND
PATRIOTS

From "Patsies" to triple Super Bowl champs

Vol I: Achievements, Personnel, Teamwork,
Motivation, and Competition

James Lavin

Pointer Press

This book is for entertainment and information only and is in no official way related to either the National Football League ("NFL") or the New England Patriots ("Patriots"). This book is written by a fan possessing no insider knowledge of the Patriots. All material in this book comes from public sources.

Pointer Press books may be purchased for educational, business, or sales promotional use. For information please contact Pointer Press.

Designed by James Lavin

FIRST EDITION

Book's website: www.PatriotsBook.com
Publisher's website: www.PointerPress.com

Printed in the United States on acid-free paper

Publisher's Cataloging-in-Publication
Lavin, James, 1969-
Management Secrets of the New England Patriots: From "Patsies" to triple Super Bowl champs; Vol. 1: Achievements, Personnel, Teamwork, Motivation, and Competition / James Lavin
p. cm.
Includes endnotes and index.
ISBN-13: 978-0-9762039-5-7
ISBN-10: 0-9762039-5-2
First edition (with revised subtitle)

1. New England Patriots (Football team).
2. Management–General.
3. Football–General / Professional.

GV956.N36
796.3326   2004099596

08 07 06 05   10 9 8 7 6 5 4 3 2

Passion, pride, poise, preparation, perseverance

Attitude, accountability, aggressiveness, awareness

Teamwork, tenacity, technique, tactics

Resolve, responsibility, resilience, respect

Intelligence, interdependence, intensity

Organization, overachieving, optimism

Training, toughness, togetherness

Selflessness, stamina, sacrifice, self-discipline

TABLE OF CONTENTS

VOLUME 1

VOLUME 2

(Expected publication: June 2005)

PRAISE FOR THE PATRIOTS

"This is as close as it gets to being an all-time great football team, and if they win [a third] Super Bowl, they will have to be classified as that."[1]
 – *Bill Walsh, Hall of Fame coach who won three Super Bowls with the San Francisco 49ers*

"Belichick, owner Bob Kraft and personnel director Scott Pioli have fashioned a formula other franchises are struggling to emulate. It is now called, around the league and in most teams' front offices, doing things 'the Patriots way.'"[2]
 – *Len Pasquarelli, ESPN*

"Bill [Belichick] has done the best coaching job in football. Bar none."[3]
 – *Don Shula, Hall of Fame coach of the 17-0 1972 Miami Dolphins*

"The Patriots… should someday occupy a historical place in the pantheon of outstanding teams."[4]
 – *Paul Zimmerman, Sports Illustrated*

"That's one of the great coaching jobs in the history of this league."[5]
 – *Ernie Accorsi, New York Giants general manager*

"[Bill Belichick]'s clearly the diamond of the coaches in this league and deserves special notice, credit and praise… Bill is probably the standard for the rest of us in the league, how he manages the game, his team… He's a Hall of Fame head coach. He may be as good as there has ever been."[6]
 – *Mike Martz, St. Louis Rams head coach*

"The Patriots' achievement is not only unprecedented but also remarkable when you consider how competitive our league is today. Congratulations to the entire Patriots organization on this extraordinary milestone."[7]
 – *Official statement of NFL Commissioner Paul Tagliabue on the Patriots' NFL-record 19-game winning streak*

"This is the preeminent organization in American team sports, providing a blueprint [for success]. It's a feat that should be heralded as a sporting miracle."[8]
 – *Jay Mariotti, Chicago Sun-Times*

"It's the most incredible thing I've seen in sports."[9]
 – *Philadelphia Eagles owner Jeff Lurie, on the 2001 Patriots' Super Bowl win*

"Their streak [is] on top of all the others. ...If you're really good today, you've got to replace a $10 million player with a $400,000 player almost every year, and the Cadillac has to keep running."
    — Ron Wolf, general manager of the Super Bowl XXXI-winning Green Bay Packers

"It's just a phenomenal thing they've done here in the past two years. It's borderline unbelievable."[10]
    — Wayne Chrebet, New York Jets wide receiver

"They do a better job of evaluating talent, developing and coaching talent ...than anybody in the National Football League, and they've done it in spite of injuries, in spite of the cap, in spite of free agency. Everybody can learn from them."[11]
    — Carl Peterson, Kansas City Chiefs general manager

"[Patriots owner Bob Kraft] brought a vision to the task of rebuilding a team... and basically rescued the franchise. He delivered a state-of-the-art, privately-financed stadium and two Super Bowl championships within a decade. ...He is a model sports owner and CEO."[12]
    — NFL Commissioner Paul Tagliabue

"We need to get as many Bob Krafts as we can into this league... He doesn't only want to build the Patriots but to build the league."[13]
    — Jerry Jones, Dallas Cowboys owner

"They play very, very, very smart. Dean Smith, in his book, *The Carolina Way*, says the underlying theme of everything he wants from his teams are play hard, play smart, play together. The Patriots are the epitome of that in the NFL. ...Their streak is phenomenal."[14]
    — Bill Polian, president of the Indianapolis Colts and 5-time NFL Executive of the Year

"There's no disgrace in losing to New England, everybody does it these days."[15]
    — Dave Bolling, Tacoma News Tribune

"[Belichick is] the greatest coach in the game and one of the greatest of all time... He has stepped into the territory of a legend."[16]
    — Vic Carucci, NFL.com national editor

"From start to finish, it's the best coaching job anyone has [ever] done."[17]
    — Bill Parcells, multi-Super Bowl winning coach, on the 2001 Patriots' Super Bowl victory

"The Rams [were] the most formidable offense the NFL's ever seen... [Winning Super Bowl XXXVI] was the best coaching job I've ever seen."[18]
  – Ron Jaworski, ESPN analyst and former NFL quarterback

"Opposing teams have to ask two questions–first, how do you build an organization like this? Second, how do you stop this Instrument Of Death now that someone else *has* built it? [Theirs is] the most impressive streak in the history of professional football... I stand in awe of what this team has done."[19]
  – Doug Farrar, Seahawks.net

"The longest winning streak in NFL history... [is] perhaps the most remarkable achievement in the annals of U.S. team sports... The Patriots are unique because their roster's neither brimming with Hall of Famers nor the product of steadfast continuity. They have no lock on the great players of the era and, in fact, have willingly rid themselves of premium talents coveted by their rivals... They often fill the gaps by shopping garage sales, by finding a use for the unwanted... They'll gladly whip your high-priced free agent with an undrafted nobody."[20]
  – Bob Dicesare, The Buffalo News

"They've really set the model for other teams to look at and say, 'Hey, if you want to win games, this is kind of how you should orchestrate it.' ...Their players get it. They understand that it is about the team. ...It's not the name on the back of the jersey, it's the emblem on the side of the helmet that you want to play for. And you want to coach for, really."[21]
  – New York Jets head coach Herman Edwards

"Belichick is currently the best coach in the league–something that's not arguable anymore. Nobody is as prepared as this group. It's almost as if they relish the challenge. Take away their star players, so what? They'll scheme you and beat you with what they have left."[22]
  – Pete Prisco, CBS Sportsline

"You know you're good when teams take satisfaction in playing you close."[23]
  – Kimberly Jones, The Star-Ledger

"Patriots players have bought into a successful system that is revolutionizing the game in a fashion that hasn't been seen in the NFL since the Bill Walsh heyday with the 49ers back in the '80s. ...In a me-first era in professional sports, [Belichick] has somehow resurrected old-fashioned notions of team and made them paramount... Nobody on the Patriots treats touchdowns, or any other on-field accomplishment, as the first step in a marketing scheme."[24]
  – Mark Starr, Newsweek

"Like Belichick, Paul Brown and Tom Landry… were dry and colorless characters, the antithesis of the classic emotional model of the American football coach, the Knute Rockne, Vince Lombardi, Bear Bryant type. But as Brown's and Landry's franchises eventually influenced all their rivals, so have Belichick's Patriots begun to change the way other NFL teams operate. …The 21st Century organization man, Belichick, has made the Patriots the bellwether franchise of this NFL generation."[25]
  – Frank Deford, Sports Illustrated

"[The Patriots' lack of obvious Hall of Famers] might define New England, in the end, as the best *team* of them all."[26]
  – Len Pasquarelli, ESPN

"It's an unbelievable thing they've done."[27]
  – Mike Holmgren, Seattle Seahawks head coach and Super Bowl-winning head coach

"New England VP of player personnel Scott Pioli [is] the state-of-the-art roster-builder in football right now, a guy who can deal with [salary] cap troubles by making smart decisions on second-day draft choices and middle-class free agents."[28]
  – Peter King, Sports Illustrated

Al Michaels: "'Genius' is thrown around too loosely, but, when it comes to defense, tell me someone better than Belichick."
John Madden: "There's no one better."[29]
  – Monday Night Football

"The machine has won 26 of 27."[30]
  – ESPN "Sports Center"

Chapter 1

PREFACE

"The strength of the wolf is the pack... On a football team, it's not the strength of the individual players but... the strength of the unit and how they all function together."[31]
– Bill Belichick, after his Patriots won their first Super Bowl

"I [played for] Cincinnati for all those years. You always wonder... is the grass really greener someplace else. [When] I got to New England, I found out it's pretty green."[32]
– New Patriots running back Corey Dillon

"More important than the will to win is the will to prepare to win."[33]
– Bill Belichick

The Patriots have won three of the last four Super Bowls. They also won an astonishing 21 games in a row (their final 15 of 2003 and first six of 2004), shattering the NFL record of 18 consecutive victories. After so much winning, it's easy to forget how horrible the Patriots were just four seasons ago and how dramatically the organization has transformed itself:

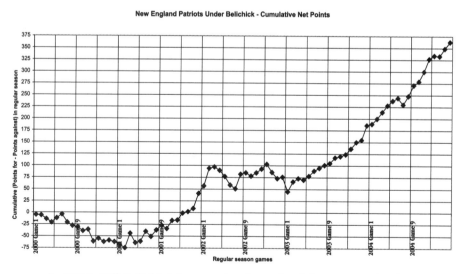

New England Patriots Under Belichick - Cumulative Net Points

In 2000, Bill Belichick became head coach of the New England Patriots, a team in shambles. Belichick needed a 53-man team, but just 36 players' salaries put the Patriots $10.5 million over the NFL's salary cap.[34] Even worse, previous management had squandered the team's 1997, 1998, and 1999 college draft picks, netting few talented young players. Belichick slashed spending by eliminating unaffordable veterans and replacing them with kids fresh from college plus 23 unheralded, inexpensive free agents. After the talent exodus, NFL personnel directors rated the Patriots' player talent the absolute worst in the entire NFL.[35] Four players failed Belichick's conditioning test. Some were so lazy that a furious Belichick declared "We've got too many people who are overweight, too many guys who are out of shape... You can't win with 40 good players while the other team has 53."[36] Belichick himself was judged by *CBS Sportsline* the 30th worst of 32 NFL head coaches.[37] His 2000 Patriots' 5-11 season exposed yet another problem: "Forget about the gaping holes of talent, ...Belichick inherited [a bunch of] losers."[38]

Heading into the 2001 season, *Pro Football Weekly* didn't exactly predict a Patriots Super Bowl victory: "Belichick better hope that Robert Kraft is a very patient owner who can still see the big picture if the team is 4-10 and playing in front of 30,000 empty seats this December."[39] *Athlon* predicted a last-place finish because "with loads of holes to fill, Belichick tried to cut-and-paste his way back to respectability with cheap free agents."[40] *Street & Smith's* also predicted a last-place finish since "The Pats signed a bunch of free agents from the NFL five-and-dime store."[41] Belichick's 2001 Patriots lost three of their first four games, the third defeat a 30-10 pounding by the Miami Dolphins, after which Belichick admitted "We just got our butt kicked today."[42] The New England "Patsies" appeared headed for another train-wreck season.

Instead, Belichick dug a hole in the practice field and ritually buried the Miami game ball while players watched. That symbolic moment marked the banishment of the Patriots' losing ways. The 2001 Patriots reeled off thirteen wins over their final fifteen games, including nine straight victories to close the season with a stunning victory over the "unbeatable" St. Louis Rams in Super Bowl XXXVI that national sportswriters judged the "Best Super Bowl of all time,"[43] "easily the greatest Super Bowl of them all,"[44] and "one of the biggest upsets in playoff history... right up there with Joe Namath and the Jets beating the Colts in Super Bowl III."[45]

Few believed the 2001 Patriots "deserved" to win the Vince Lombardi Trophy as the NFL's best team. Even New Englanders were sheepish about two games saved by dubious, obscure rules: Tom Brady's "fumble"-that-wasn't-a-fumble against the Oakland Raiders (ruled an incomplete pass when the referee correctly invoked "the tuck rule": Rule 3, Section 21, Article 2, Note 2), and David Patten's "fumble"-that-wasn't-a-turnover against the Buffalo Bills (ruled out-of-bounds because, after Bills safety Keion Carpenter knocked Patten unconscious, Patten's head lay out-of-bounds while his leg happened to touch the ball, rendering the ball out-of-bounds before Carpenter grabbed it, according to Rule 3, Section 20, Article 2, Paragraph C).

ESPN readers voted the 2001 Patriots the "worst team sports champion of all time."[46] Worse than any team that ever won a World Series, Stanley Cup, NBA Finals, or Super Bowl. To most football fans, the Patriots were simply the luckiest champions in history. How could the team be the best if no one had ever heard of the players?

"The Patriots are known only to their next of kin. They are the NFL equivalent of a brown bag."[47] Anonymous players implied lousy team.

To Patriots VP of player personnel Scott Pioli, however, players' anonymity actually makes the 2001 Patriots the *greatest* team sports champion of all time... a collection of good-but-not-glamorous football players who out-thought opponents, out-hustled opponents, out-hit opponents, played great together, and made few mistakes. Though the Patriots had few individual stars, they had character and chemistry: "These guys are good players and good people. Football is the ultimate team sport, and these guys fit our system."[48] Sure, they caught some lucky breaks, but most Super Bowl champions do.

Reflecting on that season, Pioli told students at his alma mater that Patriot players possessed championship hearts and minds, even if they lacked big name reputations and the league's greatest arms and legs:

"How we won [the Super Bowl] and who we won it with was just as important to me [as winning]. As a group we were able to validate everything that I was raised to believe in. Everything that was taught to me by my parents, coaches and teachers in life came together in that special season. As a team we overcame a great deal of adversity and countless distractions. Hard work, humility, faith, mental toughness, trust—the building blocks of any solid foundation led us to becoming the best team in football."[49]

Mike Vrabel was one of those unknown 2001 Patriots, a linebacker who had seriously considered law school after wasting away for three seasons on the Pittsburgh Steelers' bench. After joining the Patriots as his only other option and then pressuring Rams quarterback Kurt Warner into throwing an interception that Patriots cornerback Ty Law returned for a touchdown to help win Super Bowl XXXVI, Vrabel laughed: "The has-been's and never-will-be's. That's us. That's fine. We went out and proved here that football's the ultimate team game."[50]

The team's chemistry developed only after months of intensive training. New York Giants quarterback-crushing defensive end Michael Strahan later said of the Patriots' preseason scrimmage with the Giants, "They were terrible, an awful football team."[51] Patriots safety Lawyer Milloy said the Patriots' poor start in 2001 resulted from the acquisition of two dozen free agents who needed time to absorb Belichick's complex system and work together smoothly: "The first day of training camp was like the first day of school in junior high. You didn't know anyone. Luckily, we got used to each other before it was too late."[52] After months of intense effort, Patriots players and coaches found themselves working together harmoniously toward their eventual 2001 NFL championship (earned with their February 2002 Super Bowl triumph).

After Belichick's 2003 Patriots won 17 of their 19 games, outplaying the 31 other NFL teams to win Super Bowl XXXVIII over the gutsy Carolina Panthers, the football world could no longer dismiss the Patriots as "lucky." Belichick's Patriots remained unglamorous, unheralded, and virtually unknown as individuals… but were an undeniably successful team. After a shaky (2-2) start, the 2003 Patriots were unbeatable, winning their final fifteen games of the season and posting an unprecedented 10-0 record against teams with regular season records of 10-6 or better.[53] Multiple Super Bowl-winning coach Jimmy Johnson considers the 2003 Patriots the eighth-greatest team in NFL history.[54]

Super Bowl XXXVIII featured the NFL's toughest defenses, so no one was surprised when the epic battle opened with nearly 27 scoreless minutes of smothering defense. But even players and coaches were shocked when the Patriots and Panthers scored a whopping 61 points over the game's dramatic back-and-forth final 33 minutes. In the fourth quarter, neither defense could muster enough strength to prevent the other team's offense from marching relentlessly downfield. Patriots linebacker Mike Vrabel said it "was like Ali vs. Frazier. That's how it felt out there. We hit them, they hit us, we hit them, they hit us."[55] In the final minute, Patriots players dug deep and found a way to emerge victorious, as they had in 17 of their final 18 games. Football reporters (again) dubbed the team's dramatic *déjà vu* second championship (also clinched by a last-minute Patriots drive culminating in an Adam Vinatieri game-winning field goal) the "Greatest Super Bowl of all time."[56]

In the three seasons since Belichick was named one of the worst coaches in the league, he has collected two Coach of the Year awards and two Super Bowl trophies, and his 2004 team is 11-1 as this book goes to press. Nine of twelve NFL general managers and executives polled by the *New York Daily News* consider Belichick the league's best coach, one unnamed GM even saying, "Belichick is on the edge of becoming one of the great head coaches in the history of the game."[57] *The Sporting News* ranks Belichick #1.[58] And Belichick dominated in a poll of 354 current and former NFL players, receiving 45% of votes versus just 9% for runner-up Bill Parcells.[59]

The probability that an average team will win 21 straight games by chance is 0.0000477%.[60] Belichick's Patriots are a verifiably exceptional team.

WINNING WITHOUT STARS

"What's a 'superstar' if you can't go to the big game [Super Bowl]? Maybe the team concept isn't that popular in the league, but it works for us."[61]
– *Patriots linebacker Willie McGinest*

The Patriots have no darting runner like Walter Payton or Barry Sanders, no acrobatic receiver like Lynn Swann or Jerry Rice, no unblockable defender like Lawrence Taylor or Reggie White, and no rocket-launching quarterback like Dan Marino or John Elway. So, the Patriots' success has football fans scratching their heads and wondering, "*How* do they do it?" Patriots safety Rodney Harrison credits "concentration, maturity, confidence."[62] *Sports Illustrated*'s Peter King concludes the Patriots' magic derives from "knowledge, fearlessness, ruthlessness";[63] in other words, Patriots coaches know their profession, take informed, calculated risks, and decide issues unemotionally to maximize the team's chances of winning. These analyses are as good as any, but no pithy analysis can completely explain how and why the "Patsies" transformed themselves into two-time Super Bowl champs and ran off 21 straight wins. The Patriots' story deserves to be told in rich detail because it is fascinating, fun, and informative. The words of Patriots coaches, players, executives, and owners reveal many truths about great organizations.

The Arizona Cardinals franchise has won just one playoff game since 1947.[64] New Cardinals head coach Dennis Green believes he knows how to turn his Cardinals around: "we're going to outwork New England. If the Patriots work from 9 to 4, we're going to work from 8 to 5."[65] Coach Green might want to talk with Patriots rookie running back Cedric Cobbs, who reports that Patriots players are "at the stadium all day and all night. It's not an all day thing, it's an all day and all night thing. [It's hard] getting used to getting in at 6:30 am and leaving at 9:30 pm."[66] Patriots also don't perceive what they do as "work." They enjoy hard preparation and pride themselves on mental and physical toughness. According to three-time Pro Bowl running back Corey Dillon, who joined the Patriots in 2004:

> "I understand why this organization wins. They work extremely hard. *Hard*. I mean *hard*! My first couple of days here, I [would] call my agent and be like, 'Man, what'd you get me into?' It's unbelievable. After that first day, I understood why they're Super Bowl champions. I understand. It's only going to make me better. I know one thing, I'm going to be stronger and faster this year. Guaranteed."[67]

In preparing so intensely, Patriot players and assistant coaches are emulating their head coach, who leads by example. Bill Belichick has always been fanatically disciplined and passionate about every aspect of football. Phil Simms (quarterback of the New York Giants and MVP of Super Bowl XXI while Belichick was the Giants' defensive coordinator) offers this anecdote:

> "[Belichick] was the only person left [in the Giants facility]. He'd be on the bike watching film with the clicker in his hand, sweating like wild. His dedication and attention to detail are unbelievable. He ruined at least one or two bikes because he was sweating so bad... the bikes... would rust out."[68]

Current Patriots tight end Christian Fauria swears "[Belichick] can tell you everything about an offensive guy or a defensive guy when you've got a question. I think to myself, 'How the heck does he do it? There just aren't enough hours in the day.' And it's not like he's reading off a piece of paper. He knows, and the only way to know is to look at the film."[69] Belichick expects nothing less from his players and assistants. Former Patriots quarterback Drew Bledsoe says "he's a very intense guy that demands the same from his players."[70] Dedication that appears extraordinary to outsiders merely satisfies Belichick's lofty expectations. Players and assistants have internalized Belichick's standards. Each Patriot holds himself and his teammates accountable to extreme expectations. Most Patriots share Belichick's fanatical commitment to winning football games.

The Patriots' success derives from something more fundamental than "hard work." "Hard work" is a symptom. No coach can dictate a player's work habits, except perhaps during practices. Players must be motivated to work hard 365 days a year, not merely when a coach is observing them. "Hard work" is not a coaching strategy or a training camp strategy but a consequence of hiring players who love playing football and building a competitive, performance-focused organizational culture that inspires players to passionately pursue individual and collective excellence, every day of the year.

To greatly oversimplify, the Patriots have won two Super Bowls because they are a cohesive team unified by daily dedication to collective success and disregard for individual glory. They win because they love playing and winning football games. They win for their fans. They win for their families. They win for themselves. And, perhaps most importantly, they win for one another. The moment Patriots rookie tight end Benjamin Watson caught his first touchdown pass, in a meaningless preseason game, quarterback Tom Brady sprinted downfield so enthusiastically that his hug knocked Watson, who outweighs Brady by forty pounds, to the ground. A moment later, half the Patriots offense piled on top of Watson in a symbolic welcome. The Patriots are a true team of competitive guys who respect one another, love one another, and never want to disappoint one another. With nine seconds left in Super Bowl XXXVIII, Patriots receiver Deion Branch hauled in a 17-yard catch that set up Adam Vinatieri's game-winning field goal. Branch's analysis ("I just want to get as close for Adam as I can"[71]) suggests the warm feelings players have for one another. Patriots strive to set their teammates up for success.

Fittingly, the Patriots win because they best embody the ideal of John Adams, Benjamin Franklin, and Thomas Jefferson, who proposed the original motto of the United States of America, *"E Pluribus Unum"* ("out of many, one"). On July 4, 1776, our new nation tasked these three founding fathers with designing a Great Seal. These wise men proposed the motto *"E Pluribus Unum"* to highlight the binding together of the original thirteen colonies/states into a single nation. Adams, Franklin, and Jefferson emphasized national unity because they knew it would empower and enrich all Americans.

Not every player is willing to suppress his ego for the good of his team. Not everyone is willing to practice and study and watch film and lift weights from 6:30 a.m. till 9:30 p.m. Though 45% of 354 current and former NFL players polled say Belichick is the best coach in the NFL, only 10% say they would most want to play for Belichick, presumably because Belichick's system is no country club.[72] Patriots scouts and personnel executives search hard for players like wide receiver David Patten, whom no NFL team wanted but who now owns two Super Bowl rings. Patten trains with unbelievable intensity... not because he must but because he loves football and loves winning:

> "[Patten] has a heart as big as this [locker] room. You'll never outwork him. He'll never give in. He'll always have the upper hand. Back in high school, he wasn't the fastest kid in school, but he could make great plays because of his desire. Then, when he went to college, he knew he had to improve his speed and that's what he did."[73]
> – *Boston Red Sox second baseman Pokey Reese, who grew up with David Patten*

Belichick picks for his Patriots guys like himself but possessing more physical talent. Patriot players have good (though seldom NFL-best) physical traits, the ability to calculate optimal football tactics (Xs and Os) on the fly, and an indomitable competitiveness and work ethic that matches their coach's. Belichick says his 2001 Patriots won the Super Bowl not because they started the season expecting to win the Super Bowl but because each player pushed himself and his teammates each minute of each day of each week: "My whole thing with this team was, 'Let's just get better. Let's just get a little better every day.' And, you know, of all the teams I've ever been around, these guys try so hard. They really try to do what you tell them."[74]

Of the 53 players Bill Belichick inherited when he took over the Patriots, only 15 were still around to celebrate the team's first Super Bowl victory. Belichick scrounged up the other 38 players by digging through the NFL's discard bin and the college draft.[75] NFL insiders simply couldn't believe the Patriots had won the Super Bowl because Belichick's players lacked "talent," as it is traditionally defined:

> "One personnel director for a playoff team said he wouldn't want any of the Patriots' 17 free agents. Another said it wouldn't surprise him if New England went 6-10 next year [2002]. 'It will change dramatically... quickly,' one executive in personnel said, referring to the Patriots' fortunes."[76]

39-year NFL veteran Ron Wolf was amazed by what Patriots coaches accomplished with what he called "a waiver wire team,"[77] *i.e.*, a collection of other teams' cast-offs. (Wolf is a personnel genius who knows "a waiver wire team" when he sees one. As Green Bay Packers general manager, Wolf angered Packers fans by trading the team's 1992 1st-round draft pick to the Atlanta Falcons for a quarterback whose only five NFL passes had resulted in two interceptions and three incompletions. In 1997, that inept quarterback, Brett Favre, became the only player in NFL history to win three "Most Valuable Player" awards.) Belichick couldn't even keep the "best" of his 2001 team's "waiver wire" personnel on the field. The 2001 Patriots ranked second in the league in compensation paid to injured players,[78] most notably quarterback Drew Bledsoe, wide receiver Terry Glenn, and linebackers Willie McGinest and Ted Johnson.

But the Patriots had unearthed some hidden diamonds. The Pittsburgh Steelers had little use for Mike Vrabel, and no other team wanted him. This reflects poorly on NFL talent evaluators, not Vrabel, a smart, tough, talented, competitive football player. Vrabel runs *after* practices. And he's almost obnoxiously competitive: "Mike just competes. It's like, if you're playing golf with him, and you're a couple of holes ahead, you can tell how Mike's playing by the noises from a couple holes over. It's like, 'Geez, Mike, make a birdie so we can all have some fun.'"[79] And Vrabel is practically a player-coach. At Ohio State, Vrabel convinced every last teammate to stay on campus and train all summer. Former Buckeyes strength coach Dave Kennedy recalls, "He was my first real enforcer. He held everybody accountable, every single player."[80]

The only people who believed in the 2001 Patriots were the Patriots themselves. Not even the local media sang the team's praises. Players invented an unofficial mantra ("Don't talk to me!") to shout down questions from local reporters who had doubted them. After winning Super Bowl XXXVI with a 48-yard field goal as time expired, kicker Adam Vinatieri said, "We shocked the world, but we didn't shock ourselves."[81] Linebacker Roman Phifer said, "No, baby, it's not an upset. To the world it was an upset, but to us, we were confident. We believed in ourselves."[82] And cornerback Ty Law said, "Hell, no—we expected to win."[83]

But the world refused to believe the NFL's laughing stock could become its best team just one season later. How could other teams' rejects propel the Patriots from worst to first? Six months after the Rams lost Super Bowl XXXVI, *Pro Football Weekly* still called the Rams "Clearly the most talented team in football."[84] Even quarterback Tom Brady, looking back with three years of hindsight, confesses to self-doubt: "Going into that Rams game, we didn't think we'd win. Nobody thought we'd win and then it was, 'Oh my God, we won.'"[85] And Belichick admits, "The 2001 team that won, it was a miracle to win a championship with that team."[86]

Patriots fans were similarly shocked by the team's spectacular turnaround. Many still find it hard to believe the Patriots have twice conquered the NFL's Mount Everest. *Pro Football Weekly*'s Eric Edholm speculated that record-shattering sales of the 2001 Patriots' Super Bowl video *Three Games to Glory* reflected fans' desire to "make sure that they really did see the Pats win it all."[87] (I recently bought *Sports Illustrated*'s commemoration of the Red Sox's World Series triumph for this exact reason. We Patriots/Sox fans are struggling to shed the cynicism that calcified during decades of disappointment. We had grown quite comfortable with self-pity.)

Vegas oddsmakers expected the 2001 Patriots to lose each of their three playoff games. All three playoff opponents landed on the cover of either *Sports Illustrated* or *ESPN The Magazine* before falling to the Pats. In Super Bowl XXXVI, the "Patsies" were 14½-point Super Bowl underdogs[88] against the star-studded St.

Louis Rams, nicknamed "the Greatest Show on Turf" after scoring 500+ points in three consecutive seasons, an accomplishment unmatched by any NFL team before or since. The Rams' stars included: 1) quarterback Kurt Warner, MVP of the entire NFL in 2001; 2) running back Marshall Faulk, who earned his third consecutive NFL Offensive Player of the Year award in 2001 after becoming the only player in NFL history to gain 2,000+ combined rushing and receiving yards in each of four consecutive seasons; and, 3) a fleet of cheetah-fast wide receivers whom Patriots cornerback Ty Law called "Definitely the best group of receivers I ever had to defend."[89]

By contrast, the 2001 Patriots were a bunch of football misfits. The team had just two recognized "stars": quarterback Drew Bledsoe and wide receiver Terry Glenn. Neither played much in 2001 or remained with the team in 2002. Early in 2001, Bledsoe, the first player selected in the 1993 NFL Draft and a Pro Bowl quarterback in 1994, 1996, and 1997, suffered a life-threatening injury. Despite his $103 million contract, Bledsoe played only 32 minutes the rest of the 2001 season before shuffling off to Buffalo where he became a Pro Bowl quarterback again in 2002. Bledsoe's backup: a skinny, slow kid with a weak arm named Tom Brady, the 199th player drafted in 2000 who was earning the NFL-minimum salary of $298,000/year.

The team's other star, Terry Glenn, was the seventh player selected in the 1996 NFL Draft and talented enough to earn 1999 Pro Bowl honors and receive a $50 million contract extension in 2000. But Glenn always had trouble staying focused on football. Coach Belichick finally said "enough's enough" during 2001. Glenn missed most of the season and was later shipped off to Green Bay.

With the Patriots' #1-drafted quarterback and #7-drafted receiver sidelined during Super Bowl XXXVI, who caught the only touchdown pass thrown by #199-drafted Tom Brady? That would be the undrafted David Patten, whose illustrious post-college career included stints planting shrubs for his father's landscaping company, playing Arena Football, and a full-time job hauling 75-pound sacks of coffee beans; Patten had even been cut by the Canadian Football League's Edmonton Eskimos during training camp![90]

Having grown up cheering for decades of horrible-to-mediocre Patriots teams, I was astonished to witness the Patriots transform themselves from a 5-11 team in 2000 into Super Bowl champions in 2001 and 2003. Winning the Super Bowl was amazing. Winning it twice with players whose names only fanatical Patriots fans recognized was unbelievable!

LEADERSHIP, NOT LUCK

After the Patriots' first Super Bowl win, Tom Brady said, "Call it a fluke, whatever you want. But the scores are there for eternity now."[91] Winning the Super

Bowl is never a fluke. Many Super Bowl champions, including the 2001 Patriots, have benefited from an occasional lucky bounce. But 31 other NFL teams don't roll over and hand you the Vince Lombardi Trophy.

Asked repeatedly whether they had taken the Patriots lightly, St. Louis Rams players and coaches insisted they had anticipated a tough game, similar to the 24-17 regular-season game the two teams had played in November 2001 that the Patriots might have won if not for a questionable fumble by Patriots running back Antowain Smith as he stretched the ball forward for a touchdown ("I felt my knee was down. If not my knee, then my forward progress was stopped. The whistle never blew."[92]). After that game, Rams head coach Mike Martz called Smith's fumble "The telling point for the whole season no matter what happens the rest of this year; the telling point is that the defense took the ball away on the three-yard line."[93] Martz also said, "I told the guys that night they beat a Super Bowl-caliber team. They were certainly the most physical team we played."[94]

After the Super Bowl, Rams wide receiver Ricky Proehl said, "We knew coming into the game they were a good football team. Everyone else was writing them off, but we weren't."[95] Coach Martz was offended by the suggestion they had taken the Patriots lightly: "Oh, please. That's insulting to me. This is the Super Bowl. How can you overlook somebody in the Super Bowl?"[96] Those who persist in believing the Rams deserved to win forget that the Patriots nearly crushed the Rams. The Patriots almost intercepted several additional passes, and only a penalty on Willie McGinest nullifying a Tebucky Jones fumble recovery and 97-yard touchdown return kept the game close.

Belichick's rapid reconstruction of the "Patsies" into two-time NFL champions involved hundreds of informed and inspired personnel, management, organizational, and tactical decisions plus insanely hard work by players, coaches, scouts, and executives. As both a life-long Patriots fan and an economist who previously researched "high performance work organizations," I have been obsessed with the Patriots' turnaround.

Many months of research later, I now understand how the seemingly impossible happened. The Patriots' success no longer seems improbable. Instead, success seems the inevitable outcome of building a superb organization peopled with competitive individuals who believe their success is intertwined with the organization's success and with leaders who lead by example, give helpful direction and training, and constantly act in the organization's best interest.

You too will enjoy learning how the Patriots leapt from worst to first and how you can apply the Patriots' management "secrets" to improve your organization. The Patriots' "secrets" are no secrets at all. They are time-tested management fundamentals... well applied and well executed.

Chapter 2

A CHAMPIONSHIP ORGANIZATION

"Other guys say they want to be a Pro Bowl caliber player. ...But I want to be considered a championship caliber player because that is what sports is all about, winning championships."[97]
– *Patriots linebacker Tedy Bruschi*

"You can tell just walking in here, it's a great organization."[98]
– *New Patriot wide receiver Kevin Kasper, in his first days with the team*

During player introductions preceding their first Super Bowl victory, the Patriots broke with tradition. They burst onto the field *en masse* as "The New England Patriots" rather than emerge one-by-one as individual players receiving individual fanfare. This was no coaching gimmick: "The players wanted to do it that way; they wanted to come out as a team. We've been doing it since October."[99] Defensive lineman Richard Seymour explained the players' thinking: "We're not a team of individuals; we do things as a team, so it was appropriate for us to go out together."[100] The Patriots' decision to forgo individual glory symbolized their unity and epitomized their formula for victory. According to Bill Belichick, "That's the reason we won. Because we played the game as a team."[101]

The Patriots don't have the most talented players. Since the AFL-NFL merger, the average Super Bowl champion has placed seven players on its conference's Pro Bowl roster, that honors the conference's best players each season. Almost insultingly, the 2001 and 2003 Patriots championship teams each had just two Pro Bowl honorees. The Patriots have won two of the past three Super Bowls not with the best individuals but with the best team. Scott Pioli and Bill Belichick understand the difference: "Our job isn't to assemble the best players, it's to put together the best team."[102] Games are not won on paper or in "Fantasy Football" leagues. Games are not won based on individual player statistics or Vegas odds. Games are won when eleven men coordinate their actions on a football field and outscore the eleven men on the other side of the ball. When reporters asked Belichick for his response to being eight-point underdogs in the 2001 AFC Championship Game, Belichick explained: "This game will be decided in 60 minutes of football, well maybe more, you never know."[103]

Pre-salary cap dynasties (like the Dolphins, Steelers and Cowboys) had the luxury of collecting standout players who could dominate their opponents in one-on-one matchups. In the salary cap era, "talent" is much more evenly distributed across teams, so the Patriots necessarily use a different approach... training their good, solid players to play a cohesive, coordinated, cooperative, consistent brand of football. After his Buffalo Bills became the Patriots' 18th consecutive victim, head coach Mike Mularkey said, "the ball was coming out of [Brady's] hands really before the receiver was coming out of the break. He was throwing some timing routes very well."[104] Throwing a pass to a location in space to an intended receiver running in a different direction requires trust and understanding that develops only through intense, dedicated practice. Belichick's Patriots out-prepare their opponents. Phil Simms noted the team's blue-collar blueprint even before its first Super Bowl victory:

> "Do you think football's not the ultimate team game? Think it's not about teamwork and what the coaches do to help you? Just look at the New England Patriots. ...I give the New England coaching staff a lot of credit–a lot of credit. ...It's hard to look at [Patriots players] and pinpoint who the stars are–how they're getting it done, why they're getting it done."[105]

Management Secrets of the New England Patriots explains "how they're getting it done [and] why they're getting it done." The Patriots haven't achieved greatness with unknown players by accident. They built a great organization. The Patriots win because their selflessness and intense preparation enable them to perform their collective best on game day. Belichick-style preparation systematically covers every aspect of winning football games: opponent analysis, clock management, strength and conditioning, strategy and tactics, situational practice, two-minute drills, advance planning for inevitable injuries, matching player talents and skills to roles, recognizing what the opponent is doing, forcing and avoiding turnovers, managing emotions, preventing penalties, avoiding trouble on and off the field, substituting players smoothly, *etc*.

HUMBLE OWNER

The Patriots' unified collective performance encompasses not only players and coaches but also executives, scouts and owners. No analysis of the Patriots' success would be complete without noting that Patriots owner Robert Kraft entrusts all football decisions to his football professionals. For teams lacking humble owners, Super Bowls are virtually unattainable. Though Bob Kraft is in the 99th-percentile of football fans in his knowledge of the game, he's smart and humble enough to know he'll never know as much as the football professionals he pays to make football decisions. So Kraft doesn't interfere with, for example, player personnel because he recognizes that "there is a philosophy of the kind of player that fits here."[106]

It's no coincidence that the Arizona Cardinals: 1) Have lost nearly twice as many games (103) as they've won (57) over the past decade; and, 2) Have a president and four VPs with the last name "Bidwill." (During the 2003 NFL Draft, the Baltimore Ravens were prepared to trade their 2nd-round pick and their 2004 1st-

round pick for the Patriots' 1st-round pick if Kyle Boller, the quarterback they wanted, were still available after the Cardinals made their back-to-back selections. After the deal went through, Patriots director of football research Ernie Adams exclaimed, "Thank God for the Cardinals. When you need them to f--- it up, they f--- it up."[107])

A related non-coincidence is that: 1) Carolina Panthers owner Jerry Richardson stays out of football management; and, 2) Richardson's Panthers nearly beat the Patriots in the 2003 Super Bowl. Given that Richardson shares with only George Halas the distinction of having been both an NFL player and owner, you might expect him to be an activist owner. You would be wrong: "I don't [get] involved in football matters. We have personnel people and coaches for that... I think I can count only five times in our history when I addressed a coach over something that miffed me."[108]

Kraft deserves tremendous credit for evolving from a hands-on owner into an observer of football operations. Before the 1996 NFL Draft, Kraft overruled then-head coach Bill Parcells' preference for a defensive player over wide receiver Terry Glenn. In 1998, Kraft was criticized for "alighting from his limousine to scout a potential draft pick and later, after all but clicking the stopwatch himself, evaluating for reporters the player's ability as a cornerback."[109] Even the Dallas Cowboys, who won three Super Bowls in the '90s, illustrate the destructive power owners can have. Owner Jerry Jones' passion for winning and obsession with football operations prevented him from allowing coach Jimmy Johnson to coach and wrecked what might have been a decade-long dynasty. It is a paradox that recurs endlessly throughout professional sports. After many losing seasons, Jones eventually swallowed his pride and wisely handed true control to Bill Parcells who brought the Cowboys back to the playoffs in just his first season.

Like his friend Jerry Jones, Bob Kraft learned through painful experience to focus squarely on his implicit role as "chairman of the board" of Patriots football operations. Kraft describes his NFL education:

> "When I bought the team, I was a kid with peach fuzz who hadn't shaved. And I got nicks and scrapes. It's nice to learn how to shave on someone else's beard but I had to shave on my own—using Gillette products of course. ...[Y]ou have to get knocked around and see for yourself first hand. It's an intoxicating business and you can get seduced by it. ...My involvement in the trenches was something I would change."[110]

Now, Belichick is CEO. As chairman, Kraft appoints the best people and asks them tough, probing questions but never forces his answers on them. VP of player personnel Scott Pioli really appreciates Kraft's trust: "I'm thankful Robert allows us to do what we do. He understands what we have going here. We've got an owner that asks questions—but doesn't question us."[111] By serving his football professionals as a sounding board, business advisor, and devil's advocate, Kraft complements rather than undermines them. They, in turn, are completely honest and forthright with Kraft because they know he trusts their professional judgment, as Belichick explains: "Robert has gone above and beyond [giving us the tools to win]. He provides support as well as genuine friendship. Robert's the owner–the boss, but also a good friend."[112] Because Kraft had listened carefully to Belichick and bought into Belichick's principles for building a successful football organization, Kraft patiently ignored the naysayers as the Patriots lost fourteen of their first twenty games under Belichick: "People were calling me dumb and calling for me to fire him, but I believed in him. The reason I brought him here is because I thought he had a system which was bigger than any one player."[113] And Kraft's trust in his executives kept him from panicking, as many fans did, when they released long-time star Lawyer Milloy: "I trust Bill's judgment to do things that are right for the team. He explained to me what he was doing and we supported him. Did I feel bad as a fan? Absolutely."[114]

TOM BRADY: CONSUMMATE LEADER

"This guy's the best quarterback in the league right now, and one of the best ever to play."[115]
– *Carolina Panthers safety Mike Minter*

"We all felt that if Tom had the ball at the end, we would win [the Super Bowl]. He just gave us that kind of confidence."[116]
– *Patriots running back Antowain Smith*

"If I had to pick one quarterback to win one game for me, I'd take Brady."[117]
– *Troy Aikman, who quarterbacked the Cowboys to victory in Super Bowls XXVII, XXVIII, and XXX*

"Men want to be like him and women want to be with him. We're not jealous of him. We just want his life. Just for one day. Everybody wants to be Tom Brady."[118]
– *Patriots tight end Christian Fauria*

"[As a rookie, Brady] had moxie and he had character and he had that competitive fire. He had all of the qualities that allow you to develop into [a great quarterback], but there are a lot of people that have thrown abilities away [and] never reached their potential. Who knows what his potential is as a football player, but using his brain, I mean he is already right at the top of the league as far as being able to handle [the mental challenges]."[119]
– *Patriots offensive coordinator Charlie Weis*

The Patriots' 6th-round draft pick in 2000, Tom Brady, was a lonely bachelor. Girls laughed when he said he played for the Patriots, and he was forced to wait in line at nightclubs like everyone else. But Brady was supremely confident, telling Patriots owner Robert Kraft "Drafting me was the best decision the Patriots ever made."[120] Brady immediately went to work proving his bold statement. As the fourth-string quarterback, Tom Brady prepared each week as if he were the starter. Wide receiver David Patten joined the Patriots before Brady's second season and quickly noticed Brady teaching teammates how to play better: "Tom carried himself like this was his team. I thought, 'If he's this confident as a backup, I can only imagine how he'd be running the show.'"[121] When Drew Bledsoe was injured in Week 2 and Brady stepped in, even sportswriters were wondering "Who's Tom Brady?"[122] Brady began his career by throwing 162 passes without an interception, a new NFL record.

Two Super Bowl MVP trophies later, Brady walks on water, and his toughest challenge is fending off fans, including millions of female admirers. He bought Lawyer Milloy's house when Milloy left for Buffalo because "his own house is under siege–by panting female fans! They leave cookies, flowers, candy, soup, pictures, marriage proposals and thongs."[123]

Bill Belichick regularly praises players on teams he's about to compete against but seldom brags about his own players. Asked to compare then-onetime Super Bowl MVP Tom Brady with the legendary Joe Montana, Belichick said, "They're both right-handed quarterbacks. You're talking about Joe Montana. The guy is a Hall of Fame quarterback. He's won however many Super Bowls he's won."[124] So it was very revealing when Belichick, basking in his team's second Super Bowl win, answered David Letterman's question of whether he would want Tom Brady or Joe Montana in a pressure game with "Tom Brady, Phil Simms, Bert Jones."[125] Belichick now places Brady at the summit of his quarterback pantheon because:

> "He's got a lot of elements of a combination of guys. He has a charisma and a presence like Bert Jones. He has a work ethic and a sense of purpose like a Phil Simms. Simms was one of the hardest workers on the team in terms of lifting weights and all of the offseason stuff that the quarterbacks don't always do. Tom is like that."[126]

Brady listens, learns, and improves himself better than anyone Belichick ever coached: "You point him in the right direction and he runs with it."[127] Belichick says this is essential: "I don't know how you get any better if you can't take coaching. If you can't take constructive criticism, how do you improve?"[128]

Tom Brady is fiercely competitive and never surrenders. In high school, Brady's freshman football team lost all nine of its games, but Brady still couldn't get on the field as the quarterback. He stuck with the sport. The defining moment in Brady's life came at the University of Michigan. Furious about playing backup to future NFL quarterback Brian Griese, Brady nearly transferred to another school where he could be the starter. Instead, Brady impressed the hell out of Michigan head coach Lloyd Carr:

"I said, 'Tom, quit worrying about the guys you are competing against. Just worry about yourself and concentrate on being the best you can be.' So he came back the next day... and he leaned forward–now this kid is only 19 years old–and he said, 'Now I'm going to prove to you that I'm a great quarterback. I'm going to prove to you that I can take this team to a championship.' And he did, he did."[129]

Tom Brady is simultaneously supremely self-assured and genuinely humble. Greatness demands such Orwellian "doublethink." In February 2002, Brady became the youngest quarterback to win a Super Bowl. Brady was just 24½ (more than a year younger than "the Joes," Namath and Montana, when they won) when he confidently marched the Patriots downfield in dramatic fashion to set up the field goal that won Super Bowl XXXVI. Brady's childhood idol Joe Montana, whose #16 jersey "Tommy" wore everywhere as a boy, sensed their similarity before Brady's historic drive:

"I just knew that they were going to win. It was very easy to see that he was confident. That's the biggest thing–having confidence in your own ability gets you past a lot of that pressure. I think that those that are afraid that they can't do it feel the pressure more. I think Tom has that presence enough to know his own ability and his capabilities in that situation."[130]

After winning, Brady was no brash, self-obsessed Broadway Joe. Brady shared his triumphant moment with Drew Bledsoe, a Patriot who hadn't even played that day and everyone knew would never play again in a Patriots uniform because Brady had displaced him, both as the starting quarterback and as team leader. Though Bledsoe was a lame duck, Brady celebrated by running over to Bledsoe and beating on his shoulder pads while screaming, "We fucking won!"[131] In his post-game comments, Brady quickly acknowledged the help his mentor had given him: "There was a lot of emotion. He was proud of me and I'm proud of him."[132] He made sure the world recognized Bledsoe's contribution in coming off the bench when Brady was injured during the AFC Championship Game: "I'm fortunate to be on a team with guys like Drew, or else we couldn't have won the Super Bowl."[133]

For his calm heroics with the game on the line and time running out, Brady was named Super Bowl MVP. Had he displayed the arrogance of youth, Brady might have been excused. Instead, Brady epitomized the Patriots' season by waving off personal accolades: "I'm just a little piece of the puzzle."[134] He also instinctively credited his teammates: "I think our whole team is MVP. We have an MVT–a Most Valuable Team."[135]

Coping with the ceaseless outpouring of affection he receives is harder for Brady than throwing a football with accuracy while dodging 300-pound defensive linemen. Brady says "[The adulation] really embarrasses me. ...I just like to be one of the guys. ...[O]ff the field, I don't think of myself differently than I did when I was a 12-year-old kid."[136] Even after winning two Super Bowl MVP trophies, Brady feels more comfortable as "Tommy" than "Tom": "I still am ['Tommy']. It was always 'Tommy.' 'Tom' doesn't even sound right."[137] He jokes about how slowly he runs and how weak he is, even after he added more than twenty pounds of muscle. Brady jokes he has avoided injuries because "There's nothing for me to pull… I can't pull a muscle I don't have."[138] After running for a first down and getting smashed simultaneously by multiple Seattle Seahawks so hard that his helmet flew off and he fumbled the ball, Brady teased himself again: "That was disappointing because I had the first down. I was fine. Not much in that head to rattle around."[139] Paradoxically, Brady's "aw shucks" reaction to fame only further endears him to Patriots fans. One Boston College student wrote on his website, under a photo of Brady, "Although completely heterosexual with a girlfriend, I cannot help but love this man. …He is the only person in the entire world whom I can forgive for wearing a Yankees hat in public."[140]

Hall of Fame coach Bill Walsh, who coached Joe Montana's San Francisco 49ers, says Brady is "as close to Joe (Montana) as anyone I've ever seen."[141] *CBS* analyst and former NFL quarterback Boomer Esiason says "Tom Brady is this generation's Joe Montana."[142] *ESPN* analyst and former NFL quarterback Ron Jaworski's believes "By the time he's done, he may end up being the greatest."[143] Seemingly oblivious to such talk and to his two Super Bowl MVP trophies, Brady continues to talk as if he's but a minor factor in the Patriots' success:

> "[I'm] playing with a whole bunch of great players… I have the most underrated receivers in the league. I have an offensive line that has been protecting me all year… I play a role on this team and it happens to be quarterback. …Heck, I couldn't block or tackle or run with the ball or do any of that stuff. In that case those guys are the most valuable. Rodney Harrison, he is playing like the best safety in the league. There are guys up and down the roster who have really played their role at an MVP-type level. …It has been a great year because the guys on this team make it easy for me to go out there and do my job."[144]

After winning his second Super Bowl, Brady continued praising the Patriots organization he credits for making his success possible: "Right from [owner] Mr. Kraft to Coach Belichick, down to [offensive coordinator Charlie] Weis and [defensive coordinator] RAC [Romeo Crennel] and down to the players, this is a first-class organization."[145] Brady's humility and eagerness to deflect praise onto everyone around him reminds me of President Harry Truman's famous saying that "You can accomplish anything in life, provided that you do not mind who gets the credit." Such maturity and self-deprecation is rare in anyone who has achieved Brady's success, but it is astounding in a young man.

But Brady is also correct to admire the entire Patriots organization. For example, Brady credits Patriots owner Bob Kraft with helping him keep his success in perspective by advising: "Remember, you just throw a football. You don't cure cancer."[146] Though Brady's youth and movie star good looks make him the team's poster boy and Brady can't even walk around Paris, London, or Rome without attracting attention,[147] the Patriots are not *The Brady Bunch*. As Patriots cornerback Ty Law explains: "Our team isn't about stars. That's why we had a lot of the success we had. We don't feel like there are stars. We're a complete team."[148]

PLANNING FOR SUCCESS

"If one rookie is late for a meeting, [Patriots head coach] Belichick makes them all come in a half hour earlier the next day. ...That's one way to teach *team*. If one dies, we all die. If one guy blows his responsibility on the field, we all pay the price. That's because it says 'Patriots' on the scoreboard."[149]
– *Patriots inside linebackers coach Pepper Johnson*

The Patriots' recent NFL dominance without superstars proves they are a championship organization. Only a superior organization can consistently outperform its 31 rivals on a level playing field. Which "success factors" propelled the New England Patriots to victory in two of the past three Super Bowls? Like all great organizations, the Patriots have succeeded through a combination of superior vision, methodical planning, and outstanding execution.

The first step toward achieving greatness is defining greatness and committing to achieve it. After taking control of the Patriots in February 2000, the new leadership team established a mission statement that set a lofty objective, sustained success, and stated the Patriots' recipe for leaping over the bar they set so high for themselves:

"We are building a big, strong, fast, smart, tough and dedicated football team that consistently competes for championships."[150]
– *New England Patriots' mission statement*

After deciding what they wanted to achieve, Patriots management formulated a detailed plan for achieving it. Belichick and his assistants used their decades of NFL experience and their informed beliefs about what separates winners from losers to develop a concrete blueprint. Belichick, Pioli, *et al.* didn't making a series of smart *ad hoc* decisions. Many of the Patriots' top coaches and executives (including: director of football research Ernie Adams, defensive coordinator Romeo Crennel, offensive coordinator Charlie Weis, college scouting director Thomas Dimitroff Jr., and pro personnel director Nick Caserio) previously worked together and share a vision of what their winning football team would look like and, therefore, a clear framework for making decisions. Belichick's management techniques are textbook examples of how to run an organization. In fact, the best summary of Belichick's approach I have seen is actually *BusinessWeek*'s description of how CEO George David runs the $37-billion conglomerate United Technologies:

Educate	*Organize*	*Analyze*	*Track*	*Lead*
Teach... techniques to identify quality problems...	...make [work] cleaner, simpler, and more intuitive. Nothing is random...	...study the root cause of every defect and... fix the problem once and for all.	Map out every process, make people own it, and reward constant improvements...	Convert top management into disciples... Nonbelievers can head for the exits.

Table from: Diane Brady, "The Unsung CEO," *BusinessWeek*, 25 October 2004, p. 80.

Belichick implements every one of these in a football context. He also uses many other smart management tactics and reads management books while on "vacation."[151]

Belichick's original plan was superb, but Patriots coaches are perfectionists who regularly reassess their plan and review their performance to find improvements. For example, Scott Pioli doesn't just do his job; he analyzes his profession and optimizes his job performance through intense self-scrutiny. Pioli long ago committed to (and has succeeded in) becoming the NFL's best player personnel executive. Academics say you truly know a subject only if you can teach it. Pioli could not only teach a course on NFL personnel management; he could even assign the textbook he has already written on the subject:

> "Pioli's personnel prowess is held in such high regard that several of his peers around the league boasted of his personnel book—a tome that he has actually copyrighted yet allowed others to review. 'It's definitely impressive,' said one NFC personnel director who has seen the book. 'It lays out his personnel philosophies and strategies. It's just more advanced in philosophies than others that I have read. But at the same time it makes his personnel philosophies seem like such common sense.'"[152]

One of Pioli's core beliefs, which grew out of his personal experience as a collegiate football player, is the centrality of "team":

> "I am a very bad loser and unfortunately, I was a part of two losing seasons [in college]. ...[I] learned a lot about the insignificance and emptiness of personal and individual success. I was fortunate to receive some individual accolades as a player, but none of that compared to the shared thrill that came with winning games."[153]

Like the players he acquires, Pioli has repressed his personal ambition (for money, status, and power) to satisfy his overriding desire to perform an essential role within an organization that collectively achieves great things. Asked what he hopes to be doing in five or ten years, Pioli replied, "Hopefully right here at a table, answering questions at a Super Bowl."[154] Pressed about whether he aims to become a general manager, which would bring him prestige, greater control over personnel, and higher pay, Pioli expressed apathy: "Like I said, right here at the Super Bowl."[155]

Similarly, Bill Belichick regularly critiques his own performance ("I would like to think I learned a little bit over the last few years"[156]) and solicits constructive criticism from both his assistants and outsiders he trusts and respects, like LSU head coach Nick Saban. Belichick says, "We're constantly evaluating what we're doing and we make a lot of changes. We try to improve... The things that worked good for us last year or two years ago, in some cases we need to move on from that. ...We've made mistakes and then tried to figure out how to correct them and not repeat them."[157] Though Belichick does not take time to record his philosophies and methods, he certainly subjects them to rigorous analysis and refinement every off-season. The team scouts itself throughout the season and again following each season. It holds "needs meetings." Belichick obviously grew wiser in many ways during his disappointing tenure as Cleveland Browns head coach from 1991 through 1995. To cite just one:

> "I've learned that as much as the game is played on the field... there are also a lot of things on the periphery and outside, off the field, that are also important toward winning, and I'll put more time and effort into making sure those things are right for the organization than maybe I did previously."[158]

With the Patriots, "I probably spend a little more time with things that go on in the locker room, go on off the field, the players, their attitude, their motivations, the chemistry on the team and that kind of thing."[159]

Finally, and perhaps most importantly, Belichick, Pioli, *et al.* communicated their plan to others, built an organization capable of and excited about carrying out that plan, and rallied everyone to help achieve that vision. Executing a plan is always harder than devising one. Great execution requires smart, motivated people and careful coordination. An architect can design a beautiful house, but it takes a team of skilled builders to erect that house. New York Giants general manager Ernie Accorsi, who explicitly modeled his 2004 Giants on the 2001 Patriots, knows how hard it is to turn a great blueprint into a great team:

> "You can follow that blueprint, but the blueprint isn't going to win. What will win are your judgments. If you're signing 15 [free agents, as the 2001 Patriots did], they better be the right 15 guys. If there are seven good and seven misses, you're not going to win. They are operating brilliantly. They've made almost no mistakes."[160]

Belichick and Pioli are simultaneously "big picture" architects and "hands-on" general contractors. They had already built two winning teams: the 1994 Cleveland Browns, who won a playoff game using just six of the players whose arrival in Cleveland predated Belichick's,[161] and the 1998 New York Jets, whose defense they rebuilt and led to the 1998 AFC Championship Game: "the unheralded defense is playing [brilliantly]. But exactly who are these guys... They are a collection of bargain-basement free agents. Not a million-dollar acquisition among them. ...All of them were let go by their previous teams. ... [T]he Jets are using eight free agents for the bulk of the defensive work."[162]

Belichick's vision of leadership emphasizes not controlling via hierarchy, rules, and orders but ensuring that every executive, scout, coach, and player possesses the same principles, techniques, vision, and values that Belichick holds in his head. He wants his knowledge, attitude, energy, and philosophy to cascade down into the heads of everyone throughout the organization. Belichick tells his assistant coaches that he expects them to emulate his standards of professionalism and dedication because players will emulate their coaches if the entire coaching staff sets a strong example.[163] Similarly, Tom Brady feels Belichick "is passing on what he wants to communicate to me so I can communicate that to the rest of the guys."[164] It is essential that each Patriot buy into the vision and and make his daily decisions accordingly. Accomplishing this mind meld frees Belichick to attend full-time to head coaching duties.

One myth about the Patriots is that Belichick runs the defense. Defensive coordinator Romeo Crennel runs the defense. Crennel didn't earn the "2003 Assistant Coach of the Year" award by simply conveying Belichick's thoughts to Patriots defenders. He has called every defensive play for three years. Fans under-appreciate Crennel because Belichick is "a defensive genius" and because Crennel, like every Belichick assistant, shuns publicity:

> "It doesn't make any difference who gets the credit as long as we win. We've worked on this system before, the parts have come along, and we've grown together, both of us. I've been in this business for 20 years, and that's what the deal is about, winning ballgames. Maybe my being here gives him more confidence to do the head coaching job. Trying to do both jobs can spread you thin."[165]

Belichick involves himself in every aspect of his organization, but Crennel is an extremely smart and experienced football professional who runs the defense and will likely soon become a superb NFL head coach. Crennel and Belichick coached together on the Giants (1981-1990), Patriots (1996), Jets (1997-1999), and Patriots again (2001-present). Crennel's vision for "his" future team sounds like the best description of Belichick's New England Patriots I have ever heard, proving that Belichick's vision is not locked inside the vault of Bill Belichick's brain but is shared widely throughout the Patriots organization:

> "My football team would apply its strong points to the other team's weak points and take advantage. I would have a team that is fundamentally sound and that is smart, disciplined and physical in name and nature. I would have a defense that is aggressive and does not give up the big play. I would have an offense that is multiple and based on ball control that runs to win and throws when necessary. My team would emphasize the turnover game. The

special teams would be disciplined and able to handle whatever comes up in games. It would be a team that flies to the football with effort and enjoys playing the game."[166]

The story of the Patriots' success is the story of Belichick's vision, the coaches' plan for methodically transforming their heady mission statement into reality, and the organization's implementation of that plan. Like any success story, the Patriots' success derives from not only smart strategy but also meticulous attention to detail. Execution is always the most time-consuming and challenging step, as backup quarterback Rohan Davey explains:

"(Belichick will) let you know what he expects from you and what he expects you to know. He'll just pop up in the meeting room and ask, 'Davey, what coverage is that?,' 'Who is that at left corner?,' 'What number is he and what school did he go to?,' 'Who's the nickel backer?,' 'If the right corner goes down, who's coming (in) and who's his backup?,' 'If they're in this front and you see the end with his foot up, what are you anticipating?' Stuff like that. You've got to let him know you're on top of your game."[167]

The superbly coordinated performance of Patriots owners, executives, coaches, scouts, and players holds so many valuable organizational and business lessons that I know you too will find the Patriots' blueprint for success as enlightening, inspiring, and relevant as any business case study.

WINNING WITH CLASS... WINNING BECAUSE OF CHARACTER

"I basically said, 'If we need thugs and hoodlums to win, then I'm out of the business.'"[168]

— Patriots owner Robert Kraft

"The most important thing is that we have high character people representing this organization. That was the one thing I had said to Bill when he joined us: He could have full control of personnel, but... the team carries our family name, and if something bad happens, people think of our family."[169]

— Patriots owner Robert Kraft

The Patriots deserve attention not only *because* they have won multiple championships but also for *how* they have won. The Patriots' tenacity and togetherness earned them the admiration of millions. As Pats fan Laurie Jerome told a reporter during the victory parade following the team's first Super Bowl victory, "They're hardworking blue-collar slobs like the rest of us. That's why it's so exciting."[170] What does it mean to be a "blue collar" football player earning millions of dollars? Patriots safety Rodney Harrison says his teammates "pay the price."[171]

They admire competitiveness, heart, striving, and intense, inglorious preparation, not seven-figure bank accounts:

> "Every [team] has someone who comes [to work] early. When I was in San Diego, it was me, Junior Seau and Fred McCrary. Here, you have 10-20 guys in at 5:30 [a.m.] When your quarterback is here at that time running on a treadmill, it just gravitates down to everybody. It's not for show–it's real."[172]

Patriots safety Lawyer Milloy credits Tom Brady: "Tom described himself as the type of player who hasn't always been the fastest or strongest but whose competitive nature always had him racing the fastest player on the block until he beat him. I joked with him that after about the 30th time, the guy probably let him win so he could go home for supper. ...That competitive approach filters through a team when its leaders bring it into a huddle."[173]

The Patriots deliberately assembled a team of "blue-collar slobs." Patriots players always work hard and seldom cause trouble because the team's personnel people look for three "f"s: football, family, and faith. Bob Kraft always talks about the "Patriots family,"[174] and Patriots bond so tightly to their work and their colleagues that they joke about their "other" families.[175] The team hires family-friendly guys like Joe Andruzzi for whom "Family's number one, no matter what."[176] To the Patriots, "family values" is no platitude or campaign slogan. Though the Patriots were short on running backs in early 2004, they let Kevin Faulk miss the final preseason game and first several regular season games because his mother was ill:

> "When my mom was sick, I was going to be [with her]. Coach Belichick, being the coach that he is, he was like 'However much time you need to be down there with your family, or whatever you need, I grant you that.' That just goes to show how much class the organization has."[177]

Patriots special teams ace Don Davis is also impressed by the team's thoughtfulness and concern for players:

> "It's ...the small things like the way we have meals, the way we travel. The average person may not even think about, but it comes into play. There's also the fact that Mr. Kraft is an owner you actually see, he calls me by name, says 'hi.' No other owner, on any [of my previous] team[s] probably knows my name or even realizes I played on the team. You get that family feel here."[178]

No Patriot wears a bluer collar or lugs a larger lunch pail than linebacker Tedy Bruschi. If Whitey Ford, who nicknamed Pete Rose "Charlie Hustle" after Rose sprinted to first base after drawing a walk during a spring training game, were a Patriots fan, Bruschi would be "Charlie Hustle." Patriots fans are bonkers about Bruschi. The Patriots Pro Shop's best-selling player jersey is not Brady's but Bruschi's.[179] Karen Cardoza (a.k.a. "Mrs. B") built an Internet shrine to Bruschi (PatriotWorld.com). Bruschi reciprocates Patriots fans' admiration: "I relate to them. They are my kind of people. Just blue-collar, hard-working people that just work hard and love their families and do the best they can to get the job done. That's the way I would describe the people in the stands—and that's how I would describe myself."[180] Bruschi's actions speak even louder than his words. On the field, Bruschi slams into opponents with glee. Off the field, he signs contract extensions with the Patriots for millions of dollars less than he could earn elsewhere, and he doesn't even bother negotiating because he feels football players are all overpaid. Bruschi's also so loyal that he swore to his girlfriend (now his wife) the day he was drafted that he would spend his career with the Patriots: "I'm going to play out this contract with the Patriots and keep signing back with them. They're the ones I want to finish with because they're the ones I'm going to start with."[181] Bruschi's "love the one you're with" attitude isn't corny sentimentalism; it's admirable:

> "To go to another team and have all those fans who bought that No. 54 jersey with my name on the back, which to me is the biggest compliment they could give me, for me to look up and see someone wearing the 54, for me to know that they'd have to see me wearing a 54 with another team's colors, I wouldn't like that. That would be painful to me and I wouldn't want to do that to any of them."[182]

The Patriots have won with class, both on and off the field, by refusing to tolerate talented but troublesome players, always respecting their opponents, helping the less fortunate in their communities, *etc*. Five days after offensive tackle Kenyatta Jones was arrested for throwing hot water on his roommate in 2003, apparently as an idiotic practical joke, the Patriots released him.[183] Jones had started eleven games the previous season, was becoming a cornerstone of the offensive line, and had no obvious replacement. Nevertheless, the Patriots didn't even attempt to trade Jones. They simply released him because his action was inconsistent with the team's definition of "a New England Patriot." Many might assume the Patriots win "despite" giving up on talented players like Terry Glenn and Kenyatta Jones. The Patriots would tell you they win *because* they give up on such players. Tolerating selfishness destroys "team."

The 2001 Patriots' character and over-achieving so captivated and inspired fans that over 600,000 bought a copy of NFL Films' Super Bowl XXXVI highlight video. NFL Films president Steve Sabol said, "We thought that a record half million copies of our Super Bowl XXXVI highlight would satisfy the hunger that Patriots fans have for their team. We were wrong."[184] That video sold twice as many copies as any previous Super Bowl highlight video and more copies than any previous sports video of any kind.[185]

"TEAM FIRST" ACHIEVEMENT CULTURE

> "We feel [cohesion]'s the reason for our success... Why worry about individuals? Why worry about superstars?"[186]
> – *Patriots linebacker Roman Phifer*

While Patriots head coach Bill Belichick has been widely (and justifiably) hailed as a "genius" for leading a team of mostly unknown and unwanted football players to multiple NFL championships, the Patriots' true genius resides in the hearts and minds of each player, scout, coach, executive, and owner. Every Patriot, whatever his role, is dedicated to doing whatever he personally can (both off and on the field) to give his team the best chance to win football games. This selfless "team first" mentality is woven throughout the fabric of the entire organization, explains VP of player personnel Scott Pioli:

> "[W]e're all on the same page... It's an organizational-wide philosophy. In a large part it is the players, but we've got coaches that believe and understand that they have a role. I understand that I have a role. Our scouts know that they have a role. And all of us work, collectively, toward the same goal. Bill's a perfect example of that. He is, in my opinion, the best coach in the National Football League and he doesn't perceive himself that way and he doesn't [act] that way. It's part of our culture."[187]

Marv Levy, who coached the Buffalo Bills to four straight Super Bowl appearances, says Patriots players' attitudes are a key element in the team's success: "They don't have a bunch of wild guys and end-zone dancers, and that's good. It keeps them focused on the next opponent rather than [planting] a phone in the goal-post padding [as Saints receiver Joe Horn did]."[188] All the coaches share this mentality, as offensive coordinator Charlie Weis explains: "the best way that you could say something positive about yourself is to fit in within the structure of which you're already working and be successful doing that."[189]

Bill Belichick obviously played an essential role in establishing this culture, but no individual can transform an organization's culture through sheer force of will, as Belichick himself admitted within days of the team's second Super Bowl victory:

> "You can't dictate [culture]. You put people on a team and the chemistry and bonds, they all form. You can't tell 70 guys how to act, how to feel and how to respond. That's all genuine and that's how it all blends together. You can't control that, but it's remarkable how this group handles so many pressure situations and didn't crack, didn't lose their composure, played tough and smart and made plays at key times in almost every game in so many different areas."[190]

The Patriots built their achievement culture over time, through personnel changes, quality coaching, individual dedication, friendships and bonding, healthy competition, and many other factors. Each individual dedicated himself to daily improvement. As players experienced individual and team improvement, they grew hungrier for more. Success snowballed. Patriots linebacker Roman Phifer says, "When you see the results of being disciplined, and the results are wins, it's a good feeling. After the success of 2001, when free agents come in, it was easy to sell that discipline works."[191] Guys were having so much fun working that some players, like Patriots special teams captain Larry Izzo, didn't want the grueling seven-month 2003 season to end: "For me, there was a sadness it was over. It was a really enjoyable season, rolling off 15 wins the way we did. It was the most fun a lot of guys had been around. When it was over it was like, 'Jeez, I want to keep playing.'"[192] Tight end Christian Fauria describes being a Patriot in terms similar to belonging to an exclusive club, or even cult, that possesses a secret formula for winning football games:

> "You get a bunch of guys who are all in it for the right reasons, who can see what the possibilities are and see what the rewards can be, and they buy into the philosophy. They buy into the aspect of team. Anyone who's won a championship, it's just a certain bond that you have amongst the guys who are on the team. It's like you know something everybody else doesn't know. When people come into it, you don't necessarily tell them, they just kind of see how it is, and it becomes a domino effect."[193]

Defensive lineman Richard Seymour says new players quickly adopt the team's winning mindset:

> "It's just our attitude that we won't be denied, that we won't lose. We have some guys with a lot of character and experience, and we're bringing in guys, and they're feeding on that as well. When it comes down the stretch, we feel like we're going to win the football game."[194]

The Patriots' success under head coach Bill Belichick is even more remarkable when you consider the sub-par performance of the Belichick-led Cleveland Browns (37 wins and 45 defeats during Belichick's 1991-1995 tenure). Patriots assistant coach Pepper Johnson, one of many dedicated guys who helped build the Patriots' winning-focused, "team first" culture, reflected on the poisonous environment in the Browns' locker room while he was a player on Belichick's Browns:

> "I considered retiring after... 1994... because there were too many players who didn't care or seemed unaffected by losses. Like cancer, this mentality spreads... Finally, wherever you look, no one cares. ...The little creeps who were coming in and not caring—wow, I just couldn't stomach that. I tried talking to them, but it was wearing me down, almost killing me."[195]

Legendary NFL running back Jim Brown was and is a close friend of Bill Belichick. (They bonded over their mutual love for football, lacrosse, hard work, and personal responsibility.) Brown hung around Belichick's Browns and, like Johnson, was deeply disappointed by many players' lackadaisical attitude:

> "I wanted to win far more than the players. ...They were kind of just casual. I said, 'Man!' ...I'm pulling for every break. Every detail... matters. But it seems like back then some of the players didn't know that every detail counted. Every mistake can lose a game for you. I'm thinking, 'Man, is this how it is? This casual?' It's a 60-minute game and you only got so much time. The fourth quarter is running out and you had gotten two touchdowns down. There's no sense of urgency."[196]

Belichick, Pioli, and Ernie Adams extracted important lessons from their disappointing Cleveland experience and applied those lessons in New England. But their maturation cannot fully explain the performance gulf separating Belichick's Browns from Belichick's Patriots. Organizations are complex, organic entities with many moving parts. Many of those "moving parts" are human beings, each of whom possesses a complex set of emotions, strengths, and weaknesses. When so many individuals interact, outcomes are unpredictable... but they're not random. The Patriots are proof that if you select the right guys, instill the right mindset and reinforce behaviors that benefit the group rather than the individual, the whole can become far greater than the sum of the individual parts. Belichick says his Patriots prove "You can win with players who are not looking to promote themselves and be selfish. You can win with people who care about the team first."[197] Conversely, the greatest leader in the world is powerless to lead a group of selfish individualists because "It's not all about [any one individual]. ...If a player's basically selfish, then you can talk teamwork until you're blue in the face and there's going to be a high degree of selfishness in that player's performance."[198]

EVERY PATRIOT IS A LEADER

> "I didn't come here to fit in with everybody. I came to do my job. I respect people and I'm humble, but I'm not trying to be best friends with everyone. I came to be a professional and to win."[199]
> *– Patriots safety Rodney Harrison*

> "[Safety Rodney Harrison] would check around the locker room, making sure that players were getting the proper rest and nutrition. 'Are you hydrating?' was one of his popular questions. He was one of the players who instituted a fine system for mistakes in games and practices. If coaches made mistakes on calls, they would get fined too."[200]
> *– Michael Holley, Patriot Reign*

Many business books attempt to dissect "leadership." On the Patriots, everyone is a leader... and everyone is simultaneously a follower. Bill Belichick knows leadership has nothing to do with titles, power suits, fear, status, luxurious offices, brashness, or screaming. Belichick defines leadership as doing one's job to the best of one's ability and enabling others to do their jobs to the best of their abilities:

> "When a player comes to work in the morning, he is prepared, ready to go, ready to improve as a player, ready to help the team, alert, awake, and has a good attitude. You couldn't have any more leadership than that. That's what a true leader does, and believe me, some of the best leaders on the New England Patriots would never ever in 100 years stand up in front of the team and say, 'Oh guys, we've got to do this or that.'"[201]

Patriots safety Rodney Harrison doesn't order teammates to drink water. He goads and prods them into it. Defensive lineman Richard Seymour says, "He may say, 'I'm hydrating and you're not. And I'm getting the edge on you.' It's a fun thing to do, but it's relevant to the situation that's going on. It's all to get each other better. It's all part of the competitive atmosphere we have here."[202]

Many training camp sessions are run at three-quarters speed and with an attempt to avoid hitting so hard that players fall down and risk injury. After Patriots safety Rodney Harrison noticed certain players jogging through such training sessions using sloppy ball-protection techniques, he devised a tactic to force ball carriers to shape up. Since he was not allowed to hit, Harrison started trying to poke the ball loose every play:

> "It irritates them to death when I come up there and do it, but what it does is—like I tell [running back] Corey [Dillon], because I think he was getting a little agitated, but he's laughing about it now—I do it to make sure our runners secure the ball. And it works on me going to get the ball out. So now every time those guys catch the ball and they're running, they're aware. Because that's a turnover. I do it all day. I don't care if the play is 40 yards away, I run all the way to the ball and try to poke it out."[203]

That's just one example of how Patriots players devise drills and tactics and techniques that improve their team. There's no rule that only coaches can be inventive. Smart football teams, like smart companies, encourage everyone to innovate.

Another example is a drill cornerback Ty Law invented that players might have thought torture had a *coach* demanded they do it. But because a *player* pushed himself to do it, teammates joined in on the "fun," and it has spread like wildfire. Law's innovation basically consists of filling dead practice time with extra sprints. For years, Law has stayed after practice to run extra sprints ("gassers") that give him additional stamina and endurance during games. Linebacker Tedy Bruschi even added a new element: stomach crunches. Safety Rodney Harrison swears by the results:

> "Ty Law got me started doing it and it really helped me out last year. Eighth week of the season, fourth quarter, I felt like I had more endurance, I felt like I was stronger. I probably was running better than I'd ever run. During the fourth quarter, you feel like you have more energy. It's contagious. Everybody's doing it now. It's just working hard, paying the price. You figure everyone else is standing around doing nothing, you can get in a little extra stretching, a few sit-ups, some push-ups."[204]

Every Patriot, even Coach Belichick, has a role, knows his role, practices his role, believes in the importance of his role, and performs his role as proficiently and passionately as possible. And every Patriot seeks to help his teammates perform better. Therein lies the greatest genius of the New England Patriots.

Each Patriot is a leader. For example, Patriots safety Rodney Harrison advises younger players; he challenged cornerback Asante Samuel after Samuel missed the first few days of training camp with some sort of injury: "Sant, you have all the talent in the world. You just have to do it day-in, day-out. Sometimes you don't feel like it, sometimes you feel lazy. When you get in a bad mood, you still have to practice on the same level that you play.... I don't care if you have two interceptions one day. You have to come back and do it again the next day."[205] When Patriots cornerback Terrell Buckley was frustrated with his limited role in 2001, veteran defensive lineman Anthony Pleasant changed Buckley's thinking and boosted his self-worth and morale. When Pleasant noticed that offensive lineman Kenyatta Jones was, by his own admission, "out late almost every night, a rookie with money,"[206] Pleasant gave Jones a vision of the future he was creating for himself: "I told him the door [to the NFL] is a revolving door. ...I said 'Don't be an "I should have, I could have" player.'"[207] Even after his career ended, Pleasant was worrying about the development of his younger teammates: "I'm just hoping they continue up there some of the things I started with some of the younger defensive linemen."[208]

SPECIAL, BUT NOT UNIQUE

> "Our team was one-game-at-a-time. It was total preparation. It was being very focused. It was priding ourselves on not making mental errors."[209]
> – *Dick Anderson, safety on the undefeated 1972 Miami Dolphins' "no name" defense*

Belichick's Patriots are a special football team, but other special teams, including the undefeated '72 Dolphins, have earned championships after embracing a team-centric "all-for-one-and-one-for-all" mentality. Football is scarcely the only collective endeavor in which: tenacity and teamwork trump talent; passion, perspiration, and perseverance power performance; selfless sacrifice supersedes statistical superiority; and coordination, collaboration, and cooperation kill competitors.

Such truths are obvious to anyone who witnessed the U.S. Olympic hockey team defeat the Soviets in 1980's "Miracle On Ice," the Detroit Pistons crush the L.A. Lakers in the 2004 NBA Finals, the Puerto Rico basketball team destroy the U.S. "Dream Team" (a.k.a., "Nightmare Team") by 19 points in the 2004 Olympics, or low-scoring Bill Russell win eleven NBA championships while perennial scoring champion Wilt Chamberlain won only two. Belichick arranged for his Patriots to meet Russell because Russell was all about long-term team success: "[In] college, Olympic competition, and the NBA, he played in 21 winner-take-all, someone-is-going-home-tonight games, and his record was 21-0."[210]

Playing as a team propelled the 2004 Detroit Pistons to the NBA championship over a "more talented" Los Angeles Lakers "team" so laden with superstars that some stars watched from the Lakers' bench. Pistons players proudly called themselves "misfits" and admitted they weren't the league's best individual players, but they fought to prove they weren't chopped liver either, something Pistons GM Joe Dumars already knew: "The fact that... we don't have four or five All-Stars on this team, I think people can lose sight of how good of players they are. These guys are stepping up and doing it. It's not like it's the first time they're doing it."[211] The Pistons were a cohesive team of good-but-not-great players who prepared intensely and played team basketball with heart and respect for one another. Lakers players and coaches, most famously Kobe Bryant and Shaquille O'Neal, were far more "talented" but lost because their bloated egos prevented them from playing team basketball.

The Carolina Panthers

Even the Super Bowl XXXVIII-losing Carolina Panthers exemplify the power of this tenacious, blue-collar, sink-or-swim-together formula. Few believed the Panthers (1-15 in 2001 and 7-9 in 2002) had the talent to make the Super Bowl. Yet they nearly won it, losing a 32-29 nail-biter on a field goal with just seconds remaining. Tom Brady was mightily impressed: "I don't think you could be any more proud of the guys you played with or the guys you played against."[212] Brady gushed that Carolina "never gave up. They were down 11 at one point. They really played their butts off."[213] The Panthers' style, emphasizing defense, special teams, and low-risk "ball control" offense, is a photocopy of the Patriots'. And Panthers players are so competitive that defensive lineman Brentson Buckner swore the 2004 Pats-Panthers preseason game would be "a war," safety Mike Minter called it "Super Bowl No. 2," and wide receiver Steve Smith warned, "[players] are going to have to bring their lunch pails. It's going to be a construction zone."[214]

The Panthers have a Patriot-like "no name" roster. Neither Super Bowl team had a quarterback, running back, wide receiver, tight end, offensive lineman, defensive lineman, linebacker, cornerback, or safety with a top-five salary at his position,[215] except Patriots cornerback Ty Law (who signed his 7-year, $51 million mega-contract in August 1999, before Bill Belichick's arrival as head coach). Widening the analysis to the top-ten salaries at each position, the Patriots had no additional players while the Panthers had only a wide receiver and offensive lineman.[216] The one position the two teams shelled out for is kicker... the least glamorous in football. The Patriots and Panthers both paid their kicker among the NFL's top five.

Both teams evaluate and train players extremely well. When Panthers linebacker Dan Morgan says, "If you mess up, you are going to know about it, but if you are good, you are going to know about it,"[217] any Patriot would nod his head in knowing agreement. And Patriots and Panthers players all know that winning is about team, not individual stars:

> "there are absolutely no self-promoters on either team... Guys who are looking to stand out from their teammates, to get more notoriety than what comes naturally from just being a good football player. For both the New England Patriots and Carolina Panthers, the lack of self-promoters has created a tremendously productive working environment."[218]

Players, coaches, and executives on both teams share many philosophies, including "team first," confidence without arrogance, striving for continual improvement, and focusing on the task at hand rather than looking backward or forward. Each coach used his highest-ever draft pick not on a glamor position but on a defensive lineman (Julius Peppers of the Panthers and Richard Seymour of the Patriots). Panthers GM Marty Hurney has even figured out the Scott Pioli system:

> "We found out you can't keep spending the highest money for each player. We were trying to buy a Super Bowl, and you can't do it. We tried to hit too many home runs and instead we kept striking out. You need to try to hit singles instead. Just make contact and once in a while you will hit one out of the park."[219]

The teams' many similarities are unsurprising because, according to Panthers head coach John Fox, "Bill and I have been close friends for a long time. ... I am familiar with his staff. I have some close friends there."[220] Fox's offensive coordinator, Dan Henning, worked with Belichick, Patriots offensive coordinator Charlie Weis, and Patriots defensive coordinator Romeo Crennel on Bill Parcells' New York Jets in 1998 and 1999. Henning says, "I've known Romeo [Crennel] for 25 years and Bill [Belichick] for 20 years."[221] And Fox, like Belichick, is a former New York Giants "defensive genius"; he coordinated the defense of the 2000 Giants that shut out the Minnesota Vikings 41-0 in the NFC Championship Game.

Similar styles and philosophies are, not coincidentally, reflected in similar results. The Panthers had lost fifteen straight games before John Fox took over as head coach. Fox says "the players' wives were embarrassed to go to the shopping malls."[222] Both teams rapidly improved from worst to first in their respective conferences and battled each other fiercely in Super Bowl XXXVIII.

Although the 2003 Panthers embody and exemplify many of the lessons in this book, small Panthers deviations from the Patriots' blueprint cost the Panthers the Super Bowl. These include: poor clock management (leaving the Patriots too much time to win the Super Bowl), questionable strategy (regarding two-point conversions), players' boasting and disrespectful statements about the Patriots, and players' failure to keep their mouths shut regarding their game plan.

The Panthers haven't learned these lessons. As Patriots safety Rodney Harrison accurately noted following the teams' 2004 preseason "rematch": "They were hyping it up in the paper. This was their Super Bowl. They have a lot of guys that talk a lot of smack. But our motto is, 'Shut up and let's leave it out there on the field.'"[223] Some Panthers are still whining. Receiver Steve Smith calls the Patriots "a bunch of cheap-shot artists." Receiver Muhsin Muhammad says, "We watched the film of the Super Bowl and we felt there were a lot of things that were not classy."[224] Such comments serve no productive purpose.

The Patriots' rise from worst to first is compelling and inspiring but hardly unprecedented. The Patriots are following a blueprint shared by many high performance organizations that have outcompeted "superior" competitors. Because variants of the Patriots' formula have proven successful in many team sports (and non-sport organizations, like Southwest Airlines), the transformation of the "Patsies" into a championship organization admired not only throughout the NFL but even by legendary GE CEO Jack Welch[225] contains insights useful to anyone seeking to improve the performance of any team, company, or organization.

A STRONG WEAKEST LINK

The Patriots teach us, for example, the value of subordinating our egos, enjoying and respecting our colleagues, and recognizing that success derives from teamwork. A touchdown pass requires someone to throw the ball, someone to catch the ball, and offensive linemen, tight ends, and running backs to protect the quarterback long enough for the receiver to get open. A touchdown pass even requires other wide receivers to distract and/or block defensive backs so the receiver is not triple-covered. After kicking a game-winning 44-yard field goal in 2001, Adam Vinatieri credited his teammates: "The guys out front did a great job blocking. I'm just the last leg of it."[226] New Patriots absorb the team message immediately. New Patriot running back Corey Dillon, purportedly selfish and self-absorbed during his seven seasons in Cincinnati, credits his new teammates for helping him run well:

> "I'm getting a lot of help. I'm getting a lot of help up front [from my offensive line]. We have great receivers, and that kind of takes the pressure

off me because I don't see that many eight-man [defensive] fronts. We have a great quarterback. I think the running game and the passing game complement each other, so it makes my job a lot easier."[227]

After scoring his first-ever NFL touchdown in his *seventh* NFL season, new Patriots running back Rabih Abdullah deserved to celebrate but said, "Dan Klecko opened up a great hole. Every score is a team effort so I am not going to… dance around and try to take the glory."[228]

Success requires everyone playing well together, but failure requires only one person screwing up. As Belichick said of his team's poor punt returns in early 2004: "if you don't handle the ball cleanly you are not going to get very many good returns. …If you don't block well, that is a problem. If you have penalties, that is a problem. I would say everybody is joining in the party."[229] So, every Patriot knows "individual success" is a football oxymoron. Saying that any one player made a play happen is absurd. Every Patriot knows, as safety Rodney Harrison says, that "you are only as good as the other guys on the team."[230]

Because players buy into this "weakest link" philosophy, they also accept its corollary: that they help themselves by helping their teammates. In case they forget momentarily, Bill Belichick never misses an opportunity to point out how winning demands and derives from total team effort. After the Patriots defeated the Tennessee Titans in the 2003 playoffs, for example, Belichick spotlighted the unified effort of defense, offense and special teams that transformed an ugly situation (the Titans' offense with the ball at midfield in a tie game) into the Patriots' game-winning field goal: "That was an example of all of it working together… It wasn't one play. It was a multiple number of plays."[231] The pre-Belichick days when the defensive unit pointed fingers at the offensive unit following losses (or vice-versa) are, mercifully, a distant memory. Now, each unit blames itself for losses and credits other units for victories, just as each Patriot points a finger at himself following an unsuccessful play but deflects praise for his role in a successful play onto his teammates. As defensive lineman Richard Seymour said after Week 1 of 2004, "Hats off to our offense. They really kept us in this ballgame. They did a good job. If it wasn't for the other side of the ball, we wouldn't have won this game."[232] The Patriots are a true team.

Chapter 3

GOOD PLAYERS…
GREAT TEAM

"Let's face it, this isn't Joe Montana with Jerry Rice and John Taylor out there. It's just a tough bunch of guys who step up and make plays."[233]
— *Patriots offensive coordinator Charlie Weis*

"They may not be the most talented at every position, but as a team, they were the most talented. I think that's even more significant. I think they set a great standard. Not only for themselves, but for everyone, what team is about."[234]
— *New York Jets running back Curtis Martin*

On November 22, 2001, *Boston Globe* writer Ron Borges made the seemingly indisputable remark that "this Patriot team isn't going to win two Super Bowls any time soon."[235] Fans, reporters, and most NFL insiders agreed the Patriots "obviously" lacked sufficient talent to win a championship, let alone two. All were stunned when the Patriots became world champions just 73 days later. When the Patriots emerged victorious from a second Super Bowl 728 days after their first, NFL experts knew their "talent" measuring devices were broken, but they were clueless how to recalibrate them. The Patriots obviously possessed "talent" that no one could detect.

The Patriots' roster is full of good-but-not-great players who maximize their collective potential through healthy competition, selfless teamwork, meticulous preparation, mistake avoidance, smart decisions, dedication to organizational success, *etc*. Patriots coaches' performance-enhancing training and brilliant game plans would accomplish nothing without outstanding individual and collective effort within the organizational framework by players possessing solid football abilities. The Patriots' success formula was clear to *ESPN*'s Len Pasquarelli even before the magical 2001 Patriots secured a playoff spot: "[Belichick] has fashioned a roster of modestly talented players into a club that wins by playing physically on both sides of the ball and heeding the details many other teams simply take for granted."[236]

Belichick preached "collective performance" to players in June 2001 by naming thirty first-time Pro Bowl players from the 2000 season and telling his players that "all were on playoff teams in 2000. They didn't make it because every single scheme and game plan revolved around these individuals but because their teams embraced a program, chemistry gained momentum and they won. Almost seven of every 10 Pro Bowlers came off playoff rosters."[237]

Though the Patriots' "talent" level rose impressively from 2001 to 2003, new Patriots were no less tough, prepared, smart, selfless, or football-loving. Such players are "talented" in less visible traits often ignored by NFL observers. A classic example is linebacker Tedy Bruschi. When Belichick and Al Groh convinced then-Patriots head coach Bill Parcells to draft Bruschi late in Round 3 of the 1996 NFL Draft, nine months before the Patriots played the Packers in Super Bowl XXXI, they didn't even know what position Bruschi could play (because Bruschi had been a defensive lineman in college but was too small to be an NFL lineman). But Bruschi had such football passion and productivity (tying the NCAA sack record) that he was catnip to Belichick and Groh. Belichick remembers the draft room discussion: "We're taking him, we're taking a good football player. We don't know what we're going to do with him exactly, but we'll find something."[238] Groh had fallen in love with Bruschi while watching his own son play in a college All-Star game:

> "Everyone from the West team gravitated toward Tedy. They had only been together four or five days, but here was this bunch of All-Stars, looking to this guy as their leader. The second thing was his unbridled enthusiasm for the game. It was hard to miss. He performed in their practice like he was in the middle of a playoff game. ...Anyone who has ever watched Tedy walks away saying, 'There's something about that guy.'"[239]

STAR TEAM LACKS STARS

> "I asked two personnel directors, 'Who would you double-team on the Patriots roster?' After a long pause, both said no one."[240]
> – *Pat Kirwan, NFL.com*

> "It's not about talent, it's about how the team plays. That's the litmus. Let's see how we play. Let's see how we coach. What the team looks like on paper doesn't mean a thing."[241]
> – *Bill Belichick*

After outperforming all 30 or 31[1] other professional football teams twice in three seasons, the New England Patriots are the NFL's best team of the early 21st Century. In 2003, the Patriots not only won the Super Bowl (going 3-0 in the playoffs) but also had an undefeated (4-0) preseason in which they scored twice as many points as they gave up, had the NFL's best regular season record (14-2), and surrendered fewer regular season points than any other team (238, versus a league-wide average of 333.3). The 2003 and 2004 Patriots combined to string together 21 straight wins, the longest-ever NFL winning streak.

The 2003 Patriots beat Miami on a humid 84° day and again on a 28° day following a blizzard that dumped 30 inches (2½ feet) of snow on Foxboro. They beat the Jets at 71° and at 30°. They beat Philadelphia at 82°, yet won four more games in

---

[1]There are now 32 NFL teams, but the Houston Texans weren't yet competing in 2001.

sub-33° temperatures: Dallas (33°), Indianapolis (32°), Jacksonville (25°), and Tennessee (2°; -11° wind chill[242]). They beat the Giants and Browns in the rain. They beat Jacksonville and Indianapolis in the snow. They won on a foggy 35° Monday night in Denver, where it's hard to breathe and the ball carries farther. They beat Houston, Indianapolis, and Carolina in windless, temperature-controlled domed stadiums. No matter the conditions, there was no beating the 2003 Patriots after the first month.

Despite these achievements, experts see few of the league's "best" or "most talented" players on the Patriots' roster. The NFL players, coaches, and fans who vote for the 43-man AFC Pro Bowl team saw only two top players on either the 2001 or 2003 Patriots:

- In 2001, the Patriots triumphed over the AFC's three other conference semifinal teams, each of which had either five Pro Bowlers (Oakland Raiders) or six (Baltimore Ravens; Pittsburgh Steelers). Only two Patriots, Tom Brady and Lawyer Milloy, were voted onto the AFC Pro Bowl team (though Troy Brown and Ty Law were added as injury replacements). Though the Denver Broncos finished 8-8 and missed the playoffs, six Broncos (seven including replacements) made the 2001 Pro Bowl.[243]

- In 2003, the Kansas City Chiefs and Baltimore Ravens each had eight players on the AFC Pro Bowl roster, yet both teams were knocked out of the playoffs in their opening-round games. The Patriots again won the Super Bowl, but only cornerback Ty Law and defensive lineman Richard Seymour were selected for the Pro Bowl (though Willie McGinest was added as an injury replacement).

Bill Belichick couldn't care less. He doesn't believe in "individual achievement" in a football context, let alone care about it: "Our goals this year are about what our team can accomplish this year."[244] And he has convinced his players to focus on collective goals too. In his low-key-but-mesmerizing speech to the team before Super Bowl XXXVIII, Belichick placed the Patriots' first Super Bowl trophy on a table and said, "What this trophy stands for is the team. Not the guy who leads the league in punting. Not the guy with 15 sacks. It's about the team."[245]

UNPRECEDENTED DISRESPECT

The 2001 and 2003 Patriots are the only Super Bowl winners ever to have just two players selected for the Pro Bowl. For each season since the AFL and NFL merged in 1970 (Super Bowl V), I have calculated how many players each Super Bowl participant sent to that season's Pro Bowl. (I ignore the pre-merger seasons because each league had two Pro Bowl rosters.) Perhaps most astonishingly, 33 of the 34 Super Bowl *losers* had more than two Pro Bowl players! Only the 2000 New York Giants, who were crushed by the Baltimore Ravens 34-7 in Super Bowl XXXV, had just two. The disrespect shown to the 2001 and 2003 Patriots players is unprecedented in NFL history:

Season	Super Bowl winner	Pro Bowl players	Super Bowl loser	Pro Bowl players
1970	Baltimore Colts	3	Dallas Cowboys	3
1971	Dallas Cowboys	7	Miami Dolphins	7
1972	Miami Dolphins	9	Washington Redskins	5
1973	Miami Dolphins	11	Minnesota Vikings	7
1974	Pittsburgh Steelers	5	Minnesota Vikings	7
1975	Pittsburgh Steelers	11	Dallas Cowboys	3
1976	Oakland Raiders	6	Minnesota Vikings	8
1977	Dallas Cowboys	7	Denver Broncos	5
1978	Pittsburgh Steelers	10	Dallas Cowboys	9
1979	Pittsburgh Steelers	10	Los Angeles Rams	5
1980	Oakland Raiders	5	Philadelphia Eagles	3
1981	San Francisco 49ers	6	Cincinnati Bengals	5
1982	Washington Redskins	4	Miami Dolphins	4
1983	Los Angeles Raiders	8	Washington Redskins	6
1984	San Francisco 49ers	10	Miami Dolphins	7
1985	Chicago Bears	9	New England Patriots	8
1986	New York Giants	7	Denver Broncos	6
1987	Washington Redskins	3	Denver Broncos	3
1988	San Francisco 49ers	5	Cincinnati Bengals	9
1989	San Francisco 49ers	6	Denver Broncos	4
1990	New York Giants	6	Buffalo Bills	10
1991	Washington Redskins	7	Buffalo Bills	8
1992	Dallas Cowboys	6	Buffalo Bills	11
1993	Dallas Cowboys	11	Buffalo Bills	7
1994	San Francisco 49ers	10	San Diego Chargers	3
1995	Dallas Cowboys	9	Pittsburgh Steelers	6
1996	Green Bay Packers	5	New England Patriots	6
1997	Denver Broncos	5	Green Bay Packers	7
1998	Denver Broncos	9	Atlanta Falcons	5
1999	St. Louis Rams	6	Tennessee Titans	4
2000	Baltimore Ravens	5	New York Giants	2
2001	**New England Patriots**	2	St. Louis Rams	5
2002	Tampa Bay Buccaneers	5	Oakland Raiders	5
2003	**New England Patriots**	2	Carolina Panthers	3
Average	Excluding 2001 & 2003	7.06	All Years	5.76

Note: Pro Bowl rosters exclude injury replacement players. Source (1997-2003): www.supernfl.com/ProBowl.html
Source (1996 and earlier): www.pro-football-reference.com/misc/pbindex.htm

Since Super Bowl V, the average Super Bowl loser has had 5.76 Pro Bowlers, and the average winner (excluding Belichick's two Patriots teams) has had 7.06 Pro Bowlers. Even the Patriots' two Super Bowl-losing teams had many more Pro Bowlers (eight in 1985; six in 1996). The NFL players, coaches and fans who vote for the Pro Bowl have sent a clear message: the Patriots may be a great team, but they're not a collection of great individual talent. The Patriots are winning without stars, something no other champion has ever done.

Patriots players have admitted as much. Basking in the glory of his first Super Bowl win, Patriots linebacker Mike Vrabel said, "On paper you may not look as talented or as fast or as strong as your opponent, but if you get guys to buy into a system and fight to the bitter end, you can accomplish incredible things."[246]

In mid-December 2003, Patriots players and coaches answered repeated media questions concerning Pro Bowl voting by saying they weren't concerned, both because they were completely focused on team success and because team success leads to personal recognition. Bill Belichick: "I can tell you where [Pro Bowl] players come from. The teams that are winning. If you want to be in the Pro Bowl, winning will get you there quicker than anything else."[247] Middle linebacker Tedy Bruschi: "Individual accolades come with team success, and that's all I focus on." [248] Veteran fullback Larry Centers: "As you get older, you realize individual honors come as a result of team play. Teams that play well send more guys to the Pro Bowl." [249]

Historically, winning teams have indeed placed more players on Pro Bowl rosters. Belichick's Patriots are the two glaring anomalies. An argument can be made that the 14-5 (11-5 in the regular season) Patriots of 2001 needed more luck than the average Super Bowl champion and did not "deserve" the typical 7.06 Pro Bowl berths. Since the 1980 Oakland Raiders won the Super Bowl with a 14-5 (11-5 regular season) record, only the 13-6 (10-6 regular season) 1988 San Francisco 49ers have won the Super Bowl with five or more losses. But even these "weak" Super Bowl champions each had five Pro Bowlers.

Setting aside 2001, the 17-2 Patriots of 2003 were as dominant as any team since the 18-1 1985 Chicago Bears (9 Pro Bowlers). Of the seventeen most recent Super Bowl victors, only the 1989 San Francisco 49ers (6 Pro Bowlers), 1991 Washington Redskins (7 Pro Bowlers), and 1998 Denver Broncos (9 Pro Bowlers) have gone 17-2, and no team has done better. To have only two Pro Bowlers after such a dominating season is completely without parallel. In the chart below, the 2001 and 2003 Patriots are the two dots with just two Pro Bowl players. The trend line predicts that the 2001 Patriots "should" have had at least five Pro Bowl players and the 2003 Patriots "should" have had at least seven. Excluding the two Patriots Super Bowl victories, the trendline is higher, predicting the 2001 Patriots "should" have had six Pro Bowlers and the 2003 Patriots "should" have had nearly eight.

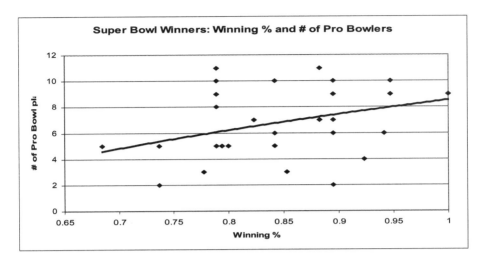

YOU CAN'T MAKE SOMETHING OUT OF NOTHING

"The good people of New England have somehow come to the conclusion that, unlike all other successful teams in the history of sports, theirs is one that wins consistently because its coaches regularly outwork and outthink the opposition while the players are little more than interchangeable parts. ...This is a grand myth that has taken on a life of its own in these parts."[250]
– Ron Borges, Boston Globe

"[Having better players] allows you to do more on offense. While I think our coaching staff is good, the difference is the level of ability of the players–both physically and mentally. By having guys who can do a lot of thinking, it allows you to do a lot of things."[251]
– Patriots offensive coordinator Charlie Weis

Many have claimed, falsely I believe, that Bill Belichick's coaching staff has achieved great performance with sub-par talent. Former New Orleans Saints GM Randy Mueller says, "I call the role players on [the Patriots and Panthers] 'get-by guys.'"[252] The 2001 Patriots overachieved due to great coaching, but the players' toughness, smarts, teamwork, and work ethic were also essential elements of that team's success. Such purported "intangibles" are overlooked by those who glorify physical characteristics but deserve to be valued as dimensions of football "talent." Belichick and Pioli used their comprehensive definition of "talent" to assemble a 2001 Patriots team that had more talent than most outsiders believed. Those who focus on a narrow, primarily physical, definition of "talent" are often surprised when "underachieving" players fail to live up to their "potential." Belichick's 2001 Patriots accomplished the opposite: startling everyone with players who "overachieved" and surpassed their "potential."

In 1998, NFL personnel analyst extraordinaire Joel Buchsbaum named twenty-six players "achievers," guys who "Pushing themselves to the limit... always get the most out of their ability."[253] These are the NFL's Larry Birds, guys whose obsessive, tenacious, analytical approach to football makes them much better players than seems possible, given their size and speed. Buchsbaum's impressive list included, for example, the undrafted Wayne Chrebet, "a real student of game who gets separation from much more talented defensive backs. In his first three years in the NFL, he had 208 catches, which is even more than [Jerry] Rice had in his first three seasons."[254] You can't find a single Patriot on Buchsbaum's 1998 list. You certainly could, however, find many worthy candidates on Bill Belichick's Patriots teams. Tom Brady would nominate Rodney Harrison, whose professionalism and passion for winning were so obvious after he joined the Patriots in 2003 that his new teammates instantly voted him a team captain:

> "We made him a captain after being here about 10 minutes. He has a lot of heart. To see him get a Super Bowl ring is special. Hopefully, he gets his arm [that he broke late in the Super Bowl] better so he can carry that ring around."[255]

With players like Harrison, the 2003 Patriots continued to "overachieve" but with even more "talent" than in 2001. The 2003 Patriots were not a collection of exceptionally talented players, but they certainly were an exceptional collection of talented players. Patriots VP of player personnel Scott Pioli put it this way:

> "Calling these guys mid-level is a disservice to them... Mike Vrabel, David Patten, Larry Izzo and others. Those are just guys who weren't in the right situation. You can't tell me that just because they weren't playing that much previously that they weren't good players."[256]

While it's true that the Patriots have no perennial Pro Bowlers, twelve of the 2003 Patriots played well enough at some point during their career to be considered among the best at their position. Though only Ty Law and Richard Seymour were chosen for the 2003 Pro Bowl team, seven other 2003 Patriots have been honored with at least one Pro Bowl selection: Tom Brady, Larry Centers, Rodney Harrison, Larry Izzo, Willie ("Big Mac") McGinest, Adam Vinatieri, and Ted Washington. Also, Damien Woody (2002) and Troy Brown (2001) played in Pro Bowls as injury replacements, and Brown was Pro Bowl-deserving in 2001: "One of the biggest [Pro Bowl snubs] occurred in 2001, when Troy Brown caught 101 passes for 1,152 yards and was the AFC's leading punt returner and didn't make it."[257]

Several Patriots played almost well enough in 2003 to make the Pro Bowl:

· Linebacker *Tedy Bruschi* was named a Pro Bowl alternate in 2003. Many New Englanders were bitter that Bruschi was only an alternate, but a poll of 22 NFL personnel directors rated Bruschi the NFL's seventh best inside linebacker.[258] #7 is indeed impressive but not quite Pro Bowl quality.

- Safety *Rodney Harrison*, with his three interceptions and 140 tackles, deserved to play in the 2003 Pro Bowl but was also an alternate. Harrison finished second on fans' ballots in 2003 but was snubbed by coaches and players for his pre-Patriots cheap shot reputation.

- Cornerback *Tyrone Poole* intercepted six passes and forced three fumbles in 2003. Safety Rodney Harrison says Poole "deserves to go... He's been a lockdown corner. Name one other corner that's played better than Ty Poole."[259]

- Guard *Joe Andruzzi* also finished second on fans' 2003 ballots.

Bottom line: Belichick's players are tenacious and scrappy, but they're not crappy. The 2003 Patriots had few great players but many very good ones:

Player	Position	Pro Bowl season(s)
Tom Brady	QB	2001
Tedy Bruschi	LB	2003 (alternate–did not play)
Troy Brown	WR	2001 (injury replacement)
Larry Centers	FB	2001
Rodney Harrison	S	1998, 2001, 2003 (alternate–did not play)
Larry Izzo	Special teams	2000, 2002
Ty Law	CB	1998, 2001 (injury replacement), 2002, 2003
Willie McGinest	DL	1995 (alternate–did not play), 1996, 2003 (injury replacement)
Richard Seymour	DL	2002, 2003
Adam Vinatieri	K	2002
Ted Washington	DL	1997, 1998, 2000
Damien Woody	OL	2002 (injury replacement)

Sources: 1996: www.infoplease.com/ipsa/A0104141.html, 1997: www.infoplease.com/ipsa/A0302523.html, 1998: www.infoplease.com/ipsa/A0771006.html, 1999: www.infoplease.com/ipsa/A0801193.html, 2000: www.infoplease.com/ipsa/A0881429.html, 2001: http://espn.go.com/nfl/s/afcprobowl01.html, 2002: www.nfl.com/probowl/2003/roster_afc.html

This conclusion is supported by one unnamed NFL team that rates every NFL player. Their analysis indicates the Patriots have only two of the NFL's 60 premier players (Tom Brady and Richard Seymour) but lead the league in second-tier talent.[260]

As former General Electric CEO Jack Welch said in refuting the notion that Belichick was manufacturing Super Bowls with inferior players, "I don't think anyone can take 6-footers and make them 6 feet 8."[261] Championship teams, whether the Patriots, the 2004 Detroit Pistons, or the 1980 Olympic hockey team, require players with solid athletic and mental potential. But potential and performance are totally different things, especially in a true team sport like football. Getting a bunch of solid-but-individually-unspectacular players to work together cohesively gives you a better chance to win football games than adding a handful of dominating players to a poorly-coordinated, poorly-motivated team. After the Patriots' February 2002 Super Bowl victory, *Sports Illustrated*'s Peter King declared coaching and coordination the keys to victory in the NFL: "Every team has enough talent. It's how the talent is coached and orchestrated, and how the coaches make the talent 10 percent better than they'd be somewhere else. Coaching in the NFL means more than in any other sport, ever."[262] Knowing this, Belichick and Pioli have stocked recent Patriots rosters with solid, motivated players and coached the heck out of them.

RISING REPUTATIONS

"I've never seen a coach go out there and make interceptions or get a sack. ...[W]hen you say 'no stars,' it depends on the eye that's looking at them."[263]
 – Patriots defensive lineman Richard Seymour

Patriots players' reputations have been rising. In 2004, *Pro Football Weekly* rated three Patriots among the league's top 34 players: Tom Brady (#13), Ty Law (#29) and Richard Seymour (#34).[264] In 2001, no one disputed Packers GM Ron Wolf's characterization of the Patriots as a "waiver wire team." By 2004, Wolf himself was raving about the greatness of Tom Brady (who had been a 4th-string quarterback in 2000 before becoming the starter early in 2001):

"The guy that makes [the Patriots] go is Brady. He wins. He's the best quarterback in the NFL. Better than all of them. He's beaten them all. That's the reason they win, because of Tom Brady. Someone has to be the best, and he's the best at what he does at the position that is most important to have someone who is the best at what he does."[265]

NFL players are also impressed with Brady, but only 14% rate him the best in the league, behind Peyton Manning (34%) and Brett Favre (23%) and slightly ahead of Steve McNair (12%) and Michael Vick (8%).[266]

L.A. Times journalist Bob Oates, who has covered every Super Bowl, insisted on Brady's greatness after his first Super Bowl victory. To my knowledge, Oates is the only reporter who did not credit Belichick's coaching for the Patriots' 2001 Super Bowl season. Oates actually criticized Belichick for underutilizing Brady, like someone who buys a Ferrari but drives it only in second gear. Oates said that the 2001 NFL season's greatest quarterback performance was Brady's completing 18 of his final 19 passes to beat the Oakland Raiders in the "Snow Bowl" playoff game. Oates argued the Patriots would have trounced the St. Louis Rams if Belichick had been smart enough to pass more aggressively:

"By waiting to green-light Brady until only 90 seconds remained, Belichick recklessly bet the game and season on the premise that he could win a Super Bowl with his defensive team–a group that failed him [late in the game]–and with a running game on offense. That group failed him too. ...Those weren't wild, fluky passes Brady launched while throwing on every down as time ran out on Belichick in the Super Bowl. Each of the five winning passes was well-calculated and well-thrown by a young quarterback playing with the poise of a 10-year veteran."[267]

Belichick and Weis may have secretly agreed with Oates. In 2002, Brady threw 45.5% more passes than in 2001... though he gained only 32.4% more yards. Where the 2001 Patriots underutilized Brady (413 attempts), in 2002, they overused him (601 attempts). In 2003, like Goldilocks, they got the balance just right (527 attempts).

Hard work and stellar results have steadily bolstered Patriots players' reputations the old fashioned way. Players have earned their reputations on the field, not by being drafted high, pulling attention-grabbing stunts, mouthing off, signing fat contracts, or making mega-million dollar endorsement deals. Tennessee Titans offensive coordinator Mike Heimerdinger, who twice (once in the regular season and once in the playoffs) failed to beat the 2003 Patriots, says the Patriots defense is no longer composed of generic, nameless, Brand X players: "The only guy people might not know is (Eugene) Wilson and he's playing fantastic; he can cover ground. But other than him, everybody knows the corners, the linebackers and the guys up front."[268]

BETTER THAN THEIR STATS

Many Patriots players are better than their statistics suggest. Individual Patriot players face an almost impossible task in trying to rack up the kind of eye-popping statistics that grab the attention of Pro Bowl voters because the Patriots freely and frequently substitute players, consciously and deliberately spread the ball around on offense, and unpredictably, almost randomly, blitz their largely interchangeable defensive players. Where some teams implement a "star system" designed to isolate their star one-on-one, the Patriots use an "anti-star system" that effectively prevents any non-quarterback from becoming a star. For example, in 2003, running back Kevin Faulk rushed 178 times, and Antowain Smith rushed 182 times.

The few Patriots who consistently got the ball in 2003 posted impressive numbers: Tom Brady, who throws every pass, was the NFL's 10th-rated passer; Adam Vinatieri, who kicks every extra point and field goal, was the 10th-highest scoring kicker; Bethel Johnson, who runs back many kickoffs, was the NFL's 2nd-rated kickoff returner; and Troy Brown, who returns many punts, was the 13th-rated punt returner.[269] Otherwise, few Patriots rank high in the NFL's individual statistical categories:

Category	Highest-ranked Patriot	Rank in NFL
Rushing yards	Antowain Smith	#30
Total tackles	Tedy Bruschi	#15
Receptions	NO PATRIOT ON LIST	N/A
Receiving yards	NO PATRIOT ON LIST	N/A
Total touchdowns	NO PATRIOT ON LIST	N/A
Receiving touchdowns	David Givens	#23 (tie)
Rushing touchdowns	Mike Cloud	#24 (tie)
Sacks	Mike Vrabel	#16 (tie)

Receptions, Tight end	Daniel Graham	#16
Receptions, Wide receiver	Deion Branch	#32
Interceptions	Tyrone Poole & Ty Law	#7 (ten-way tie)
Linebacker: Assists	Tedy Bruschi	#4
Linebacker: Tackles + assists	Tedy Bruschi	#15
Linebacker: Tackles	Tedy Bruschi	#27 (three-way tie)
Linebacker: Solo tackles	Roman Phifer	#64 (two-way tie)
Defensive line: Assists	Richard Seymour	#2 (three-way tie)
Defensive line: Tackles + assists	Richard Seymour	#19 (six-way tie)
Defensive line: Tackles	Richard Seymour	#48 (seven-way tie)
Defensive line: Solo tackles	Richard Seymour	#72 (nine-way tie)

Source: *NFL.com*, "NFL Stats: 2003 Regular Season," www.nfl.com/stats/2003/regular.

A common pattern is several Patriots in the solid-but-not-great range of a statistical category. For example, the Patriots had no Tory Holt, Randy Moss or Anquan Boldin, each of whom caught over 100 passes in 2003. Deion Branch caught 57, Troy Brown 40, and David Givens 34. Throwing the ball to different receivers keeps defenses guessing, and blitzing different defenders keeps offenses guessing.

Another telling pattern is that Patriots players rank low on solo tackles and high on assists. The Patriots play as a team, and this shows in their stats: they tackle as a team. Tedy Bruschi's 37 solo tackles put him in a three-way tie for 76th among NFL linebackers, but his 79 "combined tackles" (*i.e.*, tackles + assists) ranks 15th because his 52 assists is 4th-best among linebackers. Richard Seymour's 22 solo tackles put him in a nine-way tie for 72nd among defensive linemen, but his 57 "combined tackles" ranks 23rd because his 23 assists place him in a three-way tie for 2nd-place among defensive linemen. Tackling an NFL running back is easier with two tacklers.

Conspiracy theorists suggest financial motives for the Patriots' star-less system: "A few players… believe the coaches actually take individual statistics into account when formulating game plans"[270] because suppressing player stats presumably makes players cheaper to re-sign. Former Patriots safety Tebucky Jones, for example, believes Patriots coaches had him split playing time with Victor Green in 2002 "so when it comes to contract time, they can say 'You're not a full-time player.'"[271]

Whether intentional or a side effect, involving every player and spreading the ball around benefit the Patriots' salary cap by holding down salaries during contract renegotiations. Though individual players prefer higher pay, players also benefit because paying below-market-rate salaries enables the Patriots to field above-average players, something important to players who value playing for a winner.

CONSTANTLY UPGRADING PERSONNEL

The Patriots upgraded their personnel substantially between 2001 and 2003. The 2001 Patriots admittedly possessed less "talent" than the average Super Bowl winner, but the 2003 Patriots roster was very solid. Though remarkably similar in character, the 2001 and 2003 teams were strikingly different in personnel. Ten of the 22 Super Bowl XXXVIII starters were not Patriots during Super Bowl XXXVI, and at least four positions were clearly upgraded while none was clearly downgraded:[272]

S.B. XXXVI starter	S.B. XXXVIII starter	Position	Change
Mike Compton	Russ Hochstein	Guard	
Damien Woody	Dan Koppen	Center	
Greg Randall	Tom Ashworth	Offensive tackle	Upgrade?
Jermaine Wiggins	Daniel Graham	Tight end	Upgrade
David Patten	Deion Branch	Wide receiver	Upgrade
Marc Edwards	Larry Centers	Fullback	Upgrade
Brandon Mitchell	Ted Washington	Defensive tackle	Upgrade
Otis Smith	Tyrone Poole	Cornerback	
Lawyer Milloy	Rodney Harrison	Safety	Upgrade?
Tebucky Jones	Eugene Wilson	Safety	Upgrade?

As the following chart demonstrates, non-starting personnel turned over even more substantially. Of the 2003 Patriots' 23 non-starting Super Bowl participants, 15 were not on the 2001 team.[273] Of the eight active-roster Patriots inactivated for Super Bowl XXXVIII (because teams can activate only 45 of their 53 players for any particular game), six weren't on the 2001 team.[274] So, 31 of the 53 Patriots (58.5%) were added in the two years following Super Bowl XXXVI. Additionally, 11 of the 14 players on injured reserve, the physically unable to play (PUP) list, or the non-football injury list during Super Bowl XXXVIII were not with the team in 2001.[275] 42 of the 67 Patriots (63%) joined the team between the two Super Bowl victories:

	Super Bowl XXXVIII Patriots who joined after Super Bowls XXXVI	% who joined Patriots between Super Bowls XXXVI and XXXVII
Super Bowl starters	10 of 22	45.45%
Non-starting Super Bowl participants	15 of 23	65.22%
Active roster, inactive for Super Bowl	6 of 8	75.00%
Injured reserve, physically unable to play, or non-football injury	11 of 14	78.57%
TOTAL	42 of 67	62.69%

Only twenty Patriots played in both Super Bowls,[276] and five of these (Bobby Hamilton, Antowain Smith, Ken Walter, Matt Chatham, and Je'Rod Cherry) were not on the Patriots' 2004 opening day 53-man roster.[277]

Also significant is the improvement (from 2001 to 2003) of the twenty players who played in both Super Bowls. Two seasons of training in the Patriots' system improved players like Matt Light, Richard Seymour, Mike Vrabel, Tom Brady, Bobby Hamilton, and Tedy Bruschi. Belichick says of Brady: "Without a doubt, he has improved each and every year. It's not like he had it all down after year two."[278] In short, the Patriots substantially upgraded their talent between 2001 and 2003.

THE PATRIOTS' "SECRET SAUCE"

When Ron Wolf called the 2001 Patriots a "waiver wire team," was he: 1) Disparaging players; 2) Complimenting the coaches for maximizing the potential of players overlooked by other teams; or, 3) Complimenting players for squeezing every ounce of performance out of whatever raw potential they possessed? All three possibilities contain a kernel of truth.

Dr. Michael Roberto, Harvard Business School professor of strategy and management, argues that the Patriots' talent isn't special and that the team's magic derives entirely from brilliant coaching: "Under Belichick, the system is the star. If you pulled some of these guys out and put them on another team it is not clear they would do as well."[279] I argued above that the Patriots have more talent than many believe, thanks to the team's tremendous depth in good-but-not-great talent. And Patriots players partially create "the system," especially the great organizational culture. Nevertheless, I agree with Professor Roberto that the Patriots' personnel is not inherently better than other teams'. What Patriots players are exceptionally good at is playing Bill Belichick-style football. Many outstanding Patriots (like linebacker Mike Vrabel, defensive lineman Bobby Hamilton, and wide receiver David Patten) previously played on other NFL teams that had little or no use for them. Many Patriots players are extremely productive within the Patriots system but less productive elsewhere. Who cares whether this makes them "talented" or not?

The Patriots get great collective performance from good players because: 1) Patriots players are solid, both physically and mentally; 2) Belichick's schemes, training, and coaching are superb; and, 3) Patriots players and Belichick's system are perfectly matched. All three elements are essential to the team's success, but many overlook the importance of synergy between the Belichick system and Belichick-type players. Belichick's Browns used much the same system but with disappointing results because Browns players weren't as well-suited to Belichick's system.

Smart coaches and coachable players

In football, effort matters. Stamina matters. Avoiding stupid penalties, fumbles, and interceptions matters. Acting in concert with one's teammates matters. Out-thinking one's opponent by anticipating and observing their behavior and reacting appropriately matters. Getting out of bounds to stop the clock when losing late in a game, or staying in bounds to keep the clock running when leading, matters. Belichick says, "When you get to the end of the game, a gain of ten yards might be the worst thing in the world if you stay in bounds and keep the clock running."[280] In these and many other unglamorous areas, Patriots players excel through a combination of smart coaching and smart, coachable, selfless players.

Another example is smartly dropping an interception on 4th-down rather than grabbing it to pad one's stats. It's foolish to intercept a long pass on 4th-down. Unless you can run the ball back a long distance, it's smarter to knock the ball down so your offense takes possession at the original line of scrimmage. Nevertheless, you often see NFL players intercept such passes because they are poorly coached, oblivious to the game situation, or more concerned about padding their stats than helping their team. I can't recall ever seeing a Belichick-coached Patriot intercept a ball on 4th-down unless he was able to run it back a long distance.

Had Patriots running back J.R. Redmond not gotten out of bounds on the Patriots' game-winning drive of Super Bowl XXXVI, the Patriots might have lost because "if he had gotten tackled inbounds we would have kneeled on it and gone into overtime. He could have been tackled in bounds, but he made the play."[281] Belichick's obsessive concern with such "details" is obvious from the praise he heaps on quarterback Tom Brady. Belichick emphasizes the way Brady plays the game from the neck up. Brady's "very smart, has good game-management skills. He's instinctively a good player–knows when to throw the ball away, stop the clock, when to go out of bounds, when to audible or when there is too much crowd noise to audible."[282] Belichick also praises Brady for "spreading the ball around, taking advantage of weaknesses in the defense, and being able to recognize times to audible and change plays."[283] If Brady were obsessed with his stats, getting into Pro Bowls, and winning MVP awards, he wouldn't want to throw a 60-yard Hail Mary pass into a crowd of players in the end zone, as he did as time expired on the first half of the 2004 Patriots-Cardinals game. As former Patriots quarterback Steve Grogan said:

> "If they took out the Hail Mary passes that were intercepted I would have finished with more touchdown passes than interceptions! It just kills you as a quarterback to do that because you know the odds are in the defense's favor of the ball being intercepted."[284]

But Brady cares only that his team benefits because it's a touchdown if a Patriot catches it but no harm (except to Brady's stats) if a Cardinal catches it, as happened that day.

The world's most brilliant coach would fail without players willing and able to learn from him. As excellent as Patriots coaches are, coaches don't make tackles or intercept passes or pounce on loose balls. Players play. That's why they're called "players." Belichick pointed this out to defuse media hype before the Patriots played the Dallas Cowboys, coached by Belichick's former boss, Bill Parcells: "Someone is going to have to make some blocks out there and someone is going to have to make some tackles. It's not going to be me, and it's not going to be Bill."[285] Patriots safety Rodney Harrison says, accurately, "Bill gives us advantages and favorable matchups, but the key is players winning their battles"[286] and "The system is great, but the system is nothing without the players. The system only works if you have the players out there making plays."[287] Both the system and the players deserve credit. Success requires both. And success requires that players' strengths match coaches' plans.

Belichick's system relies heavily on smart, adaptable players. The intellectually-rigorous, team-centric Patriots system would flop without smart, selfless, passionate players. Belichick's Browns employed a similar system but played only one playoff game in five seasons because many players weren't coachable, passionate, or suited to Belichick's system. The Patriots have acquired many superb players who previously achieved little on other teams that did not utilize those players' intelligence and adaptability. Belichick's staff relentlessly squeezes maximal performance from players whose "excellence" is defined by their heads and hearts as much as their arms and legs.

Patriots coaches and players have helped each other achieve greatness. Though Tom Brady was a 6th round draft pick (the 199th player drafted in the 2000 NFL Draft), earned the league-mandated minimum salary of $298,000 in his first year as starter (versus $12 million for his backup Drew Bledsoe),[288] and was called by *ESPN* football analyst Len Pasquarelli "the modestly talented Brady"[289] even after winning his first Super Bowl MVP award, Tom Brady is one heck of a football player, as *Sports Illustrated*'s Peter King explains:

> "Brady is 26 years old. He is 6-0 in playoff games, 26-4 in games played in November or later, 7-0 in overtime games, 2-0 in Super Bowls, two-for-two in Super Bowl MVPs. If you seriously think it's premature to compare him to Joe Montana, you are high."[290]

Of course, great coaching and a great system helped make Brady the second coming of Joe Montana, and all the statistics King cites are team statistics. However, Brady clearly possesses traits (intelligence, heart, competitiveness, charisma, a disarming/self-deprecating sense of humor, *etc.*) of great value, especially in Belichick's system. Brady's career passer rating (85.9) ranks eleventh all-time,[291] even as he continues to learn and improve and despite separating his arm twice in 2002 and playing in pain throughout 2003 because he required arthroscopic surgery.[292]

Arguing whether Patriots players or coaches deserve more credit is like debating about chickens and eggs. You must credit the Patriots for seeing in part-time Michigan quarterback Tom Brady potential that other teams missed. Says Scott Pioli, VP of player personnel:

> "We weren't necessarily looking for a quarterback in that draft but we had separated Tommy from a lot of other people because from a makeup

standpoint he fit a lot of the things that we believe in this organization. The things that people refer to as intangibles, we do not see as intangible at all. A player's makeup, his character, his integrity, his leadership... are very tangible. And they have a say in how we try to build our football team."[293]

You must also credit the coaching staff for developing Tom Brady. Would Tom Brady *be* Tom Brady today if he had been drafted by, say, the Arizona Cardinals? Very doubtful. Before Brett Favre was traded to Green Bay, where he blossomed into one of the NFL's all-time greatest quarterbacks, he warmed the Atlanta Falcons' bench, was called "a car wreck" by his coach (Jerry Glanville), and tossed no completions, three incompletions, and two interceptions when he finally got off the bench. As Tampa Bay's quarterback, Steve Young completed just 53.3% of his passes and threw 11 touchdowns and 21 interceptions; in San Francisco, Young completed 65.8% and threw 221 touchdowns against only 86 interceptions. As former NFL quarterback Jim Harbaugh notes, "The quarterback can be skewed by what the talent is around him. You see a lot of Heisman Trophy winners that aren't great pros for that reason."[294] Coaching plays a giant role in a young quarterback's development, as Brady is the first to admit: "I am the recipient of a very good team and I acknowledge the fact that we wouldn't have been successful the last couple of years if we didn't have a defense or a coaching staff or a group of guys on offense that have played as well as they have."[295] As I neared completion of this book, I discovered that Brady himself answered my exact question:

> "I'm the beneficiary of a lot of stars aligning just right. ...I know how fortunate I am. If I get drafted by the Arizona Cardinals, who knows what would have happened to me. Who knows what kind of career I'd be having. What the Patriots ask me to do is contribute, not be an all-star for 75 plays a game. They ask me to be a leader, to make the throws I can make."[296]

But Tom Brady is no lump of clay passively molded by Belichick and offensive coordinator Charlie Weis. Would Bill Belichick's name be uttered in the same sentence as "Vince Lombardi" or "Hall of Fame" if he hadn't drafted Tom Brady? Even Belichick implies it wouldn't: "Tom's got to be mentioned among the best [quarterbacks of all time]. You can't deny his production. Tom's a winner. He does a great job managing the game and he makes big plays."[297]

The Patriots' 17 coaches and 53 players complement one another. The way Belichick was pilloried by Browns fans and unceremoniously expelled from Art Modell's franchise proves he is not so brilliant that he can coach any random bunch of NFL players to a Super Bowl title. Belichick requires players willing to buy into his team-first, blue-collar philosophy and smart enough to grasp his complex schemes. It took years before Browns players started to "get it," but Belichick's Patriots are solid NFL players who buy into Belichick's mentality, embrace their coaches' advice, and enthusiastically push themselves extraordinarily hard.

In August 2001, *ESPN*'s Chris Mortensen made an insightful comment: "I wonder whether Belichick is equipped to deal with the Terry Glenns of the world. They're out there. It's part of the culture that any coach inherits."[298] Belichick *cannot* win with such players. But Mortensen failed to imagine, perhaps because no NFL coach had ever done it so aggressively, that Belichick was systematically purging his team of self-absorbed players. Terry Glenn spent 2001 in Belichick's dog house.

Belichick inherited a "me" culture and transformed it into a "we" culture. Addition by subtraction. The Patriots dumped players who didn't match Belichick's blueprint (whether because they were bad apples, lazy, overpaid, or possessed skills poorly suited to Belichick's style of football) and brought in team players to create a healthy team chemistry, even at the expense of overall "talent." As Patriots assistant coach Pepper Johnson explained, "When we picked the [2001] team's final roster… we looked for guys we all felt comfortable dealing with as coaches for the entire season. No assholes allowed."[299] That strategy paid rapid dividends. Immediately following the Patriots' first Super Bowl victory, linebacker Roman Phifer said, "Part of what made this team a champion was the chemistry."[300] Belichick's Patriots place enormous emphasis on character in all their personnel decisions:

> "We personally interview prospective players now, and it really doesn't matter how much talent each one has. If we don't feel he can be one of our guys, a guy who can fit in with our overall concept, we won't sign him."[301]

Coordination: 1+1 = 3

Football is not a one-on-one sport. It is an eleven-on-eleven sport. The Patriots succeed in part because their system maximizes players' potential by getting players to play smarter, work together, and prepare more intensely.

The individual players on the 2004 U.S. Olympic Basketball Team were "better" than virtually everyone on the teams the U.S. lost to. But the U.S. lacked outside shooters, so they could not counter opponents' strategy of clogging the middle and daring the U.S. to shoot from outside. "All Star" teams often lose to "lesser" but more cohesive teams whose players possess complementary skills and coordinate their play more effectively.

The Patriots' ascendence proves that enlightened leaders can foster an environment that helps good employees produce great results. A well-managed company can dominate its industry without superstars. The Patriots demonstrate that executives and managers can foster superior employee performance by challenging employees to succeed, encouraging them to work together, directing their efforts in fruitful directions, building an organization employees are proud to belong to, *etc*. Most successful firms, like Hewlett-Packard in its heyday, hire good people and create a sense of pride and togetherness, as the Patriots have. As Northeastern University business professor Leonard Glick wrote:

"So, what is it, exactly, that makes [the Patriots] so good? The answer is rooted in their organizational practices. Don't yawn. Over the past two decades, much has been learned about what makes some organizations more effective than others. As a business professor who teaches these strategies, I'm particularly compelled by three core Patriots practices: staffing, leadership and learning."[302]

Boston College also recognized that the Patriots are a stellar organization and invited "Bill Belichick [to] speak about, obviously, football, and then combine that with leadership and management."[303]

The Patriots don't have the flashiest players, but they find a way to defeat most every opponent because they have coachable players and great coaches. The Patriots show how ordinary people can achieve extraordinary results by collaborating harmoniously and selflessly toward organizational objectives. Egypt's pyramids prove this same point (though Patriots players sacrifice for their team voluntarily).

Building an unselfish organizational culture is a tremendous challenge. Bill Belichick sold every Patriot on his "team first" philosophy by jettisoning talented players who didn't buy in (like unreliable wide receiver Terry Glenn and veteran offensive lineman Bruce Armstrong who had lost the will to lead and the passion required to win) and bringing in unheralded players possessing "team first" attitudes. Players' willingness to check their egos at the door and work with great intensity also derives from their professional respect for Bill Belichick, who always leads by example. Belichick expects players to strive relentlessly toward maximal team performance. Doing so requires hard work and sacrifice, but players respond enthusiastically because Belichick himself is boring, driven, detail-oriented, and so completely focused on winning and so oblivious to personal glory that his disregard for the Cleveland media as Browns head coach in the early '90s made him the media's punching bag. Belichick is the opposite of the flamboyant, ego-driven, limelight-grabbing coach. Early in his coaching days at Cleveland, Belichick sounded like Rhett Butler: "I don't give a damn what the fans think."[304] His rhetoric has softened, but not his intensity. Belichick's "team first" mantra resonates with players because they see him striving obsessively for team success.

Chapter 4

TWO SUPER BOWL VICTORIES IN THREE SEASONS

"We better start learning from [the Patriots] because they'll beat everybody forever. ...They've done a great job of building the roster. They've done a great job convincing all the players on the roster of their importance and when guys have a chance to step in play, they produce. That's where we're all trying to get to, but they've just done it a lot better than the rest of us."[305]
– Buffalo Bills general manager Tom Donahoe

This chapter summarizes the Patriots' 2001, 2002, and 2003 seasons. (Volume 2 will analyze the 2004 season.) To understand why general managers like Buffalo's Tom Donahoe and the New York Giants' Ernie Accorsi (who says "They've made tremendously sound [personnel] judgments and they've coached the heck out of them"[306]) so fear the Patriots, we need to appreciate the magnitude of the team's accomplishments.

2001

"We've got a whole team full of underdogs, and now we're the top dogs."[307]
– Tom Brady, after winning Super Bowl XXXVI

"[Super Bowl XXXVI] was an extraordinary demonstration of the power of 'team,' because there is no way the Patriots should be this good. They just believe they are, and for them, that has been enough."[308]
– Paul Attner, The Sporting News

As the 2001 NFL season kicked off, the New England Patriots were coming off a 5-11 season and considered 75-1 shots to win Super Bowl XXXVI.[309] They were a "dead-end bunch of players–waiver-wire alumni, discards, has-beens and wannabes."[310] The team lost three of its first four games, but by December 2001, *Boston Globe* sportswriter Ron Borges was writing that "Bill Belichick [should be] AFC Coach of the Year [because] no coach in pro football has done so much with so little this season."[311] Buffalo Bills general manager Tom Donahoe concurred: "I don't even know how you could consider anyone else as Coach of the Year. What Bill has done there is pretty incredible, really... [H]e's taken a relatively average team, and gotten everyone to play hard. That's a lot easier said than done in this league."[312]

"Relatively average team" was an overstatement. The Patriots' $49.6 million payroll was second-lowest in the NFL and $14 million below the league average.[313] After spending $85 million, nearly twice as much, the Denver Broncos finished 8-8 and didn't even make the playoffs. Bill Belichick wasn't just winning… he was winning with both hands tied behind his back!

Making the playoffs was but the beginning of the 2001 Patriots' Cinderella season. Oblivious to the accolades, the Patriots hadn't impressed themselves by more than doubling their win total from the previous season: "We're headed in a positive direction, [but] we haven't won a damn thing yet. That's the bottom line."[314]

The "Snow Bowl" / "Tuck Rule" Game

"The [Jets last week] treated [Raiders receivers Jerry Rice and Tim Brown] like Hall of Famers–they hardly hit them. When I'm out there, I'm not going to see numbers or credentials. If they come into my territory, they are going to get hit. We're going for a championship, and they're in our way."[315]
– Patriots safety Lawyer Milloy before the Raiders playoff game

On January 19, 2002, the Patriots took the field against the Oakland Raiders with a trip to the AFC Championship Game on the line. The "Snow Bowl" had drama, controversy and snow… tons and tons of snow. It became an instant classic for several reasons. First, did I mention they were playing in a blizzard? Second, with the Patriots losing 13-10 and just 1:43 left in the game, Tom Brady dropped back to pass, unaware that Raiders cornerback Charles Woodson was rumbling toward his backside on a blitz. Pow! Woodson slammed into Brady and the ball popped loose. Another Raider pounced on the loose ball. The Patriots' season was finished, done, dead. *Hasta la vista*, baby. But wait! The officials are reviewing the play. What's going on? The referee ruled it "Not a fumble"!?!? Patriots' ball again!?!? Wow!!!!!

(You can re-live the moment via the dramatic *Raider's Radio Broadcasting Network* live audio broadcast at www.cryan.com/patriots/.)

Third, Patriots kicker Adam Vinatieri lined up for a game-tying 45-yard field goal with the Patriots' season on the line. That in itself is a huge challenge for any kicker. But the four inches of fresh snow covering the grass made it treacherous for Vinatieri to plant his non-kicking foot and take a big swing with his other leg. But Adam somehow managed to squeeze the ball just over the crossbar during a raging snow storm with 27 seconds remaining. It was arguably the greatest kick in NFL history, given the Arctic conditions, playoff atmosphere, and season-ending stakes. Even great kickers Gary Anderson, Morten Andersen, and John Kasay were astounded. Cleveland Browns kicker Phil Dawson calls it "the greatest kick I've ever seen."[316] Not even Vinatieri himself was sure his kick had enough distance: "We were pushing the envelope a little bit there. I was hoping as I kicked it… Once I saw it was long enough, it was time to be happy."[317] A month later, Patriots running back

Antowain Smith joked, after Vinatieri kicked a walk-off Super Bowl game-winner, "If he can kick it through snow, I know that he can kick it through confetti."[318]

Fourth, in overtime, the Patriots won the coin toss, marched downfield on 8-for-8 passing by Tom Brady, and Vinatieri kicked the game-winner. The "waiver wire team" with the league's second-lowest payroll had beaten the Raiders, a super team that would dominate the AFC in 2002 and go to the Super Bowl.

Democrats will admit George Bush won the 2000 election before Raiders fans will admit the Patriots beat them in the "Snow Bowl." Why? The 2001 "Snow Bowl" has another nickname: "the Tuck Rule Game." Referee Walt Coleman initially ruled that Tom Brady had fumbled the ball and the Raiders had recovered. But Coleman saw only Brady's backside. After replay official Rex Stuart ordered a review, Coleman re-watched the play from other angles and knew instantly that his initial ruling had been wrong. Coleman shocked viewers by invoking "the tuck rule," a then-obscure-but-now-infamous rule that applies only when a quarterback starts throwing the ball, changes his mind and decides not to throw the ball, starts pulling the ball back in toward his body but has not yet tucked the ball back under his arm. In such a circumstance, the "tuck rule" states that a ball knocked loose is an incomplete pass, not a fumble. Consequently, the "fumble" was ruled an incomplete pass and the Patriots retained possession.

Coleman has steadfastly insisted that invoking the tuck rule was an obvious decision. After the game, Coleman said, "When I got over to the replay monitor and looked at it, it was obvious that [Brady's] arm was coming forward. He was trying to tuck the ball and they just knocked it out of his hand."[319] More than a year later, he said, "From an officiating standpoint that call was easy for me."[320] Controversy persisted more than two years later when he said, "At the monitor, I was able to see the play from the front angle, which allowed me to see the arm motion. And I had a lot of people ask me how could I make that call, but that's because they don't know the rule book."[321] As despised as the rule is, the league has never since changed it, and the league has explicitly and repeatedly maintained that Coleman's final ruling was correct. Director of officiating Mike Pereira went out of his way to explain the rule and why Coleman's ruling was correct. The rule may be dumb (though no one since has ever proposed a more popular alternative), but the ruling was correct, given the rule.

The Patriots caught a lucky break, but due to the rule, not the ruling. Experts agree. *ESPN* NFL expert John Clayton explains: "The tape showed that Brady's arm was still moving down as he decided not to pass but to tuck the ball in. Coleman made the correct interpretation of the rule, calling it a downward passing motion and calling the play an incomplete pass and not a fumble."[322] Joel Buchsbaum said, "if you go by the rules as they are written, the referees made the right call. Obviously, it was an unfair call, but it was the right call."[323]

The facts notwithstanding, immediately after the game, Oakland cornerback Charles Woodson was livid, swearing "It's bull----. I thought it was a bull---- call. It never should have been overturned."[324] Raiders receiver Jerry Rice said, "I feel like we had one taken away from us."[325] And Brady was smiling like a murderer acquitted by a jury: "I wasn't sure. Yeah, I was throwing the ball. How do you like that?"[326] It's likely neither Woodson nor Brady knew the relatively obscure rule. But the Raiders have steadfastly refused to accept that the rule was applied appropriately. One month later, Raiders owner Al Davis said, "I had no idea Walt Coleman was from France,"[327] referring to the French skating judge, Marie-Reine Le Gougne, who traded votes with Russia during the 2002 Winter Olympics. More than a half a year later, the Raiders were still steamed enough to protest the call by walking out of a preseason talk by referees to explain the new season's rule changes. Ironically, peer pressure to walk out on the NFL officials was so intense that even Raiders defensive back Terrance Shaw, who had won the Super Bowl as a Patriot six months earlier, walked out!!! (Shaw's motives were slightly different from his irate teammates': "I was hungry. And [the officials] didn't have anything to say. I was told everybody's got to [walk out]. It's a team thing."[328])

Oakland fans will always believe they were robbed... to which Patriots fans will always point to referee Ben Dreith's December 18, 1976 phantom "rushing the passer" penalty on Patriot nose tackle Ray "Sugar Bear" Hamilton, which everyone involved (except Ben Dreith) admits was a truly atrocious ruling and unfairly knocked the Patriots out of a playoff game they had just won after forcing the Raiders to punt, had Dreith not called the phantom penalty. That penalty "even shocked Raiders QB Ken Stabler, who allegedly had been roughed. Stabler will tell you to this day that Hamilton did nothing wrong on the play."[329] Moments earlier, the Patriots had just been robbed by a non-call on their preceding drive: "Steve Grogan's pass hit [tight end Russ Francis] right in the chest for what would have been a first down, but the ball fell to the ground because (Oakland linebacker) Phil Villapiano had Russ's hands pinned. But there was no call."[330] Those 1976 Raiders had lost just one game all season: a 48-17 trouncing by the New England Patriots on October 3. The Raiders went on to easy victories over the Steelers, 24-7 in the AFC Championship Game, and Vikings, 32-14 in the Super Bowl, denying the Patriots a championship title they felt was rightfully theirs. Patriots fans have never forgotten. Raiders fans will never forget "the Tuck Rule Game."

The Ketchup Stadium game

"[We] were playing at home and [we] kind of expected to win and, when [we] didn't, it hurt a little more. Everybody was looking forward to the Super Bowl."[331]

– *Pittsburgh Steelers receiver Hines Ward*

The Patriots then traveled to Heinz Field in Pittsburgh to battle the supremely confident 14-3 Steelers in an AFC Championship Game few believed the Patriots deserved to play in. Patriots players fed off the disrespect they received from the Steelers and the media. Patriots defensive lineman Anthony Pleasant said afterward, "Any time a team runs off at the mouth, you want to take it to them."[332] When the media asked Bill Belichick before the game whether Las Vegas, which favored the Steelers by a whopping 9½ points, was disrespecting the Patriots, Belichick underscored the depth of Vegas' disrespect: "The spread is the same as when Pittsburgh played 1-12 Detroit a few weeks ago."[333] But Belichick secretly harbored confidence. Bill's dad Steve says "Even I was surprised" when his son asked him on the Wednesday before the game, "When are you going to [the Super Bowl in] New Orleans?"[334] One reason for Belichick's confidence: the Patriots had discovered how Steelers receivers were lining up differently for different plays.[335] The Patriots jumped out to a 21-3 lead and held on for a 24-17 win. The Patriots' "waiver wire team" had stunned the Steelers on their home turf in Pittsburgh.

NFL "experts" like *NFL Insider*'s Vic Carucci busily ate their words:

> "I was among the legions of preseason prognosticators that had this team finishing dead last in the AFC East. I was among the many doomsayers who assumed their season was over after an 0-2 start and the loss of Drew Bledsoe to severe internal injuries after a fierce collision with Jets linebacker Mo Lewis. I said, 'Tom Who?' when Tom Brady took Bledsoe's place."[336]

David slays Goliath in Super Bowl XXXVI

As surprising as upsetting Oakland and shocking Pittsburgh were, those games were pure prelude to what is arguably the greatest upset in Super Bowl history. The 2001 St. Louis Rams were 16-2, scored an amazing 503 points while surrendering only 273 during the regular season, and then outscored their playoff opponents 74-41. Before the Super Bowl, most everyone already dubbed the Rams a "dynasty" because they were supposedly "invincible" and obviously headed to their second Super Bowl victory in three seasons:

> "A trillion words have been written and spoken down here in devout testimony to the overpowering greatness of the St. Louis Rams. The best offense ever. A stout defense. The best combination runner-receiver in the game, perhaps in the history of the game. Speed everywhere. ...a team that, on paper, can be beaten only by cosmic intervention or by quietly slipping an extra man or two on the field when the officials aren't looking."[337]

Patriots fans feared a repeat of Super Bowl XX (January 26, 1986) when the Chicago Bears steamrolled the Pats 46-10. The media and most of the football world expected a rout. Bill Belichick had a different opinion. Steve Belichick says his son told him about mid-week that "They're not going to get many points on us."[338] Right again. Seemingly miraculously, the Patriots stunned the world by besting the Rams in Super Bowl XXXVI.

Afterwards, NFL personnel guru Ron Wolf stuck with his claim that Belichick won with smoke-and-mirrors coaching and game planning, not great players:

> "If you think about the history of the Super Bowl, this would have to rank right up there as the best coaching job ever. No. 1. They won the Super Bowl with a waiver wire team. No one has ever done anything like that before."[339]

The Rams had been 14½-point (more than two touchdown) favorites to beat the "Patsies." After they lost, virtually everyone pointed to the Patriots' coaching. Former Eagles quarterback and NFL commentator Ron Jaworski called it "The best coaching job I have seen in 29 years–period."[340] Defeated Rams head coach Mike Martz concurred, "They are the most well-coached football team I have come up against since I've been coaching in this league. All three areas of the game: offense, defense, special teams."[341] Hall of Fame coach Don Shula, who led the Dolphins to a perfect 17-0 season in 1972, was flabbergasted: "Can you believe this coaching job from Bill Belichick? It's one of the best coaching jobs I've ever seen."[342] Even Patriots safety Lawyer Milloy praised not his teammates but his coach:

> "the MVP for us was Belichick, because we all knew he'd come up with something to stump them. When you've seen him do it time and time again, like we have, you come to believe in the man. A lot of people have the 'genius' label in this league, but he's one of the guys who really deserves it. We were all confident we could stop [the Rams]."[343]

Patriots linebacker Tedy Bruschi especially admired the way Belichick had so calmly navigated the team past dangerous shoals all season long:

> "There isn't a coach in the NFL that had to deal with the adversity Bill had to deal with. There was [quarterbacks coach] Dick Rehbein's death. There were injuries. There was Sept. 11. There was the quarterback controversy, and we can't forget, Terry Glenn. Think about it. He got us through all of those things. That's incredible."[344]

While the world busily heaped praise on Patriots coaches, quarterback Tom Brady offered a rare dissenting opinion, arguing the Patriots won because they were a true team: "This is the perfect example of what happens when guys believe in each other"[345] and "[Our] whole team, as far as I'm concerned, is MVP."[346] Brady repeatedly emphasized what a great and unified *team* the Patriots were: "I knew guys were going to get open. I just had to drop back and get it to them. I've got a team full of unbelievable talent, we support each other, we rally around each other."[347]

Lack of respect had been a Patriots theme throughout the season. Players seethed at the contempt they felt from opponents and the media. Even after winning the Super Bowl, players wondered whether the doubting would ever end. Basking in the glow of victory, Patriots offensive lineman Damien Woody asked, half seriously, "Now do you think we'll start getting some good publicity?"[348]

It was a fair question. Post-season computer analysis supported the naysayers, suggesting the Rams had been the NFL's dominant team and the Patriots had "lucked" or out-coached their way into a championship. (The phrase repeated throughout New England was "Team of Destiny." Patriots safety Lawyer Milloy wondered before the Super Bowl, "Who's to say we don't have magic dust sprinkled all over us?"[349]) Sagarin's ratings, the most famous of computerized football rankings, stubbornly insisted the Rams were not merely the better team but a markedly superior team, even after they lost the Super Bowl to the Patriots. In fact, the Patriots ranked only fifth in the league:

Final Sagarin ratings for the 2001 NFL season thru February 3, 2002's Super Bowl:[350]

```
RANK TEAM                      RATING  W   L   T  SCHEDL(RANK)  VS top 10 | VS top 16
  1  St. Louis Rams          = 31.03  16  3   0  20.20( 15)    7 1 0  |  8  2  0
  2  Pittsburgh Steelers     = 26.39  14  4   0  19.04( 30)    2 2 0  |  7  3  0
  3  Philadelphia Eagles     = 26.30  13  6   0  20.49( 13)    1 4 0  |  4  4  0
  4  Chicago Bears           = 25.73  13  4   0  19.53( 26)    1 4 0  |  5  4  0
  5  New England Patriots    = 25.69  14  5   0  20.05( 20)    4 2 0  |  6  4  0
  6  Green Bay Packers       = 25.34  13  5   0  19.62( 24)    4 1 0  |  7  2  0
  7  San Francisco 49ers     = 25.18  12  5   0  19.77( 21)    2 4 0  |  3  4  0
  8  Baltimore Ravens        = 23.47  11  7   0  21.13(  5)    3 3 0  |  6  6  0
  9  Miami Dolphins          = 22.94  11  6   0  20.11( 18)    2 4 0  |  4  6  0
 10  Oakland Raiders         = 22.86  11  7   0  19.65( 23)    1 2 0  |  4  5  0
     ...
 30  Detroit Lions           = 12.34   2 14   0  21.70(  1)    0 7 0  |  0 10  0
 31  Carolina Panthers       = 11.02   1 15   0  21.33(  2)    0 7 0  |  0  8  0
```

Being disrespected after a 5-11 season is one thing, but being disrespected after winning the Super Bowl is downright insulting. Belichick was only half joking when he said, after winning the Super Bowl, "We beat the number 1 seed in the AFC [Pittsburgh] and we beat the number 1 seed in the NFC [St. Louis]. But I'm sure we'll be the underdog again when we play next week."[351]

Several years later, many still see the Patriots' February 2002 triumph as a fluke. Few remember that, although the final score was close, Super Bowl XXXVI was nearly a blowout. With the Patriots leading 17-3, the Rams went for a touchdown on 4th-and-goal. Quarterback Kurt Warner fumbled, and Patriots safety Tebucky Jones scooped up the ball and ran it back 97 yards for an apparent touchdown that would have put the Patriots up 24-3. But the referees called a holding penalty on Patriot linebacker Willie McGinest, giving the Rams a first down on the Patriots' 1-yard line. The easy touchdown shrank the score differential to 17-10. Belichick later said, "The game's over if McGinest doesn't hold Marshall Faulk."[352] Also, Patriots Mike Vrabel, Ty Law, and Lawyer Milloy (twice) narrowly missed potential interceptions.[353] As McGinest observed: "We controlled this game from start to finish. This was no upset. They never had control of the game."[354]

The Patriots undisputedly outplayed the Rams in Super Bowl XXXVI and deserved to win, as Rams linebacker London Fletcher confessed immediately afterwards: "They outplayed us. They deserved to win. I was comfortable with the outcome. I was disappointed, but I understood."[355] *Pro Football Weekly* declared the Patriots had "outplayed and outexecuted the Rams at every turn."[356] Many, however, refused to accept the Patriots as the best NFL team of 2001. Before the Patriots' second Super Bowl season, *The New York Times* suggested "their run to the Super Bowl may be remembered as a brilliant but fleeting spurt of dominance and luck."[357] Patriots receiver Troy Brown later wrote: "I lost some respect for some people around football who didn't believe we were worthy of winning a Super Bowl."[358]

2002

"We executed to a 9-7 level in 2002."[359]
   – *Bill Belichick*

"I don't think we played or coached well enough. The year before, we executed better at critical times. When the bar was raised (in 2002), we didn't rise with it. ... [W]e just weren't good enough."[360]
   – *Bill Belichick*

The 2002 season was disappointing but still impressive. The Patriots' 9-7 record tied them with the New York Jets and Miami Dolphins atop the AFC East, but NFL tie-breaking criteria handed the division title and playoff berth to the Jets. The Pats' 9-7 record was below expectations but still above average, especially in a strong division, the AFC East, where even the worst team, the Buffalo Bills, went 8-8. The best record in the entire AFC was 11-5, just two games better than the Patriots' record. (That season, one reporter wrote, "I love parity. You want to call it mediocrity, fine. I love mediocrity. I'd be fine with all 32 teams going 8-8 and the final playoff spot decided by the quality of stadium bathrooms."[361]) As Belichick constantly reminds his players, the line between winning and losing is as thin as an Olympic gymnast:

"Almost every game comes down to the last possession and three points. So it's not like we win a bunch of games 60-0. We make one or two more plays at the right time, and win. And if we don't make them, like in the Washington game [one of the 2003 Patriots' two losses], you know, we lose."[362]

One problem was too many aging players. It's surprising Belichick didn't develop ulcers worrying all season about his secondary. The staff felt safeties Lawyer Milloy and Victor Green had lost speed. And running back Antowain Smith's 40-yard dash time rose from 4.44 in 2001 to 4.54.[363] Belichick believed his 2002 team's defense was atrocious: "We're one of the [NFL's] bottom five teams defensively."[364]

Repeating as Super Bowl champion is extremely difficult. The last coach to win back-to-back Super Bowls, Mike Shanahan (whose Denver Broncos emerged victorious in the 1997 and 1998 seasons), declared in 2001 that "The days of building a Super Bowl-type team for three or four years are over. It's a near-impossibility. ...[Y]ou can't keep the... team intact because of the salary cap."[365] Shanahan's Broncos had to cheat to repeat. They basically kept their team intact by underpaying players while promising to overpay them later (with interest), but they failed to report a number of side agreements with players that they were obligated to report. In 2001, the NFL fined the Broncos $968,000 and stripped them of their 2002 3rd-round draft pick for circumventing the deferred compensation fund in 1998 and 1999 regarding $29 million owed to Terrell Davis and John Elway. In 2004, after further investigation, the NFL fined the Broncos another $950,000 and stripped them of their 2005 3rd-round draft pick for cheating on the salary cap from 1996 to 1998. In 2000, infuriated Oakland Raiders owner Al Davis declared, "These people broke the rules. They circumvented the cap. ...They should be suspended from football for one year. It's worse than gambling. It's worse than other things that people have been suspended for."[366] *Denver Post* reporter Mark Kiszla confesses "the NFL championships won by the Broncos have been tarnished. ...Davis has reason to feel validated and the Broncos have reason to feel shame... The Broncos did not win those championships entirely fair and square."[367]

Repeating as Super Bowl champion is harder because winning the first...

- *Creates distractions*, like Tom Brady's invitations to judge beauty pageants and escort girls to high school proms... and even unsolicited marriage proposals.

- *Reduces hunger and breeds complacency*, which leads some players to slack off in preparing for games against weak opponents and during the so-called "off-season" so essential to success in the NFL. Super Bowl-winner Phil Simms says "[Winning] takes tremendous want, tremendous craving. It's like food: How can you crave it when you've just stuffed yourself?"[368] Troy Aikman, quarterback of the only team in history to win three Super Bowls in four seasons, explains that "When we got to the point where anything short of the Super Bowl was a disappointment... The enjoyment of winning was taken away and the lows were just enormous."[369]

- *Swells heads*, making it harder to re-sign players while staying under the salary cap, as Super Bowl-winning quarterback Troy Aikman knows: "Before you've had success, it's easier to put the team first. As you have success, individuals want more of the credit. Just look at the Los Angeles Lakers."[370] Bill Belichick cleverly explains that coaches of defending Super Bowl champions "tiptoe on the line between helping your players forget that they're the champions and helping them remember why they're the champions."[371]

- *Lengthens the season and shortens the off-season*, which reduces opportunities to heal injuries and rest up and gives coaches less time to study film, design new plays, and evaluate free agents and college players.

- *Reduces the value of your draft picks*. The Super Bowl winner picks last in each round of the annual college draft.

- *Guarantees a tough schedule*: The parity-crazed NFL gives its best team not only the worst draft picks but also one of the league's toughest schedules.

- *Motivates one's opponents*. Perhaps the most significant consequence of winning the Super Bowl, as Patriots kicker Adam Vinatieri notes, is that it paints a bullseye on the team in each opponent's schedule: "teams are going to give you their best effort when you're the defending champions."[372] Guard Joe Andruzzi says, "Everyone is gunning for you. ...We're the most important game of the season for most teams. They'll want to bring the house on us."[373] In the 2004 preseason, Patriots players understood at an intellectual level that they were marked men, but it didn't hit them in the gut until a fired-up Cincinnati Bengals team crushed the Pats 31-3 in their second preseason game. After that debacle, Patriots safety Rodney Harrison said, "We're people's playoff games. We're people's Super Bowls. They want to knock us off. They want to make a statement to the world: 'We beat the Patriots.'"[374] Belichick says defending champions must raise their performance level because "opponents know your team a little better... they'll hit you a little harder and play a little better when you show up. Deal with it."[375]

- *Leads other teams to learn your tricks*. Patriots rookie Vince Wilfork was told by his former Miami Hurricanes teammate Vernon Carey (now with the Miami Dolphins) that the Dolphins are "looking at how we (use) our hands on the New England Patriots... So we're all being watched."[376] (For this reason, I suspect GMs around the league will be among the first readers of *Management Secrets of the New England Patriots*!)

New England certainly faced all the above challenges in 2002. Given that one more win (a 10-6 record) would have put them in the playoffs, residual effects of winning the previous Super Bowl likely kept them out of the 2002 playoffs. Despite those problems, however, the Patriots lost the AFC East on a tie-breaker.

Complacency was a factor. After Tom Brady spoke out about "some guys who aren't playing like this is their livelihood" following a late October loss, some unnamed Patriots accused Brady of throwing stones in a glass house: "two veterans told ESPN.com this week that Brady may not have been the player best suited to offer such an assessment."[377] Regardless, Brady's assessment of the problem was accurate. Another unnamed player said some Patriots had gone soft following the team's Super Bowl and their dominating wins early in the 2002 season (30-14 over the Steelers and 44-7 over the Jets):

> "We have to get back to the same work ethic that earned us these rings some guys like to flash around. We have some players who bought too much into the press clippings from early in the season. Some people feel like they can

just flip a switch and make all the bad stuff go away. If that's the case, they better find the switch soon."[378]

And defensive lineman Richard Seymour undoubtedly drove Belichick into a rage when he said, following the team's first two blowout wins, going 16-0 was "realistic. It's very realistic, if we take care of our business week in and week out."[379] After hearing what Seymour said, center Damien Woody tried in vain to undo the damage: "Please don't print that. If you print that, then Belichick is going to… say, 'See that bull---- in the paper?'"[380] Tom Brady said the same thing privately to David Patten[381] but wisely hid those thoughts from the media. Reflecting on the season, former Patriots backup quarterback Damon Huard says, "we were 4-0 in preseason, started off 3-0, and we thought it's too easy."[382]

Brady now says players learned a painful lesson in 2002 that they have no intention of repeating in 2004: "you can get fat and happy, but I think that's really the lesson we learned. Not that we didn't think we were working hard a couple of years ago, but I think we realize how much harder we're going to have to work."[383]

Also, 2002 opponents exploited the Patriots' porous run defense. The team lacked a big body to clog up the middle of the field. They addressed this by acquiring 375-pound Ted Washington before the 2003 season.

The Patriots' finest moment of 2002 came in their final game. Despite their disappointing season, the Patriots would win the AFC East if they defeated the Dolphins and the Packers beat the Jets. With less than three minutes left, the Patriots were down by 11 points. But they didn't surrender. They stormed back to tie the game and then win it with an overtime field goal, knocking the Dolphins out of the playoffs for the first time since 1996.[384] Sadly for the Patriots, the Jets beat the Packers and the Patriots joined the Dolphins and Broncos as 9-7 teams watching the playoffs from the comfort of their living room La-Z-Boy recliners.

Safety Rodney Harrison, who joined the Patriots as a free agent before the 2003 season, perhaps summarized the Patriots' 2002 season best when he said, "they were a year removed from the Super Bowl and they finished 9-7. I can't remember the last time I finished 9-7—and it was disappointing to them."[385] (For the record, his San Diego Chargers' last winning season occurred in 1995.)

2003

The Patriots' 2003 season is one for the ages. The team went a perfect 4-0 in the preseason, a league-best 14-2 in the regular season, and a perfect 3-0 in the postseason. They accomplished this despite leading the league in injuries (which necessitated the use of an incredible 42 different starting players, 15 different starting offensive lineups, and 11 different starting defensive lineups during the season[386]), playing one of the toughest schedules, and relying on rookies (called "new dudes" by their veteran teammates[387]) to start 41 games (more than all but four other teams[388]).

The only teams to use more starting players in 2003 were Atlanta (5-11), Cleveland (5-11), Houston (5-11) and Oakland (4-12). The last NFL division winner to use as many starters was the 1969 Vikings. In October, as the team continued battling, despite looking like a trauma unit, Belichick described the team as "tough": "I can't say enough about these guys. They keep fighting. They keep scrapping."[389] One of the few positions where the Patriots avoided injuries in 2003 was at safety. So it was perhaps fitting that both starting safeties were knocked out of the Super Bowl with injuries (Rodney Harrison broke his arm, and Eugene Wilson ripped his left groin so badly it required surgery). Belichick noted the irony: "We finished the game with two backup safeties. That's the way it's been all year."[390]

Despite the injuries, the 2003 Patriots had one of the best defenses in NFL history. Great defenses usually require a year or two of personnel stability before players mesh into a cohesive unit. But the Patriots overhauled almost their entire secondary before the 2003 season. Cornerback Tyrone Poole and safety Rodney Harrison were free agents, while safety Eugene Wilson and nickelback Asante Samuel were untested rookies straight out of college. Nevertheless, the defense gave up a league-low eleven regular season touchdown passes, picked off a league-leading 29 interceptions, recovered a league-leading 41 turnovers, scored a league-leading 38 points, surrendered a league-low 14.9 points per game, held opposing quarterbacks to a league-low passer rating of just 56.2, gave up a league-low yards-per-pass-attempt (5.64), surrendered a league-low longest run of just 23 yards, and allowed opposing quarterbacks to complete only 53 percent of their passes (second best in the NFL behind Dallas).[391]

Before the season, few "experts" expected a Patriots Super Bowl victory. On July 30, 2003 (the day I happened to record this data), Vegas was offering 15-1 odds on the Patriots winning Super Bowl XXXVIII.[392] At 15-1, the Patriots, Giants and 49ers had better odds than half the teams in football and worse odds than the other half. 15-1 implies a 6.25% probability, but all NFL teams' probabilities summed to 221% because Vegas sets odds to guarantee that "the house" makes money. The Patriots' adjusted probability of winning was just 2.83%.

By winning their last fifteen consecutive games of the season, the Patriots accomplished a feat many believed impossible in the salary cap era. In recent years, the old saying that "any team can beat any other on any given Sunday" has become a more reliable predictor than ever before. In winning the Super Bowl for the second time in three seasons, in the parity-obsessed NFL, the Pats proved that their first Vince Lombardi Trophy was no fluke. Belichick, famous for always focusing intensely on preparing for his upcoming opponent and never feeling satisfied unless his team has won it all, was finally able to relax and look back on the season with pride, both for the results ("You win 15 in a row and win a Super Bowl championship, that's pretty good"[393]) and the team's effort and attitude ("[W]e've had around 110 practices, and every day these guys came and worked and tried to improve. It was such a group effort, to be a part of it was thrilling."[394])

Sagarin's ratings merely confirmed what everyone already knew: The Patriots were 2003's dominant NFL team. The Patriots seldom won by large margins, but they invariably had more points on the scoreboard than their opponent when time ran off the clock, and they had won all nine of their contests against the top 10 teams of 2003, including two victories over the second-best team (the Indianapolis Colts) and two victories over the third-best team (the Tennessee Titans):

Final Sagarin ratings for the 2003 NFL season thru February 1, 2004's Super Bowl:

RANK	TEAM	RATING	W	L	T	SCHEDL(RANK)	VS top 10		VS top 16
1	New England Patriots	= 28.43	17	2	0	21.27(8)	9 0 0	|	10 0 0
2	Indianapolis Colts	= 27.64	14	5	0	21.86(4)	5 4 0	|	7 4 0
3	Tennessee Titans	= 27.11	13	5	0	21.50(6)	2 4 0	|	5 4 0
4	Kansas City Chiefs	= 25.02	13	4	0	18.17(31)	2 2 0	|	3 3 0
5	Philadelphia Eagles	= 24.81	13	5	0	20.11(15)	4 2 0	|	6 4 0
6	Carolina Panthers	= 23.75	14	6	0	20.54(13)	3 3 0	|	8 4 0
7	Miami Dolphins	= 23.64	10	6	0	20.96(10)	0 5 0	|	2 5 0
8	Green Bay Packers	= 23.28	11	7	0	19.34(23)	1 4 0	|	5 5 0
9	St. Louis Rams	= 23.04	12	5	0	18.05(32)	1 1 0	|	4 2 0
10	Denver Broncos	= 22.35	10	7	0	19.97(19)	2 4 0	|	2 6 0
	...								
30	Oakland Raiders	= 13.89	4	12	0	19.76(21)	0 6 0	|	2 6 0
31	San Diego Chargers	= 13.37	4	12	0	19.72(22)	0 6 0	|	1 7 0
32	Arizona Cardinals	= 12.27	4	12	0	20.11(16)	1 3 0	|	2 7 0

ON PAR WITH THE '72 DOLPHINS?

"Sure [you can compare them to my Dolphins] when the Patriots get all their wins in one year. If they start out 17-0, then ask me that question."[395]
– 1972 Dolphins head coach Don Shula

"It's a great run for New England–one of the greatest of all time."[396]
– Hall of Fame coach Bill Walsh (San Francisco 49ers)

The Patriots finished 2003 on a 15-game winning streak, and the 2004 Patriots stretched the streak to an NFL-record 21 games. Many sportswriters began comparing Belichick's Pats with the undefeated (17-0) 1972 Dolphins. In mid-September 2004, many of those '72 Dolphins spoke condescendingly toward and dismissively of the 2003-2004 Patriots. Dolphins linebacker Nick Buoniconti offers a representative quotation: "You don't really want me to dignify that by answering the question do you?"[397] Dolphins running back Jim Kiick said he "wouldn't give a crap"[398] if the Patriots won 19 straight (breaking the then-NFL record of 18 straight). Running back "Mercury" Morris insisted, "You must win every game in a season. That's what puts the Patriots on our back burner."[399] Offensive lineman Bob Kuechenberg said the Patriots' 2003 season is irrelevant because "Perfect is perfect. Everything else is imperfect."[400]

Only one '72 Dolphin, tight end Jim Mandich, raved about the Patriots, calling their accomplishment "a monumental achievement"[401] and saying "what they've done is tantamount to what we did in 1972. Why? Because… in the NFL of 2004, there are forces that erode excellence that did not exist in 1972."[402] Mandich confessed "there were some pretty bad teams in [our] days" and "The Patriots don't get any weeks off."[403] He basically called it a tie: "Why discredit either one? Each, in its own way, is an unprecedented accomplishment."[404]

But most former Dolphins players and coaches insisted that, even though the Patriots won more consecutive games (21) than the Dolphins did (18), the Patriots' streak is not nearly as impressive as the Dolphins' because the Dolphins' streak included an undefeated season.[405]

Some former Dolphins are warming up to the Patriots. After meeting Belichick, Dick Anderson felt the presence of his former defensive coordinator:

> "It was remarkable how close [Belichick] was mentally and philosophically to Bill Arnsparger, and I consider [Arnsparger] the smartest defensive coach ever. We won because Bill Arnsparger was a brilliant coach. …he was a great chess player. He understood what the capabilities were of each of our players, and he put us in the right place at the right time. He designed our defenses so you didn't have mismatches. We were just better prepared than everybody all the time. In that way, Belichick is like Arnsparger. That's why they're winning."[406]

Defensive tackle Manny Fernandez sees Don Shula in Belichick: "He's a very focused, tunnel-vision type of guy. I don't think he takes anything from the players. They are going to conform to what he wants them to be or they can leave. And Shula didn't give us a lot of options in regards to anything."[407] But he adds: "does it remind me of our team? No."[408] Offensive lineman Bob Kuechenberg also sees Don Shula in Belichick:

> "I know enough about Belichick to respect him. He works real hard and he's very smart. He asks a great deal of his players, but first, he gives a great deal of himself. Same with Shula. He's also demanding and somewhat of a taskmaster, like Shula. …To be a champion is demanding. The people who aren't champions at heart are unwilling to pay the price. All they do is bitch about it and settle for mediocrity. Don Shula wouldn't allow it, and I believe Bill Belichick is much the same way. You need players who aspire to the 'big team, little me' attitude, and they made sure to get that kind of player."[409]

Don Shula also sees some Don Shula in Belichick: "The way he teaches and coaches, I believe there are a lot of similarities."[410] Even Buoniconti, one of the '72 Dolphins who gleefully reunite each year to pop champagne and smoke cigars after every NFL team has lost a game, now says, "I love the Patriots [because] they remind me an awful lot of our old Dolphins."[411] Such a dramatic change of tone suggests the 1972 Dolphins decided to stop circling their wagons and instead welcome the Patriots into their exclusive club… or at least cease their shameless campaign to discredit another great team's accomplishment.

The bias of many '72 Dolphins' notwithstanding, comparing the two teams is not ludicrous, for several reasons: First, the 2003 Patriots played a much tougher schedule. The '72 Dolphins' opponents had roughly a 44% collective winning percentage, whereas the '03 Patriots' opponents had roughly a 57% collective winning percentage. Until the 2003 Patriots, no team had ever gone 10-0 against teams with winning records. The previous record was the '69 Vikings who went 9-0. The Patriots went 10-0 against teams with 10-6 or better records. The Patriots beat the Colts twice, the Titans twice, the Eagles, the Cowboys, the Panthers, the Dolphins twice, and Denver (in Denver, where the thin air and noisy fans give the Broncos the biggest home field advantage in professional sports).

Second, the gap between "good" and "bad" teams was much wider in 1972 than in 2003. The standard deviation of teams' winning percentages fell from .2275 in 1972 to .1919 in 2003. And the standard deviation of teams' net points (*i.e.*, points scored minus points surrendered) fell from 119.42 in 1972 to 98.62 in 2003. In other words, no matter how you slice the numbers, the NFL is significantly more competitive in 2003 than it was in 1972. There are many likely causes for this: the salary cap equalizes spending; every team now has a strong scouting program; every team now has a sizable professional coaching staff; every team now uses sophisticated computers and digital video to improve performance; *etc.*

Many call the 2003 Patriots "lucky" because they won many close games, but the '72 Dolphins won six very close games (16-14; 24-23; 28-24; 20-14; 21-17; and 14-7) and three more games by just ten points. Consider a few more arguments: 1) The Dolphins played in a 26-team league, not the current 32-team league, so winning the Super Bowl is now, *ceteris paribus*, 23% harder; 2) There was no salary cap in 1972 to prevent the Dolphins from simply cornering the market on the best players; 3) Drafting well was a huge advantage in the early 1970s, but college players are now studied so intensively that the NFL Draft has shrunk from 17 rounds[412] to only seven rounds; and, 4) The 2003 Patriots suffered so many injuries that they became the first division winner since 1969 to start 41 different players.

So, though the 2003 Patriots blew out few teams, they played in a more competitive league, played far more "good" teams than the '72 Dolphins, suffered a slew of injuries, and were financially constrained in ways the Dolphins were not.

Only five teams ever strung together 18 consecutive wins (including playoff games) before the 2003-04 Patriots won 21 straight: George Halas' Chicago Bears in 1933-34 and again in 1941-42, Don Shula's 1972-73 Dolphins, George Seifert's 1989-90 San Francisco 49ers, and Mike Shanahan's 1997-98 Denver Broncos. The official NFL record for consecutive wins does not count playoff games. The 2003-04 Patriots now also hold that record, after winning 18 straight regular season games. The 1971-72 Dolphins and 1983-1984 Dolphins won 16 straight regular season games but lost playoff games during those streaks. The 1933-34 Bears and 1941-42 Bears also won 16 straight regular season games.

Because the NFL is more competitive today, tying either record today is an even more impressive accomplishment. *Sports Illustrated*'s Peter King argues the two-year nature of the Patriots' streak actually makes it more impressive than the '72 Dolphins' because Super Bowl victors now face astounding challenges.[413] *Chicago Sun-Times* columnist Jay Mariotti agrees that "Winning 19 straight in this day and age trumps the 17-0 season of the Dolphins in 1972."[414] *CBS SportsLine.com*'s Clark Judge agrees.[415] So does the *Orlando Sentinel*'s David Whitley because "it was lot easier to win back then than it is now."[416] Don Shula admits free agency and the salary cap make it harder to dominate today's NFL: "The Steelers won four Super Bowls in the '70s with pretty much the same team. That's hard to do now."[417] And '72 Dolphin Jim Mandich notes the extra increased media pressure: "From the number of microphones in your face daily, the number of media looking for content. Compared to that, we just merrily bobbed along."[418]

The 1972 Dolphins and 2003-2004 Patriots are similar in style as well as success. "Mercury" Morris says "It wasn't about having fun. It was about knowing what we were doing."[419] And Belichick uses Shula-like motivational tactics. Shula began the 1972 season by forcing his players to watch the Dallas Cowboys beat them 24-3 in Super Bowl VI. Like Belichick, Shula blamed himself as well as his players: "It was as much my fault as it was yours."[420] And both teams had strong defenses. By limiting opponents' scoring, they kept themselves in every game and gave themselves a chance to win each week.

One characteristic separates these two great teams: the Patriots' humility. Patriots cornerback Ty Law says, "If we don't make it to the playoffs, who's going to remember that team that won 18 games? It doesn't mean anything like the '72 Dolphins. They were unbeaten man, and there is nothing that compares to that. We've accomplished something right here and that's fine, but that (Dolphins team) was monumental."[421] Don Shula doesn't pooh-pooh the consecutive wins record: "If the Patriots set the record, that's something to be proud of. When you do something that no one else has done, that tells you something."[422] But Shula insisted that anything short of a 19-0 2004 season would leave the Patriots short of his Dolphins: "If New England can go on and win all their games this year, I'll be the first to congratulate them."[423] Does New England really require a 34-game winning streak (15 in 2003 and 19 in 2004) to equal the Dolphins' 17-0 season? 34 games is the equivalent of two full 1972 NFL seasons. That's absurd. Somewhere between 17 straight and 34 straight, the Patriots deserve to be ranked with the 1972 Dolphins. They won 21. Former Dolphins would be wise to graciously admire the Patriots' accomplishment and let history worry about comparisons. Instead, they sound like petulant teenagers lobbying for class president. If Bill Belichick's Patriots some day find themselves in the shoes of Shula's Dolphins, I am certain they will speak glowingly of the hot young team and let their accomplishments speak for themselves.

Chapter 5

TEAM

"We knew we could win [Super Bowl XXXVI] even though we weren't given much of a chance. You can look the word 'team' up in the dictionary and there should be a picture of us."[424]
– Patriots kicker Adam Vinatieri

"You have to have [all] 11 guys on the same page, not 9 or 10."[425]
– Coach Bill Belichick

"Football is the ultimate team sport. No matter how many 'stars' you have, you're not going to win games without team chemistry."[426]
– Patriots owner Bob Kraft

"The reason we're successful here is everyone is on the same page. We sing from the same hymn, the same notes. No one deviates."[427]
– Patriots director of football research Ernie Adams

"I know their mentality. …That's a team's team. You know how you have a man's man? That's a team's team."[428]
– Former Patriot Terrell Buckley, before his New York Jets played the Patriots in 2004

ESPN commentator Trey Wingo called it "the coolest thing I've ever seen in 36 years of Super Bowl history."[429] During "player introductions" before Super Bowl XXXVI in February 2002, the St. Louis Rams were introduced the traditional way: one by one, each of the team's offensive starters emerged from a tunnel and jogged onto the field to applause as an announcer blared his name over the stadium's sound system. The Patriots were given the same choice: introduce your offensive or defensive starters. They defied tradition, demanding to burst onto the field together, so the announcer simply introduced them as "the AFC Champion New England Patriots." Patriots cornerback Ty Law remembers "They tried to tell us we couldn't do it… but we did it anyway."[430]

Sacrificing their moment of individual glory epitomized that Belichick's Patriots are about one team, not 53 individual players, and collective glory, not personal glory: "The Belichick Way does not stand for individual promotion. It's a cog-in-the-machine approach, and Belichick often has said that he, his players and his coaches are merely 'shareholders in the same company.'"[431] Tom Brady explained: "We're not a group of individuals. We're not running out one at a time";[432] "We are a team, period. We win as a team, we lose as a team. That's how it's been all season long. …We [just] won the Super Bowl as a team."[433] Patriots defensive lineman Richard Seymour put it more colorfully: "We don't need a player doing his best dance. We don't care about that. We come out as a team, we're going to bloody your nose as a team, and we're going to beat you as a team."[434]

Patriots also support one another off the field. Tom Brady is a true leader who is universally popular and makes everyone around him happier. Unlike many stars, Brady isn't hung up on himself, and he cares deeply about his teammates and coaches. When offensive coordinator Charlie Weis went into the hospital for what was supposed to be routine gastric bypass surgery, Brady kept Weis' wife, Maura, company. When Weis' "routine" surgery led to severe internal bleeding, nerve damage, and sepsis that nearly killed him, Brady held Maura's hand, remaining at the hospital Saturday and Sunday. As Weis tells the story:

> "According to what everyone tells me, I was done. They told my wife to call my family, (saying) 'he isn't going to make it through the night.' This was supposed to be an overnight procedure. (Brady) came in just so he didn't have to listen to my garbage if he didn't come to visit me. The next thing you know, I'm in intensive care and extremely critical condition. He stayed there with my wife until the troops could get there and be with my wife. ...All day Saturday and all day Sunday, the one person who was there helping my wife was Tommy. He didn't need to do that. My wife and him formed a bond that remains to this day. To the Weis family, Tommy Brady is a hell of a lot more than a football player. He's a person whose character will always be treasured."[435]

Weis is tough on his players and often yells insults like "Can you see? What are you looking at?" or "What the hell was that?" Weis never goes easy on Brady, despite his Super Bowl MVP trophies: "[Tommy] doesn't like my obnoxious, sarcastic, rude, rhetorical, one-line zingers a lot of times. He gets them. He's not immune. He's getting them like everybody else."[436] As Weis battled for his life in surgery, Brady made light of Weis' gruff style to cheer Weis' wife:

> "Brady and Maura covered a wide number of topics. Brady tried to distract her from wondering about her husband's condition at first. Then he decided to do what Charlie would have done–keep it light. 'You think if he pulls through, he'll stop swearing at me,' Brady asked Maura that day. After a long pause and a few suppressed giggles, the quarterbacks in Weis' life made eye contact, smiled and simultaneously said, 'Nah.'"[437]

Not even Bill Belichick stands apart from his team. Following defeats, Patriots coaches always share responsibility: "Any player you want to mention, and any coach–head coach, assistant coach–we got beat as a team."[438] Upon taking over in 2000, Belichick explained he intended to share personnel decision-making authority with other executives and coaches because "This is not a one-man band here. I can't play all the instruments. I don't think it's important who's right. I think it's important what's right."[439]

Belichick has read widely and thought deeply about leadership and how to build a great team. His statement above sounds remarkably similar to Peter Drucker's 1954 classic, *The Practice of Management*: "A man should not be appointed if he is more interested in the question: 'Who is right?' than in the question: 'What is right?' To put personality above the requirements of the work is corruption."[440]

But no coach can force selfish players to act unselfishly. The Patriots locker room is cohesive because Belichick's Patriots sign only "team players" like linebacker Roman Phifer, whom fellow linebacker Tedy Bruschi says "has such an upbeat personality and is always cracking a joke to make guys laugh."[441] Safety Rodney Harrison admires the way "They were able to bring people in here who put the team first, and you could really see it. We have great guys. They're unselfish."[442] Tight end Christian Fauria appreciates New England's clique-free locker room atmosphere. Players on Fauria's previous team—the Seattle Seahawks—segregated themselves by race when eating meals.[443]

Before the 2004 season, Tom Brady spoke of "the team" as an entity with a human-like personality: "It's good to get out here and see what type of team we'll have, what type of work ethic it will have, and the attitude it will have. So far, it's been good."[444] Have you ever before heard anyone objectify "team" as "it" rather than "we," as if it were a living, breathing entity?

What distinguishes a true "team" from the many ordinary teams? New Patriots linebackers coach Dean Pees believes he found the Patriots' secret: "What's been ingrained into everybody is that everybody will reach his individual goals if you help the next guy to reach his goals. And we'll all get what we want if the next guy gets what he wants."[445] The power of "team" struck Pees full force while watching his first Patriots passing camp:

> "One of the players [who was rushing the passer] went out of his way to hit a running back who was going out for a pass to help the other linebacker cover him. It wasn't like anybody had to tell him to do it. He did it because he knew it would help the guy behind him. That's helping your buddy, not thinking about just you. That epitomized to me what this team is about."[446]

The Patriots provide many examples of selfless, team-oriented behavior. In a 2004 game against the Buffalo Bills, for example, Patriots linebacker Tedy Bruschi stripped Bills quarterback Drew Bledsoe of the ball. Instead of trying to pick up the ball himself, Bruschi tackled Bledsoe so he couldn't recover his fumble. Bruschi calculated that his teammates would have a better chance of scoring a touchdown if he knocked down Bledsoe than he would have had trying to pick up the fumble himself. With Bledsoe on the ground, defensive lineman Richard Seymour scooped up the loose ball and ran 68 yards for the touchdown. This is no isolated example. In an August 2002 preseason game against the Eagles, for example, Willie McGinest passed up a fumble recovery to instead block the only nearby Eagle player, allowing linebacker Rosevelt Colvin an unimpeded opportunity to scoop the ball up and run downfield with it. This mindset is endemic. Seymour offers this hypothetical example:

> "if Mike Vrabel has two guys on him and I may be free to go make the play, if that's what it takes to win, then that's what he's willing to do and vice versa. ...It's for the better good of the football team. ...To have a good team, you're going to have to make [personal] sacrifices."[447]

Mike Vrabel compliments his fellow linebacker Willie McGinest for doing the unnoticed things that help win ballgames but go unnoticed on stat sheets: "He ping-pongs receivers and tight ends into each other. If you are willing to do that, you're not going to get a big contract or a whole bunch of stats, but you are going to help your team."[448]

Every Patriot knows success on the football field requires eleven teammates coordinating their performance. Consider Patriot offensive lineman Tom Ashworth's explanation of why Tom Brady had been sacked only once in the two previous games. Casual fans would credit the offensive line, but Ashworth credits his quarterback, his offensive linemates, his coaches, and even his defense:

> "Tom was getting hit a little bit. He does such a great job of getting rid of the ball. He realizes where the pressure is and gets rid of it, so much of the credit is on him. I think we work on it a lot. I think the coaches do a good job on that. They've always got us prepared for what [opponents] can bring. We also practice against our defense, where we see a lot of different things, so that helps. We take a lot of pride in knowing what to do. That's one of the strengths I feel of our offensive line. We have an intelligent bunch of guys, plus we don't want to get Tom hit. It's unbelievable Tom's pocket presence. He makes us look good."[449]

Preventing sacks is a team task, not the responsibility of any single player or position. In that same game, Brady and David Givens demonstrated how quarterbacks and receivers help avoid sacks when Miami Dolphins cornerback Patrick Surtain blitzed Brady from his blind side. Scanning the field, Brady detected Surtain rushing unblocked toward him and reflexively threw the ball over Surtain's head to David Givens, whom Surtain would have been covering. Instead of running his route, Givens stood and waited for Brady's pass, then turned it into a 12-yard gain. The speed with which receivers get open affects how long the quarterback must hold the ball. The Patriots had sustained so many wide receiver injuries that they were playing Kevin Kasper, whom they had signed just four days earlier. Kasper's poor understanding of the playbook contributed to Brady's getting hit and to one of Brady's worst NFL performances. Running backs also help prevent sacks by serving as either extensions of the offensive line or additional receivers. Corey Dillon demonstrated both roles on one impressive play early in the 2004 season. Dillon dove at a pass rusher's legs, then leapt up, caught Tom Brady's pass, and ran for a substantial gain. And, of course, the offensive line is essential, as Brady acknowledges: "I can tell you there's no way we get to the Super Bowl if those guys don't play as great as they did. ...Our linemen just don't get enough credit."[450]

Patriots players' faith in "team" was tested after Belichick and Pioli released veteran safety Lawyer Milloy for financial reasons just days before their 2003 opening game. Players were angry. Linebacker Tedy Bruschi was emotionally shaken: "I wish... I could put my heart on the line for something. But, how do you do that in a place where guys who've established what this team is about just come and go?"[451] But Milloy' departure was not capricious: Milloy had placed his salary above his team, refusing a pay cut Belichick and Pioli felt his diminished performance warranted. When Milloy refused, Belichick decided the team couldn't afford him. Players met to discuss their anger and disillusionment. They concluded they weren't slaves on a plantation; each player benefited from the team's success. Players weren't playing for paychecks. They weren't playing to please owners or coaches. They were playing to win...for themselves and for each other. They knew they needed to stick together as teammates and continue winning through selflessness. If players had started acting selfishly, the team would have collapsed, to everyone's detriment. "Team" is both a community to which a player belongs and a mechanism for winning.

There is perhaps no tougher way to be a team player than to be inactivate for the Super Bowl. (A coach can activate only 45 players on his 53-man roster for any particular game.) A disappointed Dan Klecko trusted his coach had made the best decision for the team:

> "I would never, ever complain about that or question it. It was tough not playing, I'm not going to lie, but we won a Super Bowl ring and I would not complain about that. That's selfish. If the best thing for the team is sitting down that week, you have to sit down."[452]

THE WHOLE CAN BE MORE (OR LESS) THAN THE SUM OF THE PARTS

> "They have the kind of people here that make you play better and make you look better."[453]
> *– Pro Bowl offensive tackle James "Big Cat" Williams, who joined the Patriots in 2004 (but was cut in training camp)*

> "This team has really meshed... We may not be the most talented team in the league. But we play well together."[454]
> *– Patriots offensive lineman Tom Ashworth*

> "There are several teams that may have more pure talent than New England on a player-by-player basis, but the only other time I've seen a team play in

concert at this level is when I treat myself to highlights of the 1972 Miami Dolphins–the only undefeated team in NFL history. Those Dolphins, like these Patriots, were the smartest team in the league–by far."[455]
– Doug Farrar, Seahawks.net

"[Patriots running back] Corey [Dillon] was running harder than anyone I've seen in a long, long time. Whenever you see something like that, it just makes you want to block better. When you see him break tackles, it makes you want to work harder."[456]
– Patriots center Dan Koppen

Patriots owner Bob Kraft gushes that Bill Belichick turned the New England Patriots into winners, both on and off the field, by building "a true team": "My family and I are proud of this man, Coach Belichick, who instilled the values of the power of team. And because of that today we have seen a true team and a true champion."[457] Players take great pride in and derive great enjoyment from being Patriots. 36-year-old linebacker Roman Phifer is having too much fun to hang up his shoulder pads, despite enduring a weekly pounding from men ten or fifteen years younger than him:

"Yeah, some days I wake up and say, 'What am I doing?' But when you get around the guys and you win, you have success, it's such a great thing. It's hard to really substitute that as far as the feeling that you get when you see your kids and they know what you do. It's a great feeling."[458]

3-time Pro Bowl running back Corey Dillon is giddy about being a Patriot:

"I'm honored to be here. The whole atmosphere in this locker room is special. I've only been one other place, and all I can say is the difference is night and day. I'm glad I'm here. This is a first-class organization. Everybody goes out and fights for one another. There is so much of a team concept here."[459]

Best team, not best players

Football is less about individual talent than golf, tennis, swimming, or baseball. Many teams with "more talented" players have lost to the 2001-2004 Patriots. No team has excelled more consistently than Belichick's "less talented" Patriots. In the February 2002 Super Bowl, scrappy Patriots defenders stymied the 2001 St. Louis Rams, known as "The Greatest Show on Turf" for their virtually unstoppable passing attack, especially on Astroturf. Patriots players and coaches together beat the Rams (on artificial turf), primarily by bumping Rams receivers to disrupt the meticulously-practiced rhythm and timing between quarterback Kurt Warner and his receivers. As Rams receiver Tory Holt said after the Super Bowl:

"It's pretty frustrating. We're so used to moving the ball and doing what we like to do. You have to credit Coach (Bill) Belichick and his defensive staff and the players for going out there and executing their game plan, slowing us down, and not allowing us to do what it is that we like to do."[460]

Cornerback Ty Law laughed after his Patriots' aggressive coverage smothered Rams receivers, rendering them an ineffectual shadow of their normal selves: "They say it's the best track team in the National Football League, but I never saw anybody win a 100-yard dash with someone standing in front of them."[461] Linebacker Mike Vrabel explained the strategy that neutralized the Rams' greatest strength: "They are faster than we are. We bumped anyone who could catch a pass. We tried to make them stop [dead in their tracks] and start over again."[462] Another tactical advantage the Patriots created was discovering that the Rams almost always ran the ball with Marshall Faulk lined up in the "I" formation (behind the quarterback) but usually passed when Faulk lined up elsewhere. Even before the Rams snapped the ball, Patriots defenders were thinking "run" or "pass."

The Rams were neither the first nor the last opponent with "more talented" players that Belichick's Patriots have out-thought and out-executed. The 2003 Patriots, with just two Pro Bowl players, were one of the NFL's all-time great teams. In the franchise's second Super Bowl-winning season, the 2003 Patriots won 21 of their 23 games (including preseason). They were an unprecedented 10-0 in the regular season and playoffs against teams with regular season records of 10-6 or better.[463] The Patriots defeated the NFL's second- and third-best teams[464] of 2003 (the Indianapolis Colts and Tennessee Titans), led by NFL co-MVPs Peyton Manning and Steve McNair, twice each... once in the regular season and once in the postseason. And they achieved all this "Despite the league-high 87 games that its starters lost to injury in 2003."[465] For example, in late November the *Eagle Tribune* pointed out that "Bethel Johnson is the only receiver that has a regular season catch for New England this fall and actually practiced this week."[466] NFL commentator Phil Simms said the 2003 Patriots, like the 2001 Patriots, won through teamwork, not individual greatness:

> "They may not have the explosive or big-name players, but you have to look at that group as a team. Opposing teams can't believe what they are doing. I can see it in guys like Peyton Manning's face. They start twitching because they know how much work they have coming up when they go up against Belichick and the Patriots."[467]

Before the 2003 AFC Championship Game, the Indianapolis Colts offense, led by Peyton Manning's apparently unstoppable aerial attack, trounced the team's first two playoff opponents, scoring 41 points against the Denver Broncos and 38 against the Kansas City Chiefs. It averaged an insane 456.5 yards of offense in those playoff games. The Colts' punter hadn't punted in either game, and Manning had thrown no interceptions and been sacked just once. The team was blowing out playoff opponents with such ease that Colts tight end Marcus Pollard proclaimed, "If we keep playing like this, then you can just go ahead and hand us the [Super Bowl] rings."

Tom Brady was amused by the comment ("I don't think you will hear that come out of our locker room"), implying it would inspire his teammates: "You always want to know the mind-set of your opponent. If that happens to be his mind-set, then [we] have 53 guys that will do everything possible to change it. So, ultimately, it comes down to the way we are playing on the field."[468]

Entering that AFC Championship Game, Manning had passed for 4,948 yards and 37 touchdowns while throwing only ten interceptions in 622 attempts (one per 62.2 attempts). Against the Patriots in the Championship Game, the Colts managed only 14 points, and Manning was sacked four times and threw four interceptions versus just one touchdown. The Colts' punting team was so rusty that when it finally lined up to punt the ball away, long snapper Justin Snow's toss sailed over punter Hunter Smith's head. When Smith caught up to the ball at the 5-yard line, he was forced to kick it out the back of his own end zone, gifting the Patriots a two-point safety and a 15-0 lead. The Patriots played disciplined, smart, coordinated defense and hit Colts wide receivers after the ball was snapped to disrupt the timing between Manning and his receivers, as Patriots safety Rodney Harrison explained after the victory:

> "When you saw their receivers on film scoring all these touchdowns, it was because they were untouched, unscathed because no one really played physical with these guys. Our aim was to play physical, hit these guys in the mouth and let them know that we're here."[469]

2003 was *déjà vu* all over again. In 2001, Belichick's Patriots shut down the "unstoppable" Colts offense after the Colts had run up 87 points in Weeks 1 and 2. Week 3, the Colts fell to the Patriots 44-13.

Only team defense can defeat quarterbacks as smart and skilled as Kurt Warner or Peyton Manning, who quickly spot and connect with open receivers. Similarly, Patriots linebacker Tedy Bruschi says only team defense can stop elusive runners like the Jets' Curtis Martin: "it was a matter of remembering to stay in position. We know Curtis. We know his game. If we overpursue and both of us wind up on the same side of the center, we're in trouble. That's when Curtis will cut it back to where neither of us is and break down the field on the other side. Giving up 3 or 4 yards is better than 20. You know if you vacate your gap too soon, Curtis will see it and be gone."[470]

In the 1980s and early 1990s, the New England Patriots were the NFL's Rodney Dangerfield. No one took the "Patsies" seriously. By 2003, the Patriots were so dominating that several bitter rival coaches and general managers who control the NFL's Competition Committee pushed through a rule enforcement change–informally dubbed "the anti-Patriots rule," "The Patriot Act," and "The Ty Law Rule"–in an attempt to blunt the Patriots' aggressive, physical disruption of opposing wide receivers' passing routes. The #1 cause of the Patriots' turnaround is Belichick and

Pioli's replacement of the Patriots' star system with a team-oriented culture of selfless individuals dedicated to winning.

If the Patriots prove that a cohesive team of non-Pro Bowlers can win Super Bowls, the Washington Redskins prove that a random collection of Pro Bowlers can lose more games than it wins. The Redskins are notorious for dangling fat signing bonuses to attract "big name" players: Dan Wilkinson, Jeff George, Adrian Murrell, Mark Carrier, Deion Sanders, Bruce Smith, Andre Reed, Mark Brunell, Shawn Springs, Clinton Portis, *etc*. Though the 2004 salary cap is $82 million, the Redskins' payroll exceeds $110 million.[471] They have lured many stars with outsized contracts without violating the salary cap by handing each star a giant signing bonus that is paid immediately but pro-rated, for salary cap purposes, over the life of the contract. These bonuses lock future Redskins teams into "Salary Cap Jail," forcing future payrolls below the salary cap. Leaving aside the fact that the Redskins are mortgaging their future, their tactic hasn't worked, even in the short-term. The Redskins have not contended for a Super Bowl championship since the early 1980s. One problem: the Redskins assume players who starred in the primes of their careers will continue starring in the twilight of their careers. A second problem: the Redskins assume a player yanked out of one system and plopped into their system will perform equally well. A third problem: no Redskins coach has survived long enough under owner Dan Snyder to build a true team. Snyder dumped Norv Turner (now head coach of the Raiders) during the 2000 season while the Redskins (then 7-6) had a shot at the playoffs. He fired coach Marty Schottenheimer after two seasons and Steve Spurrier after another two. Now it's Joe Gibbs' turn as miracle worker, and his 2004 Redskins have lost five of their first seven games. Because many celebrated free-agent signings prove disappointments with their new teams, smart teams focus on maximizing output (team performance), not spending.

The best football team does not necessarily have the most "talented" football players, at least according to the standard definition of "talent" that gives short shrift to intelligence, work ethic, cooperativeness, perseverance, *etc*. Patriots offensive coordinator Charlie Weis says the 2004 Patriots are "the best group of football players we have had since I have been here. That doesn't mean they are going to be the best team, but they are the best group of football players."[472] Scott Pioli explains the Patriots' philosophy:

> "Football is the ultimate team sport. We believe that. Individuals go to Pro Bowls, and teams win championships. And that's something we always try to keep in the back of our minds as we try to build a team. My job, and what I do, is not simply trying to collect talent. It's to build a team."[473]

The Patriots don't even attempt to define "talent" independent of context because a player's performance depends on how he is utilized. All scouting evaluations explicitly attempt to predict how the player would perform in the Patriots' system and mesh with the Patriots' personnel. Redskins owner Dan Snyder apparently fails to appreciate the importance of a good fit between a team's strategy and its personnel. He traded star cornerback Champ Bailey to the Denver Broncos for a running back, Clinton Portis, who "is really not a Joe Gibbs power back. He's a cutback runner. He's not a perfect fit for their offense"[474]:

> "How they blocked in Denver for Portis ...well, that's not how [Redskins offensive line coach] Joe Bugel does it. This is almost a classic case where a guy was a star in one system who wanted a lot of money, got traded and now isn't the runner everyone thought he would be for his new team."[475]

Quick 310-pound defensive tackle Brentson Buckner stars because the Carolina Panthers ask him to penetrate the offensive line and cause havoc in the opponent's backfield; Buckner might be a liability on a team like the Patriots that uses a single heavy nose tackle and asks him to stand his ground, clog the middle of the line of scrimmage, and prevent opponents' running backs from running down the middle of the field. (Buckner might fit at defensive end in the Patriots' system.) An outside linebacker who records countless sacks for a team that asks him to rush the passer every play might flounder on a team that asks him to drop into pass coverage. A short, speedy receiver who thrives when thrown long passes that enable him to run away from defenders might struggle in goal-line situations where out-leaping defensive backs is more important than speed. (Belichick says "Speed actually in that area of the field is limited. Some of the best red area players aren't the fastest players, because their speed is neutralized. You're only dealing with a 10-, 15-yard area."[476]) Many teams that sign free agents who posted impressive statistics in one system are surprised when those free agents don't duplicate their past statistics in their new team's system. Patriots personnel evaluators predict how each player would perform in the Patriots' system and also consider the need to field a team with a comprehensive mix of complementary skills that equip the team to handle every situation a football team faces:

> "[Often] one guy does one thing better and the other guy does another thing better and sometimes it comes into the overall mix of how you are putting them together [into a team], what skill or what set of skills or what roles are more important to you based on maybe what other people can do."[477]

Kansas City Chiefs general manager Carl Peterson says the Patriots do a superb job of finding players who fit their scheme:

> "Belichick and Pioli are very much in tune with each other on the type of player they want, they seem to have a very good understanding scheme-wise, what players fit their scheme and they have great patience in finding that player. They don't run and grab the first guy, and when they bring a player in, he has a full understanding what his role is and that's what he's going to do. That's why he's there."[478]

Finally, the Patriots spread their dollars across all positions. They realize a single player can't win them a Super Bowl. A team can sign the world's greatest left cornerback, but that one player does little good if the right cornerback is lousy because opponents will simply exploit the right cornerback. A team that signs two great cornerbacks but has no money left to sign decent backups is extremely vulnerable to injuries. As multiple Super Bowl-winning coach Jimmy Johnson says, "Some teams' starting 22 players might be better, but New England's second 22 are better than anybody in the league. Some teams go from a superstar to a zero. Well, the Patriots go from one good player to another good player. That's what a lot of teams are trying to emulate."[479] Patriots players appreciate the importance of quality depth. Cornerback Ty Law says "we don't want to be good one to 22. We want to be good one to 53."[480] Because high-speed collisions between some of the strongest men in the world cause injuries every week, no NFL team can ever have too much depth. Even the Patriots' famed depth appears insufficient seven games into their 2004 season, after they sustained multiple injuries at each of five positions (cornerback, offensive line, halfback, fullback, and wide receiver).

COLLEAGUES SHOULD BE FRIENDS

"It doesn't get any better than winning championships while being around some of your closest friends."[481]
 – VP of player personnel Scott Pioli

"I'm proud it happened with this bunch of guys."[482]
 – Bill Belichick, after the Patriots won their first Super Bowl

"Work is *social bond* and *community bond*. In the employee society, [work] becomes primary access to society and community. It largely determines status [and is] the means to satisfy man's need for belonging to a group and for a meaningful relationship to others of his kind. When Aristotle said that man is a *zoon politikon*, i.e., a social animal, he said in effect that man needs work to satisfy his need for community… companionship, group identification, and social bond. …[One's] fellow worker can also be a close friend with whom one spends as many hours away from work as possible, with whom one goes hunting or fishing, spends one's vacation, spends one's evenings, and shares much of one's life."[483]
 – Peter Drucker, father of management science

I cannot possibly overemphasize the importance of Bill Belichick and Scott Pioli bringing in hard-working, competitive, team-oriented players. Patriots players love training and playing together because they admire one another's passion for and dedication to winning football. Patriots teammates bond tightly, prepare thoroughly, and play cohesively in large part because the Patriots scouting process selects only players who love football, detest losing, and discipline themselves.

Play together; win together

Patriots players tease each other relentlessly. After linebacker Mike Vrabel played a remarkable game, a lectern appeared in front of his locker: "I knew it was Tedy [Bruschi]. I didn't even have to ask."[484] Hours after besting the Colts for a trip to Super Bowl XXXVIII, Tom Brady and Willie McGinest were ripping on each other in a way only great friends can:

Brady: "Not bad for an old linebacker who was washed up a couple of years ago."

McGinest: "Hey, not bad for a fourth-string quarterback who can't throw deep."[485]

After winning the Super Bowl two weeks later, special teams captain Larry Izzo mocked Matt Chatham for knocking down the naked guy who danced an Irish jig on the field and held up the start of the second half: "I didn't want to get too close to the guy. Obviously, Chatham wanted to get on TV a little bit more than I did, and he accomplished that."[486] An embarrassed Chatham felt compelled to respond to Izzo's barb: "I've got to clarify: I didn't form him up [tackle him properly]. He was half-naked. I just gave him a nice shot and he went out. There was no form tackling. It was clean. I looked at the officials and they (flashed thumbs up)."[487]

Izzo is basically a wise ass who keeps his teammates from taking themselves too seriously. Before the Super Bowl two years earlier, Izzo derided Patriots kicker Adam Vinatieri for growing a beard during the playoffs: "When he walked on the field today, I saw a bunch of security guards move over to check him out. I told him he looked like John Walker [Lindh], like he was ready to go fight for the Taliban."[488]

Patriots left tackle Matt Light is another wise ass. Listening to a message from "Bill Belichick" on his answering machine after a 2003 game, offensive lineman Mike Compton grew increasingly concerned. "Belichick" harshly critiqued Compton's performance and blocking methods. "Bill Belichick" was actually Light, Compton's offensive linemate, who had learned to impersonate Belichick's speaking style. A delighted Light warned his teammates: "From now on, when you hear from the coach, it might not be him. It could be me, my friend."[489] Light is hardly the only Patriot who enjoys poking fun at his serious head coach: "[Linebacker Mike] Vrabel is noted for... having a great deal of fun using Belichick's signature line, 'I've been in this league for 30 years, and I've never seen...'"[490]

On Media Day before the Super Bowl, Light carried around a video camera, calling himself "Mitch Snodgrass." His interview of Dan Klecko hinted at the good-natured ribbing Pats players give one another:

Light: "How does that double chin affect your pass rushing?"

Klecko: "You should talk with that ugly goatee, the only thing that hides yours."[491]

After Light returned from an off-season appendectomy and reporters suggested he seemed smaller, Light fired back: "You think I'm skinny? You guys are terrible judges of weight. If you guys were at a circus, I would be winning the largest stuffed animal in the entire place. I'd have 'em all."[492] Late in both the 2003 and 2004 training camps, Belichick gave Light a chance to earn his teammates a day off by catching a punt. Light succeeded both times. After catching his 2004 punt, Light made light of Belichick's efforts to build depth at various positions by teaching players multiple positions. Though there is zero probability Belichick will ever call on 305-pound Light to field a punt in a meaningful game, Light spoke straight-faced as if he were auditioning for the role of backup punt returner: "If somebody goes down and you need a specialist, you don't want to bring somebody in off the street who hasn't been in the system. You need somebody who has been around and knows what to expect."[493] Mocking the modesty and humility expected of Patriot players, Light added, "This is just one small step forward in that whole process."[494] When a teammate is giving an interview, Light sometimes gangs up with his fellow offensive linemen Dan Koppen and Joe Andruzzi to plant an alarm. When it rings or buzzes, they laugh, calling it a "BS meter."[495]

Offensive lineman Russ Hochstein learned the hard way not to compete with his jokester linemates: "I sit back and watch it happen because I can't match wits with these guys. They're smart alecks. I learned my lesson. I try to match wits and I get outdone so I don't try to get involved with that stuff."[496] But Light's other teammates enjoy teasing him. Brady says "He's goofy as hell."[497] Asked to describe Light's style, fellow offensive lineman Brandon Gorin calls it "stylish hillbilly" while tight end Daniel Graham thinks the question makes no sense: "What style?"[498] Linebacker Rosevelt Colvin suggests Light needs to "Botox those lips."[499] Offensive lineman Tom Ashworth says Light "doesn't slump enough."[500] Center Dan Koppen basically calls Light a pussy: "He's too skinny."[501]

Patriots enjoy imitating their more outspoken teammates. Defensive lineman Richard Seymour says his rookie class (2001) was forced to entertain veterans every other day: "We would always make fun of Ty Law and Lawyer Milloy–how they talked in practice or in the meeting rooms. They were so confident that they'd be telling the coach, 'Nah, that's not the way it's supposed to go.' They knew it all and they would get into it with each other arguing how a play should be executed. So we [imitated] that."[502]

Patriots are good-naturedly funny without being mean-spirited. After Patriots defensive back Victor Green intercepted a pass thrown by his former Jets teammate Vinny Testaverde and ran it back 90 yards for a touchdown early in 2002, Green said: "Vinny's a great guy. But I can't drop the ball on purpose and not score a touchdown because he's a great guy."[503] Patriots cornerback Ty Law poked fun at Green, joking that Green ran so slow he was afraid the game would end before Green crossed the goal line.[504] In 2004, 33-year-old Willie McGinest intercepted a pass and ran it back 27 yards before getting tackled. Fellow defender Richard Seymour had returned a fumble for a touchdown two weeks earlier and was eager to get into the film room and tease his teammate for not scoring: "He said he had a lot of speed, but I don't know. It was a big play, a momentum-changing play for us. I just hope it wasn't an offensive lineman [who caught him]. I hope it was a running back who got him. If it was, I'll let it slide a little bit."[505] (It was a running back, but I doubt that stopped Seymour from having fun at McGinest's expense.)

Patriots players aren't too proud to poke fun at themselves. Linebacker Mike Vrabel caught a touchdown in Super Bowl XXXVIII during a rare appearance as a tight end. Several months later, Vrabel jokingly expressed concern his offensive days had come to an end: "I think when they drafted a tight end in the first round, that pretty much told me that my days as a tight end are numbered."[506] One of the funniest and most self-deprecating Patriots is new punter Josh Miller. Every time someone pushes a microphone in front of Miller, he makes me laugh: "every time I get dressed, I look at myself, and say, 'You're stealing.' ...I've definitely out-punted my coverage as far as expectations. ...I married above me. My job's above me. I'm like that loose tooth that hasn't fallen yet, so I'm happy."[507] The former Pittsburgh Steelers punter initiated and fueled rumors about swirling winds in Heinz Field: "it's amazing how quick [the rumor] went around. It's not bad at all. ...the rumors grow, and suddenly we have the Loch Ness monster roaming the field."[508] He describes his punt in the 2001 AFC Championship Game that the Patriots' Troy Brown returned for a touchdown as "The worst athlete on the field gave the ball to the best athlete, and I never touched him."[509] After Miami Dolphins wide receiver/punt returner Wes Welker (who missed his only college extra point attempt) filled in as the Dolphins' field goal kicker following a game-time injury to their kicker, and Welker kicked a field goal, Miller joked, "That actually put all the kickers and punters back ten years because it makes it look like anybody can do it... They may say, 'screw kickers and punters; we're going to go with just the athlete.'"[510] After Miller was told about Tom Brady's 36-yard punt against the Dolphins in 2003 (that the Patriots successfully downed at the 1-yard line, leading to a Jarvis Green safety), he said, "Well, that's my point. That's a shame. You got these returners coming in and kicking field goals; you have quarterbacks punting the ball. Hopefully I get a couple more years in before they're clever enough to realize they really don't need us."[511] Before returning to Pittsburgh to play his former team, Miller was asked about reports he and Steelers coach Bill Cowher never got along: "You don't stay in a bad marriage for eight years. [Pause] Well, maybe you do. A lot of people don't. But there were no kids involved. ...So, he went his way and... I mean, I went my way."[512]

Linebacker Roman Phifer, now in his 14th NFL season, complains about "old fart" jokes: "I get all the jokes—18 years, they always want to add years to my career."[513] While linebacker Rosevelt Colvin, the NFL's top free agent in the 2002-

2003 offseason, was preparing to take the field for his first preseason game after missing nearly the entire 2003 season with a fractured hip, "Everybody made fun of me. Everybody was like, 'New dude.'"[514] A week later, Colvin was dishing it out. As Corey Dillon told a crowd of reporters for the millionth time that the team's upcoming game with his former team (the Cincinnati Bengals, for whom he rushed over 8,000 yards) was "just another game," Colvin shouted, "Corey Dillon is a liar! Write it!"[515] Dillon joined reporters in a good laugh. When a reporter asked about Tedy Bruschi's saxophone playing, Willie McGinest saw it as ammunition: "I've never heard him play the saxophone, but we're going to tease him about it now that you told us."[516] Media-friendly tight end Christian Fauria feeds reporters juicy lines like "There are a lot of [quarterbacks] that come out of college hyped like Tarzan. And they come out and play like Jane."[517] Because Patriots players tease any teammate who receives outsized media attention, Fauria complains that "Bobby Hamilton [says] that every time I put on my socks there's a microphone in my face."[518]

Not even the most senior Patriot, wide receiver Troy Brown, now in his twelfth season with the team, is immune from ridicule. When the coaches asked Brown in 2004 to learn to play nickel back, presumably for emergency situations like when both starting safeties had to leave Super Bowl XXXVIII with injuries, his fellow wide receivers teased him mercilessly: "I've been called a little bit of everything, things I can't repeat. I've been called 'traitor' and 'Little Benedict.'"[519]

Nor is the Patriots' star, Tom Brady, immune, despite his humble, down-to-Earth persona. After a two-page Brady ad appeared in *ESPN the Magazine*, the offensive linemen who protect his pretty-boy face had their fun. Center Dan Koppen: "Little subtle hints and making sure the other guys in here were aware of the photo situation. The slogan of the ad campaign is 'The way you wear it.' Whenever you can get a comment here or there using that phrase, there's no harm in that."[520] Tight end Christian Fauria: "I still had my doubts [the guy in the photo was Tom]. When I looked closer, it looked like the guy had chest muscles, I thought, 'No, that can't be Tom.'"[521] (Brady is also kept humble by his three older sisters and his father, Tom Sr., who teased "Tommy" after *Men's Health* put Brady on its cover, joking "he was first person in the magazine's history to be asked to wear a T-shirt over his chest."[522])

After the Red Sox lost the first three games of the 2004 American League Championship Series and then won the last four, Patriots players (and even support staff) teased several teammates who grew up cheering for the Yankees. Dan Klecko discovered his name and number on a Red Sox banner above his locker. Asked by a reporter whether his teammates had mocked him for supporting the Yankees, offensive lineman Joe Andruzzi was anticipating a long day: "the day is young."[523] When a reporter asked Patriots punter Josh Miller about the Sox making the World Series, kicker Adam Vinatieri chimed in with: "You're asking a guy who's been here six minutes about the Red Sox?"[524]

Rookie running back Cedric Cobbs says Patriot players genuinely enjoy being together: "The teammates are all great. I can see where they get their togetherness, everyone treats everyone with respect."[525] You can tell Patriots players love each other by the many nicknames they affectionately give one another: "Chompers" (Tyrone Poole, a reference to his teeth); "Chief" (David Patten); "Moses" (Anthony Pleasant); "O.G." and "Phife" (Roman Phifer, "O.G." stands for "old guy"); "Kleck" (Dan Klecko); "Geno" (Eugene Wilson); "Big Sey" (Richard Seymour); "Big Mac" and "Old Man" (Willie McGinest); "Bru" (Tedy Bruschi); and, "Vrabes" (Mike Vrabel).

It's no accident Patriots players love each other and get along so well. Bill Belichick has repeatedly said something to the effect of "Every year is different. I don't think you can orchestrate chemistry. You can't tell people what their relationships are going to be or how they are going to feel about each other."[526] You indeed cannot compel a particular culture on an organization, yet in 2001, 2002, 2003, and 2004 a different group of players wearing "Patriots" jerseys has bonded and worked selflessly toward a winning season. Belichick, Pioli, and Patriots scouts can't dictate culture, but they very effectively create conditions conducive to a healthy culture by bringing together "good," hard-working, hungry guys who love winning football games. They also wisely bring in a mix of veterans and youngsters. Implementing a rigorous, demanding, and meritocratic training-and-evaluation program staffed by highly skilled coaches ensures that the best players play, but it doesn't ensure that players enjoy each other, hold one another accountable, help one another improve, and communicate well. Patriots players deserve most of the credit. But coaches also help by ensuring the smooth flow of information and addressing problems early. Belichick admits that:

> "In Cleveland, I might also have been a little too 'football-oriented.' I felt that so much of the game was determined between the lines [on the field], and a high percentage of my focus is still there. But there are a lot of things that go on outside the white lines that affect the chemistry of the team. I'm trying to be more aware of and sensitive to those."[527]

Smart hiring is essential to building a strong team culture. Linebacker Mike Vrabel is a perfect example. 2nd-year linebacker Tully Banta-Cain says, "Mike's a pretty outspoken guy. You make a mistake, and he lets you know right away. And I think that was good for me, because I kind of keep things in, and now I'm a little more vocal with the guys, too."[528] Bill Belichick didn't need to light a fire under Vrabel. Vrabel played the same leadership role in college, terrorizing any Ohio State football player who failed to give 100%.

The Patriots sign only high-character players. Before the 2004 NFL Draft, most draft boards ranked Ben Troupe as that draft's second-best tight end (after Kellen Winslow Jr.), but the Patriots instead grabbed Benjamin Watson, in part due to his great character:

"[Watson's high school coach Jimmy] Wallace almost laughs when NFL scouts and executives call to do background checks. 'My response is you don't have to do an FBI check on this young man,' he said. 'You most definitely don't have to drug test him. He's an awesome kid. Impeccable character.'"[529]

...and his astounding work ethic:

"Watson's father... recall[ed] how his son came home from a workout in the weight room at school and went to the local gym to lift some more. 'When we first got here, he couldn't bench 180 pounds,' Watson's father said. 'He came out doing 450. It was because of hard work. He carried that straight across academically and athletically.'"[530]

Another indication of the Patriots' emphasis on signing "good guys" is the number of Patriots who spontaneously mention God. I do not intend to equate religiosity with morality because many evils, including 9/11, the Holocaust, and the Crusades, have been perpetrated in the name of religion, and because many agnostics and atheists possess strong moral compasses and behave with great concern for others. But many Patriots' concern for God appears to reflect concern for leading good lives and for behaving as responsible and caring husbands, fathers, and sons:

- Defensive lineman Richard Seymour: "The man upstairs and my family comes first. [Football]'s a game and something I love to do, but first is God and my family."[531]

- Cornerback Tyrone Poole: "My situation is God first, then my family, then everything else."[532]

- Defensive lineman Anthony Pleasant, who retired after the February 2004 Super Bowl, has seriously contemplated attending seminary. There's a reason teammates call him "Moses."

- Linebacker Roman Phifer says of his great play and two Super Bowls with the Patriots, "I just give thanks to God."[533]

- Fullback Fred McCrary: "I believe God works in mysterious ways."[534]

- Wide receiver Deion Branch after catching 105 yards and a touchdown against the Kansas City Chiefs in his first game back after eight weeks out with an injury: "First of all, I'd like to thank God for blessing me and have the opportunity to come in and play again."[535]

- Wide receiver David Patten: "every time when you undergo surgery–and especially two surgeries–you really don't know whether you're going to come back. That's totally in the Lord's hands."[536]

- Linebacker Rosevelt Colvin: "It's just a blessing from the Lord that I had the opportunity to [recover from my shattered hip socket] and to be in the place I am now."[537]

- Wide receiver Bethel Johnson (whose locker has a "Real men love Jesus" sticker on it[538]): "I believe prayer changes things. When you say a little prayer, and calm yourself down, God comes through for you."[539] Johnson seems to believe he benefits from divine intervention. After catching a 48-yard pass that sealed a victory over the Seattle Seahawks, Johnson said, "I was talking to Him the whole game, and when it was my time He let it happen. I'm grateful."[540] Many, myself included, would scoff at the idea that God takes sides in football games, but this might seem natural to a player who grew up in Corsicana, Texas, where football and religion intertwine.

- Even running back Corey Dillon, who developed a bad reputation through repeated trouble with the law and his teammates, credits God for mellowing him out: "It took me a long time to get out of the stage of, 'If you mess with me, I'm going to mess with you.' It took me a long time to get out of that mold. Just being born again and putting God in my life, it lifted all that anger and that madness, that revenge-type attitude."[541] Few would place Dillon high on their list of "high character" individuals. But Dillon appears to have genuinely improved himself. Dillon answered a pastor's 1999 Easter Sunday invitation to the congregation to come up and get baptized, but only after some soul-searching: "I'm thinking about all the dirt I did… and finally I just got up and went up there. Ever since then, I've been a totally different person. … [J]ust getting to know Him, it's humbled me. It took away a lot of built-up anger I used to have toward certain things. …Just coming to know Christ saved me from a lot of strife. … [M]y focus and things I valued back then I don't value now."[542] After five games with the Patriots, he says, "God is very good. I just thank Him for giving me an opportunity to be in a different situation. I'm pretty sure he saw my struggles and my tears down there and answered. He put me in a totally different situation and in an organization where things are done the appropriate way. And I'm having fun."[543]

Patriots safety Rodney Harrison believes religion is one reason the Patriots are "the closest team I've been around":

> "We have a lot of Christian guys in this locker room that are helping guys with broken relationships, marriages and stuff like that. Those are things people don't see behind the scenes that are going on in this locker room. Guys support one another. We have a lot of fun, but there are a lot of positive things going on."[544]

Off-field friends = On-field success

"Everybody just plays for each other. I don't think people are giving us enough credit when they say we play well as a team. We really play well as a team. Everybody has a really good relationship with each other. That's what makes this thing work."[545]
– *Patriots running back Corey Dillon*

Why and how do the Patriots benefit because players like one another? First, "working" with people you like makes "work" feel more like "play." Whether something is "work" or "play" is subjective and depends entirely on the doer's mindset. Weightlifting, for example, is much more fun with friends. On your own, lifting heavy weights can be both unpleasant and dangerous. With friends urging one another on and spotting for one another, lifting weights can be fun. With friends, you can lift heavier weights while perceiving less discomfort. The same is true of running. Over the past two off-seasons, a group of Patriots wide receivers (Deion Branch, Troy Brown, David Givens, Bethel Johnson, and J.J. Stokes) has worked together to improve their running technique to better catch passes at full speed to maximize YAC ("yards after the catch"). Deion Branch says the training sessions would feel more arduous if players did not run together: "The best thing about this group is that everybody pushes each other."[546] Even longshots to make the team, like wide receiver Michael Jennings (who didn't make the 2004 roster despite catching a preseason touchdown pass), rave about the support they receive from players whose jobs they're trying to steal:

> "All those guys have been helpful and kind of taken me under their wings. This is the best group of guys I've ever been around in any sport. David Patten in particular has really helped me spiritually and mentally and that's made it so much easier working with these guys. This is like a dream come true."[547]

Because the Patriots' wide receivers are friends as well as teammates, they perceive competition positively as something that makes each of them better, not as a zero-sum game. Their mutual respect for one another's abilities and contributions also squelches egos. Deion Branch was the Patriots' #1 receiver in 2003, but don't bother asking him to admit it: "You'll have to ask Brady that. There is really no No. 1 or No. 2 in our group. But in my heart, Troy Brown is our No. 1, and I'm pretty sure that's in everybody's heart. The guy has been playing 12 years. He's more deserving."[548]

Second, employees who like one another are more reluctant to change teams or retire. Peter Drucker wrote that "every company that has polled its retired employees has found... 'What we miss isn't the work; it's our colleagues and friends. ...Send me the gossip. I miss even the people I couldn't stand.'"[549] Male bonding motivates and encourages players to stay with the Patriots, and many have stayed for far lower salaries than they could have earned elsewhere.

Third, it's easier to communicate with friends and more fun to be around those you like. Scott Pioli credits his friendship with Belichick as a reason for their success:

> "I think that's why we've been able to make it work, because we're around each other so much and it's important that you're around people you care about. He's an incredibly loyal guy. I think the reason we get along so well is we have the same values. Quality of life is important. This isn't just about football."[550]

Players who like one another and enjoy hanging out together communicate and collaborate better. Patriots guard Joe Andruzzi believes the Patriots' horsing around helps the team succeed because players who joke around together can more easily say tough things to one another:

> "We can fool around with [Brady] because he'll fool right around, too. He gives it right back to us. This is a close-knit group. We've been with Tommy since his rookie year and everybody fits in together. Nobody tenses up when we joke around. That's one reason why we are what we are. We all know there are superstars but on this team they don't perceive of themselves like that. We're all on the same wavelength."[551]

Tight end Christian Fauria agrees that Brady's humility makes everything work. Fauria notes this similarity with Joe Montana: "NFL Films …showed [Montana] in training camp sitting down with all the guys black guys, white guys, O-linemen, D-linemen, DBs, whatever. You need a guy like that to be just one of the guys."[552]

Camaraderie is especially valuable in an intrinsically team sport like football, where eleven men must coordinate their actions to outperform eleven other men acting in concert. Backup quarterback Rohan Davey explains the critical importance of coordination:

> "There are so many little things that go unnoticed that are very important, especially for a quarterback. These things are really stressed in New England… Small things that might not seem like a big deal like taking my drop and making sure I wind up in the right place. If you drift one way or the other it can affect the [offensive linemen's] protection schemes. The tackle might be expecting you to be one place and he might block it a certain way accordingly and then I drop back to the wrong spot and make him look bad when I get sacked."[553]

Communication is obviously easier among players who know, respect, even love, one another than among players who distrust and despise one another. Since football is the ultimate team sport, even a team of Hall of Famers would lose if they couldn't work together, as Belichick says:

"You can take an all-star team and still not be a good defensive football team because it all has to fit together. There only needs to be one hole. Five guys can be doing a great job, but if there is a hole there, they only need to make two blocks and the guy is through it. Only one guy needs to be open. The other four could be covered like a blanket. If one guy is open, you have a play. Playing good team defense means everybody on the team playing good defense, not one guy. One guy cannot stop an offense."[554]

During the 2003 season, Patriots nose tackle Ted Washington created cool "Homeland Defense" T-shirts and sweatshirts depicting him with some of his defensive teammates. The 2003 Patriots took such collective pride in winning their home games that Washington created a special shirt, and that shirt further motivated players to complete an undefeated (10-0) season at Foxboro with three shutouts. In their ten home games (including playoffs), the Patriots surrendered 16, 30, 6, 3, 0, 0, 13, 0, 14, and 14 points.

Fourth and finally, players will go to great lengths to help those they respect and love. In war, soldiers often bond so tightly that one will try to save his comrades by knowingly throwing himself on a live hand grenade or willfully drawing a hail of bullets or carrying a wounded soldier for miles. In sports, lives are not at stake, but the potential for male bonding and self-sacrifice for the good of the team is no less real. For example, after Patriots linebacker Mike Vrabel broke his arm in the third week of 2003, he missed just three games. It's not that Vrabel has miraculous healing powers. In fact, his fracture never fully healed the entire season, presumably because he kept smashing it. But Vrabel played… and played extremely well, making nine sacks and 68 tackles and playing brilliantly in the Super Bowl, where he separated Panthers quarterback from the ball and later caught a touchdown pass. Why did Vrabel play with a broken arm? "There are a lot of guys who play hurt in this league. And they don't do it for their owner, unfortunately, they do it for their teammates."[555] After stuffing the 2004 Seattle Seahawks' attempt to score a touchdown from the 1-yard line on the game's final (and meaningless because the Patriots won 30-20) play, Vrabel explained his teammates' intensity: "You're out there fighting with 10 other guys that you'd cut your foot off for."[556] Safety Rodney Harrison added, "We're a very proud unit."[557]

Even Patriots whose jobs aren't secure help their teammates. After the Patriots released veteran fullback Fred McCrary, fullback Malaefou Mackenzie raved about the help McCrary gave him: "Fred was awesome. He helped me learn my position. Fred helped me as much as he can every day. We'll miss Fred."[558]

Players and coaches who like each other and enjoy being together will not only strive to maximize their collective performance but also help one another off the field. The Patriots' star defensive lineman Richard Seymour idolized and was devoted to his father. To the shock of everyone who knew Richard's father, he murdered his girlfriend of three years before killing himself. Richard was horrified. Most everyone, including Coach Belichick and owner Robert Kraft, traveled to the funeral, a gesture Richard's mother says "helped Richard so."[559] Richard later spoke about the importance of his football family: "Football is a part of my life, but my life is also part of the lives of the people I know, and their lives are a part of mine. It's all together, and that's a good thing. That's the way it's supposed to be."[560] After his rookie season, Seymour had said, "The guys on this team made me feel at home by asking about my family, my home and my upbringing. They wanted to know more about me and it showed they were human beings rather than just sports machines that play football. They were caring people... That's one of the reasons our team has such terrific chemistry."[561]

NO ONE IS INDISPENSABLE

"No player is bigger than what we've established here."[562]
– Patriots VP of player personnel Scott Pioli

"I don't think one guy is going to come in and save the world."[563]
– Bill Belichick

"Everybody has a little ego, but nobody's ego is so large that it overshadows anybody else. We preach that and, as a result, our guys play as a team."[564]
– Patriots defensive coordinator Romeo Crennel

"I played against them, and you could see they were a team without egos."[565]
– Patriots safety Victor Green, who played for the Jets in 2001

Safety Rodney Harrison says, "We have good, quality people. It's a tough locker room if you're a *prima donna*. There's not one guy who singles himself out as being better or different than anyone else."[566] Every Patriot understands that no one is indispensable. When star quarterback Drew Bledsoe was knocked out in early 2001 with a sheared blood vessel in his chest (that threatened his life, though no one realized it at the time), the team didn't forfeit the rest of the season... literally or psychologically. Players pushed themselves harder to support then-unknown backup quarterback Tom Brady. Months later, they celebrated their first Super Bowl victory.

Before the 2003 season, expectations and energy were high in the Patriots' locker room... until the team suddenly cut four-time Pro Bowl safety Lawyer Milloy, who had played sixteen games a year for the Patriots for seven straight seasons without missing a game. Assistant coach Pepper Johnson had called Milloy "the heart and soul of the defense"[567] and pointed out that "Milloy was the only guy on defense [in 2001] who didn't rotate [share his position with another player during a game] all season. He came out only when we were way ahead or he had to tie his shoe."[568] Many in the media branded Milloy's release insane and suicidal:

"Stunning. Just plain stunning. In my three years on board and in charge of the AFC East at *Pro Football Weekly*, never have I seen such a terrible roster move. The Patriots... have made a flat out mistake this time. ... Milloy's departure leaves a massive, massive void in defensive and team leadership. It's hard to emphasize that enough. ...[H]ow did this blunder happen?"[569]

Even worse, Milloy quickly signed with the Buffalo Bills, a division rival led by Drew Bledsoe. Weaker-willed teams would have collapsed following such a loss. On *ESPN*, Super Bowl-winning quarterback Steve Young said Belichick had "ripped the heart out of the team."[570] *ESPN* analyst Tom Jackson was so certain Patriots players were wounded by the loss of such a talented teammate to a division rival just days before the two teams played each other to start the season that he told viewers, "Let me be very clear about this... they hate their coach."

But not even the sudden departure of Milloy, captain of the Patriots defense, and an opening day 31-0 pummeling by the Bledsoe/Milloy Buffalo Bills to start the 2003 season prevented the team from going 17-1 the rest of the season and winning another Super Bowl. Players rallied to Belichick's defense. Patriots safety Rodney Harrison said, "I respect Tom Jackson, but that is one of the stupidest things I ever heard. He has no idea what we think about Belichick."[571] Jackson was forced to admit he hadn't actually talked to any hate-filled Patriots players and had simply assumed players in such a circumstance must hate their coach. Belichick described the team's response as: "We have mentally and physically tough players here who have already shown they can deal with adversity. In the end they saw that we made a business decision that affected a player everyone likes and respects, including me."[572] Several months later, even Patriots cornerback Ty Law, Milloy's long-time buddy, confessed Harrison brought more to the table than Milloy: "He's definitely brought an attitude, which was something Lawyer Milloy brought, too. But Rodney has brought another aspect–he's a physical presence."[573]

The Patriots' anti-superstar philosophy is also obvious from the normally poker-faced Belichick's unprecedented public denial of a rumor the Patriots might trade both low 1st-round draft picks and one or more lower-round picks to the Detroit Lions for the sixth selection in the 2004 NFL Draft: "That is just not something that we would be interested in doing. ...No. I think you can rule out five, four, three, two and one too. ...I don't even want it out there that we would be considering that. To me it would be embarrassing to even think about that."[574] Belichick was so embarrassed by the idea of trading two or three very good players for one superb player that he broke his own vow of silence regarding team strategy.

The Patriots are so confident in their system's solidity that they believe they can survive the loss of any individual. Belichick intentionally designs redundancy into his organization to reduce risk:

"There's a lot to be said for being able to spread the production around. If it's one or two who are giving it to you, and they can give it to you consistently, you can still have a chance to thrive. But if you ever get shut down there, the big question mark is if you can get it from somebody else. Sometimes, that's not too certain."[575]

Redundancy and substitutability

"We've tried to build the depth all the way through the system. The preparation comes earlier rather than the week a crisis hits."[576]
 – Bill Belichick

"I call [football] the modern day, Roman gladiator-type sport. Injuries, you've got to have depth. We have guys on this team who can go out and play. If they could not play, I'm pretty sure the coaches or the front office would not have put them on the roster or signed those guys to this team. Anytime you come to this team you're expected to be able to perform your duties, not only in practice but on the field."[577]
 – Patriots cornerback Tyrone Poole

"We [linebackers] had a revolving door… I got hurt in Miami, Bryan Cox broke his leg in Denver, and Ted Johnson got hurt the week of the Rams game. Each of us, at one time or another, was healthy but not playing as much as we wanted and had to bite our tongues for the betterment of the team."[578]
 – Patriots linebacker Tedy Bruschi

Injuries. Illnesses. Free agency. Off-field temptations. Contract disputes. Personal problems. Suspensions. Deaths in the family. NFL coaches can't expect any particular player to be available every week of a season or to remain with the team from season to season. No single player's unavailability should kill a team's season. No player should hold his team hostage and eat up a large fraction of its salary cap. And no player should be so important that he is given special treatment that erodes "team." As Belichick said in refuting the notion that the Patriots live or die by Tom Brady's health, "You can't single guys out. This is not a one-man show."[579] For all these reasons, redundancy and substitutability are essential to NFL success. Patriots like Tedy Bruschi want to win more than anything, so they *want* to be redundant:

"Football is the ultimate team game, and we know there are going to be injuries and that's when guys have to step up. It's a long season. We know everybody isn't going to play every game. The key then is preparing for when they don't. And that's what this team does. We're ready for every situation."[580]

Smart teams ensure that every player is replaceable. This requires skilled backups who know the playbook. It also requires that starters and backups practice together often enough that they can play together comfortably. Ideally, a backup entering a game does not force the starters to change how they play. Belichick says,

"When a player comes in, I don't think you want to change the other 10 for the one guy who is coming in."[581] After the Patriots' starting cornerbacks both fell to injuries and were replaced by an undrafted rookie (Randall Gay) and a 2nd-year player (Asante Samuel), Patriots linebacker Tedy Bruschi insisted the defense would play no differently: "We're still going to run what we run. They've been in the system now for months since they've been drafted, in minicamps, so we expect them to know what we do and we can throw anything at them."[582]

Many teams feel compelled to adjust when substitutes come in. If, for example, backups are less talented than the starters they replace, then the starters will have to pick up the slack by compensating for the substitutes' weaknesses. Even if a backup is as talented as the starter he replaced, he may play with a different style or approach. If so, the starters must adjust their play when the backup enters the game. Finally, because NFL teams can activate only 45 players per game, no team can have a dedicated backup for every position. The more players capable of playing multiple positions a team has, the better prepared that team is to adjust when injuries strike.

Belichick's Patriots have fewer superstars and more talented backups than other NFL teams. Patriots coaches also ensure that everyone practices and everyone plays. Coaches seldom leave the same eight players off the 45-man active roster two weeks in a row. And they rotate the 45 active players in and out of each week's game, keeping everyone involved.

The Patriots' player rotation helps protect against injuries to starters because the more players play together, the better they understand one another and the more effectively they coordinate their play. For example, virtually every dominant offensive line has had personnel stability for years. It is a cliché that "continuity [is] necessary for a cohesive running and passing game."[583] Jerry Fontenot, a 15-year NFL veteran and New Orleans Saints center, says, "Playing offensive line teaches you the principles of [teamwork] because if you're on your own program, the team won't be able to function."[584] Minnesota Vikings tight end Hunter Goodwin concurs: "Your best lines are the ones that stay together, and those are usually the best teams. There are so many calls to be made, so many times when you need to intuitively know how the guy next to you is going to react, that continuity is everything."[585] In 2003, the Kansas City Chiefs had the best offense in football. Their 30.3 points per game ranked #1 in the entire NFL, and their 369.4 yards per game ranked #2 behind the Minnesota Vikings.[586] One reason for the Chief's offensive domination: "[They] had started the same five linemen for 28 consecutive games, the longest such streak in the league in 11 years."[587] In 2004, John Welbourn replaced John Tait at right tackle, and the offensive line temporarily lost some of its dominance because, according to offensive line coach Mike Solari, "If you don't have the unity and cohesiveness, there's disruption, a breakdown—sacks, negative-yardage plays. John is an outstanding fit. He brings attitude and toughness to the group. We're behind in the sense of his foundation of the offense, the [repetitions] and knowing adjustments and techniques."[588] After starting 2004 with four losses in its first five games, the Chiefs busted out for 56 points (on an NFL-record eight rushing touchdowns) against Atlanta and 45 against Indianapolis, thanks to its offensive line regaining its former greatness. It took five games before John Welbourn assimilated with his teammates.

Coordinated players play bigger than they are. For much of the past decade, the Denver Broncos have had one of the smallest and best offensive lines. In 1998, "while every other NFL team [had] at least two starting offensive linemen weighing 300 pounds or more, the Broncos ha[d] none."[589] That smallest of offensive lines played among the best, thanks to great technique and exquisite coordination. San Diego Chargers GM Bobby Beathard said, "They rank at the top of the league. I don't mean that individually but as a unit. Their strength lies in their ability to play together."[590] The Broncos' trench players made stars of running backs Terrell Davis and Clinton Portis. And even late-round draft picks Mike Anderson and Orlandis Gary each had 1,000-yard seasons running behind that line. It sometimes seems as if anybody could be a good running back for the Broncos. Bill Williamson believes "Mike Shanahan could make a 1,000-yard rusher out of Martha Stewart."[591] The Broncos obviously felt that way when they traded away Clinton Portis to the Washington Redskins in 2004. On week 1 of the 2004 season, Quentin Griffin made them look like geniuses, running for 156 yards and three touchdowns. When Griffin went down with an ankle injury, mystery man Reuben Droughns came in and ran for 193 yards and 176 yards in his first two games. Cohesive offensive lines make running backs look great.

In theory, standardizing the responsibilities of each position and the expected behavior of each position in every conceivable scenario can eliminate the style-of-play performance drop when a substitute replaces an injured starter. However, few teams are sufficiently disciplined and detail-oriented to precisely specify performance expectations, drill players so intensely, and monitor their technique closely. Patriots coaches know exactly how they want each position to be played, and their careful coaching and evaluation/feedback cycle enables the Patriots to mix-and-match players, including offensive linemen who rarely rotate in the NFL. The Patriots have been rotating offensive lineman since at least 2002 when, in their opening game against Pittsburgh, the Patriots played four different guards. Offensive tackle Kenyatta Jones said, "We've got some chemistry out there together, no matter who's out there. The way we shuttle guys in there is almost like defensive lines do."[592] Standardization and training give the Patriots something better than offensive line stability... offensive linemen who play well together, on and off the field, *plus* quality depth. Patriots offensive linemen accept rotation because they get along great. They regularly play practical jokes on one another and laugh together. Says left tackle Matt Light, the biggest practical joker of the bunch, "We laugh constantly. We're kind of like hyenas."[593] Also, Patriots linemen worry not about their personal performance in isolation but about how their performance affects their linemates and overall line blocking. Russ Hochstein says, "I want to make sure that they're comfortable–everybody in this system, the guys that I play with... with me being in there."[594]

Standardization, training, and rotation pay huge benefits when an offensive lineman goes down with an injury. The Patriots can recover without skipping a beat, as they proved when Russ Hochstein subbed for injured star Damien Woody in the 2003 AFC Championship Game and Super Bowl. Belichick feels substitutability is essential because "inevitably... you have to be prepared at some point to play guys other than the guys that are in the starting lineup on opening day. You better have everyone ready to play. Whether you need them or not, you better have them ready, and that's what we're trying to do."[595]

Another way Patriots coaches create redundancy and substitutability is by training most players to play multiple positions. Defenders Richard Seymour, Mike Vrabel, and Dan Klecko have all played at either fullback or tight end in games. (Vrabel even caught a touchdown as a tight end in Super Bowl XXXVIII.) In 2004 training camp, wide receiver Troy Brown practised as a nickel back (*i.e.*, the team's third cornerback). Players who can play multiple positions expand the effective size of the Patriots' game day roster and help protect against injuries. The Patriots wisely teach players who have already mastered their existing position(s) to play new positions:

> "We saw many situations last year when we had to move people around and that comes from having a background in it. Training camp is the best time to do it and Troy [Brown] is a pretty experienced player on offense. Not that he doesn't need the practice over there, but I think he can afford a little bit of time trying to help learn to do something else."[596]

This creates flexibility so that if anyone goes down with an injury, the best reserve can come into the game, even if he doesn't happen to play the position of the injured player, by shuffling players around: "You build a good foundation in the spring and in training camp so that you have flexibility and you're not locked into one thing where if you lose a couple of guys at a spot, the whole thing comes apart."[597] Belichick has said of his offensive linemen: "We'll give them a chance and put them out there and see what they can do. In the end we'll try to put our best five on the field, whoever those five are."[598] After Damien Woody played center in the Pro Bowl in February 2003 (as an injury replacement for Raiders center Barrett Robbins), he moved to guard during the 2003 season so the Patriots could start rookie Dan Koppen at center. The Patriots can shift offensive linemen around because centers learn to play guard and vice-versa, left tackles learn to play right tackle and vice-versa, *etc*. Learning to play other positions also helps offensive linemen coordinate their blocking because each understands the responsibilities of the other positions.

The Patriots could not have won either Super Bowl without personnel redundancy. For example, three of the Patriots' five offensive linemen in Super Bowl XXXVIII (Tom Ashworth, Russ Hochstein, and Dan Koppen) were backups early in

2003 who took over following injuries to starting players. "Experts" said the Patriots' "patchwork" offensive line was its Achilles Heel, but the Patriots didn't surrender a single sack in its three playoff games. In Week 7 of 2004, the starting offensive line was, from left to right, "Light, Andruzzi, Koppen, Neal, and Ashworth." When a back injury kept Ashworth out of Week 8, Gorin came in at right tackle, and Neal slid from tackle to guard: "Light, Andruzzi, Koppen, Neal, and Gorin." During the game, Light reportedly got the wind knocked out of him (though it sounded more like a concussion). Gorin flip-flopped to left tackle, Neal slid over to right tackle, and Russ Hochstein came in at right guard: "Gorin, Andruzzi, Koppen, Hochstein, and Neal."

In their ceaseless quest for flexibility, the Patriots prefer to draft players who have displayed the ability to play multiple positions. Belichick drafted strong safety Guss Scott, for example, because "He's played both free and strong safety. He's also played some nickel back. I like him on all four downs."[599] The Patriots also prefer flexible players so they can attack in different ways with the same personnel. They shy away from unidimensional players who play a position well in certain situations and poorly in others. Inside linebacker Ted Johnson, for example, saw his playing time diminish under Belichick because Johnson is super against the run (a "slobberknocker") but a liability in pass protection. Johnson is primarily used in "running situations." More flexible insider linebackers Tedy Bruschi and Roman Phifer stay on the field against a "hurry up offense" because there is not enough time to substitute heavier defensive linemen and linebackers in "running situations" and lighter, quicker, faster players in "passing situations." The more personnel-swapping a defense does, the more incentive an opposing offense has to use a "no huddle" / "hurry up" attack. Also, Patriots coaches don't want their personnel choices to tip opponents off to their plays. For both reasons, Patriots coaches love the flexibility of their tight ends, Daniel Graham, Christian Fauria, and Benjamin Watson:

> "All three players have shown that they can be productive in the running game and the passing game and that really helps the balance of the offense. It is not, 'Well, we put this guy in to run. We put this guy in to throw. Then, we have to take that guy out and we are going to run.' It is just so hard to call plays or to get into any kind of flow offensively when you are in that type of a mentality. I have been in that before. It is not where you want to be."[600]

Even Belichick is dispensable

"The thing that gets me about them is outside of Tom Brady, Tedy Bruschi and Ty Law, I can't name a lot of their players off the top of my head. I mean, they don't have a lot of famous names like Dallas when they had the Doomsday Defense and our [Pittsburgh's] Steel Curtain."[601]
– Terry Bradshaw, multiple Super Bowl-winning Steelers quarterback and Fox NFL analyst

I even dare say the Patriots could survive the loss of Tom Brady, Scott Pioli, or Bill Belichick. This is absolutely not a claim that the Patriots will win Super Bowls forever or that they wouldn't initially hiccup if Brady vanished. Winning a Super Bowl is a tremendous feat. In a 32-team league engineered for "parity," each NFL team begins each season as a longshot to win the Super Bowl. A crush of injuries quickly reduced 2003's NFC Champion, the Carolina Panthers, to a 1-6 team in early 2004. My claim is that "the Patriots Way" has become self-perpetuating. Only wholesale management turnover or a new, meddlesome owner could derail the strong culture Belichick has established and return the Patriots to mediocrity.

Saying Belichick is dispensable is not a knock on Belichick; quite the opposite. Jim Collins' blockbuster best-selling business book *Good to Great* presents persuasive evidence that the greatest leaders achieve greatness not through force of will or personality but by constructing institutions that embody their principles and beliefs. Such institutions continue thriving after their creators depart. *Good to Great* would classify Bill Parcells as a "Level 4" leader because Parcells threatens, scares, and goads players to greatness but fails to build an institution capable of sustaining success beyond his (inevitable) departure. "Level 4" leaders are self-absorbed headline-grabbers. Bill Belichick, a.k.a. "Monotone Man"[602] and the "Human Snooze Button,"[603] perfectly fits *Good to Great*'s characterization of "Level 5" leaders:

- "embody a paradoxical mix of personal humility and professional will. They are ambitious, to be sure, but ambitious first and foremost for the company, not themselves"

- "set up their successors for even greater success"

- "display a compelling modesty, are self-effacing and understated"

- "fanatically driven, infected with an incurable need to produce sustained *results*. They are resolved to do whatever it takes to make the company great, no matter how big or hard the decisions"

- "display a workmanline diligence—more plow horse than show horse"

- "attribute success to factors other than themselves. When things go poorly, however, they look in the mirror and blame themselves, taking full responsibility"[604]

Good to Great cites Abraham Lincoln as a classic "Level 5 leader" because he was "humble and fearless [and] never let his ego get in the way of his primary ambition for the larger cause of an enduring great nation. Yet those who mistook Mr. Lincoln's personal modesty, shy nature, and awkward manner as signs of weakness found themselves terribly mistaken."[605]

Bill Belichick is another textbook "Level 5 leader." He shares blame for defeats and insists "if the Patriots win a game, it's because the players went out there and made a few more plays than the team they are playing. All of the games that we've won, that's been the case."[606] And Belichick intends to remain in New England for the remainder of his career: "I can tell you from my experience, when you put in several years building a program up to a level that you're comfortable with, the last thing you want to do is walk away from that."[607] Unlike Parcells, Belichick is not interested in duplicating his success elsewhere to prove his greatness or auctioning his services to the highest bidder every few years to stroke his ego or maximize his salary.

Belichick's primary concern is sustaining the Patriots' success. His secondary concern is helping his assistants succeed, whether in New England or elsewhere. (As Belichick's former Cleveland Browns offensive coordinator was coaching his Iowa Hawkeyes to a 37-17 bowl game victory over Florida, Bill proudly called his father, Steve Belichick, and asked, rhetorically, "How's my boy doing?"[608]) Belichick's pride in the institution he has built also shows in his excitement when players, like Tedy Bruschi and Matt Light, accept less-than-market pay to remain Patriots: "I think it's great when players want to stay in a situation with the team they're with; it makes you feel good about what you're doing and the fact they want to continue to be part of it."[609]

Belichick also displays the humility and reserve typical of "Level 5 leaders":

"In contrast to the very *I*-centric style of the comparison leaders, we were struck by how the good-to-great leaders *didn't* talk about themselves. During interviews with good-to-great leaders, they'd talk about the company and the contributions of other executives as long as we'd like but would deflect discussion about their own contributions. When pressed to talk about themselves, they'd say things like… "Did I have a lot to do with it? Oh, that sounds so self-serving. I don't think I can take much credit. We were blessed with marvelous people." …It wasn't just false modesty. Those who worked with or wrote about the good-to-great leaders continually used words like *quiet, humble, modest, reserved, shy, gracious, mild-mannered, self-effacing, understated, did not believe his own clippings*; and so forth."[610]

Belichick's final challenge will be setting up his Patriots to succeed following his eventual retirement. As a seven-year-old, "Billy" Belichick met the man who has now become his ultimate measuring stick: George Halas, whose Chicago Bears achieved *two* 18-game winning streaks, in 1933-34 and 1941-42. Halas built the Bears into a great institution "so well put together that even when Halas went into the Army in the middle of the '42 season, they kept right on winning."[611] *CBS*' Jim Nantz related this story Belichick told him:

"[Belichick] had a chance as a young boy to meet all of these legendary coaches, including George Halas… at the age of seven… He went in the locker room, escorted by his dad after the game, and he said 'Congratulations, Coach Halas, for the win.' Halas said, 'Young man,' he whipped out a dollar bill, signed it, and said 'I give a dollar to the first person who congratulates me on a victory, and this is yours.'"[612]

Phil Simms added that the Halas-Belichick connection was especially poetic because "George Halas was known to be a little tight with the money." Belichick's Patriots have all the hallmarks of a team built for sustained success. But the Patriots still rely on Belichick's unparalleled knowledge of football to prepare game plans that exploit opponents' weaknesses. He must train his successor to find an edge every week.

Because the entire Patriots organization accepts the "no one is indispensable" mantra, the team refuses to throw suitcases of cash at any single player. Ty Law, with his $9.46 million 2004 salary, is an exception, but Law's contract predated Bill Belichick's arrival as head coach, and Law's play (discussed below) has justified his top pay. Tom Brady's pay is also high, but most teams would gladly pay Brady twice what what Patriots are, and far less accomplished quarterbacks are earning much more. Scott Pioli says the Patriots would rather have a team full of "A-minus" guys than a team with a mix of "A" guys and "B-minus" guys: "We're trying to build a team, and if you deviate too much and go too much on the high end with too many players, you're not going to be able to build a team and spread available cash out to be strong in all positions."[613]

Bill Belichick seemed less excited about winning his second Super Bowl than the selflessness and humility his players displayed:

> "Here's all you have to know about our team. We won all those games in a row, and not one person wants to take credit for it. Not one guy. Brady credits the offensive line. The coaches credit the players. Ty [Law] got three interceptions in the AFC Championship game, and he says the pressure from the defensive line made it possible. How cool is that?"[614]

Never pay a king's ransom

Tom Brady earned a combined salary and prorated signing bonus of $314,960 in 2000, $387,800 in 2001, $1,019,600 in 2002, $3,323,450 in 2003, and $5,062,950 in 2004.[615] This is *mucho dinero* to you or me but pocket change for a two-time Super Bowl MVP. Brady's five-year earnings total roughly $10 million, about what the Indianapolis Colts' Peyton Manning, who has led his team to exactly zero Super Bowls, earns each season. Brady's cap figure is scheduled to jump to about $10 million/year in 2005 and 2006, but this will likely fall when Brady signs a contract extension.

Peyton Manning is a great QB, but he is eating up a huge percentage of the Colts' salary cap because the Colts organization had no choice but to re-sign him. Indianapolis agreed to pay Manning $98 million over the next seven years, $34.5 million totally guaranteed, meaning the Colts won't get it back even if Manning suffers a career-ending injury in his first training camp practice. It's not like Manning needed the money: Over the past seven seasons, the Colts have paid him over $54 million in signing bonuses alone, not including salary. The New York Jets gave Chad Pennington a 7-year $64 million contract. Even previously-unknown Carolina Panthers quarterback Jake Delhomme now has a 5-year $38 million dollar contract.

A contract analyst at the NFL Players Association believes "The Patriots are basically stealing Tom Brady... whose contract is so far below market value. ... Brady's agent should be demanding a renegotiation."[616] Brady is quite aware he's underpaid. His buddy Peyton Manning says, "I always tell Tom he's underpaid. Don't see how he puts up with it."[617] Aside from Brady being a team player, Brady and his agent are also being very sophisticated and taking a long-term view of Brady's financial opportunities. A mega-contract would reduce the Patriots' ability to hire other great players. Brady loves winning. He also knows that his non-contractual financial options expand with his team's success. Each Super Bowl championship brings larger marketing opportunities. Brady signed multi-million dollar contracts to pitch *Sirius Satellite Radio* and *The Gap* but has also rejected many millions of dollars in endorsement opportunities to avoid overexposure or association with products he does not believe in. If Brady demanded a new contract or sat out in a contract dispute, his marketability would plummet and he would undercut his ability to lead the Patriots. If Brady continues being a team player and can win another one or two Super Bowls, he might surpass his childhood idol, Joe Montana, before reaching his 30th birthday.

The Patriots hate paying megabucks to any single player when the team's total salary is capped at $80.5 million per year. Brady and "shutdown cornerback" Ty Law ($10,206,965) are the only Patriots making more than $3,667,300 (Willie McGinest) in salary and prorated signing bonus for 2004.[618] The Patriots pay Law that much because Law's contract pre-dates Belichick's arrival and because Law, effectively, single-handedly takes the opponent's top wide receiver out of the game. After Law intercepted a Seahawks pass, announcer Cris Collinsworth said, "One of the things Seattle was worried about was Law running their routes better than the Seahawks' receivers."[619] Consider also the 2003 playoffs:

> "The Titans threw to his side just once in the entire game. The Panthers followed their lead by concentrating on [the Patriots' other cornerback, Tyrone] Poole. The only team that took the business-as-usual route was the Colts, and Law burned league co-MVP Peyton Manning for three interceptions. Law didn't have the numbers over the course of the three games, but that was only because the Titans and Panthers avoided him at all cost."[620]

According to Patriots defensive coordinator Romeo Crennel, Law's ability to nullify the opposing team's best receiver effectively makes the other Patriots defenders play better by freeing them to worry only about stopping the offense's other ten guys:

"That's why the corner position is so important in the NFL. You need guys who can cover one-on-one and not need to have help. That makes calling the game easier. If you don't have that, you need to take that into consideration and tilt your coverage one way or another because you have to be able to hold up on both sides."[621]

Law's skill also enables the Patriots to be very creative with their defensive schemes. Law's importance was obvious from the instant collapse of the Patriots defense after Law's injury forced him from the 2004 Week 8 Patriots-Steelers game. Before Law's injury, the Patriots forced the Steelers to punt twice without gaining a single first-down. After Law left, the Steelers scored 34 points. In the 76 games Belichick's Patriots played (2000-2004) before the Steelers game, they surrendered 34 points only four times: to the Jets (34) and Lions (34) in 2000, to the Chiefs (38) in Week 3 of 2002, and to the Colts (34) in 2003, the last two being shootouts the Patriots won.

Many consider Tom Brady the one indispensable Patriot, but I suspect the team would have let him walk if he had demanded a Manning-like $14 million/season. One reason the Patriots drafted quarterbacks Rohan Davey and Kliff Kingsbury and signed veteran Jim Miller, despite having a superb starter, is to avoid the desperation that forced the Colts to open their vault at gunpoint. Davey earned NFL Europe MVP honors and opened many eyes with his dazzling performances while leading the Berlin Thunder to a World Bowl championship, and Davey's arm is stronger than Brady's. Jim Miller led the Chicago Bears to a 13-3 season in 2001 before separating his shoulder in their playoff game. I expect the Patriots and Brady will agree to another below-market contract extension beyond 2006. If not, the team will go to its "next best option." The Patriots' emphasis on quality depth at every position gives them a strong bargaining position entering every contract negotiation. If the team knows it can afford to walk away from the negotiation, and if the player knows that too, the team is likely to get a better deal. The Patriots can make credible take-it-or-leave-it offers because they have repeatedly demonstrated their willingness to walk away from star players, including Lawyer Milloy, Ted Washington, and Damien Woody. The Patriots have also traded away former stars Tebucky Jones and Drew Bledsoe, so Brady knows he could become the next Bledsoe. The only question is how much of a "home town discount" Brady is willing to offer the Patriots to stay. Brady will set his demands, and the Patriots will either acquiesce or let him go. I expect Brady to stay long-term because he wants to win and New England offers the best chance to win, in part because many Patriots are willing to accept below-market salaries. Accepting lower pay is tough for many players, but it is just another realm in which Patriots sacrifice for the good of their team. Players who stay are less concerned about maximizing their income than winning and belonging to a special organization.

The Patriots wisely let their best offensive lineman, Damien Woody, leave for a mammoth free agent contract from the Detroit Lions, and let another experienced lineman, Mike Compton, walk away too, because they had younger, cheaper replacement offensive linemen waiting in the wings. Woody's six-year, $31 million contract includes a $9.5 million signing bonus, 33% more than any previous free agent interior offensive lineman:[622]

> "the $9 million signing bonus handed to Damien Woody by the Lions is more than triple what New England's entire starting line in Super Bowl XXXVIII is scheduled to earn in 2004 salary. Left tackle Matt Light and Russ Hochstein will earn $455,000, center Dan Koppen is slated for $305,000, right guard Joe Andruzzi $1.2 million and right tackle Tom Ashworth $380,000."[623]

Even after Woody and Compton departed, the Patriots still have an abundance of promising low-paid linemen. Stephen Neal, who became a starter in 2004, earns $455,000, and Brandon Gorin $386,850. (Another, Adrian Klemm, is on injured reserve.) The Patriots also figured they could get substantial performance for vastly less money out of less heralded free agents like six-year veteran Bob Hallen, whom they signed May 11th, probably for the veteran minimum of $535,000 (but Hallen didn't make the final roster).

As great as Woody is, he isn't $28 million better than Russ Hochstein or Dan Koppen, especially since Woody never learned to long-snap as center (much to the chagrin of Bill Belichick who, as a center/longsnapper in his youth, learned through intensive practice to long-snap so consistently that he never once mis-snapped a ball[624]) and had to swap places with a guard in long-snapping situations.

NO ONE IS IRRELEVANT

> "Every single person in this locker room is doing something to help the team. And that's something that really excites me about this sport."[625]
> *– Patriots offensive lineman Stephen Neal, a former wrestler with no football experience*

> "It takes everybody to win... The opportunity comes and you make things happen, no matter who you are."[626]
> *– Patriots running back Kevin Faulk*

> "Every player on this team is important. Every player has a role. If we could take [all] 53 players to the game [rather than 45], if they were all healthy, I am sure we would use all of them."[627]
> *– Bill Belichick*

> "Nobody rots away as a special teams player on the Patriots. Every player gets at least one-third of the practice reps, and almost every player has a role on offense or defense. Belichick likes to have three players ready to play every two positions."[628]

– Sporting News journalist Dan Pompei

Just as no Patriot is indispensable, no Patriot is irrelevant. If you make the Patriots' roster, the coaches know you can play and trust you will play well. You may not play every game, and you certainly won't play every down of every game, but you won't waste away on the bench as a permanent backup (unless you're a quarterback) because the Patriots find ways to get every non-quarterback into games. The Patriots find roles on special teams for backup players and stress the importance of special teams. Belichick also de-emphasizes the distinction between "starters" and "backups" by instead focusing on who plays in which situations. The "starter" may play on first downs, but the "backup" may play on third downs. Typically, "starters" get the glory, but not in Belichick's mind. In 1997, Belichick explained that he and Bill Parcells see things differently:

> "We looked at third-down players rather than first. We looked at Tedy Bruschi, Scooter McGruder, Jerome Henderson. Otis Smith is the best example. We brought him in as a third-down back. We started looking at the team from third-down play to first down rather than the other way around. Some people value first-down players more. But in reality, when you stop them on third down, you're off the field."[629]

Perhaps most importantly, the Patriots rotate at many positions so starters don't play every snap. 42 of the 53 players on the Patriots' 2003 opening day roster started at least one game that season.[630] As Patriots linebacker Mike Vrabel puts it,

> "When guys make this football team, they understand they are going to play some time during the season, and they don't know when. Your job as a football player is to be ready to play. It might not be this week, but it's going to be some time. It might not just be on special teams but it could be expanded roles."[631]

Patriots defensive lineman Jarvis Green was largely invisible all season before his three-sack performance in the 2003 AFC Championship Game. Green's monster game against Indianapolis illustrates how, according to Carl Banks (who played many seasons for Belichick's Giants and Browns), "[Belichick] understands how every person on his team can be put into an optimum role to have success."[632]

TEAM FIRST

> "We're a selfless team that enjoys being around each other. You don't see that very often."[633]
> *– Tom Brady*

> "I'm a winner. I'm a champion, man. I'll do whatever it takes to win. If [coach] feels like [playing me on defense] will help the team and give us some depth and really believes I can do it then I'll do it."[634]

– Ageless Patriots wide receiver Troy Brown, the longest-tenured Patriot player

"If [Belichick] understands you are passionate about football, that you love the game for the right reasons–the competitiveness of it, the purity of it and not the trappings of it–he respects that and will bend over backwards for [you]. If he feels you have a big ego or personal agendas, [you're] not going to last very long."[635]

– Patriots VP of player personnel Scott Pioli

When Bill Belichick asked Troy Brown, the longest-serving Patriot, now in his twelfth season with the team, to learn a totally new position, Brown didn't grumble or second-guess his coach: "I'm an employee here, so I do what the boss tells me. ...He's trying to build a little depth at that position and I told him I'd give him the best I had."[636] Brown already played on offense (wide receiver) and special teams (punt returner) and now had to train to play on defense (defensive back). It is unheard of for a veteran and star to be asked to learn a completely new position. But Brown, a true professional and team player, is proud to help his team in any capacity. He never grumbled: "Man, I welcomed it with open arms. I'm a football player, and any chance I have to get on the field, I want to be out there. But I didn't want to be out there just taking up space. I wanted to go out there and play well."[637] Belichick says he checked with Brown during the Rams game how he was handling playing on offense, defense, and special teams. Brown replied "Look, I'm a football player, it's football season, I'm going to play football. Put me in wherever you want me."[638]

Troy Brown lives up to UPS's tagline, "What can Brown do for you?" If Bill Belichick believed the Patriots could win more games by Brown taking charge of delivering Gatorade, Brown would sprint up and down the sidelines with the jug. Patriots linebacker Rosevelt Colvin says exactly that: "I just play where they tell me. They tell me to sweep the floors, and I'll get the broom."[639] Offensive lineman Stephen Neal agrees: "The job I have to do is simple. Whatever coach asks you to do, do it to the best of your ability."[640] Linebacker Mike Vrabel, who has caught three touchdown passes after lining up at tight end, loves helping out the offense: "What defensive player doesn't like scoring touchdowns?"[641] Brown might want to start bulking up because Belichick told the media: "[Brown] has always been one of the most cooperative and unselfish players I have coached. So, what we have asked him to do, he has done... I'm sure if we went in there and asked him to play tackle, he would go in there and play it the best he could."[642] Longsnapper Lonie Paxon says this makes his Patriots a true team: "I think what a championship football team is all about is people going above and beyond what they thought they were going to and doing everything the coach asks you to do. That's the way all of our guys are. They want to help the team and do whatever it takes."[643]

Owner Bob Kraft is proud of his players' selflessness, on and off the field. He cares deeply about the image players project, so he insists that every player involve himself in community service. Hiring "good guys" who act responsibly and with concern for others isn't mere marketing, do-gooding, or projecting a positive image to young fans. Kraft, like Belichick and Pioli, insists it's smart business:

> "We have a terrific locker room. By the way, what I've learned in 10 years of ownership is that most games are won in the locker room before you go on the field, with the kind of balance you have or don't have. And I think we have a wonderful balance with a lot of great men."[644]

The 2001 season made believers of many skeptics. By 2004, every NFL coach was scrambling to emphasize teamwork, but transforming an ego-driven locker room into a team-centric culture is a long process. Comparing the raw talent of his new team (the Detroit Lions) with the success of his former team (the Patriots), offensive lineman Damien Woody says, "The thing we had in New England is team chemistry among the players that I'd never seen anywhere before. I think that's what we [the Lions] have to develop."[645]

One of the newest Patriots, former Cincinnati Bengals star running back Corey Dillon, also noted the Patriots' unity: "It was just one heartbeat, offense and defense. The chemistry here is great and they know how to win football games."[646] He says joining his new team has been...

> "Everything and a bag of chips. ...You can't ask for more. This is a class organization top to bottom. You've got great coaches here that prepare you well. You've got guys that are on the same page and work hard and share one common goal of winning. ...You want to be around guys that you share the same goal with and guys who are thirsty and ready to hunt and get victories."[647]

Before joining the Patriots, Dillon had acquired a reputation as a selfish player. One unnamed NFL GM said, "That coaching staff's ability to keep players focused on what's good for the team will be tested now that Corey Dillon is there. He's one mean, selfish (jerk) who cares only about himself. Always has been."[648] Dillon repeatedly insisted that he wants to fit in as just another Patriots role player: "We have Tom Brady, one of the best quarterbacks in the NFL. We have a great receiving corps, a great offensive line, our defense is excellent. All I have to do is fit in and be one of the guys and play football."[649] He says, "I'm now just an extra ingredient to this big pie— and it's sweet."[650] Is he worried about getting the ball less in the Patriots' pass-heavy offense? He's talking like every other Patriot:

> "Well, that's no problem. Like I said, this team was already set. I am just going to be one of the guys and how many times they want to run it is up to them. I am just going to go by their guideline and be a team player. I am not even concerned about that. I am just happy to be a part of the team and help them try to win some football games."[651]

ESPN's Brian Murphy was shocked by Dillon's transformation:

"The guy was a bitching, whining moaner in Cincinnati. Now, in Patriots' blue, he is Audie Murphy with a helmet, all about the larger goal, not at all about individual glory. I heard him interviewed after the win over the Jets, and he sounded like he'd been injected with serum from 'The Manchurian Candidate.'"[652]

After seven seasons of losing, Dillon has a desperate passion to help a team win: "This whole game is predicated on winning… I just wanted to be part of an organization that thrives on winning."[653] On Dillon's first day of training camp, he continued to emphasize that all he cares about is winning: "I'm not trying to impress nobody. I'm just trying to play football. I ain't got no personal goals. I've just got one objective, and that's to win football games."[654] Dillon's teammates are convinced he's a team player. Said fullback Fred McCrary, who hoped to open gaping holes for Dillon to run through (but was cut before the season began):

"You'd be pissed too [if your team had suffered seven straight losing seasons]. Forget about him being selfish and all that. People are going to love that dude. He comes to work. You see him out here soaking wet every day. Plus he's got a little chip on his shoulder. …Thinking Rudi [Johnson] took his job and the whole nine. Watch him this year. That guy's on a mission."[655]

Team chemistry is the hallmark of recent Patriots teams. According to Cincinnati Bengals assistant coach Chuck Bresnahan, who has known Belichick since 1973 when their dads coached together at Navy:

"The thing about Bill is he's blue collar, which I really love… Look at what Bill did last year with that team, and how many high profile, big name players did they have? They weren't about the individual. They were about a 53-man roster. Playing as a group. Playing as 11 on defense. That's hard to beat. That's why they've won so many close games the last three years."[656]

If Patriots players epitomize "team first," Ryan Leaf is the poster child for "me first." A head-turningly great college quarterback and the second player taken in the entire 1998 NFL draft, Leaf had an insanely powerful arm, tremendous size, and spectacular productivity in college. The only question many scouts had about Leaf was whether he should be the #1 or #2 pick in the draft. Despite Hall of Fame physical potential, Leaf was a complete bust in the NFL. The major cause of his downfall was his towering ego. Leaf's arrogance was no secret. Draft guru Joel Buchsbaum wrote in the *1998 Pro Football Weekly Draft Preview* that Leaf was "Very self-confident to the point where some people view him as arrogant and almost obnoxious." Leaf placed himself above his team, and his Chargers teammates despised him. They didn't want to play with him. They wanted him to fail. And fail he did, spectacularly!

Career NFL statistics of Ryan Leaf

Year	Team	Games	Complete Passes	Pass Attempts	Comp %	Yards	TDs	Ints	Fumbles
1998	Chargers	10	111	245	45.3%	1,289	2	15	8
1999	Chargers	11	161	322	50.0%	1,883	11	18	12
2000	Cowboys	4	45	88	51.1%	494	1	3	4

The Patriots would never draft a player with an ego like Leaf's. Any player who fails to appreciate that his success is utterly dependent on the success of his teammates cannot survive on Belichick's Patriots. Contrast Leaf's attitude with that of Tom Brady immediately after being named Super Bowl MVP at the tender age of 24½: "[Our] whole team, as far as I'm concerned, is MVP. I always say a quarterback is as good as the team around him, and we have some unbelievable talent."[657]

On Day 2 of the 2003 NFL Draft, Belichick wanted to take a flyer on a player with obvious talent who had character issues. If that player didn't work out, Belichick figured, the team could cut him. VP of player personnel Scott Pioli convinced Belichick not to send his team the wrong message and risk re-creating the poisonous locker room atmosphere a handful of character-challenged Browns players had created in Belichick's days as Cleveland's head coach.[658] Eighteen months later, that talented but character-challenged player "isn't playing for the team that picked him, and he's in his team's doghouse."[659]

Patriots backup quarterback Rohan Davey parrots Brady when discussing his incredible 2004 success (league MVP and World Bowl championship) in NFL Europe: "I feel as if whatever a situation calls for and throwing in any situation, I can make the best of it along with my teammates and people around me. No one does it on their own."[660] Everyone associated with the Patriots talks this way. After becoming the youngest-ever winner of the NFL Executive of the Year award,[661] VP of Player Personnel Scott Pioli said, "The award truly represents the ownership, coaching staff, scouting staff and players. To me, it's a statement about the organization"[662] and "This award is a direct reflection of the trust and support given by Robert and Jonathan Kraft... The award is also a by-product of great teamwork within our organization, starting with Bill Belichick and including our assistant coaches, our players and our entire scouting staff."[663] How excited was Pioli to be singled out for his achievement? "You enjoy these things when you retire, I've been told."[664] Pioli has also said, "I don't care that people don't know who I am."[665] But success speaks louder than words, and every NFL executive is very familiar with Scott Pioli.

The Patriots' ubiquitous humility and near denial of individual achievement emanates from Bill Belichick. Belichick's official statement after being named 2003 NFL Coach of the Year (with 35½ votes compared with 7 for runner-up Marvin Lewis of the Bengals) highlighted the important contributions of virtually everyone in the organization... except himself:

"I am honored to accept this award as recognition of the tremendous work of our entire coaching staff, personnel department and Mr. Kraft. Coaching is always a collective effort that depends on the assistant coaches' preparation and direction and the players' performance on the field. More than anything, it was the players' exceptional resiliency, toughness and execution under pressure that allowed us to have a successful regular season."

Asked by the media about winning Coach of the Year honors, Belichick continued spotlighting scouts and video people, not himself:

"the award is something that a lot of people in this organization should share and take part of starting with the assistant coaches, the scouting department, the people that help the coaches like the video people and guys like that who put in countless hours to give us an opportunity to do what we have to."[666]

Pressed further, he insisted on looking forward, not back, explaining, "It is not that big of a deal. I am more concerned about what the team does."[667]

After a 2003 season full of highlights, Belichick was most impressed that no one within his entire organization had ever placed himself above his team:

"The thing that stands out as much as anything–[in addition to] the accomplishments, the 15 wins in a row, the Super Bowl victory, the records and performances in all the types of games we won–is that nobody wants to take the credit for it. Nobody's saying, 'It's because of me and I'm the guy.' To me, that's as rare as anything else that happened. They want to spread the credit to everyone but themselves."[668]

Belichick predictably minimized Tom Brady's role in earning his second Super Bowl MVP trophy: "The MVP trophy in the Super Bowl usually goes to the winning team. That's what's most important to Tom, and I know it's what's most important to this team."[669] After Brady won the Cadillac Escalade that came with his first Super Bowl MVP trophy, he announced the SUV belonged to all the players.[670] After safety Eugene Wilson was named AFC Defensive Player of the Month for September 2004, Belichick didn't tear up with pride for his second-year player because "We're not that big on individual awards around here."[671] No kidding.

Arrogant players can thrive in sports like tennis and golf because outcomes are determined by individual performance. Even baseball involves far less teamsmanship because team performance is approximately the sum of players' individual contributions. In baseball, the optimal strategy for each position can be written down for a finite list of situations, like "if the batter bunts the ball toward third base." In football, eleven men work together on every play against another eleven men who are coordinating their actions. As Gregg Easterbrook writes, "Academic-trendy figures who speak of baseball as the intellectual sport may do so only because football is too complicated for them to understand. ...a baseball player cut because he could not remember the playbook is rare indeed."[672] (I suspect many academics were too small and frail to participate in and fall in love with football.)

Football is inherently a team sport; you can't judge a football team by adding together players' individual contributions.

Because football involves far more strategic and tactical complexity than baseball, teamsmanship is far more important. Football demands players and coaches who bond together, both emotionally and mentally. Without strong ties, the whole is less than the sum of the parts. On the Patriots, strong bonds improve everyone's performance. Patriots players understand this. For example, veteran linebacker Willie McGinest so valued the coaching he received from outside linebackers coach Rob Ryan (who helped McGinest earn a selection to the Pro Bowl after the 2003 season) that McGinest paid for Ryan's Hawaiian honeymoon.

Patriots players enjoy joking around and teasing each other. They also enjoy working hard together. This positive group dynamic keeps egos in check and boosts collective performance. Patriots linebacker Ted Johnson says Patriots players bond during training camp: "[Training] camp is also about the camaraderie, the downtime, the jokes, and the tricks you play on each other. That piece, those team-building activities, are essential."[673]

As friends and teammates who share a passion for winning, Patriots help one another focus on preparations for winning each upcoming game. After winning Super Bowl XXXVIII, Patriots linebacker Tedy Bruschi said, "we're a team. Fifteen in a row speaks for itself. If we had a game next week, we'd be focused on winning it."[674] Any player who places personal needs above team needs or lacks the discipline to perform his role in preparing the team for its next game (whether as a starter, backup, special teams player, or even a scout team participant emulating the upcoming opponent) does not last long as a Patriot. Players who excel in New England instead believe, as Tom Brady does, that "You can't do everything you want to do if you still want to be the best at what I want to be the best at." "Be all you can be" could be the Patriots' recruiting slogan.

The Patriots acquire "team first" individuals and feed them their "team first" philosophy. Players drink the Kool Aid. 340-pound rookie defensive tackle Vince Wilfork, the team's 2004 #1 draft pick from the Miami Hurricanes, already "gets it":

> "If they want me to penetrate, I'll penetrate. If they want me to sit back and hold up the line, I'll do that. It's about the team. It's not about me. That's what I'm looking forward to. To look in the playbook and see what type of schemes they have so I can get to work on my end."[675]

The Patriots seek out players eager to bust their butts to achieve their full potential and to help their teammates do the same. Countless talented players flounder in the NFL because they fail to maximize their potential or to work smoothly with their teammates. The Patriots love guys like rookie tight end Benjamin Watson who is humble and hungry enough to know that his eye-popping ability to run a 4.4-second 40-yard dash and bench press 560 pounds "doesn't mean you can go out on this grass and play football."[676] Raw "talent" must be trained to a professional standard and fit into a team framework before it can yield success in the NFL.

BE A ROLE PLAYER... DON'T TRY TO BE A BIG HERO

"There is no getting away from the assignments. You just can't put 11 guys out there and let them run around and think that everything is going to work."[677]

– Bill Belichick

Everyone in the Patriots organization, including Belichick, knows his role, believes in performing his role to the best of his ability, and ignores anything that doesn't impact his ability to perform his role:

"Every person on the team has a job to do. A coach has a job to do. The quarterback has a job to do. The left guard has a job to do. The middle linebacker has a job to do. I can't do his. They can't do mine. They can't do each other's. They have to do theirs. How the team comes together and everybody is able to perform in their role and maximize their capacity in their role, that is what having a good team is all about."[678]

This is no throw-away line. It's practically a Belichick stump speech:

"I have a job to do, Charlie [Weis] has a job to do, Romeo [Crennel] has a job to do, Pepper [Johnson] has a job to do, Corey Dillon's got a job to do, and none of us can do each others' jobs. You wouldn't want me doing some of the things that other people are doing, and other people are a lot better at doing the things that they do. So that's what a team is–everybody goes out and does their job. I don't think anybody deserves any credit for anything other than their individual role in the team. It's the team that's been successful, when it's been successful, and whether it's successful or not in the future will depend upon how well everybody handles their individual responsibilities. That's really what I try to focus on, and what I think our team tries to focus on–is just taking care of your job, and having confidence in everybody else that they'll get theirs done."[679]

Success is easier if you know your role and focus on it. Three-time Pro Bowl running back Corey Dillon always felt pressure in Cincinnati to carry his Bengals on his back. He felt he had to be Superman or his team would lose. In New England, Dillon knows his teammates have won two NFL championships without him, so he simply needs to do his job well. He feels liberated knowing he can rely on his teammates: "To me, this is less pressure, because these guys have done it already. I don't have to carry the load. Brady's a great quarterback, and we've got great receivers. I can just sit back, relax and worry about getting those tough yards."[680]

Trust your teammates and play within the scheme

"We never give up, never lose poise as a team. We look to each other for support."[681]
— Patriots cornerback Ty Law

"Hopefully, what everybody is thinking about at [crunch time] is executing the play. 'Here's what we have to do. This is what my job is on this play. I have to make sure I get that taken care of. I can't worry about what the guy next to me is doing. I have confidence in him that he's going to do what he's supposed to do.'"[682]
— Bill Belichick

"There's no 'I' around here. I've seen a lot of teams say, 'There's no 'I' in team.' They talk about it a lot. But they don't just talk about it here. I've never seen a team with such humility as this team. A team where players are willing to play within the system, and understand that if we win, everyone will get the accolades."[683]
— Patriots veteran special teamer and backup linebacker Don Davis (who played on the Rams Super Bowl team the Patriots defeated)

"[Success] means everybody taking care of their responsibility. Everybody has a responsibility to take care [of] and defensively, once you show vulnerability in one area, then a lot of times that leads to problems across the board because you try to plug that up and then you end up softening yourself in other spots and pretty soon you have holes all over the place."[684]
— Bill Belichick

Many teams get in trouble when Player A worries about Player B's responsibilities. The Red Sox demonstrated this during the 2004 World Series when their catcher and third baseman, each of whom could easily have caught a Cardinals foul ball, both insisted on making the catch and wound up preventing each other from catching it. If coaches design roles (responsibilities) properly, intelligently match players to roles, and adapt roles according to players' strengths and weaknesses, then the team maximizes its odds of winning if each player focuses exclusively on performing his role. A player will focus on his role if he understands it and trusts his teammates to perform their roles properly. Each Patriot knows his responsibilities, knows his teammates' responsibilities, and trusts his teammates. So he never tries to be a hero by doing a teammate's job because that would leave his job undone. Says Belichick: "Teamwork is the ability for you to count on somebody else, and them to count on you. Whether it's two people or 100 people, it's all the same. We have a term: 'One die, all die.' If somebody makes a mistake, everybody pays a price."[685]

Patriots players know they're in one boat and will sink or swim together. When the Patriots run defense was sinking in 2002, players accepted collective responsibility. A major reason why they couldn't stop the run was poor coordination resulting from players attempting to handle others' responsibilities. Linebacker Mike Vrabel explained that as each defender pressed individually to tackle the running back, the run defense became less coordinated and less successful:

> "Little things, stuff like 'gap control' …We aren't a team that can get by with athleticism. We have to be coordinated in what we do and that hasn't been the case. And when you start losing, well, everyone seems to try to do too much, you know? Everybody wants to be the guy who makes the play and, invariably, you make mistakes instead. You dig the hole a little deeper."[686]

Linebacker Ted Johnson understands this too:

> "Coordination is so important in the front seven. If you have one or two guys who aren't where they're supposed to be, the offense can gash you pretty good. Sometimes in an attempt to make things happen, somebody will get outside the framework of the defense, which creates more problems. We need to work together, with everybody taking care of his assignment and not trying to do too much."[687]

Safety Rodney Harrison says, "In football, everybody has a job to do. You have to take care of your responsibilities and not try to go above and beyond the call of duty. That's when you get exposed."[688]

In 2004, the Patriots' run defense looked lousy on opening day (allowing Edgerrin James to gain 142 yards on 30 carries) but stiffened as rookie nose tackle Vince Wilfork learned to play the Patriots' two-gap style. Wilfork's primary responsibility is "gap control": standing his ground against the run. Wilfork understands he's playing a team sport and must focus on his responsibilities and let his teammates worry about theirs: "I have my linebackers in back of me who can scrape up everything. Anything [that gets] behind me, they're going to knock your head off. A lot of people want to run at us, but starting today, I think we showed that we are capable of stopping the run."[689] Even as a rookie, Wilfork's prodding the Patriots' veteran linebackers: "I've told them, 'If I'm going to be up there holding up guys, you better make the tackle.' But they have. They've been working like dogs."[690]

Belichick explains to players the danger of succumbing to the temptation to do a teammate's job:

> "'Okay, I am covering this guy, but some guy isn't playing [well] over there. What am I going to do–go cover that guy?' I mean, it is impossible. If a player really wants to help the team… the best thing he can do is do his job as well as he possibly can. That is the best thing a player can do for this football team. As soon as he starts to do everybody else's job, there is no way he can be as effective doing his job. To try to get into that type of game, 'I am

supposed to be here, but I am going to be over there,' then who is here? It just doesn't work."[691]

Belichick reinforces his team-centric message through team-building exercises. During an August 2003 training camp session, Belichick noticed players had grown cranky and tired. He injected excitement by challenging left tackle Matt Light, who had never caught a punt in his life, to catch three consecutive punts and promising to cancel the next day's session if Light succeeded. What happened? Players flooded Light with advice, showing him how to block the sun with his hands, for example. "Troy Brown is telling him to put his hands here, and Deion Branch is showing him how the ball spins and where it'll come. You talk about a team coming together over one guy catching punts."[692] Light amazed everyone by catching all three, and players went nuts. "When they knew they didn't have to go back on the field the next day, [Light] could have run for governor."[693] A year later, Belichick gave Light another chance to end the training day by catching a punt, and Light again thrilled his teammates... this time making a difficult over-the-shoulder catch on the run. He then sprinted to punter Josh Miller and hoisted him into the air... yet another example of Patriots acknowledging that personal success derives from teamwork. (Sadly, during that same session, Light attempted a 25-yard field goal that he somehow managed to line drive in the wrong direction.[694] Light, mocking the Patriots' tradition of never pointing fingers, blamed his miss on the long-snapper: "The snap wasn't the best snap but that's why you practice. If that was in game, I'd be upset. I'd probably throw my helmet off. Thank God we were just having some fun."[695])

Patriots players appreciate that Belichick's system spells out each player's responsibilities, letting each player focus on performing a well-defined role. Players trust their teammates to perform their roles because their teammates' skill and professionalism and their coaches' high standards and teaching skills instill confidence. Linebacker Rosevelt Colvin, for example, says he has the luxury of not rushing his return from his fractured hip:

> "Last year before I got hurt we had a good group of linebackers, so even then there wasn't a lot of pressure on me to make a lot of plays. The group of guys I was coming into were pretty good already. It [now] helps that I don't have to go out and play the whole game... I'm fortunate to be in the situation I'm in, where I don't have to take on a large load at this point."[696]

Patriot players are constantly saying how much they trust their teammates. Offensive lineman Tom Ashworth after Super Bowl XXXVIII: "I'll put my faith in Brady and our receivers any time. And tonight you saw why."[697] Tom Brady on receiver David Givens: "As a quarterback you always want to trust the receiver and the dependability and the consistency of the guys you throw to. You just want to know where they're going to be and how well they're going to do what they're going to do and that if you throw it to them they're going to catch it. That's David."[698] "Whenever you throw it past the first-down sticks, [Givens] catches it, and if he catches it short of the first-down sticks, he will turn around and run over some guys."[699] Safety Rodney Harrison says, "We believe in each other, we believe in our coaches and we believe if we all do our jobs we will win as a team."[700] Corey Dillon: "I look out at my [offensive] line, which did a great job, and they've got my back, and I have theirs. That's what makes it work."[701]

Patriots trust their teammates because they like them as people and respect them as football players. Patriots differ in many ways, but they are all upbeat, nice guys who love football and love winning. Tom Brady says, "We're a selfless team. You have 22-year-old guys and 38-year-old guys. You have guys who are married with kids, and guys right out of college. Everybody is different. But we enjoy being around each other, and we really enjoy playing football."[702] They also practice together, practice togetherness, and know that Belichick's meritocracy tolerates no slackers or poor performers.

Linebacker Mike Vrabel believes "It's silly to say that we don't have the players that everybody else has, but this team does understand what each other can do better than any other team I've been around."[703] Knowing and trusting their teammates' talents and tendencies allows each Patriot to focus on his responsibilities. Playing within the team's scheme is crucial because players who try to win games on their own often end up losing games on their own, according to Arizona Cardinals head coach Dennis Green:

> "The quarterbacks that have success are the guys who are able to kind of stay the course on what's expected of them and don't try to make incredible plays. They will occur when they occur, but you have to go out and make solid plays and get other guys to do their part. It's what I call carrying their own water."[704]

After the Patriots' star defensive lineman Richard Seymour recorded zero tackles and zero sacks against the Arizona Cardinals, he was disappointed but noted he's part of a team defense and that his occupying blockers frees up his teammates to make plays:

> "Everything is not going to be predicated on me. You just have to be patient and when something comes your way you have to make [the play]. I don't want to play outside of the scheme to get things done. In the opener we had a three-man rush, and we were concentrating on [the Colts'] passing game, and rightfully so. Then [against the Cardinals] we had outside linebackers and safeties coming down and making plays. It's just important for us defensively, especially up front, to be solid in our techniques. Rodney Harrison had two sacks, and he's a safety. He's coming down and making those type of plays, where usually it's a defensive lineman."[705]

In that Cardinals game, safety Rodney Harrison and outside linebackers Willie McGinest and Mike Vrabel racked up five sacks and fifteen tackles while the defensive linemen made few tackles. This was by design, not because the defensive linemen played poorly. Fans often judge players by their stats, but Patriots judge one another by whether they help win games. Belichick points out, for example, that "If you're a defensive back and you're covering your guy and they don't throw him the ball, that's doing your job [better] than having them throw the ball and making the tackle after the catch."[706]

Patriots also embrace the "role" Belichick hopes they will take toward the media: 1) speaking only positively about opponents; 2) speaking only positively about their teammates; and, 3) never bragging about their own "individual achievements." At the start of the 2003 training camp, for example, the media tried to goad Tom Brady into expressing frustration toward the few players who showed up out of shape (*i.e.*, unable to complete twenty 50-yard sprints in under seven seconds each). Brady, focused on his responsibilities and too smart to create an unproductive public controversy, didn't take the bait because he knew coaches would discipline out-of-shape players in private:

> "Q: What are your thoughts on the guys who didn't [complete] the conditioning run? Is that very disappointing…
> Brady: That's really one of those things that you just let Coach take care of…
> Q: But… as you said, you can't waste a day of practice…
> Brady: …for me to worry about that is not really helpful. I try to work and be in the best condition I can be.[707]

As head coach, Bill Belichick isn't a role player, right? Wrong. Belichick entrusts coordination of the team's offense, defense, and special teams to his coordinators. He delegates many personnel and contractual matters to front-office executives. For example, Belichick doesn't worry about draftees who haven't signed, even draftees who hold out beyond the start of training camp, because Belichick delegates responsibility for contracts to the superb team of Scott Pioli, Andy Wasynczuk (COO, senior VP, and "capologist"), and Jack Mula. Wasynczuk is a Harvard Business School graduate (as are Bob Kraft and Jonathan Kraft) and a former Bain consultant who began managing the Patriots' salary cap in the 1990s. When three players remained unsigned after the start of training camp 2004, Belichick answered a reporter's question with a non-answer: "When both sides agree, that is when there will be a contract and that is when they will be here. Until that point, they won't. …It is what it is."[708] Asked later about the status of contract negotiations with first-round draft pick and hold-out Benjamin Watson, Bill deadpanned, "I was going to ask you guys about that."[709]

RESPECT YOUR COLLEAGUES AND SHARE CREDIT FOR SUCCESSES

"Do we [wide receivers] get enough respect? Yes, we get it from us. We like the position we're in. You're not going to have everyone standing out on a team. It's OK with us."[710]
— *Patriots wide receiver Deion Branch*

"Turn on the TV and watch the highlights and you see a bunch of individuals making plays and celebrating as individuals. We don't play to make highlight shows. Watch how we celebrate—with our teammates. Always."[711]
— *Patriots linebacker Tedy Bruschi*

Patriots players voted linebacker Mike Vrabel the team's 2003 Ed Block Courage Award winner after he played most of the season with a broken arm. Vrabel sounded more honored and excited to receive this obscure award, because it was voted by his teammates, than he would a Pro Bowl start, which is determined by the NFL's fans, coaches, and players:

"When [your teammates] recognize you and when they appreciate what you do, that's what means a lot to me. You want to win the Super Bowls and make the Pro Bowls and bring home the big bucks, but at the end of the day, if your teammates recognize what you're doing, that's the thing."[712]

Vrabel says his fellow linebacker Tedy Bruschi feels identically:

"Justice would have been served if he had made the Pro Bowl this year. But he is no less of a player just because he didn't. He's heralded among the guys on the team. When you can garner the respect of the teammates and coaches, then with players like Tedy and I, that's all you need."[713]

Bruschi confirms that, to him, team success trumps individual recognition:

"[P]layers can get sort of engulfed in their place among the best and forget about team goals. They worry about Pro Bowls and they worry about being All Pro, and they forget what it takes to win football games. To be the best linebacker in the league or to be a member of the best team in the league, I'll take the latter."[714]

Patriots cornerback Terrell Buckley similarly craves only his teammates' respect: "When you walk into a place full of athletes, your peers, and the respect is there immediately, that's all you need, that's all I needed."[715]

A famous quotation holds that you can accomplish anything as long as you don't care who gets the credit. The Patriots are living proof. When journalists praise a Patriot player's performance, that player invariably deflects credit away from himself onto just about everyone else. To a Patriot player, public credit is a hot potato, something to be passed immediately to other players and coaches. For example, after Patriots cornerback Ty Law intercepted a pass in Super Bowl XXXVI and ran it back 47 yards for a touchdown, Law said: "Credit [linebacker] Mike Vrabel on that one. He got in Warner's face on the blitz and made him hurry the pass. It was right there for the taking and I got it and ran."[716] Vrabel refuses the credit: "To me, that play with Ty Law–that wasn't a contribution. They didn't block me. Let's be honest. I thought it was a screen or a draw. I got there late, I didn't even get the sack."[717] Similarly, after wide receiver David Patten made a brilliant, acrobatic touchdown grab in that same Super Bowl so impressive the Rams challenged the ruling that Patten had control of the ball with both feet in-bounds, all Patten could talk about was how great Tom Brady's throw had been: "Tom threw the ball before I turned around, which is the right thing to do in that spot as the quarterback. But I saw the ball coming at me at like 100 miles an hour and all I wanted to do was just catch it and fall in bounds. I knew I had a step on the d-back, and the ball was there. It was a tremendous throw by Tom."[718] After the Patriots won their second Super Bowl, running back Kevin Faulk became a broken record regarding the offensive line's performance: "All running back Kevin Faulk could say to me early Monday was: 'How about that offensive line? How about that offensive line, man? How about that offensive line? How about that offensive line, man?' It didn't stop there. But, I got his point."[719]

Tom Brady is the Patriots' best facsimile of a superstar, but Brady insists he's surrounded by superstars who make him look good:

> "My receivers, they always catch the ball. We expect them to run the right routes, find the holes, and get open, and that's what they do… Our offensive line, they don't get enough credit, and I don't know why not. …What we've accomplished, it starts with our offensive line."[720]

As quarterback of 2004 NFL Europe's Berlin Thunder, Patriots backup quarterback Rohan Davey did his best Tom Brady imitation, both on and off the field. After Davey won league-wide "Offensive Player of the Week" honors three of the first five weeks, Thunder coach Rick Lantz praised him as "just outstanding… the complete package and… always in command."[721] With many calling him the greatest player in NFL Europe history, Davey credited his coaches and teammates: "It's a combination of having a good position coach in Steve Logan, a good offensive coordinator in Don Eck and good players around me."[722] The next week he wrote, "I'm surrounded by good coaches and I have such a good team around me and good teammates that it's made my job easier… When it's time to play ball [my teammates] really come to play. The receivers are terrific and the offensive line is smart and tough and they keep me clean every week."[723]

Bill Belichick and the coaches are just as modest. They don't forget to point fingers at themselves following losses, and they make sure to credit the players following victories. Belichick friend and rock musician Jon Bon Jovi asks, rhetorically, "Have you ever seen him wear any of his Super Bowl rings? …I work with Jaws [Ron Jaworski] and he wears his NFC Championship ring like it's his wedding band. And he won that thing 23 years ago!"[724] The following exchange between Belichick and David Letterman is representative:

> Letterman: "Are you smarter than everybody else coaching in the NFL?"
> Belichick: "No. No. I don't think so. I'm fortunate. I've got a great group of assistant coaches, we have a tremendous support staff and an outstanding group of players. They're the ones who make the plays. That's why I'm here. I just take the credit. ...Just around the home, Dave, I get brought down to Earth right away. When I do something dumb there, my kids will say, 'You moron! What did you do that for?'"[725]

Bill inherited his modesty from his parents. Bill's father Steve, an innovative football coach for many decades, says, "I'm number three in our family when it comes to brains. And I'm a distant third. My wife and son are kicking dust in my face. I used to be able to say I was number one in football, but I can't even say that any more."[726]

Belichick displayed a different form of respect by not replacing popular quarterbacks coach Dick Rehbein following his sudden passing in early August 2001. Belichick and offensive coordinator Charlie Weis wisely assumed Coach Rehbein's responsibilities, partly because finding and instructing an appropriate replacement would have taken time and energy and partly because rushing to "replace" Rehbein would have seemed disrespectful. Rehbein was, in a sense, irreplaceable. Not replacing him inspired everyone else to work that much harder in his memory. That dignified decision may have helped propel the 2001 Patriots to Super Bowl victory.

Chapter 6

ACQUIRING TALENT

"We've got good players. We've got smart players. We've got humble players. We've got guys who love to play ball."[727]
– Tom Brady

"When you take a player onto your team, you get everything that that player has. You get his mental makeup. You get his physical makeup. You get, to a certain degree, his work ethic. You get his confidence. You may be able to improve some of those things marginally, but in the end, you're getting the whole package, and you'd better be comfortable with that or you're probably going to end up looking for another player."[728]
– Bill Belichick

HIRING WELL IS JOB #1

"Among the effective executives I have had occasion to observe, [some] make decisions fast, and [some] make them rather slowly. But without exception, they make personnel decisions slowly and they make them several times before they really commit themselves...People decisions are time-consuming [because] People are always 'almost fits' at best."[729]
– Peter Drucker, father of management science

Hiring well is essential to success because no team can win without capable players. It's obvious from the Patriots' heavy investment in personnel research that they understand the importance of hiring well.

The NFL salary cap restricts spending on players but not on non-player personnel. Smart teams invest heavily in coaching and scouting. The New England Patriots have a top-notch scouting program. Since a rookie's pay is based heavily on the draft slot in which he is selected, a team's spending on rookies is largely pre-determined, but the quality of the drafted rookies varies substantially. Teams that draft wisely, like the Patriots, get better players for their money. Late in the 2003 season, NFL expert Rick Gosselin wrote an article, "Redrafting the class of 2003." It begins: "Too bad all the NFL teams couldn't pick from New England's draft board last April. Then everyone might have had a good draft."[730] Gosselin believes three of the Patriots' draftees (center Dan Koppen, defensive lineman Ty Warren, and cornerback Eugene Wilson) were among the top 22 players available in the 2003 Draft. On Draft Day, the Patriots believed they had grabbed three of the top eighteen players in the draft (Ty Warren, Eugene Wilson, and Bethel Johnson)[731] with their first three picks (the #13, #36, and #45 picks overall).

Asked to explain the secret to their drafting success, Scott Pioli cited clear objectives and hard work:

> "I don't know if there is any special secret in what we do here–other than a lot of people being on the same page, looking for the same kind of players. It's just a lot of people here pouring hard work and passion into something. I'm just not sure I'd call that a secret."[732]

The NFL Draft has long been considered "a crapshoot." Scott Pioli disagrees. He insists intensive, disciplined research and consistent evaluation methods eliminate most uncertainties:

> "For as much time as we put into it, as much work as we do, I can't believe anything about the success in the draft has to do with luck. We may make some good decisions and some wrong decisions. I'm just not going to say there's any luck involved."[733]

As one example of the intense effort the Patriots scouting system exerts to find just the right college players, consider that the Pioli-led scouting system considers 4,000 players each season. The system eliminates 3,900 before Bill Belichick begins looking at the remaining hundred players.[734] Because the system screens out so many players, Belichick can make optimal use of whatever time he has to watch film of potential Patriot-type draftees.

Unfortunately for Patriots fans, the quality of the Patriots scouting system is no longer a secret. The Philadelphia Eagles have raided several Patriots scouts. Jason Licht became the Eagles' assistant director of player personnel in May 2003, and Sean Gustus became the Eagles' Northeast region scout in May 2004.[735] But the quality of and emphasis on the Patriots scouting program demonstrate the importance Belichick and his organization place on identifying and hiring the most suitable players.

KNOW YOUR NEEDS

> "Our way won't work for a lot of [teams]. But just because a player doesn't make it in our system doesn't mean he won't fit in another system. To me, it's all about an organization understanding how they want the environment to be. You have to get players who can fit in with the leadership structure, especially the head coach."[736]
>
> – *Scott Pioli*

A Joe Jackson song says, "You can't get what you want till you know what you want." Bill Belichick's Patriots know what they want... and get it... at the right price. Belichick's Patriots don't make *ad hoc* personnel decisions. Each player is, in effect, a bundle of skills (plus potential to improve on those skills, given training and experience). Patriots coaches seek to maximize collective performance by optimizing the portfolio of skill bundles possessed by their 53 players (plus non-roster players cut in training camp but potentially available for re-signing, should injuries occur). Because injuries are inevitable and unpredictable and because a football team must perform many different roles (on offense, defense, and special teams, with situational substitutions at many positions), the Patriots believe winning as many games as possible requires a flexible, resilient, energetic, competitive, cohesive team with quality throughout its roster, not concentrated in its starting lineup or in a handful of stars.

But winning requires more than skills. Each player also possesses a bundle of attitudes, beliefs, and behavioral tendencies. Because personalities are harder to change than muscles or knowledge, Patriots VP of player personnel Scott Pioli paints a clear picture for his scouts of the mental/behavioral characteristics Belichick craves. Pioli leaves nothing to chance, providing detailed criteria for filtering out players who won't fit the grueling, starless Patriots system. The objective is winning... with class. As Pioli puts it: "We want to win the right way with the right kind of people. And that's paramount. It's not just going out and getting players that have great skills and have wonderful tools. We're looking for players that fit the personality of our organization."[737] Unlike every other dominant team in NFL history, the Patriots are not loaded with future Hall of Famers. No team in the salary cap era can field an All Pro team. The Patriots are smart shoppers who find bargain players because they know which talents and traits are essential for their system and which are luxuries. Pioli says, "Some people term [our players] 'second tier' or the 'next level [down].' We don't see them as that type of player. They're the right player for he way we want to construct our team."[738]

"The personality of our organization" is no cliché. Belichick's father (author of the highly-regarded book *Football Scouting Methods*) says the Patriots have succeeded because "They got rid of the wrong kind of people and brought in the right kind."[739] The Patriots' scouting manual, written by Scott Pioli and Ernie Adams, asks scouts to answer football questions tailored to whatever position a prospect plays. But the manual pushes scouts beyond football to determine of each prospect: "Is he ready to act like an adult? Would you let this player spend time with your family? How important is football to him?"[740] Patriots scouts are not permitted to provide general impressions of a player or wishy-washy, ass-covering "opinions." Patriots scouts must provide detailed answers to questions tailored to assess each player's suitability to and likely performance in the Patriots' system. They must also express (and defend with evidence) a clear opinion on each prospect. Every potential Patriot is graded both on how well he plays his position and on seven "major factors": athletic ability, behavior and personal, competitiveness, durability and injury, mental and learning, strength and explosion, and toughness.[741] Non-athletic traits are critical because they determine a player's coachability, reliability, competitiveness, ability to assist and motivate teammates, and the speed with which he will grow toward his full potential. Tellingly, Belichick mentions "physical skills" *after* mental traits he seeks: "work ethic, intelligence, physical skills, playing style, versatility."[742]

Scott Pioli explains that smarts and self-discipline are essential because Patriots coaches spend their limited time analyzing, strategizing, and teaching, not monitoring and disciplining:

> "If we bring in players that aren't smart, they're going to have a very difficult time lasting in our environment. If I bring in players that are high-maintenance, they're going to have a very difficult time lasting in our system. We're all business; that's the way it's going to be. So if we bring in immature players, they don't have a very good chance."[743]

Toughness, selflessness, and love of football are also essentials, according to Patriots linebacker Roman Phifer: "Coach Belichick gets guys in here who are hungry, smart and tough. There's so much individual hype in the game today, and there's the ego factor, but we've found guys who are committed to winning no matter what it takes."[744] The Patriots find such players. Admiring former Dallas Cowboys personnel director Gil Brandt confirms that "[The Patriots are] a model for getting smart guys, character guys and competitive guys."[745]

Match skills to job requirements

> "If you're a player, they'll figure out a way to use you. That's why I'm here. That and, truthfully, to win one of those [Super Bowl] rings these guys are wearing."[746]
>
> *– Patriots safety Victor Green*

"Beauty is in the eye of the beholder." "One man's trash is another man's treasure." The Patriots have put these truisms to work in quilting together a cohesive, dominant team from a collection of unheralded individuals. They unearth overlooked talent through in-depth research and a clear vision of how each player's particular bundle of skills, traits, strengths and weaknesses matches the team's needs. They're not merely looking backwards at past performance but projecting forward to estimate how a player would perform within the Patriots' system:

> "[Scott Pioli]'s one of the top young personnel guys in the league as far as sniffing out low-rent guys… He gets a ton of guys who can contribute right away… He does an extremely thorough job of researching guys and getting in players who fit the schemes the coaches want. He gets guys who fit the criteria the coaches are looking for. Not everybody does that. …[Belichick and Pioli] really understand value of players in their system."[747]

In other words, the Patriots don't ask, "How good is this player?" They ask, "What contribution would this player make within our system?" This is essential because football performance is not about individual talent; it's about the fit between individual and system.

This section highlights one example: the Patriots' need for smart, adaptable players because they use complicated schemes and insist that players learn multiple positions (to maximize personnel flexibility). The Patriots defense is notoriously complex and confusing. After Belichick took over in 2000, cornerback Ty Law admitted the intellectual demands had lept up:

> "I've been doing a little more thinking than I usually have to do. ... [W]e'll pick [the new scheme] up sooner or later. ...We've got a lot more tricks and a lot more terminology. We have a lot more zone blitz schemes and things like that."[748]

The Patriots have a slew of linebackers (including Tully Banta-Cain, Tedy Bruschi, Rosevelt Colvin, Dan Klecko, Willie McGinest, Mike Vrabel, and Justin Kurpeikis) who were outstanding collegiate defensive linemen but converted to linebackers in the pros because they lacked the mammoth size typical of NFL linemen. Tedy Bruschi, for example, holds the all-time NCAA Division 1 sack lead, having sacked college quarterbacks 52 times. McGinest and Vrabel were also great college linemen, as Miami fullback Rob Konrad pointed out: "Look at those guys, you see two All-American defensive ends. They're huge. They create mismatches and they do a lot with them."[749] Vrabel's 36 sacks as a defensive end set the Ohio State record.[750] So did his 66 tackles for a loss. And Dan Klecko, whom the Patriots are now grooming as Tedy Bruschi's backup at linebacker, was Defensive Player of the Year in the Big East Conference (which includes nationally-ranked teams like Miami, Pittsburgh, Syracuse, and Virginia Tech) as a nose tackle, even though Klecko's Temple Owls were atrocious. Belichick loves repurposing fast but undersized collegiate defensive linemen as linebackers because, he says, there are simply too few college linebackers with the size to play in the pros: "You look at guys in college that are 6-foot-3 or 6-foot-4, and 250 to 255 pounds, and they are playing down [as defensive linemen]. They are not playing on their feet [as linebackers]."[751]

Another reason Belichick loves defensive-line-to-linebacker converts is their ability to drop down "in the dirt" as defensive ends. Interchangeable players enable coaches to design complicated schemes that confuse offenses. Similarly, some Patriots defensive linemen, like Richard Seymour, are fast enough to occasionally drop back into pass coverage as linebackers. Belichick's Patriots have drafted virtually no college linebackers, instead drafting defensive linemen whom they project as sufficiently strong, smart, fast, and agile to morph into NFL linebackers. The Patriots look especially hard for such players at colleges employing "zone blitzes" (which require defensive linemen to occasionally drop back into pass coverage) because players with demonstrated pass coverage ability: 1) are easier to project as linebackers; and, 2) already have experience in linebacker-like roles. Consider former Penn State defensive end Justin Kurpeikis:

"[Kurpeikis] picked off two passes [in his senior] season when the [Penn State] defense called for him to drop into pass coverage. He knows how to read pass plays and break on the ball. He also has quickness to get the top job done after picked up 18 tackles for losses last season."[752]

Fortunately for Patriots rookies, so many veteran linebackers have made the defensive-line-to-linebacker transition that advice is plentiful. After the team's first 2004 preseason game, linebacker Tedy Bruschi said of Dan Klecko, "I saw Kleck making the same mistakes I made at that point in my career. Actually it was sort of eerie watching him out there. It was like, 'Wooooo! I remember doing that too.'"[753] Klecko leans so heavily on Bruschi for advice that Bruschi said with a laugh: "He's really eager. He comes and asks me a lot of questions, sometimes too many. Sometimes I just wish he'd leave me alone."[754] After that same preseason game, the Chicago Bears were so enamored of 265-pound Quinn Dorsey, whom the Patriots were converting from a defensive end (for the Oregon Ducks) into an outside linebacker, that they traded an undisclosed draft pick for Dorsey, who had recorded a sack and three tackles in early preseason action.

Casual fans don't appreciate how different the inside and outside linebacker positions are. Patriots linebackers, like Tedy Bruschi, are unusual because they are fast enough to play outside linebacker and cover receivers but tough and strong enough to play inside linebacker where they must block linemen and tackle running backs: "In this defense, it doesn't matter [what position I play]. We use a lot of guys. We move guys around. I just want to be out there, that's all."[755] Learning to play both inside and outside linebacker is much harder than it sounds: "I went from the [defensive] line to outside linebacker, then to the inside. Even that time on the outside didn't help me [at inside linebacker] at first. I still didn't know what I was doing."[756]

Interchangeable players and complex scheming (in which players constantly move around to different positions and line up in different formations) require smart players. Executed well, the Patriots' inscrutable defense plays havoc with opposing offenses' blocking schemes. Patriots linebacker Willie McGinest says:

"You have to be kind of versatile to play in this system. That's what makes us a good, sound group. Everybody depends on everybody else to do certain things. When you think we are going to do one thing, we can switch and do something totally different."[757]

It's virtually impossible for offensive linemen or quarterbacks to guess what each Patriots defender will do once the ball is snapped. Because the Patriots' linemen and linebackers are so flexible, any player (except the free safety) might blitz on any given play. McGinest again:

"We don't always have the same guys in the same place. There are a lot of interchangeable players that can do a lot of different things and move around, pass rush, pass drop, cover guys. That gives the coaches the ability to do a lot more things like blitzing certain guys or show that one guy is coming and then he's not, it's someone else blitzing."[758]

From Day 1 as Patriots head coach, Belichick emphasized "position flexibility": the ability to play multiple positions and to use multiple techniques (*e.g.*, cornerbacks who can play both bump-and-run "man" coverage and "zone" coverage). This enables defensive coordinator Romeo Crennel to reconfigure his defense almost instantaneously... to compensate for injuries, confuse the offense, exploit an offensive vulnerability, or react to an unexpected move by the offense. The Patriots do not need to bring in heavier players to stop the run and lighter players to stop the pass. Instead, their base defense can reconfigure itself on the fly, based on what the offense appears to be doing. Listen to NFL quarterbacks complain about the Patriots defense:

"When you prepare for New England you study, you watch film, but then most importantly you understand that what you see is probably not what you are going to get."[759]
– *New York Jets quarterback Chad Pennington*

"I gave up a long time ago trying to figure out whether I'm going to get zoned or manned or blitzed. Bill Belichick changes it every single week."[760]
– *Former Miami Dolphins quarterback Dan Marino*

"It's hard to prepare when you don't know what they are going to throw at you."[761]
– *Pittsburgh Steelers quarterback Ben Roethlisberger*

"More than any other team in football, the Patriots can line up near the line of scrimmage and time it just right so that the players retreat or move up to get in position just as the ball is snapped. The key to blitzing is having terrific timing–not only to catch the quarterback by surprise, but to catch the blockers and not give them time to react. The Patriots do this very well."[762]
– *Super Bowl-winning quarterback and NFL broadcaster Phil Simms*

Most NFL teams line up in a "4-3" defense (with four defensive linemen and three linebackers). Because the Patriots use a base "3-4" defense and often mix in "4-3" and even "4-6" defenses, a defender who starred at the University of Miami (or Ohio State or the Pittsburgh Steelers) might perform poorly with the Patriots because his talents are best utilized in a traditional "4-3" defense. Conversely, someone who performed poorly elsewhere might be a standout on the Patriots if his skills match the role he is asked to play within the Patriots' scheme. An obvious example is Mike Vrabel, who languished as a Pittsburgh Steelers backup before emerging as a Patriots star.

Coaches must either find players compatible with their schemes or modify their schemes to better utilize their players. The Patriots' "3-4" defense requires beefier defensive linemen. In a "3-4," linemen are responsible for controlling the line of scrimmage while linebackers step up into the holes and make plays. Conversely, "4-3" defenses emphasize quicker, lighter linemen ("only" 300 pounds or so, versus 340+ pounds for a "3-4" nose tackle) who aggressively push upfield toward the quarterback.

Switching between the "3-4" and "4-3" requires players sufficiently big, strong, and quick to play on the line yet fast enough to play linebacker and cover a tight end running a pass pattern. Belichick says the Patriots draft few college linebackers because college linebackers are too small to play on the line in the NFL but that such players can fit well on other NFL teams that never ask their linebackers to line up as defensive linemen:

> "if you're playing an off-the-line linebacker, you don't need as big of a player. You can afford to take the 220- to 235-pound guys that don't run well and let them scrape and flow to the ball. A team like (the Dolphins) that almost never has their linebackers on the line of scrimmage, then those (small college linebackers) flow pretty smoothly into their system."[763]

The Patriots instead seek "tweeners," like Willie McGinest and Tedy Bruschi who lined up as defensive ends in college but are undersized for defensive end in the NFL yet larger than average NFL linebackers. Such players are ideal for the Patriots' system which emphasizes flexibility, adaptability and interchangeable parts and regularly requires defensive linemen to drop back into coverage as linebackers and linebackers to line up as defensive linemen. The Patriots' love of tweeners led to reduced playing time for run-stuffing middle linebacker Ted Johnson, a Patriots star in the '90s. Before a 2000 Jets-Patriots matchup, New York Jets star running back Curtis Martin, who knew the Patriots defense intimately from his early years with the Patriots, called Ted Johnson "a brick wall,"[764] but Johnson was long a backup under Belichick because the Patriots defense stresses mobility.

Defensive lineman Richard Seymour is another kind of "tweener." He is powerful enough to play tackle and quick enough to play end. End is the position that takes maximal advantage of Seymour's size and speed, but he is flexible enough to play anywhere along the defensive line in either a "3-4" or "4-3." The same is true of linebacker Roman Phifer, whose physical and mental talent enables him to play outside linebacker or inside linebacker. Phifer can play on the line of scrimmage (as a "3-4" strongside linebacker) or off the line. By fielding players who can play on or off the line, the Patriots defense can trick offenses into screwing up their blocking assignments and misreading the defense's intentions. A Patriot may line up along the line as a down lineman but then drop back and play like a linebacker or vice versa. Two offensive players may each assume the other is responsible for blocking a defender, leaving the defender unblocked. Or both may block the defender, leaving another defender unblocked. Sowing confusion in offensive players' minds results in big defensive plays.

The Patriots' offense is pretty tricky too. Patriots tight end Daniel Graham says, "Learning this offense was tough. It took me a whole year to understand it, then another year to comprehend it."[765] Tom Brady admits:

> "There is a lot that we put on our receivers. There is a lot of plays for them to learn. We ask them to learn a lot of different spots [to line up] and a lot of different route adjustments. It's not as easy as I think maybe some other places are."[766]

In praising Patriots wide receiver Deion Branch, Belichick explains that intelligence is important for his team's wideouts because they are asked to "read" the defense and adjust their routes accordingly:

> "[Deion] has a good understanding of pass concepts. When you talk about different coverages, 'Here is the way they're playing,' he picks that up very quickly. [He] knows how they're trying to defend him. [He] knows and can comprehend very quickly how to change the route or how to run the route to attack the technique that the defense is playing or to beat the coverage they are in."[767]

Patriots receivers cannot creatively improvise but must intelligently analyze the defense within the framework of the playbook because the quarterback must make the same "read" to get the ball to them. If the receiver runs in one direction and the quarterback throws to another, the result is incompletions or interceptions.

Personnel must match specific roles within your organization. If you know your needs with clarity, you may be able to hire talented individuals who thrive in your organization but have modest salary expectations because they aren't job market standouts: "It's all about fit. They defined their team and really knew what they needed. It's not a question of what their names are or how other people classify them."[768] Explains Scott Pioli: "History and experience has taught us that chasing and pursuing high-profile names isn't necessarily the way to go. We're going after players that fit our system and our overall philosphy. Some people term that second-tier or next-level. We don't see them as that type of player."[769] Pioli knows that high pay in no way guarantees high performance: "just because a player has made a Pro Bowl or has a marquee name because of his salary doesn't mean the player is necessarily a good football player… Sometimes perception and reality are two completely different things."[770] Pioli also warns that cheap in no way implies a bargain: "We evaluated a lot of football players. We didn't go, 'Oh, Mike Compton, let's sign him because we can get him cheap.'"[771]

Know yourself to know your needs

"If I said a guy was a first-round pick, the Colts picked him, and if he turned out to be a bust, [the Patriots] wouldn't have looked down on me. They wouldn't have said I was a bad grader. Because that player in the *Patriots'* system might have been successful."[772]
— *Patriots scout Jason Licht (now assistant director of player personnel with the Philadelphia Eagles)*

Scott Pioli is considered the NFL's best personnel executive because he knows exactly what kind of players Coach Belichick wants and how to find them. The results are extraordinary: "Of Pioli's 26 picks since 2001 only three are out of the NFL and six of last year's picks made a significant impact on the Super Bowl squad."[773]

Role players

"They surround themselves with people who are good at [their role]. They don't pay attention to all these other things people obsess over. If a guy can play football, and do [the tasks] they want, they'll find them."[774]
— *CBS analyst and former 49er Randy Cross*

You don't need an expensive Swiss Army Knife to open a can. A simple can opener lacks sex appeal but gets the job done. Rather than field eleven Swiss Army Knives, each of whom can do it all, Belichick uses a toothpick, screwdriver, corkscrew, pair of tweezers, can opener, saw, magnifying glass, fork, knife, and spoon. It's much cheaper. Why pay extra for tools you won't use?

The Patriots acquire and productively utilize "role players." The Patriots make maximal use of specialists who perform certain tasks extremely well, even if they are not considered "talented" because they cannot perform other tasks.

Patriots scouts and coaches worry about what a player can do, not what he can't do. Every year, Patriots fans beg the team to draft a 1st-round, "can't miss" wide receiver. And every year the team drafts receivers in the 2nd through 7th rounds. Every one of these receivers has flaws and weaknesses. Most lack the height and strength of top receivers. But the Patriots would rather overwhelm the defense with many fast, smart receivers and rely on Brady to find the open guy than spend high draft picks on tall, strong receivers who are marginally better at getting open and catching balls.

Similarly, many outstanding college defensive linemen are available in the mid-to-late rounds of the NFL draft because they're "too short" or "too light" to play in the NFL. If the Patriots find such a player who is smart and mobile, they scoop him up and convert him to linebacker. Such a player perfectly fits the Patriots system which requires smart, adaptable linebackers who can absorb a thick playbook, prepare meticulously for each opponent, and switch effortlessly among multiple positions. Tedy Bruschi, for example, is a very bright linebacker who performs brilliantly within the Patriots' system but has never made a Pro Bowl appearance and "some within the league question whether he would be as effective in another system."[775]

The Patriots won two Super Bowls without a star running back. They got by with a combination of a Buffalo Bills castoff (Antowain Smith, who lacked the cutback agility required to elude tacklers and break long gains but proved adequate on first and second down and in short yardage situations because he seldom fumbled and had the power to crash into a defender for an extra yard or two) and a quick but undersized third-down back (Kevin Faulk, who is good at pass blocking and catching short passes out of the backfield but is not an every-down back). In 2001, one reporter wrote of Antowain Smith, "his fumble on the 3-yard line last Sunday night reminded people why the Patriots got him for nothing."[776] Smith failed the beginning-of-training-camp conditioning run three consecutive years because he didn't keep in shape during the off-season. Instead of arriving at camp in shape and passing the test, "Smith often complained that as a 232-pound back, he should be allowed to run in the slower group with the fullbacks."[777] After Smith signed with the Tennessee Titans for the veteran minimum salary after the 2003 season, an unnamed Patriot player suggested Smith lacked the Patriot-standard ration of heart and will: "You get what you pay for. From Week 9 to Week 16 is when he may show up. Other than that, it's his own pace."[778] (Not a single Patriot failed the conditioning test on Day 1 of training camp 2004.)

Despite their inadequacies, Smith and Faulk together generated enough production from the running back position to win two Super Bowls. The beauty of Smith and Faulk was not their play but their pay. The Patriots paid low salaries to two situational role players rather than a king's ransom for a "great" running back. Also unnoticed, the Patriots measured "production" comprehensively: not just as yards gained but also as pass protection, ability to hold onto the football, ability to catch the ball out of the backfield before Brady was sacked, *etc.* Every team lusts after a "great" running back, but the Patriots squeezed good value from the position at a bargain price by utilizing two complementary role players rather than one flashy and expensive every-down star.

But a lackluster Patriots running game in 2001 deteriorated further. In 2003, the Patriots gained only 100.4 yards/game, ranking 27th of 32 NFL teams. Even worse, the Patriots gained only 3.4 yards/rush, ranking 30th of 32. Only the Tennessee Titans and Pittsburgh Steelers, each of whom gained 3.3 yards/rush, were worse. The fourth-worst team, the Detroit Lions, gained 3.6 yards/rush; the best team, the San Diego Chargers, gained 5.1 yards/rush. 2002 was little better, with the Patriots gaining 94.3 yards/game (28th of 32) and 3.8 yards/rush (27th of 32). After watching Antowain Smith's performance deteriorate from 3.9 yards/rush in 2002 to 3.5 yards/rush in 2003, the Patriots let Smith go and upgraded the position by acquiring an every-down star, Corey Dillon, who averaged 4.3 yards/rush in Cincinnati from 1997 through 2003 (despite being the "go to" guy and primary focus of opposing defenses) and accumulated 1,482 yards receiving (vs. Smith's 767 yards over the same period). This decision resulted from a cost/benefit analysis. Smith's "cost" was rising as his "benefit" was falling. Smith was let go days before the Patriots were obligated to pay him a $500,000 option payment if he remained on their roster, an expense the Patriots chose to forgo. Because the Patriots had dug themselves out of "Salary Cap Jail," they could afford to upgrade to Dillon at an acceptable cost: a second-round draft pick, a relatively low salary (because Dillon wants to win so much he accepted a pay-cut to be traded to the world champions), and a low-risk contract (enabling the Patriots to cut Dillon without little salary cap hit because the Patriots paid Dillon a minimal signing bonus).

Employee diversity

"I think it's about keeping your core guys, your veteran leadership, the guys you can count on to make the plays, and bringing in solid young guys who are willing to learn, who don't have too much attitude–be seen and not heard and just follow along. But you have to keep the guys who are used to doing it a certain way. We have a lot of core guys here... They probably call us old. We say we're experienced."[779]
    – *Patriots cornerback Ty Law*

"We have some young players, and then we have some guys that have played a lot of games in the NFL... I think that is kind of a good blend. The young guys have people they can learn from, and I think our young players... are receptive to that. They have their ears open. They listen to what the veterans say, and they take the advice that those guys give them and try to apply it."[780]
    – *Bill Belichick*

For the whole to become more than the sum of its parts, the parts must complement and enhance one another. Employee diversity is necessary, though not sufficient, for employees to help one another achieve. One important way the Patriots balance their employee portfolio is through a mix of veterans and youth at every position. Says Belichick:

"[Y]ou would like to have at every position... some veteran experience, some guys that are kind of right there in the prime of their career, then some younger players to keep that cycle going. It is hard to keep that smooth cycle at all of the positions. ...In an ideal world, you would like to have that kind of flow so you have new people coming in and experience at the position."[781]

Young players are necessary because they cost less and are often more athletic. But veterans are necessary to make difficult on-field decisions on coordinating the team and to impart their experience and wisdom to the younger players. Patriots safety Rodney Harrison believes veterans are like extra coaches who are closer to the players:

> "The veteran leadership helps [coaches communicate well with players]. With guys who have been in big games before, who have been through adversity, it helps the young guys. We can talk to them and keep them humble and get them prepared for what is expected."[782]

Belichick expects veterans to advise younger players, and Patriots veterans, like 36-year old linebacker Roman Phifer, enjoy helping the younger players:

> "Anyone who has a problem or just wants to talk, I'm here. I've seen a lot of things. I know people always have questions about my longevity and how I do it. I'm glad to offer advice, tips, what have you, to them. [I tell them] I'm having a good time. I still feel like a kid. That's part of what keeps me yearning, having these young guys come in and just bonding with them and see yourself when you were 21 or 22, try to sit down with them and try to give them wisdom and try to be a role model for them."[783]

Second-year Patriots linebacker Tully Banta-Cain appreciates Phifer's guidance:

> "He's a stalwart, but he's a real humble guy. He doesn't put up a wall. He's open. He shows you how to take care of your body, tells you what to say and what not to say. If I have a question I want to ask a coach, I ask him how to say it. …If a [young player] has a question, I always send them to him for advice. He'll help anybody."[784]

Patriots linebacker Willie McGinest quizzed Earthwind Moreland during practice the day Moreland re-signed with the team (after being cut in pre-season): "I was on the sideline with Earthwind last week and I asked, 'What play did they just call?,' just to see if he was paying attention. [Then] I was like, 'What if you're out there, what are you going to do?' He said, 'I'll play [well].' [The next day] two guys go down [with injuries] and he's out there."[785] Patriots rookie defensive lineman Marquise Hill says veterans, even without saying anything, help rookies by serving as role models: "My role now is to sponge as much as I can and learn from the veterans… You see how they do things. You realize that they work hard and it pays off by them winning the Super Bowl. You just kind of look at them and follow what they do."[786]

The Patriots wisely adjust the mix of experience and youth by position. Belichick generally prefers young defensive linemen (DLs) but veteran linebackers (LBs) and defensive backs (DBs) because LBs and DBs must process more information than DLs. Young players are usually cheaper and more athletic, but inexperience makes them mistake-prone, something Jets tight end Anthony Becht noticed:

"[Belichick] likes to have smart, veteran players around him. I wasn't surprised at all when he signed Victor Green (away from the Jets). Victor knows how to play the game. He's been around a long time. Rather than have all these young, talented guys who can make great plays, but also make mistakes, he likes guys who are going to be consistent."[787]

EMPLOYEE CHARACTER & PERSONALITY

"You know why they win [after watching them practice]. From the coaches on down to the players, it's noticeable–the attitudes. Compared to where I came from, you can see a big difference, and it's a pleasure to be here. I just assume this is the way it's always been. It's just a lot different from what I'm used to. Like day and night."[788]
  – Veteran punter and former Pittsburgh Steeler Josh Miller, after joining the Patriots in 2004

Many coaches say, "You can't coach height." The Patriots know you can't coach personality, so Patriots scouts place great weight on character issues in player evaluations. According to VP of player personnel Scott Pioli, "There have been some young guys who have been immature and gone through our environment and grown up. But guys who are flat-out selfish and that was a true part of them, those things generally don't change."[789] Belichick agrees: "You're better off with a player who looks like he already has some of those elements in his makeup rather than thinking you're going to take a 26-year-old and suddenly mold him into something he's never been."[790] Pioli adds:

"It's not guesswork. It's research, and it's knowing what we're looking for, which are certain dynamics and certain things about a person, and a lot of that has to do with the fact that I know what kind of player Bill wants in his system. The word we use is 'makeup.' We're very concerned about a player's makeup. My job is to find players who are compatible with our head coach."[791]

Belichick knows enough about human nature to realize how critically perception shapes performance:

"I think that the main ingredient with a player on a team is the player's attitude. A player's attitude can make his situation whatever he wants it to be, and the player controls that. However they want to feel about what they're doing, they can either feel good about it or bad about it, no matter what it is. I've had guys where they play every snap and aren't happy with their role, for whatever reason, and other guys who don't play every snap, and they try to make the most of their opportunities when they come, so I think that's all in the player's control."[792]

The Tennessee Titans and New England Patriots have a mutual admiration society regarding their personnel decisions. Neither team is mesmerized by physical attributes or college stats. And both teams care deeply about a player's heart and personality. Says Belichick,

> "When Tennessee's turn comes up to [draft], it's not good for us; it's usually a direct hit to the values on our [draft] board. That's not necessarily true of every team. ...[Titans general manager] Floyd [Reese] is trying to build a football team, not just take talent. He takes into account everything that comes with the player, not just the vertical jump but all the other qualities as well."[793]

The Patriots and Titans realize that character (a player's heart and mind) lies at the root of many brilliant personnel decisions. Football talent expert Joel Buchsbaum spotlighted the Giants' drafting of Phil Simms and the Packers' acquisition of Brett Favre, two fiercely competitive and brainy quarterbacks who later led their teams to Super Bowl victories, as superb personnel moves:

> "An example of a great pick was when the Giants took Phil Simms over some players who were graded as sure-fire superstars because they were convinced he could become the type of quarterback who could lead them to a Super Bowl. Another great pick, or at least use of a pick, was when Ron Wolf, in his first year as Packer GM, traded a first-round pick to Atlanta for QB Brett Favre, who had been the Falcons' second-round choice a year earlier and was viewed as a bust as a rookie. Wolf, who rated Favre as the top player in the entire '91 draft, was convinced he would become a great quarterback."[794]

What personality does the Patriots seek? For example, Belichick says "Troy Brown is without a doubt one of the best leaders I've ever been around, and he never says a word. It's not about who talks the loudest, who says the most. It's about attitude. To be a leader, have a good attitude, be positive, help out your teammate."[795] Though Brown caught 101 passes in 2001 and 97 in 2002, he is the opposite of the NFL's many *prima donna* receivers who demand coaches put them in the game and quarterbacks throw to them. Brown has handled his diminishing role with grace:

> "I just go out and run the plays, and we'll see what happens. I get myself ready as if I'm going to be out there playing every play. That's what you've got to do. My job is to help the team, no matter what it is. Whatever that situation is, I'll be ready. ...[I] run every route like I'm getting the ball. That's what you've got to do. I do a lot of things other than catching passes that keeps me involved in the game. Rushing field goals, returning punts, whatever."[796]

Safety Rodney Harrison says the Patriots now have a team full of guys with hearts like Troy Brown's: "We have good people in the locker room, real good character guys."[797]

Too many teams overemphasize "measurables," such as 40-yard-dash times and bench press repetitions, relative to intangibles such as a player's coachability, likability, selflessness, perseverance, and effort. The Patriots acquire players for their overall potential as football players, not their raw physical ability. By contrast, the Arizona Cardinals were losers for many years, in part because they drafted players for their skills, with insufficient concern for character. Again, Buchsbaum:

> "Another awful pick was the Cardinals' selection of Michigan State OLB Anthony Bell with the fifth overall choice in the 1986 draft. Virtually everyone else had Bell rated as a second-round pick at best. Bell was a great workout guy but a mediocre player who lacked instincts. However, the Cardinals loved his workout and let his college coaches convince them that Bell had fine instincts and looked the way he did on film because that was the way he was told to play things and he was just being a loyal soldier."[798]

The Cardinals also made David Boston their #1 draft pick in 1999. Character is the only reason a guy as physically gifted as David Boston has now played for three different NFL teams.

Hire guys who love their work

"My best advice to you is to pursue the things you're passionate about... That's the foundation, in my opinion, to anything great."[799]
 — *Patriots owner Robert Kraft, speaking to graduating college seniors*

"It's the self-starter in each of us that's really important. I don't think you can count on somebody else to motivate you to do something. You have to want to do it personally, and you have to provide that energy. It's unrealistic and unfair to expect someone else to push you in a positive direction. So you better pick out something you really like to do, because you will have to be your own driving force."[800]
 — *Bill Belichick*

"I wouldn't go out and make myself feel the way you feel at training camp if I didn't love playing football, and with these guys in particular."[801]
 — *Patriots linebacker Mike Vrabel*

"Bill doesn't have a lot of patience for players that don't view football as being very important to them. All these guys are passionate about the game.

We definitely thought there were some things about the personality of this team [we inherited] we had to change."[802]
– Scott Pioli

The hilarious Tom Lehrer song "Fight fiercely, Harvard"[803] includes the line, "Albeit they possess the might, nonetheless we have the will." Young "Billy" Belichick first witnessed passion defeat talent as a boy cheering for his hometown team, the Navy Midshipmen. Billy's dad, Steve, remembers those Navy teams he helped coach: "Guys that were 165 pounds would hit a 200-pounder like he was a 125-pounder... They're gung ho about the whole thing. Football [at Navy] is different than anything else. ...I had never seen so many small players knock the hell out of big players."[804]

Because Belichick has reached the peak of professional football only after decades of devotion to his profession, he knows from personal experience that: 1) You must love your work to grind away at it every day; and, 2) Grinding away day after day, week after week, year after year is the only way to achieve success. Belichick advises Boston College students accordingly:

> "I would not take the job that pays more than the other one. That's the wrong reason to take it. Do something that you really love. If you can find something you love to do, it makes it easier to come to work everyday regardless of what you are getting paid."[805]

As an employer, Belichick hires only players who, like Patriots offensive lineman Stephen Neal, can say, "I'm here doing my dream. I've always dreamed of playing football."[806]

Tom Brady's success demonstrates both the necessity and efficacy of passion in professional development. When Brady arrived in the NFL, he lacked the physical attributes associated with quarterbacking greatness, but he strengthened his arm and body and improved his mental game to compensate for other weaknesses (especially his non-existent "speed"). Brady jokes that if you keep grinding long enough, you too may become an "overnight sensation." Success sneaks up on those who unceasingly strive to better themselves. Outsiders, oblivious to the daily grind, see only the apparently rapid results. Those who succeed remember the long struggle:

> "[E]ight years removed from high school... being a professional quarterback on a team that's been as successful as we have. You don't even dream of stuff like that. At least I don't think you do. It all seems like it's been such a progression. I've just been taking the next step. What do I need to do to get better? What do I need to do to find an opportunity? Just continuing to take coaching."[807]

Belichick, who has been grinding away at football his entire life, knows his success derives from his unquenchable love for the game. Belichick's passion is obvious to everyone. Jim Schwartz, who worked for Belichick in Cleveland and now serves as the Tennessee Titans' defensive coordinator, bonded with Belichick through their shared passion:

> "It's a not a job to us. That's what we struck on. People always said Belichick would burn out and I would burn out. But imagine making a living with something you love to do. It's not work for me to be at the office at midnight. It's never a job where I say, 'Hey, I've got to go to work.' I'd rather watch game tape than watch 'Spin City.' We had a common bond."[808]

New York Giants general manager Ernie Accorsi says, "Here's a guy who wanted to be a head coach when he was like 6 years old. That's all he wanted to do in his life. It's not a guy who said, 'Oh, I think I'll get into coaching.' This was obviously his goal. His passion. His complete understanding of the game was amazing."[809]

Belichick knows Patriots coaches can teach tactics and techniques but can't instill passion in someone who is just collecting paychecks: "If a player has a high level of desire, we can mold his work habits or the methods that he uses so that he'll be more productive."[810] Patriots fullback Fred McCrary agrees: "I just love football. I absolutely love the game. If you don't love it, the NFL has a way of chewing you up and spitting you out."[811] Barry Sanders, Ricky Williams, and Robert Smith are three outstanding running backs who suddenly retired from the NFL while still highly productive because they lacked passion.

Realizing how essential passion is, Belichick and Pioli hire players as passionate about football as they are. Belichick's Patriots are physically gifted men with childlike enthusiasm for playing football. Pioli's scouting system digs up players who love not only playing and winning games each Sunday but also the year-round hard work that separates winners from losers. Consider the reverential tone of Patriots players' childhood NFL memories and their addict-like obsession with playing football:

- Offensive lineman *Damien Woody* grew up worshiping the Washington Redskins offensive line. He loved watching "the hogs" part a sea of Miami Dolphins defenders for running back John Riggins in Super Bowl XVII: "You had to love that team. The way those guys ran the football. They just pounded people. ...[M]y favorite part was watching those boys blow open big holes for Riggins to run through."[812]

- Cornerback *Ty Law* envisioned himself playing wide receiver while growing up in Pittsburgh "watching Lynn Swann making those acrobatic catches. I had dreams of doing that in the NFL."[813]

- As a youth, wide receiver *Troy Brown* threw passes to himself, imagining himself catching balls in the Super Bowl. After sitting out four games in 2003 with a leg injury, Brown caught his first pass and threw the ball in the air because "I was ecstatic about coming back. I love playing the game, that's what I love to do."[814]

After winning his second Super Bowl ring, Brown, now in his 12th season with the Patriots, swore "the fire will never die out, no matter how old [I] get."[815]

· Wide receiver *David Patten* missed the second half of the 2003 Super Bowl season due to injury. After recovering, he became overwhelmed with joy before the Patriots' first 2004 preseason game: "I felt like a rookie all over again, like it was my first game. That first series, I was so out of breath because my adrenaline was up so much. There was so much excitement. It hit me 30 minutes before we went out, just to be in pads again."[816]

· The day after his father died, special teams captain *Larry Izzo* helped the Patriots beat the Cleveland Browns:

> "Losing [my father] the day before the Cleveland game, I mean that wasn't a question of whether I wouldn't play–he would've wanted me to play. He would've been disappointed if I didn't play. My career has always been very important to him and my family, so for me to not play in that game, was not even a factor. ...I've dedicated this whole season to him and his memory. He's the reason I'm [playing in the Super Bowl]. He taught me to play football at a young age. Football's always been a good part of our lives and our family. It's going to be a tough deal, but I know wherever he is, he's watching. He's proud."[817]

· Rookie defensive tackle *Vince Wilfork* practically pinched himself before his first preseason game: "All my life I wanted to play in the NFL. Before the game I actually took a minute to realize where I was and look at the fans and realize I am actually here. A dream come true. Every game I will appreciate. I don't care if it is preseason or Super Bowl."[818] Wilfork has been focused on the NFL for decades: "I can think back to when I was 5 or 6 years old and telling my father I'm going to be a professional football player."[819]

Decades later, these players' passion remains undiminished. Tom Brady swears he even loves off-season training: "There's always room to improve. There's always room for progress. I just enjoy playing football. I like lifting weights. I like training in the offseason. I love training camp. I know that's sick, but I do. I like practicing and I like playing."[820] Hearing this, a grinning Bill Belichick told a reporter, "I can't wait to remind Tom sometime this August about how much he loves training camp."[821] Brady is so dedicated he actually squeezed in a full workout, starting at 5:00 a.m., the day the team visited the White House and met the President, even though coaches had exempted players from working out that day.[822]

Admittedly, not every Patriot masochistically loves the daily torture of training. An unnamed player, reminded that training camp started a week later, said, "Oh [expletive], don't remind me."[823] That unnamed Patriot might have been guard Joe Andruzzi, who said of training camp: "My favorite part? Going to bed. This is a trying time of year. It takes a lot out of you. It seems the turning point is when the (preseason) games start. You finally get to hit someone else. After a while you just get tired of hitting the same guys. It's refreshing to get some fresh meat in there."[824]

Because Belichick and Pioli know you can only become great if you enjoy your work on a daily basis, the Patriots draft and sign only players who love football and are dedicated to improving themselves in every way possible. Cyclist Lance Armstrong, for example, was an excellent cyclist until he nearly died of cancer. After beating cancer, Armstrong fell in love with training in a way he never had before. Armstrong has since won six consecutive Tours de France and is the Tour's only six-time winner.

Patriots safety Rodney Harrison is a football fanatic who fits the Belichick-Pioli profile perfectly:

> "I've been playing this game since I was 6 years old. And it's just a great opportunity. I love it. Just play with passion. Play around, make sure your teammates play as hard as they can play. And just be an example... Being able to go out there and do something that you've been doing your whole life and just have fun doing it–the camaraderie with the guys, just the hours you spend, the sacrifices you make around your family. It's just wonderful to be able to go out there and play a violent sport and just kick butt."[825]

Belichick first noticed Rodney Harrison was special when Belichick coached the 1999 AFC Pro Bowl team (as a stand-in for his then-boss Bill Parcells). Belichick was frustrated because players weren't taking game preparation seriously: "we had a couple of guys that didn't wear their shoes out to practice. They came out in sandals. A lot of other guys didn't even bother to tie them. A lot of guys weren't too interested in the game plan or the plays–just pick them up at the game or whatever."[826] Harrison's motivation lept out at Belichick: "At practice he was out there trying to get it right. It was important to him. You could tell that it may have been a meaningless game, but it wasn't meaningless to him. He was competing in it."[827] Belichick added: "He was very intense in terms of [asking], 'What are we doing, how are we doing it, how do you want us to play this?'"[828]

In his commencement address at the New England Institute of Technology, Belichick told graduating seniors that he seeks "passion, commitment and staying power"[829] in prospective Patriots. Belichick is living proof: he has studied football literally his entire life because the game excites him. He loves winning, but all coaches and players do. Belichick loves sweating every detail. After decades analyzing football footage, Belichick is a master at understanding the intricacies of what he sees on film or on the practice field. Patriots linebacker Mike Vrabel is astounded by his coach's ability to instantly interpret what he sees: "I can watch the film for an hour and not come up with [the insights] he comes up with."[830] Ray Mickens, who played safety on Belichick's New York Jets defense, is similarly amazed: "You can't get anything past that guy. I've seen him in action when he was here. He sees things that nobody else sees. He confuses people. I've never been around a guy like him."[831] Vrabel, who hopes to become a football coach after retiring as a player, jokes of the Patriots' tactical guru, "I never game planned against us, and hopefully I'll never have to against a Bill Belichick-coached team."[832] Belichick would tell you Vrabel is being modest: "He'll be a good coach some day."[833] Vrabel's in the right place. Fresno State head football coach Pat Hill, tight ends coach during Belichick's tenure as Cleveland Browns head coach, insists that "The preparation you get from [Belichick] is the preparation you need to be a head coach."[834]

Former New York Giants punter Dave Jennings says, "it's funny to be with Bill in a movie theater. You can see his fingers start to twitch, because he wishes he had a remote so he could replay a scene that he likes."[835] Ernie Accorsi recalls flying to four schools in a single day while he and Belichick were scouting together in Cleveland. Accorsi, who was exhausted, says "I heard Bill arguing with the motel clerk because there was no VCR in the room so he could watch film."[836] Accorsi adds that Belichick insisted on talking business on the plane the next day: "He won't stop working. We got on the airplane and instead of relaxing, he wanted to go over everybody we saw. He's relentless."[837] Belichick really does watch that much film and learn that much from it, according to Patriots linebacker Roman Phifer: "He's a football genius, like a whiz kid at football... I can just picture him watching film at all hours of the night."[838]

Belichick's prowess at dissecting football derives from his analytical mind, his long experience watching film, his respect for and knowledge of football history ("He speaks of Clark Shaughnessy... He speaks of Halas, Don Shula, Sid Gillman, Bill Walsh, and Paul Brown"[839]), and his incredible memory ("He still remembers, exactly, what defensive calls he made in games several years ago"[840] and "on the sidelines, he has no notes. It's all in his head"[841]). Sheer brilliance is not enough. Even the greatest mind in the world can only become a great NFL coach through decades of passionate devotion to football.

While playing college football, Patriots VP of player personnel Scott Pioli learned that winning football teams require committed individuals and positive peer pressure:

> "[Pioli's college football team captain] Bouressa taught [Pioli] a valuable lesson when he caught Pioli losing focus on his weight training program... 'He was trying to tell me to grow up. He was telling me, it's time to take some responsibility, it's time to do some things that maybe your mind is telling you that you don't want to do,' Pioli said, his voice briefly cracking with emotion. 'Mike hit me with some tough love. And I want to thank you in front of all these people.'"[842]

Consequently, a bedrock Patriots hiring principle holds that success requires loving your "job" and admiring the competitiveness of those you "work" with. Coach Belichick told graduating seniors "I don't feel like I've worked a day in my life"[843] and attributed his success in part to his love of the game: "Belichick described coming into work at 5 a.m. to review tapes of punt returns while with the Giants in the 1970s. 'I guess I really did love what I was doing,' Belichick said."[844] Asked once how many hours he works, Belichick replied that being a football coach "Beats working."[845] Scott Pioli says the same:

> "I have a GREAT job because I love what I do. I never consider what I do 'work' because I love it so much. ...[E]ven when we were 5-11 two years ago, I couldn't wait to get to work. I have an opportunity to compete every single day–and compete in an arena that I love. ...People are often shocked by the hours that we 'work.' However, I always keep it in perspective–my father 'WORKED' for a living... I'm doing something that I love."[846]

That Patriots players love football and love competing provides two additional benefits: players don't retire early, and they get high on the game, not on drugs:

- The Patriots have employed many veterans who have eagerly played well into their 30s: Otis Smith, Roman Phifer, Willie McGinest, Anthony Pleasant, Larry Centers, *etc.* Aside from a bizarre string of veteran offensive linemen who retired during their first Patriots training camp, *few Patriots choose to retire before they're over the hill.* Roman Phifer, for example, says "It's hard at 36 to wake up and chase around guys who are 21, 22 years old, but this is what I love doing."[847] Other teams have been hit hard by early retirements. Star running backs Barry Sanders, Robert Smith, and Ricky Williams shocked the Lions, Vikings, and Dolphins, respectively. All retired young, apparently because they: 1) Didn't revel in full-speed collisions with powerful defensive players; 2) Were uncomfortable with the idolatry and unrealistic expectations that come with earning a fortune to play a game; and, 3) Felt they had earned plenty of money. Williams felt trapped in football, saying after he decided to retire, "I'm finally free."[848] Williams has many joys in life. According to his agent, Leigh Steinberg, "He's someone who talks about philosophy and spirituality and the meaning of life, what it means to be a person, and friendship. ...Many of the discussions I've had with him have been about philosophy, comparative religion. He's had a struggle with the consequences of fame. At times, he's extremely uncomfortable with it."[849] Williams also liked marijuana, and failing his third drug test precipitated his decision, though he said: "I didn't quit football because I failed a drug test. I failed a drug test because I was ready to quit football."[850] (Williams later decided to un-retire after learning he would have to pay back $8.6 million he had already earned.) Barry Sanders, who retired at age 31 while just 1,457 yards shy of the all-time NFL rushing record, seemed to understand Williams' decision: "he always seemed like football wasn't the most important thing in his life. He didn't seem as excited about it as everyone else. I know in Miami... they saw him as a savior in Miami. Maybe he didn't see himself that way."[851] The warning signs that Williams was not in love with football reach back to his college years at Texas where "he appeared and sounded genuinely shaken by the sight of Longhorns legend Earl Campbell. Campbell is 49 going on 69. Campbell can barely walk. ...Williams always seemed horrified by that prospect."[852] Pat Tillman left the Arizona Cardinals for what he considered a more important mission: protecting America as an Army Ranger. He was killed in Afghanistan. For these four players, football was a way to earn a living, not their reason for living. Patriot players, for the most part, are passionate about football and play for the enjoyment and challenge the game gives them. Patriots are more likely to confront a different challenge which Patriots special teams standout and 9-year veteran Je'Rod Cherry describes as "you don't want to think... 'This could be over.' To some, it's a defeatist attitude in your psyche. You want to stay on the affirmative, that 'I'm going to make it and walk away when I'm ready to walk away.'"[853]

- After repeatedly violating the NFL's drug policy, Tampa Bay defensive tackle Darrell Russell received an indefinite suspension, which may become a lifetime ban. The Oakland Raiders largely wasted the #2 pick in the entire 1997 draft on a player who, according to the man who recruited him and mentored him at USC, partied too much and "was pretty much a mama's boy who never really loved playing football the way you have to love playing it. His primary motivation for going early to the NFL draft was so he could sign a big contract and be more popular with the girls."[854] Ricky Williams retired from football in part because he insisted on his right to smoke marijuana, while the NFL insisted on punishing him for doing so. *Drug use has not been a problem for the Patriots because they sign players who get high on striving to win football games, not on drugs.*

Players must love not only playing on Sundays but, more importantly, preparing all year in many unglamorous ways. Patriot Dan Klecko is smart enough to know passion is essential to success. Asked to switch positions (from defensive line to inside linebacker), Klecko initially considered the task "work" before quickly deciding it was "fun": "When [Belichick] first told me, I thought, 'Wow, this is going to take a lot of work,' but as I think about it more and more, it's just something I've got to sell myself on, it's got to be fun and I've got to love it."[855] Klecko succeeded in loving his new job. In fact, he makes it sound great compared with his old one: "You get out there and get to make the calls [for the defense]. I just find it more fun than sticking a hand in the dirt and hitting someone, but they both are fun."[856]

Hire hungry, goal-oriented guys

"You're looking at a team that has some f----- guts, man."[857]
  – St. Louis Rams defensive end Chidi Ahanotu, after losing Super Bowl XXXVI to the Patriots

"Of all the teams I have watched over the years in pro football, the quality [the 2001 Patriots] had that no other team had was that all three areas of the game–offense, defense, special teams–were played at a high level of intensity. There was no drop-off and they carried this through the entire game."[858]
  – St. Louis Rams head coach Mike Martz

"Coach Belichick says it's tough to run with tears in your eyes. That word ["tough"] is used a lot around here. We are tough."[859]
  – Patriots linebacker Mike Vrabel

"We don't have guys on this team that are going to let down… The guys we have here want to be out there."[860]
  – Patriots offensive lineman Joe Andruzzi

Just hours after becoming the youngest person to ever win two Super Bowl MVP trophies, Tom Brady told the world he was looking toward his third. He shared a story about the veteran trainer at his alma mater, the University of Michigan, which has won more than its share of national titles:

> "I asked him once, which was his favorite ring, you know? And he kind of thought about it for a little while and finally said, 'The next one.' That's how I feel right now. This is great but you already want to start thinking about the next one."[861]

Brady was already excited about working hard in the "off-season":

> "There are still a lot of things to improve on. There is still a lot of room for growth. The thing is, I enjoy playing football, I enjoy the game. I like being in the weight room. I like training camp. I like practicing. And I hope to be doing this for a long time."[862]

As the 2004 season began, Brady said, "The last two have been great, but… Heck, I want as many as I can get. I'm going to be selfish about this."[863] How does he stay so hungry? One motivator was forcing himself to watch the 2002 Super Bowl as a spectator: "I remember how miserable it was being [at the Super Bowl] and not playing."[864]

While this book heavily credits the Belichick system for the Patriots' success, not any player could achieve greatness under Belichick's system. The system demands players who are dedicated to doing everything possible to constantly improve themselves. Talented but low-effort players from the pre-Belichick era were quickly replaced. As Pepper Johnson describes the 2000 Patriots under first-year head coach Bill Belichick, "there were so many bad elements on that team. …We had a lot of people bucking the system. Some guys were just collecting a check… [W]hen the camera was off, it became me, me, me."[865]

Belichick expects Patriots players to be hungry but not greedy. Each Patriot wants to be the best player he can be. He wants to do everything he can to help his team win. But each Patriot channels his competitive hunger into performing his best, not into lobbying coaches for more playing time, quarterbacks for more passes, or reporters for publicity. Patriots wide receiver David Patten explains the compatibility between hunger and selflessness:

> "I want the ball thrown to me 10-15 times a game. I want the quarterback looking at me every play. But that's not my call. My call is to go out there, run the route, run the play as they call it. And when the ball comes, I get paid to make that play. Hopefully, I can do that when my number is called."[866]

Patten understands "I can't control what people think. The only thing I can control is when I get an opportunity to go out and do my job on the field."[867] On some teams, players can talk their way into larger roles than their performance justifies.

Several holdovers from the Pete Carroll regime, such as Ty Law, were natural Belichick-type players and achieved greatness under Belichick. Under Carroll, Law refused to attend the Patriots' off-season workouts because they were a country club equivalent of what he put himself through:

> "I was going to train like a boxer. I got some Muhammad Ali tapes and said, 'I want to do something like that.' Then I saw a story on Gail Devers (a track star who trains with Kersee) a couple of years ago. I'd been hearing about Bob Kersee and said, 'I want to do that one day.' …And the workouts he put me through. At times, I thought, 'Man, this guy is trying to kill me.' But I kept saying, 'I'm not going to let him break me.'"[868]

After Law's insubordination, Coach Carroll admitted "He had a great offseason,"[869] and Law went on to have an excellent season. When Belichick took over, he acknowledged that Law put himself through intense off-season training but still pushed Law to join the team during the off-season: "I've talked to Ty about that. I respect what Ty's doing, but at the same time, we're planning on having a later discussion on that."[870]

Law was also a Belichick-type player in his enthusiasm for studying game film and in his setting of lofty goals for himself and striving to achieve them:

> "I could sit and watch tapes of Deion [Sanders] all day. He's that kind of special cornerback to me. He's on another level. To me, Muhammad Ali is the greatest athlete of all time. Deion is the Muhammad Ali of cornerbacks.

He has so much respect from every cornerback, every quarterback and every receiver in the league. That's where you want to be."[871]

Through goal setting, dedication, and sweat, Law ratcheted his game up several notches and made himself an elite cornerback. Belichick admired such traits in Law and brought in more players with Law-like traits.

Patriots wide receiver Troy Brown was drafted in the 8th round of the 1994 NFL Draft. The NFL doesn't even bother with an 8th round any more! Troy Brown overcame (or ignored) minimal expectations to not only make the Patriots roster (after Bill Parcells cut and later re-signed him) but remain a key player a decade later. Brown has achieved excellence because he is a consummate professional who pushes himself day in and day out and does whatever necessary to improve himself and help his team. Before becoming the Patriots' "go to" wide receiver in critical situations, Brown made his mark returning punts and kickoffs, tasks at which he continued to excel even after he became the team's #1 wide receiver. "Tireless" should be Brown's middle name. On his twelfth birthday, Brown began loading watermelons onto trucks ten or eleven hours a day in Barnwell, SC because his single mother and siblings needed the money: "When you're a have-not, you're wearing your brother's shoes and pants. You're trying to find something to eat."[872] After working all day, Brown then went weightlifting, so you believe Brown when he says, "The way I grew up just wouldn't allow me to quit."[873]

Coming out of college, was Tom Brady considered a likely two-time Super Bowl MVP? *The Sporting News*' scouting report on Brady said "Decent arm. Could be an NFL backup."[874] Draft guru Mel Kiper Jr. judged Brady the tenth-best quarterback prospect of 2000 (behind future NFL "greats" Joe Hamilton, Tee Martin, and Chris Redman), writing, "his lack of mobility could surface as a problem, and it will be interesting to see how he fares when forced to take more chances down the field... doesn't have the total package of skills."[875] New Orleans Saints general manager Randy Mueller scouted Brady and concluded: "Skinny kid, average arm, average athlete, average physical skills. Not much there."[876] Had teams seen Brady's true potential, he would have been the #1 overall pick. Instead, Brady lasted until the 6th round. Even the Patriots admit they underestimated Brady: "I wouldn't say we're geniuses. We didn't see [Brady's talent] for five rounds, either." [877] Super Bowl-winning quarterback Phil Simms says teams were rightly skeptical of Brady: "Look. The guy ran a 5.2 40[yard dash] coming out of college. That worries people."[878] Brady's greatest asset, that makes him special, is his incredible competitiveness and drive to dominate. At age 8, Brady threw the remote at his TV after losing a video game; and, at age 12, a wall savagely struck Brady's fist after Brady's basketball team lost a game.[879] His refusal to lose drives him to improve himself and prepare for games. Scott Pioli says Brady "has worked himself into one of the best quarterbacks in the National Football League. His hard work, dedication ... Tom's a special guy."[880] Wide receiver Donald Hayes marveled, "I've seen him work extremely hard in the offseason. He's still competing like he doesn't have the starting job, even though it's his."[881] Brady's focus comes from his ambition and refusal to coast on his reputation: "I don't know of any great athlete who says, 'I've done it. I've proved it. That's all I've got to do.'"[882] Brady even coined a phrase for how he prepares: "I'm trying to geek myself up for that opening game, which means everything I'm doing now is preparation for that."[883] In 2001, Brady was already as anal a perfectionist as his mentor:

> "It's a midweek practice before the Jets showdown. Coleman runs a slant to the wrong spot–right into the linebacker–so Brady pulls him aside. 'If you do that again, that's an interception,' he tells Coleman. 'You've gotta get behind him.' Coleman would do exactly as he was told on the critical 46-yard reception that Sunday."[884]

> "During one practice, [Brady] was coach as much as quarterback, instructing receiver David Givens how to run a route against different coverages and running the route himself to demonstrate, and then telling receiver Deion Branch to run a hook-in about a yard deeper than he was running it. Brady might have a future in coaching, considering both receivers scored touchdowns [that Sunday in the Super Bowl] and Branch had 10 catches for 143 yards and Givens five for 69."[885]

In 2004, the Patriots surprised almost everyone by selecting tight end Benjamin Watson with the final pick in the 1st round of the NFL Draft. Watson has great strength, size, speed, and smarts but had only so-so statistics in college (partly due to injuries and because he transferred from Duke to Georgia). Most draft "experts" felt Watson wasn't the best tight end available to the Patriots with that pick. Almost everyone rated Ben Troupe above Watson. But, even after missing eighteen days of training camp due to a contract dispute (due to his agent's stubbornness, not his... Watson eventually fired his agent), Watson played brilliantly before seriously injuring himself early in the season. (I'm convinced Watson will emerge as a star in 2005.) Brady said, "He's come in and picked up the offense much faster than I ever did."[886] Meanwhile, Troupe struggled:

> "Ben Troupe has been a disappointment so far in Tennessee. The Titans had hoped Troupe would be an immediate starter in place of the recently retired Frank Wycheck. But Troupe has been outplayed by unheralded tight end Dwayne Blakley and might be a game-day inactive when the season starts."[887]

One reason the Patriots chose Watson is his demonstrated passion for football. Watson was smart enough to attend Duke but transferred to Georgia because he was hungry to play big-time football:

> "I went to Duke initially because of the academics... I just wasn't happy with the football aspect of it, with the winning aspect of it. We worked so hard every day at practices, then on Saturdays we struggled a lot of times. I

wanted a chance to play for the national championship, play in big bowl games, do all the big-time college football things. So that's why I decided to go to Georgia."[888]

Many Patriots have blue-collar backgrounds and Ph.D.s from The School of Hard Knocks. No team drafted Patriots wide receiver David Patten, so he lugged 75-pound bags of coffee beans for $8 an hour at a factory in Columbia, SC. Co-workers laughed when he insisted he would make the NFL; he later played for the Albany Firebirds to keep his football dreams alive. When just six years old, defensive lineman Richard Seymour began working every summer with his father. Seymour says his background helps him in the NFL:

"It's a constant battle. You have to push yourself to levels where you don't feel like going. That's what the great ones do. It's not easy. If it was easy, everyone would be doing it. My father always says, 'Nobody beats you when you work hard.' It was the only thing I knew as a kid. I got tired of hearing him say it; he was talking like he was Muhammad Ali. It was inbred in me. I've always had ability. I've seen guys rely on that. At this level, everyone's got ability. It's only this [touching his heart] that separates players."[889]

Tight end Christian Fauria's father was also a bricklayer and also made his three sons work: "My father had his rules. No one ever sat down. If someone else is working, you had to be working. We used to toss these 16-inch blocks at each other to see if we could scratch each other's legs."[890] Offensive guard Russ Hochstein's family runs a concrete business in Nebraska, and Hochstein reports "We had to do manual labor when I was growing up. ...I was always taught to work hard and keep plugging away at things."[891] Fullback Fred McCrary worked as a corrections officer at a maximum security prison in Louisiana. Wide receiver David Givens has a stern Army father: "You know how military men are. ...he was very demanding. Now I just try to prove to myself I can do what other people say I can't do."[892]

Adversity conquers many, but the Patriots love players, like New Orleans native and Pats rookie Marquise Hill, who have persevered through adversity and overcome challenges:

"The murder capital. You see dead bodies every day. You drive around the neighborhood and see someone laid out, yellow tape everywhere. It's just common. It's really going to be a culture shock here [in New England] because nothing happens. ...[Size] doesn't prevent anybody from (bothering) you, especially in New Orleans because everybody has the equalizers–the guns. It doesn't matter how big you are. Just keep yourself out of harm's way. You know where to go and where not to go. So that was the big thing for me, getting out of there with no problems."[893]

Running back Kevin Faulk's brother died in a gang fight.

Challenges need not be life-and-death. What matters is players' willingness to confront them. Patriot special teamer Je'Rod Cherry is very serious about his football career but preparing for life after football because he grew up around "guys with all the potential in the world [who] didn't take school serious or got hurt."[894] Scott Pioli says the Patriots drafted Tom Brady out of Michigan because he had competed hard against several future NFL quarterbacks: "We saw a guy who is very accurate, a guy that's a tremendous leader. A guy who had a difficult situation–he handled it like a man. He kept his eye on the prize and won a bunch of football games."[895]

Patriots special teamer Shawn Mayer, who made 17 tackles in 12 games during 2003, worked through many adversities: "At Penn State, I had back surgery and I had knee surgery. I've just been overcoming obstacles my whole life. Growing up, it was the same deal. Money situations. We weren't the wealthiest family. My dad got fired, stuff like that. We had our times with no electricity, no heat, and no water. ...You don't complain about it. You just work and work, and that's all you can do. That's all I know how to do."[896]

Many Patriots are devoted husbands and fathers. Tedy Bruschi adores his kids, Tedy Jr. and Rex. Mike Vrabel returned to Ohio State in the 2004 offseason to complete his degree to set an example for his sons, Tyler and Carter: "You're going to have to raise your kids, and you want them to go to college. ...[Y]ou're going to... want to say, 'Hey, you've got to go to class.'"[897] Even Patriots who aren't parents act like parents. After a training session, Dan Klecko made time for "tackling drills" with Vrabel's sons.

It's no coincidence several recent Patriots draftees are already married with children. Patriots management apparently believes that young men who commit to marriage are likely to commit to their jobs and that marriage matures young men and makes them more serious, professional football players. Maturity is critical because, as rookie tight end Benjamin Watson learned immediately, "it's a business and everybody here treats it as such."[898]

2003 #1 pick Ty Warren has a wife and family. 2004 #1 pick Vince Wilfork has a son and a daughter and is a devoted, doting husband who volunteered to the Boston media that he checks with his wife before making any important decision. He also fought through the death of both parents in 2002 (his dad, David, to diabetes-related kidney failure in June and his mom to stroke complications in December). Wilfork wears a locket containing his parents' high school prom picture,[899] and his college teammate Willis McGahee, now a superb Buffalo Bills running back, calls Wilfork "a teddy bear."[900] Each of Wilfork's arms bears a "One life to live" tattoo.[901] (Another Patriots draftee, safety Dexter Reid, has motivational tattoos saying, "Only Warriors Survive," "Built for this," and "Don't knock the hustle."[902]) Having become a father and lost his parents, Wilfork has a "take charge" attitude: "I can't do anything but step up and be a man. And that's what I am today."[903] He says his troubles "forced me to mature a lot earlier than other people. A lot of kids my age are still kids. With that, losing both parents and having a daughter I had to do something and my wife and I turned it around and basically that is how I became the man that I am."[904] Wilfork is not merely mature beyond his years. Wilfork quickly became the starter at nose tackle and appears headed for stardom because he combines great size, good speed, a tremendous attitude, stamina, and tenacity. Like every Patriot, he loves playing football:

> "When someone looks at a guy my size they think of a fat slob or a guy who can't move, but right here there is none of that. If you saw my game tape down in Miami I was everywhere on the field. I played 60 minutes. I never took a play off and always played full speed and I think it is hard for defensive tackles my size to do that. Either they are getting taken out of the game for a breather or they are not in condition. I never had that problem. I was always in great condition and always had fun playing football."[905]

Wilfork has proven himself a dexterous athlete, quite a feat for a 340-pounder:

> "As a high school senior in Lantana, Fla., Wilfork had the third-best shot put in the country at 67-7. If that burst of energy doesn't impress you, his footwork in guiding him to the 20th best discus throw of that same year (187-8) should."[906]

But it is Wilfork's heart that spurs him achieve his potential:

> "When you're talking about a pass rush, it's a matter of how much do you want it. When you're one-on-one, man-to-man, it comes down to every move there is. You might have to use three or four moves just to get to the quarterback–and sometimes that's not enough. Sometimes you can beat a guy with one move. It's a matter of how bad you want it and what you're willing to do to get it."[907]

The maturity that so often grows out of marriage, fatherhood, or the loss of one's parents seems especially relevant in the Patriots' evaluation of players who have gotten into trouble in their pasts, like rookie running back Cedric Cobbs: "I'm more grown up now. I have responsibilities. I have a fiancée, I have a child, and I have another child on the way. I now have to take care of my business or else I'm going to be out on the streets."[908]

On October 22, 2000, Cincinnati Bengals running back Corey Dillon ran for 278 yards against Denver, breaking Walter Payton's all-time NFL single-game rushing record. Despite Dillon's prodigious physical talent, no one envisioned Dillon wearing a Patriots uniform because his poor attitude and life-long tendency to find trouble made him seem a classic anti-Patriot. Since his teen years, Dillon repeatedly landed in legal scrapes. In the NFL, he acquired a reputation as an egomaniac. So, many were startled in Spring 2004 when the Patriots traded a 2nd-round draft pick for Dillon. Belichick and Pioli hadn't lowered their standards; they had recognized and admired Dillon's newfound maturity. Dillon had avoided trouble for most of the past four years, no longer drinks, and steers clear of his old friends who had a knack for getting themselves and him in trouble. Dillon has become a family man, with a wife, Desiree, and 5-year-old daughter Cameron. In the Dillon family, "little [5-year-old daughter] Cameron, whose arched eyebrows give her the same quizzical look as her father, is running the show. 'She's unseated me as leader of the house,' he jokes."[909] On January 30, 2000, Dillon married the mother of his daughter, born in January 1999. Around that time, he started putting his troubled past behind him:

> "He said after reporting to camp [in 2000] that his life was great and that he enjoyed 'sitting back' and looking at his gorgeous wife and daughter. He also recently told a Bengals media relations employee that he has become a born-again Christian."[910]

One way to know whether a guy is hungry is to analyze whether he improves each year. Asked to point to "one thing that stood out" about a particular draftee, Belichick said such a question is naive because players are complete packages and must be evaluated on many criteria and over time to see whether they're learning and growing and maturing:

> "I don't think with any one player there is any one play or any one thing. It is the whole picture of the player, the whole evaluation from when he started in college whether it was in junior college, Division I, whatever it is, and what his progression is. You try to evaluate it all the way through as much as you can."[911]

Hungry guys want to win

> "No. 1, you have to be committed to winning. Everybody here [and everyone] that's been here before, is 100 percent committed to winning. Football is important to the guys. If you want to fit in, that's the best way to do it, commit yourself 100 percent to this team, do what it takes to win, and then you'll gain the respect of the other guys."
> – *Special teams captain Larry Izzo*

Sales managers often hire hungry, driven salespeople because they sell aggressively and successfully. The Patriots also love hungry players. In 2002, *ESPN*'s Len Pasquarelli suggested the Patriots' motto should be "Give me your tired, your poor, your hungry, yearning to… win a championship."[912] The Patriots are stocked with such players. The night Pro Bowl safety Rodney Harrison received his Super Bowl ring, he explained he joined the Patriots for a chance to earn a championship ring: "Ty Law, Richard Seymour, Troy Brown; they all told me: Come and win a championship. Come to the Patriots. Here I am."[913] What's Richard Seymour's goal? To be one of the best defensive linemen in the NFL? No. To be absolutely #1: "My goal is to be the best, period. I said that from Day 1. Ain't no joy being No. 2."[914] Seymour has become a dominating player who occupies two blockers, makes tackles, sacks quarterbacks, and uses his long arms to knock down passes (ten in 2003) and block field goal attempts (one in 2003). Seymour recently raised the bar on himself: "you have to want to be the best that ever played the position. I still have a long way to go for that, but that's one of my goals."[915]

The Patriots' emphasis on character produces great results not only in the NFL but also in NFL Europe. Five Patriots played on the 2004 Berlin Thunder. (Only one, Rohan Davey, made the final 2004 Patriots' roster, but all were players the Patriots thought highly of.) The Thunder won the World Bowl after losing only one game all season (on a last-play touchdown). Offensive lineman Jamil Soriano pointed to locker room chemistry as a key to the Thunder's success and implied that Patriots players helped foster that team chemistry:

> "We came in here having a kind of winning attitude. Rohan is doing a great job leading the team and leading the offense. Chas (Gessner) is doing well as well as the other guys, (Lawrence) Flugence and Scott (Farley). They are all doing pretty well. The biggest thing about our team is that I think we click pretty well and jelled pretty well. We get along with everyone else. So we are playing good football."[916]

Hire reliable (tough) guys

"There are two kinds of toughness. Mental toughness and physical toughness. Those are the kinds of football players we want here."[917]
  – Bill Belichick

"We don't quit. We never quit."[918]
  – Patriots fullback Jermaine Wiggins, after the Patriots beat the Oakland Raiders in the January 2002 "Snow Bowl"

"I'm a machine. I'm going to give you everything I got. I don't boast to be anything great. I don't boast to be this and that. But the one thing you're going to know when you line up across from D.P. is that you're going to get everything he's got."[919]
  – Patriots wide receiver David Patten

"I know when I'm out on the field I'm the best player out there. There is no [defensive back] who is going to outwork me."[920]
  – Patriots wide receiver David Givens

"I haven't been afraid to run into anything. I'll run into a brick wall if I had to. My mom taught me the value of work ethic, that no one is ever going to give you anything in life. You always have to work harder than the next person."[921]
  – Patriots safety Rodney Harrison

"You see guys 250 pounds and they don't want to hit anything moving. Then you see a guy like [Patriots safety] Eugene [Wilson]–185, 190 pounds–who'll hit anything moving. It's just a matter of heart and being committed to what you want to hit and not being afraid to hurt yourself."[922]
– *Patriots safety Rodney Harrison*

In September 2003, Patriots linebacker Tedy Bruschi lay motionless on the field after a crushing collision with the Washington Redskins' Ladell Betts. Moments later, Bruschi popped up, to everyone's relief. After the game, he joked: "No matter what the situation is, when you go down, get up. The wife is watching and you don't want to worry her too much."[923]

You know Patriots rookie safety Dexter Reid is tough when he tells you his idols are two of the hardest-hitting safeties in NFL history: "I love Ronnie Lott. I was a Ronnie Lott fan coming up. I love Steve Atwater."[924] Mental toughness and a drive to excel are prerequisites for becoming a Patriot. Scott Pioli and his scouts focus exclusively on such players and ignore many other talented players who may become stars on other NFL teams, as Pioli has explained: "Just because a player is right for us doesn't mean he's right for someone else. We have a demanding system, and we expect a lot for our players. We have to get a certain type of player that fits with our coach."[925]

Before Super Bowl XXXVIII, Patriot linebacker Willie McGinest predicted there would be "a lot of eye-gouging, hair-pulling and leg-whipping" before adding "No, these are two classy teams... But it's going to be violent."[926] Carolina Panthers defensive lineman Kris Jenkins predicted "a street fight."[927] Panthers safety Mike Minter agreed the game would play out "like two trains colliding."[928] Early in that war... I mean game... Panthers defensive lineman Mike Rucker's knee smashed Patriots wide receiver Troy Brown's nose, and blood came pouring out. Brown went to the sidelines, stuffed a wad of cotton up his nose, then came back onto the field to return a punt. He also caught eight passes, gaining 76 yards. The next day, Brown "was sporting a tremendous black-and-blue bulge where the left part of his nose should have been."[929]

Patriots linebacker Tedy Bruschi's love of smash-mouth football is obvious from his response to the media's suggestion that football pitting the cerebral Belichick against smartypants Colts quarterback Peyton Manning is like a chess match (in which Belichick is the grandmaster because Peyton's Colts usually lose): "I don't like to use the word 'chess.' That's too much of a finesse word for me. I like 'Rock-'em Sock-'em Robots,'"[930] referring to a children's game involving two plastic boxing robots who try to knock each other's heads off. After Bruschi won his first Super Bowl, he exclaimed, "I feel like Rocky!"[931] Bruschi's passion makes him the prototypical Belichick player. Belichick paid Bruschi the ultimate compliment, calling him "the Troy Brown of our defense."[932] Patriots cornerback Ty Law says "Bruschi would be a good guy [for NFL Films to put a microphone on]; he's intense, into the game, and always doing some crazy scream. He does some 'E-yayayaya' scream. I don't know what the heck [he's] doing. You wouldn't be able to interpret what he's saying, but you'd get some good sounds out of him."[933]

Patriots cornerback Tyrone Poole agrees with Bruschi that "Football is tackle. It's not tag. You have to go out and be physical. It's a modern-day Roman gladiator event."[934] Before opening day 2004, Patriots safety Rodney Harrison was excited about hitting opponents, not enjoying the star-studded hour-long NFL pregame show saluting the 2003 Patriots: "When it comes down to it, at 9:07 [kickoff time], you've got to go and crack some heads."[935]

Inside linebackers coach Pepper Johnson, a former player with Super Bowl rings to prove it, encourages his players' physicality. Before the Patriots countered the St. Louis Rams' speed with their power in Super Bowl XXXVI, Johnson said, "The Rams' way is a lot more finesse than offense. It is good by them because you have finesse guys on that team. Myself, when I think about football, you are not just tired when you finish a game, you are worn down and beat up and have a couple of bruises."[936]

Professional football players must be tough because the NFL is brutally violent. As Patriots rookie nose tackle Vince Wilfork says, "it's a contact sport. If you don't want to get hit don't play football."[937] Asked about dirty tricks players pull when a pile of players forms (after a fumble, for example), Brady said, "Aw, man. I'll tell ya. I've had just about everything punched. I've had things grabbed that just shouldn't be grabbed."[938]

Growing up in Sacramento, Tedy Bruschi had two loves: football and jazz saxophone. Though Bruschi still plays his alto sax regularly and has performed several times at Symphony Hall, he chose to pursue a football career because "I couldn't use my saxophone to hit anybody. So I sort of liked the helmet better."[939]

Every Patriot seems to love the sound of two giant men crashing into each other at full speed. Patriots offensive lineman Damien Woody says "[Matt Light]'s a tough guy Bill felt would fit the system. He's got a nice little mean streak."[940] Super Bowl XXI MVP quarterback Phil Simms says "the Patriots are battle-tested. They are the worst kind of opponents–they just like the action. I never liked playing teams that just enjoyed the action. Everybody wants to win, but some teams just like to fight, and the Patriots are one of them."[941]

Bill Belichick loves Corey Dillon for many reasons: "He's got power, he's got quickness, he's got speed to outrun guys. He uses all those."[942] But a major reason Belichick loves Dillon has nothing to do with running or catching passes. It's Dillon's powerful pass protection: "He's tough. I thought he stepped up three or four times and made solid contact on the blitz. He's a tough guy. It's one of the things I liked about him in Cincinnati."[943]

The Patriots wanted to draft Illinois quarterback Kurt Kittner in the 5th round of the 2002 draft, but the Atlanta Falcons grabbed him earlier in that round. After two undistinguished seasons in the NFL (2 TDs; 6 INTs; 38% completion percentage), Kittner was signed and later released by the Falcons, Bengals, and Giants. The Patriots tried repeatedly to grab Kittner off waivers and finally got their hands on him in the summer of 2004 after no other NFL team wanted him. Why were the Patriots so high on Kittner? His toughness is one reason. Diving into the end zone during the third game of his senior season in high school, Kittner tore ligaments and tendons in his thumb so severely it ended his season. But Kittner insisted on playing, despite his broken thumb. His coach explains:

> "He couldn't play quarterback because of the cast. He asked me if he could play linebacker, because he could play with the cast. I told him he had a scholarship to Illinois and why mess with it. But he said he wanted to do it. So I let him. That's him in a nutshell. He's tough and he's fearless."[944]

Kitner did not make the 2004 Patriots roster, but Belichick indicated Kittner might have made the team if the Patriots had acquired him earlier.

On the recommendation of LSU head coach and Belichick confidante Nick Saban, the Patriots brought in undrafted LSU cornerback Randall Gay, who played most of his senior season as LSU's third cornerback ("nickel back"). Gay caught no interceptions as a senior and was overshadowed by starters Corey Webster and Travis Daniels. But Gay impressed the Patriots by knocking down eleven passes while playing in pain after breaking his left forearm in the first game. Gay handled his injury and his demotion with tremendous team spirit:

> "With me getting hurt, guys like Jessie and LaRon got more reps and some experience. ...If I don't get hurt, then maybe they don't develop like they have and maybe we wouldn't be undefeated. ...The first game LaRon was out there, I don't think he knew anything. The pressure was on him to learn, he had to be out there. The last game he played, that's the best I've seen a freshman go out there and play in a while. Usually freshmen come in and are ready to quit in fall camp. I never heard that from either one of them."[945]

Gay's talent and attitude helped him earn a spot on the 2004 Patriots' final 53-man roster.

The Patriots are suckers for tough guy stories. Tom Brady is certainly tough. Without complaint, Brady played the entire 2003 season in need of shoulder surgery (on his AC joint) due to an easily-inflamed shoulder: "Everybody plays in pain. You deal with it. A lot of guys play with worse injuries than I had."[946] He says, "[surgery]'s something I probably should have done last year, but I didn't. I kind of paid for it all year."[947]

The Patriots are also suckers for guys who love to train, train some more, and then train again. Offensive lineman Russ Hochstein's ability to pass block has been questioned in high school, college, and the NFL because he's a self-confessed "300-pound slow guy," but Hochstein strives relentlessly to improve himself:

> "I'm a very determined person. I know I'll never be able to run a 4.8 40 or bench press 520 pounds or something like that, but I know the one thing they can't take away from me is how hard I work. Determination and hard work will get you a lot of places."[948]

The Patriots can't resist guys like linebacker Ted Johnson who embraces the pain of training camp because it's a callous that makes regular-season and post-season pain bearable: "Camp is your rite of passage. It gets you battle-hardened, it really does. Your body needs to feel that, the bruises, the pain, the aches that come with camp, so when it's for real, you can push through it."[949]

Hire pleasant guys

> "Tom has a real good personality for a quarterback. He is confident, but he is not cocky. He is assertive, but he is not overbearing. He can come on pretty strong and ...get a point across without being antagonistic or offensive in doing it."[950]
> *– Bill Belichick in 2001, before Tom Brady's first start*

> "[Patriots linebacker Rosevelt Colvin] has got an upbeat personality. I think he comes across as a guy who likes to play football and is having fun out there playing football on the field and that is a little bit contagious defensively. ... He does have a little bounce in his step and has a little spark when he is on the field and I think that is good for him but it's good for the other players that are out there with him too."[951]
> *– Bill Belichick, before Colvin suffered a season-ending hip fracture the second week of the 2003 season*

Enthusiasm is infectious. Belichick's even-keeled disposition notwithstanding, the Patriots are loaded with happy, optimistic, perpetually upbeat guys: happy-go-lucky Tom Brady, the always-smiling Deion Branch, Rosevelt Colvin, Dan Klecko, Tedy Bruschi, Rohan Davey:

> "Brady seemed to go through Super Bowl week with a perpetual smile on his face. Whether he was trying to talk referee Ed Hochuli out of a penalty or signing autographs for a youth football team, the smile never left. It was even bigger than usual after the Thursday practice when Brady claimed victory over receiver Bethel Johnson in a punting contest. Brady screamed and ran around as if he had won his personal Super Bowl."[952]

At the Super Bowl, Patriots tight end Christian Fauria acted like a kid in a candy shop:

> "I was almost becoming a complete idiot. Like a court jester, I was so giddy. You know, I wasn't going to hide my feelings. I was happy and I was going to

show it. I didn't want to act all cool just because I was at the Super Bowl. Forget about hiding my emotions, this is freakin' awesome."[953]

Such upbeat, positive attitudes lift the whole team and make being a New England Patriot enjoyable. Players bring professional attitudes but view football as fun. They work hard not because they have to but because they enjoy preparing to win football games and enjoy each other. They remind one another, "If you're going to play like a champion, act like a champion."[954] After Belichick took over the Patriots, offensive lineman Damien Woody noticed a difference between his pre-Belichick and post-Belichick teammates: "[Belichick and Pioli] brought in guys you want to play with, guys you want to be around, guys you want to hang around with after work."[955] Patriots linebacker Rosevelt Colvin, for example, brings his mouth and sense of humor to practice with him. After returning to practice after a year-long hip fracture, "Rosey" said: "After I got the first couple of reps out of the way, I was back to my old self–talking and letting people know this and that. I had fun. That's what I've been trying to get back to for almost a year now, trying to have fun again."[956]

Positive attitudes not only motivate preparation during the dreary, drudgery-filled off-season but also spur performance during games. After the Patriots offense rallied to win the "Tuck Rule" playoff game in the snow against Oakland, wide receiver David Patten singled out Brady's charisma and infectious enthusiasm:

> "You can't say enough about him. Just the way he comes in the huddle. We were down, it was the start of the fourth quarter, and he had just so much confidence, so much excitement. You know, you can't get down in our offensive huddle, because if you get down, Tom's going to jump you. He's a true leader in every sense of the word. He leads by example. It's not so much his talk. It's his excitement, his passion for the game."[957]

Patten adds that Brady was equally inspiring before the final drive of that season's Super Bowl:

> "When he got into the huddle to start the drive, he said, 'OK, we need to go down the field now, so Adam can win it for us.' He said it like he knew it was going to happen and when he did that, you could actually see the offensive linemen perk up. That's how he's been all year."[958]

> "He said, 'Here we go.' He said we have to go down and win the game here. He just has such a tremendous amount of confidence and it revs us up. If you look in his eyes and hear him talk, you think, 'We have to go out and get it done for this kid.'"[959]

Two years later, with another Super Bowl riding on another final drive, Brady said in the huddle: "Let's just do it."[960] Players respond because, as Patriots tight end Christian Fauria puts it, Brady has "a JFK presence around him. People want to be around him."[961] Patriots center/guard Damien Woody says, "He knows he's going to win, and he makes you believe it. ...I'd die for the man. ...He's the kind of guy who makes you want to bust your ass."[962]

Most of the coaches' and players' wives and girlfriends have crushes on Tom Brady. Even Coach Belichick's daughter does. In fact, half the women in Massachusetts swoon for him, and girls have been spotted around New England wearing "Mrs. Brady" tee shirts. Former Patriots defensive end Dave Nugent, who shared an apartment with Brady as he was rising to prominence, shares this funny story:

"We had a high school girl stop by the house. Usually I answer the door when we're both home, but I wasn't home this time, so he had to open the door. It was this high school girl, and she asked him if he would go to her prom with her. And I mean the guy seriously hates saying no to people. He couldn't say no to her face, so he's like, 'I'll let you know.' So she goes home, and obviously he had to call up the next day and, you know, tell her no. Actually, he had to talk to her parents, because they're the ones who answered the phone-he had to explain why he couldn't take her to the prom."[963]

Brady's cheerfulness and confidence in 2001 impressed not only teammates and adoring female fans but also Super Bowl XVII-winning quarterback Joe Theismann, who participated in a Patriots practice that season:

"[Brady] always looks like he has a smile on his face. He has a wonderful calm demeanor. Talking to him, I sensed a quiet confidence... Brady answers questions in a positive way. He talks in terms of what the team is capable of doing. He seemed to have little doubt he could do the job. He was very calm, not in an egotistical way."[964]

Brady's attitude inspired confidence in teammates, from the day he took over from Bledsoe. Troy Brown said, "People listen to him. He gives you a look that makes you know if you do what he tells you, it'll be fine."[965] Even while Bledsoe's backup, Brady was impressing the starters: "[Wide receiver] David Patten was stunned when Brady, between reps in the weight room, [told] the newly signed free agent how to adjust his routes on the fly."[966]

Perhaps most valuably, Brady uses his popularity to motivate his teammates. He prods them when necessary and celebrates with them when warranted. A fan wrote:

"one thing that typifies Tom Brady is his reaction to Patten early in Sunday night's game. After chewing Patten out... Brady was the first to congratulate Patten after he caught a touchdown pass. It just showed how his intensity never got personal and was all about professionalism and improving the team."[967]

Hire smart guys

"In pro-sports competition, you have to make a lot of decisions in a very short amount of time."[968]
– Bill Belichick

"We're a thinking man's team. And if you're going to try to think along with us, to match wits with Belichick, man, you're going to come out of the game with a headache."[969]
– Patriots safety Rodney Harrison

"The whole key to [this] defense is whether or not you can get everybody to understand what everybody else is doing, and should be doing, on every play. Do that, and you can be very good."[970]
– Patriots linebacker Mike Vrabel

"The rookie camp was hectic, long hours. We were going from 7:30 a.m. till 9 at night, it was an information overload. ...My goal for now is just to learn what to do. The biggest difference [from college] is the amount of information and the new terminology."[971]
– Patriots rookie tight end Benjamin Watson

"I am trying to stay on top of it, even if that means I have to lose an hour's sleep at night to learn the playbook. ...[I]n college it's kind of hands on, now they throw the playbook at you and it's up you to catch on." [972]
– Patriots rookie wide receiver P.K. Sam

"In college, the linebacker just called everything, while here I have to know what the guy next to me is doing and know different positions."[973]
– Patriots rookie defensive tackle Vince Wilfork

The three NFL teams with the most college graduates in 2003 (Patriots, 35; Colts, 37; Panthers, 42) were three of the final four playoff teams.[974] This is no coincidence. A college degree indicates persistence, dedication to achieving goals, love of learning, and intelligence. The Patriots hire for smarts because they rely on an extraordinarily thick playbook and complex schemes that require intelligent players. After the Patriots call "a play," players position themselves on the field with several possible plays in mind. One play is the default, but players retain flexibility to quickly change to any of several backup plays if their opponent shows them something unexpected. One player may change the play and communicate the change using shouting or hand signals. Sometimes, individual players switch based on what they observe the opponent do after the ball is snapped. "Field generals" on offense (quarterback and center) and defense (middle linebacker and safety) hold primary responsibility for calling plays and making last-second adjustments based on what the opponent is showing. Field generals must interpret the opponent's pre-snap behavior and intelligently change which variation of the play to run and instantly communicate any change to their teammates.

Before the ball is snapped until the play ends, each player must constantly interpret the opponent's behavior and react accordingly, within the framework of his responsibilities (even as opposing players attempt to disguise their intentions by moving around before the snap, running reverses, double reverses, play-action passes, draw plays, *etc.*). Hiring smart players enables Patriots coaches to use their complex schemes and helps Patriots players react well to opponents' trickery. Philadelphia Eagles head coach Andy Reid says the formula works: "The whole [Patriots] defense just knows what they're doing better than anybody in the N.F.L. They execute that defense. Everybody knows how to adjust. They're physical. You don't see a lot of mess-ups."[975] Three-time Emmy-winning NFL analyst (and former three-time Pro Bowler) Cris Collinsworth agrees: "the group that gets very little credit is the linebackers. Roman Phifer, Mike Vrabel and Tedy Bruschi jump out at me every time I watch the film. They are just smarter than the offenses they are playing against."[976]

In July 2003, Bill Belichick treated the media to a simulated two-hour training session. He asked reporters to imagine themselves playing the strong-side linebacker position (the "Sam" position). Reporters were impressed by the complexity of the Patriots defense, even though Belichick showed only a single defensive alignment:

> "As Belichick said… the extreme base 3-4 cover 2 defense that he used throughout his examples would be considered a single scoop of vanilla ice cream when compared to something like the six-flavor, three-topping banana split that players will have to quickly digest."[977]

One of the biggest misconceptions casual fans have is the "simplicity" of playing on the offensive line. To the uninformed, it seems straightforward: line up and block the guy in front of you. Grunt work, right? Twenty or thirty years ago, it was simple. But, as defenses have evolved countless tricky schemes for attacking the quarterback (most famously a million different "zone blitzes" in which the defense seeks to overload part of the offensive line with more defensive players than the offensive linemen can block while rotating other defensive players from elsewhere to even out the defense), defending one's quarterback (not to mention blocking for one's running back) has become as mentally taxing as it is physically straining:

> "in 1981… a team usually went into a game with one protection for a deep drop, one for a quick drop, a couple for play-action passes and one for a bootleg. Twenty-two years later, the Chiefs are prepared to use 30 protections in a game, and sometimes teams must resort to protections that aren't even in their game plans."[978]

Defending one's quarterback is so difficult and so essential that starting left tackles (who protect the blind sides of right-handed quarterbacks) are among the best-paid players in the NFL. Tackles in particular often have a split second to decide which of two or even three guys they will block. If a tackle knows a running back is behind him with pass protection responsibility, for example, he may allow a (smaller) safety or linebacker to run around him and instead block the (larger) linebacker or defensive lineman. But if he knows there is no running back behind him to block, he may need to slide over and block the speedy edge rusher who would otherwise have an unimpeded path to the quarterback. Rams coach Mike Martz, who begins crafting each game plan with unsexy-but-crucial pass protection schemes, says much of a team's offense revolves around the intelligence, experience, and intuition of a team's tackles: "If you get a guy on the edge who never has played, it really limits what you can call. You're going to get mental mistakes, and you're going to get the quarterback hit."[979] Offensive lines use many blocking schemes each game so defenses can't anticipate a particular scheme and exploit its vulnerabilities. And each scheme requires each player to rapidly interpret what the defense is doing and adjust his actions accordingly.

Players at every position must make last-second matchup-determined adjustments. Such "hot routes" and "sight adjustments" require smarter players. A programming analogy can help us appreciate the difficulty adjustments create for players. Calling a play before seeing what your opponent is doing is a "compile-time" decision, meaning that behavior is coded directly into the program. Executing such plays is easy because the instructions are simple and unambiguous: "Block the guy nearest you" or "Run this route" or "Stand in this part of the field and knock down any passes thrown there." Adjusting behavior during a play requires "runtime" decisions, meaning that the program decides what do based on conditions existing during the play. Executing such plays is difficult because instructions are complicated and ambiguous: "If you see X, then do A; if you see Y, then do B; if you see Z, then do C; *etc.*" Since it is impossible to spell out every situation, players must interpret and adapt on the fly... and those individual decisions must be compatible. Executing a coordinated defense well requires both art and science. This is why Patriots linebacker Ted Johnson objects to the notion that Belichick, Crennel, and Weis "program" players who then simply take the field and behave like Xs and Os on a chalkboard. Johnson says his teammates coordinate their runtime decisions well because they know and like one another:

> "It's not that we're Pavlov's dog, but we're conditioned to think a certain way. It's not that [our schemes] are so crazy or innovative, but we work well together. We're a humble group. We like each other, we hang together. No one strays from the group."[980]

Obviously, "runtime" programming demands more of players than "compile-time" programming but potentially yields superior results. Smart players enable coaches to rely more on "runtime programming" and less on "compile-time programming."

Tight ends and running backs are also integral elements of blocking schemes, and their responsibilities vary according to whether the quarterback will fake a hand-off to a running back ("play-action") and whether the quarterback will drop back short or deep behind the center or roll out to one side of the field or the other. It's even more complicated. Mike Martz says defensive coordinators have become so inventive that "You have to be able to [adapt on the fly] versus a blitz you've never seen before. The offensive line has to be great problem solvers."[981] In the language of my earlier programming analogy, Martz is saying that offensive linemen *must* use runtime programming. Offensive lineman Gene Mruczkowski made the 2004 Patriots roster because, Belichick says, "he's a pretty smart guy who reacts well to different situations, which, there are a lot of out there."[982]

Smart players not only grasp complexity but also embrace and enjoy it. Belichick says of linebacker Mike Vrabel: "He's a very smart and versatile guy. Mike's one of those guys, when you give him something to do, it's like he's been doing it for a while. You can tell he's comfortable doing a lot of different things, and he enjoys it."[983] Enjoyment helps because the Patriots' complex schemes confuse even the smart rookies the Patriots draft. For example, wide receiver P.K. Sam struggled with adjusting his route based on which coverage the defense is showing:

> "right now I feel robotic. I'm thinking too much right now. I'm listening in the huddle and then when I get to the line, I want to make sure I'm lining up properly with my splits. I'm reading coverage a lot more. That's important, because we change routes for certain coverages. It's a new aspect of the game for me."[984]

A player must understand his teammates' responsibilities in every situation because such knowledge is necessary to know what kind of help he can expect on any given play. For example, a cornerback must know whether his teammates are playing "man-to-man," in which case he is fully responsible for covering his assigned receiver wherever he runs, or "zone," in which case he should "pass off" a receiver running a deep pattern to a deep safety. If offensive players shift around in a way that causes the defense to shift from zone to man-to-man but the cornerback misreads the situation and assumes the defense is still in zone, he will pass the deep route-running receiver on to a non-existent safety and that receiver will be wide open for an easy touchdown pass.

Even offensive players must understand defensive strategy and tactics... to exploit it. Brady says Patriots wide receiver Deion Branch is brilliant at exploiting defensive weaknesses: "he's got a quarterback's mentality. He knows when he's getting the ball based on the coverage. He knows how to run routes, he knows how to set defenders up."[985]

Running the ball sounds simple, and it was at the University of Arkansas for Cedric Cobbs, the Patriots' 2004 4th-round selection. But the running back playbook of the New England Patriots is far thicker: "We had maybe two or three different routes we had to run [in college]. Here, I don't know how many we have, probably 20. And then you get into the different names, numbers and colors."[986] Patriots running backs also have heavy responsibility for pass protection and catching the ball out of the backfield. Explained Cobbs following a disappointing practice early in his Patriots career:

> "In college we just didn't have a lot of different pass schemes, especially dealing with the running backs. Here, if you're not getting the ball you have to block a certain guy or go out for a pass, every play. It's a lot more complicated. I didn't quite have the playbook down."[987]

What happens to slow learners in Belichick's system? They're confused and don't survive long. Impressed by wide receiver Donald Hayes' 113 catches for the Carolina Panthers in 2000 and 2001, the Patriots signed Hayes to a two-year, $2.4 million free agent contract. The Patriots weren't dumb to sign the tall and physically talented Hayes. Panthers coach John Fox actually wanted to re-sign Hayes, but Hayes lept from the 1-15 Panthers to the Super Bowl champions. New England saw Hayes as a starting wide receiver, but Hayes had a learning disability, flailed around in early practices, and never established himself in Tom Brady's mind as a reliable receiver who would run the right routes (*i.e.*, appropriate to the defensive coverage) and run them with precision. Even Hayes admits it took him a long time to pick up the Patriots' system:

> "the coaches were expecting me to perform at this high level–which I was myself, too–and then I found out that the way I knew how to learn things was totally different than how they were teaching it. I would say, 'OK, I need to learn how to do it like this. Can someone teach me in a way that I can understand how I'm supposed to go about learning that?' I didn't have that, and that kind of hurt me a little bit. …Once I got to a point where I knew the offense and everything, they already had a couple of guys in front of me who were having success. They weren't going to make any changes."[988]

Learning the playbook is even more daunting because the Patriots teach players to play multiple positions. The Patriots lost their 2003 opening game to the Buffalo Bills 31-0. Rookie cornerback Eugene Wilson was told before the second game that he would be playing safety… as the starter! "Josh (McDaniel, a defensive assistant) told me I was going to be playing safety starting that week. I asked him if it would mean I'd have less playing time. That's when he told me that I'd be starting."[989] Wilson says, "I thought it was a joke… The thought of [playing] safety never crossed my mind."[990] But the Patriots had enough trust in Wilson's ability and intelligence to toss him into the fire at a position he had never played before, even in practice. They knew Wilson was versatile when they drafted him because "I led the nation in passes broken up and also had six interceptions"[991] his junior year when Illinois played man-to-man and then played well (though without the eye-popping stats) in zone coverage his senior season. Wilson responded with solid play and four interceptions in 2003. Such flexibility enables the Patriots to put their best eleven healthy guys on the field at any moment. But it places a great intellectual burden on players who must know the playbook inside and out, as Patriots linebacker Tedy Bruschi points out: "A long time ago, [Patriots assistant coach] Dante Scarnecchia told me that the more positions I could play, the more valuable I'd be. The key is you have to be on your game mentally."[992]

But not every Patriot can devour the Patriots' thick playbook at multiple positions. After playing his rookie season as the "Y" tight end, Daniel Graham was asked to also learn to play the "F" position (involving heavy fullback-like blocking responsibilities and substantial pre-snap movement). After that second season, coaches determined Graham had been less effective than he might otherwise have been and suspected he had become tentative and occasionally confused because they had asked him to think too much. After drafting another tight end in the first round (and a brilliant one, Benjamin Watson, who started his collegiate career at Duke before the lure of playing big-time college football drew him to Georgia), Patriots coaches decided to reduce the mental demands on Graham by letting him play just the standard tight end role (the "Y") where he can concentrate on using his superb blocking skills and improving his pass-catching.[993] After an inconsistent first two seasons (catching many difficult-to-catch balls while dropping many easy-to-catch balls), Graham spent his offseason catching hundreds of throws a day from the automated JUGS® machine rather than studying the "F" position. Rookie Benjamin Watson was taught to play the "H." And the Patriots will retain flexibility because tight end Christian Fauria can already play both "Y" and "H."

Potential NFL draftees are given twelve minutes to answer as many of the fifty questions (of increasing difficulty) in the Wonderlic Test as they can. The average American worker answers 22 correctly, while the average NFL prospect scores 19. (Harvard punter Pat McInally, drafted by the Bengals, famously scored a perfect 50 back in 1975.) Teams worry about players who score in the single digits or low double digits. Patriots rookie tight end Benjamin Watson scored a 41! Recent Patriots quarterbacks have scored as follows on the Wonderlic:

Quarterback	Wonderlic score
Drew Bledsoe	37
Tom Brady (current #1)	33
Rohan Davey (current #2)	17
Kliff Kingsbury	31
Kurt Kitner	31
Jim Miller (current #3)	?

Source: Data posted by "Mac Mirabile" on www.unc.edu/~mirabile/Wonderlic.htm.

It seems most of the Patriots' quarterbacks are smarter than average. Does that help? Just ask Belichick why he loves Tom Brady:

> "I'll get mad at him and say, 'Why did you do that?' And he'll say, 'Well, I saw the corner here, I saw the linebacker there. It looked like the receiver slipped a bit on his cut and I didn't want to throw it to him. I had a guy in my face, so I came back late and tried to throw it in the flat. I should have thrown it away.' But then I go and look at the tape and I see all that's happening, just as he sees it."[994]

What teams really want in a quarterback is not the ability to answer math problems but to juggle the X's and O's of football. The Wonderlic is not a test of football intelligence, but it provides useful information about how well a player thinks. Brady scored well and certainly has great football intelligence: "Football's always come easy to me. I've always been able to focus downfield. I think I know where everyone is on every play."[995] Conversely, Davey's low score may partly explain why, according to *Eagle Tribune* reporter Hector Longo, "Davey reads defenses like most Americans read Sanskrit … very slowly."[996]

A perfect example of an anti-Belichick player is former Ohio State linebacker Andy Katzenmoyer whom the Patriots drafted late in the first round of the 1999 draft, when Belichick worked for the Jets. Katzenmoyer was an astounding physical specimen who dominated his freshman year at Ohio State before coasting and under-performing the next three years. Katzenmoyer was lazy, arrogant, and not the brightest bulb in the pack, the unholy trinity of The Book of Bill. Here's how *Pro Football Weekly* assessed "Big Kat"'s NFL prospects immediately before the draft:

> "If a team turns Katzenmoyer loose and tells him to just get after the ball, the chances for success improve. If a team asks Katzenmoyer to be a thinking man's linebacker in a complicated defensive scheme, then I think it is asking for trouble."[997]

Also, "Perhaps instead of strutting around as God's gift to football, he [will develop] a little humility, a little hunger."[998]

You don't need a crystal ball to predict Katzenmoyer wouldn't thrive in a complex, cerebral Belichick defensive scheme requiring players to out-think and out-hustle opponents while subordinating personal glory to team success. After Katzenmoyer went AWOL just days into 2001 training camp, the *Eagle Tribune* opined:

> "Maybe things under Belichick, year two, got a little tough for the Big Kat. Regardless, he's been dead weight around here. The problem with Katzenmoyer has been he's never showed that fire, like he did at Ohio State. You never knew if he actually wanted to be out there, beheading halfbacks or not."[999]

Aside from perhaps quarterback, linebacker is arguably the most mentally intensive position on the Patriots because linebackers must defend the run and the pass. Under Belichick, the Patriots have drafted only a few linebackers, and all were late-round picks taken primarily for their projected contributions on special teams. The Patriots use only experienced, veteran linebackers who have seen it all, know how to react appropriately to any situation, and digest very thick playbooks. (I hope the smart Dan Klecko, transitioning from defensive line to linebacker, proves an exception.)

The intellectual demands of playing on the Patriots' ever-changing defense are obvious to Tennessee Titans offensive coordinator Mike Heimerdinger: "Not everyone can play all those looks. You need experienced veterans to do that; otherwise you're probably going to have breakdowns. They really game-plan almost like an offense does."[1000] As an example, it's easy to coach a player to play man-to-man defense. You just point the defender at the offensive player he must cover. But offenses have tricks for defeating man-to-man defenses, like using a tight end to block ("pick") a cornerback who's covering a wide receiver (or criss-crossing two receivers' routes so the two defenders run into each other). Patriots defenders are responsible for noticing picks and swapping defensive responsibilities, as Patriots cornerback Terrell Buckley explains:

> "Some coaches will keep telling you to run with the receiver, even though you know the tight end is going to pick you and the receiver's going to be running free. We don't do that here. If the tight end is going to pick me, somebody's going to be waiting on that receiver on the other side, and I'm going to pick the tight end up. Common-sense defense."[1001]

It's easy to say, "Just cover your man." It's more effective to teach as the Patriots do. Cornerback Ty Law says, "You could be a little mind-boggled at first, because there are so many different things to know in his system. It's pretty complicated, and you have to be pretty intelligent to understand it. But once you buy into it, it's actually pretty easy and allows you to go out there and do your job."[1002] Belichick is always tweaking and modifying schemes in preparation for upcoming opponents, so "You never know what he's going to do. It makes it fun for everybody because you are constantly learning."[1003] Veteran and Pro Bowl safety Rodney Harrison, who joined the Patriots in 2003, agrees both that the Patriots defense is extremely complicated and that Patriots players are very smart: "All of these guys can flat-out play. And you know they know the game. This is the most complicated system I've played in. You can't be an idiot or a dummy and play in this defense."[1004] After defensive lineman and former NFL Defensive Player of the Year Dana Stubblefield joined the Patriots in 2004, he sounded lost: "they're throwing the whole playbook at me. It's like speaking Chinese."[1005]

The position Belichick has spent a boatload of high-round draft picks on is physically gifted defensive linemen: Richard Seymour #6 overall in the 1st round of

2001, Jarvis Green in the 4th round of 2002, Ty Warren #13 overall in the 1st round of 2003, Vince Wilfork #21 overall in the 1st round of 2004, and Marquise Hill in the 2nd round of 2004. Belichick also surrendered a 2004 draft pick to the Pittsburgh Steelers for 24-year-old defensive lineman Rodney Bailey and signed veteran free agent Keith Traylor (nicknamed "Truck" by his former Chicago Bears teammates). Belichick places obvious importance on defensive linemen. His reliance on the draft for defensive linemen may also partly reflect that defensive line play is relatively more physical and intuitive and relatively less tactical and scheme-driven. Therefore, defensive linemen can be effective with less training and experience than players at other positions and their talent is more discernible from their performance in college. Because attacking the quarterback and running back requires less coordination than protecting a quarterback or blocking for a running back, defensive linemen can perform at a high level with less mental training, experience, preparation, and grooming than, say, offensive linemen who love pointing out that "It's not like we're a bunch of dumb guys, like most defensive linemen. Instead of just lining up in the three-gap and hitting the hole, we have to know what's going on."[1006] New Orleans Saints head coach Jim Haslett is more diplomatic but agrees "[Defensive line]'s the easiest position to play quickly. There isn't a lot of thinking to it."[1007] Second-year Patriot Tully Banta-Cain, who has converted from a college defensive end to an NFL linebacker, agrees defensive line is less mentally challenging than other positions:

> "At D-end, you just kind of pin your ears back and you've got to face a 300-pound lineman in front of you. He's either going to run-block you or pass-block you. Whereas at linebacker, you're standing up, trying to get an overall view of what's in front of you. D-end is a lot easier than linebacker."[1008]

But, even along the defensive line, the Patriots' system demands more intelligence from its players than most teams do. Most teams ask their defensive linemen to be disruptive and "shoot the gap" between offensive linemen to quickly attack the quarterback or running back. The Patriots are one of a handful of teams that give defensive linemen "read-and-react" responsibility. Each lineman is responsible for holding his ground and occupying a blocker so linebackers can "hit the hole" and stop runners as they come through the hole. Whether a DL moves left, right or forward depends on how they see the play developing. According to Patriots rookie defensive tackle Vince Wilfork, "You can easily pick a side, but if you guess wrong, it's your butt, and you don't want it to be your butt right there."[1009] Much of the glory goes to linebackers who "shoot the gaps" and make many of the tackles. Two-gapping also creates flexibility because offensive linemen must guess whether each defensive lineman will move to their left or right after the ball is snapped. But it creates mental challenges that "one-gap" defenders don't face. Further, the Patriots don't play a pure "3-4." Though the Patriots drafted defensive lineman Ty Warren high in the first round of the 2003 NFL Draft because of his experience playing "3-4," Warren admitted a year later he faced a learning curve: "Even though we played a 3-4 at Texas A&M, this was really coming into a different style of 3-4. I like to call it a chameleon type 3-4, where you never know how Coach and his staff will utilize it."[1010] However, Belichick agrees that defensive line is more physical and less mental than linebacker, safety, or cornerback:

> "When you are lined up on the line of scrimmage with a hand on the ground you are usually about 'this' far away from your opponent and things happen quicker. Fewer people can really get to your position than when you are back further off the ball you can be threatened by more people, different angles, it happens slower, but there are a lot more multiples [complex situations involving "if… then…"]. Then, when you get into pass coverage and they have five receivers, you have seven defenders, there are a lot of combinations there, a lot of different routes, a lot of different coverages, a lot of different matchups. The multiples of those are almost infinite."[1011]

Hire experienced guys

To be successful over the long term, football teams, like other businesses, require a mix of experience and youth. Experience is necessary in as cerebral a game as football. After his veteran-heavy "immovable force" defense shut down the "unstoppable object" Indianapolis Colts offense in the AFC Championship Game, surrendering only 14 points while sacking Peyton Manning four times and intercepting him four times, Belichick credited his veterans' experience and intuition for the win: "I am very fortunate that we have a lot of experienced defensive players."[1012]

Veterans are also player-coaches who help young players fulfill their potential. Rookie running back Cedric Cobbs says he has learned a lot from the Patriots' veteran running backs, Corey Dillon and Kevin Faulk: "They've been real helpful. On certain plays, there's just a certain way to cut, a certain timing on everything. By watching those guys, I've learned a lot and learned to be patient."[1013] Some veterans, like cornerback Terrell Buckley, are so helpful and so successful at teaching the younger players that they teach their way out of a job. After undrafted rookie Randall Gay made the 2004 team and Buckley was cut, Gay said, "I learned a lot from Terrell. He took time to help the younger guys, and I appreciate that."[1014] (Buckley landed with the Jets.)

Hire coachable guys

After being asked to learn to play inside linebacker in addition to the four other positions (defensive line, fullback, outside linebacker, and special teams) he has already been asked to learn as a Patriot, Dan Klecko didn't question why but set about doing what the coaches asked of him: "I'm a professional athlete. I have to come out here and learn it… that's my job. The biggest thing for me making the team is shutting my mouth and doing what they tell me to do."[1015]

Talented coaches benefit from players eager to learn, and vice-versa. The Patriots' entire offensive line has just one player (left tackle Matt Light) whom scouts projected as a solid NFL offensive lineman coming out of college. The rest were unknown or unappreciated guys. But the Patriots believed they had the intelligence, toughness, coachability, and team-centricity to become NFL linemen. The players who have stuck with the team have all worked their butts off. Matt Light believes that's the team's magic formula: "We're very well coached, and all these guys are coachable, which is a big plus. No one is bigger than the next guy. Off the field, we're a group that kind of sticks together."[1016] The importance of intelligence, toughness, coaching and team-centricity is obvious from the tremendous coordination required of effective offensive lines:

> "We learn a lot from [offensive line coach] Dante [Scarnecchia], he works harder than anyone. The attitude that we have probably get us through all these games. There's a lot of times, physically matching up, that it looks like it might be hard for (us) to open up any holes and create protection, but we find a way to get it done. ...We're not looking to dominate, go out and destroy people, although that happens every now and then. Consistency for us is more important than one guy making one huge block."[1017]

Seattle Seahawks quarterback Matt Hasselbeck, now emerging as a star after a rough first few NFL seasons, holds himself up as a negative example of the importance of coachability:

> "I came in and didn't allow myself to be coached. When I came [to Seattle], I tried to run Green Bay's offense. It all sounds the same, the words are the same, but the way that [Seahawks coach] Mike Holmgren wanted me to run it at that time was not the same. I just didn't listen well, I didn't allow myself to be coached. On offense, we had 10 guys doing one thing and me doing something else. That hurt our team and that hurt me. ...For example, Mike yelling at me during the game. Instead of taking it as constructive criticism, I would get angry at him. I watched how Trent [Dilfer] handled that... like a pro, and I didn't."[1018]

FIND WHAT YOU WANT

Hire or train?

> "There is also an important factor that I would call 'process mix.' Is it more productive for a company to buy a part or to make it, to assemble its product or to contract out the assembly process, to market under its own brand name through its own distributive organization or to sell to independent wholesalers using their own brands? What is the company good at? What is

the most productive utilization of its specific knowledge, ability, experience, and reputation?"[1019]
— Peter Drucker, father of management science

Before Super Bowl XXXVIII, many reporters, and even NFL players, talked about how the completely outclassed, no-name, bargain basement Patriots offensive linemen would cringe in fear as the Panthers' overpowering defensive linemen blew by them on the way to sacking Tom Brady: "The Patriots offensive line appears overmatched. While Carolina's front four is made up of first- and second-round picks, making gobs of money, New England's blockers are a collection of undrafted free agents and veteran castaways."[1020] Patriots offensive linemen are admittedly low-paid and largely unknown, but that does not imply low quality. They're like generic, house-brand products sold by discount retailers like Costco. They're cheaper not because they're lower quality but because they were manufactured in-house and lack the sexy branding of better-known products. Of the Patriots' five Super Bowl starters, Joe Andruzzi and Tom Ashworth were never drafted and Russ Hochstein and Dan Koppen were drafted in only the 5th round. Only Matt Light was a 2nd-round draft pick.

Teach what you know; buy what you can't

Well-run businesses know their "core competencies." They focus on their strengths and outsource functions others can do better and cheaper than they could internally. This logic guides optimal decision-making regarding "make vs. buy." "Making" is doing something internally using in-house resources and personnel. "Buying" is going to the external marketplace to find someone else to do it for you. What to "make" and what to "buy" should be determined by comparing your organization's capabilities with external options.

The Patriots' belief in their ability to "make" interior offensive lineman factored into their decision to allow star guard/center Damien Woody leave for the Detroit Lions. The Patriots loved Woody and considered him their best offensive lineman but knew that re-signing Woody to a giant contract like the Lions offered would have hamstrung the team in too many other areas. Management decided to instead continue grooming offensive linemen who may perform a notch or two below Woody's level but for a much lower sticker price.

The Patriots believe certain positions and certain skills are easier to "make" than others. Patriots coaches believe they can take a raw, rough diamond of an interior offensive lineman (guard or center) and cut-and-polish him into a gem. But they believe it virtually impossible to coach a blazingly fast guy to play running back in the NFL because running well demands hard-to-teach split-second instinct.

Other traits and skills are also unteachable: "You can't teach speed" is one famous football aphorism. (There actually are now trainers who teach players how to run faster, but no trainer can teach any player to run faster than their inherent maximum speed, a trait that varies from athlete to athlete.) That's why the Patriots surrendered a 3rd-round draft pick in 2003 to better their 2nd-round pick from #50 to #45 and select Bethel Johnson, whom *The Sporting News* projected as a 7th-round draft pick: "He's got a couple of things you just can't teach. We know he can run. He's as fast, if not the fastest receiver, in the draft."[1021]

You can't teach "big" either, which is why the Patriots traded the Chicago Bears a 4th-round pick in 2003 for aging veteran 375-pound nose tackle Ted Washington, who later left New England after playing just one (Super Bowl championship) season. Before trading for "Mount Washington," the Patriots had tried plugging different defensive linemen (Jarvis Green, Ty Warren, Richard Seymour, and Dan Klecko) into their gaping hole at nose tackle, but none had sufficient girth. After Washington's departure, the Patriots acquired 340-pound Keith Traylor, who had played alongside Washington in Chicago, and spent their top 2004 draft pick on 340-pound Miami Hurricanes nose tackle Vince Wilfork.

Similarly, you can educate smart players to make more effective football decisions with their brains, but you can't coach a low-intelligence player to become a high-intelligence player. Coaches must work with whatever raw speed, size, and intelligence any player has.

Intuition is not always a reliable guide to which skills are coachable. I would have guessed "arm strength" is less coachable than "throwing accuracy," but Belichick remembers great quarterbacks who lacked great arms: "There have been a lot of great ones through the years. The Billy Kilmers and the Fran Tarkentons of the world, the guys like that who were great quarterbacks but they weren't going to throw the ball through any wall."[1022] The Patriots' experience and research suggests "Arm strength is important, but getting the ball in the right place is probably more important."[1023] As Super Bowl XXXV-winning quarterback Trent Dilfer puts it, "There's a lot more to being a quarterback than throwing the ball 80 yards in the air and jumping high at the [scouting] combine."[1024] "Getting the ball in the right place" sounds easy but requires five hard-to-master talents: 1) Scanning the pass defense and "reading" how defenders are defending; 2) "Feeling" the attacking defensive players (esp. those on your "blind side" or behind you) and sensing how long you can hold the ball before they sack you or knock the ball loose; 3) Identifying the most appropriate receiver, given the defense's strategy, the offense's play, and the quarterback's guess about how each receiver will read-and-react to the defense; 4) Figuring out where and how to throw the ball so the receiver and ball arrive simultaneously at the same place before any defensive player; and, 5) Accurately throwing the ball to that exact location (where the most effective pass may require "touch," not power, such as when the ball must arc over a defender's outstretched arms). Brady has mastered all five:

> "He is seamless in his decision-making. There is no indecision. I'm watching him against Arizona. He starts to pass, the defensive back closes [on his

intended receiver], he pulls back, moves just enough in the pocket to buy some time and then finds the open guy and puts it right on his hands. It's all so fluid that you forget how hard it is to do that consistently. But he does it all the time."[1025]

Steve Szabo, who coaches the Buffalo Bills' cornerbacks and safeties, was amazed that Brady made "no errant throws"[1026] against his defense, despite the Bills' strategy of forcing Brady to throw quickly by blitzing on 42 of the Patriots' 56 plays.

Patriots' personnel decisions embody their emphasis on "getting the ball in the right place" and de-emphasis on throwing strength and running speed. They traded star Drew Bledsoe, who possesses an amazing arm but gets himself into trouble by pressing to throw downfield rather than dink-and-dunk for low-risk short gains. They won two Super Bowls with a 6th-round draft pick and poster boy for smarts over a world-beating arm and track speed. They acquire all their unglamorous quarterbacks in late rounds of the draft (Rohan Davey, 4th round, pick #117 in 2002; Kliff Kingsbury, 6th round, pick #201 in 2003) or in the low-rent free agent market (Damon Huard, Kurt Kittner, and Jim Miller).

The Patriots distinguish between teachable and unteachable football skills. If a running back shows poor instincts or fails to cut quickly into holes the offensive line creates, no coach in the world can turn him into a great (or even adequate) NFL running back. But if a running back has always run well but fumbles too much or was never taught to pass block or catch passes out of the backfield, such skills are teachable. You can cure "fumble-itis" (by strengthening the player's arm, holding the ball in a more secure position, *etc.*) and teach blocking skills, but you can't teach running the ball. By the time a runner enters the NFL draft, he either can or can't run.

The Patriots' drafting of Cedric Cobbs in the 4th round of the 2004 NFL draft reflects this logic. Cobbs is an immensely talented runner: "You watch the Alabama game [when Cobbs carried 36 times for 198 yards], he pretty much carried the [Arkansas] team on his back."[1027] But Cobbs was never expected to or taught to pass block or catch passes. Many draft "experts" predicted the Patriots would use a 1st-round pick on a "complete, well-rounded" running back like Michigan's Chris Perry, who demonstrated in college an ability to not only run but also to catch passes and to pass block. The Patriots apparently decided such skills are sufficiently coachable that they could use their 1st-rounder on another position and grab in the 4th round a guy (Cobbs) possessing great "uncoachables" and coachable deficiencies.

Ease of evaluating talent

At the so-called "skill positions" (running back, quarterback, and wide receiver), players' talents are showcased and obvious for all to observe. A receiver either runs fast, precise, predictable routes or he doesn't. He either catches every ball thrown to him or he doesn't. Consequently, it is hard for skill position players to slip too far in the draft. At less heralded positions, especially interior offensive line positions, it is easier for talented individuals to get overlooked. They may play great but look lousy because their linemates screw up. Offensive tackles, because they play on the outside of the line, are harder to misjudge than interior linemen (guards and centers). Consequently, as Belichick points out, "If you look at the starting tackles in the NFL, there are not many tackles in the league that weren't high draft choices."[1028] On the other hand, Belichick and Pioli have not drafted a single guard since taking over drafting for the Patriots. And the one center they drafted, Dan Koppen, was a major steal. A mere 5th-round pick (#164 overall), Koppen stepped right into the starting job as a rookie and significantly helped the team win its second Super Bowl.

The harder it is to evaluate talent at a position, the riskier it is to spend high draft picks on that position and the easier it is to find and develop undrafted NFL-capable players. The Patriots seldom draft interior linemen, partly because they are hard to evaluate based on college game films. Even if the Patriots know a player has great potential, other teams may overlook him. So it's smarter to spend draft picks on positions at which little talent escapes undrafted.

Capacity to transform potential into performance

The Patriots have great coaches who teach technique and tactics to smart, motivated, coachable players. Tom Brady is in awe of Belichick's encyclopedic football knowledge:

> "[Belichick] points things out that you would never even think about. He comes in and breaks down coverages for us. He probably knows what they're doing better than they know what they're doing. You know he watches so much tape and he really has an understanding of their tendencies and the keys that we should be looking at from a quarterback's standpoint."[1029]

Knowing they can teach techniques and tactics, the Patriots are willing to grab guys with raw potential, like Stephen Neal, and mold them into NFL players. Stephen Neal is a world champion heavyweight wrestler: "In 1999 Neal was the World Freestyle Champion, Pan-American Games Champion, USA Freestyle Champion and repeat NCAA Champion." After Neal mailed NFL teams a video of wrestling highlights, the Patriots first signed him in July 2001 because he obviously possessed great raw potential for playing offensive line. But Neal had not played football since high school. The Patriots released Neal but later re-signed him. After training Neal, the Patriots expected great things from him until he injured himself early in both the 2002 and 2003 seasons. Like every Patriot, Neal is a tenacious guy. He worked hard to become healthy and is an impressive starter on the 2004 Patriots.

Neal is hardly the only raw talent the Patriots have attempted to mold. Two of the Patriots' starting offensive linemen (Tom Ashworth and Joe Andruzzi) and seven of their nine backup offensive linemen were never drafted. After Damien Woody suffered a 2003-ending injury, backup Russ Hochstein stepped in and helped the Patriots win every playoff game without surrendering a single sack in 126 pass attempts. Hochstein played superbly, another indication of the value of Patriots coaching. On the January 21, 2004 broadcast of *ESPN* talk show *Pardon the Interruption*, star defensive lineman Warren Sapp dissed the entire Patriots offensive line and openly attacked Hochstein, brashly predicting the Patriots would lose the Super Bowl because Hochstein stunk so bad that he couldn't block even *Pardon the Interruption*'s middle-aged TV personalities:

> "I think this defensive line of Carolina will dominate the front five of New England. I don't even think it's a fair matchup. I don't see how they're getting it done because… Russ Hochstein started for them in the AFC Championship game and I've seen Russ Hochstein block, and he couldn't block either one of you two fellas."

Instead of backing off, Sapp continued hurling insults at Hochstein:

> "Sapp began to talk to the Panthers' linemen about which had to play the role of Hochstein during the team's practices. When Mike Houghton said, uh, no, he wasn't Hochstein, Sapp said, 'So, you don't have to tie your shoelaces together during practice?'"[1030]

Sapp made the classic mistake of underestimating the Patriots by extrapolating from an individual's pre-Patriots reputation to the team's collective performance following coaching by the Patriots staff. Hochstein and the other unheralded Patriots offensive linemen did a brilliant job in the Super Bowl: "The only times we noticed Panthers All-Pro defensive tackle Kris Jenkins were the three occasions he jumped offside."[1031] Brady threw 48 passes without a sack while completing a Super Bowl-record 32 passes for 354 yards. And the Patriots were able to run the ball for 127 yards and a healthy 3.6 yards-per-carry. (The running stat would be more impressive without a 10-yard loss on a trick play the Panthers stuffed.) Sapp based his prediction on past experience playing against Hochstein while they were both in Tampa Bay (where Hochstein had been a practice squad player): "I've seen Russ Hochstein block, and he can't. So this is a mismatch, plain and simple."[1032] Confronted by Patriots linebacker Tedy Bruschi, Sapp stood firm: "I've been with Russ Hochstein a lot longer than you have. I wouldn't go there with me."[1033] Sapp was blind to Hochstein's improvement and learning to perform well as part of a cohesive, unified offensive line. He had also grown stronger: "Since signing on with the Patriots in October 2002, Hochstein has added 20 pounds of muscle."[1034]

Wide receiver Troy Brown defended his teammate, laughing that the Jacksonville Jaguars had run through Sapp:

"He says [the Panthers'] defensive line is going to kill our offensive line, Hochstein sucks and all of that. ...Go get the Jacksonville tape and watch (Tampa Bay) play Jacksonville and watch what they did to [Sapp]. He's talking about somebody (who stinks)–they drove him 20 yards down the field in the other direction. Go get that tape and put that one on. They were chippin' on them and knockin' them on their butts."[1035]

Hochstein stayed out of the fray, saying later:

"My O-line coach [Dante Scarnecchia] had me in one afternoon and told me, 'Expect to get a lot of heat. You're the most unproven guy here as far as experience.' Then he goes, 'I believe in you, the guys around you believe in you, and that's all that matters. Whatever those guys say to you, it's all lip service, because they're not playing the game.' And it's true. The only people that mattered to me were my teammates and the Carolina Panthers."[1036]

Sapp's comments had no impact on the Super Bowl because Patriots players knew their coaches had polished Hochstein from a rough diamond into a sparkling gem. No one in the Patriots locker room lost any sleep over Sapp's ignorance.

Only after winning that Super Bowl did the Patriots attack Sapp. A tongue-in-cheek Damien Woody thanked Sapp for "his motivational speech on national television" which "I [took personally] and I'm not even playing. Those guys took it personal"[1037]:

"I'd like to thank Warren Sapp for helping me get another ring. The ring is going to really look good on my finger. You think what he said didn't play a part in our performance? If I could, I'd like to thank him personally for his comments on national TV."[1038]

Focus on "functional ability"

"What we want are football players–not guys who blow away the tests. ...The people who come and fill these stands won't be here to watch guys lift weights, run the 40, or make some incredible vertical leap. Maybe some of the guys we get don't fit the prototype the rest of the world has, but they're our kind of players, and they're the guys we want on the field."[1039]
– *Patriots VP of player personnel Scott Pioli*

Incredible athletes don't win football games. Incredible football players win football games. Belichick says, for example, that a nose tackle must be strong enough to hold his ground against two offensive lineman, but "strong" does not equate to bench press stats: "That player has to... play strong regardless of what his lifting strength is."[1040] Linemen must have muscles, of course, but they must also master leverage and balance. A Hall of Famer has said of former Patriot great Andre Tippett "A lot of guys thought he was better than Lawrence [Taylor]. He's definitely one of the best outside linebackers who ever played."[1041] One reason Tippett played so spectacularly was his black belt in karate. (Tippett is now a Sensei [instructor] in Uechi-Ryu Karate-Do and the Patriots' Assistant Director of Pro Scouting.) When linemen crash into each other, the battle is more like karate than weightlifting. For that reason, Belichick believes former wrestlers have an advantage as linemen:

> "There is... the balance aspect of it–being on your feet, but being in a lot of different contorted positions where, if you are not good at that, you are probably not going to be a very good wrestler. You are going to be on the mat too much and the other guy is going to be on top of you. I think there is a degree of balance, and, to a certain extent, training or whatever you want to call it–self-discipline–that generally goes with that sport."[1042]

Offensive linemen must also be smart and team-oriented to coordinate their blocking to stop blitzes designed to confuse them and exploit gaps in the offensive line:

> "Guys [that] get drafted at the top of the rounds, as far as offensive linemen, [are] those height-weight-speed guys, the guys with the measurements. The stud athletes. [But it's] how do they play and how do they play with the other four guys? ...The chemistry of the offensive line has a lot to do with your success and failure."[1043]

Consequently, Patriots offensive coordinator Charlie Weis believes "Intelligence in the offensive line is greatly underrated. A smart lineman can compensate for a lot of things."[1044]

Unlike many teams that get mesmerized by prospects' 40-yard dash times and other measured statistics, the Patriots tell their scouts to focus on "functional ability":

> "the Pats ask their scouts to emphasize the practical. On the offensive line, for example, players must be as aggressive and physical as they are big and strong. At receiver, where some teams focus on speed or height, the Pats' most critical factor is a simple one: 'Be a playmaker.' Pioli said the receiver checklist also includes a quotation from offensive coordinator Charlie Weis: 'We can't run the ball with soft receivers.' ...Before Pats scouts evaluate [a quarterback's] physical skills such as arm strength, size and mobility ...the quarterback must be the 'mentally toughest and hardest-working player on the team.' Then it lists the critical factors at the position: leadership, decision-making, accuracy and clutch production."[1045]

The Patriots scouting manual says a quarterback must be tough enough "to take a big hit and then walk into the huddle and call the next play" and "to handle the pressure and scrutiny to which all NFL QB's are subjected."[1046] The manual even suggests where to look for evidence of a quarterback's toughness: "watch the passes they complete under a heavy rush. Watch the first downs they get on third and long, passing into heavy coverage. Listen to what their teammates... say."[1047] At least one

Super Bowl-winning quarterback, Joe Theismann, shares the Patriots' belief that toughness is a quarterback's most important attribute.[1048] With other teams blinded by "top" quarterbacks' arm strength and leg speed, the Patriots stole the physically unimpressive Brady in the 6th round. The Patriots' reasoning? "He's a good tough player."[1049] He sure is. Former NFL quarterback Jim Harbaugh says "He's as cool as they come. The thing about Brady is that nothing rattles him and I love that about him. He's just as tough as nails."[1050]

Brady is but the best-known example of a Patriot overlooked by other teams because he lacked the incredible physical talent and attention-grabbing stats of 1st-round draft picks. There are many such Patriots. The Patriots' leading receiver, Deion Branch, was a steal at the end of the 2nd round. In just two seasons at Louisville, Branch gained 2,204 yards on 143 catches, and he has the biggest grin you'll ever see, a grin that never disappears. NFL teams overlooked Branch because he didn't attend a top school and because he's, at most, 5´9˝ and teams prefer taller receivers. Current backup quarterback Rohan Davey has an incredible arm, but the Patriots drafted Davey as much for his leadership talent: "he's led [LSU] to an SEC championship. He was a captain of the team as a junior when he wasn't starting, so I think that speaks a bit to his leadership abilities."[1051]

More often than not, the eleven men wearing Patriots uniforms outplay eleven more physically gifted opponents because, as Scott Pioli points out, football isn't the Decathlon:

> "We're not focused on data. We're not fixated on what a guy can bench-press or how fast he can run the 40. It's simple: We want good football players. We want 'em big and strong and fast. That said, how many times do you see a 300-pound guy who doesn't play like a 300-pound guy? You want guys who are football strong, who are football fast. It's awareness. It's skills. It's knowing leverage and the angles."[1052]

> "Bill and I aren't great numbers guys. We don't get hung up on height-weight-speed. We want football players, because, come Sunday at 1 o'clock, football players play football. What they did in the 40-yard dash one day in shorts, or in the vertical jump, is not what the fans pay to see and not what we're asking them to do."[1053]

Belichick doesn't confuse great athletes with great football players: "Running around doing sit-ups and jumping jacks is not the same as football."[1054] Patriots linebacker Ted Johnson says football isn't weightlifting:

> "[Succeeding in the NFL]'s more about maintaining and staying healthy. [I realized that] after two or three years in the league and seeing it doesn't matter how strong you are, if you can't make a tackle they'll get rid of you. I saw the strongest guys in our weight room get cut so I realized then it wasn't that important."[1055]

Tedy Bruschi, another Patriots linebacker, says, "if you're a defensive lineman, [Belichick and Pioli] don't care if you can press 400 pounds. They care if you can press a guard."[1056] Belichick terms this "playing strength." As Patriots wide receiver prospect Michael Jennings, a former track star attempting to catch on with the Patriots, explained: "There is a difference between track speed and football speed. That's one of things I have to work on, my bursts, the power of my running, getting in and out of my cuts."[1057]

Belichick distinguishes between "quickness" (acceleration, or how quickly a player moves during his initial burst from a stationary position) and "speed" (velocity when running at full speed). A quick-but-slow defensive end can dart around an offensive tackle toward the quarterback before the tackle moves into position to block the defensive end. Conversely, a fast safety with sub-par quickness can still play well if he anticipates receivers' movements and the quarterback's decisions. His "top-end speed" or "catch-up speed" enables him to get back into position while the ball is in flight. Because Belichick understands which skills each particular role on his football team requires, he is able to identify which overlooked players possess the functional ability to play particular roles:

> "The one thing about track guys that you really have to take a look at is just their ability to change directions laterally. They can run fast. They can be the fastest guys in the world for whatever their distance is, but there's only a certain amount of football that is played in a straight line. A lot of football is played with a change of direction or two. If we're talking about guys that are fast, can change directions quickly and have some size and are tough, now we're talking."[1058]

Every Patriot player must be intelligent because the Patriots throw complex schemes at players and expect them to adjust their play according to their constantly-shifting interpretation of what their opponent is throwing at them. Recognizing they need intelligent players, the Patriots have more college graduates than most NFL teams. A bachelor's degree indicates intelligence and "shows commitment and follow-through,"[1059] two traits essential to success within the Patriots' system.

But the Patriots want functional football intelligence, not Mensa members, spelling bee champions, or rocket scientists. Says Belichick: "[Intelligence is] definitely important. Our players have a lot of responsibilities and adjustments they must handle. (But) we're not doing an IQ test here. We're just trying to play football."[1060] The Patriots' scouting manual explains the difference: "Just because a person is smart does not necessarily mean they can make quick decisions under pressure."[1061] Scott Pioli expects his scouts to infer football intelligence from on-field performance more than IQ scores, SAT scores, Wonderlic scores, *etc.*:

> "You can see the level of a player's intelligence on film, what his team is trying to accomplish and how he grasps it. When the process is finished, you

must try to determine functional football intelligence and functional football physical ability."[1062]

How do you "see" football intelligence on film? Belichick says they noticed, for example, North Carolina safety Dexter Reid (whom they drafted in the 4th round in 2004) telling his teammates what to do every play: "He's a sharp kid. ...Ran the defense [at North Carolina]. Not just the guy that verbally called it, but I think they relied on him on a lot of the checks and adjustments, and we noticed that on film."[1063]

The Patriots don't want players who run the fastest, hit the hardest, win chess tournaments, or become *Jeopardy!* champions. What matters is the player's complete package of physical and mental traits. The Patriots want players who can work smoothly with ten other men to collectively outplay eleven men wearing different color jerseys at the game of football for sixty minutes. In short, Belichick wants whichever players give the Patriots the best chance to win: "When you make the final roster decisions, it comes down to in the end, who are the... best players for the team. I don't think we've ever made a decision here based on height."[1064]

Hunt for overlooked talent

"You have to exhaust every resource [for] finding players."[1065]
– Scott Pioli

"As an organization, you look for every avenue to improve your team, and we've spent a great deal of time and energy on [evaluating talent]."[1066]
– Scott Pioli

The Pittsburgh Steelers valued linebacker Mike Vrabel so highly that Vrabel didn't start a single game during four years in Pittsburgh (1997-2000) and languished as a special teams niche player. Vrabel averaged nine tackles per season during his four years in Pittsburgh. In his first year with the Patriots (2001), Vrabel made 60 tackles. In 2002, he made 75. After forcing Kurt Warner into throwing an interception that Ty Law ran back for a touchdown in Super Bowl XXXVI and then catching a touchdown, making two sacks, and forcing a fumble in Super Bowl XXXVIII, Vrabel noted, "This is a long way from the days in Pittsburgh when I just covered kicks."[1067] It sure is. Vrabel nearly quit the NFL:

> "I thought seriously of going to law school, because my career with Pittsburgh wasn't working out. I didn't think anyone would find a way to use me. But I was amazed how much Bill knew about me. One day he came up to me and said, 'Remember in that Miami preseason game last year, how you played the power block? That's how we want to do it here.' In situational football, which is basically what the NFL is today, he's got to be the best mind out there."[1068]

Fortunately for New England, Pioli and Belichick recalled Vrabel's 36 sacks at Ohio State and envisioned Vrabel-the-special-teams-player as Vrabel-the-starting-linebacker. His role later expanded to Vrabel-the-tight-end who nearly stole the Super Bowl XXXVIII MVP trophy from Tom Brady. Vrabel's smarts and versatility have made him "the chameleon," capable of playing any defensive line or linebacker position, not just the strongside (tight end side) linebacker position the team recruited him to compete for.

How do the Patriots find such hidden gems? They watch tons of film and evaluate players contextually. Belichick says a safety with few tackles, passes defensed, or interceptions may be better than a safety who makes many "big" plays:

> "Sometimes the best thing a safety can do is not be involved in any plays. That means he's in position. That means that the quarterback isn't trying to challenge him in that part of the field because it looks like it's pretty securely defended... It's hard to evaluate a safety just on production alone. ...A guy has a lot of production, well, sometimes that's good thing, and sometimes that isn't a good thing. It just depends on the circumstances that that production is coming in."[1069]

Also, because football is a team sport, certain players underperform because they're in the wrong system, used improperly, or surrounded by teammates who hamper their performance:

> "You do your due diligence and go back and watch the player perform and take into consideration what the circumstances were in his performance. Sometimes, he was being utilized in a different scheme. There could be a lot of factors: who his teammates were; how much of [his play] was the function of one person; how much of it was the function of the entire unit. A lot of times, that can make a player look good or bad relative to how the people around him are performing. You try to evaluate all of that. It's an inexact science."[1070]

Some Pioli pickups weren't on anyone else's radar. Stephen Neal didn't play football in college. Neal was the nation's best wrestler in 1999, winning the Dan Hodge Award. As a wrestler, Neal won 156 of his 166 matches. He was undefeated in his final 88 matches and won two NCAA Division 1 individual championships. When he arrived in New England, "Steve didn't even know how to put his equipment on. You're talking about starting from scratch. I mean, he was at the bottom of the barrel. You know, 'Where is the field?' and that kind of thing."[1071] That's Belichickian exaggeration, but Neal didn't know where the huddle was or what a "snap count" was.[1072] Offensive lineman Joe Andruzzi says "He didn't even know if a football was pumped or stuffed."[1073] After overcoming injuries in both 2002 and 2003, Neal has become a monster. Blocking on one sweep during the Cardinals game, Neal knocked two defenders on their backs simultaneously! Watching the game, I shouted "Wow!"

when I saw one guy totally flatten two NFL starters. That requires impeccable leverage, power, and positioning. Not bad for a guy ignored by the NFL because he didn't play college football.

In March 2004, the Patriots signed a wide receiver who, like Neal, never played college football and had just failed to make the roster of NFL Europe's Berlin Thunder. Michael Jennings was a track star at Florida State but ineligible to play football because the NCAA prohibits athletes with track scholarships from playing football. Had he stepped into even a single football scrimmage, Jennings would have surrendered his track scholarship. After the Thunder cut Jennings, Thunder quarterback (and Patriots backup QB) Rohan Davey raved to Belichick that Jennings "was as fast as anyone he's thrown to."[1074] (Jennings clocked a 4.3-second 40-yard dash that wowed NFL scouts.) The Patriots agreed Jennings had the raw unteachables to be a pro wide receiver. And they believed he showed sufficient football passion and promise at the teachables to merit a chance to continue growing into an NFL wide receiver. After five months training with the Patriots, Jennings caught a touchdown pass in the 2004 opening preseason game. Fittingly, that touchdown was thrown by Patriots scout... I mean backup quarterback... Rohan Davey. Jennings did not make the final roster, but the fact the Patriots gave him a legitimate shot demonstrates how many rocks the Patriots turn over to find players to improve their team. Even Jennings was startled when the Patriots came to meet him: "We were talking and I was looking at him and [wondering], 'Who is this?' And he said, 'I'm Bill Belichick,' and I said [to myself], 'Isn't this the Super Bowl coach?' But he's been great and he's given me a great opportunity."[1075]

There are many examples of the Patriots finding value by thinking differently. The players listed below were overlooked because they were injured, unsuited to the scheme they played in, overshadowed by other great players, or simply unappreciated by their team. In the case of Corey Dillon, everyone acknowledged his ability but overestimated his "character issues" and misinterpreted as disloyalty his burning desire to win.

Injured players:

- *Rodney Harrison*: The San Diego Chargers believed Harrison was washed up. The Patriots correctly believed Harrison was slowed in 2002 by his groin injury and had come back too quickly because he's a tough football player.

- *Bethel Johnson, Benjamin Watson*, and *Randall Gay*: Each was injured for a significant portion of his college career. Watson was also underutilized by his team's system. When the Patriots drafted Johnson in the 2nd round, even he was startled: "Yeah, I was surprised, being taken in this position."[1076] Draftnik Mel Kiper Jr. said no one imagined Johnson being drafted in the 3rd round, let alone the 2nd.[1077]

Talent not obvious because previous team's system did not give player an opportunity to shine:

- *Eugene Wilson*: After an exceptional junior year in man-to-man coverage, Wilson's stats suffered while playing zone coverage senior year. After snaring six interceptions and knocking down 30 passes as a junior, Wilson entered his senior season as the nation's top-rated college cornerback.[1078] But he grabbed only two interceptions and defended only 14 passes his senior year due to the switch to zone and because, Wilson says, teams started throwing away from his area of the field: "I could count on my hands the number of times they threw deep balls on me."[1079]

- *David Givens*: Notre Dame seldom threw the ball, so wide receiver David Givens got few opportunities to show his stuff.

- *Matt Light*: Never got opportunity to stand out because his Purdue Boilermakers seldom ran the ball. Belichick says "their offense pretty much was 50 or 60 passes in a game, plus about 15 draw plays."[1080] Offensive linemen get noticed for run blocking (especially "pancake blocks" where an O-lineman knocks a defender onto his back), not pass blocking. But the Patriots noticed that Purdue surrendered only 38 sacks in 1,690 pass attempts with Light at left tackle: "we didn't have to pick [our quarterback] up off the ground too much."[1081] And they projected from Light's aggressiveness that he would become a solid run blocker. (Defensive line star Richard Seymour says of Light, "He's a high motor guy with that nasty offensive lineman's mentality. He's a tough guy."[1082])

- *P.K. Sam*: Florida State rotated all its wide receivers in and out of games, and quarterback Chris Rix was less than stellar.

Overshadowed because he played with other great players:

- *Tom Brady*: Never locked down the starting job at Michigan because he overlapped with Brian Griese (who has since played for the Denver Broncos and Miami Dolphins and is now with the Tampa Bay Buccaneers) and Drew Henson (now with the Dallas Cowboys after earlier passing up the NFL for the New York Yankees). After 2003, Brady's NFL passer rating was 11th-best in NFL history, even as he continues to improve and had no legitimate running threat to force opposing defenses to defend the run before 2004. (Belichick says Dillon's presence "really adds bite"[1083] to Brady's play-action passes.) At Michigan, Brady competed against Brian Griese, whose NFL passer rating (through 2003) was 18th-best in NFL history.[1084] The odds that two of the top-rated quarterbacks in NFL history would play at the same university at the same time are pretty low, but it happened, and Brady was overshadowed.

- *Mike Vrabel* and *Rodney Bailey*: Neither Vrabel nor Bailey could break into the Pittsburgh Steelers' starting lineup because the Steelers had so many strong defensive linemen and linebackers. Scott Pioli says of Vrabel: "No one thought much of him. We thought he could be a starter and/or a major contributor. He's one of the smartest players I've ever been around. He has a pain threshold that's off the charts."[1085] The Patriots were thrilled to get Bailey, but he suffered a season-ending injury in preseason.

Lacks NFL-typical strength/size:

· *Asante Samuel:* Weighed only 185 pounds and was among the weakest of NFL hopefuls.

· *Dan Klecko:* At only 5´11´, Klecko was much shorter than the typical NFL defensive lineman. (After 2003, the Patriots told Klecko he would instead play fullback and linebacker.)

· *Dan Koppen:* Has short arms. Most teams want offensive linemen with long arms. Patriots offensive coordinator Charlie Weis was more focused on Koppen's intelligence: "Koppen... makes all the calls on the line. Having a guy who can handle that at such a young age, that's unusual. It doesn't happen often."[1086]

Saddled with "trouble-maker" label after cleaning up his life:

· *Corey Dillon:* When the Cincinnati Bengals decided to go with the younger Rudi Johnson and trade Dillon for a draft pick, other teams were interested but unwilling to part with a 2nd-round draft pick. The Patriots did their homework on Dillon and decided he was no longer the trouble-maker his reputation made him out to be and that he had a Patriot-like passion for winning and eagerness to be a team player.

Patriots swear Dillon has been the perfect teammate, and Dillon swears he's in heaven:

> "I'm just having fun. It's been a long time since I felt like this. I'm playing with great guys, I'm playing for a great owner, playing for some excellent coaches. And I'm having fun. We're doing things as a team, and when you get wins like this, you have to smile. [Our linemen] do a great job. They don't get a lot of praise, but I'm going to give it to them. They do an excellent job protecting Tom and opening up holes for me to get into and make something happen. They deserve a lot of credit. They really go out there and bust their butts every Sunday. They're doing a wonderful job."[1087]

HIRING PROCESS

Hiring objectives shape hiring process

"A lot of guys like to be football players, but they don't like to be around everything that goes into being a football player. This group had as good an energy and attitude as I've been around."[1088]
– Bill Belichick

"Bill and I have a rule. If a guy needs the sizzle, he's not for us."[1089]
– Patriots VP of player personnel Scott Pioli

Once an organization envisions the kind of people it seeks to hire, it must design a process that finds and hires them while screening out people who don't fit the desired profile. Because the Patriots desire only players to whom winning football games is intensely important, they use an unglamorous hiring process that screens out players with "un-Patriotic" mentalities and priorities.

For aspiring Patriots, Scott Pioli says, "football better be among the two or three most important things in their life."[1090] Patriots coaches and personnel executives believe players obsessed with winning are too focused on issues that impact winning to worry about glitz... or even college grades. Pioli's still mad he drafted Notre Dame tight end Jabari Holloway in 2001. The warning sign was flashing neon: Holloway arrived late for practice his senior year because he was stuck in chemistry lab. To Pioli, that demonstrated football was not Holloway's top priority.[1091]

The Patriots screen out players by underwhelming potential hires in every way except their dedication to winning football games. Pro Bowl safety Rodney Harrison signed with the Patriots after "they really wined and dined me"[1092] at a burger joint, *The Ground Round*. I recall *The Ground Round* from my youth for the mounds of discarded peanut shells littering its floor. If not the burger or the peanuts, what about New England impressed Harrison, who had been excited about signing with the Oakland Raiders before Scott Pioli started ringing his agent's cell phone every few minutes and begging Harrison to visit the Patriots before signing with Oakland?

"The first thing Coach Belichick told me was, 'I like the way you warm up, the intensity of it.' I'm thinking, Damn, this guy really knows football. So we sat there and talked, the coach, Scott Pioli and me, and they told me, 'You give us a chance to win,' and that's what I needed to hear. No b.s., no wining and dining, just straight football."[1093]

Harrison's decision to join New England was half about being part of a great team. He wanted to recapture the rush he felt playing on the 1998 San Diego

Chargers' defense when the Ryan Leaf-"led" Chargers' offense was so atrocious it handed the ball to the opposing team an astounding 51 times:

> "our defense had this thing going, and it just snowballed. Guys working, working, coming in at all hours, lifting weights, studying. The offense would throw an interception. Boom, we stop them, three and out. We're on the bench, we don't even get our helmets off, and our offense gives them the ball back again. Clap hands, let's go. We stop them again, three and out. What a feeling! That's what I came here for, to get the feeling back." [1094]

The other factor in Harrison's decision was respect... feeling appreciated and welcomed. The Chargers, for whom Harrison had played at a Pro Bowl level and given his all for nine years, had just cast him off. Belichick and Pioli had done their homework and knew what a hard-working and tough (both mentally and physically) player Rodney Harrison was. They knew he was a perfect fit for their organization, and they let him know how much they wanted him. "[Belichick] knew exactly what he wanted from me. He said, 'These are our expectations. I know what you can do.' ...Coach told me he was bringing me in here to be a leader."[1095] Harrison was thrilled to be so wanted and respected by a Super Bowl champion coach like Bill Belichick after being so disrespected by his former team: "The [Chargers] figured that, at 30, I couldn't run anymore. I'd suffered a groin pull in the first game last year. The muscle was 30 percent off the bone. The doctors told me I'd miss eight weeks. I missed two. I guess the Patriots feel I can run well enough."[1096]

Harrison didn't care that the Patriots didn't take him for lobster at Legal Seafood: "I didn't mind. I liked it, in fact. There was no b.s. about it."[1097] What impressed him more was seeing free agent linebacker Rosevelt Colvin visit the same day he did and hearing they would soon bring in free agent cornerback Tyrone Poole. It was obvious to Harrison that "They were making the commitment [to win]."[1098]

The Patriots' evaluation of Harrison was spot on. He ran and hit plenty well in 2003... well enough to lead one of the great defenses in NFL history to a Super Bowl trophy. And Harrison's leadership and attitude were so admired in the locker room that his new teammates elected him a team captain in his first season.

Rodney Harrison was lucky to get a burger at *The Ground Round*. The most heavily recruited free agent in the NFL in 2003, linebacker Rosevelt Colvin, didn't even get a meal:

> "It was not a glamorous visit. I went to Bill's office and talked to him for an hour. Then Scott came in, and we talked another hour. Bill asked if I wanted to see the locker room. He opened the door a crack and said, 'There it is.' There were no lights on. He took me to see the club seats—in the dark. The whole place was deserted. There was nothing to see. Just a bunch of sand, dirt, and snow."[1099]

So, what did they discuss that impressed Colvin? Achieving greatness:

> "I sat in their office, and Scott Pioli was excited, and Coach Belichick was excited, and after a while, so was I. The coach talked about the great linebackers he had on the Giants, Pepper Johnson and Carl Banks and Lawrence Taylor, and all the plans he had for me and how I'd fit into their defense. Some of the other teams I'd talked to wanted to take me out for dinner and show me a good time, but you can keep all that stuff."[1100]

Despite being the hottest commodity on the free agent market and being treated like royalty by the Texans, Jaguars, Lions, Cardinals, and Giants, Colvin signed with the Patriots–reportedly turning down millions of dollars more from at least one other team–because "I was looking for basic things... Like a plan to win." [1101] Belichick admired Colvin passing up more money to play for the Patriots: "With most guys, it's all about not leaving the last dime on the table."[1102]

Special teams captain Larry Izzo decided to join the Patriots for the same inglorious reason: "Scott and Bill told me when I came in that they were looking for a certain kind of player [and] I was the kind of player they were looking for."[1103]

The Patriots' no-frills hiring process exemplifies what economists call a "screening mechanism," *i.e.*, a filter that screens out those who want the job for the wrong reasons. Belichick understands this and intentionally makes internships painful experiences:

> "When I hire young people, it isn't like I haven't done the jobs I'm asking them to do. ...I made the airport runs and picked up the towels and all that crap. I know what 'entry level' means. So... I try to make it as bad as possible. I fight with my coaches all the time because they say we can pay these guys more so they could be more comfortable. I don't want them to be comfortable. I don't want them to make ends meet. Will you make the sacrifice? I don't know what that sacrifice is for you, and I don't care. ...Are you willing to make the commitment this job takes?"[1104]

After long-time Patriots star safety Lawyer Milloy refused a pay-cut Belichick felt his diminished 2002 production warranted, Belichick released him days before the 2003 season opener. A Buffalo paper called Belichick a "cold-hearted ogre." Hardly. Belichick believes the great ones in every profession succeed by doing whatever success requires and work their hardest because they love what they're doing, not for financial rewards or glory. Belichick forced Milloy to choose between maximizing his income and being a champion, and Milloy chose top dollar.

As a young man, Bill Belichick was in heaven earning $25-a-week to work for the Colts: "I left [home] at 7 in the morning and usually got back around 11 or 12 at night. It was pretty much 17, 18 hours of football on a daily basis. ...It was awesome."[1105] He says, "I was happy to work for nothing. I was ecstatic to work for nothing."[1106] He appreciates that Colts coach Marchibroda expanded his responsibilities as he proved worthy:

"Even though I was the low man on the totem pole–by a lot–he would say, 'Billy, take care of this' or 'take care of that.' As one thing was done or another thing was done, he felt confident giving me other responsibilities, things like running the scout team on offense for the defensive team or running the special teams kick team for our special teams unit."[1107]

Fifteen years ago, Belichick was using this tactic on men who now serve in top positions on his Patriots. Patriots offensive coordinator Charlie Weis says, "My first year, 1990… All I did was break down film for him. I was his form of a graduate assistant, like they have in college."[1108] Belichick did the same to current Patriots VP of player personnel, Scott Pioli, when Pioli was a 25-year-old considering an offer to become a 49ers scout and Belichick was head coach of the Cleveland Browns. Remembers Pioli:

"I told Bill that I had this opportunity. And he said to me, 'Well you have one here, too.' Now, he couldn't tell me the duties, or the pay, or anything else about the job. But the next morning, I woke up, went right to his office and told him I'd take it. I didn't know what it was–but I knew I'd be with someone that I would respect and trust, and in turn would respect and trust me."[1109]

Belichick lavished Pioli with a princely salary of $14,000 a year for his all-consuming sixteen-to-eighteen-hour days full of chauffeuring people to/from the airport, entering data, watching endless reels of film, lugging bags, and photocopying ("I had a tan from standing over a copy machine for hours and hours"[1110]). Pioli proved to his mentor that he wasn't in it for the money or the glory but for the thrill of football. Belichick kept telling Pioli, "the more you can do, the more you can do."[1111] Pioli, who knew Belichick was testing him, now laughs about his sacrifice and $14K salary:

"You know, we're not talking 1968 [dollars] here. But anyone who gets into this solely because of the money–other than a passion for football–might as well just forget it. At the kind of money I was making, heck, I didn't want to go back to the apartment at night–the office was a better place to sleep."[1112]

Belichick so admired the fearlessness and resourcefulness of Sir Ernest Shackleton's 28-man crew in surviving a 21-month shipwreck in 1914-15 (after their ship, *The Endurance*, was enveloped and crushed by a drifting ice pack 350 miles from shore and 800 miles from a whaling station) that Belichick brought his entire team to watch the *IMAX* film "Shackleton's Antarctic Adventure" before the 2001 season. Linebacker Willie McGinest felt the movie's message:

"If they wouldn't have been a team out there, they wouldn't have survived. If they hadn't believed in their captain, they wouldn't have survived. (Belichick) is the captain of our ship and we're the crew members. Everything hasn't gone perfectly for us, obviously, but we've believed in him, we've followed his direction and he's gotten us to the Super Bowl."[1113]

I mention Shackleton here because Belichick would no doubt also applaud the no-nonsense "help wanted" ad Shackleton ran before the voyage (aimed at exploring Antarctica, though Shackleton's crew never reached the continent): "Men wanted for hazardous journey. Small wages, bitter cold, long months of complete darkness, constant danger. Safe return doubtful. Honor and recognition in case of success."[1114] By describing a worst-case scenario, Shackleton screened out all but the hardiest and bravest of souls. Had Shackleton not warned applicants of life-and-death challenges, his crew would not have been mentally prepared to confront them. He and they would have perished. Belichick takes the same approach with the Patriots. Most coaches roll out the proverbial red carpet for and toss cash at potential hires, but Belichick gives no free agent the Hollywood treatment because "If that's what a guy cares about, then he's come to the wrong place."[1115]

Find passionate employees by de-emphasizing money

"Everyone has a mutual respect for everyone. I don't see jealousy about guys' salaries and stuff like that. You see it around the league, but here you don't see the bitterness about one guy getting paid this and the other guy getting paid that. They really don't care. Guys go out there and they play football."[1116]
— *Patriots safety Rodney Harrison*

"No one but the ...worker himself can [decide] what in work, job performance, social status, and pride constitutes the personal satisfaction that makes [him] feel that he contributes, that he performs, that he serves his values, and that he fulfills himself." [1117]
— *Peter Drucker, father of management science*

"Each day I work as if I'm a rookie. I don't take anything for granted because I'm now financially secure, because it's not about money. It's about passion. It's about love for the game."[1118]
— *Patriots safety Rodney Harrison*

To attract the right players, the Patriots use an unusual approach to hiring. They use an intentionally understated approach, rather than wining and dining players and puffing up their egos. Belichick says:

"A guy who comes in and wants his name on a scoreboard that says, 'Joe Blow, No. 28,' is probably not going to be a... Patriot. A guy who wants to play for a team and not worry about being a star is likely to be one."[1119]

Similarly, the Patriots don't entice free agents with false praise or false promises. Wide receiver Donald Hayes knew before signing that no Patriot is guaranteed playing time:

"They basically look you in the eye and tell you, 'If you're the best player, well, then you'll play.' ...A lot of teams will try to (deceive) you, but these guys are straight shooters, OK? Guys seem to want to play for them. Just look at all of the veterans on the roster, guys who maybe could have made more money somewhere else, but came here because they know (coach Bill) Belichick will find a way to use them."[1120]

If Hayes had any doubts, he learned the hard way when his poor performance led to little playing time and eventually cost him his job.

The living embodiment of the Patriots' quest for players who intrinsically love the sport is Tedy Bruschi, who fell in love with the rough-and-tumble of football playing on a dangerous scrap of grass full of sprinkler heads and potholes: "Street ball. It was tackle football, ripping people's shirts off, bringing others down. I loved to get dirty. ... Ripped clothes, muddy clothes, bloody knees–those were fun times. I'm the same guy."[1121] Bruschi was joyous after getting his first taste of an organized game: "Once I put on that helmet and those shoulder pads, I just let it all go, didn't care who I was hitting or how hard it was. I just wanted to hit people. After that first day, I remember thinking, 'This is fun.' I was whooping and hollering. It's been a joy ride ever since."[1122] Bruschi's passion for football has led him to outsized success. His brother Tony reports that "[after] his last high school football game, he cried his eyes out because he didn't know if he'd play in college. Then his last college game, he cried his eyes out again, because he didn't know if he'd play in the NFL."[1123]

Bruschi's football addiction leads him to value winning and playing for a winning organization above all else. Unlike virtually every other NFL player, Bruschi has no agent. He represents himself and loves being a New England Patriot: "I'm comfortable to go in there, we look each other in the eyes, and we'll work it out. The Patriots have always treated me with respect."[1124] Even more amazingly, Bruschi willingly and happily signs contract extensions with the Patriots for well below fair market value. Bruschi will receive $8.1 million for the 2005-2008 seasons. That averages to $2 million/year, less than half the 2004 rate for linebackers of his quality, a rate that rises each season:

"The NFL 'transition' number (the average of the 10 highest-paid players at the position) is just over $4 million. ...As a 2003 Pro Bowl alternate and an essential cog in two Super Bowl championships, it's inconceivable (barring injury) that Bruschi wouldn't have done better as a free agent following the 2004 season. Word is that a few of Bruschi's teammates implored him to get an agent to help in the negotiations. ...Bruschi admitted in a radio interview that he probably could have gotten more in free agency, but that it was more important to him to remain in New England. Bruschi went on to say that all NFL players are probably overpaid anyway."[1125]

After teammates and journalists told him he had signed for too little, Bruschi explained that it wasn't about money:

> "How much is enough? How much do you need? I live in North Attleboro. I don't live glamorously. I live in a nice home and we're happy where we are. You really have to look yourself in the eye and say, 'Do you want to go out there and chase every single dime?' Or do you want to stay somewhere and establish something. I chose to stay and establish something."[1126]

Bruschi's decision to negotiate his own contract seems smarter when he explains that he simply wanted to stay in New England: "If I had an agent I wouldn't be here. Agents tell you, 'I can get you more.' But after they say that, it's always, 'But it's going to have to be somewhere else.' ...I didn't need to make that decision."[1127]

Bruschi's love for the game is painted on his face. During games, he's got a goofy grin... while sacking quarterbacks or flying over 6'5" offensive linemen. I have no idea how he gets above the fully-extended arms of offensive linemen, but he does so while smiling and focusing intensely on the opposing quarterback. The photographs are unbelievable. (Also unbelievable is the way Bruschi in mid-2004 survived a knee wrenching so ugly that I couldn't watch replays. I feared Bruschi's career was over because his feet got trapped in a pile and then his knee bent in a horrible way as he fell backwards. Bruschi himself was scared but popped up and flashed a "wow, how the hell did I escape disaster?" look to his teammates. Later, he said, "The guys call me a bunch of things. 'The contortionist.' They call me 'Gumby.' They say I'm double jointed. I was just lucky. I rolled with it a little bit and here I am talking to you."[1128])

After Bruschi intercepted a pass and ran it back for a touchdown to clinch the 2003 AFC East title, fans went bonkers, hurling snow (left over from a 30-inch snowstorm so powerful the stadium could not be cleared before the game) into the air in sync with the raucous music. Bruschi ate it up: "That was incredible, wasn't it? Throwing the snow up in the air with the music. It got me into the holiday spirit."[1129] Bruschi's love for New England fans is one reason he's willing to earn less to stay here: "I'll tell you something that would just kill me. To go to another team and then come play a game here and see all those people wearing No. 54 jerseys in the stands. That's something I couldn't take."[1130]

Getting bargains requires patience

In 2000 and 2001, the Patriots did not rush to sign high-priced free agents at the start of free agency. Instead, they signed several low-priced free agents but kept much of their powder dry and waited for the initial chaos to die down. They then evaluated those players who had not been scooped up and signed a bunch of talented players for relatively few dollars. In 2000, they grabbed three key players (Joe Andruzzi, Bobby Hamilton, and Otis Smith) in July or later. In 2001, they signed six key contributors (Terrell Buckley, Je'Rod Cherry, Bryan Cox, Roman Phifer, Antowain Smith, and Ken Walter) in June or later. If your heart is set on a particular player, you risk getting caught in a bidding war. If, however, you focus on getting good value, you can achieve this with diligence and patience. Journalists joke the Patriots shopped at Kmart, but a better analogy is liquidation sales, *Overstock.com*, *Filene's Basement*, and *Building 19* because the Patriots found quality players at bargain prices.

Gamble on greatness

"While it is futile to try to eliminate risk... it is essential that the risks taken be the right risks. The end result of successful strategic planning must be the capacity to take a greater risk... To extend this capacity, however, we must understand the risks we take. We must be able to choose rationally among risk-taking courses of action rather than plunge into uncertainty on the basis of hunch, hearsay, or [personal] experience." [1131]
– *Peter Drucker, father of management science*

There is no job security in the NFL. If there were, Belichick and Pioli would seldom gamble on unproven players and would be even more obsessive about pre-hiring screening. But NFL players know that signing a contract and attending training camp guarantees nothing, and Belichick never promises anything more than a fair evaluation. Given the NFL reality of tenuous employment and non-guaranteed contracts, Belichick and Pioli smartly gamble on players with great potential but significant uncertainty. Belichick's Patriots take chances on players like wrestling star Stephen Neal and track star Michael Jennings, neither of whom played football in college. Neal is now a starter on the offensive line. Jennings is out of football. This is "heads-we-win, tails-so-what" gambling.

Trying out undrafted LSU cornerback Randall Gay was a similar "gamble." Gay wasn't even a starting cornerback his senior season in college, but his coach recommended him to Belichick, and Gay now starts on the 2004 Patriots defense (following injuries to starting corners Law and Poole). Not even Belichick could have known Gay would make the roster. For every Randall Gay, there are many hopefuls who don't work out. After the 2002 season, the Chicago Bears decided not to re-sign their long-time right tackle, James "Big Cat" Williams. After Williams sat out the 2003 season nursing injuries, the Patriots signed him in 2004. As a 6'7", 330+ pound former Pro Bowl tackle, Williams might have helped the Patriots, but they released him after evaluating him for several weeks.

Patriots owner Bob Kraft is impressed by his head coach's personnel prowess: "Bill Belichick manages a roster like a stock portfolio. He's always trying to upgrade the bottom of a roster, like you try to upgrade your bottom five or six stocks."[1132] More than any other NFL coach, Bill Belichick stresses getting production (especially on special teams) from the "bottom" of his roster. Because Belichick gets every player (except his backup quarterbacks) onto the field and squeezes performance from each one, he describes his approach to personnel as: "You can never have... too many good football players."[1133] Sentimentality never prevents Belichick from upgrading his roster. As he says of the painful necessity of cutting well-liked veterans, "For some, the time has come for them to step aside and they don't get to retire on their own volition. The coach has to tell them because you represent the interests of the other fifty-three players. You owe it to the team to make the decisions that are best for the team and the team's best opportunity to win."[1134] (Don't confuse sentimentality with concern for team chemistry; Belichick does not make minor "upgrades" that harm team cohesiveness because such "upgrades" don't benefit the team.)

But Belichick is not obsessively focused on the bottom of the roster. In fact, he also takes calculated gambles to improve the top of his roster. After winning two Super Bowls with the solid-but-unspectacular Antowain Smith at running back, Belichick rebalanced his portfolio, replacing the blue chip, dividend-paying Smith with two "speculative stocks" (high-risk, high-potential-return running backs). First, Belichick traded for one of the NFL's all-time best running backs, Corey Dillon, whom the Cincinnati Bengals were willing to trade because of his long history of getting into trouble and his visible frustration (after eight years of losing). Dillon's on-field talent is beyond question, but his off-field behavior marked him as a major gamble. Second, Belichick drafted Cedric Cobbs, another talented-but-troubled running back in the 4th round of the 2004 NFL Draft. Many, ironically, compared Cobbs with Dillon. Cobbs' stock fell due to college injuries and his being sentenced "to 20 hours of community service and six months' probation, and fined $700 for driving under the influence of drugs [marijuana] in August 2002."[1135]

Are the Patriots insane for signing not just one risky running back but two? Not at all. First, the Patriots conducted exhaustive research into each player and determined that the actual risk was lower than the perceived risk. Second, avoiding risk entirely is impossible. There are no guaranteed stars available late in the 4th round of the NFL Draft. After 32 teams have each selected three or four players, every unselected player is either risky or uninspiring. Choosing a potentially great, but risky, player in the 4th round (or later) can be wise.

Third, unlike a stock portfolio, Bill Belichick's portfolio "return on investment" (ROI) is not his average return. The Patriots' roster is so solid that Belichick must cut talented, NFL-capable football players late in preseason, something NFL players call "getting whacked." Other teams drool over whatever scraps the Patriots toss them. When wide receiver David Patten, who caught a beautiful touchdown pass in the Patriots' first Super Bowl win, was rumored to be on the bubble, one AFC general manager said, "The Patriots are stacked, and if a guy like Patten is out there he won't be unemployed very long."[1136] Indeed! After the Patriots cut cornerback Terrell Buckley at the end of 2004 training camp, Buckley joined the

Jets. Due to the Patriots' great roster depth, a solid-but-uninspiring late 4th-round selection might not even make the Patriots roster. And, even if he makes the team, he would only marginally boost overall team talent. Taking a "riskier" guy with greater upside potential and greater downside risk is actually a safer decision. The "riskier" player may have a lower probability of making the team than a "safe" late 4th-rounder, but the "riskier" player will boost overall team performance much more if he makes the team. Thus, the "risky" player (when judged by probability of making the team) is actually the "safe" player (when judged by expected contribution to the team's performance)!

Fourth, signing multiple risky running backs greatly reduces your overall risk. Since only one running back can run with the ball at a time, Belichick's primary concern is "How talented is our *best* running back," not "What is the average talent level of *all* our running backs in training camp?" By signing two "risky" running backs, the Patriots greatly increased their odds of finishing training camp with at least one great running back. This can be seen using simple math. Assume that a "risky" running back has a 50% chance of being "great" and a 50% chance of being "lousy" while a "safe" running back has a 10% chance of being "great," an 80% chance of being "solid," and a 10% chance of being "lousy." If you have two running backs, how good will your best (better) running back be?

	Best running back is "great"	Best running back is "solid"	Both running backs are "lousy"
2 "safe" running backs	19% (.1+.1·.9)	80% (.8·.9+.9·.8-.8·.8)	1% (.1²)
1 "safe" running back & 1 "risky" running back	55% (.1 + .9·.5)	40% (.5·.8)	5% (.1·.5)
2 "risky" running backs	75% (.5 + .5·.5)	0%	25% (.5·.5)

If you have three running backs, how good will your best running back be?

	Best running back is "great"	Best running back is "solid"	All running backs are "lousy"
3 "safe" running backs	27.1% (.1+.1·.9+.1·.9·.9)	72.8% (100%-27.1%-0.1%)	0.1% (.1³)
2 "safe" running backs & 1 "risky" running back	59.5% (.1 +.1·.9+.5·.9·.9)	40% (100%-59.5%-0.5%)	0.5% (.1·.1·.5)
1 "safe" running back & 2 "risky" running backs	77.5% (.1 +.5·.9+.5·.5·.9)	20% (100%-77.5%-2.5%)	2.5% (.1·.5·.5)
3 "risky" running backs	87.5% (.5 + .5·.5+.5·.5·.5)	0%	12.5% (.5³)

From these tables, it's clear that "risky" running backs maximize your chances of having at least one "great" running back. But having at least one "safe" running back largely protects you against having only "lousy" running backs. The Patriots already had two "solid" running backs (Kevin Faulk and Patrick Pass). So they gambled that either Cedric Cobbs or Corey Dillon would be "great" while fully aware that either could stumble, on or off the field. Even if they both stumbled, they had two "solid" runners. Thus, the Patriots' decision to sign two "risky" running backs was very smart.

Stockpile obvious talent, even in the absence of need

After drafting quarterback Kliff Kingsbury (who threw for an astounding 12,429 yards and 95 touchdowns with only 40 interceptions at Texas Tech), the Patriots sat him down and told him he would be "injured" in 2003. The Patriots wanted to retain Kingsbury and let him learn their offense, but they couldn't sacrifice an active roster spot for a rookie quarterback who would never make it off the bench. A year later, they signed Jim Miller, whom they considered an upgrade, and released Kingsbury.

The Pats' draft philosophy is generally to take "the best player available," regardless of team needs. In 2004, the Patriots hardly needed more defensive linemen but grabbed two top talents because they felt they were the best players available. Had the Patriots drafted for need rather than value in the 6th round of the 2000 NFL Draft, they wouldn't have drafted two-time Super Bowl MVP Tom Brady:

> "For the second straight year, the Patriots felt compelled to draft a quarterback despite having one of the best active quarterbacks in Drew Bledsoe. … When asked why the team would select a quarterback two years in a row, Belichick explained Brady's selection as being a 'value pick.'"[1137]

The Patriots went even further in 2000, choosing their final roster for value, not need. Teams virtually never keep four quarterbacks, but the Patriots kept Tom Brady as their fourth-string quarterback in 2000 (behind Drew Bledsoe, Damon Huard, and Michael Bishop) because they believed his potential justified sacrificing a valuable roster spot that would otherwise have been filled with a lesser talent who would have played in 2000.

When the Patriots picked tight end Benjamin Watson with their second 1st-round pick in 2004, the media read this as dissatisfaction with their current tight ends, but Belichick insisted the Patriots simply draft according to perceived value, not need: "We don't evaluate players based on what others did."[1138]

Coming out of college, Tedy Bruschi was a great football player who didn't even have an obvious NFL position. Belichick grabbed him, despite not knowing how to use him. The Pats similarly grabbed Dan Klecko because they loved his aggressive, enthusiastic style and productivity. Said Belichick, "he was clearly one of the most productive players in college football last year. Why he was there in the fourth round and not taken in the third or the second, I'm not really sure."[1139] It was likely because teams thought Klecko undersized for an NFL lineman, especially at nose tackle, his position in college. But the Patriots consider Klecko "a football player" and have tried him at all sorts of positions. Heading into 2004, Patriots coaches began teaching him to play interior linebacker. Belichick hopes to use Klecko's versatility to drive offensive coordinators mad: "He's got the athleticism to play linebacker, but he'll definitely play down [on the defensive line] in some situations, or maybe all of them. [Linebacker] may or may not be permanent, but it at least gives him a chance to do something he hasn't done."[1140]

COMPENSATION

Focus on value (performance/pay)

The Patriots have few superstars, aside from Tom Brady who rode a rocket to superstardom after Drew Bledsoe went down with an injury early in the 2001 season. The Patriots believe spreading their salary cap dollars more evenly than most teams helps them win more games.

The Patriots started tossing stars overboard the moment Belichick seized the ship. They had to. In early 2000, the Patriots were $10.5 million over the salary cap. Even worse, Tedy Bruschi and Troy Brown became free agents on February 11th. (Belichick re-signed Brown February 28th and Bruschi March 23rd.) Belichick dumped or chose not to re-sign many big-name players with inflated contracts or salary expectations: six-time Pro Bowl offensive lineman Bruce Armstrong ($3.5 million), five-time Pro Bowl tight end Ben Coates ($3.456 million), Pro Bowl running back Terry Allen, Zefross Moss, Todd Rucci, Vincent Brisby, Shawn Jefferson, and Max Lane. After cutting Armstrong and his $3.5 million salary on February 10th, the Patriots re-signed him in July for $440,000 plus incentives.[1141] A year later, in early 2001, the team was again $6.5 million over the salary cap[1142] and "whacked" Pro Bowl linebacker Chris Slade, two-time Pro Bowl defensive lineman Henry Thomas, Bruce Armstrong, backup quarterback John Friesz, and special teams standout Larry Whigham. The Patriots reluctantly surrendered talented defensive tackle Chad Eaton to the Seattle Seahawks because they couldn't afford to match the Seahawks' $10.7 million offer that included a $3.5 million signing bonus.

Chad Eaton's signing bonus exceeded by nearly $1 million the aggregate signing bonuses ($2.6 million) the Patriots paid to acquire all sixteen of their "value" free agents in 2001. The largest bonus the Patriots handed out was $625,000 to offensive lineman Mike Compton.[1143] Most NFL personnel executives felt the Patriots' sixteen "Blue Light Special" signees were all anonymous retreads. Few thought the Patriots had acquired even a single "good" player.

But there was a discernible method to the Patriots' "madness." Mike Lombardi (currently senior personnel executive for the Oakland Raiders) phoned Belichick "and he told me what a good job he thought we'd done. He told me, 'You'll be successful and other teams are gonna look at this and build teams like you did.'"[1144] Lombardi's observation was more accurate than even he knew. Those "anonymous retreads" helped the Patriots win the Super Bowl that very same season! Despite not signing a single well-known player, the Patriots acquired sixteen players who probably constitute the greatest crop of free agents any team has ever signed in one season. Many of the team's "waiver wire" signees excelled within the Patriots' system because Belichick and Pioli had "systematically studied every veteran to find low-priced fits."[1145]

Belichick's Patriots have generally shunned fat free agent contracts because "there's not always a direct correlation between marquee names, marquee salaries, and good football players."[1146] But they aren't afraid to sign an occasional big name if they believe he's worth the money. Safety Rodney Harrison and linebacker Rosevelt Colvin have been Belichick's biggest splashes. Harrison was a cornerstone of the Patriots defense in 2003. Colvin played well in early 2003 before shattering his hip socket.

After watching the Patriots dominate, NFL teams now appreciate the wisdom of signing value players rather than chasing superstars with super-sized salary demands:

> "At the scouting combine a week ago, I heard coach after coach—and GM after GM—talk about how they want to make sure they don't overpay for free agents. NFL team people always say that, but this time I think they mean it. The lesson of the Patriots' two Super Bowl wins in the last three years is a simple one: Don't become entranced by the big-money free agents. Get the value guys, as New England did."[1147]

Buy low

> "When [the Patriots] go shopping, it's at Wal-Mart and Kmart, for the Blue Light specials."[1148]
> – *Super Bowl XVII-winning quarterback Joe Theismann*

Scott Pioli is always looking for value acquisitions because big-bucks guys don't always make big-time plays:

> "I hate the words 'high-priced.' I hate that whole concept. We're going to go after good football players. We're not going to go after some guy because he has a high price or because he's a Pro Bowl player. Hey, if we can get another Mike Vrabel, if we can get another Marc Edwards, if we can get another David Patten [or] another Mike Compton—we're going to get those guys. But just because a guy has a marquee perception? No."[1149]

> "You can find good players everywhere. One of the many things Bill and I are in agreement on is that just because a player has a marquee name or a high price tag, that doesn't necessarily mean he's a good football player. There are good players out there, at every financial level—and it's a matter of looking hard and long at all of them, figuring out what's good about them,

what's bad about them, and then figuring out if or how they fit into your organization."[1150]

Just as some homebuyers fall in love with a particular house and pay far above market value for it, so too some NFL teams zero in on a guy they want for their team and pay a king's ransom to sign (or re-sign) him. The Patriots look as hard at a player's sticker price as his performance. The Patriots don't want the best players at any cost; they want the players who provide maximal "bang for the buck": strong performance at low cost. Bill Belichick was an economics major, so he naturally looks for bargains that squeeze extra value from a fixed salary cap. By focusing on performance-per-dollar, the Patriots find solid values, like Tyrone Poole, who not only started at cornerback but had his best year ever in his first season with the Patriots, helping his new team win its second Super Bowl. Even before his superb season, Poole already looked like a good bargain:

> "In acquiring Poole, who the coaches hope will vie for a starting cornerback job while, at the very least, filling the nickel back role, New England spent about $2 million less in signing bonus money than many other teams paid for starting caliber corners, and that doesn't include the Lions ridiculous $6.5 million paid to Dre Bly up front. The more typical bonus paid to starting level corners this year was $3.5 million to $4 million."[1151]

An even bigger value acquisition was Patriots safety Rodney Harrison who, based on his lights-out 2003 season deserved to play in the 2003 Pro Bowl. Most believe Harrison was robbed of Pro Bowl honors because many players around the league dislike him for his not-wholly-undeserved reputation, "earned" while with the Chargers, for playing dirty. With the Patriots, Harrison has played aggressively but within the rules. However, his reputation precedes him.

Another brilliant strategy the Patriots employ is avoiding the mad dash at the start of free agency. In 2000 and 2001, they waited for talented players to fall through the cracks. As free agency wears on, unsigned players become increasingly worried, even panicked, and willing to sign contracts they would have rejected a month or two earlier. The Patriots scooped up many key free agents, who played essential roles in their Super Bowl season, during the last few months before their 2001 opener.

Belichick and Pioli have spent many high draft picks on defensive linemen. This is a wise investment strategy because quality veteran defensive linemen command giant salaries while young defensive linemen can play extremely well for far less. The Patriots' defensive line is one of the NFL's best, but not one Patriot defensive lineman earns anything close to what top defensive linemen earn:

Player	Position	Team	Year	Income	Salary cap
Bryant Young	DT	49ers	2003	$4,500,000	$8,418,049
Jason Taylor	DE	Dolphins	2003	$5,671,100	$7,866,100
Robert Porcher	DE	Lions	2003	$3,504,000	$6,836,745

Warren Sapp	DT	Buccaneers	2003	$6,600,000	$6,600,000
Trevor Pryce	DE	Broncos	2003	$4,800,000	$6,566,667
Gary Walker	DE	Texans	2003	$4,500,000	$6,300,000
Phillip Daniels	DE	Bears	2003	$3,750,800	$5,600,800
Chad Bratzke	DE	Colts	2003	$5,251,500	$5,438,500
Courtney Brown	DE	Browns	2003	$3,700,000	$5,383,000
Travis Hall	DE	Falcons	2003	$3,200,000	$5,378,571
Jevon Kearse	DE	Titans	2003	$4,103,500	$4,873,500
Fred Robbins	DT	Vikings	2003	$4,454,400	$4,700,650
Richard Seymour	DT/DE	**Patriots**	2003	$984,200	$2,528,200
Ty Warren	DE	**Patriots**	2003	$3,765,000	$1,265,000
Vince Wilfork	DT	**Patriots**	2004	$5,825,000	$1,241,666
Marquise Hill	DE	**Patriots**	2004	$1,380,000	$ 460,000
Jarvis Green	DE	**Patriots**	2003	$304,700	$ 386,366

Source of 2003 data: "USA Today Salaries Databases," *USA Today*,
http://asp.usatoday.com/sports/football/nfl/salaries/default.aspx?Loc=Vanity.
Source of 2004 Patriots data: www.patscap.com/capfootnotes.html.

The best approximation of the true price a team pays for a player is that player's "salary cap" figure, *i.e.*, the sum of his current salary and the prorated fraction of his signing bonus. (Ty Warren, Vince Wilfork, and Marquise Hill have high "income" but low "salary cap" figures because the year listed happens to be their rookie season. Rookies receive a large signing bonus that is prorated over the length of their contract for salary cap purposes.) The Patriots' Richard Seymour is the best defensive tackle in the entire NFL, according to a May 2004 poll of 22 NFL personnel directors,[1152] but Seymour earned only one-third of what the top defensive linemen earned in 2003 because he's still playing under his rookie contract. (Seymour is disappointed with his contract and fired his agent. His new agent, Eugene Parker, also represents Corey Simon, the defensive tackle picked #6 overall in 2000, the year before Seymour was picked #6. Simon refused to play under his existing contract but eventually relented.) Warren, Wilfork, and Hill may quickly join the ranks of the league's best linemen but will still be playing under rookie contracts that pay them only a fraction of what top defensive linemen earn. Hall of Fame coach Don Shula says NFL coaches today must engage in "coaching in a hurry"[1153] because the salary cap does not allow coaches the luxury of grooming players slowly. One way the Patriots deal with "coaching in a hurry" is by spending high draft picks on positions (like defensive line) where they can get a quick and substantial return on investment. On positions requiring substantial grooming (like offensive line and quarterback), the Patriots either sign low-priced veterans or spend time and energy developing low-round draft picks or undrafted players, saving themselves draft picks and salary.

In short, the Patriots wisely spend early-round draft picks on defensive linemen because quality defensive linemen playing under their rookie contracts provide tremendous performance-per-dollar. Also, defensive line salaries are inflating rapidly. Jevon Kearse nearly doubled his salary when he signed with the Philadelphia Eagles who are paying him $24 million over the first three seasons of his eight-year, $66 million contract.[1154] That's $8 million/season from 2004 through

2006. Grant Wistrom signed for $33 million (6 years), Cornelius Griffin $25.5 million (6 years), Robaire Smith $26.3 million (6 years), Rod Coleman $28 million (6 years), Warren Sapp $36.6 million (7 years), Bertrand Berry $25 million (5 years), *etc.*[1155] Signing Vince Wilfork to a deal worth $9 million (plus possible incentive bonuses) over six years is a tremendous bargain. Scott Pioli realizes getting productivity from young players is essential: "You always have to have an infusion of young players who can contribute to keep you in good cap shape. If you are purely a veteran team, you won't be able to have a complete team."[1156]

Sell high

The Patriots have received good value for players they no longer wanted and/or could no longer afford, like Terry Glenn, Drew Bledsoe, and Tebucky Jones. In several cases, the team insisted it would find a way to keep the player, if necessary, despite actively shopping him. Avoiding the appearance of desperation to rid themselves of unwanted players improves their bargaining power. The Patriots extracted a 1st-round draft pick for aging quarterback Drew Bledsoe, even though the Bills were bidding against themselves. That pick became defensive tackle Ty Warren. Wide receiver Terry Glenn, an unending source of discord and distraction, became 4th-round pick Asante Samuel (after the Patriots moved up eight spots in the 2003 Draft). After slapping safety Tebucky Jones with the team's "franchise player" tag (guaranteeing Jones one of the highest salaries in the league at his position), the Patriots traded him to the New Orleans Saints for their 3rd-round and 7th-round draft picks in 2003 and 4th-round pick in 2004. Instead of using the 3rd-rounder in 2003, the Patriots traded it to the Miami Dolphins for a 2nd-round pick in 2004. While other teams seeking three-time Pro Bowl running back Corey Dillon were willing to trade only a 3rd-round pick for Dillon, the Patriots used the extra 2nd-round pick from Miami to pick up a proven star who transformed the Patriots offense in 2004. The Patriots effectively traded Jones for three players:

· Saints' 2003 3rd-round » Dolphins' 2004 2nd-round » running back Corey Dillon

· Saints' 2003 7th-round » defensive end Tully Banta-Cain

· Saints' 2004 4th-round » free safety Dexter Reid

Know the market

In a 2004 NFL Draft that witnessed a record twenty-eight trades, the Patriots stunned many by not making a single draft-day trade. In every previous draft since Bill Belichick took control, the Patriots traded with seemingly reckless abandon ("16 trades involving 49 picks in the previous three drafts"[1157]). Their abrupt behavioral shift was not arbitrary, fickle, or inconsistent. Before trading away a draft pick or staying put and selecting a player, the Patriots always study their complete opportunity set (*i.e.*, all available options) and make an informed, fact-driven decision, choosing whatever option maximizes their benefit. Before the 2004 Draft, the Patriots thoroughly investigated potential trading opportunities:

> "A lot of teams that are ahead of us have talked to us about it. A lot of teams have talked to us about moving back in exchange for multiple picks. I think those will all be draft-day decisions. You only have 15 minutes on the clock so you don't want to be calling around asking: 'Do you want to make a trade?' We... have heard a lot of ideas the last few weeks and maybe we will call a team and ask them if they are still interested in something that was brought up a week ago."[1158]

On Draft Day, the team received many offers to trade their picks. Each time, though, they decided they preferred taking the player they selected: "We felt like for the most part when we were picking the value was there... We felt like the draft just kind of came to us at various selections."[1159]

The Patriots don't guess on Draft Day. Any team that relies on hunches and public information is headed for failure. No team can waste draft picks. Teams must know every potential NFL player graduating from college because building a quality team using only free agents is prohibitively expensive. In the salary cap era (where each team's aggregate annual salary is capped), making the playoffs requires finding talented but inexpensive players in the college draft. Consider, for example, the importance of Patriots left tackle Matt Light. Light's four-year rookie contract paid him $260,000 in 2001, $325,000 in 2002, $390,000 in 2003, $455,000 in 2004, plus a $1.3 million signing bonus[1160] for a four-year average of $625,000 per season. This is an incredible bargain for a starting left tackle on a two-time Super Bowl champion. Many offensive tackles around the league earn at least $5 million per season: Walter Jones (Seahawks): $7.021; Jonathan Ogden (Ravens): $6.875; Chris Samuels (Redskins): $6.714 mil; Orlando Pace (Rams): Rejected offer of $6 mil/year; Chad Clifton (Packers): $5.4 mil; Kyle Turley (Rams): $5.3 mil; Tarik Glenn (Colts): $5 mil; Wayne Gandy (Saints): $5 mil; Luke Petitgout (Giants): $5 mil; Flozell Adams (Cowboys): $5 mil.

Know your price

> "The New England Patriots are absolutely, positively not cheap. In fact, I've found them to be one of the few organizations that will step up and create extra money when needed."[1161]
>
> *— Agent Steve Feldman, after the Patriots signed his client (Rodney Harrison) who had been on the verge of signing with the Raiders*

The NFL "salary cap" imposes a long-term hard budget constraint on each team. Consequently, teams must analyze not only a player's performance but also his price tag. There is an "opportunity cost" to handing Player X a fat contract... You won't be able to afford Player Y. So, salary is very important when acquiring "free agent" players on the open market or trading for players under contract to other teams. Teams cannot avoid to be too lavish… or too cheap.

After Ted Washington anchored the Patriots defense to victory in Super Bowl XXXVIII, the Patriots let Washington walk because they weren't willing to offer a long-term contract to an aging player who had broken a leg each of the past two seasons. The Patriots offered Washington a shorter contract than the Raiders offered, frugality that led to comedy in the White House Rose Garden:

> "I'm going to be back here next year with the Raiders!" said Washington, who signed a free agent deal with Oakland in March.
> "The Raiders?" replied Bush. "What's that all about? What happened to the Pats?"
> Washington then turned and pointed to vice president of player personnel Scott Pioli, who happened to be standing nearby.
> "Blame him," said Washington.
> The exchange drew hearty laughs from Pioli and the gathered players.[1162]

Draft position is a non-cash "price," and the Patriots always avoid overpaying. In the 2003 NFL Draft, "Belichick and Pioli knew they wanted cornerback Eugene Wilson with their [second] selection. They were sitting with the No. 19 pick, but they knew Wilson would be available in the second round. So they traded out of the pick (getting Baltimore's 2003 second-round pick and their 2004 first-rounder in the process) and then maneuvered to take Wilson at No. 36. … Wilson wasn't deemed good value at 19. He was at 36."[1163] By trading down, the Patriots got a player they valued highly at a bargain price. They also saved themselves salary cap money because the value of a newly-drafted player's rookie contract declines rapidly with his draft position.

Just days before the start of the 2003 season, the Patriots waived safety Lawyer Milloy, a fan favorite, because he wouldn't accept a pay cut and the team felt Milloy's performance had slipped and no longer justified his salary. Milloy had a public reputation as a team leader, but the team was full of leaders. And Milloy's enthusiasm was apparently too shrill for some teammates and coaches. Pepper Johnson admitted "He might grate on us a little bit."[1164] Milloy played his music too loudly for some of his teammates, enjoyed making fun of others, and displayed less trust in and deference toward his coaches than his teammates.[1165] The team's post-2001 self-scouting report on Milloy said, "A negative leader sometimes… Over-aggressive, doesn't wrap up, inconsistent leadership, selfish."[1166] In 2002, Milloy's stats plummeted: zero sacks (after three in 2001); zero forced fumbles in 2001 and 2002 (after four in 2000); and zero interceptions (after 19 over his first six NFL seasons). Milloy signed with the rival Buffalo Bills who, ironically, played the Pats in the 2003 season opener just days later. After Milloy's Bills triumphed, 31-0, the media slammed Belichick for his decision, but he was (as usual) right. The Patriots not only didn't collapse but, instead, pushed forward as a team, losing only one more game the entire season and winning their second Super Bowl. In Buffalo, meanwhile, Milloy didn't catch a single interception in 2003.

Belichick's ability to make "gutsy" personnel decisions, such as trading star quarterback Drew Bledsoe to a division rival and handing the starting QB job to a 6th-round draft pick, is grounded in his (and his staff's) careful analysis of each player's capabilities, strengths, and weaknesses. Belichick did not let Bledsoe's reputation, past performance, or popularity sway his decision. Belichick compared Bledsoe's projected future performance with Brady's and concluded Brady was his QB and Bledsoe's huge salary and insistence on being a starting quarterback were unaffordable luxuries. Many New Englanders despised the trade because Bledsoe is a great guy who raised the Patriots from mediocrity to respectability. As a stunned Tom Brady accurately said, "Drew Bledsoe *was* the New England Patriots."[1167]

Belichick does not factor sentiment into his decisions. For Belichick, the only relevant question is, "What is Player X's likely future performance, and at what price?" He made the right call. Brady is now a two-time Super Bowl MVP and one of the league's best quarterbacks. Bledsoe is in the twilight of his career. In 2003, Brady was clearly the AFC East's best quarterback and "threw more touchdowns passes than [Buffalo Bills quarterback] Drew Bledsoe and [Miami Dolphins quarterback] Jay Fiedler combined with 23, and he did it with 258 fewer attempts."[1168] Bledsoe has not come close to leading his Buffalo Bills into the playoffs, and 2004 looks like his last as a starter. He continues making the kind of characteristic mistakes that so pained Belichick. Belichick's confidence that he could exploit such weaknesses in Bledsoe's game likely factored in to his decision to trade his star to a team in his own division that he plays twice a year. Again, smart move: Bledsoe is 1-5 against the Patriots, with 11 interceptions, just five touchdowns, and 211 yards/game.[1169] Bledsoe still refuses to take the easy, short completions and continues to rely on his arm to force difficult, long passes to well-covered receivers. After Bledsoe threw the Patriots four interceptions in a 27-17 Bills loss in December 2002, for example, Bledsoe said, "If I could have one back, it would be the [intercepted] throw in the end zone. I should have thrown it out of the end zone."[1170] That errant pass occurred while Bledsoe was scrambling. Belichick's defense emphasized forcing the slow Bledsoe to leave the pocket where he is most dangerous and to throw on the run. In the second Patriots-Bills game of 2004, Bledsoe recorded his worst-ever quarterback rating, a ghastly 14.3. Afterwards, Bledsoe said what Belichick probably told him repeatedly in 2000: "Just looking at the pictures (of formations), I should have thrown more (short) check-downs. They did a good job covering us down field. So I should have dropped more underneath and looked for the shorter gain."[1171]

CREATE A REWARDING WORK ENVIRONMENT

Top organizations attract top people

"To make a living is no longer enough. Work also has to make a life. This means that it will be more important than ever to make work productive. ... [Workers] expect work to provide nonmaterial psychological and social satisfactions. They do not necessarily expect work to be enjoyable but they expect it to be achieving."[1172]
– Peter Drucker, father of management science

"I've been to three Super Bowls and won two of them... It's a great organization and a great team and when you have that, sometimes you have to sacrifice a little bit of the money for something special and that's what a lot of guys here do."[1173]
– Patriots linebacker Willie McGinest

"When the guys won [the Super Bowl] again last year, I was rooting for them all the way. It's almost like, you never realize what you have until it's gone. I didn't realize how much fun I had with this coaching staff, the game planning. You really appreciate that."[1174]
– Cornerback Terrell Buckley, who played on the 2001 Patriots and the 2002 and 2003 Miami Dolphins, upon re-signing with the Patriots in June 2004

"We have people who want to come here and play here. We have people calling our organization who want to come and want to be a part of a winning (program)."[1175]
– Patriots owner Robert Kraft

For Patriots-type players, belonging to a great organization is more valuable than cash. Former Cincinnati Bengals star running back Corey Dillon was so hungry to join a winner that he accepted a substantial pay cut to be traded to New England. "Money couldn't buy me happiness anymore,"[1176] so Dillon lowered his $3.3 million salary by $1.55 million and accepted incentives instead.[1177] He agreed to base salaries of just $1.75 million in 2004 and $3.85 million in 2005. But he can earn back his salary by producing as he has in past years. Those incentives are: $100,000 for 700 rushing yards, $250,000 for 850 yards, $625,000 for 1,000 yards, $1,000,000 for 1,150, $1,375,000 for 1,300, $1,750,000 for 1,450, and $2,250,000 for 1,600+ yards.[1178] Dillon later agreed to lower his 2004 salary even further, to the veteran minimum of $660,000.[1179]

Asked why he rejoined the Patriots in June 2004, Terrell Buckley answered "Super Bowl."[1180] As VP of player personnel Scott Pioli says, "Fortunately, we have some players that are willing to make some quality-of-life decisions."[1181] Guys who love to win will make great sacrifices to play for a winner. Some former Patriots have left for the pot of gold at the other end of the free agency rainbow. But many others have sacrificed financially to play for the team they love and believe in. Consider middle linebacker Ted Johnson, a former star who has accepted both a backup role (to Tedy Bruschi) and many rounds of pay cuts:

> "Johnson, who was drafted in the second round in 1995, signed a five-year, $25 million deal in 1998. Since then, his contract has been restructured six times. He agreed to have his base salary cut down from $3.1 million to $650,000, although he still received a $1 million roster bonus in March."[1182]

Ted Johnson's not collecting paychecks. He loves playing football and must hate standing on the sideline. He has twice grabbed running backs with one arm and held on so tightly that he injured himself: tearing a pectoral muscle in December 1998 tackling Jerome "The Bus" Bettis, and rupturing a bicep in Summer 1999 tackling Kevin Faulk in practice. Guys as tough and proud as Ted Johnson seldom swallow their pride as Johnson has for the good of his team.

Is Johnson stupid for accepting pay cuts and less salary than he could receive elsewhere? Hardly. While there's nothing wrong with joining whoever offers you the most money, players like Johnson want to play with great teammates, win games, and bring happiness to fans. It's not about money. Johnson says, "The guys are such good guys and high-quality guys that it's easier to make concessions for the greater good."[1183] Winning is fun, and having fun leads to winning, said Patriots defensive lineman Richard Seymour during his 2001 rookie season: "If you play with intensity, if you play with pride, if you go out there and have fun, that's what happens. It makes it fun for everybody, Coach included."[1184]

Different people have different objectives. While some workers will switch jobs for more money, others need more than money to be "happy." Psychologist Abraham Maslow famously defined a "hierarchy of needs" and argued that human beings crave whatever helps them ascend to the next level in the hierarchy. Maslow's levels were: 1) Physiological (shelter, food); 2) Safety; 3) Love; 4) Esteem; and, 5) "Self-actualization." Most professional football players are focused on love, esteem, and/or self-actualization. They don't need money to eat or to protect themselves. Some (like Ty Law) perceive money as indicative of the love they feel from their team and as an affirmation of their self-esteem. Such players value money highly. Others (like Ted Johnson, Tedy Bruschi, Tom Brady, and Matt Light) are quite secure in feeling love and esteem (and receive these from their teammates and coaches and from belonging to a winning team), so they focus on "self-actualization" and believe that playing for a winning team and classy organization like the Patriots enables them to maximize their football potential and achieve things (like winning Super Bowls) they could not achieve while maximizing their income elsewhere. They also enjoy making fans happy, something money can't buy. Sacrificing some income to achieve "higher" life goals is not at all dumb and generally indicates a self-assured, successful individual focused on self-actualization and achieving true happiness, not the false happiness that many assume more money will give them.

Ted Johnson is motivated by chivalry and "team" more than money. After visiting the Rose Garden, where President Bush congratulated the team on their Super Bowl victory, Johnson joined six other Patriots in visiting injured soldiers at Walter Reed Medical Center. Johnson was impressed by the soldiers' optimism and concern for one another:

> "You couldn't help but be humbled by what you were seeing ... [W]e saw soldier after soldier and they were very candid about their injuries and how it happened. Most of the people we saw were amputees, and the way they talked about it, I couldn't believe how open they were about their injuries... What put me away was the spirit of the guys. One of the first people we met was walking outside for the first time (since being injured). It was a huge step and one of his fellow soldiers was helping him. You could see how protective he was of him. There's a common bond through shared experiences. It's a little like football, except football is about winning and losing, not life and death."[1185]

Johnson is also very impressed by his coach, undoubtedly another reason he has accepted lower pay and a lesser role to remain a Patriot: "[Belichick] has to be considered among the best [coaches] of all time now. I don't think there's any doubt about that now."[1186]

The Patriots offer players riches money can't buy... the biggest being a realistic chance to earn a Super Bowl ring. During the playoffs, Belichick tells players: "Nobody *hands* you a ring. I don't care how much money you have, you can't buy one."[1187] Pepper Johnson drilled this point after the Patriots won the 2001 AFC Championship Game: "How often do you see guys proudly wearing AFC Championship rings, I asked them. That's embarrassing."[1188] Players respond. Cornerback Tyrone Poole signed with the Denver Broncos before quitting football in 2001. After signing with the Patriots in 2003, Poole nearly quit again. Instead, he started opposite Ty Law and helped his new teammates win their second Super Bowl. Poole's back again in 2004, seemingly hungrier than ever after talking with his friend and three-time Super Bowl champion, Shannon Sharpe: "your goal coming into the league is to be a champion. The money will come and go, but being noted as a Super Bowl champion stays forever. [Sharpe] has three (rings) and now I look at this as an opportunity to catch up with him and pull away from the other guys who haven't had a chance."[1189]

A Super Bowl ring brings pride and prestige no amount of money can. Patriots defensive end Jarvis Green's hometown in Louisiana was thrilled by its local hero: "We have 10,000 people in my home town. ...Everybody wants to see the ring. Everybody wants to take a picture of the ring. The kids want to hold the ring. It's fun for everybody to share the experience."[1190]

Does a ring matter? Just ask former greats, like Dolphins quarterback Dan Marino, who never earned one. After John Elway's Denver Broncos lost three Super Bowls, the legendary quarterback became desperate as he neared retirement. He closed out his career by winning two Super Bowls after slashing his salary to almost nothing to maximize his team's chances: "Elway chose to restructure his contract from $4.65 million to somewhere in the neighborhood of $300,000, so the Broncos could sign more talented free agents to help them defend their title."[1191] After the Patriots defeated the heavily-favored Rams in Super Bowl XXXVI, Rams defensive tackle Tyoka Jackson admitted, "For a long time, this is going to be painful. I was really looking forward to that parade."[1192] Nearly three years later, Jackson added, "I still remember turning around and watching the ball sail through the uprights, and that confetti falling down in the wrong color. That's the memory I will always carry with me."[1193] Another Rams defensive tackle, Ryan Pickett, agrees completely: "It's the worst feeling I've ever had. I hated to lose that kind of game, that kind of way. A game that we thought we could've won and should've won."[1194]

Ask Carolina Panthers players whether losing the Super Bowl by three points matters. Defensive tackle Brentson Buckner says, "Nobody remembers second, so it's all a bust. Right now we're losers. We're one of the 31 losers in the NFL. If you don't win, it doesn't mean anything. It's painful. You can't take anything away from this except you lost the chance to be the best in the world at what you do."[1195] Receiver Ricky Proehl, on the losing end of both Patriots Super Bowl victories, once with the Rams and once with the Panthers: "Brady going down the field. The same thing–and Vinatieri kicking the field goal. When it was over, I had the sick feeling again."[1196] He also said "I will have nightmares about Adam Vinatieri for a long time."[1197]

Or you could ask veteran Patriots who suffered through many lousy seasons, like linebacker Roman Phifer who played in 168 regular season games (most with the St. Louis Rams and the New York Jets) without ever reaching the playoffs. After Phifer's 2001 Patriots not only made the playoffs but defeated the heavily-favored Rams in the Super Bowl, Phifer was an emotional wreck:

> "Oh man. I cried, dude. Really, I've never been that emotional for a game in my life. I've never cried–maybe in Pop Warner when we lost a game real bad. I grabbed my [5-year-old] son [Jordan], and I cried, and he started crying. He understood. I mean, I even asked him, 'Why are you crying?' I thought he was crying because he saw me crying. So I thought I frightened him or whatever. He said, 'I'm crying because I'm happy.' I thought, 'Wow, I didn't know a 5-year-old could cry because he was happy.'"[1198]

Even one of the toughest football players in the NFL, Patriots safety Rodney Harrison, who spent ten years in the league before winning a Super Bowl, lost control of his emotions:

> "I was in so much pain [after breaking my forearm during the game]. And all I could think about was all my previous nine years [in the NFL]. I've been playing football since I was 6 years old. All my dreams, all my hopes coming down on one kick. And I was on the sideline, and once he kicked it and it went through, I just broke down."[1199]

Even Bill Belichick, who seldom seems excited about anything, confesses to giddiness: "You're the best, and few can ever say that. Wait until you see the ring! You can count on one hand the moments that top putting that baby on."[1200]

Great people love great organizations

"There's no question players are your best recruiting tool."[1201]
– Bill Belichick

"Ask any guy in the league where he would most want to play, and this is the place. This is a franchise right now that gets it, you know, and it's a team that everyone else wants to kind of copy."
– Three-time Pro Bowl running back Corey Dillon, who joined the Patriots in 2004

"It's a wonderful place to play, to come to work each day. You're surrounded by great people, top to bottom, and I think those things come into the equation when you're making a decision on where you're going to be."[1202]
– Patriots special teams captain Larry Izzo

"The second task of management is to make work productive and the worker achieving. ...Business enterprise[s] ...are increasingly the means through which individual human beings find their livelihood, find their access to social status, to community and to individual achievement and satisfaction. ...Making the worker achieving implies consideration of the human being as an organism having peculiar physiological and psychological properties, abilities, and limitations, and a distinct mode of action. It implies consideration of the human resource as human beings and not as things, and as having–unlike any other resource–personality, citizenship, control over whether they work, how much and how well, and thus requiring responsibility, motivation, participation, satisfaction, incentives and rewards, leadership, status, and function."[1203]
– Peter Drucker, father of management science

In early 2002, NFL tight end Christian Fauria was absolutely certain the Rams would defeat the Patriots in Super Bowl XXXVI. His confidence was shattered the moment he heard the Patriots had insisted on being introduced as a team rather than one-by-one, as every previous Super Bowl participant had been introduced. Fauria suddenly realized he had ignored team chemistry:

> "The game was about to start and I was willing to bet [my father-in-law] anything the Rams would win ...[A]ll of a sudden these guys come out of the locker room together and weren't introduced. When you're a little kid you watch how each of the players comes out and everybody has their own little routine or dance. The Patriots were different and I knew right then I had lost my bet. I even tried to welsh on my father-in-law before the game started. ...Football is about more than just offense and defense. That was their moment. It was huge."[1204]

Fauria, a free agent, was so moved that he decided to become a Patriot: "I was trying to decide where I was going to play the next season but I had already made up my mind. If I had the opportunity to come [to New England], I was going to jump at it."[1205]

Fauria is hardly alone. Linebacker Roman Phifer says New England attracts veteran players sick of losing like honey lures ravenous bears:

> "The bottom line is winning. Most of the guys here–most of the veterans that come to New England like this year–they come because they want to win. They want to have a ring. And there are some guys who haven't had that kind of success. When I see [the NFL's all-time leading pass-catching fullback] Larry Centers or [Pro Bowl safety] Rodney Harrison, you know, they remind me of me when I came here in 2001. And it's like, 'Man, I'm laying my career out. I'd love to go to the playoffs or win a Super Bowl.' So here they are and I tell them, 'I thought the same way and you're in the right place.'"[1206]

Running back Corey Dillon cut his 2004 salary by $1.55 million to play in New England because he was frustrated with losing: "I needed someone to feed off of, to get energy. I couldn't feed off myself. And I just felt like, 'What's the point of sitting here, making all this money, if I wasn't happy?' I wanted to be happy as a person and a player."[1207] Dillon later slashed his salary even further, to the veteran minimum of $660,000 plus incentives, to help the Patriots' salary cap.[1208]

Special teams star Larry Izzo left the comfort of sunny Miami, where he played five seasons for the Dolphins, to join the Patriots because he wanted to win: "that was a tough decision for me... But I knew when I left that I was going to an organization that knows how to win, that Bill Belichick and Scott Pioli were building something, and I knew I wanted to be a part of that. I'm just thankful that I made the right decision."[1209]

After the Pittsburgh Steelers cut their outstanding punter, Josh Miller, many teams expressed interest in signing him. Flooded with opportunities, Miller knew exactly what he wanted… until Bill Belichick insisted on eating dinner with him: "I told my wife, 'I'm either going to be in a dome, or I'm going to be kicking in nice weather.' I come home and I said, 'I'm a Patriot.'"[1210]

As a St. Louis Ram in Super Bowl XXXVI, linebacker Don Davis personally witnessed the teamwork and solidarity that enabled the Patriots beat his Rams. Davis later joined the Patriots because he admired their professionalism:

> "The type of veterans, the type of coaching staff, the success they have had. You know you're going to be coached, you know you're going to be well-prepared and you know you're going to a team where they take away all the distractions and there's no crap. It's all football. They do a good job of getting players in here who just want to win, not players with their own individual agenda. As I'm getting older, I wanted a chance to play for another Super Bowl team. Here, there aren't different rules for different people. … They were very up front with me [about my role]. A lot of times, teams fill your head with stuff they have no obligation to fulfill."[1211]

Even before the Patriots won any Super Bowls, Bill Belichick was attracting to the Patriots hard-working players he had previously coached and who believed in him. Former Jets defensive lineman Bobby Hamilton played in all 70 Patriots games from 2000 through 2003 and started 68 of them: "I'm the only player since coach Belichick took over to never miss a game, never miss a practice. I did everything they asked. I never said a bad word."[1212] Hamilton followed Belichick to the Patriots because he trusted him:

> "I saw the guy for three years when I was with the Jets. He's organized. He has a plan. He works hard. I knew when he came to the Patriots that he was going to be a winner. Did I predict two Super Bowls in three years? No. But I knew we would win a lot. It's why I wanted to join him here in New England."[1213]

Because the Patriots are a great organization, they not only attract talented players but also convince many, though not all, of their players to extend their contracts for lower pay than they could receive elsewhere, as left tackle Matt Light explains:

> "Some guys want to be the highest-paid player at their position. Some say, 'I want to get a respectable amount but I don't care to break the bank.' And then you have some guys who do whatever it takes to stay on this team. There are different philosophies."[1214]

A few months after saying that, Light proved he wasn't out for every last buck. One of the league's better left tackles, Light gave up his chance to score a massive free agent payday after the 2004 season and instead re-signed with the Patriots for millions less than he could have earned elsewhere. Light's agent says his client's love of New England left him no leverage: "The simple fact is, he didn't want to leave. The Patriots have a way of doing that sometimes. They do a good job of maintaining continuity."[1215] Hearing that news, Patriots kicker Adam Vinatieri said, "I can see why he wanted to stay. There are a lot of great guys in here."[1216]

The Patriots are a favorite free agent destination because even former Patriots spread good news about the team. When veteran defensive lineman Keith Traylor was considering an offer from the Patriots, his former Bears teammate Ted Washington (who had recently joined the Oakland Raiders for more money than the Patriots had offered) told Traylor he would love the Patriots. When fellow defensive lineman Bobby Hamilton followed Ted Washington to the Raiders, also because the Patriots would not pay him what he wanted, Hamilton also said great things about his about his experience:

> "They wanted to get younger and you can't complain about that. I had four wonderful years there. They gave me the opportunity to show everybody what I was about after the Jets wouldn't. They showed me how to compete and how to win. How can you be mad about that? ...I loved my time with the Patriots. I loved my teammates and I loved the fans most of all. I'll miss them."[1217]

Former Miami Dolphins starting quarterback Damon Huard fell to third on the Patriots depth chart behind Bledsoe and Brady and never played a game for the Patriots, who decided in early 2004 not to re-sign him. Bitter feelings? Resentment? Hostility? Hardly:

> "Overall, it was a great experience. I would have loved to have played, but it was a great team with great coaches, great teammates, and there were so many positives that by no means am I bitter. It was too good of an experience not to come away with positive feelings"[1218]

Former Patriots center Damien Woody, who left after the Detroit Lions begged him to accept their $31 million offer, has only positive comments about the Patriots:

> "I didn't have any hard feelings. Not at all. We had a disagreement on terms. That's all. The heart and soul of that team is the middle-class player, so when I became a free-agent, I figured they probably wouldn't offer me as much as other teams would. To me, this is the American way. ...The thing I like about Bill is he was straight up with me through the whole process."[1219]

Even punter Ken Walter, who was released in the middle of the 2003 season, re-signed a week later, and permanently released after the Super Bowl, took time to give tons of advice to his replacement, former Steelers punter Josh Miller: "He told me everything, the ups and downs and what it's all about. Told me how to deal with Adam [Vinatieri], how to deal with Lon [Paxton]."[1220]

Many teams and firms overemphasize money. What the best employees want most is respect, growth opportunities, empowerment, collegial colleagues, challenges, trust, a plan for winning, *etc.*, in other words... a great work environment. Though "high performance work organizations" raise both worker productivity and employee satisfaction, most firms are overly bureaucratic. Having built a "high performance work organization," the Patriots now attract and retain talented free agents and pay below-market rates for that talent. Also, because their system generates a consistent "profit" (wins), Patriots fans, owners, and reporters are a trusting corporate board: they seldom second-guess their "CEO," leaving him (and his staff) free to decide personnel matters without worrying about public perception.

Chapter 7

MENTALITY

"They play well for 60 minutes. They don't let up at 58 minutes or 59 minutes."[1221]
   – Indianapolis Colts quarterback Peyton Manning on the Patriots

"We [get] in some situations, man, but we come through."[1222]
   – Patriots running back Corey Dillon

"We won one game fifteen times in a row."[1223]
   – Bill Belichick, after winning Super Bowl XXXVIII

Since December 24, 2000, Belichick's Patriots have led thirty-two games at the end of the third quarter. They won all thirty-two of those games. 32-0! They also won two of three games that were tied after three quarters and snatched victory from the jaws of defeat in four more games they were losing at the end of the third quarter.[1224] In a league where 48.4% of games in 2003 were decided by seven points or less,[1225] the Patriots' mental edge translates into victories.

The Patriots' ability to hold a lead and to come from behind to win games derives from mental preparation and exceptional physical conditioning, both Belichick trademarks. CBS analyst and former Super Bowl-winning Giants quarterback Phil Simms says, "It's like they just wear other teams out. It's like their opponents eventually just say, 'Hey, OK, here, you can take it.'"[1226] Patriots tight end Christian Fauria says: "It's kind of like a boxer. He gets in the ring, not really sure what he can do. The guy gives him his best punches, and he's like, 'I can stand up to this guy. Let me do my thing.' Nobody ever panics."[1227]

Patriots are mentally tougher than average NFL players because toughness is a top criterion in personnel decisions and because the Patriots' tough guys push one another to be even tougher. Patriots embrace physicality and take pride in self-discipline and grittiness. Mental strength helps Patriots overcome disappointments, push past pain and weariness during rough-and-tumble games, and relentlessly challenge one another to grow and improve throughout the season and offseason.

This chapter details the sources of the Patriots' mental strength.

"THE SHORT TERM IS WHAT IT'S ALL ABOUT"

"We weren't thinking Super Bowl [in early 2001]. We were thinking, 'Let's win a game.'"[1228]
   – Bill Belichick

"What streak? We're just trying to win a game."[1229]
— Bill Belichick, on the team's 17-game winning streak

"I'm just sick of talking about the streak. When people ask, I change the subject."[1230]
— Patriots tight end Christian Fauria

Bill Belichick preaches that "The short term is what it's all about."[1231] Patriots players know they can't win Week 9's game in Week 6, they can't clinch a playoff spot in Week 6, and they can't win the Super Bowl in Week 6. All they can do in Week 6 is everything possible to win their Week 6 game, so that's what they focus on. Belichick believes instilling a sense of urgency in his players is essential. He agrees more with R.E.M. ("The only thing to fear is fearlessness") than FDR ("The only thing we have to fear is fear itself"). When the 2002 Patriots were struggling following a 2001 Super Bowl season, several players told the media they needed to recapture their swagger. Belichick disagreed epithetically: "We didn't have a 'swagger' last year. What we had was a sense of urgency about playing well, being smart, and capitalizing on every opportunity and situation that came our way. ...It wasn't about a f----- swagger. You can take that swagger and shove it right up your a--."[1232]

Live in the present

"We've experienced the success we've experienced by... not focusing on the big picture but [instead] focusing on what's in front of [us]."[1233]
— Patriots linebacker Tedy Bruschi

"You just have to win one game a week."[1234]
— Tom Brady

The Patriots are neither historians nor futurists. "Right now" permeates every aspect of Bill Belichick's coaching. As obvious as staying focused on the present sounds, players and teams often lose sight of the here-and-now, instead worrying about events beyond their current control.

Most NFL coaches preach "one game at a time," but the entire Patriots organization lives and breathes what many consider a trite platitude. Every game is the most important of the Patriots' season because players and coaches adopt a *Crosby, Stills & Nash* mindset: "if you can't be with the one you love, love the one you're with." Explains Belichick:

"What matters to me is... what we can do this week. We're playing one game [this week]. The ones that we have played don't matter. The ones down the road, that will all take care of itself in due time. There's nothing we can do about any of those right now. …It doesn't really get any bigger than than this."[1235]

Each week, players study and prepare diligently for their upcoming opponent. After winning 14 consecutive games, Patriots middle linebacker Tedy Bruschi didn't view the accomplishment as "a streak." He corrected a reporter before the Super Bowl: "It's all about attitude. *You* say 14 straight. We say one straight."[1236] After the win, Bruschi insisted, "We didn't win 15 in a row, we won one in a row 15 times."[1237] Tom Brady made the obvious, but profound, comment that "You can't win all those games in one week."[1238]

As the Patriots prepared for their 17th-consecutive victory, there must have been lots of excitement about being tantalizingly close to the all-time record, right? Adam Vinatieri: "Honestly, no. There really isn't. Coach Belichick is pretty good at nipping that really quick before anybody talks about that stuff. One game at a time, and it's a long season."[1239] Safety Rodney Harrison actually beat Belichick at his game of pithy, apparently meaningless tautologies when he said, "Last year's last year."[1240] Though the Patriots had won the championship game of the 2003 season and their 2004 season opener, the only "streak" Bill Belichick admitted to was the Patriots' three-game preseason losing streak. Players like linebacker Willie McGinest love their coach's logic: "The streak was last year."[1241] The next week, before facing the Buffalo Bills, Belichick said, "a streak of one division win is what I'm looking for."[1242] Not until the Patriots broke the NFL-record 18-game winning streak did Belichick even acknowledge the streak. He says he "told the team they should be proud of what they accomplished, something that no other team in pro football has done."[1243] Players followed their coach's lead: "Him acknowledging it, I think that gives us a little green light to acknowledge it a little bit–but, at the same time, not to dwell on it, to get ready for next week."[1244] Linebacker Mike Vrabel says players celebrated their collective achievement in the locker room: "Bill acknowledged it. Everybody kind of shook each other's hands. And we clapped. For each other."[1245]

The Patriots have a philosophy more valuable than "one game at a time." They train and perform "one day at a time" and even "one play at a time" because, as Belichick says, "Football is a lot of short-term goals"[1246] and "Each play is a game within itself."[1247] A Patriot player told Phil Simms that his teammates "don't think about winning and losing; they just keep playing hard."[1248] Looking ahead is useless because you can't win two games at once… let alone fifteen. Even if you could, the objective is not fifteen straight. The objective is winning a championship. And the best way to win a championship is to always focus on winning your upcoming game. After winning 14 in a row to earn a spot in Super Bowl XXXVIII, Brady pointed out, "To win 14 in a row, that's unbelievable. Still, the goal really hasn't been achieved. Winning 14 in a row is great, but if there's not a 15th, then it's all for naught."[1249] After winning 17 straight, linebacker Tedy Bruschi said, "You try not to focus on things you did last year. You move on and realize that we've won two games this year and try to make it three."[1250] After winning 19 straight, Bruschi said, "The formula for how we got here was simple: focusing on practices, focusing on opponents, step by step."[1251]

Bill Belichick keeps himself, his coaches, and his players focused on their upcoming game. He looks ahead only during the preseason, when everything Belichick does is preparation for the first meaningful game: "Right now, I'm thinking about this week's game and the opener against Indianapolis. That's long-term for me."[1252]

Don't look backwards

"If you look back instead of forward, people are going to track you down and beat you. Then we'll all feel like crap."[1253]
– *Tom Brady*

"I'm not answering any more questions about winning a world championship. We don't care about last year. It's this year and that's what we are focused on. We are not going to be complacent and we are not going to be content. It's all about what are we going to do this year."[1254]
– *Patriots safety Rodney Harrison*

No matter how your team performed last season, on opening day, every team has zero wins and zero losses. And, no matter how your team performed last week or what your opponent's record is, at kickoff the score is 0-0 and winning requires outscoring your opponent over the next sixty minutes. Nothing else matters. Patriots defensive lineman Richard Seymour: "The past is the past. It's all about what have you done for me lately and what can you do for me now? [Our opponent's] past history and our past history doesn't matter."[1255] With the team's winning streak at 18 games, Tom Brady said any Patriot dwelling on the team's streak was inviting trouble: "Anyone who is thinking about last year or our first three games is not doing this team any justice and doesn't deserve a spot in this locker room if (they) start thinking about stuff that makes absolutely no difference in a game."[1256]

The same holds true even for a team entering the 2003 AFC Championship Game on a 13-game winning streak, as Belichick soberly reminded his players. He warned that if they played against Indianapolis as they had in their first playoff win against Tennessee that their season would be over.

Belichick says, "We're not really in the reflection business."[1257] The Patriots seldom look backwards, even during the offseason, because they know how meaningless the past is to winning their next game. Just days after winning Super Bowl XXXVIII, wide receiver David Patten skipped the victory parade and instead hit the team's gym at 6:30 a.m. because "Those things are fine, but I don't get caught up in them. I don't really need that."[1258] Backup quarterback Rohan Davey missed the White House visit because he was busy leading the Berlin Thunder in NFL Europe. Was he disappointed?

"I'm not missing anything. We win another championship in a year or two and I'll get to visit the White House then… Right now, I'd rather be here getting the experience that it takes to become a quarterback rather than visiting Bush. It would have been a good experience but this is the kind of experience I need right now."[1259]

Bill Belichick celebrated the Patriots' first-ever Super Bowl victory in 2002, but not for long: "Because of the playoffs and Super Bowl, we are a month behind in preparation. We have to find a way to squeeze four months (of preparation) into three months. It's going to be difficult."[1260] Asked in 2004 whether he had taken time to reflect on his team's achievements, Belichick said "We had a parade last year, you may have seen that one, so we took care of it then,"[1261] as if Super Bowl victory parades are necessary evils, like Kiwanis Club or Rotary Club speeches that keep Bob Kraft and the Patriots' public relations staff off his back.

Have Patriots players watched the slick *3 Games to Glory II* double-DVD set commemorating their 2003 season? Few players have watched it even once!

· Tom Brady: "Haven't watched it. I know the outcome."

· Ty Warren: "It's still in the wrapper."

· Matt Light: "I've never seen any of either one."

· Mike Vrabel: "I got a lot going on. That's a lot of time for me to sit. I could watch golf for that long, but no I haven't watched it."

· Rodney Harrison: "After it was all over and done with I wanted to leave it like that and I want to stay focused and not become complacent. My goal is to go back."

· Adam Vinatieri: "Maybe in 15 years when my kids start talking to me, I'll tell them to sit down and I'll show them a few things when I'm old, fat and gray."[1262]

Patriots center Dan Koppen refuses even to utter the word "Super Bowl": "I don't say [Super Bowl] any more."[1263]

It's easy to get trapped by the trappings of success. But Patriots know that reminiscing about past glory distracts and demotivates. Winners stay hungry and humble. Linebacker Mike Vrabel was flabbergasted just to be asked how history would judge his Patriots team:

"History? That's not a factor around here. The only history I worry about is what I did on the last play. And 30 seconds later, that's a memory, too. Uh-uh. I'll worry about history when I'm sitting in a rocker somewhere."[1264]

The message is so clear in the clubhouse that new Patriots catch on immediately. Before running back Corey Dillon returned to Cincinnati to play his former Bengals teammates, he swore "It's just another preseason game… I'm serious when I say this... [I]t's really not a big deal. I'm a Patriot now. I'm with my new teammates, and we're jelling. I'm as happy as ever. I'm not even trying to look back."[1265] Because Dillon was, for many years, the Bengals' only star, he was inundated with questions about his feelings about returning to Cincinnati and whether he holds grudges. Dillon said all the right (*i.e.*, unprovocative) things, prompting reporter Geoff Hobson to credit "the old, 'I-have-nothing-bad-to-say-let's-move-on-and-it's-just another game' cue card straight from Bill Belichick Non-Productions."[1266] In fact, Dillon maturely apologized to Bengals offensive lineman Willie Anderson, with whom he had earlier had a public spat, even though Anderson had started the spat: "I said what I said out of frustration for that last ball game and [Corey] had to respond to it."[1267] They wound up joking around, Dillon saying the Patriots planned to line him up in a pass-rushing role opposite Anderson.

Even Mrs. Deb Belichick illustrates this point. After living through years of journalists attacking and ridiculing her husband, Deb was asked, following her husband's first Super Bowl victory, whether the win was "a little revenge for what happened in Cleveland?" Her reply: "We are so past that!"[1268]

Don't worry about the day after tomorrow

Fans may daydream about hypothetical playoff scenarios: "We're better off losing this week but winning next week than winning this week and losing next week." But if Patriots ever waste time fantasizing about the future, they keep such thoughts private. Belichick has drilled into each player's skull the pointlessness of looking beyond his sphere of control.

Belichick embraces the advice of management guru Peter Drucker who says worrying about the future is productive only insofar as the shadow of the future impacts current decisions and actions:

> "Strategic planning does not deal with future decisions. It deals with the futurity of present decisions. Decisions exist only in the present. The question that faces the strategic decision-maker is not what his organization should do tomorrow. It is, 'What do we have to do today to be ready for an uncertain tomorrow?' ...There are plans that lead to action today–and they are true plans, true strategic decisions. And there are plans that talk about action tomorrow–they are dreams."[1269]

Daily improvement

"I don't think you go from the bottom of the mountain to the top in one week. It's little incremental [improvements]."[1270]
– Bill Belichick

"I always keep a positive outlook and I'm thankful for every day I wake up. It's another chance for me to show, in a football sense, what I can do. It's another opportunity to get better."[1271]
    – *Patriots linebacker/special teamer Tully Banta-Cain*

"There's so much to learn in this game. You work to get better. You never can be too good at run blocking or pass blocking or with your mental game."[1272]
    – *Patriots center Dan Koppen*

"Unless [Brady]'s completing 100 percent of his balls, he's not going to be complacent."[1273]
    – *Patriots wide receiver David Givens*

Former Giants legend Lawrence Taylor redefined the position of linebacker. Asked why Bill Parcells' teams so often beat him, Hall of Fame coach Joe Gibbs replied, "Lawrence Taylor. Lawrence Taylor. Lawrence Taylor."[1274] Taylor was so physically gifted that he could spend all week doing cocaine and God-only-knows-what-else and then show up, without practice, and win that Sunday's football game for the Giants. But there has only ever been one Lawrence Taylor. Unless you happen to be a completely dominating physical freak of nature like Taylor, you can't just show up and make 325-pound NFL offensive linemen look like girlie men. You must prepare–constantly and intensely–just to play competitively each week. Belichick points to Brady as Exhibit A: "He's gone from as low as you can go in the National Football League to a two-time Super Bowl winner. It was made in gradual steps, like going up a flight of stairs, with very few setbacks."[1275] Former Patriots quarterback Drew Bledsoe says Brady is always improving himself:

"[Brady] has worked so hard to be where he is. He has put on a ton of weight. He is a much stronger, bigger guy now than he was. When he was a rookie, and early in that second year, he was a guy who was always paying attention whenever anything was happening. ...He was a guy who very early on I sensed would be around for a long time, just because of his attitude and his work ethic."[1276]

After Brady played an especially impressive game, Patriots left tackle Matt Light said "[Tom]'s going to take this game and he's going to find 100 things he didn't like. That's the kind of guy he is. He's always pushing himself."[1277] Former Saints GM Randy Mueller, who had zero interest in Brady after scrutinizing his college career, is astounded by Brady's never-ending improvement:

"He has improved his skills light years, even from the first Super Bowl win. That doesn't happen. But it has with him. He could have sat back after the first ring, but it was like he went back to the drawing board and said, 'I am going to keep doing what I am doing, but even better.' He has improved his arm strength, his fundamentals. Before now, he's gotten most of his credit for the way he manages the game. But that isn't appropriate anymore. Now he is a playmaker. He is not afraid to take chances."[1278]

Now that Brady's name appears so frequently in sentences alongside "Joe Montana," he's finally satisfied, right? "Oh, man, where do I start? There's so many things that I'd like to improve on."[1279] Brady can even be disappointed at himself following a nice pass completion: "If there was [potential for] a 10-yard completion or a 20-yard completion and you threw the 10-yard completion when you should have thrown the 20-yard completion, then that's 10 yards you left on the field."[1280] Tom Brady was even disappointed after completing a 48-yard pass on 3rd-and-7 to Bethel Johnson that sealed a victory over the Seattle Seahawks. Because Johnson is the fastest Patriot and one of the fastest players in the NFL, Belichick says "we always tell Tom [to] just throw it out there as far as you can and make him run for it. He can't overthrow [Johnson, but] he almost did."[1281] After Johnson leapt in the air and made a spectacular stretched-out catch, Brady was less than thrilled with his throw: "I wish I led him less and let him walk into the end zone but I'll take it."[1282] Safety Rodney Harrison offers insight into what drives Brady (and the rest of the team after finishing 2003 with a 15-game winning streak): "he is smart enough to understand that the more he achieves, the more people want him to fail. So he needs to do everything he can to keep getting better."[1283]

Surely three-time Pro Bowl running back Corey Dillon, who has rushed for over 8,500 yards in the NFL, is an old dog who knows all the tricks, right? The Seattle Seahawks were startled by the guy who showed up wearing the "Dillon" shirt:

> "Many of Dillon's runs were on cutback plays, where the offensive line would block one direction, and the running back would cut the other. 'He's a good cutback runner,' Seahawks linebacker Isaiah Kacyvenski said, 'and he didn't show that on film at all.'"[1284]

A Chinese proverb says, "You can't become fat in one bite." The Patriots hold the same philosophy regarding talent development. After the Patriots defensive line played brilliantly against the Rams in 2004, Jarvis Green said, "I think we can still get better... That's the goal for us every week."[1285] Players strive for constant, year-round, incremental improvement, as Belichick stated during spring rookie camp:

> "What we want to try to do, and I think what each player's goal should be, is to maximize his potential, to put everything into it to give himself the best chance and to get as much out of it as he possibly can in the experience. Where that leads and what happens within that, a lot of things affect it. Right now that is the main goal. Not about what somebody did last year or even about where they are going to be in November but actually what they can do today and tomorrow and Sunday and where they can be when they leave here and what they need to do when they come back."[1286]

Every Patriot strives to make each day count. Patriots receiver David Patten says "I feel I could do so much more, do so much better."[1287] Raves Patriots left tackle Matt Light, "look around at this team now. The one thing that stands out is the fact you have 53 guys who want to get after it every day."[1288]

Linebacker Tedy Bruschi is a great example. As a rookie, Bruschi worked hard to carve out a niche role for himself. Ever since, he has persistently carved out increasingly larger roles until he not-so-suddenly emerged as a bona fide star, an incremental process Bruschi says parallels the Patriots' 2003 Super Bowl season:

> "When I look at my career, it was a lot like the approach we've taken as a team this year, a step-by-step process. I came in at 6-1, 245. I wasn't going to play defensive end in the NFL, but I had to show I could play football. I was lucky to make myself a role and then it was all about showing progress, consistently getting better, taking that next step."[1289]

Players who demonstrate potential to grow are more likely to make the Patriots' roster. No one expected undrafted LSU cornerback Randall Gay to make the team in 2004, but he did. One likely reason: He loves criticism. "If a coach is getting on me, I take it as a lesson that he's trying to make me better. I never get down about it."[1290] Another reason: Gay is smart and inquisitive. Belichick says "he's picking [our system] up quickly."[1291] Star cornerback Ty Law says "He's eager to learn"[1292] and "Randall pays attention and asks some good questions. It's not like, 'Will you shut up?'"[1293] (Law confesses he himself was so brash and obnoxious as a rookie that "I might have told myself to shut up."[1294])

Before he tore his Achilles' tendon and was lost for the 2004 season, first-year Patriot defensive lineman Rodney Bailey (formerly of the Pittsburgh Steelers) said Patriots players take preparation to another level:

> "Everyone puts their nose to the grindstone. They have blinders on and they work constantly. Not saying that doesn't go on anywhere else, but since I've been here I've watched and learned from a lot of different people and seeing the attention to detail has been a tremendous boost to me to see people working that way."[1295]

Belichick demands daily improvement from himself too. He knows he's not perfect and seeks to perform better by learning from his mistakes. After the Bills crushed the Patriots on opening day 2003, Belichick accepted personal blame and immediately committed to improving: "I'll be the first to admit it. I made some mistakes. As many as anybody. My job is to look at the mistakes, try to correct them and not make them again."[1296] Confessing to fallibility is nothing new for Belichick. He admitted to excessively micromanaging the Browns: "I've definitely delegated more [with the Patriots]. There are other things I need to concentrate on. I'm kind of a detail-oriented person and I probably had a tendency to do too much."[1297] Likewise, he realized that he needlessly relied on dramatic stunts to convey to players his disappointment and anger:

> "I think I've mellowed since then. ...When I look back at some of the things we did as coaches on those Giants teams, we went too far... There were times when during meetings we would take cannisters of film and throw them across the room, to make sure the players knew we were upset. That was unnecessary."[1298]

Belichick has been observing and analyzing football coaches ever since he was five or six. Former Navy coach Rick Forzano, who knew "Billy" at Navy and later hired him as an assistant coach on his Detroit Lions staff, says of young Billy: "he was always observing, and he'd go back to his room and make a list of ideas to bring to the staff. He knew his place because he was so young, but he was so observant of everybody."[1299] So he possesses perspective that enables him to scrutinize his own performance.

After each season, Patriots coaches and executives study the past season with a critical eye to identify weaknesses and areas of potential improvement:

> "[We look back at] not just the last game, the last two or the last three but it's a look back at the whole season. We'll evaluate performance trends and figure which ones we want to improve or modify and that'll be in full swing when the coaches come back [after attending the NFL Combine]. We'll try not to leave any stone unturned in trying to improve before next year."[1300]

Belichick is never satisfied. After his team won its first Super Bowl, Belichick was dissatisfied with the offense, defense, and special teams:

> "Offensively, we need to put a few more points on the board. ...Defensively, we probably gave up too many yards last year. Even though we were good in the red area and on third downs, we didn't give up a lot of points but the yardage and the amount of time our defense was on the field was more than we would like it to be. In the kicking game, our No. 1 target will be kickoff returns. We were poor in that area."[1301]

Belichick also appreciated that standing pat with the team that won the Super Bowl would not likely bring another Super Bowl victory: "We've spent quite a bit of time trying to keep pace with the rest of the league because everybody is improving."[1302] He embodies the song by *Rush*: "He doesn't worry about yesterday, knows constant change is here to stay."

It's a profession, not a seasonal hobby

> "It seems like the only time we had to really step back and take a break was right after the Super Bowl. Then it was right back to work and you kind of

lose track. Plus, part of what makes coach Belichick so good is he keeps you focused on what's right in front of you."[1303]
– Patriots fullback/linebacker/defensive lineman Dan Klecko

"[David Givens'] first year was long and clanky, with every [ball] making that oh-so-familiar clank of pigskin rifling off of shoulder pads. But Givens worked on that in the offseason, catching hundreds of balls in rapid-fire succession from the Jugs machine."[1304]

Winning as many games as possible requires that players exert intense effort not merely during the sixteen to nineteen meaningful games an NFL team plays each season but also on each of the 346 to 349 non-game preparation days each year. Patriots players and coaches set short-term goals and objectives throughout the off-season, as well as the regular season, and constantly strive to build a solid foundation for success. Many NFL players give their all on game days yet underachieve because they prepare poorly during the off-season. It's easy to push hard from September through January. What separates winners from losers is pushing hard from February through August. Which players train year-round like professional athletes and which succumb to couch potato-itis?

To outplay your opponent in today's NFL, simply playing games intensely is not enough. You must practice intensely and effectively. Training intensely and effectively requires arriving at training camp in shape because, as Belichick notes, "You don't have 21 other people [unless you're participating in training camp]. You're not getting coverage reads. You're not seeing fronts. You're not seeing the adjustments. There is just no way to simulate it."[1305] Professionals arrive at camp in shape. Getting in shape is remedial work. If you waste training camp riding stationary bikes and treadmills, you're in trouble because you're not learning new plays, improving your technique, practicing under simulated game conditions, and advising rookies. And excelling requires more than being in shape. Patriots tight end Daniel Graham is having an outstanding 2004 after deciding after the 2003 season that "I wanted to work harder in the off-season, to get more film in, to do things I needed to do to get better."[1306] And Tom Brady notices Graham isn't dropping passes he dropped as a rookie: "you throw it to him and he catches it."[1307] Graham is thrilled: "All the hard work I put in the off-season has paid off."[1308]

A seasoned Tedy Bruschi now advises players at his alma mater, the University of Arizona, that winning football requires tough off-season workouts and dedication, even when coaches and fans aren't watching:

"The work isn't just going to be done in summer camp when the players report a few weeks before the season starts. ...If they haven't started working by now [February] for next year, it is too late. ...it is more important what they do this summer, this summer when it is not expected of them, when they are not expected to be in the workouts. It is important to see what they do when the eyes are not on them. Are they going to take it upon themselves to say 'I'm going to be here four days a week, five days a week and train as hard as I can.'"[1309]

Tom Brady aims to squeeze maximal improvement out of each day. He pressures himself to improve even during training months before the start of real competition: "[Y]ou really have to take advantage of every practice. Because you only have so many days to prepare… Over the course of a long season and a long training camp, the important thing is to just focus on the short-term goals."[1310]

Seeing stars like Brady busting their butts during the "off-season" inspires everyone to admire and emulate their work ethic. Says special teams captain Larry Izzo:

"[Brady] works as seriously as anybody out here. He's here at seven in the morning throughout the off-season… throwing the ball, running. He works like he's a sixth-round draft pick out of Michigan still, not the Super Bowl MVP. And that's good. When you see a guy like that–a leader of your football team–doing all the hard stuff the hard way, [it generates] a level of respect from everybody in the locker room."[1311]

Since taking over, Belichick has aggressively "encouraged" players to work out together in Foxboro during the offseason where players push one another and coaches and trainers advise and motivate players. Competition threatens the jobs of players who don't train hard year-round:

"They need to understand how important it is to their development. If we thought the best place to train was somewhere else, we'd hold it somewhere else. We're trying to specifically improve their skill level. The players who attend will gain too much of an advantage over the one's who don't. And eventually they'll push them out."[1312]

After winning their first Super Bowl in February 2002, many Patriots were distracted during the 2002 off-season, a significant factor in their narrowly missing out on the playoffs the following season. (They lost on the third tie-breaker after going 9-7.) Angry Patriots rededicated themselves to hard work in early 2003 to prepare for the fall 2003 season (that culminated in the team's second Super Bowl win):

"turnout for the so-called voluntary program is outstanding and features newcomers like Rosevelt Colvin and Rodney Harrison, the latter who rarely attends such programs. 'This is the second offseason program I'm participating in,' Harrison, who is entering his 10th season, said. 'Normally I would stay back home in Chicago or Atlanta and train there.'"[1313]

Inside linebacker Tedy Bruschi was blown away by the participation: "the 8:30 running group was absolutely huge. We were stretched all the way across the field from sideline to sideline. So it's nice to see mostly the whole team here."[1314] Such dedication builds camaraderie and a sense of togetherness that can pay giant dividends months later:

> "I think [the] most important [value of off-season workouts] is being around all your buddies, being around all of the guys that you are going to play with. When you are out there running and you got 10 other guys with you... and everyone is sweating together and everyone is going 'this sucks' or you're cussing out your strength coach, that's what it's all about, the camaraderie. And so, [you can draw on that shared experience] when... it's third-and-two and you're looking at the same guys in the huddle, you say 'hey it's really time to do it.'"[1315]

In the 2004 off-season, veterans like Roman Phifer pushed younger players by letting them know how quickly and painfully the Patriots crashed-and-burned following their first Super Bowl triumph:

> "We went through that in '01 and it wasn't a good feeling not making the playoffs after winning the Super Bowl. We're aware of that and more in tune with not letting that happen again. Everyone's trying to keep a tight focus and Coach Belichick has emphasized that."[1316]

Patriots players aren't just going through the motions. Everyone has either experienced or heard first-hand, as Bruschi puts it, that the off-season and training camp is the "time to do the things that will get us through a 16-game season"[1317] and, as Patriots fullback Fred McCrary said, "It's important we improve every day and that every day we are getting something out of practice."[1318] Rookies quickly sense the intensity of Patriots practices. According to running back Cedric Cobbs, "Practice with New England has been good but tough. I can see why they're the best–it's three times harder than college. Coach Belichick and Coach Weis are all business–no fun and games here."[1319]

EXPECTATIONS

"Past performance is no guarantee of future results"

> "If you want to make history, then you've actually got to forget about history."[1320]
> – Patriots defensive lineman Richard Seymour

Worrying about the past–or glorying in it–serves no purpose. Was Patriots safety Rodney Harrison excited by his team's 14-game winning streak? "I kind of forgot about it. We understand there is a streak, but we're out here to win the [Super Bowl], regardless of what we've done the past 15 or 16 weeks."[1321] Before the 2004 season, Harrison wouldn't even admit his Patriots had won 15 straight: "Ted Washington's not here, Bobby Hamilton's not here, it's not even the same team. There's no such thing as the streak to me. We're 0-0."[1322]

Asked by the media "How much does the fact that [the 2003] season ended on such a successful note [help]?" Belichick answered:

> "We haven't played anybody, we haven't won a game, and we haven't scored a point. I don't know what we have. I don't know what anybody else has. We are just trying to get it ready for the point when we start competing against them. But we haven't done anything. ...I don't think you can worry too much about how many games you won or didn't win [last season] or how productive one part of your team was or wasn't. All of that is going to be reevaluated on a whole new basis the following year so you are always starting from scratch no matter what your results were the year before. You are starting from scratch and you are trying to build it to the highest level you can."[1323]

Living and breathing "one game at a time" was, not coincidentally, a key to the success of the Miami Dolphins who went 17-0 in 1972 and 15-2 1973. Explains former Dolphins coach Don Shula:

> "You can't get caught up in thinking that it's a streak. Just one more game to win. I used to get all over the team's butt when I thought that kind of thinking was seeping in. After games, I would find one or two things I didn't like and hammer them on it. I remember one time I was ranting and raving and Csonka said to [Jim] Kiick, 'Shula is crazy. You'd think we'd lost the game.'"[1324]

It took Bill Belichick just hours after winning Super Bowl XXXVIII to note that the 2004 season had begun and that "everyone is 0-0."[1325] On the opening day of training camp in August, every Patriot was saying it. Wide receiver Troy Brown said, "Everybody in the league is 0-0 right now, man."[1326] Each player had his slight variation on the theme.

The Patriots know their winning streak won't help them win their next game... but dwelling on it might help them kill it. So they ignore the streak and focus on the next game: "Bill is doing the right thing, not thinking or talking about the streak, and always focusing on the next game. The minute you think two games down the road, you're not going to be there [in the Super Bowl] at the end."[1327]

"Predictions are bullshit"

"If we listened to the experts, we shouldn't have even bothered showing up."[1328]
> — *Patriots linebacker Willie McGinest, after the Patriots stunned the St. Louis Rams in Super Bowl XXXVI in February 2002*

"A lot of bookies are probably pretty mad at us right now, but we don't give a damn. We're the champs!"[1329]
> — *Patriots cornerback Ty Law, after Super Bowl XXXVI in February 2002*

"Don't let other people tell you what you're capable of. As long as you believe in yourself and work hard to achieve whatever you set your mind to, you just keep plugging away. It may not be up to your timetable, but you can get it done."[1330]
> — *Tom Brady, after winning his first Super Bowl*

"There have been people hating on me since I've been in the league. Everybody is entitled to their opinion. I just use it as steppingstones. When they doubt me, that fuels me."[1331]
> — *Patriots wide receiver David Patten*

"We know what kind of team we are so we don't need anybody else to tell us how good we are. ...When [you] hear people say, 'You're not going to do this' and start listening to the so-called experts then you'll start believing it. The same goes for when people tell you you're this good. Pretty soon you'll start believing that and you'll think you're better than what you really are."[1332]
> — *Patriots cornerback Ty Law*

After winning his first Super Bowl, Tom Brady said, "Believe in yourself. Only you know what you are capable of. No one else does."[1333] A corollary to "one day at a time" is "predictions are bullshit" ...or, less profanely, "don't let other people define you." If you work as hard as possible, whether the media or fans expect you to win one game or fifteen is irrelevant. What matters is going out and doing everything you can to win each week's game. What journalists write and fans say is irrelevant. Odds posted by Vegas bookmakers are irrelevant. The only thing that matters is what happens on the field every week.

Patriots inside linebackers coach Pepper Johnson says the Patriots' 5-11 season in 2000 resulted partly from self-fulfilling low expectations:

> "guys came in with their expectations already low, especially after reading all the media predictions and listening to the barrage of negatives that went with them. That's the time when the leaders are supposed to step up, take the

initiative, and tell everyone that the predictions are bullshit. If they don't, everyone else will fold up. The young soldiers are too weak. They look up to the veterans who have been there, done that, and seen it all."[1334]

In the 2001 playoffs, Vegas predicted the Oakland Raiders would defeat the Patriots. After the Patriots won, Vegas said the Pittsburgh Steelers would beat the Patriots in the AFC Championship Game. After the Patriots won again, Vegas said they would lose to the St. Louis Rams. Asked to comment on being underdogs to the Steelers, Belichick joked about the irrelevance of Vegas' point spread: "Can we get those points, will they put them up on the board for us?"[1335] Even after beating the Steelers and then winning the Super Bowl, the Patriots found themselves 4½-point underdogs against those same Steelers on opening day 2002, despite home field advantage. After beating the Steelers 30-14 and beating the Jets 44-7 in Week 2, another game where Vegas had picked against the Pats, Patriots safety Tebucky Jones explained, "It doesn't matter what other people think of us. We don't doubt each other."[1336] When Vegas finally began picking the Pats to win, the team started believing the hype and lost a bunch of games.

Before the Patriots' first 2003 playoff game, Bill Belichick was asked to comment on the Patriots being 2-1 favorites to outplay the eight remaining playoff teams and emerge victorious in the Super Bowl. His response was classic Belichick: "There couldn't be anything less relevant than that to me."[1337] For emphasis, he repeated himself: "I couldn't think of one single thing less relevant than that."[1338] Tom Brady was equally excited to be favored to win the Super Bowl: "Whether we're the underdog or the favorite, [our opponent] Tennessee doesn't care and we don't care."[1339] Contrast this we-determine-our-destiny attitude with the Patriots of old. Just three hours before the Patriots took the field in Super Bowl XXXI against the Green Bay Packers, Patriots linebacker Chris Slade was so upset that a *USA Today* reporter had predicted the Packers would win that he called to complain: "Yo, I thought you were my boy and here you are picking the Packers to kick our asses."[1340] That reporter had better perspective than Slade:

> "I asked Chris then what I'll repeat to you now: What cotton-pickin' difference does it make what I think is going to happen? (This was just before I wondered aloud, 'Hey Chris–don't you have somewhere you need to be right about now?')"[1341]

While the Patriots never succumb to we're-better-than-you thinking, they have benefited. Special teamer Don Davis, whose Rams lost Super Bowl XXXVI to the Patriots before Davis joined the Patriots in 2003, remembers the Rams locker room being "very stunned. We thought we were going to win that game."[1342]

The Patriots' star defensive lineman, Richard Seymour, tattooed "Faith" onto his arm to remind himself that "You gotta have faith [in yourself]. There are a lot of things going on in the world and you need to believe when nobody else believes.

That's my approach. If you don't have faith in yourself, nobody else will have faith in you."[1343]

Tedy Bruschi is a prototypical Belichick Patriot. Not a highly recruited athlete coming out of high school and too small to play defensive line in the NFL (as he had in college, where he tied the NCAA sack record), Bruschi never worried about what others thought of him:

> "I'm going to do whatever I can to be successful. I'm not going to let anything stop me. Certainly, not any of the doubters or naysayers. There have been a lot of opinions and predictions put out on me and who I can be as a player. What I can be as a player in my mind is totally different than what other people say."[1344]

External expectations are more often dangerously high than insultingly low. Fans expected great things from both the 2002 and 2004 Patriots. In 2002, the team bought into the hype and missed out on the playoffs by not preparing for and playing every game as if it might lose. Not the 2004 Patriots, according to backup quarterback Jim Miller:

> "Anything can happen in the NFL. ...If you don't prepare week-in and week-out it doesn't bode well for you on Sunday. I think we all know that and understand that in this locker room. Again, I think that goes back on Bill [Belichick] and the offensive and defensive coaches pretty much hammering that in our heads. I think for the most part, guys believe it and they understand it and go with it."[1345]

The 2004 Patriots have learned to completely tune out expectations. Players realize it doesn't matter what anyone expects, except to the extent that players' expectations affect their preparation for games. Safety Rodney Harrison says, "It doesn't matter what they expect. It's all about what we expect out of ourselves. We're the ones out here working, we're the ones out here busting our tails, and we're the ones here 10 hours a day. It doesn't matter what people think."[1346]

Expect greatness

"All [Belichick] wants is perfection. If you can give him perfection, you'll be all right."[1347]
– Patriots outside linebackers coach Rob Ryan

"[When linebacker Mike Vrabel plays as a tight end, he] always comes back to the huddle and tells you he's open. There could be eight guys on him, but in his mind he was wide open. He's got a lot of confidence in himself."
– Bill Belichick

"We win this one today, but I get called for a penalty that takes away a Willie McGinest sack. That's what's going to haunt me the next couple of days. It's

never about what we did well with this team. It's always about what we screwed up."[1348]
     – Patriots safety Rodney Harrison

If you expect great things, your people may amaze you. But if you accept average, your people will never surprise you with greatness. Tom Brady admires Belichick's expectation that Patriots will play aggressive, mistake-free football, and he credits that high standard with spurring players to execute at a level higher than their opponents: "[Belichick] expects perfection out of us. I think you see that when we go out and play smart, tough, disciplined football. That's what he prides himself on and that's what he expects out of us."[1349]

Immediately after becoming the Patriots' head coach, Belichick made clear that three-quarters effort was no longer acceptable:

> "If you can't [pass] the conditioning [test], then you can't pass the physical, and you can't play. ... The things we're doing are designed to hit a high standard. We're not going to just roll out the ball, play at 50-60 percent, and keep everybody happy."[1350]

After Belichick sent a strong message, players responded by participating in his "voluntary" mini-camp. He singled out the one player (veteran defensive lineman Henry Thomas) who didn't attend the full "voluntary" minicamp ("all the players... except one being here for the entire minicamp"[1351]). And he cut veteran offensive tackle Ed Ellis on Day 1 of training camp after Ellis showed up out of shape.[1352] Belichick so respects superior performances that he'll go out of his way to congratulate competitors, like Buffalo Bills cornerback Terrence McGee who ran a kickoff back 98 yards for a touchdown and nearly intercepted a Brady pass: "He was telling me that I gave him hell. He told me what a good athlete I was. I was surprised that he came up to me, shook my hand and told me that. I thought he'd be doing something else besides coming to me and telling me how good I played."[1353]

The Patriots set equally lofty expectations at an organizational level. Before the 2001 playoffs, Scott Pioli was already talking about winning multiple championships:

> "We don't want to sit here for the next five years and finish second in the division. We don't want to sit here for the next five years and just make the playoffs. That's not what the goal is. The goal isn't just to keep your job. The goal is to win championships. ...[U]ntil you win a flat-out championship, you can't be totally pleased."[1354]

Perhaps the most important fact about expectations is that every player has the same high expectations Belichick does. The Patriots have brought in players passionate about improving themselves and about winning football games. Consequently, Belichick says, players don't need their coach telling them how disappointed he is. They're already disappointed with themselves:

"Players have high expectations, too. They sit here and go through hours and hours of meetings and a lot of hours on the practice field, a lot of film study, a lot of preparation time, and their expectations are to go out there and play well. When you have opportunities to be productive and, for whatever reason, it just doesn't happen, that's not satisfying to the player, it's not satisfying to the coach, it's not satisfying to the team, and there's a certain level of frustration."[1355]

RESPONSIBILITY & OWNERSHIP

Everyone's a coach

"[Employees] at practically every level of the organization... make, by necessity, risk-taking decisions, that is, business decisions. Every one of these men bases his decision on some, if only vague, theory of the business... Common vision, common understanding, and unity of direction and effort of the entire organization require definition of 'what our business is and what it should be.'"[1356]

– Peter Drucker, father of management science

"We would hang out together, have fun, and hold each other accountable."[1357]

– Patriots center/guard Damien Woody

"The thing I admire about them is that within the players, they're pushing each other, whether it's a scheme where a guy's not getting it done right–you can see it on tape, the players are saying, 'You've got to get it done right'–or if you're not playing hard enough."[1358]

– Buffalo Bills head coach Mike Mularkey

Getting players to motivate themselves and one another separates Belichick from what Charlie Weis terms Bill Parcells' "button-pushing": "[Parcells] knew how to play to the psyche of every player, every coach. He'd tell me I wasn't working hard. It's 11:30 [at night] and he'd say, 'Are you trying to get out of here?'"[1359] Belichick wants players and coaches who push themselves and enjoy doing so. VP of player personnel Scott Pioli says he and his scouts look for players with the mindset he and Belichick share: "We're both highly, highly competitive people. And we don't have patience for high-maintenance people or people who do dumb things."[1360] Belichick can't waste time cajoling and threatening people to do what they don't want to. So he built his New England team around competitive, self-disciplined players, and this gives the team a huge advantage. Asked whether players "give [each other] crap" when they screw up, quarterback Tom Brady replied, "Oh yeah. They hear plenty of it from everybody. It's probably a lot easier from the players than what the coaches give them."[1361]

The contrast between Belichick and the many constantly-screaming NFL coaches is so stark that *Sports Illustrated*'s Peter King, the only reporter allowed inside the Patriots' nearly six hours of pre-Super Bowl training sessions in early 2002, was "amazed... that not once in three afternoons of working his team did he raise his voice. ...Belichick and this team were at one. They knew what he wanted. They knew how to give it to him."[1362] Relying on self-discipline rather than externally-imposed discipline paid off in another way during the 2001 season. It likely prevented a team meltdown following challenges that included: the shocking death of quarterbacks coach Dick Rehbein, 9/11, and "situations" involving several troublesome star players. Because Belichick and Pioli had stocked the Patriots with character guys and because Belichick refused to cater to the egos of "star" players, said an admiring Patriots wide receiver Charles Johnson, "You didn't have guys in the locker room taking situations and running with it to the media and everything. For him to do that at this level was unbelievable. Those situations were enough to tear a team apart."[1363]

Any sizable organization is like the proverbial iceberg: its leader can see only the small portion above the water's surface. No leader can be everywhere and see everything, yet every organization's success is heavily impacted by what employees do when their leader isn't looking. Recognizing how much of the iceberg they cannot perceive, wise leaders: 1) hire self-motivated employees; 2) foster organizational buy-in to an overarching philosophy and vision; and, 3) cultivate enthusiasm and excitement for the organization's work and success.

The Patriots have built an organization where everyone focuses 100% on winning. John Lynch, star safety of the 2002 NFL-champion Tampa Bay Buccaneers, was blown away during his free agent visit to New England in early 2003:

> "[I]t's really clear as to why this organization is so successful. A lot of times when you talk to different people in an organization, they're on different pages, but when you talk to a lot of people in this organization, it's clear they're all on the same page and know what they stand for. I heard the same thing from [owner] Mr. Kraft as I heard from [defensive secondary coach] Eric Mangini as I heard from the scout who drove me from the airport. Either they really rehearsed it or they truly believe it, and I think it's the latter."[1364]

Running back Corey Dillon, who joined the Patriots in 2004, was similarly struck by the maturity and focus of his new teammates and coaches:

> "That's what a championship team is, it's people with heart who still have a desire to go out there and compete and win. I see it in everybody here, from the owners on down, from the coaches to the players. That's what you need. That's the kind of organization you want to be a part of."[1365]

Such praise illustrates a core element of the Patriots' success. Bill Belichick knows that self-discipline and peer pressure are more effective than screaming coaches, so he signs disciplined players and leverages the power of peer pressure to get players to cajole and encourage one other.

The Patriots search for disciplined players who are their own worst critics and do the right thing even when no one's watching. According to Scott Pioli, "We're looking first and foremost for players that are low maintenance. Do players get it? Do they know what they know? Do they know what they don't know?"[1366] Former New Orleans Saints general manager Randy Mueller says self-discipline is responsible for the success of Tom Brady and Seahawks quarterback Matt Hasselbeck: "There are a lot of players in this league that until they're accountable in their own mind, they are not going to get to the next level. These two guys are accountable to themselves, first. You've got to hold yourself in the same regard that others do. But you've also got to be hard on yourself, too."[1367]

After hiring the right players, Belichick uses peer pressure to reduce mental mistakes (like jumping offsides) by punishing everyone when anyone makes an avoidable error. After Belichick switched tactics from ineffectually yelling at each offender to making the offender's entire unit (offensive, defense, or special teams) run laps, he found that players "were doing my work for me. It hasn't been all that much of a problem since."[1368] This was as close to a "Eureka!" moment as Belichick has likely experienced during his five decades in football.

Another example is Belichick's oral exams. Like a law professor, Belichick stands before his team aiming this question at this player and that question at that player about the team's upcoming opponent:

- "Which defense will they likely use on 3rd-and-long?"

- "Which player uses the two technique [three technique, four technique, five technique, *etc.*]?"

- "In [a certain defensive formation], which blitz are they most likely to run?"

- "On [a certain offensive play call], how do you determine which defensive player is the weakside ('Will') linebacker, which is the strongside ('Sam') linebacker, and which is the middle ('Mike') linebacker?"

- "If they call [a certain play], what do you expect [a certain player] will do?"

- "If we're running [a certain play] and our opponent is running [a particular play], how should we attack that?"

Tough questions. Players are expected to answer correctly. If not, they are immediately embarrassed in their teammates' and coaches' eyes. Belichick also gives his players written exams with similar questions. If a player isn't studying effectively, his coaches and teammates will know almost immediately. Everyone studies hard.

Running back Rabih Abdullah joined the Patriots during the 2004 season and "as soon as I got here, I just noticed how together everybody was as a team and how everybody worked hard together and studied and just prepared for the game as a team."[1369]

Such preparation pays off. Early in the Patriots-Jets game on Week 7 of 2004, five seconds before the Jets snapped the ball, Belichick began madly waving at his pass defenders to back up in preparation for a long pass; after the snap, Jets quarterback Chad Pennington lofted a deep pass that defenders Randall Gay and Ty Law were in position to break up.[1370] With 2½ minutes left, the Jets were losing by six but had marched to the Patriots' 27-yard line and were threatening to take the lead. On 3rd-and-5, Patriots linebacker Willie McGinest smelled a draw (an apparent passing play that becomes a run several seconds after the play starts), prepared to defend the draw, and stuffed it for a 3-yard loss: "That's [Jets running back Curtis Martin's] favorite play—the draw. Against them, you always have to account for Curtis first. So they handed the ball off and we were playing it."[1371] On 4th-and-8, Pennington tried to force the ball to a triple-covered Wayne Chrebet. One New York reporter suggested "The Patriots reacted as though they knew Chrebet was the target all the way. Why else would cornerback Ty Law leave [Santana] Moss all alone and squeeze the middle as the third man surrounding Chrebet along with nickel back Randall Gay and safety Rodney Harrison?"[1372] Patriots safety Rodney Harrison said afterwards he had helped cornerback Randall Gay because "We knew [Chrebet] was getting the ball all along. He's a fantastic receiver."[1373] Belichick confirmed "When [Chrebet] went in motion, we went into double coverage."[1374] Double coverage apparently became triple coverage because Pennington looks too much at his intended receiver and the Patriots took advantage: "Cornerback Ty Law, who was on outside receiver Santana Moss, went into his backpedal with his eyes on Pennington. Seeing Pennington looking dead at Chrebet, he left Moss the instant both receivers made their breaks."[1375] Whether Patriots players knew the Jets would throw to Chrebet in that critical situation or read Pennington's eyes, three defenders surrounded Chrebet. Ballgame.

Tight end Christian Fauria explains what happens to teammates who refuse to give 100% or display poor attitudes: "When 50 guys are all on the same page and one guy's trying to rock the boat, it's not going to happen. We're not going to let it happen. Either you're going to get onboard, or we're going to leave you behind."[1376]

Belichick is no longer the foul-mouthed disciplinarian of his early Cleveland years. Patriots center/guard Damien Woody says, "As the years have gone by, he's more comfortable. He's letting his hair down a little bit more with the team. He's a business-as-usual guy, but he jokes around with the guys in the meetings or at practice, so he has his lighter side to him."[1377] But Belichick hasn't gone soft: "I've yelled at every player. That's my job."[1378] Belichick's lack of hysterical shrieking stood out in a montage of NFL coaches during 2004 training camp; other coaches were all screaming at their players. The *Providence Journal*'s Bill Reynolds says the harshest, loudest thing Belichick said was a matter-of-fact, "If you don't know what you're doing, I can't put you in [the game]."[1379] *60 Minutes* thought it had uncovered Belichick's secret, never yelling at players, but Belichick says, "Oh, I think they've heard me raise my voice a couple times ...when things aren't going well."[1380] Belichick's secret is not never yelling. It's knowing when to yell. Constant screaming is like overuse of exclamation points... it quickly loses its impact. Cornerback Ty Law once compared Belichick to E.F. Hutton,[1381] alluding to a once-famous ad with the tag line, "When E.F. Hutton talks, people listen." Paradoxically, because Belichick rants and raves less than earlier in his career, his players now pay closer attention. Patriots tight end Christian Fauria says Belichick expressed his displeasure over an embarrassing 31-3 preseason loss to the Cincinnati Bengals in 2004 in a matter-of-fact, business-like manner:

> "He [was] pretty even-keeled. ...[H]e just kind of did what he always does. He just treats us like we are normal people and says, 'Listen, look at this. This is just unacceptable.' And if you are a player who cares about his performance then you are like, 'Yeah, you are right. We need to step it up a little more.'"[1382]

Tom Brady offered the same assessment: "Coach kind of warned us. He said, 'You guys have to start practicing better. If you want to execute better on game day you have to go execute better on practice days.'"[1383] Belichick is not players' babysitter. He doesn't waste time yelling to vent anger or get players' attention. He speaks to convey information, and his players listen because they value Belichick's knowledge. Belichick also uses other, often more effective, methods to make his point. He wields his wry humor like a rapier:

> "Do we have to see that again next week, and the week after that? When is it going to get fixed? When? When are we going to run 'Toss 38 Bob' at least for no gain? Forget about gaining yardage. When are we going to run it at least back to the fucking line of scrimmage? How long is that shit going to take?"[1384]

Patriots defensive players love and respect their defensive coordinator, Romeo Crennel. Crennel says he is even less likely to yell than Belichick:

> "Part of [Bill Belichick and Bill Parcells] are in my makeup, but I am more low-key. I demand and expect a certain performance, and I can put my arm around a player and say, 'This is what I need,' and put pressure on them in a different way. I've been known to raise my voice from time to time, and I have never had a problem getting the attention of a player."[1385]

Belichick has succeeded not only in teaching his players to know what he knows but also in convincing them to think and even act like him. Each player feels responsible for his team's success. Each player prepares for each game with complete professionalism. And each player reacts with restraint following victory and with determination following defeat. Tom Brady says, "We respond a lot of times to the things he speaks to us. ...We take on his personality. ...There are things that are important to him and things that aren't... [U]s being prepared, us playing hard and us playing smart and tough are important."[1386]

Belichick expects his veteran players to coach and advise the team's younger players, especially those who play their position. Former practice squad offensive lineman Jamil Soriano found it easy to get help from the experienced linemen: "If I have any problems or want to know what to expect I always talk to those guys in the locker room."[1387] Doing so is part of veteran players' informal job description, and players who help rookies are the kind of players Bill Belichick wants around:

> "Christian [Fauria] has been great. He is really the ultimate professional player. He has a great work ethic, totally team-oriented, has been great to work with both as a coaching staff and also his interaction with the other players offensively and the other tight ends. We have a couple young guys playing that position and he has been a great role model and source of information and guidance for those players. I can't say enough good things about Christian and what he has meant to this team. ...he has been a good addition to our organization both on and off the field."[1388]

Two of the few Patriots remaining from the 1990s are linebackers Tedy Bruschi and Ted Johnson. Linebacker Vernon Crawford, who played his first two NFL seasons with the Patriots in 1997 and 1998, still "smiles when talking about how helpful Patriots linebackers Tedi Bruschi and Ted Johnson were in teaching him the nuances of pro football."[1389] Veteran defensive lineman Anthony Pleasant grew tired of hearing black players call each other "nigga," so he called a meeting of the team's black players and told them to stop.[1390]

Veterans teach younger players because: 1) coaches expect it of them; 2) they received similar guidance when they were younger; and, 3) they desire to do whatever they can to strengthen the team. Tom Brady, for example, says he enjoys helping the backup quarterbacks because "The better they are, the better we'll be on offense. The better we are on offense, the happier I'll be, so I'm trying to be happy and get a few more of these wins."[1391] Brady knows the Patriots wouldn't have won their first Super Bowl if Drew Bledsoe hadn't been ready to go when Brady was injured during the AFC Championship Game. If Brady gets injured, he wants the team to continue winning.

Veterans also motivate their teammates. Tom Brady demands top performance from his teammates, but no player feels Brady is bossy or arrogant because Brady works as hard as anyone else and lightens the atmosphere by poking fun at himself. Running back Antowain Smith says Brady, the slowest Patriot, challenges teammates to races Brady knows he'll lose:

"He just has fun with it. It keeps everyone loose. When your quarterback is a big jokester, it sets the tone. He gets excited in games, he jumps around and makes noise and it's great. He's the first one to congratulate you in the end zone and the first one in your face if you don't run the route the way you are supposed to."[1392]

When Brady orders his offense to run a lap as punishment for a lousy practice, Brady doesn't watch. He leads the run. And when Brady tears into the end zone to congratulate you, tight end Daniel Graham warns, beware: "I say to Tom, 'Tom, if I ever score, I need to run from you because you are dangerous.'"[1393]

Focus on what you control

"I tell [players] this at the beginning of the year… We don't write the rulebook and we don't make the calls. The only thing we can do as a football team, I'm talking about the coaches and the players, is try to play the game the way that the rules are written. However the officials determine to call it, they call it. Some call it tighter than others. Some call it looser than others. Whatever it is we have to play within that framework."[1394]
– *Bill Belichick*

Belichick tells his Patriots not to waste time and energy worrying about things beyond their control. Asked whether playing the pass-happy Rams the week both starting cornerbacks are out with injuries was bad timing, Belichick shrugged, saying, "We play 'em when they're scheduled."[1395]

Belichick often answers media questions with seemingly tautological, but actually quite revealing, statements like "It is what it is" and "Whatever it [the weather in Phoenix when we play the Cardinals] is going to be, that is what it is going to be."[1396] He puts all his energy into things he can control. For example, asked about the Patriots' late start preparing for the 2004 season because their 2003 Super Bowl season lasted until February 2004, Belichick said:

"It doesn't really matter. We are where we are. I think we have to make the best of our opportunities in the future and we have tried to maximize the time that we have had even though it was a later start than everybody else.… What is more important to me, again, is to try to take advantage of all of the opportunities that we have, the off-season conditioning program, passing camps, mini-camps, the conditioning heading into training camp and try to have the team as ready as we possibly can for training camp."[1397]

Patriots players and assistant coaches share Belichick's philosophy of ignoring potentially distracting subjects over which they have no control: injuries to teammates; personnel problems; insults from the media; inflammatory rhetoric from opponents; teammates who might "steal" their job; bad officiating; stupid rules; *etc.*

"When the going gets tough, the tough get going" is a corny *cliché*, but the Patriots live it.

Patriots wide receiver David Patten was angry when an injury ended his 2003 season after just six games. Instead of moping around and feeling sorry for himself, Patten threw himself into rehab and preparing for 2004. Belichick says, "Even last year when he was hurt, I remember seeing him just about every day coming in and he would tell me, 'I will be back next year. I am working hard. I am going to be there.'"[1398]

The Patriots' proactive, you've-got-no-one-to-blame-but-yourself attitude is easy to preach but hard to practice. Don Shula, who coached the Miami Dolphins to their miraculous undefeated season in 1972 and achieved an NFL-best 347-173-6 career coaching record, admires Belichick's Patriots because he knows how hard it is to stay positive and proactive as roadblocks repeatedly arise:

> "The thing I'm impressed with, more than anything, is the way he has handled it this year [2003]. He had a lot of injuries. He had a lot of situations he had to overcome, but you never heard any excuses. You never heard him complaining about anything. All you did was see him plug people in to certain situations, and these guys responding to that opportunity and they somehow found a way to win."[1399]

Injuries no excuse for losing

"We have a motto. 'You are only one play away from being a starter.'"[1400]
   — Patriots safety Rodney Harrison

"They're not going to cancel the season because some guys are banged up."[1401]
   — Bill Belichick, on his 2004 team's injury problems

"It's not a matter of who's down but who's in there and are they going to get the job done."[1402]
   — Patriots linebacker Tedy Bruschi

"What are [we] going to do, sulk that Ty [Law] is not here? We lost Ty Law. He's the best cornerback in the game. But what can you do? We've still got to play the game."[1403]
   — Patriots safety Rodney Harrison

The Patriots dominated the NFL in 2003, despite leading the league in injuries. When players were lost to injuries, their backups took over. Rather than dwell on the loss of their teammates or feel sorry for themselves, healthy Patriots remained focused on what they could control, their own performance. After linebacker Rosevelt Colvin was lost for the season in Game 2 and nose tackle Ted Washington broke his leg in Game 3, linebacker Tedy Bruschi said, "I don't know who was hurt or who wasn't. I just have got to worry about the guys that are out there playing."[1404] Asked by the media for the word that best epitomizes the team's "never surrender" attitude, Bruschi explained that players just go out and do the best they can: "We leave all the adjectives to you [media] guys. When guys go down, we don't hang our heads. We expect whoever is in there to do the job."[1405]

Patriots safety Rodney Harrison says players love stepping up, taking more responsibility, and filling their fallen comrades' shoes: "That is the great thing about this team, man. Everybody in here wants the responsibility. Everybody in here is (sharing) a common goal."[1406] When #1 receiver Deion Branch was knocked out of the Patriots-Cardinals game with an injury, others proudly stepped in for their fallen friend. David Givens became Brady's #1, hauling in six passes for a career-high 118 yards and saying afterward, "I think all of our receivers have the ability to start anywhere in the league. If you watch film, we all get open every week, so if one guy goes down, we have ammunition to back him up. We have five guys who can all play."[1407] Winning with backups requires quality backups, trained backups, and mentally strong backups. Patriots linebacker Willie McGinest explains the team's attitude toward backups:

> "I don't look down on guys who aren't starting. I just say, 'When it's your time [be ready]. Any given Sunday you never know what's going to happen. You have to be prepared. That's being a professional. If you're backing up a guy, you're supposed to know what to do when you get in. There can't be a letdown. You can't say, "I'm shook. I'm scared. I don't know what to do. They're going to eat me alive.""[1408]

Witness the 40-22 victory in mid-2004 over the speedy Rams on their fast Astroturf in St. Louis. Both Patriots starting cornerbacks, Tyrone Poole and Ty Law, missed the game with injuries. On the second defensive play of the game, #3 cornerback Asante Samuel was injured. A sticky situation? "Tell me about it,"[1409] Belichick admitted afterwards. Would the Rams' great receivers exploit the Patriots' depleted secondary? Hardly. The Patriots slowed the Rams offense with a defense that included a wide receiver (Troy Brown), an undrafted rookie who hadn't even started for his college team the previous season (Randall Gay), a special teams player (Don Davis), and a cornerback they signed the day before who hadn't stuck with the Canadian Football League's Montreal Alouettes and "whose career highlight was an interception for the Duesseldorf Rhein Fire... in World Bowl X"[1410] (Earthwind Moreland). On offense, the field goal kicker (Adam Vinatieri) tossed a touchdown pass, and a linebacker (Mike Vrabel) caught a touchdown pass... on a difficult fade pattern! Patriots players enjoy that Belichick uses them in unusual ways; says Vinatieri, "It's great for the team and all that, but I also think it's fun. Doing something you're not used to doing adds a little excitement to it."[1411] Perhaps the Army should hire Belichick's Patriots to cook gourmet dinners from surplus rations.

The team's resilient attitude reminds me of a farcical scene in *Monty Python and the Holy Grail*. As a knight's limbs are hacked off one by one, he keeps coming back for more:

> Black Knight: "'Tis but a scratch."
> King Arthur: "A scratch? Your arm's off!"
> Black Knight: "No it isn't. ...I've had worse... Come on, you pansy!"
> King Arthur: "Look, you stupid bastard. You've got no arms left."
> Black Knight: "Yes, I have. ...Just a flesh wound... Chicken!"
> [Arthur lops off one of Black Knight's legs]
> King Arthur: "What are you going to do, bleed on me?"
> Black Knight: "I'm invincible! ...The Black Knight always triumphs! Have at you! Come on, then."
> [Arthur chops off Knight's remaining leg and heads off]
> Black Knight: "Oh. Oh, I see. Running away, eh? You yellow bastards! Come back here and take what's coming to you. I'll bite your legs off!"[1412]

In fact, cornerback Ty Law might *be* the Black Knight: "I always try to block [an injury] out mentally, whether it's pain, a strain or a tear. Playing on one leg is not fun. I've done that for a whole year."[1413]

Offensive line coach Dante Scarnecchia takes a proactive, "no excuses" attitude toward molding and melding a group of guys, most of whom drew little or no interest from NFL teams, into a stalwart offensive line. Asked about the fact that three of his five Super Bowl starters were opening day backups and had little time to work together and develop the chemistry and mutual understanding that every great offensive line possesses, Scarnecchia replied: "We don't have that luxury. We haven't had it all year, so I don't subscribe to that. What am I supposed to say? 'It's going to take a year,' and surrender?"[1414]

Loss of star players no excuse for losing

> "The coaches always say, 'When your number's called, you've got to cash in.'"[1415]
> *– Patriots wide receiver Deion Branch*

The same attitude helped the team ignore the soap opera of flaky, unreliable star wide receiver Terry Glenn. Safety Lawyer Milloy in 2001 told his teammates not to waste time worrying about Glenn's status: "Hey, if Terry is here, then fine, but if not we go on and stop worrying about it."[1416] Linebacker Bryan Cox similarly felt Glenn's absence was "a non-issue. It's been like this all year. What's the difference now? If it was Troy Brown, it would be a different story. Whatever. Since I've been here, I haven't said more than hello to him."[1417] When starting quarterback Drew Bledsoe was knocked out early in 2001, the team rallied behind an unknown former fourth-string quarterback named Tom Brady.

When veteran linebacker Ted Johnson got angry with his diminished role at the beginning of the 2002 season and went AWOL (after asking Belichick to release him), Bill Belichick said simply, "He's made his decision. We're preparing for the game. We're moving forward... People that are here are preparing for the game and that's what we can do. It's going to be just like any other situation where a player wasn't available, whether because of injury or whatever the circumstances. We're going to move on with people who are here."[1418] To Ted Johnson's great credit, after reflecting on his situation, he rejoined the team and began worrying only about what he could control... his performance. Coaches' decisions regarding playing time were out of his control, so he let go of that worry. Johnson is a proud man who takes pride in his performance on the football field. In his mind, diminished playing time and loss of his starting job meant he was a less worthy human being. He apparently concluded he had been placing unhealthy importance on his personal football achievements. Johnson realized that his personal worth could not be measured by how many minutes he played, how many games he started, or how many tackles he recorded. He matured and discovered more joys in his life than just football. Perhaps most significantly, he discovered that he could extract joy from football, even without being on the field, by mentoring and encouraging and helping his teammates. He had grown into the next phase of his football career, later saying:

> "I'm not going to say [2003] was rewarding statistically, but I felt good I did everything I could up to the point of my injury to get myself ready to help the defense be prepared. You find a silver lining in that, maybe you had something to do with the success of the defense even if you weren't always out there. That's key, to find a silver lining in a situation. Even if you're not a main cog in a Super Bowl run that you can be a productive person and help out in other ways."[1419]

Officiating no excuse for losing

Belichick insists that players play and let coaches coach and officials officiate. He doesn't want players wasting time and energy fuming over what they believe to be bad calls. Belichick warns players in advance that there *will* be bad calls and that players must keep their minds on the next play, not the previous bad call:

> "[A]s a football coach and as a football player, that part of the game is out of your control. There is just nothing you can do about it other than understand what the rules are, understand how the game is being played and play it within that framework. ...There are plenty of calls that come up during the year that I personally don't agree with and I'm sure our players that are involved in the play don't personally agree with the way they were called, but that doesn't make any difference."[1420]

"Our approach... is to know the rules and to play within them. It doesn't matter what they are. It doesn't matter what we think of them. It doesn't matter whether we think something should or shouldn't be a foul. Again, I emphasize that to the team as well. It doesn't matter what I think, and it doesn't matter what they think. It only matters what the guys in the striped shirts think because they are the ones calling the game. It is our job to play the game within the framework of the rules as they are calling the game."[1421]

If a player believes challenging an official's ruling may successfully overturn an unfavorable call, he should inform coaches of his belief, but he should never get angry and lose concentration for the next play. If an official's ruling determines the outcome of a game, the Patriots believe it has only itself to blame because, as Brady says, "you just don't want to let it come down to such close plays at the end of the game."[1422]

The Oakland Raiders might have beaten the Patriots in the infamous January 2002 "Snow Bowl" if they had possessed the Patriots' *c'est la vie* attitude toward referees' calls. Instead of playing hard the rest of the game, Raiders players became bitter and indignant. They fixated on the "fumble" that was (correctly) ruled an incomplete pass. They moped around, wallowing in self-pity, rather than exert themselves to the max. Afterwards, Raiders cornerback Charles Woodson seemed to blame the refs not only for "blowing" the call (which they did not) but also for taking the wind out of the Raiders' sails: "Ball came out, game over. [That call] kind of took the air out of a lot of guys. We knew the game was over. We were celebrating."[1423] So did Raiders linebacker William Thomas: "We didn't lose this game. It was taken from us."[1424]

But the Raiders, not the refs, are responsible for keeping the Raiders pumped up. Only the Raiders can control the Raiders' state of mind. When the refs made the (correct) call, the Raiders still had the lead. Instead of trying to hold their lead, they rolled over... twice! Immediately after the ruling, 1:59 remained in regulation, but the Raiders failed to prevent the Patriots from tying the game with 32 seconds left. They barely attempted to block Adam Vinatieri's 45-yard line-drive field goal. The ball flew low and straight and could easily have been blocked, but not a single Raider bothered to raise his hands into the air: "if someone had stuck a hand up, he might have tipped it. In a do-or-die playoff game, somebody should have been clawing and scratching [to block the kick]."[1425] Also, that kick—which *NFL Films* president Steve Sabol considers "the greatest kick in NFL history"[1426]—merely tied the game. In overtime, the Raiders defense rolled over again. Tom Brady completed all eight passes in a snow storm, marching the Patriots downfield for the easy game-winning 23-yard field goal.

The 2004 Patriots are taking the same *c'est la vie* attitude toward the crackdown on overly aggressive defensive tactics. This tightened enforcement is designed to stop the Patriots, but cornerback Ty Law says the team will just have to adapt: "No one will ever [admit] we are the reason [for the change], but if I was a betting man, I'd say they brought up some films of the Patriots. That's OK. We're good enough athletes to evolve."[1427] (We have since learned that those urging the enforcement change did splice together lots of film in which the Patriots appeared prominently... though many other teams also were shown doing similar things.) Despite saying his team has no choice but to adjust, Law confesses to being nostalgic for the good ol' days when "you got to beat the hell out of the guy until the ball got there."[1428]

Tough schedule no excuse for losing

Some teams play easier opponents, while others play tough ones. Some teams enter a game after ten, or even fourteen, days of rest and preparation (if they played in the previous week's Thursday game or had a "bye"), while their opponent may have had only six days rest (if they played the previous Monday night). Some unfortunate teams have their "bye week" (off week) as early as the third week of the season, when they don't need it, while others have it late in the year. Bill Belichick doesn't want to hear whining about scheduling challenges. He expects his team to be prepared and play its best, no matter the circumstances. A typical response to a scheduling-related question from the media is: "We are not going to worry about it. We are going to look at whatever it is and try to make the most of what we can with the opportunities in the time frame that we have to work in. When the games are scheduled, we will show up and play them."[1429]

Sticks and stones may break my bones, but words...

Words can hurt, but only if you're insecure and weak-willed enough to let them hurt you. The Patriots ignore inflammatory rhetoric from the media and opponents. Players and coaches want to win football games, not word wars, so they don't bother revealing their thoughts or justifying their actions, except when doing so might help them win. After the Patriots released star safety Lawyer Milloy, *ESPN* analyst Tom Jackson reported Patriots players "hate their coach." The team did not dignify Jackson's unsubstantiated comment with an official response, but one unnamed Patriot player said:

> "[Negative] comments [from outsiders] aren't going to disrupt us. Who in here would give that issue a second thought? It's only talked about because reporters ask about it. It's not distracting. It's just somebody's opinion. If we ever let something like that distract us, we wouldn't be a very strong team, would we?"[1430]

In the days before Super Bowl XXXVIII, star defensive lineman Warren Sapp (whose team hadn't even made the playoffs) injected himself into the pre-game hype by insulting Patriots offensive lineman Russ Hochstein, who had been a backup until Damien Woody suffered a season-ending injury. Sapp predicted the Pats would lose the Super Bowl because, Sapp claimed, Hochstein (whom Sapp practiced against when they were both on the Tampa Bay Buccaneers) couldn't block even non-athletic TV personality Tony Kornheiser. Hochstein's response was, "I don't care"[1431] and "All I care about is the Carolina Panthers and the Super Bowl that's coming."[1432] When Sapp, who was covering the Super Bowl for *The NFL Network*, had the *cajones* to approach Hochstein with the line, "How did you like me making you the center of attention?" Hochstein displayed class and self-control. After glaring at Sapp while holding back the vitriol he must have felt and been tempted to unleash, he said simply, "No more questions."

Other Patriots defended their teammate. The injured guard/center Damien Woody made clear he would not allow Sapp to distract the Patriots' focus: "We're not concerned about guys who didn't even make the playoffs. All we're concerned about is the Carolina Panthers."[1433] Tom Brady also poked fun at the fact that Sapp's Buccaneers hadn't even made the playoffs: "He'll get a good view from wherever he's sitting."[1434] Brady fired off a great double-meaning one-liner after Sapp (a quarterback-sacking machine) approached him for an interview:

> Brady: "Why are you talking about our offensive line?"
> Sapp: "I just came over to say hello, and I can't get close to you."
> Brady: "That's the way I like it."[1435]

Bill Belichick believes fervently in avoiding unnecessary, unproductive controversies and distractions. Asked in 2000 to comment on former boss Bill Parcells' new book that criticized Belichick, Belichick laughed it off: "Book selling can be a good business, as we all know."[1436] Later in 2000, Belichick's predecessor as Patriots coach, Pete Carroll, said of the Patriots (then with a 3-9 record): "Was [hiring Belichick] the right decision? Look what's going on here now. It's a joke."[1437] Belichick has a sarcastic/sardonic sense of humor but was too mature to fire back. Instead, he said simply, "I'm not going to comment on that remark because I don't know the context or anything about it."[1438]

Belichick's no-excuses attitude is shared by his close friend and former defensive coordinator, Nick Saban. The 3-8 LSU Tigers team Saban inherited in 2000 had suffered through eleven straight losing seasons. Saban guided his Tigers to a share of the 2003 NCAA Division 1 national championship, earning NCAA Coach of the Year honors for his efforts. A decisive moment came when he ended players' griping over their then #7 BCS ("Bowl Championship Series") ranking:

> "I said we're going to talk about the BCS and where we're ranked. This is the time to talk about it. I told them when we leave this room we'll focus on what is and not what was. Rankings are what was. Rankings are what happened last week, we had to worry about what will happen this week. We

knew we had no control of the BCS but we knew that if we didn't win we didn't have a chance. We could only control what we could do."[1439]

An incident before Super Bowl XXXVI vividly illustrates Belichick's tunnel vision on matters of importance. As coach, Belichick had every right to a better hotel room, but when safety Lawyer Milloy complained that a few veteran players had worse rooms than some of the younger players, Belichick swapped rooms with Milloy and then jabbed Milloy light-heartedly:

> "Belichick took one for the team, switching places with Milloy–from spacious room 692 at the Fairmont Hotel to the cramped quarters of room 533–and persuaded several assistants to do the same for other players. 'You think I need a sofa or a dining room table? Who gives a s---?' Belichick said to a reporter, smiling, the day before the game. 'Then again, every time I see Lawyer, I ask, "How's that nice, big room? Are you getting a good night's sleep?"'"[1440]

Build yourself up; don't tear others down

Many professional athletes worry about other players "stealing their job." Belichick has done a remarkable job of convincing Patriots that: 1) No player "owns" his job and must continually earn it; 2) A player can best succeed by worrying exclusively about making himself the best he can be, not on what others are doing; and, 3) Being a member of a winning team requires everyone helping everyone else become the best they can be. The Patriots locker room has little or no back-stabbing. Quite the contrary. Players support one another. Asked whether veteran Troy Brown was worried about younger players, Belichick said:

> "I don't think he really cares who else is out there. If he goes out and does what he does well, I don't see why he can't continue to be productive. If somebody else can go out and do something else… great. …I don't think they really care what somebody else is doing. It doesn't really matter what anybody else does. They just need to control what they can control. I think that is really what the whole team should be thinking about, is to get themselves ready to go. Whatever somebody else is or isn't doing is beyond their control. There is nothing they can do about it."[1441]

Take pride in contributing

Many football players think of themselves as playing a particular position. Great players contribute to their team's success in any and every way possible. They don't think special teams are "beneath" them. They want to get onto the field on every play, and they want to make a difference in the game's outcome. They take pride in contributing, not in performing a specific role. They take pride in winning, not in puffing up their personal stats by taking heads-I-win-tails-my-team-loses gambles that either make them look great (when they get a sack or an interception) or hurt their team (when their opponent makes a huge play exploiting their over-aggressiveness that has taken them out of position to handle their responsibilities). Bill Belichick says "outside linebacker" Mike Vrabel is that kind of player: "Mike takes a lot of pride in what you ask him to do, whatever it is, whether it's the punt team, whether it's kickoff return, whether it's short yardage and goal line or a defensive play."[1442] Tedy Bruschi is the same way:

> "Everything I try to do is just based on winning football games. That's all. Whatever sacrifice I need to make, whatever I need to do, I will do to help the team win. Coming in playing special teams–where do I line up? Third down–what do you want me to do? You want me to play Mike [middle linebacker], Will [weakside], Sam [strongside], whatever it is. That's the attitude I have. I've never gone up to a coach and said this is where I want to play. They've always put me where they felt was best and I've always accepted it as, I trust them and that's where I need to be and I need to do my best to help the team win."[1443]

YOU DON'T WIN FOOTBALL GAMES WITH YOUR MOUTH

> "We kept our mouths shut and got the job done when nobody gave us a chance in hell of doing it."[1444]
> – *Patriots wide receiver Troy Brown after beating the Rams in Super Bowl XXXVI*

> "Just shut up and play. That's what I keep telling these young guys. Just shut up and play football."[1445]
> – *Patriots safety Rodney Harrison*

You don't win football games with your mouth. You don't win football games in the newspaper or on *ESPN*. You don't win football games by becoming Vegas' favorite or by being the better team "on paper." You win football games by winning football games. After winning Super Bowl XXXVI, Tom Brady said telling the world you're confident serves no purpose: "You just have to go do it."[1446] Because players who shoot off their mouths usually distract and detract from their team's ability to win football games, you won't witness the Patriots doing so... at least while Bill Belichick remains head coach.

You also don't win football games with the most provocative touchdown dance. To Bill Belichick, insulting your opponent and bragging about yourself are the football equivalents of digging yourself a deeper hole. Why needlessly put your team at a disadvantage? Folk wisdom advises: "If you're in a hole, stop digging." Another cliché warns against "digging your own grave." But, because American society glorifies outlandish, outspoken attention-grabbers, the celebratory restraint Belichick demands is a throwback. American sports has glamorized bragging at least since Babe Ruth pointed to the location in the bleachers where he would hit a home run on the upcoming pitch. By 1965, the NFL had banned throwing the ball into the stands following touchdowns, so Homer Jones invented "the spike." After Joe Namath "guaranteed" victory over the heavily-favored Baltimore Colts in Super Bowl III and backed up his boast on January 12, 1969, all hell broke loose. Few NFL players are shy about running their mouths or celebrating big plays, sometimes even when their teams are losing! We've witnessed the Ickey Shuffle, the Dirty Bird, the Lambeau Leap, the Sack Dance, the Throat Slash, the Heisman, the Fun Bunch, the Mile High Salute, the Sprinkler, Billy "White Shoes" Johnson dancing in the end zone, Joe Horn calling on a cell phone he stashed in the goal post, Terrell Owens whipping a Sharpie out of his sock to autograph the ball, *etc.* Depending on your perspective, these are either fun celebrations or self-indulgent forms of taunting that teach kids the wrong lessons. It's obvious which view Bill Belichick holds. And his Patriots probably win more games because they play with class.

Don't get mad... Get even!

"Sometimes you get tired of people not seeing what you really bring to the table. But you just keep your mouth shut and try to prove people wrong."[1447]
– *Patriots defensive lineman Bobby Hamilton*

"Most veterans have been around long enough to know to just play football. You don't have to talk through the media. Just show it on the field."[1448]
– *Patriots cornerback Ty Law*

"[Seattle Seahawks players] did some talking this week, but as a unit, we do our talking on the football field. When you talk, you just give the other team more motivation. It doesn't matter what type of football team you have, it matters what you do every Sunday."[1449]
– *Patriots defensive lineman Richard Seymour, after the Patriots' 20th straight win*

When the Patriots feel disrespected, they keep their mouths shut. Instead of exploding with a barrage of words, they stew and wallow in silent rage... and explode with indignant anger when the game starts:

"People close to [Patriots wide receiver David] Patten said he headed into [Super Bowl XXXVI] with a chip on his shoulder after Vikings receiver Cris Carter questioned Patten's status as a starter on a television show. [Patten] used the additional motivation and came up big by providing the Patriots with their second touchdown, an 8-yard touchdown reception with 49 seconds remaining in the first half."[1450]

Pittsburgh reporters and fans helped motivate Patriots safety Lawyer Milloy for the 2001 AFC Championship Game: "All the questions directed at us... were about whether we thought we had 'a chance' to win. That was a slap in our face. I had to count to 10 because I was so furious. I made a joke out of it, but I didn't really think it was funny."[1451] To make matters worse, when Milloy went to dinner at IHOP with relatives who wore some Patriots gear, the restaurant manager pointedly brought a bottle of Heinz ketchup and a plate of Steelers-colored cookies to their table, rubbing it in with "this is the last decent meal you'll have before we crush you tomorrow."[1452]

Arrogant NFL players often talk smack or "dis" their upcoming opponent. Such blather doesn't help win games; it helps opponents win by supplying an emotional boost. Before the 2001 AFC Championship Game, Steelers wide receiver Plaxico Burress called Patriots cornerbacks Ty Law and Otis Smith "average corners." The Patriots came to Pittsburgh and beat the heavily favored Steelers, then went on to win Super Bowl XXXVI. After the two teams faced off again on opening day 2002 and the Patriots trounced the Steelers, a humbled Burress admitted the obvious: "We didn't lose this one. We got whipped."[1453] Tom Brady explained "we let our play do the talking. Eventually, you've got to go out there and line up and play for 60 minutes."[1454] Bragging about how great you are or how crappy your opponent is energizes opponents and distracts you from whatever you should be doing, as Tom Brady explains:

> "Not only do we not say anything stupid, but we don't think anything stupid. We don't think like that, so because of that, it keeps us focused. You know, we don't need to go out and talk. We let 13 games in a row talk for itself and that's how we approach it. People can say what they want. I saw something one of the Tennessee players said. They are the best team in the league or something, you let them talk and you go out and do your business."[1455]

Astoundingly, the Steelers have still not learned this lesson. Before facing the defending Super Bowl champions and their NFL-record 21-game winning streak on Halloween 2004, Steelers defensive end Kimo von Oelhoffen said, "I don't know [whether New England is the AFC's best team], I really don't. Ask me Monday, I'll let you know... Individually, I don't think they have that much talent."[1456] Receiver Hines Ward said of the 2001 AFC Championship Game, "We actually won the ball game. We didn't win, but giving up 14 points off special teams, that's tough to overcome."[1457] Steelers reporters agree: "What was forgotten in the confetti and Tom Brady's trip to Walt Disney World, is that the Pittsburgh Steelers were the better team that season."[1458] Huh? Special teams points don't count in determining which team is better?

Unlike many Steelers, who display neither humility nor respect in victory or defeat, the Patriots are gracious toward their opponents (at least off the field). After the Patriots lost that Halloween game to the Steelers, Belichick admitted "We got beat. We got killed"[1459] and "they certainly deserved to win, and they won convincingly."[1460] Every Patriot credited the Steelers, even though the Steelers had three giant advantages: 1) Coming off two weeks rest, the Steelers had had an extra week to prepare for the Patriots, time that enabled Steelers defender Deshea Townsend to intercept a Brady pass and return it for a defensive touchdown: "I saw the route [on film] earlier in the week. It was a curl and I jumped it."[1461] The extra week also helped the Steelers install new plays the Patriots hadn't seen on film, including a touchdown pass to Plaxico Burress: "It was surprising because the pattern Burress ran was a fade, something the Steelers have rarely used… 'We've been working on that more and more in practice,' offensive coordinator Ken Whisenhunt said. …the Steelers have avoided calling the play for nearly five years."[1462] 2) Injuries kept ten Patriots starters out of the game or knocked them out early: starting running back (Dillon), top receiver (Branch), both starting cornerbacks (Law and Poole), starting nickel back (Gay), both fullbacks (Klecko and Pass), starting tight end (Watson), starting left tackle (Light), and the top two right tackles (Klemm and Ashworth). And, 3) The Steelers' "groundskeepers" (sic) keep Heinz Field in miserable shape to benefit the home team's running game, and the crappy field caused three Patriots slip-induced blunders: a slip by Dexter Reid caused him to knock a punt into the end zone for a touchback rather than down it at the Steelers' 2-yard line; a slip by receiver Bethel Johnson led to Deshea Townsend's interception that he returned for a Steelers touchdown; and a slip by cornerback Ty Law early in the game broke a bone in his foot, forcing him out of the game. The Patriots refused to make excuses:

- Safety Rodney Harrison: "Give them credit, they played a great game. They played their tails off."[1463]

- Linebacker Willie McGinest: "We're not going to make any excuses, like blame the refs, or injuries, or anything like that. It's disappointing we got our butts kicked and got outplayed. We have to come in tomorrow and look in the mirror and make sure each and every one of us can see what we did."[1464]

- Defensive lineman Richard Seymour: "We're not going to make any excuses about what happened, why it happened. We just took one on the chin and we have to bounce back from it."[1465]

- Belichick: "It was pretty obvious the Steelers were the better team. They outcoached us, outplayed us and we weren't good in any phase of the game. We didn't do much of anything right."[1466]

- Tom Brady: "When you don't play the way you're capable against a good team, you lose."[1467]

- Receiver Troy Brown: "You have to play football. Everybody on this roster is here for a reason, to come in and play. It's football, people get hurt and you never know when it's your time to come in and play. Not having those guys is no excuse at all."[1468]

The Patriots were gracious in defeat, while Steelers were sore winners. As the game ended, Steelers fans taunted the Patriots by chanting "Who's your Daddy?"[1469] as if the Patriots hadn't whipped the Steelers in their previous meetings. Steelers running back Duce Staley said their offensive line had carved up the Patriots defense "like a Halloween pumpkin."[1470] Classy team. Classy fans. (The best-spoken Steeler, by a mile, was rookie quarterback Ben Roethlisberger, who made gracious comments following the game, impresses me in every way, and plays and behaves like a "super-sized" Tom Brady.) I don't begrudge the Steelers their victory dance for beating the Patriots. But I resent their disparaging pre-game remarks. Beating a team that had won 21-straight is an impressive accomplishment. Disrespecting that team *before* ending their 21-game streak is not. Had the Patriots been healthier, those comments might have cost the Steelers. Perhaps they will. One unnamed Patriot told a reporter, "God, I hope we get those guys again."[1471]

Consider Indianapolis Colts kicker Mike Vanderjagt as he lined up for a game-tying field goal attempt with just seconds remaining against the Patriots on opening night of the 2004 season. Vanderjagt "never misses." In fact, this kick would have extended Vanderjagt's own NFL-record 42 straight successful field goal attempts. Vanderjagt hadn't missed a field goal attempt since 2002! A kicker that good is mentally focused with the game riding on his foot, right? Not this kicker. Vanderjagt, whom Colts quarterback Peyton Manning once called "our idiot kicker," cockily taunted the Patriots... *before* his kick: "he turned toward the Patriots' sideline before setting up for the kick and rubbed a few of his fingers together," indicating that his kick was as certain as "money in the bank." Vanderjagt (who nicknamed himself "Money") missed, and his Colts lost.

You'll even hear NFL players dis their opponent after *losing*. Again consider Colts kicker Vanderjagt. After his Colts lost to the Patriots both times they played in 2003 and again in the 2004 season opener, Vanderjagt insisted the Patriots, who have beaten the Colts five of their past six meetings, are "clearly not a better team than us."[1472] It's OK to believe that, but saying so publicly is just embarrassing and will likely haunt his team if the Patriots and Colts meet again in the 2004 playoffs.

Vanderjagt is hardly the first sore loser to moan after losing to the "inferior" Patriots. After losing Super Bowl XXXVI, an embittered St. Louis Rams linebacker London Fletcher said, "Sometimes, the better team doesn't win."[1473] After the 2003 Patriots beat the Tennessee Titans in a playoff game, the Patriots' second win over the Titans in two meetings that season, Titans guard Zach Piller said:

> "I think we are the best team in the NFL and I stick by that. I don't think anything could have stopped us, but we hurt ourselves. ...I will not leave this stadium thinking we got beat by a better team. I think that that team is not a very good team and it sickens me that we lost to them."[1474]

Piller elaborated: "Everyone was talking about their defense. I thought it sucked. It'd be a shock to me if they were holding the trophy at the end of all this."[1475] The Patriots, of course, went on to beat the Colts and Panthers and hold the trophy at the end. After losing to the Patriots 30-20 in 2004, Seattle Seahawks safety Terreal Bierria blamed the referees for correctly ruling that Patriots receiver Bethel Johnson had caught a 48-yard pass: "They're at home, they're going to get the call. I saw it kind of hit the ground, but it was too close, just like the referee said, to overturn it."[1476] Every camera angle showed that Johnson caught the pass.

After the Patriots defeated the heavily-favored Pittsburgh Steelers in the 2001 AFC Championship Game, bitter Steelers quarterback Kordell Stewart said, "The best team doesn't always win."[1477] The Steelers had already booked hotel rooms for the Super Bowl and felt entitled to win the AFC Championship Game because they had the best record in the AFC in 2001 and were playing the Patriots at home in Pittsburgh.

If the Steelers weren't embarrassed enough after saying the Patriots didn't deserve to beat them, they made a mockery of themselves in the opening game of 2002. With the Patriots leading 27-7 and just 10½ minutes left to play, "Jason Gilden celebrated after a tackle on wide receiver Troy Brown on a meaningless first down play."[1478] Down 30-7 with just several minutes left, the Steelers refused to accept reality. Instead of kneeling down to end the game without risk of needless injuries to players on both teams (as almost any team would do in that situation), Pittsburgh called two timeouts on the final drive and feverishly drove downfield before Stewart scored a meaningless touchdown on fourth down with just one second left in the game.

Contrast the Steelers' behavior with that of Patriots defensive lineman Vince Wilfork. Though just a rookie, Wilfork already typifies the let-your-performance-do-your-talking mentality the Patriots' personnel people seek and the Patriots' coaching staff teaches: "I don't run my mouth on the field. I don't do that because I believe that when you make a tackle, you're supposed to do that. There's nothing else to say. That's what you get paid to do."[1479]

Teams that blame defeats on "bad luck" or referees always seem to find a way to lose. When the Patriots lose, they compliment their opponent and blame themselves. They don't make excuses for losing or for performing poorly. Following an embarrassing August 2004 shredding at the hands (claws?) of the Cincinnati Bengals, Patriots cornerback Ty Law didn't rationalize defeat by calling it "only a preseason game" or any other excuse. He said, simply, "They beat us like we were some kids. They were the grown men on Saturday night."[1480] After a 31-0 loss to the Buffalo Bills on opening day 2003, the Patriots went 17-1 the rest of the season and the Bills 5-10. Nevertheless, Patriots players never called that 31-0 defeat a "fluke" or blamed it on the obvious: a shell-shocked Patriot locker room after coaches cut starting safety Lawyer Milloy days before the game and Milloy wore the Bills' uniform on opening day. Patriots receiver Troy Brown makes no such excuses: "They just pounded us. They just beat us. They were a better team than we were, and they just took advantage. They beat our heads into the ground and never let up."[1481] Ty Law: "We got hammered."[1482] Belichick: "We... got hammered in every phase of the game. We got outcoached, outplayed. ...The game could have been a lot worse than it was."[1483]

Anything you say can and will be used against you

"There's no upside in putting your foot on the fallen carcass and smiling for the camera."[1484]
– Tom E. Curran (Providence Journal) on Belichick's philosophy

"[Belichick] pointed out before our game with the Jets [that] their star cornerback, Aaron Glenn, was already talking about them positioning themselves for the playoffs and trying to get home field advantage. ... Belichick doesn't want any of his players talking about home field advantage with four or five games left... That kind of talk goes no further than the locker room."[1485]
– Patriots inside linebackers coach Pepper Johnson

Players who "talk trash" about their upcoming opponent or about what they're going to do against their upcoming opponent are asking for trouble. At best, such boasts become bulletin board material in the opponent's locker room, free motivational material to focus one's opponent on playing their best game to embarrass and discredit the boaster. Consider this boast from Carolina Panthers defensive tackle Brentson Buckner before Super Bowl XXXVIII: "We're the best defensive line in the NFL, point blank, by far."[1486] Do you think the Patriots defensive line might have been a tad insulted? Do you think the Patriots offensive line might have seen that as a challenge worthy of stepped-up effort? Of course! Patriots offensive lineman Joe Andruzzi says, "Two weeks straight, we heard how we were supposed to get dominated, get our asses kicked. We kept our mouths shut when other people were talking and shoved it right back at them and came out with the victory."[1487] How about Panthers safety Deon Grant predicting "Us winning"[1488]? How about Panthers defensive lineman Julius Peppers saying, "[Patriots running back] Antowain Smith runs the ball hard, but they're not an overpowering group. I don't think they can overpower us up front"[1489]?

Bragging and insulting one's opponent before a game is particularly stupid. You'll never see such self-defeating behavior from a New England Patriot, at least until Bill Belichick retires some day. Belichick insists his players let their play on the field do their "talking" for them. It's not what you say but what you do that counts. Buckner's boast is even stupider given that the Panthers were second in the league in sacks. What does it accomplish to boast about the obvious (that you've got a great defensive line)? Perhaps a player, unit or team that felt unfairly criticized or underrated might want to boast to boost its confidence or challenge itself by raising the rhetorical stakes (as Joe Namath arguably did before the Jets stunned the Colts). But when you're already acknowledged to be the best, boasting is like declaring you're so good you'll just play the game with one shoe and no helmet. You handicap yourself when you hand emotional ammunition to your opponent to turn around and shoot you. Before the Patriots played the Seattle Seahawks, former Seahawk and current Patriot tight end Christian Fauria refused to compare Belichick and former coach Mike Holmgren: "No, I'm not going to compare him to Belichick. I'm not going to go there. That's a little land mine waiting to blow up in my face."[1490]

Even after a victory, bragging can lead to trouble. On December 22, 2001, the Patriots grabbed the AFC East lead away from the Dolphins, winning 20-13 by forcing and recovering three Dolphins fumbles.[1491] Defeated and disappointed Dolphins cornerback Sam Madison was furious: "year after year it's the same thing. Once we get into the month of December, we always fall apart. I don't know what it is. We've got to find some kind of cure for it."[1492] I can't explain the Dolphins' annual late-season swoon, but the mouth of Dolphins running back Lamar Smith contributed to his team's 2001 swoon. Asked, after the Dolphins trounced the Patriots 30-10 on October 7, whether he was tired after running for 144 yards and a touchdown,[1493] Smith answered, "There's a difference if you're hit hard." Before the teams' December 22 rematch, Patriots coaches reminded players that Smith had dissed them for their light hitting. Hearing that, Patriots safety Tebucky Jones declared, "Well, he's gonna know he's been hit this time!"[1494] In the rematch, Jones collided fiercely with Dolphins all game long and jarred loose two fumbles the Patriots recovered: first by tight end Jed Weaver (recovered by Otis Smith), and second on a smack-down of Lamar Smith himself (recovered by Roman Phifer).

Bill Belichick always respects and compliments his opponents. Even after the Patriots obliterated the Jets 44-7 in 2002, Belichick said, "We're fortunate we didn't catch them on their best day."[1495] Belichick does not tolerate his players denigrating other teams. Soon after Patriots tight end Rod Rutledge helped win the February 2002 Super Bowl, Patriots coaches decided to let him go.[1496] One possible reason: Rutledge mocked the Rams before Adam Vinatieri's game-winning kick. Holder Ken Walter told Rutledge to "shut up" because his obnoxiousness was upsetting Vinatieri.[1497] Belichick cut defensive tackle Steve Martin in 2002 a day after Martin said, "[New York Jets center Kevin Mawae] plays dirty. Somebody probably got mad because he did something dirty to them. That doesn't surprise me. He used to do that all the time when I was there."[1498] Mawae does play dirty. In 2004, NFL players voted Mawae one of the league's dirtiest players.[1499] Long before joining the Patriots, nose tackle Ted Washington believed Mawae played dirty, and Washington's agent said an intentionally dirty hit from Mawae broke Washington's leg in September 2003.[1500] Mawae's response: "Tell [Washington] to keep his fat ass off the ground."[1501] But the fact that Steve Martin was right about Mawae was irrelevant. Belichick expects Patriots to refrain from even truthful disparaging statements.

What does Belichick want his players to say? Before Mawae and the Jets visited Foxboro in 2004, even New York papers were talking openly about Mawae's dirty tricks:

> "Is Kevin Mawae dirty …? The center has played three straight weeks with a hard cast covering his fractured right hand. In his first week wearing the cast, a 17-9 victory at Miami on Oct. 3, Mawae upset several Dolphins defenders and was warned by officials for wielding his injured hand like a club. Yesterday, Mawae drew an unsportsmanlike-conduct penalty for whacking 49ers defensive tackle Tony Brown across the head."[1502]

Another New York paper called him "Kevin (Clubber) Mawae."[1503] Mawae wasn't apologizing for bashing opponents' heads with his cast: "If you don't like the way I play, don't step on the field."[1504] Nevertheless, the Patriots had only wonderful things to say about him. Safety Rodney Harrison: "I love the way he plays."[1505] Defensive end Ty Warren: "We could be here all day if we're talking about a guy like him. …He plays hard. …He's a special player."[1506] Defensive tackle Keith Traylor: "Let's go play football, whine later. Dirty is someone's perception. I've [battled Mawae] over the years and it's a good physical game. Whoever's saying [he's dirty] is probably upset because they got the [stuffing] blocked out of them."[1507] Linebacker Mike Vrabel praised Mawae's cast-wielding and after-the-whistle-blows hitting with the same charm John Edwards used to praise Dick Cheney's love for his lesbian daughter: "if [Mawae] has to put [a cast] on and it happens to find its way into somebody's facemask or in the helmet or whatever, you know, this is professional football. He can't grab with it, so he might as well punch you with it. But he's a guy who plays through the whistle."[1508] Belichick says, "He is tough. He is the kind of guy you like to have on your team."[1509]

Another reason to keep your mouth shut is to avoid giving away secrets, such as your game plan. In a game as close as Super Bowl XXXVIII, which was decided by a field goal in the game's final seconds, any little edge helps. It's possible the Panthers' pre-game blabbing cost them the game, much like businessmen drunk in airport bars revealing corporate secrets. Patriots offensive coordinator Charlie Weis explained after the game how they took advantage of information Panthers' players revealed before the game:

> "We listened to what their players were saying. They were saying how we throw off of three-step drops, so they had to have their hands up [to knock down quick passes] and try to hit Brady. We knew they were going to be attacking at the line of scrimmage. But we also knew if they were going to do that, the immediate zone behind the defensive line was open. So we were attacking that area."[1510]

"[Panthers players] said, 'We're going to hit Brady. We're going to knock down the three-step drop passes.' It doesn't take a brain surgeon to figure that means you can throw behind the linebackers. They helped us out a little bit by telling us what they were going to do." [1511]

Belichick himself keeps his mouth shut to avoid talking his way into trouble. After walking away from a job as New York Jets head coach and instead becoming Patriots head coach, Belichick refused to answer media questions regarding the Jets, instead saying simply "I've moved on." [1512]

If you must gloat, wait till you've won

"I was confident we could win. We didn't have to tell anyone that. We just knew it ourselves." [1513]
– Tom Brady, after beating the Rams in Super Bowl XXXVI

"We don't have a bunch of clowns. We don't have a bunch of guys doing push-ups and sit-ups [after scoring a touchdown]. …We're not trying to have guys draw attention to themselves and get singled out, flexing their muscles and stuff. Just play football and win some games." [1514]
– Patriots safety Rodney Harrison

There's nothing more ridiculous than some self-absorbed football player strutting around after a big play while the scoreboard says their team is losing by double digits. You'll never hear a Patriot compare his team's upcoming opponent unfavorably to a Pee Wee football team. You'll never see a Patriot celebrate while his team's heading for defeat. You'll never hear a Patriot guarantee a victory. Loud-mouthed players often hurt their teams and embarrass themselves:

"Bengals Pro Bowl receiver Chad Johnson perked up Cincinnati's rivalry with the Browns by shipping each of Cleveland's four defensive backs a bottle of Pepto-Bismol last week, a not-so-subtle hint that covering him would leave them feeling sick. Only it was Johnson's stomach that was turning after having more dropped passes (four) than receptions (three) in a 34-17 laugher. 'This is my most frustrating game ever,' he said. 'I made the challenge. I didn't perform.' Browns safety Earl Little told Johnson to expect a package in return. 'I told him, "Hey, I'm going to FedEx that stuff back to you, because you really need it,"' Little said. 'He didn't have much to say after that.'" [1515]

Legendary Cleveland Browns coach Paul Brown once said, "If you get into the end zone, act like you've been there before." Belichick probably absorbed this lesson as young "Billy" attending Browns training camp with his father.

The only time you'll catch sight of a celebrating Patriot is during the brief interval following victory and preceding the start of preparations for the next game. Offensive coordinator Charlie Weis waited for the appropriate moment to respond to

Warren Sapp's insulting prediction that the Patriots would lose Super Bowl XXXVIII to the Panthers because Russ Hochstein, an offensive lineman playing in place of injured star Damien Woody, "couldn't block either one of you two fellas [sports prognosticators Tony Kornheiser and Michael Wilbon]." After Weis' patchwork offensive line cruised through the entire postseason without surrendering a sack and helped the Patriots win Super Bowl XXXVIII, Weis told the media, "Tell Warren, it's Russ Hock-stein (pronounced HOK-steen)."[1516]

But mouthing off, even after the fact, can come back to haunt you. After the Patriots handed reporter Michael Holley an "backstage pass" throughout 2002 and part of 2003, coaches' "private" words returned to haunt them in 2004. The book, containing derogatory statements about quite a few Buffalo Bills players, was published before the teams played. "News cameras caught [the Bills head coach] needling Clements and the offensive linemen about Belichick's disparaging remarks."[1517] Bills coaches didn't have any problem motivating players. They just handed out copies of *Patriot Reign*. Bills running back Travis Henry said, "It's really motivating from a guy like Belichick who has won two Super Bowls. It's motivating. That's how everyone is using it."[1518] The Patriots won anyhow.

The best marketing is a great product

Too many players and coaches exhaust themselves trying to shape how the media portrays them. Such behavior stems from insecurity. Confident people don't define themselves by their media coverage or by how well their player performs in the *Madden Football* video game. The Patriots don't worry about anything irrelevant to winning football games, so they certainly don't worry about comments from outsiders who know far less than they know. The Patriots worry about winning because the Patriots' players, coaches, executives, and owners all believe the best marketing is a winning team. So they throw all their effort into improving their team, not slapping lipstick on a proverbial pig.

Before Super Bowl XXXVIII, offensive lineman Russ Hochstein was asked whether all the talk about the the Patriots' offensive line being their Achilles Heel upset him and whether the offensive line deserved more respect. Hochstein displayed the Patriots' intense focus on winning and complete lack of concern about everything else, replying, "None of it means anything unless you win. I just want to win so bad I don't care about anything [else]."[1519]

In Belichick's first head coaching interview, the Arizona Cardinals made clear they wanted their head coach to travel around Arizona generating excitement for the team that have relocated from St. Louis a year earlier. Belichick says, "I figured winning would generate the interest as opposed to going out and doing little rallies."[1520]

STAY MENTALLY STRONG

"Being tough is not just physical. It's mental, too. Character and toughness are the first two things we look at when we scout a player. That's the kind of player Bill likes. It's the kind of player I like."[1521]
  – VP of player personnel Scott Pioli

"I stopped stretching out on the field before games a few years ago. I don't want to see anyone I'm playing against, be all friendly with them, and then have to be like: 'Oh, by the way, I'm going to try to knock your head off today.' So I avoid that."[1522]
  – Patriots tight end Christian Fauria

Staying mentally strong requires fighting fiercely till the end and maintaining your composure and focus, win or lose.

"Finish the play"

"They just keep fighting. They don't know any other way to do it."[1523]
  – Bill Belichick, after his Patriots won Super Bowl XXXVI

"We just were trying to keep our poise. You realize in games like this you've got to play for 60 minutes. We made enough plays toward the end to win it. … That's what happens in Super Bowls."[1524]
  – Tom Brady, after winning Super Bowl XXXVIII with a field goal with mere seconds left on the clock

Becoming champion in a league as competitive as the NFL requires that every player perform his job as professionally and thoroughly as possible. If you're going to do something, do it properly. The Patriots call this "finishing the play." During practice, players go easy on one another. But, in games, players don't merely tackle; they smash into opponents, seeking to separate player from ball. They don't just block an opponent; they try to knock him on his [expletive deleted]. After catching a pass, they squirm and spin and lower their shoulder pads to avoid getting tackled. In pursuit of the quarterback, they may leap over a player who has been knocked to the ground. When the opposing quarterback throws a pass, they'll wave their arms and leap into the air to bat the ball down. They go all out to make good things happen. And they scratch and claw for 60 minutes, not 58 or 59. After Cardinals quarterback Jake McCown was sacked five times, knocked down five more times, hurried eleven times, intercepted twice, had four passes batted down, and completed just 13 of 29 pass attempts for 160 yards and zero touchdowns,[1525] he was awed by Patriots defenders' hustle:

"Everyone runs to the football. I got outside the pocket a few times, and there were people coming from everywhere. It's rare to see guys coming from the other side of the field at full speed. They are all coming and they play the whole play."[1526]

Though both Patriots Super Bowl victories were heartwrenchers, I reacted completely differently to the two. In the first, I couldn't believe my eyes. Could my Patriots possibly defeat the mighty Rams? Two years later, I knew so much about the Patriots' hearts and minds that, even after the Panthers tied the game near the end, I was supremely confident the Pats would find a way to win. My wife (who had lent her heart that fall to the Red Sox only to have it crushed by a Yankees extra-innings walk-off home run in Game 7 of the American League Championship Series) was panicking, but I kept assuring her that these Patriots are *not* the Red Sox and would find a way to *win*, not a way to lose. Our conversation mirrored a conversation between Patriots defenders Bobby Hamilton and Willie McGinest. McGinest assured a worried Hamilton, "We're going to kick a field goal. Relax man, you're gonna have a heart attack!"[1527]

The Patriots have great physical stamina and mental toughness. It shows in their 29-game winning streak when leading after three quarters of play. The Patriots haven't blown a late-game lead since 2000, yet they can and have come from behind to win. In his three seasons, Tom Brady has led fifteen game-winning drives in the fourth quarter or overtime. In the Patriots' first Super Bowl victory, the Rams came back to tie the game, 17-17. NFL guru and former Super Bowl-winning coach John Madden, who was broadcasting Super Bowl XXXVI for Fox, insisted the Patriots had too little time left (1:21) and too much distance to score (83 yards) and, therefore, shouldn't take the risk of throwing a game-losing interception and should just run out the clock and take their chances in overtime: "Brady should take a knee and get this to overtime! I don't like this strategy at all. The Patriots shouldn't be taking these chances!"[1528] As Madden was preaching conservatism, Belichick was telling Brady to "Go win the game"[1529] and Drew Bledsoe was urging his former understudy to "Drop back and sling it!"[1530] Brady methodically drove the Patriots 53 yards down field, taking a bunch of short completions to running backs J.R. Redmond and Jermaine Wiggins plus a 23-yarder to Troy Brown, whatever the defense allowed him while conserving the clock. Then Adam Vinatieri drilled the dramatic game-winning 48-yard field goal as time expired.

Two years later, like the odds-makers in Vegas, I expected a comfortable Super Bowl victory over the Panthers and was surprised when the teams played a tight, back-and-forth game. A rash of atypical events (some of which the Panthers deserve great credit for) conspired to complicate the Patriots' quest for a second Super Bowl victory:

· Although no offense had scored a 30+ yard touchdown play against the Pats' defense the entire season, the Panthers hit *three* (of 33, 39, and 85 yards) during the Super Bowl! Kudos to the Panthers, *esp.* quarterback Jake Delhomme who played a heck of a game. The 33-yarder, a DeShaun Foster run, was the only run of more than 23 yards the Patriots defense surrendered all season.

· Adam Vinatieri missed a field goal and had another blocked. This was especially shocking because he had previously missed only one indoor field goal in his entire career.

· The Patriots defense forced a fumble that Ty Law scooped up and probably would have run back for a touchdown but for a *dreadful* call (ruling it an incomplete pass, even though the receiver clearly had possession). *Boston Globe* reporter Nick Cafardo later reported, "Muhammad definitely fumbled... The ref blew that one. The replay clearly showed Muhammad had caught the ball, was looking to turn up field, and lost it."[1531]

· Just before halftime, the Patriots kicked a poor squib kick, giving the Panthers excellent field position, and then played poor defense, thus gifting Carolina a late 50-yard field goal and an emotional boost entering the locker room.

· Tom Brady threw a completely uncharacteristic interception in the end zone when all he had to do was throw the ball away and kick the "easy" field goal to put the game out of reach and cement a Patriots victory. (Admittedly, there were no "easy" ones that day!) I was screaming to Tom at the top of my lungs as he rolled out to pass, but he apparently didn't hear me.

· The Panthers' game-tying touchdown came from picking on backup safeties (Shawn Mayer and Chris Akins) after *both* of the Patriots' starting safeties were injured during the game... Rodney Harrison broke his arm and Eugene Wilson tore his left groin muscle.

· The Patriots' final game-winning drive nearly stalled after a "questionable pass interference call on receiver Troy Brown"[1532] cost the Patriots thirty yards (giving the Patriots 1st-and-20 at their own 43-yard line instead of 1st-and-10 at the Panthers' 27-yard line). Tom Brady said that after that flag was thrown, "I was yelling at the ref and telling him he was full of crap."[1533]

Despite mistakes/blunders, bad calls, injuries, and superb play by the Panthers, the Patriots still came away with the Vince Lombardi trophy. Great teams dig deep and find a way to win, even on bad days when playing strong opponents.

What made the 2003 season truly amazing was the Pats overcoming countless injuries. The Patriots' opening day starters missed a collective 103 games in 2003 due to injuries.[1534] 42 different guys started games this season. Few teams start 42 players, and almost every team that does start so many different players finishes with one of the worst records in the league. Since at least 1970, no NFL team had won its division while starting 42 different players that season.[1535] Through it all, the Patriots refused to whine about their injuries or mistakes or get mad when referees made terrible calls that cost them touchdowns. After each injury, they just plugged in the next guy and ratcheted up their effort. And after each bad play, they just ratcheted up their resolve to do better on the next play.

The Patriots' ability to block out misfortune and adversity to focus squarely on making optimal use of whatever time remains in a game is a hallmark of the team, a trait very deliberately instilled by Coach Belichick. Patriot players concentrate on each and every play because Bill Belichick prepares them to be mentally tough and to focus on whatever they can do each instant to help their team win. He tells them, for example, "You can't control what the refs call. Don't get involved. Let me do the bitching and bickering. You guys still have to play the game."[1536] Cornerback Ty Law says, "When our backs are to the wall, that's when we feel most comfortable, because we trust ourselves and we trust our coaches. We look at all 11 guys and know we can get it done."[1537]

That mental stamina paid off. Many narrow Patriot victories, including Super Bowl XXXVIII, might have been losses if players had let down emotionally, even slightly. Admitted Belichick: "[Super Bowl XXXVIII] was a terrific game to watch, but a heart attack to coach. It was a great team effort. We've done it 15 weeks in a row. And I'm really fortunate."[1538] Patriots defensive tackle Richard Seymour explains that Patriot players look forward to adversity because they know that's when winners separate themselves from losers:

> "everybody fights for the ultimate goal. That's why you play the game and strap it up every week. ... [E]arly in the season is like the first quarter of a game. Anybody can be good then, but in the fourth quarter, that's when the elite players step up and make plays. When you're tired, some guys want to quit or won't perform well under pressure. Some guys can't cut it. But we've been a team that, when it's crunch time, we step up and embrace it when other teams crack. We love the challenge where you have to go out and prove you're champions again."[1539]

Every Super Bowl champion has been lucky during the season, but great teams seem to conjure up good fortune. As Branch Rickey said, "Luck is the residue of design." Luck is also the residue of playing a full sixty minutes of smart, impassioned football... sometimes even more than sixty minutes. NFL.com's Vic Carucci was amazed by the Patriots' tenacity in Miami:

> "The Patriots are amazing. They keep losing front-line players and they keep on winning. ...this club thrives on adversity. ...the players actually raise their performance level whenever another starter goes down with an injury. Given their depleted roster and the South Florida heat, they could have easily wilted. Instead, they persevered, battled back to push the Dolphins to overtime and won."[1540]

Be tough

"People who are successful are ones who, when it doesn't work out, continue to give their full effort and continue to battle regardless of how many times things don't work out their way."[1541]
– Patriots linebacker prospect Justin Kurpeikis

"Of course it's personal. They're trying to score touchdowns. They're trying to end your livelihood. Their success is your downfall. They don't have any love for me."[1542]
– Patriots safety Rodney Harrison

Patriots players are both mentally and physically tough, often playing on Sundays despite excruciatingly painful injuries or illnesses. Patriots players are so tough the team has been accused by its hometown media of manipulating its injury reports. For example, after "most of the 18 names on coach Bill Belichick's entry to the Week 9 NFL Injury Report 'miraculously' gained the good health go-ahead to play yesterday," Hector Longo concluded, perhaps correctly, that the injury report was "a Belichick ruse."[1543]

But the fact that a Patriot plays in a game doesn't mean he's healthy. Many Patriots, including Tom Brady, have played with secret injuries that required off-season surgery. And players play through pain. Patriot cornerback Ty Law played brilliantly in 2003 despite playing most of the season with a high ankle sprain and later suffering an abdominal problem. Patriot linebacker Mike Vrabel also had a great 2003 season, even though he missed three games with a broken arm and played much of the season with an arm cast, an act of courage admired by fellow linebacker Tedy Bruschi: "Quarterback sacks, forced fumbles, interceptions, he's nice to have around. And the thing is all this he's doing in pain, and he's still not 100 percent."[1544] As injured cornerback Ty Law said days after begging Coach Belichick to let him back into a game:

> "This is football, and you're not ever going to be 100 percent. …I want to be out there on the field. I get paid to play. …I usually disregard how my body is feeling and go with what my heart tells me. My heart tells me to play regardless of the situation. But you have to be smart about it and do what's best for the team. But if I can try to go out there and play, I'm going to try to go. As long as I'm not hurting my team, I feel good about playing."[1545]

One of the toughest Patriots is 315-pound offensive lineman Joe Andruzzi. Andruzzi comes from a tough family. His three brothers are all New York City firefighters who were at the Twin Towers on 9/11. They all survived, though one had reached the 23rd floor before escaping. Andruzzi says "my brothers are my heroes."[1546] His fellow lineman Stephen Neal says of Andruzzi's toughness: "He'll get hit on one of his injuries and you can see he's in a lot of pain and it doesn't matter.

He gets back out there. This is his job and he gets it done. The stuff he's been through, sticking it out no matter what it is, everybody on the offensive line respects him for that."[1547]

The Patriots practice hard and in adverse weather, and refuse to blame poor performance on the weather, so they are prepared to play under any conditions. After one training camp practice when temperatures hit 90 degrees, Belichick explained that training in heat and humidity is necessary because the NFL doesn't cancel games due to heat and humidity: "Yeah, somebody turned [the heat] on. There's no other way to condition for it other than to play in it. You talk about it, but you know you got to get out there and sweat. Your body's got to get acclimated to the heat and the humidity."[1548]

Practicing and playing under any conditions and refusing to use the weather as an excuse build mental toughness that helps the team win. After beating the Raiders in the "Tuck Rule" playoff game, Tom Brady said the Patriots thrive in bad weather: "We've played in bad weather. We've played at night. We've been in a lot of situations and it made us stronger. There's four inches of snow out there. You just do whatever you got to do to win."[1549]

Adam Vinatieri, who kicked two huge field goals in that "Tuck Rule" game, including an instant NFL Films classic—a 45-yarder into a blizzard to tie the game—says simply, "Good guys find a way to get it done."[1550] While the Californian Raiders looked less than thrilled about the snow, Patriots like Troy Brown felt like little kids:

> "It was like playing old school football again. I was thinking back to the 'frozen tundra' and the Green Bay Packers winning the Super Bowl. It was fun being out there playing. We just found a way to pull out the game. It wasn't the prettiest game you've ever seen because of the weather, but it was still fun to get out there and play around in the snow. You felt like a big kid again."[1551]

Don't ride an emotional roller coaster

"[I]t's important as a team that we just don't get too high when we win or too low when we lose. If we avoid that, we'll be fine."[1552]
– Patriots defensive lineman Richard Seymour

"[Belichick] preached to us that one week had nothing to do with the next."[1553]
– Patriots special teams captain Larry Izzo

NFL teams in the salary cap era are seldom as good as they look after a victory and seldom as poor as they appear after a defeat. Recognizing this, smart teams don't wallow in self-pity or self-loathing following defeats and don't strut like peacocks following victories, no matter how big. Smart coaches find encouraging words to buoy spirits when things are going poorly and find nits to pick when things are going great.

Looking at Bill Belichick's face during a game won't tell you whether the Patriots are winning or losing. He wears a "game face" that lasts till the game ends. Even after big victories, you'll seldom see Belichick celebrate for more than a second or two. He once flung his headset into the air following an improbable overtime victory in Miami (where the Patriots almost always lose), but such celebrations are rare. As one player joked after catching a fleeting Belichick smile following a close victory, "I didn't think he had those muscles."[1554] By the time a game ends, Belichick seems to skip "relish victory" and jump immediately to "think about next game." So it was real news when he waved to the crowd and cracked a smile after the Patriots won their 21st-straight. Reporters demanded that Belichick account for his human-like behavior: "Well, I was just waving to the kids. I usually try to do that."[1555]

After winning Super Bowl XXXVIII, his team had seven months off, so Belichick relaxed long enough to joke, "We're on such a high, I don't think we [need a] plane to get back to Boston."[1556] How long did Belichick celebrate his second Vince Lombardi trophy?

"Two days after the game, Pioli and Belichick were in a meeting at 6 a.m. That was followed by the team's parade through Boston, which was followed by another meeting. On the Wednesday after the Super Bowl, the Patriots began a 13-day stretch of staff sessions in preparation for the draft."[1557]

Tough times and silver linings

"[Football]'s very unforgiving when things don't go right. You're in a man's game and you get bumped around. ...You need to really stay with it and you have to work it all the time because it's changing all the time."[1558]
— *Patriots owner Robert Kraft*

"You don't marvel at your accomplishments. You marvel at your disappointments and think about ways we can get better."[1559]
— *Patriots safety Rodney Harrison*

"I'm still picking the Eagles in a romp... This is a game I had the Eagles winning anyway when I made my 10-6 prediction for the Pats. I feel so distant from that 10-6 right now. Imagine the guys who were picking 12-4 and 13-3?"[1560]
— *Boston Globe reporter Nick Cafardo after the Patriots were crushed in their first game of 2003. The Patriots are 26-2 since Cafardo's column*

In Belichick's first season as Patriots head coach, the 2000 Patriots went 5-11. Nine losses were by eight points (a touchdown and 2-point conversion) or less.

Belichick became the team cheerleader. After the 2000 Patriots lost their first four games then won two, cornerback Ty Law noted Belichick's positive attitude: "He's been telling us good things were going to happen. It was almost to the point where we were asking ourselves, 'When?' Bill gives you that feeling that you're going to succeed. And we feel it. I know I do."[1561] (In 1995, Belichick similarly said of his struggling Cleveland Browns, "We're not that bad. But when you don't win, people lose confidence."[1562]) Belichick attempted to will his players into adopting a "never surrender" attitude:

> "The message I'm trying to send to the team is that every week, every game, we will do everything we can to win. We will not accept losing. The fans have been very supportive. I know the fans are frustrated. I don't blame them. Believe me, nobody is more frustrated than the players and the coaches of the New England Patriots. There's been a lot of blood, sweat and tears put into this season and we don't have much to show for it. We're going to win. We are going to win. We're going in the right direction."[1563]

After his 2000 Patriots were crushed 34-9 by the Lions on Thanksgiving, bringing their record to 3-9, Belichick gave players the long weekend off. Belichick knew that punishing players with additional practices might have demoralized them. His encouraging attitude was intended to buck up the team's confidence in the face of disappointment. After the Patriots lost their 2003 season opener 31-0, Belichick immediately put the game out of mind: "We've had the autopsy. We're past it. You can't kill it again. How many times can you pump bullets into a dead body?"[1564] His quarterback, Tom Brady, must have gotten the memo because he also was upbeat and proactively looking forward to the next game: "I think it is time to take those things we have learned and to put them to good use next Sunday. It's not like you can wipe it all away with a magic wand."[1565]

Proof of the value of shoving aside past disappointments is the miraculous way the Patriots rebounded from a 5-11 season in 2000 and a 1-3 start in 2001 (plus the loss of their star quarterback, Drew Bledsoe, to a life-threatening injury) to win the Super Bowl just months later. After going 6-14 as head coach of the Patriots, Belichick could have hit the proverbial "Panic" button. Instead, he focused everyone on game #21:

> "There was no ranting and raving, no finger-pointing, no threats to bench guys–none of that. In fact he didn't even show the team the entire game tape the next day. He made the coaches aware of what happened so we could all go back and tell our respective units. We [coaches] took the blame, showed them a couple of plays, and then moved on. ...Belichick's theme was 'It's done; let's put it behind us and get ready for San Diego.'"[1566]

That focus was essential because "We were on the verge of cracking. If [Chargers quarterback] Doug Flutie had come to town and won another ball game, I can honestly say I don't think we would have been able to overcome it."[1567]

Don't let the good times roll

"Congratulations on a good regular season."
   – *Bill Belichick after his team won its twelfth straight game to finish the 2003 season 14-2*

"We are a long way from being a good football team right now."[1568]
   – *Bill Belichick after his team won its 17th-straight game*

"If you look at the film, we've struggled. We've committed too many penalties. We've committed too many bone-headed plays. We've been fortunate to win these ballgames. But eventually it's going to come back and bite us in the butt."[1569]
   – *Patriots safety Rodney Harrison, after winning 18 straight games*

"Congratulations on the [NFL-record 19-game winning] streak. Great job. Now we've got to think about Seattle."[1570]
   – *Bill Belichick*

The *Lowell Sun*'s David Pevear calls Bill Belichick a "killjoy coach"[1571] because, following success, Belichick quickly lances any ego bubbles. After the Patriots shocked the Rams (a team whose success led to arrogance, complacency about turnovers, and a feeling of invincibility) to win Super Bowl XXXVI, the Patriots returned to Boston for a parade and celebration attended by 1,250,000 hysterical fans.[1572] Belichick knew his next challenge was preventing complacency and resting on laurels:

"The day after the big parade, Coach Belichick scheduled a staff meeting… Everyone was pretty much still riding high, still in the celebration mode. Belichick came in, and as soon as he started to speak we knew. The business voice was back. Listening to him, you never would have thought we had just won the Super Bowl."[1573]

After winning his second Super Bowl in three seasons, Belichick spent two days with his old Cleveland Browns defensive coordinator, Nick Saban, devising new defenses: "He had just won the Super Bowl, for crying out loud, but here he was. We went at it for two days."[1574] Then Belichick picked Jimmy Johnson's brain about how to hold together a Super Bowl winner: "Jimmy's really the only guy in this era who's lived it, who's dealt with what we're dealing with, and more. Who else am I gonna talk to?"[1575] After returning to Foxboro, Belichick went negative on his players, according to running back Kevin Faulk:

"You don't hear [talk about "dynasty"] a lot in the locker room. We know we still have a lot to work on to get to that point. As a matter of fact, we recently met to watch film and coach put up all our bad plays from last year. It's to remind us who we are. We are no better than the next team if we don't go out there and try to get it right on every play."[1576]

When he finally took a real vacation (in Nantucket, where he owns three homes), Belichick "relaxed" with audiotapes of D. Michael Abrashoff's *It's Your Ship: Management Techniques from the Best Damn Ship in the Navy.*

After the 2004 Patriots whooped the Philadelphia Eagles (participants in three consecutive NFC Championship Games and preseason favorites to win the NFC) 24-6 in their opening preseason game, Belichick sounded like a coach in agony:

"[W]e struggled in the passing game. We really didn't do a good job defensively with the quarterback, gave up some easy running yardage, struggled on the punt returns, stuff like that. ... [W]e've got a long way to go, let's put it that way, in every phase of the game."[1577]

After watching tape of the game, Belichick spent an entire day of practice on remedial passing drills because he purported to be horrified by the team's inability to properly execute a pass... despite his quarterbacks' very impressive 114.8 quarterback rating:

"All the passes that we completed were ones that [the quarterback] scrambled around on or broke a tackle in the pocket or some loose play where we got it out to somebody. At some point during the year you have to drop back, block 'em, throw it and catch it. This isn't junior high school football with everybody running around and going different directions. ...We got guys coming through the line of scrimmage unblocked."[1578]

By mid-week, Belichick's displeasure had players apologizing for their "poor" game and promising to improve. Center Dan Koppen said, "The coaching staff expects more from us. There's no reason they shouldn't. When little things break down, we've got to go back to the board and try to fix them."[1579] Receiver David Patten said:

"It's training camp. We all believe in perfection, but let's face it—we're only human. I don't believe we ever feel like we've arrived, and that's why we enjoy the success we have. We have to work hard week in and week out on the things we're not doing well, and hopefully in this next game, we can show that we've got it corrected."[1580]

After his team extended its undefeated streak to 17 games, could Belichick find things to complain about? "We can put together a pretty good list."[1581] To start, Belichick was upset with eleven costly penalties resulting from poor concentration:

"We've been emphasizing [penalty-avoidance] from the first day of training camp, and we'll continue to emphasize it... because those are all negative plays. We want to eliminate every one of them; some are really careless.

Jumping the snap count, jumping offsides, going in motion, jamming a guy too far downfield, hitting [an opponent] out of bounds, that's not acceptable, and it's not good football. ...You just can't keep doing those things and think it's not going to catch up with you because it will. "[1582]

Patriots players always seem to drag out historical examples that keep them humble and worried. After winning their 19th-straight game in 2004, Tom Brady said, "we win 15 in a row last year and then begin 4-0 this year. ...But you know things can change really fast. Remember two years ago we were 3-0 and then we were 3-4 after seven games."[1583]

In 2001, the Patriots became champions after successfully challenging themselves to overcome mediocrity. In 2003, the Patriots became champions again after overcoming the burden of success. The next two sections elaborate on "Overcoming adversity" and "Overcoming success."

OVERCOMING ADVERSITY

"You find out a lot about players when they face adversity."[1584]
– *Patriots safety Rodney Harrison*

"They can be beat. They put their pants on just like we put our pants on. We can compete. We can play. We can win. I'm looking to knock [their quarterback's] head off. That's point-blank football. You can't make them out to be Supermen. You can give them some credit; they've put up a lot of points this season. But I'm not built like that."[1585]
– *Patriots linebacker Bryan Cox, before the 0-2 Patriots faced the 2-0 Indianapolis Colts in 2001, the game that launched their Super Bowl season*

Overcoming adversity requires: 1) embracing challenges, not running from them; and, 2) productively learning and improving, not counter-productively pointing fingers or dwelling on mistakes.

Enjoy the challenge

Patriots players are on a mission. They're out to prove themselves play after play. If they lost last week, they are even more motivated to prove themselves this week. To proud players who don't tolerate defeat, adversity is a stimulant. Patriots defensive lineman Richard Seymour explains his teammates perform well late in games because they're out to prove that their opponents are bigger sissies:

"That's when the elite players step up and make plays. When you're tired, some guys want to quit or won't perform well under pressure. Some guys can't cut it. We've been a team that, when it's crunch time, we step up and embrace it when other teams crack. We love the challenge."[1586]

"Stress" and "choking" are two words seldom used to describe Belichick's Patriots. Belichick's boys love training, practicing, playing, and winning. They don't play to not lose. They play to win. They enjoy every minute of every game because they're doing what they love. And when you're doing what you love, you don't worry about screwing up. You focus on making plays.

For example, Tom Brady has won both Super Bowls he has participated in, each time by driving the length of the field in the closing minute of the game. After the Carolina Panthers tied up Super Bowl XXXVIII, Brady didn't think, "Damn! We could lose. Now I've got to try to score again, and our season's on the line." He thought, "Let's go score the game-winner!" Where most mortals would panic, Brady thrives on the excitement while remaining calm enough to execute brilliantly:

> "To be honest, if you're a quarterback at any level, those are the kinds of moments you live for. It's like basketball. You want the ball in your hand for the last shot. I knew, after [the Panthers] scored (the tying touchdown) that we had enough time, because we've been running our two-minute drill so well. Our offense is so well-designed for those situations. You just try to follow the blueprint, make your reads, make the throws."[1587]

Adversity is an opportunity

> "I've failed many times since graduating [from Columbia] in 1963. ... On the other hand, I wasn't afraid to dream big. Hard work opens doors."[1588]
> – *Patriots owner Bob Kraft, in commencement address*

> "Will [playing without Ty Law and Tyrone Poole, our starting cornerbacks] be a challenge? Yes it will. But that's what you look forward to when you play in the National Football League."[1589]
> – *Patriots cornerback Rodney Harrison*

Nobody ever ever achieved anything great without overcoming adversity. But it's essential to take a problem-solving approach to adversity. As Belichick says, "One of the things I learned in college is how to solve problems, and that's really what football is–challenges and solving the problems."[1590]

Winners overcome disappointments because they see opportunity in every crisis. The Chinese, with their thousands of years of history, so appreciate the close link between crisis and opportunity that their word for "crisis" (weiji) literally means "danger" (wei) + "opportunity" (ji). Where others see danger, Patriots like backup quarterback Rohan Davey see opportunity:

> "We trailed the whole game this week. They beat us up for 52 minutes and then we pulled it out in the last eight minutes... I think it is good for me to experience a game like that though, to come back through the adversity of the ankle injury and mistakes. It's good to get some experience with that

adversity because basically all the games in the NFL come down to that situation. From being in New England and being there for two years I have seen those games. All of them come down to the last drive or the defense has to stop them or the offense has to score, something like that late. It's definitely good to experience something like that and to come away with the win."[1591]

Everyone must cope with setbacks and disappointments and frustrations. How you handle adversity is a key determinant of both your overall effectiveness and your happiness in life. After losing his grandfather to cancer in December 2003 and then his father (after his father murdered his former girlfriend before fatally shooting himself) in April 2004, defensive lineman Richard Seymour could have let his trauma destroy him. Instead, he fought mightily to continue living, despite his heavy heart:

> "I think if you (go through adversity,) that's when you really determine the character of a person. When it's good, anybody can do it. People always talk about my character and what type of guy (I am), but I really haven't been in tough, adverse situations. ...You have to keep pushing on. I know my dad, he would be the type to tell me to go out and handle your business just like a man. It's a process. I'm an emotional guy. There's a process of grieving and not holding anything in." [1592]

Seymour didn't let his father's horrific April murder-suicide derail his May wedding. His father had always counseled him that "nobody beats you when you work hard"[1593] and was probably Seymour's closest friend. Despite deep pain and confusion over his loss, Seymour believes he has gained perspective on life and will emerge stronger:

> "I have two beautiful kids and a lovely wife now. I'm just (realizing) how important it is to spend time with them. This whole offseason, at the end of the day, when it's all said and done, I think it's going to make me a better person and a better man."[1594]

When struggling, breathe deep and regroup

Patriots punter Ken Walter had his worst season in 2003 (37.7 gross yards-per-punt; 33.6 net YPP) and isn't back with the Patriots in 2004. Walter has been replaced by Josh Miller, a consistently excellent punter who averaged 41.9 YPP and 36.0 net YPP with the Pittsburgh Steelers in 2003.[1595] Late in the 2003 season, Walter was reportedly stressed out and letting past mistakes haunt him. Coach Belichick apparently tried to clear Walter's head by releasing him and re-signing him a week later. The following game, Walter played well, booting four punts that averaged over 40 yards. Walter blamed that season's punting mistakes on stress: "It's all mental. That's probably 95 percent of it. I probably put too much pressure on myself at times. You know I don't take my job lightly. I did let some things affect me. That's only natural. I definitely have a better mindset now."[1596] Walter had a spectacular season with the Patriots in 2001, placing 49% of his punts inside the opponent's 20-yard-line and gaining 38.1 net yards per punt. It's a shame Walter could not regain that form. But Walter's solid performance a week after the Patriots released him shows that taking a deep breath can sometimes improve performance. Trying too hard and over-thinking can cause as many problems as laziness and lack of concentration.

Take pride in being an underdog

"That underdog mentality is always dangerous."[1597]
  – St. Louis Rams linebacker London Fletcher, after losing to the Patriots in Super Bowl XXXVI

Throughout the Patriots' 2001 season, virtually no one thought the Patriots could win it all. Late in the regular season, I personally thought the best the Patriots could hope for was a Super Bowl appearance because the St. Louis Rams appeared invincible. But Patriots players thrived on their underdog status all year. They reveled in the low expectations. They viewed disrespect from Vegas, football fans, and the media as a challenge to their manhood and did everything in their power to prove the world wrong about them. Said Patriots center Damien Woody:

> "Tell the truth now, honestly, do you think most people from outside this area can name even five or six guys on our team? Nobody knows who we are, but that's OK with us, because they'll find out soon enough. Bill did what he had to do. It's like day and night around here compared to last year, because we have so many veteran leaders now. And they're good players, too, which people tend to overlook."[1598]

Patriots coaches extracted maximal motivational advantage from their underdog status in 2001. Before the AFC Championship Game in Pittsburgh, Steelers were talking brashly about crushing the Patriots and talking openly about the Super Bowl. And the Steelers organization was openly making plans for a Super Bowl trip. This became bulletin board fodder for the Patriots. Richard Seymour: "We felt we were disrespected."[1599] Players even developed their own slogan, a phrase that deepened in meaning and motivational power as the season wore on. During the February 2002 victory celebration in Boston, attended by roughly 1.2 million appreciative fans despite frigid weather, kicker Adam Vinatieri whipped the crowd in a frenzy by letting the fans in on the team's inside joke:

> Adam Vinatieri: "We started off [2001] a little slow. Some of the reporters didn't think we had much of a chance, and we kind of adopted a little motto. …Reporters would say something, and if they didn't believe in us, we'd just say, 'Don't talk to me.' And as the season went along, some of the people said, 'Yeah, they're doing a little bit better, but I don't think they got what it takes,' and all we said is…"

Fans: "Don't talk to me!"

Adam Vinatieri: "That's right. We kept going, we won more games, the Oakland Raiders came in to us and a lot of people didn't think we could win. But what?"

Fans: "Don't talk to me!"

Adam Vinatieri: "That's right. We got to Pittsburgh, and we were 9 1/2-point underdogs. They were already printing Super Bowl tickets. And what did we say?"

Fans: "Don't talk to me!"

Adam Vinatieri: "We go down to New Orleans, and ain't anybody give us a chance? Nobody! And what did we say to them?"

Fans: "Don't talk to me!"[1600]

Individual players similarly use disrespect (real or imagined) to motivate themselves to prove their doubters wrong. Diminutive wide receiver David Patten says those who doubt him spur him on:

"It's been that way my whole career. I honestly believe if I knew I had it made, that's when I would begin to decline. When everyone doubts me, I use it as fuel, not as animosity. I don't use it to want to prove anybody wrong. Just to go out there and show that David Patten is going to give you everything he's got."[1601]

Patriots coaches certainly never miss an opportunity to tell a player, "Did you hear that so-and-so called you a pussy?" or "So-and-so says you've lost a step," or "So-and-so told reporters he would run right by you on Sunday." They probably even make stuff like that up, just to pump players up.

Patriots safety Rodney Harrison has always been a ferocious hitter. A painful incident in high school led him to stumble on the value of an underdog mentality:

"I went to this pretty prestigious high school, very expensive to get into, most of the kids come from well-to-do backgrounds, and I was about the poorest thing up there. I was driving my mom's Chevette one day when it broke down. Back then, I was the so-called star athlete, and [other students] pulled over and started laughing at me. They started throwing stuff, teasing me. It really hurt my heart so much, it devastated me. After that, I told my mom, 'You're never going to have to worry about anything.' I promised her I would go to college. I told her, 'I don't know what I'm going to do, but I'm going to buy you a nice new house, I'm going to buy you a nice new car, and no one's going to ever laugh at us again.'"

After that incident, Harrison became even tougher on the football field because he had something to prove.

Learn from mistakes and move on

"I've learned in every game and in every season. ...I've tried to observe [everything] and learn from either the mistakes I have made–and there have been plenty–or the things that have gone well."[1602]
– *Bill Belichick*

Success demands striving for perfection by examining past mistakes and learning from them, but flagellating yourself over mistakes is counterproductive. A team that dwells on yesterday's mistakes isn't making optimal use of the present and won't be prepared for tomorrow. The most productive approach is to admit your mistakes, learn from them, and move on with resolve to not repeat them. The objective is not masochistic self-punishment but analyzing mistakes to extract actionable insights that will help avoid similar mistakes in the future. No matter how good you are, you will make mistakes. The goal is learning how not to repeat them.

Don't make excuses... Improve

"I don't brush off the preseason. If we'd won I'd be as happy as a tick on a dog, but we didn't."[1603]
– *New Patriots running back Corey Dillon*

In the 2003 AFC Championship Game, Colts cornerback Nick Harper stepped in front of a Brady pass and was about to intercept it before the intended receiver, Troy Brown, immediately punched the ball with his right hand and Harper lost control. The Patriots don't assume everything will always go their way. They know things will go wrong, and they're prepared to respond to mistakes and misfortune, not throw their hands in the air. Because mistakes happen, avoiding interceptions is not just the quarterback's responsibility; it's a team responsibility. Belichick said of that play: "It's the receiver's responsibility if they're anywhere near the ball on a pass to make sure, number one, that the defense doesn't get it. If we can't get it, then no one can get it."[1604]

The first rule of overcoming adversity is: "Mistakes happen. Accept responsibility. Don't make excuses." Patriots coaches insist players step up and take responsibility. Belichick does not tolerate players excusing failure by pointing to the refs, the weather, other players' mistakes, *etc.*: "The only thing we care about is the result. If the result is a function of an excuse then you have no leadership, no team, and no ability to improve because everything is rationalized by something [beyond your control] that went wrong."[1605] Coaches take the same approach. After the Patriots lost four straight games in 2002, Belichick warned his assistant coaches not to complain or point fingers at anyone else: "Talk about yourself, either say something constructive or be supportive. Otherwise, shut the [expletive] up. ...Either you get better, you support someone else who is trying to get better, or you have a constructive suggestion. …Stick together as a team. Support each other as a team."[1606]

When Tom Brady screws up, as he did in throwing three interceptions to the Washington Redskins that resulted in one of the Patriots' two losses in 2003, he takes full blame. He doesn't blame his receivers for running bad routes or misreading the defense. He takes the blame: "It was just bad throws, bad decisions, plays I should have made."[1607] Brady even beats himself up following victories, like a 23-12 win in Arizona in September 2004:

> "Turning the ball over on that pitch [backwards toss to Corey Dillon who mishandled Brady's pitch] will get you beat. Throwing interceptions will get you beat. Missing open receivers, like I did on that throw to [a wide-open] Troy Brown late in the game will get you beat. …We have to get better. Too many of our plays aren't at the level they need to be. That's why a game like this is so frustrating and leaves such a sour taste. We could have performed so much better. We need to start scoring touchdowns instead of settling for field goals."[1608]

That victory, the Patriots' seventeenth straight, really upset Brady: "We left a lot of plays out there and we have stuff we're going to have to correct. …The way we're playing is not going to be good enough much longer."[1609]

Patriots running back Antowain Smith pointed at his fumble as the reason the Patriots lost their 2001 regular season game against the St. Louis Rams. Smith said, "I lost that game against the Rams. I take responsibility for it. I'm happy for the chance to play against them again."[1610] Smith ran superbly in Super Bowl XXXVI, helping his team win its first-ever championship. New running back Corey Dillon does the same. After a superb running performance (158 yards on 32 carries), Dillon was mad at himself for bobbling and losing a ball Tom Brady tossed him that the Cardinals turned into a field goal: "It was [my fault]. My gloves were kind of slippery, and I didn't get a good handle on it. It gave up three points, and I'm kind of disgusted about that. Even though it was a good day, that kind of brings me back down to earth, because I did make some mistakes out there."[1611]

The Patriots care only about striving to eliminate mistakes. Explains Tom Brady, "what gets you motivated for a fourth training camp [is] try[ing] to eliminate a lot of bad plays. All the mistakes you have made in the last three years, you try to eliminate all those."[1612]

Bill Belichick made a coaching mistake soon after arriving in New England. He had great expectations and attempted to teach complicated schemes to players who weren't prepared to absorb such a thick playbook. (Once such a scheme is in place, it's easier to bring new players up to speed because veterans can help "new dudes" out, but when everyone is new to a scheme, it takes longer for the team to learn it.) The result was confusion and poor performance. In a self-assessment that off-season, coaches admitted they had been overly ambitious. The coaches decided that, next season, they would install new schemes progressively, rather than all at once, at whatever pace players could learn them.

Belichick's willingness to admit and learn from his mistakes has deep roots. He absorbed it from his father, Steve, who coached football at Navy for a remarkable third of a century, starting in 1956:

> "[Steve Belichick] told [Bill] that players don't lose games—coaches do—and that coaches don't win games; players do. He believes [coaches] can put players in a position to win [or lose], but they're the ones who have to execute the game plan, make the plays, and ultimately win the game."[1613]

Former Navy running back and Heisman winner Joe Bellino agrees that Navy taught Bill that failure results from coaches not setting their players up for success: "It's all about preparation. [Bill]'s a leader. [He feels] if his troops aren't well prepared, he's letting them down. [Patriot players] feel they're going into a game with the best 'General' and the best chance to win."[1614] Patriots players feel great confidence in their "General": "We trust that when we go out there and play the way we're capable and do the things that we're coached to, then we're going to win."[1615]

Because no one enjoys admitting they screwed up, many teams (foolishly) allow players' draft order to affect roster decisions: "I saw higher draft picks who couldn't get it right but who were kept around, while lower round choices who had more potential were released if they said a wrong word. It's pretty much that way around the league."[1616] Not in New England, where coaches place the team's interests above their egos. "Who's the best?" is the only criterion. For example, in 2004, undrafted cornerback Randall Gay made the final roster while the team's 7th-round pick, also a cornerback, did not.

Patriots owner Bob Kraft shares Belichick's emphasis on correcting mistakes rather than rationalizing past decisions. Three days after then-head coach Bill Parcells drafted the talented but trouble-causing defensive tackle Christian Peter in the fifth round of the 1996 NFL Draft, the Patriots renounced Peter's rights because, as Kraft said, "I'm not interested in bringing in players here who we're not going to be proud to have in the New England community. And (we're concerned) with how they're going to represent us off the field."[1617]

The most important lesson Bob Kraft learned (the hard way) as owner is to let proven football professionals make football decisions. Bob Kraft refused to give legendary coach Bill Parcells final authority over player acquisition, entrusting that job to Bobby Grier. Kraft interfered in player acquisition decisions he was unqualified to make. The final straw was Kraft overruling Parcells' decision to trade down in the 1996 draft and select a defensive player (probably for Duane Clemons[1618] who has had a good NFL career). Kraft backed Bobby Grier's insistence on drafting wide receiver Terry Glenn. (Bobby Grier supposedly stared at Parcells and said, "We'll do it my way."[1619]) At that moment, Parcells says, "I made up my mind I was finished here... I didn't want to have anything more to do with this guy [Kraft]."[1620] (To Parcells' great credit, he didn't hold any grudge against Glenn. In fact, Parcells and Charlie Weis showered Glenn with the tough love he needed, spurring Glenn to a 90-catch and 1,132-yard rookie season. Many difficult years later, Glenn reunited with Parcells in Dallas. Ironically, the player Parcells didn't want and the coach who said of Glenn's preseason hamstring injury "She's making progress" really complement each other. Glenn, who never knew his father and whose mother was brutally murdered when Glenn was just 13, may look to Parcells as a father figure.) After leading the Patriots to Super Bowl XXXI, Parcells quit to take over the Jets, complaining on the way out that "If you have to cook the food, they should at least let you shop for the groceries."[1621] Parcells was so angry with Kraft that his possible departure from the Patriots was a giant distraction the week leading up to the Super Bowl and may have cost the Patriots a chance at victory. Belichick said:

> "There was a lot of stuff going on prior to the game. I mean, him talking to other teams. He was trying to make up his mind about what he was going to do. Which, honestly, I felt [was] totally inappropriate. How many chances do you get to play for the Super Bowl? Tell them to get back to you in a couple of days."[1622]

Before the Super Bowl, Parcells phoned Hampstead, NY, which happens to be the headquarters of the New York Jets, dozens of times.[1623] Patriots linebacker Tedy Bruschi admitted he was angry that his former coach, who preached "team, team, team" had acted so selfishly:

> "In looking back at it now, it was a little selfish on his part, throwing the story out (that he was leaving the Patriots after the Super Bowl). I wake up the day of the game and see this big headline, 'Parcells is leaving.' Not to have a team meeting to address it, that in my mind is selfish."[1624]

Looking back, former starting quarterback Drew Bledsoe agrees, "You'd like to... at least say goodbye. But... From the get-go, Bill is about Bill."[1625] But Parcells was that steamed at Kraft. The defection of Parcells, Belichick, Weis, *etc.* to the Jets may have denied the Patriots a chance at greatness during the late 1990s, according to star quarterback Drew Bledsoe. After coming off the bench to defeat the Steelers in the January 2002 AFC Championship Game, Bledsoe said, "in '96 there was a feeling that we had a pretty good team and that, even after we lost, we were going to get a chance to go back. That has not happened until today."[1626] When a craftier Bob Kraft hired Bill Belichick as head coach in 2000, he ensured that Belichick could buy whatever groceries he damn well pleased.

Kraft also made mistakes because he grew fond of certain players and over-payed to extend their contracts, a mistake he has not repeated since handing Ty Law a $49 million contract extension in August 1999, Lawyer Milloy a $35 million contract extension in February 2000, Terry Glenn a $50 million contract extension in November 2000, and Drew Bledsoe a $103 million extension in early March 2001. In 2000 and 2001, Belichick lacked the power to block those contracts but hardly offered a ringing endorsement after Bledsoe's new deal: "We have a lot of needs. The key is to spend those dollars wisely."[1627] After winning the February 2002 Super Bowl, Belichick had all the control he wanted. Glenn and his contract found themselves in Green Bay with the Packers, and Bledsoe and his contract wound up in Buffalo with the Bills. The following year, Milloy also landed in Buffalo. Law is the lone survivor. Kraft admits he needed time to mature into the role of NFL owner: "The head coach is probably the most important person in the system, and I'm not sure I felt that when I came into the league ten years ago. I probably did [think the quarterback was most important]."[1628]

Kraft's maturation was rewarded when Belichick brought home the Vince Lombardi Trophy in just his second season as Patriots head coach. With just four teams (the Rams, Patriots, Eagles and Steelers) remaining in the 2001 playoff hunt, NFL commentator and former NFL quarterback Joe Theismann noted that "The one thing that has become so blatantly obvious is that the four remaining organizations allow the football people to run the football operation. Maybe that's a clue for other NFL owners who want to enjoy the fruits of multiple Super Bowls."[1629]

Collective responsibility (Don't point fingers)

"When we came there the players were saying they wanted to be treated like men because Parcells had too much of a thumb on them. And then we left and they said they needed more discipline. At some point, the players have to take some damn responsibility."[1630]
— *Ray "Sugar Bear" Hamilton, assistant coach under former Patriots head coach Pete Carroll*

The second rule of overcoming adversity is: "It's counterproductive to assign blame, fend off criticism, and point fingers." Everyone is fallible, and everyone makes occasional mistakes. While it's essential to learn from mistakes, arguing over culpability is worse than a waste of time. If you make a mistake, admit it and move on. Analyze the problem to do better in the future, not to decide who screwed up in the past. If someone is constantly screwing up, that will become clear over time. It's unwise to worry about assigning blame for isolated incidents.

Patriots players admit their mistakes, and the team forgives occasional lapses but has little tolerance for regular offenders:

"guys were standing up, admitting [their mistakes], and taking responsibility for their [blown] assignments. ...If a guy said 'my fault' on a particular play, that's fine. If he said it three times, we stopped him and reminded him he had better start doing his job."[1631]

Unlike many executives who never admit making a mistake, the Patriots coaches are also quick to accept blame, even when they may not be culpable. Defensive coordinator Romeo Crennel: "When we lose, I always feel like there's something I did wrong. There's something I could have done better. There's a call I should have made to help us."[1632] After the Patriots were embarrassingly trounced by the Cincinnati Bengals in a 2004 preseason game, Belichick pinned blame on both coaches and players: "We didn't coach well, we didn't play well. We got totally outclassed tonight."[1633] After a 30-20 victory over the Seattle Seahawks, Belichick was mad at himself for the Seahawks gaining 443 yards. He called them "coaching problems" and confessed "I did a poor job, and a lot of the yards and points they got were just–I should take the responsibility and will take the responsibility."[1634] He elaborated: "It was bad, bad coaching, period... There was a guy wide open and there was nobody covering him because I screwed the thing up."[1635] He even explicitly exonerated his defenders who had let Seattle complete a 37-yard pass: "The players did a good job on it, I just screwed it up."[1636] (Hearing that, cornerback Ty Law joked, "No comment on that. For him to say that, maybe we won't get chewed out as much when we're watching the film this week."[1637] Safety Rodney Harrison's response suggested the defensive play call was sent in by the coaches too late: "It's not the coaches' fault. It's about communication. We have to be on the same page whether the play comes in early or late."[1638]) Offensive coordinator Charlie Weis says Tom Brady is "the closest thing to a coach... Not that he is error-free, but I certainly make plenty of mistakes myself."[1639] This fosters a constructive, communicative environment where mistakes are analyzed eagerly for clues on how to improve future performance rather than to point fingers and assign blame. Tom Brady appreciates that coaches accept partial responsibility for losses:

> "When we come in after the games, [Belichick] is the first person to say, 'Well, I messed this up,' and 'This was bad coaching on our part.' And the players, we …sometimes want to take credit for the bad plays too. It's like, 'No Coach, we messed that up.'"[1640]

So did former Patriots defensive lineman Rick Lyle:

> "[E]verybody takes accountability, good or bad, players and coaches. It's about being accountable for what happened and owning up to that instead of pointing fingers. [Belichick's] always been that way. …[W]hen you start having coaches point fingers at their players, it makes an adverse situation. It's not good for chemistry and it won't get you where you need to go. He was clear about it."[1641]

An unnamed Patriot said, "When a leader can do something like that and prove he's human, it's appealing and can make a difference. When you admit it, it can bring a closeness to the team and creates a bond."[1642]

It's far more productive for teams to take collective responsibility, as the Patriots do. After the Buffalo Bills blew out the Patriots 31-0 on opening day in 2003, Patriots defensive back Antwan Harris said, "We play a team defense. If they make a play on us, it's a team mistake, not an individual one."[1643] That was somewhat self-serving of Harris, who made serious mistakes that day. But that was a team loss. Tom Brady threw four interceptions that day, one of which the Bills returned 37 yards for a touchdown. On another Bills touchdown drive, the Patriots defense forced the Bills to punt, but the Patriots special teams gifted the Bills a first down when Fred Baxter was called for holding. Nevertheless, the defense didn't point fingers at the Patriots offense or special teams. Everyone accepted that the team had screwed up. More typical is Patriots deflecting blame from their teammates, as safety Rodney Harrison did after the Steelers burned undrafted rookie Randall Gay on Halloween 2004: "[Gay] got beat on one play. If the defense had been run [correctly] by me, it probably would have been a quarterback sack. I had a free lane at the quarterback. I hesitated. I should have blitzed. If I had done my job, I would have gotten to the quarterback. ...I'm going to take the blame for it."[1644]

Collective responsibility is essential in team sports because success requires intricate choreography among many players and many coaches. Football players are human beings, not programmable robots. No coach can teach players what to do in every conceivable situation. A coach can get the right players on the field, help them line up optimally against their opponent, teach them valuable techniques, and give them guidelines on how to react to different situations, but football involves exponentially more strategic complexity than even chess, a game that no one has ever fully mastered (even though, in theory, there is an optimal strategy for playing chess). So no coach can "program" his players. Winning requires that teams find smart, intuitive players and train them properly, and players must exercise wise judgment:

> "You have to know what your assignments are. Even if you recognize the play, if you don't do the right thing or fit properly in a team defensive system, then the system is going to break down. Instinct... is a big part of the game too. Guys have to make multiple decisions on every play whether to take on a guy [hit him] whether they can slip him [evade him], whether they have an angle to play over the top of them when they have to play underneath them, whether they can tell by a player's stance or his initial reaction that it is a run or a pass or he is pulling or whatever it is. There is a lot of that instinctiveness that goes with it."[1645]

Patriots coaches and players spend much of their time anticipating situations that may arise during games, forming contingency plans, and practicing them. Breakdowns can result from poor anticipation, poor planning, or poor execution. Smart, creative players can sometimes cover up poor anticipation and planning. Conversely, great anticipation and planning can be ruined by poor execution. Because losses likely involve a mix of coaching and execution mistakes, coaches and players should share the blame for defeats. Trying to untangle who screwed up is just not as important as working together to prepare for your next game.

Don't dwell on mistakes... Look forward

"You don't ever want to think about the last kick, good or bad. The only one you should ever care about is the one in front of you."[1646]
  – *Patriots kicker Adam Vinatieri*

"Ty Law has been beat [for a touchdown]. Every cornerback in football has gotten beat. It's part of it. You play the corner position long enough you're going to get beat, more than once. It's just a matter of how you come back."[1647]
  – *Patriots safety Rodney Harrison*

I was depressed after the Buffalo Bills trounced the Patriots 31-0 in Week 1 of the 2003 season. I feared the horrifying defeat might suck Patriots players into an emotional black hole from which they might never return. Instead of looking backwards, however, Patriots players simply began preparing for their Week 2 opponent (the Philadelphia Eagles, whom they defeated with ease). Belichick insists his team didn't waste a minute dwelling on defeat:

"After the Buffalo game, we thought about Philadelphia because that was the next game. It was the only thing we could do anything about. It was the only thing we had any control over. That's where all of our focus was, to play better against Philadelphia. And after Philadelphia we went through the same process again with the Jets. ... [The Jets game] was the one we could control, that's the one we could prepare for and that's where we put our energy. It's week to week."[1648]

Linebacker Mike Vrabel says Adam Vinatieri is the "Clutchest kicker of all time... Uh, is that a word? 'Clutchest?' Whatever. Most clutch."[1649] Though the appropriate adjective is in doubt, Adam Vinatieri should head to the Hall of Fame in Canton as the most clutch kicker in the history of the game. Despite playing in cold, windy, and snowy Foxboro, Vinatieri has one of the top field goal percentages in NFL history. And he has drilled unbelievably difficult kicks in astonishing situations, such as two late field goals (of 45 yards and 23 yards) in the snow to defeat the Oakland Raiders in the infamous "Tuck Rule" / "Snow Bowl" AFC Semifinal and a 48-yarder as time expired to win Super Bowl XXXVI. He kicked another game-winner in Super Bowl XXXVIII. Vinatieri is always mentally prepared for pressure situations because he anticipates pressure and visualizes himself succeeding. The night before his first

Super Bowl, he dreamed not about failure but about kicking the game-winner "about a thousand times."[1650]

In the 2003 AFC Championship Game against the Indianapolis Colts, Vinatieri tied the NFL postseason record by hitting all five field goal attempts. Given Vinatieri's clutchness, the world was shocked when, in Super Bowl XXXVIII, Vinatieri missed an easy field goal and later had his second field goal attempt blocked. A lesser kicker might have dwelled on his two uncharacteristic failures and stressed over the many problems he was facing that day:

- Both misses were attempted from parts of the field that had been painted with logos, making them slicker than other areas. *Sports Illustrated*'s Peter King later wrote, "I'd suggest the NFL use different paint on the Super Bowl fields. It looked to me like Vinatieri and punter Ken Walter both slipped, untouched, on the dark-green-painted turf."[1651] One Patriot said on the *3 Games to Glory II* DVD that he switched to longer cleats just minutes into the game after deciding the field was slippery. Vinatieri apparently put on longer spikes at halftime.[1652]

- Vinatieri had missed a career-high nine field goal attempts in 2003, partly because "Vinatieri has been battling lower back pain and 'other nagging things.' He certainly hasn't been pain-free. There have been some things he's been getting treatment on."[1653] But Vinatieri never used these problems as an excuse.

- A reliable snap is critical to a field goal kicker's timing, but Vinatieri had had to deal with three different long-snappers and several different holders in 2003. This undoubtedly impacted the timing and placement of balls he kicked.

- The Patriots' longsnapper throughout the 2003 playoffs was Brian Kinchen, who hadn't played in the NFL since 2000 and had been teaching Sunday School in Louisiana when the Patriots contacted him:

> "He had a high snap in the playoff game against Tennessee, then struggled during Super Bowl week practices. ...'I was scaring Bill [Belichick] half to death.' ...hours before the game, Kinchen sliced his finger while cutting a slice of bread. The deep wound was on the inside of the finger next to his right thumb—the finger he needs to grip and control the ball on his snaps. ...There were several poor snaps during the game."[1654]

Despite his two failures earlier that game, a slippery field, back problems, and consistently erratic snapping and holding of the ball for his field goal attempts, Adam Vinatieri was completely mentally prepared to drill the game-winner through the uprights with just four seconds left on the clock because, he says, "On any field goal, not just one like that, you have to put whatever came before it out of your mind. Selective amnesia is a good thing to have. So is good focus. All I wanted was one more shot."[1655] While Vinatieri was running onto the field for the final kick, he was all business: "I just wanted to get the ball down, get it up, and get it through."[1656] Vinatieri's ability to concentrate and focus under such pressure is astonishing. Patriots linebacker Mike Vrabel said, "When [Adam] was lining up for that kick, I couldn't even see the goalpost, there were so many flashbulbs going off. I would have needed a visor to kick it."[1657] Kicking it through the uprights after missing two earlier in the game was even more impressive: "Adam's got the mentality of Deion Sanders. If he ever gets beat, he can't wait for another chance."[1658]

Patriots get mad at themselves for mistakes, but players cheer each other up because dwelling on mistakes leads to more mistakes. After Patriots running back Corey Dillon fumbled against the Bills, his teammates needed to calm him down: "I'm highly upset. They had to come calm me down. They came to me and said, 'Hey, we're going to need you, so you're going to have to let that go and move on. Get your mind right and hold your composure and get back out there and play football.'"[1659]

OVERCOMING SUCCESS

"We do a pretty good job around here of suppressing success."[1660]
– Patriots linebacker Tedy Bruschi

"We'll come in tomorrow and Coach Belichick will be standing up here with a list of things that we didn't do right."[1661]
– Tom Brady, following the Patriots' 20th consecutive victory

"It is far more difficult to abandon yesterday's success than it is to reappraise failure. Success breeds its own hubris. It creates emotional attachment, habits of mind, and action, and, above all, false self-confidence. A success that has outlived its usefulness may, in the end, be more damaging than failure."[1662]
– Peter Drucker, father of management science

Handling success is harder than coping with adversity. Adversity provides a built-in motivator and reveals a team's weaknesses. Success breeds arrogance, overconfidence, and obscures problem areas. This section explains how the Patriots have handled their success by respecting their opponents and not believing the praise. They also never take anything for granted. Half-way through the 2004 season, reporters were projecting a Patriots-Steelers AFC Championship Game. Belichick said, "Being 7-1, we're in a decent position at this point in the season [but] Minnesota was 6-0 last year and they weren't even in the playoffs, so it really doesn't mean anything."[1663]

Respect your opponents

"Bill never says he is smarter than the guy he is playing."[1664]
– Baltimore Ravens VP Ozzie Newsome

"You play a great team every week in the NFL."[1665]
  – *Patriots defensive tackle Vince Wilfork*

"It's not always going to be pretty out there. Those guys get paid to play too."[1666]
  – *Patriots left tackle Matt Light*

"We always expect our opponents to play well. We have a lot of respect for every team we play, as well as the players and coaches in this league. You can look at the scores every Monday morning, and there are games that probably come out differently than the way most people thought they would. So if you play well in this league, you have a chance to win. If you don't, you have no chance."[1667]
  – *Bill Belichick*

"If you've been around Bill long enough, you know the routine. You know he's going to pump up [the opponent], whether he thinks they're good or not. It actually helps the younger guys to get ready. They walk out of here thinking, 'Man, he's crazy,' and we tell them, 'No, that's just Bill.'"[1668]
  – *Patriots cornerback Ty Law*

"He isn't a coach who says, 'You guys played great, way to go, take the day off.' ...As long as we don't overlook the fact any team is capable of beating [us], we believe we can win each week."[1669]
  – *Tom Brady*

In the salary cap era, "parity" reigns. The tired phrase that "On any given Sunday, any team can defeat any other team" has never been so accurate. Ironically, Belichick believes this aphorism to the core of his soul and has convinced his players of its truth, even though Belichick's Patriots' play has made them the exception to this oft-stated rule. Brady says, "It's so challenging every week that no matter who you play, or where you play, it is always tough and it's always a challenge."[1670] Before playing the 0-2 Buffalo Bills, safety Rodney Harrison said, "They're only a couple of plays away from being 2-0. ...You have to show up each and every Sunday and be prepared, because they can kick your butt out there if you take it for granted."[1671] He asked, rhetorically, "Who thought Houston was going to beat Kansas City? It doesn't matter what record you have."[1672] Patriots defensive lineman Richard Seymour added, "They could easily be 2-0. They're probably the best 0-2 team in the league."[1673] Constant fear of defeat drives the Patriots to great performances and victories, making the Patriots' embrace of this philosophy a self-unfulfilling prophecy.

Every Patriot knows there are no easy weeks in the NFL. Strong college teams can trounce inferior rivals by 40, 50, or even 60 points, but every NFL team is challenged every week. The salary cap ensures that teams have roughly equal talent on the field. And Bill Belichick knows he is hardly the only experienced and meticulously prepared coach with deep understanding of what it takes to win in the NFL:

> "when [Philadelphia Eagles head coach Andy] Reid interviewed for the Eagles job, he brought a thick notebook, compiled over many years, containing his ideas on everything from football plays to training and conditioning, player travel arrangements, lodging, pep talks, team public relations, administration and more. ...[T]he micromanaging Reid once noticed the difference when his assistant changed the brand of card stock used for his sideline game chart by 'a couple millimeters.'"[1674]

Every Patriots player and coach knows that, because parity reigns, arrogance kills. Home Depot CEO Robert Nardelli says the formula is "Arrogance breeds complacency, and complacency breeds failure."[1675] After Patriots backup quarterback Rohan Davey led his Berlin Thunder to win its first five games of the 2004 NFL Europe season, he sounded anything but complacent:

> "Guys around here are... workmanlike really. The talent level here and the competition is so close, I mean we haven't won a game convincingly yet. We've been fortunate because we have good players and we've made big plays down the stretch. But we still haven't put together a complete game. So it's not like we can just get comfortable and say we can run through the league."[1676]

As if to prove Davey's point, the Thunder lost their sixth game by one point when their opponent scored a touchdown on the final play of the game. (That was the Thunder's only loss that season.)

Before virtually every game of the Patriots' 15-game winning streak of 2003, Coach Belichick told the media that the defensive line the Patriots would face the upcoming Sunday was "fearsome," "dominating," "one of the best in the league," *etc*. Belichick makes every upcoming opponent sound like the second coming of Vince Lombardi's Green Bay Packers. And he's not spouting truisms. He says it with conviction and illustrates his claims with specific details because he truly respects every team in the league and sees sparks of greatness in each of them. In describing opponents, Belichick accentuates the positive because doing so gives his team the best chance to win. (Of course, in analyzing his own team, he seeks to eliminate the negative.)

Patriots players have learned from their coach to view each upcoming opponent not as half empty or even half full but as full to overflowing. Before facing the perennially poor Arizona Cardinals, an organization with one winning season in 19 years, defensive lineman Richard Seymour said, "they also have a lot of high draft picks. They've been drafting at the top of the draft for a while, so they definitely have some talent on that side of the ball."[1677] In other words, the Cardinals have been so bad for so long, they must be a great team!

The NFL is full of professional athletes and professional coaches. A game's outcome can hinge on just one or a few plays. A team that is focused, disciplined, and prepared will, on average, outplay their opponent just enough to win. But every game is winnable and every game is losable. Players and coaches who, even unconsciously, disrespect their opponent are likely to slightly lower their preparation and effort, thus substantially reducing their chance of victory. If they also make a public display of their lack of respect, they will fire up their opponent and their fans, further increasing their opponent's victory odds.

Patriots players embrace their coach's respect for every opponent. Instead of trash talk and boasts, Patriots players and coaches hurl superlatives at their opponents: Before the 2001 AFC Championship Game, Troy Brown wanted to put the entire Steelers defense in the Pro Bowl:

> "Their defense is just outstanding and they have a whole bunch of great young players. A lot of those guys should have made the Pro Bowl. Their linebacking group is just tremendous. They definitely know how to stop the run and get after the quarterback. Their secondary is also playing great. They have good corners and they could have taken their whole defense to the Pro Bowl if it was possible."[1678]

Before the 2003 AFC Championship Game, Patriots cornerback Tyrone Poole sounded ready to enshrine the entire Colts offense in the Hall of Fame: "They're explosive, real explosive. ...The bottom line is yardage production, touchdown production and they rank right up there with all the top offensive teams that have played in the NFL."[1679]

Linebacker Tedy Bruschi sounded almost ready to concede defeat while describing their upcoming Super Bowl opponent, the St. Louis Rams, even though the Patriots had nearly beaten the Rams in their regular season meeting and had prepared a brilliant defensive plan that would handcuff the Rams' offense a few days later in the Super Bowl:

> "It really is amazing to watch. It's like a track meet. You have to be prepared to run a lot because of their speed. Their quarterback, Kurt Warner, is the coolest quarterback I've ever seen in the pocket. And, in my opinion, they have the best back in the game in Marshall Faulk. Man, we have a tough job on Sunday."[1680]

Listening to Patriots offensive coordinator Charlie Weis describe the Carolina Panthers defense, you never would have guessed the Patriots would score 32 points against them that Sunday:

> "There are no holes, and that's what worries you the most. You look at some teams and you say, 'Well, that's not very good.' This is not one of those defenses. Start with the front four. Which end do you want to pick on? Normally, you can find some guys and say, 'I'm picking on him.'"[1681]

Though the aging Jets running back Curtis Martin had gained an underwhelming 3.2 yards per carry before the Jets and Patriots clashed in early 2003, Patriots safety Rodney Harrison refused to believe the Patriots would face anything other than the once-formidable Curtis Martin: "Anyone is crazy if they think Curtis Martin has lost a step. That's the thing about guys like him. When people start bad-mouthing him and saying he lost a step, and he comes back and steps up even more."[1682]

The Patriots praise each upcoming opponent as predictably as swallows return to Capistrano every March 19th. Players emulate their coach, who portrays each upcoming opponent, no matter how poor their record, as the 1985 Chicago Bears. Before his defense stymied Steelers quarterback Kordell Stewart in the AFC Championship Game, ending Stewart's Pro Bowl season, Belichick said of Stewart, "He has had a fantastic year both running the ball and throwing it... He beats you with his arm. He beats you with his feet. And he beats you with his head."[1683]

Belichick's barrage of praise for each opponent is a kind of "sandbagging." Belichick enjoys sailing and must know how sailors use tricks (like weighing their boats down with excess weight) to make their boats appear slower than they really are until that extra speed is needed. In talking up an opponent, Belichick is trying to convince that opponent that his boat is faster than it really is. Belichick massages opponents' egos as well as any grifter moving in for a big sting. But, unlike a huckster or swindler, Belichick may be more concerned with scaring himself and his team than lulling his opponent into an inflated sense of security.

Whatever the motivation, the Patriots' respect for and fear of each opponent help the Patriots win. Before the Patriots-Panthers Super Bowl rumble, Panthers defensive tackle Brentson Buckner seemed to think the Patriots were just another team, not a Super Bowl team and arguably the toughest-hitting team in the NFL: "I don't think they're going to hit any harder than Philly hit. I don't think they're going to hit any harder than Tampa Bay hit."[1684] Such talk sounds arrogant and disrespectful, suggests Buckner was not taking his opponent seriously enough, and quickly becomes potent bulletin board material for Patriots players... a challenge to hit Panthers with even more than their normal fury. It's impossible to say whether such loose talk cost the Panthers a Super Bowl victory, but in a game determined by three points, little things can make all the difference. No Patriot talked like Buckner. Instead, Patriots players issued a flood of praise for the Panthers. This quotation from Patriots wide receiver David Givens was representative: "I think this is going to be one of the most physical games of the season, if not the most physical. The defense we are playing against has consistently shown that they can be physical and jam guys and make big hits."[1685] What did Patriots offensive tackle Matt Light say about Brentson Buckner and his fellow offensive linemen? "They are all-world. You can't really paint them any differently than that. If you let them, they'll definitely wreck the game."[1686]

Givens, Light, *et al.* said all the right things before the game, then they went out and beat the Panthers with their play, not their mouths.

Before 1999, only once in NFL history (1988) had neither of the previous season's Super Bowl participants made the playoffs. But the league is now so competitive that it has happened in three of the past five seasons (1999, 2002, and 2003). The margin for error in today's NFL is so thin that even a hint of complacency can end a team's season. Can the Patriots repeat in 2004? Can the Patriots become a dynasty? Belichick recoils from the temptation to even consider the possibility: "To think that one team out of 32 could consistently beat the other 31 ...I just don't know. Every year is a new one."[1687] Maintaining a fear of defeat in the face of constant success is an immense challenge, but one the Patriots have managed better than any other team because the entire organization, top to bottom, is focused so squarely on winning and so quickly squelches arrogance and complacency. A reporter tried to goad new Patriots running back Corey Dillon into agreeing that he had been able to easily penetrate the Bills defense in running for 151 yards on 26 carries. Dillon sounded like he had played for Belichick his whole career: "That's a great defense over there. They play hard. When you gain 100 yards against them, you've earned it."[1688]

Don't "play down to the competition"

Cheering for the Patriots in my youth, I was astounded by how often the Patriots lost to "bad" teams but beat "good" teams. "If they're capable of beating 'good' teams," I wondered, "why do they lose so often to 'bad' teams?" The answer is probably that "good" teams often play down to the competition. They don't bring their "A" game effort because they're already looking ahead to their next opponent and assume they can beat a weak opponent with just "B" game effort.

Although Belichick's Patriots blow out few opponents, they seldom lose a "should win" game. Their success in "easy" games is a result of refusing to view any game as "easy." Because they never look beyond their upcoming opponent, Belichick's Patriots never show up with their "B" game. They can be outplayed, but never due to poor preparation or lack of effort. As an example of their mentality, consider why Belichick feels his 2004 team's preparation should be unaffected by the fact that every opponent will be hyped up with extra adrenaline and intensity to outplay the defending Super Bowl champions:

> "We expect every one of our opponents to play their best. That's what we expect every week and that's what we prepare for. We never expect anything less than that, because then you're setting a low expectation for your opponent. And I never think that's a good idea."[1689]

Don't believe the praise

"You start messing up when you feel like you're at another level."[1690]
  – Patriots defensive lineman Richard Seymour

"As soon as I congratulated [Belichick after the Patriots won Super Bowl XXXVIII], he said, 'Did you ever see a worse defense than ours in the fourth quarter?' He was all worked up. So I don't think there's any chance of him or his team being satisfied."[1691]
  – NFL analyst John Madden

"Come ask me about [our NFL-record 21-game winning streak] when I'm in my rocking chair."[1692]
  – Bill Belichick

To Bill Belichick, praise is like Kryptonite... a potential killer to be shunned. Before the infamous January 2002 "Tuck Rule" playoff game against the Oakland Raiders, Belichick was showered with praise for guiding to the playoffs an unheralded team that had been 5-11 the previous season. Belichick rebuffed such admiration: "But just let us lose one game, and you'll see how popular I am. That's when you'll hear the questions about the quarterback, or that we should have run more, or whatever. I know how that goes."[1693] Before his Patriots won their second Super Bowl, Belichick reacted to the oft-applied "genius" label with "I've heard 'Belichick' and 'genius' together. I've also heard 'Belichick' and 'moron' together."[1694]

One of the first things new Patriot tight end Jed Weaver noticed in Foxboro was the many "Don't believe the hype" signs adorning the walls.[1695] Flattery can kill. Naive leaders let false praise skew their judgment. Belichick knows sincere praise can be equally harmful. Hubris and ego have driven many of history's great (and not-so-great) leaders to make dumb decisions based on feelings of invincibility or slanted information. Optimism is a recipe for disaster. Paranoia is healthy. When a leader relies on wishful thinking rather than objective facts and reasoned analysis, "yes men" are rewarded, honest people grow embittered, and no one bears bad news. It is far safer to underestimate one's strength than to overestimate. Belichick's Patriots are paranoid:

> "Everybody's been patting us on the back saying how great we are, but we have to forget it and start a new season. And it is a new season. We've got to forget about what happened. My rookie year, I thought it was going to be [a Super Bowl trip] all the time. I'm like, 'This is easy. You win every week, you go to the playoffs, you go to the Super Bowl. No problem.' You need a group of veterans to relay the message that you can't take this for granted. As soon as you start feeling good about yourself, that's when you're going to get your butt kicked."[1696]

– Patriots safety Rodney Harrison

Belichick would likely reject the "paranoid" label on the grounds that "You're not paranoid if they really are out to get you." Asked whether the Patriots became a "dynasty" after winning their second Super Bowl in three seasons, Belichick claimed he can scarcely imagine a dynasty in the salary cap era: "The NFL is so competitive, has so many great players and great coaches, it's so hard to win. Conceptually, it's hard to understand how it could happen."[1697] Hall of Fame coach Bill Walsh disagrees, saying what the Patriots are accomplishing is "all the more impressive, because I think all of us felt, the way the game is today, there's no more room for dynasties. It's a great run for New England—one of the greatest of all time."[1698] Ironically, the only way Belichick and his Patriots can become a dynasty is by denying that they are a dynasty!

Patriots safety Lawyer Milloy once highlighted the importance of fighting complacency by saying the Patriots defense needed to "bounce back from [last week's] win."[1699] To motivate himself for the 2004 campaign, Tom Brady reminds himself of the team's 9-7 season in 2002: "You think you have a good team and that it will carry over into next year and (you think), 'We can't get worse.' But you can. It can go the other way if you don't do what you need to do to play at a championship level."[1700] Throughout 2003, "remember Buffalo" echoed throughout the Patriots locker room, a reference to their 31-0 opening day defeat: "a lot of the guys in the locker room still remember that game very well. Every time you see the tape of that game, you cringe. …There's a bad taste in our mouth from that game."[1701] Special teams captain Larry Izzo says the only impact last season's Super Bowl ring has is increasing the difficulty of earning a Super Bowl ring this season:

> "You can't dwell on what you accomplished last year because it does you no good except to realize that it affects how other teams play you. You are the bar now. Teams will test themselves against you, your team. Teams think, 'Let's see how good we are, and if we can beat them that means we're pretty good.' You face that every week, and that means you have to raise your level. Looking back to last year is pointless."[1702]

The Patriots' 2003 Super Bowl rings are about as helpful to players in 2004 as Frodo's ring was to him in Mordor. Though representing great power, those rings are burdens you must lug around.

When things are going well, players must keep themselves grounded by fixating on whatever has gone poorly. They must harbor pain over occasional losses. Brady says his teammates are still depressed about losing to the Washington Redskins… more than a year ago:

> "That was so disappointing, because when you look at those last three plays it's just ridiculous that we didn't do anything with that ball. That was something throughout the rest of last season that just gnawed at this whole

team. That was an embarrassing loss. That was an embarrassing performance. All the corrections we've made are based on a game like that, where you walk off the field and you're sick to your stomach. You know, how could you give up a game like that?"[1703]

Patriots linebacker Tedy Bruschi still dwells on a pass he dropped on a fake punt in his 1996 rookie season: "I can't tell you how many times I've gone back to that play against Denver. Whenever I start feeling really good about myself, I remember that game. I remember where I came from, and I get to work again."[1704]

Players must also realize that, no matter how many games they've won, they have won some squeakers. After a close win over the Colts on opening day 2004, Patriots left tackle Matt Light pointed out that "Good teams learn from their wins."[1705] When a reporter suggested the Patriots were dominant, after winning their eighth game in a row in 2003, Belichick responded with disdain, pointing to a game they had won only after a heroic goal-line stand against Indianapolis: "I think that's a joke. The ball's inside the one yard-line on the last play of the game. Who's dominating whom?"[1706] Soon after winning the Super Bowl in February 2002, Belichick sounded anything but complacent, hinting at big changes ahead: "I am not saying this is a rebuilding situation."[1707] Six months later, he nearly took a reporter's head off for naively asking, "Hey Bill, do you have any concerns or worries like you've had in other camps?" Bill responded the Patriots had "plenty of issues and plenty of problems":

> "Were you here Monday? …We've had a couple players leave camp. We have a couple guys banged up, and we're short in a couple positions. You should go out there and watch us practice. We drop balls. We give up passes. We get hit in the backfield on running plays. We run the ball through the defense. We drop punts. We get them blocked."[1708]

Such messages are aimed at players, who hear them loud and clear.

As the 2003 Patriots appeared to be cruising toward the playoffs, Belichick cautioned that the Patriots hadn't yet won anything: "We've put ourselves in a position to do something, but being in position and actually doing it are two completely different things. …You're only as good as your last game."[1709] Players echoed their coach. After one victory, linebacker Tedy Bruschi said, "No one is jumping around in here like it was a playoff game. It was win number eight. We got it. It's over. Now we need to get ready for number nine."[1710]

Pretend you're the underdog

Underdog status motivated the 2001 Patriots. Unfortunately, by 2003, no one was demeaning the Patriots. In fact, sportswriters were openly discussing whether the Patriots had become a "dynasty," something many considered impossible in the salary cap era where "parity" is the name of the day. Nevertheless, *en route* to their second Vince Lombardi trophy, the Patriots continued to tell themselves they were the underdogs, that they were the ones with something to prove, that the world still wasn't taking the Patriots seriously. They seized on any scrap suggestive of disrespect. Patriots defensive lineman Richard Seymour was disgusted by the media's unrelenting focus on Peyton Manning in the week before the AFC Championship Game: "It got a little monotonous at times just hearing, 'Peyton Manning, Peyton Manning.'"[1711] So was Ty Law (who intercepted Manning an amazing three times that day):

> "After the game, he praised Manning and wished only that the Patriots received more attention. 'I just wanted to go out there and play,' he said. 'What about us? What about our team? [The Manning talk] added fuel to the fire, so we just wanted to go out there and put a little silence on the situation.'"[1712]

Patriots defenders played that game like bitter, angry men. According to safety Rodney Harrison, "We were really ticked off because no one gave us credit. It was all about Peyton Manning."[1713] "All it really did was fuel a fire. No one really gave us a chance. It was just (about) Mr. Inhuman. We got tired of hearing that. It really created a great opportunity for us to overcome some adversity."[1714] Harrison went on and on about disrespect (perhaps also because the Chargers had disrespected him personally by releasing him): "I got so tired, every time I turned on (*ESPN*'s) 'SportsCenter' and not getting any credit."[1715] That attitude helped Harrison & Company neutralize the Colts' star wide receiver, Marvin Harrison. They basically took Harrison out of the game; he caught just three passes for a measly 19 yards. Ty Law, who covered Harrison, intercepted three passes from Peyton Manning, making himself look like Manning's intended receiver half the time Manning threw in Harrison's direction.

Before Super Bowl XXXVIII, Belichick told his players he took offense at the media and football fans calling the 2003 Carolina Panthers the 2001 New England Patriots: "It's a bunch of bullshit. They're not what we are. They can't be what we are. *We* are what we are."[1716] Belichick had found a brilliant argument that instantly transformed his team into an underdog. Belichick angrily implied that the Panthers: 1) were the media's darling; 2) had usurped the Patriots' crown even before playing the game; 3) were disrespecting the 2001 Patriots; and, 4) were "really" the favorites because we all know the 2001 Patriots won the Super Bowl as underdogs. Belichick's speech gave players plenty of motivation. Center/guard Damien Woody was out for the season with an injury but wanted to play anyhow after Belichick's speech: "This is going to sound weird since [his speech] was a lot of expletives, but it was touching. We saw a different side of him. We had never seen him that emotional before. He got me ready. I felt like going out there, strapping it up, and playing on one leg."[1717] I mentioned elsewhere in this book that overuse of yelling or emotion weakens its impact. This was the opposite. Because Belichick's speeches are normally emotionally restrained, this speech packed extra punch.

Though the Pats were heavily favored to win Super Bowl XXXVIII, linebacker Mike Vrabel (who can always motivate himself by remembering his inability to crack the Pittsburgh Steelers' starting lineup before being plucked away by the Pats) sounded bitter after victory, as if the whole world had expected the team to lose, as if the Patriots were a bunch of Rodney Dangerfields: "[F]or a bunch of non-stars, non-celebrities and non-football players, we have accomplished something [fifteen consecutive victories] only one other team in the history of the league has ever done."[1718] Wide receiver Troy Brown also showed his disgust at the "disrespect" the Patriots received:

> "We bit a hole in our lip for two weeks and stood silent [in the face of insults]. Everybody taking shots at us. We can't do this. We can't do that. And we had met our match because we can't handle [the Panthers' defensive line]. Hochstein (stinks). The Patriots are too small. Ricky Manning Jr. is better than Ty Law. We can't get off the jam and he's going to shut us down. *Please!*"[1719]

By 2004, after winning 19 straight games, not even the Patriots saw themselves as an underdog. So Patriots safety Rodney Harrison acts like Nixon and imagines villains conspiring against him: "We know there are a bunch of Patriots haters who want us to lose."[1720] And the Patriots' mutts devour any scraps their opponents throw them. Seattle Seahawks receiver Darrell Jackson tossed a giant bone: "We should be 4-0, everyone knows it. ...We'd like to be 4-1 and end that streak that those guys have been hoopin-hollerin' about. ...I know we can beat them. They're beatable and that's enough for me. ...I don't really think they're that good. I think we're good."[1721] During the game, Patriots safety Rodney Harrison yelled at Jackson, "Why don't you just shut up and play?"[1722] Harrison hounded Jackson all game:

> "Having to take all that talk, we were ready. All game I was in [Jackson's] ear. I was like, 'You're not doing anything today.' I just said, 'Hey, this isn't a mistake, man. This is 20 in a row for us. You've got to start respecting it. You earn your respect right here.' And he shut up. What can you say when you have two catches?"[1723]

After the Patriots won, Harrison said Jackson's "disrespectful chatter" had been "fuel for the fire."[1724] In that same game, cornerback Ty Law took special offense to another quotation Belichick showed players concerning the age of the Patriots defenders: "The one that stuck out in my mind was [the quotation] that said we were old. Well, this old man had to show you something."[1725] Amazingly, Jackson was still talking trash after losing: "They're a good team, but they're still not that good. If they ran into us again, we will beat them."[1726] Jackson also talked trash about Harrison's trash-talking: "He told me to watch comments I make in the paper and all that stuff. ...Even when he's talking trash he's preaching."[1727] Patriots players will have no problems with motivation if they meet the Seahawks in the Super Bowl.

Be humble

"The Patriots also haven't been carried away with themselves. They're not a bunch of chest beaters."[1728]
— *Marv Levy, who coached the Buffalo Bills to four straight Super Bowls*

"Maybe when he's done with his career, he might look back on his records and accomplishments and they'll mean something to him, but frankly, they don't mean a lot now to him. He only cares about the moment–winning one game at a time."[1729]
— *Former Patriots assistant coach Steve Szabo, discussing Bill Belichick, whom Szabo has known since Belichick was 10*

"[Belichick] doesn't turn on the game film and say, 'You guys are the best in the world.' He tells you the good things you did, but there are a lot of 'buts.' …[B]ecause of that, I think the team is just focused on the short-term goals and the short-term goals are winning one game each week."[1730]
— *Tom Brady*

Humble teams prepare more aggressively. The Patriots are perhaps better equipped to remain humble following success than any other NFL team because they have consciously built humility into their system. Humility is an important personnel criterion. Players deflect praise as Superman deflects speeding bullets. Asked how it felt to play on "the team of the decade" (after the Patriots won their 19th straight game), Ty Law fired back "It's only 2004."[1731] Safety Rodney Harrison said:

"It's a long, long journey. You can't get so high on yourself that you come back and have a letdown. I think that's what we are afraid of. That's why we work so hard. It's why we try and keep our mental focus on each game at hand and not get caught up in the media. When you are winning, people pat you on the back and tell you how great you are. As soon as you screw up, those pats become stabs. So you have to be careful and be consistent in all that you do."[1732]

Humility begins with Bill Belichick. Asked about the "genius" label people frequently hang on him, Belichick responded, "I've been called a lot of other things, too, that would balance that off."[1733] Another time, he answered the question with: "I was called a lot of things in Cleveland and ["genius"] wasn't one of them."[1734] Asked about making *Time* magazine's list of 100 most powerful and influential people, Belichick said his family "thought it was a joke"[1735]: "It was flattering to be on that list when I can't even get my dog to come when I call him. I'm not able to influence things in my own household, like what show we're going to watch on TV. I take out the trash like everybody else."[1736] (There he goes again, understating. Belichick has *two* English white golden retrievers.[1737]) Patriots running back Antowain Smith explains: "Everything trickles down from Coach Belichick. He's not going to let us get too high. The main thing he told us was to be humble."[1738]

Belichick has been humble his whole life. Before the February 2002 Super Bowl, Belichick was forced to stand for a media photo with the Vince Lombardi Trophy. He was in obvious discomfort and kept his distance from the trophy until the media insisted he move closer and put his hands on the table. In contrast, St. Louis Rams head coach Mike Martz eagerly scooped up the trophy, waved it in the air, and playfully asked, "Can I take this with me?"[1739] Though Belichick had earlier won two Super Bowl trophies as New York Giants defensive coordinator (and therefore had more right to hold the trophy than Martz), he revered that trophy and didn't want to associate himself with it unless and until his team had earned it. Coach Martz, on the other hand, felt comfortable joking about keeping it. Did the coaches' different attitudes play a role in their teams' performance that Sunday? No one can say for sure, but I doubt Martz' mindset benefited his Rams. Martz said "great confidence [is] something we try to instill in our players."[1740] His players continued displaying their characteristic cockiness and looseness, and that likely played a role in the three Rams turnovers that cost them the trophy. Nevertheless, Rams receiver Tory Holt insisted "You have to have some swagger if you want to be champions,"[1741] even after losing to the less swaggery Patriots.

The Patriots lack swagger because Belichick and Pioli won't tolerate it. After the Patriots secured the 2003 AFC East title with a 12-0 shutout of the Miami Dolphins, Patriots running back Antowain Smith said Belichick was already working to keep players humble: "He's not going to let us get too high. The main thing he told us was to be humble, that it's a great victory for us... But the job is not complete yet."[1742]

Humility comes naturally to most Patriots. When Tom Brady heard that Panthers quarterback Jake Delhomme said he aimed to emulate him (because "All he does is win. I'd rather be known as a Tom Brady than any [other quarterback] because his teammates respect him and he gets the job done. ...I'm not the big 6-4, 6-5 guy, sit in the pocket, chuck it all over the field. I do it any way–fight, scratch, claw just to get it done."[1743]), Brady self-deprecatingly joked, "Why would he want to be a guy that is slow and has an average arm? I want would want to be Michael Vick. That is an aspiration."[1744] Brady realizes he has become a New England legend ("Two years ago, it was much more focused on football. Now I have to figure out how to get to the mall to get some T-shirts. It's much more difficult to deal with."[1745]), but he feels like just another guy who happens to throw a football very well: "When people ask me for an autograph, I'm like, 'Why do you want my autograph? I'm just a guy.'"[1746] Perhaps it's because the only other "guys" on the planet who have won at least 70% of their games as NFL quarterbacks over the past forty years (Brady has won 74.5% of his games) are named "Roger Staubach" and "Joe Montana"?

Patriots personnel people love humble players. They drafted defensive lineman Richard Seymour near the top of the NFL Draft, even though he recorded only 1½ sacks his senior season, because "The Pats found... Seymour to be a humble, tireless worker at Georgia even though he knew the riches of the NFL awaited him."[1747] Belichick says, "when you spent time with him, you could see his maturity. He was just a real solid kid, professionally and personally."[1748] Tom Brady's so humble that his rock-star status hasn't gone to his head. Former apartment-mate and former Patriots defensive end Dave Nugent said, "He's so modest that I'll kid about it, and he'll say, 'Nuge, it's just the position. If I was anybody else on the team, they wouldn't even care.'"[1749] After driving his team down field for the winning score of Super Bowl XXXVIII, Brady characteristically pointed fingers at everyone else: "The guys made some great catches there on that last drive. And Adam drove that sucker right down the middle to win it."[1750] He even claimed "None of this would be possible without the fans back in Boston."[1751] (Later, Brady made that seemingly absurd claim sound credible: "We were undefeated at home last year and a big part of that is the fans and the advantage they give us."[1752]) Brady's father, Tom Sr., says:

> "He really doesn't think of himself that way [because] he's one of 53 guys in that locker room. ...[H]e believes that he is one of 53 spokes in the tire. He said something that I found to be profound. He said, 'I would never want to be Tiger Woods because when he wins, he has no one to share it with. I have 52 other guys to share this with. It's so neat to be part of a team as opposed to being *the* man on *the* pedestal who people want to knock off. They have to knock off the New England Patriots, not Tom Brady.'"[1753]

Brady does an admirable job being friendly with the hordes of complete strangers who approach him daily, partly because he never forgot how pained he was when the San Francisco Giants' Chili Davis once refused to give him an autograph.[1754] But Brady will never be confused with Joe Namath, who loved the limelight. Brady finds the adulation both overwhelming and unnerving:

> "Sometimes you don't want to be polite. You just want to be a human being. I walked in to get takeout last night... and people [said], 'Oh my God! It's Tom Brady!' And I'm standing right there. I cringe. It's like, 'How can I hide now?' I get so embarrassed because you're not trying to make a scene or a statement, you're just trying to slide in and get dinner and that is the stuff that, in a sense, can become very suffocating."[1755]

Brady's so popular that Donald Trump practically begged him to date his daughter Ivanka and Jay Leno joked, "Britney Spears said she could see herself married to him for a whole week." Brady also finds it odd because "I just don't have [a starry] opinion of myself. I've been where I've never been thought of like that so I don't really feel comfortable with it. I'm clawing, fighting and digging and being that underdog. That's the only thing I know and that's the only way I've found to be successful."[1756] Brady sometimes feels he's suffocating under the weight of inexplicable hero-worship. He says he has more trouble visiting a mall than he does leading Super Bowl-winning drives: "I do everything I can to go to the mall and try not to have anyone recognize me. But as soon as someone does, I start sweating. I break out in a cold sweat and I just leave."[1757] If you see Brady, please just smile and move on.

Chapter 8

COMPETING AND DISCIPLINING

"You have to compete in practice, you have to compete in the weight room, you have to compete in meeting rooms. And ultimately it transfers over to when we are playing those games."[1758]
– *Tom Brady*

"You play for Belichick and every week's a tryout."[1759]
– *Patriots linebacker Mike Vrabel*

"We might not be a good fit, as a team, for some players. This is a demanding program. Bill is a demanding coach. We're not for everyone. You come to us, you'd better be ready to compete."[1760]
– *Patriots VP of player personnel Scott Pioli*

Earning a roster spot with the Patriots requires winning Bill Belichick's annual *Survivor: Foxboro* contest known as training camp competition. At every position, Belichick and Pioli deliberately bring in more quality players (80) than can make the final roster (53). And then Belichick puts everyone through a grueling series of physical and mental trials that test every aspect of their ability to perform on a football field:

"Every time a player steps on the field he gets evaluated. You're in this business to be evaluated, that's what your performance is. It's evaluated on a play-by-play and week-by-week basis for all of us. Anybody that's not looking for that [should] go deliver mail."[1761]

Patriots rookie P.K. Sam says not even rookies are given a grace period; they must contribute: "There are no red-shirts here, just pink slips."[1762] (Sam was referring to the way college freshmen are often "red shirted," sacrificing their chance to play during their first year to retain four years of eligibility.)

This chapter analyzes competition and discipline together because spirited competition, not yelling, screaming, threatening, intimidating, bribing, or punishing, is the Patriots' primary disciplining device. Belichick says that in training camp, "I don't think anybody is solidified in any job. Ultimately, it is about performance and that is what everybody is going to go up against."[1763] Competition, he says, brings out the best in his players:

"They know that there are a lot of other [players] right there that are looking for the same [roster] spot that they are looking for, and they have respect for them and recognize their abilities. In the end, everybody is trying to get the most out of themselves. You can't really control what anybody else on the team does or doesn't do. As a player, what you can control is your performance and do everything you can do make it good. ...I think [competition] motivates competitors to try to compete at a higher level. So I think that's a healthy thing."[1764]

Belichick's belief in the value of competition has been reinforced throughout his life: watching his dad's Navy team, competing in high school and college football, studying his college economics textbooks, and observing decades of NFL winners and losers. Even in Belichick's youth, his dad Steve was constantly demonstrating for his son the value of striving: "I never let Bill beat me at anything–checkers or whatever. My wife said, 'Let him win,' but I wanted him to be competitive."[1765] Belichick learned the value of meritocracy while playing football at Annapolis High School, which had just been racially integrated: "We had a great coach who didn't see color. All he saw was performance. If you did it his way, you were OK. If you didn't, you were in trouble. ...I took [that] with me. I don't see color; I see football players."[1766] And Belichick felt the power of competition to stimulate discipline and weed out laziness and sloppines during his post-high school prep year at Phillips Andover where he found himself greatly challenged:

> "I think the biggest adjustment was being around so many talented people. You see so many kids with talents in music and art. You had kids whose parents ran Fortune 500 companies. ...Those were things I never really thought about. I realized early on in Andover that if I was going to fit in I would have to work harder and discipline myself. ...I left there a different person."[1767]

Bill Belichick is so competitive he once left a tempting slice of pizza in Scott Pioli's desk during an office weight-loss contest while Pioli and Belichick worked for the Jets.

COMPETITION BOOSTS PERFORMANCE

The Patriots improve not only by bringing in "better" players but also by bringing in many solid players who push one another for limited roster spots. Competition boosts performance both at the individual level (through its impact on players' minds) and at the team level (by ensuring that the team concludes training camp with solid players at every position and with solid reserves it can later re-sign if injuries or other personnel problems occur).

Boosting individual performance: The Patriots believe competition brings out the best in players. A player who must earn his roster spot is more likely to work hard than a player who is guaranteed a spot. Scott Pioli says a team can boost performance simply by creating competition, even without bringing in "better" players: "By virtue of some of the competition alone at some positions, we will be better."[1768]

Players do respond. While entrenched starting left tackle Matt Light missed much of 2004 training camp after having his appendix removed, he was eager to get back as quickly as possible before the coaches could fall in love with other players: "Everybody feels pressure. When you're not involved in what everyone else is doing out there, you feel like you're missing a step and there's always somebody there to take your spot, so you're always anxious to get back. They're always there."[1769] In Light's absence, backup tackles Adrian Klemm and Brandon Gorin reportedly played great. Light commented, "There's your pressure. ... [Y]ou never know who's going to step in, and when they do, they're usually great. In our system, everybody is ready to go. We've proven that the last couple of years. These guys have definitely stepped in and impressed everyone."[1770]

Assembling the best team: Even ignoring the impact of psychological pressure on player performance, competition boosts the team's odds of fielding a strong team. Having a talented and healthy 53 players at the start of training camp does not ensure having 53 talented and healthy players at the end of training camp or throughout the regular season and playoffs. Training camp competition reduces a team's vulnerability to the inevitable injuries and other problems that can derail any player's season. To perform consistently throughout a 16-game NFL season (plus the playoffs), a team must build redundancy and substitutability into its personnel. As Belichick explained, after using wide receiver Troy Brown on defense and linebacker Mike Vrabel to catch a touchdown pass, "We only have so much depth on the team. It's not like college where you have 80 guys and you have three backups at every position. We have to double up. That's part of what a team is."[1771]

No coach can know which particular players will be injured (or retire, *etc.*) in any particular season, but every coach knows with certainty that at least some players will be injured (or retire, *etc.*) every season. Given this, smart coaches train up a pool of potential replacement players who can re-join the team and help it recover from unanticipated personnel losses. By training such players in advance of trouble, a team's reservists know the team's system and the team's players and can step right in when trouble arrives: "It is not like high school where you have a graduation day and everyone gets their diploma and that is it. It is the final cut, but you are going to be hearing from a lot of these guys again, one way or another, either on this team or in the league. So it is another game to evaluate that."[1772]

Many problems can end a player's season prematurely:

- *Injuries and illnesses*: Many players become injured or sick every season. The 2003 Patriots resembled a M*A*S*H unit. The 2004 Patriots lost four players (defensive linemen Rodney Bailey and Dana Stubblefield, safety Guss Scott, and tight end Zeron Flemister) to season-ending injuries during training camp. And 1st-round draft pick Benjamin Watson played only one game before his season ended due to a knee injury.

- *Family illnesses*: Early in 2004, running back Kevin Faulk's mother, Mary Vivian Faulk, became seriously ill with leukemia. The Patriots allowed Faulk to leave the team for nearly a month to be with his sick mother who, most regrettably, passed away: "[Belichick] basically told me to go do what I had to do, to be with my family, to take as much time as I needed. He said my family came first and that football would be here for me. It was a classy thing to do."[1773] Had the Patriots not had Corey Dillon, it really would have suffered from Faulk's absence and Faulk himself would have felt guilty for abandoning his teammates. Because the Patriots had another top running back, Faulk could take time to be with his mom and then grieve for her.

- *Retirement*: As Miami Dolphins star running back Ricky Williams' sudden retirement reminds us, you never know when a player will retire. Patriots cornerback Tyrone Poole, a family man, nearly retired before the 2003 season. Fortunately for the Patriots, Poole convinced his wife to move to New England to spend the season with him. In 2004, the Patriots signed free agent cornerback Jeff Burris, but Burris didn't show up for training camp. Most bizarrely, the Patriots suffered a string of veteran offensive guard signings followed by training camp retirements (Joe Panos in 2001; Rich Tylski in 2002; and Brenden Stai in 2003). Shell-shocked Patriots fans now hold their breath whenever the team signs a veteran O-lineman. Free agent right tackle James "Big Cat" Williams had to assure the media at the opening of 2004 training camp that "My fire's not close to going out."[1774] (The Patriots later cut Williams.)

- *Trouble with the law*: Though Patriots players land in legal trouble less frequently than players on many NFL teams, Belichick has cut good players (like Hakim Akbar, Marquise Walker, and Kenyatta Jones) after they ran afoul of the law.

- *Suspensions and bans (for violating NFL rules, its drug policy, etc.)*: Patriots are not often suspended, but the league issued four-game suspensions for drug policy violations to Patriots wide receiver Terry Glenn in 2001 and to running back Mike Cloud (who served his suspension for failing a steroids drug test as a Patriot though it was handed out before Cloud joined the team).

- *Greedy salary demands*: Belichick's Patriots have had no star player hold out for more money and had signed every rookie since J.R. Redmond in 2000 within hours of the start of training camp. In 2004, however, the team grew concerned that their 1st-round tight end selection (Benjamin Watson) might prove difficult to sign, so they quickly signed two free agent tight ends, Zeron Flemister and Matt Cercone. Watson sat out eighteen days before signing. Fortunately, Watson (who attended Duke) is smart enough to contribute as a rookie even after missing weeks of training camp, but such rookie holdouts usually reduce the rookie's effectiveness. (Flemister, whom the Patriots had given a tryout on April 1, was having a strong training camp before he ruptured his Achilles tendon.)

· *Underperformance due to aging, laziness, overeating, off-field distractions, etc.*: Players who played well one season may not play well the next. Past performance does not guarantee future performance. The Patriots cut former star safety Lawyer Milloy before the 2003 season after determining that his performance had slipped somewhat (probably for age-related reasons) and no longer justified the large salary his contract called for. The Patriots team Belichick inherited in 2000 reportedly had many lazy and overweight former stars.

Assess, Advise, Repeat

Realizing the myriad ways a player's season can come to a screeching halt, or his performance can plummet, Bill Belichick wisely does not pin his team's hopes on the continued health and performance of any particular player. He stockpiles high-potential players and immerses them in a competitive environment. He and his assistants then engage in a cycle of watching each player's performance carefully and offering that player advice on how he can improve. Some players apply the advice and greatly improve themselves while others fail to grow. While Belichick can't count on any particular player, he can feel confident that whichever players emerge victorious from that tough competition will perform and compete well on the playing field that fall: "We have a lot of players working on the defensive line, a lot of good players. I think the competition there will be good. How will it turn out? That will be up to the players."[1775]

MERITOCRACY NO TURNOFF TO MERITORIOUS PLAYERS

Players who sign with the Patriots are under no illusions that they have locked up a starting job or even a roster position by signing a contract. In mid-July 2004, the Patriots signed their fourth and fifth quarterbacks (only three of whom made the final roster). As the agent for NFL veteran Jim Miller, the fifth quarterback to sign, said: "They made us no promises. It's a great organization that has a chance to go to the Super Bowl... All they're committing to is camp pay for five weeks."[1776]

After helping the 2001 Patriots win the Super Bowl and then playing two seasons in Miami, cornerback Terrell Buckley chose to return to New England fully aware signing did not guarantee making the roster or playing: "everything will be determined on how you play and what you do. I've been in situations like that, and I've realized one thing: you can't hold a playmaker down."[1777] Buckley chose the Patriots over "four or five teams"[1778] that included the Cardinals (who offered a multi-year contract) and Buffalo (where his friend Troy Vincent plays) because he hopes to return to the Super Bowl. (Buckley didn't make the final Patriots team but landed with the New York Jets.) Patriots running back Mike Cloud was equally unconcerned by the need to compete:

> "You can't [worry about making the team]. You've just go out there and perform when you get the opportunities and let management take care of [the final roster]. It's all about opportunity. When you get it, you just have to make the best of it."[1779]

(Like Buckley, Cloud also missed the final Patriots roster but also landed on his feet with the New York Giants.)

Patriots training camp is, as Patriots special teams captain Larry Izzo terms it, "opportunity camp." Signing a contract with the Patriots gives you a chance to...

· Prove yourself to Patriots coaches who are experts at assessing football talent.

· Enjoy being part of a great organization with professional and personable teammates.

· Improve yourself against top talent and receive top coaching, something hungry players like Patriots safety Shawn Mayer appreciate: "I feel like I'm getting better and recognizing things better. That's all you can ever ask for–a chance to improve."[1780]

· Sign with another team if the Patriots release you because the Patriots have a reputation for personnel depth. The players the Patriots release generally have solid NFL potential and have received months of quality coaching.

· Re-sign with the Patriots later in the season even if the Patriots cut you. Because professional football is a violent, injury-producing sport, players who learn the Patriots' system but are released may get an opportunity to rejoin the team later.

Many NFL veterans would resent the need to compete for a roster spot, but every Patriot accepts that personnel decisions are made based on current performance, not past performance. Belichick and Pioli tell players looking for guarantees to look elsewhere because the Patriots' system is a meritocracy, not an aristocracy. Competition is inescapable, as Patriots backup quarterback Damon Huard (who recently joined the Kansas City Chiefs) explains, "I learned a long time ago that you just have to be thankful for every day you get in this league. There's always competition, always guys fighting for jobs and sometimes things happen. You just have to be ready to play when you get the chance."[1781]

Although the Patriots don't roll out the red carpet for experienced veterans, many (including former NFL Defensive Player of the Year Dana Stubblefield and three-time Pro Bowler Corey Dillon) eagerly join the Patriots because they want to join a winner and appreciate that the Patriots' meritocratic approach helps build a consistent winner. Meritocratic competition builds winners. As quarterback Jim

Miller's agent noted, "[Belichick and Pioli] didn't get to be coach of the year and executive of the year by accident."[1782] Many Patriots veterans have played on teams that lacked the Patriots' competitiveness, and they have seen and felt the unpleasant consequences.

FOSTER HEALTHY COMPETITION

> "There's always competition. We are always out there competing for a job, but we're also competing for the same thing and that's to make the team win. I think that's the key to our offense, the fact that even though we are all out there competing for time, we're all doing it with the team in mind."[1783]
> – Patriots running back Kevin Faulk

No Patriot is guaranteed a spot on the 53-player active roster or on the 45-player game day roster, let alone a starting position. Coach Belichick often says, and the players all understand, that he will keep on the roster those players he feels give the team the greatest chance of victory and he will play those players each week whom he feels maximize the team's chance of victory: "If you take a look at my history and our history here with the Patriots, we've kept the players that have performed the best."[1784]

Belichick is forthright that no player should ever feel immune from competition and that the team will never hesitate to bring in new players: "If there is an opportunity for us to improve our team, with adding a player to any position, then we will always consider it."[1785] Repeatedly asked whether the Patriots would consider acquiring Player X or Player Y, Belichick always replies with some version of "we'll try to improve our team whenever and wherever we can."[1786] Asked how he communicates this message to the players, Belichick says there's no value in sugarcoating reality: "Just tell them as directly as possible. There is no need to say it any way other than the way that it is."[1787]

Players get the message. Even kicker Adam Vinatieri, one of the NFL's best, was forced to compete for his job when the Patriots drafted kicker Owen Pochman in the seventh round of the 2001 NFL Draft. (In that case, the team was also using competition to try to pressure Vinatieri, who was entering the final year of his contract, into signing a Patriots-friendly contract extension.[1788])

Even the rawest rookies know the Patriots are a meritocracy and that it's up to them whether they make the team and get onto the playing field. Patriots rookies see this as an opportunity. Where some teams automatically sit their rookies on the bench their first season, the Patriots care only about performance:

> "We are going to max out each player's performance and their potential. We are not looking to bring anybody along at any pace other than the one that they are going at and try to get them ready to contribute as much as possible for the team. We are not going to say, 'Let's just coast along here and let

things run their own course.' We are going to push it with Vince, with Marquise, with all of them, and see how quickly they come along and what they are able to do."[1789]

In 2003, rookie center Dan Koppen and rookie safety Eugene Wilson were regular starters and essential contributors to the team's Super Bowl season. The opportunity to compete for playing time on an even footing is appreciated by Patriots rookies like defensive tackle Vince Wilfork:

> "New England is a fair team. They play the good players. ...Whoever can put us in a position to win football games, that's who they're going to put on the field. It's how you take it. If you go out every day and be aggressive, and play with your heart, good things will happen."[1790]

...and rookie tight end Benjamin Watson:

> "They already told us they're going to play the best players, whoever that may be. But I've got a long way to go before I'm able to compete with the guys that have been here for years and know the system. I definitely have to do my learning. I definitely have to pay my dues."[1791]

...and rookie running back Cedric Cobbs:

> "I know this team plays talent. Whether you're a rookie or not, they're going to play the best player. That's something to look forward to. I just want to continue to work hard and show them that being a rookie doesn't mean anything."[1792]

Cobbs missed out on most of training camp with an injury, but Wilfork and Watson both contributed to the team's 2004 opening night victory over the Indianapolis Colts. Watson caught several passes, and Wilfork recovered a fumble late in the game.

Constant competition keeps players on their toes. The Patriots drafted no offensive linemen in the April 2004 NFL Draft, so reserve offensive lineman Jamil Soriano knew he had a chance to make the team and to play if he could prove himself, but Soriano did not see the news of no rookie competition as any reason to relax. Soriano knows the Patriots always seize every opportunity to strengthen the team by replacing weak links with stronger links:

> "They are basically giving the guys who they have a chance to show what they have and what they can do on the field. But by no means does it take any real pressure off me because if I don't live up to their expectations and play up to their expectations then they will bring in someone new. There are always people out there and so I just have to maintain my focus and play well in camp and get things done."[1793]

While Soriano was busy trying to prove himself in NFL Europe, on this side for the Atlantic, offensive lineman Stephen Neal had exactly the same response to the news:

"That doesn't mean anything. There is an opportunity but there are still some free agents out there. And this team is always making moves. You never know who could come in. There's nothing I can do about that. I'm just trying to make this team in whatever role I can. Whatever they want me to do, I'll do it. Backup tackle. Swing guard. Whatever."[1794]

Patriot players also believe competition enables them to learn more from their teammates. Was long-time Patriot running back Kevin Faulk disappointed that star Corey Dillon joined the team, likely reducing Faulk's playing time? Not at all:

"He's a great addition to our offense and to our team. He's a Pro Bowl back, it just makes us that much better. When you see him working and you see his work ethic, you can see why he's that type of football player. I'm really looking forward to working with him. Anytime you can get out there and work with a Pro Bowl back, maybe pick up some things and he can pick up some things from me, it's only going to make you a better player."[1795]

Competition never ends. After becoming the first undrafted rookie to make the Patriots' opening day 53-man roster since 2001, cornerback Randall Gay wasn't rushing out to buy a house: "It's harder to stay here than to get here. I now know I've got to work twice as hard because there'll also be somebody trying to take what I've got."[1796]

"COMPETITION" NEED NOT BE A DIRTY WORD

"I like a challenge this time of year [during training camp]. That's what keeps you going after 10, 11, 12 years. The competition is good, and it's going to be good during the season when you've got somebody going down [with an injury] and somebody can step in who's just as good."[1797]
– New Patriot and 12-year NFL veteran defensive lineman Keith Traylor

"It's a great group of guys here, especially the receivers. Everybody is helpful, there's no jealousy."[1798]
– Patriots rookie wide receiver P.K. Sam

Many assume "competition" is zero-sum: if I win, you lose, and vice-versa. Patriots players see things very differently. To them, competition is good. Competition is fun. Competition strengthens both the team and each individual. Healthy competition pushes each player to maximize his potential. Each player embraces competition because he wants to win and understands that having multiple talented players at each position gives coaches flexibility to overcome injuries, exploit advantageous matchups against different types of opponents, and rotate players in and out of the game to keep players fresh. (Making a regular practice of rotating players is especially beneficial when playing in oppressive heat and/or humidity, like the 100° Arizona weather during the 2004 Patriots-Cardinals game. The Patriots even rotated seven offensive linemen in and out of that game with no noticeable performance degradation.) Also, even if a player doesn't earn a spot on the Patriots' roster, competition should have helped him become a better football player and increased his chances of eventually landing an NFL job, as Belichick makes clear: "we have had players that we released go on to play for other teams. We have also had players who we released, that we brought back and have played well on our team."[1799]

Backup safety and special teams player Shawn Mayer is a good example. During the critical final minutes of Super Bowl XXXVIII, Mayer was on the field at safety after both of the Patriots' starting safeties were injured. Mayer had been waived by the Patriots earlier that season... not once but twice!

Patriots VP of player personnel Scott Pioli (who was voted "class clown" by his 1983 high school classmates) appreciates the value of tough love because he lived it:

> "I was a bit of a cutup in high school, kind of a knucklehead when I got to Central [Connecticut State University]. By far the one person who had the biggest effect on me was [high school football coach] Frank Leonard. If not for him, I'd probably be back in Washingtonville flipping pizzas. He straightened my life out. He was a coach. He was a friend. He was a nasty SOB and one of the most caring people I ever met. He... taught me about second chances."[1800]

Players who respond to competition by striving daily to improve themselves are more likely to be chosen for the final Patriots team and more likely to become successful NFL football players. Consequently, the Patriots use competition as a central organizing principle that energizes and motivates and strengthens, not merely as a device for choosing the final roster or deciding who will start each game. A few examples of how the Patriots use competition in almost everything they do:

· Inside linebackers coach Pepper Johnson lines up the linebackers and chucks footballs at them as hard as he can. If a player drops a ball, he must do ten pushups. If Johnson makes a bad throw or each player catches the ball, Johnson does ten pushups. Everyone enjoys the drill so much that even "the offensive coaches were standing around gleefully watching it."[1801] Players even egg Johnson on, claiming he isn't throwing hard enough.

· During the Friday intra-team scrimmage preceding Super Bowl XXXVIII, Tom Brady swore he would throw a touchdown pass over safety Rodney Harrison's head, and Harrison swore he would intercept Brady. They laid down a wager: two first-class round-trip tickets anywhere in the world. When Harrison picked off Brady during that practice, Brady said, "It ruined my weekend."[1802] That might be slight hyperbole. I suspect winning the Super Bowl and being named MVP provided some consolation.

· Even "Scout Team" players (whose job it is to simulate the team's upcoming opponent) compete for "playing time" on the Scout Team! In preparing for a 2001 regular season game against the St. Louis Rams (whom the Patriots would defeat in the Super Bowl later that season), Bill Belichick brought in former NFL quarterback Joe Theismann (who led the Redskins to victory in Super Bowl XVII) to simulate Rams quarterback Kurt Warner. Theismann took turns throwing passes for the Scout Team with Patriots backups Drew Bledsoe and Damon Huard. The three Scout Team quarterbacks didn't throw a predetermined number of passes. They competed. Each quarterback stayed in until they threw an incompletion, at which time one of the others replaced them.[1803]

Finally, competition can be a lot of fun. During their 2001 Super Bowl run, competitive dominoes games were the locker room rage with guys yelling "slap the domino, motherf---er" at each other.[1804] Backgammon is also popular. Patriots players were even trash-talking with each other before the charity bingo event "Troy Brown Celebrity Bingo" because "We're all competitive. When we play something, we play to win."[1805] The pressure was too intense for offensive lineman Matt Light who attended but chose not to participate because "I'm not very good. It doesn't make me feel too good when I lose."[1806] Troy Brown was flexing his mouth muscles: "Oh yeah. I'm one of the best. Rosevelt Colvin says he's the best but we'll see. Just concentrate on the numbers you want to be called and… use the right color marker."[1807]

DON'T BE A BAD GUY, MAKE THE SYSTEM THE "BAD GUY"

"If he cut me, I'm sure there'd be a good reason."[1808]
– *Cornerback Antonio Langham, who played for Belichick in Cleveland and New England*

Though Belichick doesn't slap guys on the back or go out for drinks with the team after games, he's also no longer a whip-cracking, foul-mouthed disciplinarian (though he *was* during his first years in Cleveland when he tried to emulate Bill Parcells without Parcells' endearing *je ne sais quoi*… a serious mistake Belichick has since acknowledged and corrected). Belichick relies on competition and mature, dedicated players to police and discipline themselves. He doesn't have time to be a disciplinarian or a babysitter or a parent. He has instead implemented an egalitarian system that automates disciplining for him.

A MERITOCRACY REQUIRES METRICS

By definition, a "meritocracy" requires objective assignment of merit and demerit. You can't treat everyone fairly if you're playing favorites. And you can't choose winners and losers unless you know a winner when you see one. The only way to run a meritocracy is through careful, honest assessment of each player/worker's productivity.

The Patriots film everything, even rookie camp practices: "All the coaches were around, and they filmed each and every practice session."[1809] And the coaches watch all the films, multiple times. Coaches watch each film individually and again collectively. And they don't relax in comfy chairs with soda and buttered popcorn. They constantly "rewind" (everything's now digitized) and re-watch because they assign each player a grade on each play. Assistant coach Pepper Johnson explains:

> "after I view the entire [game] tape, I grade my guys. ...By [9:00 the morning after game day], all the coaches should have graded their players. For example, I will give plus and minus grades for each inside linebacker on each play. Then each one ends up with a score. We keep count of how many plays each played [and] how many tackles they made, how many they missed, if they knocked down a pass, picked up a fumble. Each defensive coach has to be ready to talk about his players individually with... the defensive coordinator. Then we watch the tapes again as a unit, and talk about every single play."[1810]

Because Belichick attends practices and watches and re-watches practice and game film and knows precisely what he's seeing (after spending decades breaking down film), he doesn't have to guess about a guy's effort or talent. He knows. As Baltimore Ravens VP Kevin Byrne, who worked for Belichick in Cleveland, said during Belichick's first year as Patriots head coach, "One thing [players will] learn up there is [Belichick] sees everything, and he knows more than you think he knows."[1811]

The entire staff constantly and intensively monitors and assesses player performance. And coaches constantly tell each player precisely what they think of his performance. No one is ever stunned to learn the Patriots have released him. Bill Belichick despises grade inflation and never offers false praise because he believes doing so harms players:

> "I am not going to tell a kid, if I don't think he can play for us or play in the league, 'I think you should spend the next two or three years of your life training for something that in my opinion I don't think is realistic.' If he wants to do it, he can do it but really if I think it is time for him to move on, I will tell him it is time for him to move on and do something else. That doesn't mean that he has to do it, but I would tell him that as an honest

opinion. He can do whatever he wants with it. If it were different, then I would tell him differently."[1812]

Conversely, Belichick will stand up for you if his evaluation indicates you're good enough for the NFL but not quite good enough to make the Patriots' roster. Chad Lee was an undrafted linebacker who survived the Patriots' 2003 training camp until the final round of cuts:

> "Pioli and New England coach Bill Belichick thanked Lee for his effort, commended him on his ability to move from inside linebacker to outside linebacker in a matter of weeks and wished him well... Lee said Belichick and Pioli made it a point to tell him he didn't make the team because the Patriots had better linebackers and not because he performed poorly. They said he could use them as a reference."[1813]

Belichick doesn't play favorites. Star quarterback Tom Brady admires the fact that he receives no special exemptions or privileges because he's a two-time Super Bowl MVP:

> "[Belichick] treats everyone the same way. He expects out of the first year guys the same thing he expects out of the ten year vets: that you come out and practice, you know what to do, you show up on time, and you have a good attitude. ...It's nice to know that... you are going to get that same toughness out of every player you play with."[1814]

Consequently, players know that lobbying or sucking up to coaches is a waste of time. As Sean Mayer put it, "You have no control over what they do and whom they pick. You just go out there and try to play your [butt] off."[1815]

Finally, Bill Belichick and his assistants refuse to prejudge any player based on reputation or past performance. What a player did last season is ancient history. Patriots coaches even heavily discount how a player is currently performing if fall roster decisions are weeks or months away. Asked in June 2004 to comment on veteran cornerback Terrell Buckley's belief that he had improved, Belichick said: "Well, we'll find out. I'm glad he feels that way... but how you feel you are in June is one thing, and how you actually play in the fall is another story. ...[T]he proof will be in the performance in the fall."[1816]

What role will Corey Dillon, the most talented running back ever to wear a Patriots uniform (except perhaps Curtis Martin), play in 2004? "That will be determined by what he is able to do and how effective[ly] he is able to do it."[1817] The Patriots are a true meritocracy because they tape every moment of every practice and Patriots coaches skillfully and precisely evaluate each player's performance on every play of every practice by watching and re-watching film. As Belichick says, "I've attended all the practices this year. I've watched the tapes of them. I don't sleep during those film sessions."[1818] But coaches wisely use their evaluations weeks and months before personnel decisions primarily for teaching/training purposes. They base personnel decisions solely on "fresh" data.

DON'T TOLERATE INTOLERABLE BEHAVIOR

The Kraft family hands almost complete authority over football operations to Bill Belichick and Scott Pioli. The Krafts believe in hiring the best football coaches and executives and letting them run the team. But they make one exception. They refuse to tolerate players they would be embarrassed to associate with their family. The New England Patriots are an extension of the Kraft family, and the Krafts expect players to act accordingly.

During the Patriots' second Super Bowl championship season, several starting offensive linemen suffered season-ending injuries. Nevertheless, when one of their promising young offensive linemen (Kenyatta Jones, whom Pepper Johnson wrote "might be our most athletic offensive lineman"[1819]) threw scalding water on a close friend in what was apparently an idiotic prank, the Patriots did not hesitate in dropping Jones from the team. They didn't try to trade him. They dumped him. (Jones later received one-year probation for the incident and became the 2004 Washington Redskins' starting right tackle.) Before entering the NFL, Jones had been involved in a gun possession incident. And Jones confessed to not showing much maturity as a Patriot and not learning the mental aspects of playing offensive line as quickly as he should have:

> "I just didn't know how to study the plays, learn the plays. In college, it was just, 'You knock this man out of the play.' Here, there are a lot of [blocking] schemes to know. I needed to be home studying, but I was out riding around. Or I'd come home early, but leave my playbook in the car. Come in and sit around."[1820]

It's actually surprising Jones remained with the team following the 2002 season. As Patriots coaches conducted their annual assessment of each player, virtually everyone advocated releasing Jones. In 2002, Jones' blocking was dead last on the team, scoring just 72%; and Jones led the team in mental mistakes, committing 23 mistakes on 661 plays, far worse than the team's best linemen: Damien Woody (6 mistakes on 957 plays) and Matt Light (12 on 1,030 plays).[1821] Jones' laziness and sloppiness drove his position coach mad. Offensive line coach Dante Scarnecchia told his fellow coaches that some days "you just know [Jones] ain't gonna fuckin' work."[1822] The Patriots must regret drafting Jones, so his release shocked no one within the organization. The scalding water episode was the final straw. In 2004, Joe Gibbs' Redskins regretted signing Jones and cut him after Week 7, saying "we had given him every opportunity to be successful."[1823] A change of environment can improve a player's behavior but not his underlying character. A player who acts immaturely in

Belichick's locker room, with its inspiring role models, strong peer pressure, and high expectations, is not going to become an upstanding citizen elsewhere.

The Patriots similarly dumped their 1996 draft pick Christian Peter after Bob Kraft learned more about Peter's off-field problems. Kraft chose to dump Peter outright rather than accept a trade to the Kansas City Chiefs who offered the Patriots a draft pick for Peter.[1824] Kraft explains his philosophy as follows:

> "[Past Patriots teams] had a few other folks floating around here that had a lot of off-the-field antics. It wasn't something we, as fans, could feel proud about. With us, reputation is important. You always run a business for the bad times. If you stress quality, your customer base will stay with you."[1825]

In 2001, the Patriots dumped defensive back Hakim Akbar, whom some had dubbed "the next Lawyer Milloy."[1826] Akbar sustained life-threatening injuries after he was "ejected [forty feet] from [his SUV] and landed in a marsh" after he drove off the road while speeding (and driving without a license) at 1:30 a.m.[1827] As stupid as that was, the Patriots kept Akbar on injured reserve. They released him only after he committed another, even stupider, transgression. On the Friday night before his team played in the Super Bowl, he "got caught leaving his room after curfew."[1828] Akbar is talented enough that he still plays for the Jacksonville Jaguars.

The day after Patriots wide receiver prospect Marquise Walker (a 2002 3rd-round draft pick of the Tampa Bay Buccaneers who caught a record 176 passes for the Michigan Wolverines) was arrested at 3:09 a.m. on July 20, 2004 for driving under the influence and hitting a car and then two trees,[1829] the Patriots released Walker. The Patriots' decision to release Walker was so predictable that I wrote the preceding sentence (except for the first two words) before Walker's release.

One of Coach Belichick's boldest moves sent a clear signal to every Patriot that he would not tolerate unreliable players or players who placed themselves above the team. Wide receiver Terry Glenn was one of the team's few stars. Glenn was amazingly physically gifted, but he would dazzle one week and fail to show up the next. Glenn's performance seldom matched his ability because he was not a focused football player. Said quarterback Drew Bledsoe, "Terry can change the way a defense prepares for us. He is so fast and so good, and can score at any time, that teams have to spend a lot of time preparing for him. We need him now more than ever to step and take over games."[1830] Instead of begging Glenn or babying him, Belichick lost patience, benched him, and later traded him. The Patriots won their first Super Bowl that same season... without Glenn's help. Patriots players were pumped up by the implicit message that their coaches valued tenacity and toughness over "talent."

Belichick left Bethel Johnson off the active roster of a game against Jacksonville in 2003 to send him a message. Johnson claimed "I learned when you have the opportunity to be out there, you can't take it for granted. ...My goal is to be more professional."[1831] Belichick reportedly felt compelled to repeat the lesson by sitting Johnson for Game 4 of 2004, even though Patriots receivers Deion Branch and Troy Brown were out with injuries, after Johnson complained about being asked to learn some new plays.[1832] Belichick denied holding Johnson out for disciplinary reasons,[1833] but it's quite reasonable to infer that Belichick sat Johnson to prevent him from taking playing time for granted since Johnson has apparently not matured as the Patriots hoped and is not as diligent as many of his teammates.[1834] Johnson also seems to lack his teammate's respect for his head coach: "He had his reasons, I guess. I have no idea, really. I just go out and do my job. If he likes it, he likes it. If he don't, he don't."[1835] Belichick told reporters that coaches "pick out the [45 players] you think will give your team the best chance to win."[1836] Leaving Johnson off the team implied coaches felt Johnson was less helpful to his team than Kevin Kasper, a player signed just days earlier and unfamiliar with the Patriots' playbook. The day after Johnson told reporters that he didn't know why he was held out of the game, Belichick made a point of commenting: "I have a hard time understanding how he could say that. That is all I have to say. ...if you can't recognize where there is a problem and address it, I don't know how it could possibly get improved."[1837] That same day, Johnson annoyed reporters and teammates by playing "baseball" with teammate Patrick Pass in the locker room while reporters tried to interview players. One ticked-off veteran wondered "Isn't there some film they could be watching?"[1838] Veteran linebacker Willie McGinest put an end to it, telling the players to "Go read your book."[1839]

Johnson apparently got the message. The next week, Belichick activated him, and he threw himself into the air like Superman to make a fully-extended, game-winning 48-yard catch on 3rd-and-7.

DON'T TOLERATE SLOPPINESS

"I believe in making certain players know what techniques we're going to demand. I feel that if something's worth doing, it's worth doing right. If that means we have to stop practice to correct a mistake, so be it."[1840]
– *Bill Belichick*

"[Belichick's] attention to detail and his focus is so strong that those who don't recognize that high a standard have trouble with him. The hardest-working people we had in Cleveland had the best rapport with him. ...If you're a guy who doesn't work hard or tries to fake it, you have no chance with him. He will do the job himself or replace you. But if he sees you set a high standard for yourself, you'll have no problems. ...If you don't have enough respect to do your job, he dismisses you, often in a profane way."[1841]
– *Baltimore Ravens VP Kevin Byrne, who worked with Belichick in Cleveland*

Belichick uses various techniques to signal that sloppiness is unacceptable and to make players perform properly. Consider this example from his days as Giants defensive coordinator, as told by former New York Giants linebacker Pepper Johnson:

> "We were in preseason, and we didn't play our technique right on a defense, so the next time we go in, I look to him for the signals, and it's stack defense, cover 2. We play it and stop them, and I look for the signal for the next play, and it's stack defense, cover 2. We weren't in situations for that defense, but he kept calling it because we hadn't run it right. After a few plays, I kept looking over, but I knew what was coming: stack defense, cover 2. And finally we stopped 'em. We were jumping around like we just won the Super Bowl. When we get back to the sidelines, he says, 'You SOBs don't want to run it right, we'll play it the whole [expletive] game.' We got the technique right after that."[1842]

In early June 2000, Belichick broadcast a warning to his new team that slacking and laziness would not be tolerated: "When the conditioning program began, we emphasized the importance of team preparation from March through July. Most players understood that and acted appropriately. The fact others didn't disappoints me."[1843] So, how did he set the tone on the first day of summer training camp as Patriots head coach? "Thirteen players showed up overweight... All 13 were fined, four were banned from practicing and one was waived."[1844] Wide receiver Troy Brown said the players heard the wake-up call: "Man, we've released guys already. I think guys got the message right away that this is not a game. It's your job now. You have to go out and take it serious. [Players] are sitting on pins and needles, not wanting to mess up."[1845]

If Belichick believes you can "get it," he'll give you a second and, if you're lucky, a third and even fourth chance. But he eventually loses patience with unfocused players. Wide receiver Keyshawn Johnson said of Belichick when they were both with the New York Jets, "He says some things to you and if you don't get it... I've seen guys who didn't get it, and the next day they were gone."[1846]

DON'T LET PEOPLE WASTE OTHER PEOPLE'S TIME

Bill Belichick hates it when Patriots waste other players' and coaches' time. Having ten or twenty guys sitting in a room waiting for one or two guys is a major waste of time. So one of the team's few formal rules is to never be late to a meeting. Ryan Ferguson, whom the Patriots gave a shot to try out with the team in 2004, explains: "'Patriots time' means that five minutes early is on time. So Coach Belichick could be starting a 5:30 meeting at 5:25. I made it a point to get everywhere 10 minutes early."[1847]

APPLY RULES CONSISTENTLY

In a controversial move, Coach Belichick made superstar defensive lineman Richard Seymour (arguably the Patriots' best player) sit on the bench for the first thirteen defensive plays of a December 14, 2003 game against the Jacksonville Jaguars. Why? Seymour had missed two days of practice during the week preceding the game while attending his grandfather's funeral. Jarvis Green, who replaced Seymour in the starting lineup, had not missed any practices. Seymour apparently requested and received permission to attend the funeral, but Belichick apparently believed Seymour would miss only one practice, not two. Seymour was bitter after losing his starting spot for returning at the end of the second practice: "Getting benched made it tougher" especially because "I was going to play [that game] for my grandfather."[1848]

Belichick's unpopular decision to bench Seymour was apparently based on his principle that only players who practice during the week are eligible to start that Sunday and that no player, no matter how good, "owns" their starting spot but must earn it each week. The unwritten rule was that missing more than one practice during a week for any reason other than an injury disqualifies a player from starting that week's game. However, special teams captain Larry Izzo had previously missed four practices over a two-week period after his father died, yet Izzo had started both weeks.

This story illustrates the only "negative example" in this book. Although Belichick has never fully explained what he termed a "coaching decision" and has insisted that Izzo's and Seymour's cases "were different" (possibly because Izzo lost a father while Seymour lost a grandfather), the public facts of this case suggest to me that its lesson is: "Once you make an exception to a rule, application of that rule becomes arbitrary, selective, and subject to management whim and favoritism." Making exceptions to rules can easily create bitterness and resentment. Belichick is right to establish rules and principles, but rules and principles must be applied across the board. Standing on principle is difficult when precedents exist that violate that principle. A clear, well-known, hard-and-fast rule would have spared Seymour some of the additional bitterness he felt due to his surprise benching.

I believe there was a smoother way to handle that situation. Patriots coaches could have added a principle that the normal rules will be applied more leniently in situations arising from deaths in a player's family. Such a meta-principle would not water down the standard rules and procedures, except when a player's family member has died. Most everyone would have accepted such a meta-principle because "Seymour thought his benching was unwarranted. Many of his teammates agreed. Some of the Patriots' assistant coaches did, too."[1849] I suspect Belichick has learned from this controversy. He gave running back Kevin Faulk as many weeks off in 2004 as he needed to be with his terminally ill mother.

EVERYONE'S A MANAGER

Each Patriot manages himself and helps manage his teammates. In fact, players also help manage the coaching staff. In weekly Friday meetings, player representatives make clear to coaches the issues that are troubling players. Patriots coaches' responsibilities differ from Patriots players', but coaches want players to monitor themselves and do not relish the task of disciplining or wielding authority over players to motivate or punish them.

NO ONE IS IMMUNE FROM CRITICISM... OR WORSE

> "[Current University of Iowa head coach Kirk] Ferentz remembered the time Belichick dressed him down in front of everyone after running a shoddy offensive line drill. 'It made me realize that everything I did had to be of the highest quality,' Ferentz said. 'It also made me realize that he was watching everything that was going on.'"[1850]

Patriots coaches are not immune from the need to constantly scrutinize and improve themselves. Coach Belichick may appear the only Patriot immune to competition, but he views himself as competing against other coaches ("I love the competition against other great coaches like [Bill] Walsh or Tom Landry"[1851]), and every NFL coach operates under a microscope. Belichick strives to improve and has obviously learned from the many mistakes he made in Cleveland during his first stint as head coach:

> "I tried to look back at those five years and take some of the things I thought were good and build on them and take some of the things I can improve– budgeting my time and being involved in different aspects of organization that I cut short a little bit in Cleveland. I'm kind of a detail person and I had a tendency to get caught up in some details in expense of the big picture at times."[1852]

Pete Carroll inherited an 11-5 Patriots team and led it to records of 10-6 in 1997, 9-7 in 1998, and 8-8 in 1999. Bob Kraft fired Carroll, saying, "This is a business of accountability."[1853] Within months of becoming Patriots head coach, Bill Belichick fired Bobby Grier, whom Kraft had promoted to VP of player personnel in 1997, and national scout Dave Uyrus, presumably because they had directed three horrible drafts and helped Belichick to a mediocre draft soon after becoming head coach in 2000. (Former head coach Pete Carroll said, "The Chris Canty draft? That was one of the worst picks ever. He never did a thing."[1854]) Belichick did not fire Grier and Uyrus to increase his power but to improve the team. Belichick has proven very happy to share personnel decision-making with Scott Pioli. But Belichick will not tolerate continued poor performance, especially in an area so essential to success as personnel acquisition. Belichick went out of his way to say some nice things about Grier. But, reading between the lines of his press release, Belichick was clearly dissatisfied with Grier's overall performance after drafts in 1997, 1998, and 1999 yielded, according to the *Eagle-Tribune*'s Hector Longo, just three "legitimate, usable NFL talents. That's three picks out of 27"[1855]:

> "This decision is unrelated to any specific event, performance or personal relationship. It is more a reflection of my general feeling to proceed in a new direction with regard to the structure and operation of our personnel department."[1856]

Firing people for a consistent behavioral pattern rather than a single incident is a hallmark of the Patriots' approach to personnel management. Belichick has said, for example, that no player would ever lose his job following a preseason game based solely on his performance in that one game but that a player might well lose his job if his performance during a preseason game reinforced pre-existing concerns the coaches had entering that game.

Chapter 9

BILL BELICHICK: DEVELOPMENT OF A COACHING LEGEND

"Nobody achieves anything by themselves."[1857]
— *Bill Belichick*

"As a kid, I was very fortunate to watch my dad coach and to watch [many] teams practice... Collectively, these people had a tremendous influence on me in terms of work ethic, teamwork, and their unselfish drive. I've never known team effort any other way. ...A big asset was the volume of coaches I was able to observe from age twelve to twenty-five. I saw hundreds."[1858]
— *Bill Belichick*

"Belichick can look back on a 30-year pro football career... Belichick is perhaps the best-prepared football man since Vince Lombardi, who labored for 16 years as an assistant before taking Green Bay to a record five NFL championships in the 1960s. ...There are some who remember Belichick as the best scout they ever worked with–the first to insist on rookie candidates with detailed, individualized credentials for each of the 22 different offensive and defensive football positions. ...Belichick has had a more valuable in-depth football education than most of his adversaries."[1859]
— *Bob Oates, L.A. Times*

Many kids fill their days with fun and frivolity. Many graduate from college with little career direction. Many adults grind away for years before finding their niche or achieving a measure of success and recognition in their field. Some people never find their passion.

Not Bill Belichick. Born into a football family, "Billy" was assisting players and coaches at Navy while still in grade school. In junior high, Billy was practically a member of the Navy coaching staff:

"He's a genius. Ten years of age, little Billy, that little son of a gun was in there breaking down films. He had a knack for it. ...I don't think that anybody ever thought he'd be anything but a coach. ...Billy saw his dad breaking down the films, and naturally, it rubbed off on him. ...He had [an] uncanny ability not to have to write things down. He could keep it all in his head."[1860]

Bill Belichick has always loved analyzing football and been great at it.

If football were chess, Belichick would have become a grand master long ago because football coaching became his *de facto* profession at age 6. But football isn't chess. Serving as a head football coach involves more than moving X's and O's around a board. Chess pieces don't have personalities or egos. They don't break their legs, demand higher salaries, or move to other chess sets as free agents. Chess pieces don't need to memorize playbooks, read-and-react to their opponents in real time, or communicate effectively with their "teammates" …because only one piece moves at a time. Also, chess masters don't worry about personnel acquisition or talent development because there's no college draft for chess pieces and lifting weights won't help one pawn out-muscle another. Being a head football coach requires knowing more than the physics and mechanics of coordinating eleven athletes on a field. Belichick has learned it all, but rising to the top of his profession required decades of continuous learning.

Like all great leaders, Belichick is more than gifted. He has continually expanded his industry knowledge, cultivated his abilities, acquired and assimilated knowledge from his experiences, and surrounded himself with and listened attentively to other great football minds. Bill Belichick was an analytically-oriented only child of an analytically-minded football coach. He grew up intensely devoted to dissecting the game of football and displayed uncanny talent at a tender age. His present greatness reflects both inherent mental gifts and life-long curiosity, determination to excel, and passion to understand not only the technical nuances of football but every other aspect of the game, both on and off the field. With the help of the countless football coaches he has surrounded himself with throughout his life, Bill Belichick has distilled his life experience into a clear strategy for building great football teams.

GENIUS OR MORON?

"The Smart Coach/Moron Coach Meter… can be very moody."[1861]
– *Bill Belichick*

The same Bill Belichick who so rapidly transformed the Patriots into two-time Super Bowl champs was previously despised by many players, fans, and journalists in Cleveland, where Belichick's Browns finished with losing records in four of his five years (1991-1995) as head coach. Near the end, "fans pound[ed] on his door yelling, 'Bill must go'"[1862] and some players begged owner Art Modell to fire their coach. Belichick's Browns experience "proved" to many that Bill could not coach. How can a coach win when so many players dislike him? Fearing this, one *Boston Herald* reporter welcomed Belichick to New England by calling him "duplicitous pond scum,"[1863] and a talk-show host called him a "despicable human being."[1864] A national columnist wrote, "why any team would want to hire this man as a head coach is baffling."[1865] Patriots owner Bob Kraft says, "I had a lot of people on my back when we hired him"[1866] and "when I hired Bill, we gave up the No. 1 pick to Parcells, and people thought I was insane."[1867]

Many then suspected Belichick of being "just a defensive guru miscast... as a head coach."[1868] An *Eagle-Tribune* journalist wrote: "The more I think about it, the worse his past seems. The Cleveland problem doesn't go away... I see problems in New England."[1869] *The Buffalo News'* Larry Felser is big enough to confess to his readers that he said in 2000:

> "Bob Kraft made a crucial mistake. Belichick can't get along with people and he proved it when he was head coach in Cleveland. He has the personality of a dial tone. He'd alienate the Good Humor Man. You want him in a small, dark office with the door closed, making out your game plan, not dealing with other human beings."[1870]

In short, as Steve Belichick put it (with the same wry irony his son inherited from him), "[Bill] was an idiot five years ago."[1871] *Sports Illustrated's* Peter King wrote "Belichick is fortunate he landed on his feet."[1872]

Is Bill Belichick the "failed" coach of the Cleveland Browns or the "genius" coach of the New England Patriots? Where did he come from? And why did so many doubt him for so long?

As a teen, Belichick was already a talented X's and O's tactician, but only in his forties did he appreciate that his low-key coaching style and complex playbook required disciplined, self-motivated players. As Browns head coach, Belichick discovered he was poorly suited to coach selfish, lazy players who lacked passion for the hard work required to prepare to win NFL games. Belichick can yell and swear with the best of them. In fact, he practically became Bobby Knight in his early Cleveland years, angering many players. (Interestingly, Knight had recommended Belichick for the job.) Further, disciplining players steals time from training and watching film, two Belichick strengths. Belichick seemingly attempted to emulate the tough guy routine of his long-time boss, New York Giants head coach Bill Parcells, and flopped. Belichick eventually found his groove. Along the way, he discovered that a coach can build a great team only if his players possess skills suited to their coach's style of play and respond well to his style of leadership. Bill Belichick expects players to be as hard-working, detail-oriented, competitive, and self-motivated as he is. Belichick's players must also be smart and adaptable to properly execute his complex schemes.

Belichick also learned in Cleveland that he could not run a one-man show. Like many intelligent, capable, hard-working people thrust into their first-ever leadership position, Belichick initially found it difficult to delegate to others and focus on helping them succeed rather than attempt to do everyone's jobs for them. Making the Browns a success required hiring smart assistant coaches, relinquishing control over details to them, and trusting them to do their jobs.

In New England, that same Bill Belichick has succeeded beyond anyone's expectations because he learned during his Cleveland tenure to sign players eager to be coached and smart enough to digest his thick playbook and to hire great assistants and facilitate their success. For example, Patriots VP of player personnel Scott Pioli says the Patriots would never sign a self-centered, attention-grabbing wide receiver like Terrell Owens, as the Philadelphia Eagles did:

> "That's not the kind of guy we're looking for here. Bill and I understand how demanding his program is. I know his personality well... We make sure we don't bring in the kind of people he's not willing to tolerate. People who are lazy, people who underachieve, people who don't get it, they aren't going to make it. People who are high-maintenance are not going to make it in our program."[1873]

Belichick and Pioli lacked this clarity of vision when their Cleveland Browns signed Andre "Bad Moon" Rison, just one example of how Belichick has continued growing and learning throughout his life.

"BILLY": SON OF A NAVY FOOTBALL COACH

> "I felt comfortable breaking down film as a teenager."[1874]
> – *Bill Belichick*

> "Billy and his dad were really tight, so he just hung around with his dad all the time... Billy, he's a bit of a no-nonsense guy. That's the way his father is. Looking back, he was so close to his father. They were always so much alike."[1875]
> – *Roger Staubach, Super Bowl-winning quarterback who knew the Belichicks during his college days at Navy*

Bill Belichick's life has revolved around football. Bill was named after his father's college football coach, Bill Edwards, and his birth was celebrated with a flower-filled football.[1876] "Billy" grew up devoted to and inseparable from his father, Steve, who was himself devoted to the game of football. Even Belichick's mom, Jeannette, could have coached a football team, according to Steve:

> "I don't think there's a woman in the country who knows more about football. She can tell you the second-string quarterback with the Rams or who coaches at Texas-El Paso. I'd come home from a scouting trip and she'd tell me who was good or who wasn't in the Navy game that day. I'd look at the films and she was right."[1877]

Growing up the son of an assistant football coach at then-great Navy, "Billy" Belichick loved football. His father, Steve Belichick, was a Detroit Lions fullback/linebacker in 1941 before serving on a Navy ship at both Normandy and Okinawa during World War II.[1878] After the war, Steve coached football for a remarkable 43 years, including a third of a century (1956 through 1989) as a defensive assistant coach and chief advance scout at Navy. Steve traveled weekly, often with his son, to study and film every upcoming Navy opponent and design plays to defeat them. The only Navy games Steve ever watched live were the season finales against Army.

When "Billy" was just six years old, he was already displaying powerful pattern recognition prowess, identifying car makes (Lincoln, Buick, Pontiac, *etc*.) from a greater distance than his father.[1879] And when Navy's offensive line coach, Ernie George, began delivering six-year-old Billy a copy of Navy's weekly game plan,[1880] Billy memorized Navy's entire playbook:

> "He would take [the game plan] up to his room–and he may still have some of 'em. He knew how we called plays. He knew 28 was a sweep, and 26 was off tackle, 30 and 31 were for the fullback. And all the pass plays–hook, Banana X, Banana Y–he knew 'em all."[1881]

When just 8 or 9, "Billy" was hanging out with then Navy quarterback (and future Super Bowl-winner) Roger Staubach who often practiced particular passes by throwing repeatedly to little Billy. Steve says, "I'd bring film home too, and when he was supposed to be studying, he'd be drawing up plays instead."[1882] When ten-year-old Billy accompanied his dad on weekend scouting trips, "[Dad] gave me little jobs–'What's the receiver doing? What's that guy doing?' It was a great help."[1883] Bill recalls fondly being "incredibly impressed by my father's ability to go to a game and write down, not just the [player] substitutions, but diagram the play, in time for the next play."[1884] Bill says "one of [my] great learning experiences" was accompanying his father on scouting trips and "Just watching him work during the game and understanding how he could see what all 11 players were doing on both offense, defense, and special teams."[1885] Under the tutelage of his dad and his dad's colleagues, Billy got better and better:

> "I didn't start by breaking down films. More like writing down the down and a distance and trying to get that right. One thing led to another, and a lot of the coaches at the Naval Academy were very supportive and tried to encourage me and give me things to do. They were little bitty things. But as time went by, there were projects."[1886]

Billy became further fascinated by the nuances of football when he began seriously studying and dissecting film alongside Navy coaches… at age 10! Ever since, he has lived and breathed football. Says Steve:

> "I would bring [Bill] with me for the scouting meetings. He would be there, watching me talk about the opposing team. I'd say, take a look at the tight

end on this play and tell me what he does. After doing it for a long time, he got better and better at it."[1887]

The young Belichick was a sponge: "He'd sit in the back of the room, maybe for 90 minutes a session. I never had to say a word to him about his behavior. He'd stare at the front of the room and not say a word."[1888] His mother, Jeannette, remembers Billy listening in on countless coaches meetings, some held right on the Belichick's porch: "When the other coaches were around, he didn't ask a lot of questions. They liked having him around because he wasn't a pest. He was very, very good at listening and learning and remembering."[1889] Belichick often listened as coaches devised the weekly game plan (which Navy called its "ready list"). He was so serious about understanding every nuance of Navy football that Ernie Jorge kept sending Billy the team's entire game plan every Thursday. Upon becoming head coach of the Cleveland Browns nearly three decades later, Belichick recalled traveling with his dad to Browns training camp: "My father used to take me to Hiram College when I was a boy to watch the Browns practice. I remember seeing some of the greats like Jim Brown, Lou Groza and Gary Collins."[1890]

The young Belichick was also a leader. After his mom overheard Billy bossing other kids around while playing baseball, one of them explained that it was OK because "If Bill didn't tell us what to do, we wouldn't know."[1891]

Navy football coach Rick Forzano, who as head coach of the Detroit Lions later hired 25-year-old Belichick into his first "real" job (as the Lions' assistant special teams coach), knew Belichick was special when he was just ten years old:

"He could break down film at 10 or 11 and understood what he was looking at. He had a great mind even then. He could see things others didn't. His father was a great scout. That was part of it. He learned from a great coach, like Tiger Woods did as a boy. But he also has a gift like Tiger Woods has."[1892]

As a teen, Bill needed no adult supervision: "We gave him a film and put him in a room. He always had that ability to break it down."[1893]

Young Billy learned to create and exploit mismatches by watching his father. As Navy's advance scout, Steve filmed and observed each upcoming Navy opponent and then devised plays to defeat them. Steve even wrote a 1963 book, *Football Scouting Methods*, that Hall of Fame coach Paul Brown (whose Cleveland Browns won 167 games and lost just 53) "thought was the bible for young assistants and scouts"[1894] and Houston Texans GM Charley Casserly (formerly Washington Redskins GM) "calls the best on the subject he has ever seen."[1895] Bill observed his dad studying Navy's upcoming opponent, identifying weaknesses, and developing strategies to exploit vulnerabilities. Former Navy running back Joe Bellino, who was young Billy's #1 idol while Bellino was playing his way to All-American, Heisman, and

College Hall of Fame honors, describes Steve's ability to dissect an upcoming opponent in terms often used to describe Bill Belichick:

> "[Bill]'s a chip off the old block. (Steve) ran our Monday-evening skull sessions. The game plan for the upcoming game was designed to beat that team. We were convinced going into every game that we had the right game plan to win. (Steve) would pick out the weakness of the other team and exploit that weakness."[1896]

At Navy, Belichick learned the value of attentively observing one's opponent and adopted his father's passion for perceptive, precise preparation. Steve says his son's football education was non-stop: "He was around superior people and coaches at a very early age. ... [C]oaches would come by the house and we'd sit on the porch and talk football and Bill would sit right there and just listen."[1897]

Belichick became a master at breaking down film through trial-and-error and feedback from his father:

> "When I first started doing it, he would look at it, and there were a lot of mistakes and he would say, 'Do it this way' or 'Do it that way.' But then there came a point where it wasn't that way. He would look at it and maybe not find anything, or just a couple of things wrong with it."[1898]

Bill had no physical gifts for football. Steve had his son play center at his football camps because "I could see he couldn't run fast."[1899] Steve still treasures a photo of Billy snapping a football to legendary quarterback Johnny Unitas. But what Bill really took away from those camps was not a photo but knowledge:

> "My dad... would bring in fifteen coaches to work the camp. During the season, he would scout and I would go on scouting trips with him and sit in the press box. ...The spectrum of people I came across was amazing. It was an incredible opportunity. It was unbelievable to be able to observe all the different levels and styles of football and football coaching. A lot of those people would get me information because they knew I was interested in it— game plans, scouting reports, articles about different techniques."[1900]

ANNAPOLIS HIGH

Bill's dogged pursuit of perfection was obvious from his non-stop long-snapping practice in high school: "Bill spent hours in the basement, snapping the ball between his legs against the wall, where we had drawn a target. Bill shook the entire house with that ball banging against the wall."[1901] And Bill learned about "team" from Annapolis High coach Al Laramore:

> "There was no individuality on his team, other than the number you wore. I learned a lot about the team concept and about toughness from him. We used to have one bucket of water at practice. Everyone drank from it. If he

didn't like the way we were practicing, he'd walk to the bucket, kick it over and say, 'You guys ain't gettin' a water break today.'"[1902]

PHILLIPS ANDOVER

Belichick spent just one post-high school year at Phillips Andover, but it had a life-long impact on him. Belichick played center on the undefeated (8-0) Phillips Andover football team that won the New England Prep School Championship. Since 175-pound Bill was undersized for an offensive lineman, his teammates nicknamed him "Weak Link."[1903] But his understanding of the game and of his teammates' assignments kept him on the field. And Belichick played much "bigger" than his physical size because he was, as he now insists of his Patriots players, dedicated to achieving his full (albeit limited) potential:

> "Bill wasn't the best athlete on the team, but nobody worked harder in practice and nobody was in better shape. ...Bill [always] knew where everybody was supposed to be. He was solid all the time. ...I remember seeing him always staying late working on his long-snapping. He never once mess[ed] up a long snap on a punt or kick. We never worried when he had the ball in his hands."[1904]

Bill also loved squash and lacrosse and played on the Andover lacrosse team that won the New England Championship after losing only one game, to Brown University's junior varsity team. Though not physically talented enough to earn a starting position on the lacrosse team, Belichick nevertheless impressed lacrosse coach Paul Kalkstein: "Bill was a very smart player. He would watch the game from the bench and seem to be taking mental notes. I didn't know he was doing something scientifically. All I knew was, whenever he went into the game, he scored."[1905]

Andover was an intellectual awakening for Belichick. He was startled by the quantum leap in difficulty between his public high school and his prep school year: "I had taken four years of French, so I sign up for French 4... and they said, 'Maybe you better try French 3.' I figured: All right, easy. The first assignment was to read *Les Miserables*... in French! I'm looking up every [expletive] word!"[1906]

Bill formed a life-changing friendship at Phillips Andover with his fellow offensive lineman Ernie Adams, a young man so obsessed with football strategy that he had already read Steve Belichick's book, *Football Scouting Methods*, before meeting Bill.[1907] The two spent countless hours watching football film and playing bridge together. Adams later served as an assistant coach with the New York Giants throughout the 1980s and as Bill's "Special Assignment Coach" with the Cleveland Browns in the 1990s. Adams is currently the Patriots' director of football research. Andover's former trainer Al Coulthard recalls that Adams and Belichick "were better X's and O's men than most college coaches. I loved talking football and all sports with those two."[1908]

WESLEYAN

Despite his small size, Belichick toughed out college football at Wesleyan too, where he switched to tight end and linebacker. Recalls a former assistant coach, "Bill hung in there for four years without ever starting a game. He stood out because of his attitude toward the game, which was very serious."[1909] But "his career was so anonymous that the school does not even have a picture of him on the field."[1910]

Bill Belichick has always been a tenacious worker, so he unsurprisingly tried his darnedest to mold himself into the best football player he could become. He simply lacked the physical talent to ever be a good football player: "He was too small and too slow... But he took the pounding for four years."[1911] But Belichick's striving instilled in him a core belief that every football player should strive to maximize his ability. It's no coincidence that Belichick's Patriots engage in the hard-core preparation that the young Bill Belichick prided himself on.

In college, Belichick continued analyzing film and studying football strategy. At Wesleyan, one side of Belichick's notebook had class notes and the other had football plays he doodled.[1912] His positional coach in college remembers "he had a special talent and ability to analyze the technical aspects of football. He... was interested in the 'Why?' of things, and even interested in the 'What if?'"[1913]

Belichick majored in economics, a subject he credits with teaching him to think logically and analytically and to solve problems. Belichick has stayed in touch with his former economics professor, Richard Miller, and even hand-wrote him a letter thanking him for teaching him fundamental economic optimization techniques (like cost-benefit analysis and incremental analysis) that Belichick believes help him manage the salary cap intelligently. Two obvious ways Belichick now optimizes according to the principles of cost-benefit and incremental analysis are: 1) Focusing on good-but-not-great players who help the team on the field without handcuffing the team financially at other positions; and, 2) Refusing to pay megabucks to retain "star" Patriots (like Lawyer Milloy, Drew Bledsoe, Chad Eaton, Brandon Mitchell, and Damien Woody) who are excellent and popular players but not worth their inflated price tags.

(Belichick's personnel philosophy reflects not only his economics training but also his deep knowledge of NFL history, acquired through personal experience and through reading virtually every football book ever written. Former Green Bay Packers GM and NFL personnel guru Ron Wolf sees the fingerprints of 49ers Hall of Fame coach Bill Walsh all over Belichick's decisions: "[Walsh] let Montana go and Craig go and Lott go before their last couple of years. You've got to let them go and then you've got to replace them... Unfortunately, we all fall in love with our players. ...You have to take emotion out of the equation."[1914])

As Belichick was preparing to graduate, his dad recalls, "Bill [had done] so well in his business courses, that Procter & Gamble twice visited him on campus trying to recruit him for its management-trainee program."[1915] Belichick's NFL career might never have happened without his friend Ernie Adams. Ernie and Bill, fast friends at Andover, stayed in touch after Ernie headed to Northwestern and Bill to Wesleyan. At Northwestern, Adams had "served as a team manager and constantly hung around the coaching offices until he earned the staff's trust and basically became an unpaid student coach. By the time he earned his undergraduate degree, he was breaking down film and helping to crunch some game plans."[1916] Before graduation, Bill decided to pursue coaching instead. His dad recalls that "Second semester his senior year is when he told me he wanted to be a football coach."[1917] Bill got the idea of approaching an NFL team after Adams led the way by landing an unpaid position with the New England Patriots in the spring of 1975:

> "I met with [Patriots coach] Chuck Fairbanks and I talked my way into a job with them. It wasn't for low pay, it was for no pay. But it was a foot in the door. Bill saw what I did and managed to set up the same deal with the Baltimore Colts."[1918]

Belichick asked his dad for help getting his foot in the door with the Baltimore Colts. Steve knew Colts special teams coach George Boutselis who convinced the Colts' head coach to give Belichick a chance to prove himself. Bill claims he "didn't deserve" the job that he got by being in the proverbial "right place at the right time"[1919] (when the Colts general manager's cousin, who was supposed to have the film-breakdown job, became unavailable), but the Colts were lucky to get him. And former Navy coach Rick Forzano tried and failed to entice Bill to Detroit, where Forzano had become head coach of the Detroit Lions.[1920]

A few years later, in 1979, Adams became the first assistant hired by New York Giants head coach Ray Perkins. After Adams recommended Bill for an opening, Bill and Ernie reunited in New York (where Ernie served as the Giants' pro personnel director). Adams now says, with Belichickian understatement, "After 33 years, we're real comfortable with each other."[1921]

NFL ASSISTANT (1975-1990)

Bill Belichick was so eager to become a coach that he wrote several hundred letters seeking an entry-level position. But it was through his father's connections that 23-year-old Bill Belichick convinced then-Baltimore Colts head coach Ted Marchibroda to give him his first NFL "job" (initially unpaid) in 1975. The "job" involved, among other things, calling players to the coach's office before the team cut them, a task that earned Belichick the nickname "Bad News Bill."[1922] No task was too mundane or too demanding for young Bill: "He worked from 6 in the morning to 11 at night, breaking down film, making up tendency charts and serving as a chauffeur for Ted. Bill would ask a lot of questions and Ted had the patience of a saint."[1923]

Though his parents' home in Annapolis, MD was just 45 minutes away, he put in such long hours that he started crashing on a sofa:

> "It was a great opportunity for a guy with no coaching experience. I started breaking down film like I'd done with Dad, but they gave me more and more responsibility. I worked diligently, so they kept giving me more. I didn't have a place to live, so I slept on a sofa. It was a 7-to-midnight shift every day. It was like a tutorial in coaching. ...it was my chance."[1924]

Belichick lived with Coach Marchibroda and his other two assistant coaches (Whitey Dovell and George Boutselis). Recalls Bill's dad: "Bill lived at the Howard Johnson's motel by the airport. Ted Marchibroda would drive Bill to the complex every day. He bought Bill dinners. He should have been allowed to write Bill off as a dependent on his income tax."[1925]

Helping run an NFL team with just three other coaches, Belichick received a baptism by fire. His responsibilities were hardly limited to the mundane and thankless:

> "I worked primarily with the defense, broke down all the film, did all the scouting reports, then worked with the special teams coach to help set up things with him, ran the scout team in practice, ran the special teams scout team in practice. Then I did the practice schedules, and between 11 and 12 (at night) I would drive Ted and Whitey and George back to the hotel. It was 18 hours a day of solid football, nothing but football. From 7 a.m. until midnight."[1926]

Belichick obviously loved every minute because Marchibroda says "He was willing to work round-the-clock for nothing"[1927]:

> "[Bill] had just come out of college, and we were looking for a guy to break down films on defense. I was impressed with him immediately. When we gave him an assignment, we didn't see him until he had it completed. And once we got to know him, we never had to double-check it. He was a very quick learner. ...The work ethic is the thing. He always enjoyed the detail work. It seemed that he really enjoyed what he was doing."[1928]

Belichick displayed all the intensity, single-mindedness, and humility he now expects from his players and assistant coaches: "the only thing I was worried about was breaking down film. Trying to do my little job and stay out of the way."[1929] Marchibroda remembers that "The [primary] thing Billy did was prepare himself so well... He knows what an [opponent] will do, but he also knows what a team won't do... [I]f another team's tendency is not to throw to the running back in the flat, then he won't waste manpower covering it. He'll use [his players] somewhere else."[1930]

Looking back, Belichick says, with characteristic modesty, "I was getting paid nothing because I wasn't worth anything."[1931] After observing Belichick, Marchibroda was desperate to retain him and asked the Colts to pay Belichick $50/week.[1932] The team instead agreed to pay a whopping $25/week:

"[Colts GM] Joe Thomas came up after about the third or fourth week of training camp and said, 'You're doing a pretty good job, we're going to start paying you.' Great. Twenty-five bucks a week. After taxes, it was $21.22 or something like that. As Joe Thomas said when he handed me the check, 'Don't spend it all in one place.'"[1933]

Belichick's insights helped the Colts improve from 2-12 in 1974, before Bill's arrival, to 10-4 in 1975... including nine straight wins following a 1-4 start! It was the first time a team had gone from worst to first in just one season. The detail-obsessed 23-year-old Belichick was not only noticing things others ignored but also devising ways to exploit them. After noticing that running backs often tipped off their plans before the snap, he made sure Colts defenders communicated amongst themselves where the play was going:

"You had your normal position of the backs, then you had it where one [running back] would cheat wide, or one would cheat in. Then one guy cheated wide, one guy cheated in, or one guy cheated back. So we had our signals. If he cheated out, it was 'Chow,' if he cheated in, it was 'Chill.' If he cheated up, it was 'Chew.' And if he cheated back, it was 'Chubby.'"[1934]

Belichick's former college coach heard great things, not just about Belichick's dedication but also his productivity: "I remember Earl Morrall was one of the coaches with [Belichick] up in the press box, and he told me that Bill did everything exactly right."[1935] Though one report says the Colts doubled Bill's pay to $50/week before the season's end,[1936] New York Giants GM Ernie Accorsi says the Colts' general manager fired Bill rather than pay him another $25/week:

"Ted [Marchibroda] said Bill is such a great kid. [Colts GM] Joe [Thomas] calls me and said, 'Do you know this kid Belichick? Marchibroda's asking for 50 bucks a week. Let me tell you something. He's not getting 50–and he's out of here.' He fired Belichick over 50 dollars a week. And let me tell you something, Belichick's never forgotten it."[1937]

Belichick needed to eat and sleep in the off-season and requested a $4,000 annual salary for 1976 that the cheap Colts management rejected.[1938] After Belichick departed, a furious Marchibroda vented his anger on the Colts general manager.

But after Belichick's intensive research helped the Colts improve so dramatically, word spread. Belichick accepted the Detroit Lions' offer of a $15,000/year job with use of a Thunderbird to serve as special teams assistant and reunited with Lions' head coach Rick Forzano, who had thought so highly of ten-year-old Billy while Forzano was at Navy. Belichick was only 24, but "[Players] respected him immediately. And my other assistants would come back and say, 'Jiminy, this guy can coach.'"[1939] A sports writer who watched Belichick scout the Chicago Bears was mightily impressed:

> "Belichick... told Bannon about the Bears' tendency to run all of their kickoffs toward the center of the field. When the Packers' second-half kickoff rolled toward the right sidelines, as predicted by Belichick, the Bears returner went to the middle.... Bannon wrote on one play, a second and long, that Belichick correctly guessed the Packers would run the ball. 'The Packers are giving it away when they run on long yardage,' Belichick told Bannon. When Bannon asked Belichick how he knew, he responded, 'To tell you the truth, I'd rather not tell you. They've been doing it for a long time.'"[1940]

Belichick continued his football education in Detroit. Steve Belichick says Bill's fellow Lions assistant coach Jerry Glanville had a profound impact on his son: "Bill learned much of what he knows when he worked with Jerry Glanville."[1941] That speaks volumes about Glanville, given the many coaching influences Bill had in his life. (Steve Belichick was obviously Bill's most important coaching influence.) The other Detroit assistant coaches were also great: Joe Bugel (later an NFL head coach), Jim "Gummy" Carr (innovative defensive coordinator whose blitzes were "like a prison break"[1942]), Floyd Reese (current Tennessee Titans general manager), Ken Shipp (former Jets head coach), and Fritz Shurmur (defensive coordinator of the 1996 Super Bowl-winning Green Bay Packers).

After two years in Detroit, Belichick spent 1978 with the Denver Broncos as special teams assistant and assistant to the defensive coordinator, helping the Broncos win their division. But Belichick was unhappy and quit. In 1979, he was hired as special teams coach of the New York Giants by then-head coach Ray Perkins (at the urging of former Andover teammate and best friend Ernie Adams who had been Perkins' first hire). Over his first five NFL seasons, Belichick worked for four teams and five different coaching staffs. By 1985, Belichick became the Giants' defensive coordinator. The very next season, he coached the Giants defense to victory in the Super Bowl. He says his varied experience was invaluable:

> "I was influenced by a lot of different people. The biggest value was seeing a wide range of coaching styles. Because I saw so many successful styles, I became confident that there wasn't just *one* style. I didn't try to be Vince Lombardi or Tom Landry. I tried to be Bill Belichick."[1943]

In 1989, Belichick almost landed a job as Cleveland Browns head coach after George Young urged Ernie Accorsi (currently New York Giants general manager) to interview Belichick and Bill wowed Accorsi: "Bill came in and blew me away. It was instantaneous. He was meticulously prepared. He knew everything and he was ultraconfident."[1944] In 1990, the Giants again won the Super Bowl with

Belichick coordinating the defense. Throughout, Belichick usually worked "from 5 or 6 a.m. until 11 p.m. He often slept in his office. His wife and three children would schedule in time during the day to come visit him."[1945] Belichick has always worked harder than anyone else because he loves football and has an exceptional body that seems to require little sleep.

CLEVELAND BROWNS HEAD COACH (1991-1995)

"We took a bad team, made it pretty good, made the playoffs, had a bad year in the most off-the-charts negative situation maybe in football history, got fired. It just wasn't a good mix between [owner] Art [Modell] and me."[1946]
– *Bill Belichick*

Just 38 years old, Bill Belichick became the NFL's youngest head coach when he took over the Cleveland Browns in 1991, but he didn't let it go to his head. In presenting Belichick to Cleveland, Browns owner Art Modell called Belichick a young Don Shula. Belichick was characteristically embarrassed by the comparison: "To be compared to Don Shula really is a joke. I mean, the guy's a Hall of Fame coach. I haven't coached one game in this league. I hope he's not insulted."[1947]

Super Bowl victory that got away?

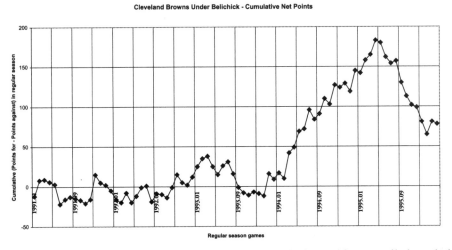

Cleveland Browns Under Belichick - Cumulative Net Points

A substantial case can be made that Bill Belichick would eventually have led the Browns to a Super Bowl championship if Art Modell had not announced in the middle of the 1995 season that he would move the Browns to Baltimore. Belichick inherited a horrible football team (the 3-13 Browns of 1990 who had scored 228 points while surrendering 462) and needed time to grow into the position of head coach. Despite a rough start, by 1994, Belichick had transformed the atrocious team he had inherited into an 11-5 playoff team in 1994. Belichick's Browns even won their first playoff game, ironically defeating the New England Patriots, coached by Belichick's former and future boss Bill Parcells, and finishing 12-6.

Further, Belichick had assembled an incredible staff that included two future "NCAA Coach of the Year" winners and many executives and coaches who subsequently helped lead the Panthers, Patriots, Raiders, and Ravens to the Super Bowl. The Browns' 1995 season started off well (a close 17-14 defeat followed by three solid victories of 22-6, 14-7, and 35-17). Despite a September *Boston Globe* article by Will McDonough that the Browns might leave Cleveland,[1948] after eight games, Belichick's Browns were 4-4, with three close losses (14-17, 19-22, and 15-23). On November 4th, before the Browns' ninth game, *Boston Globe* reporter Will McDonough broke the story that the team was moving to Baltimore. That news shocked players, fans, coaches... even Belichick, who had been kept in the dark by owner Art Modell. Belichick says:

> "The departure announcement put team morale in the tank. ...The people of Cleveland felt like they had been abandoned. If you were part of the Browns organization, you felt more like a deserter than an outcast. We were still there... but we were leaving, so it was worse than if we had actually left... Tremendous animosity developed against the team. In no way is this intended as an excuse for our record... because we didn't play well enough, and we had to fight through it. But it was a huge obstacle to overcome... The ownership left town and participated in the welcoming festivities in Baltimore. The players on the team felt abandoned with a lot of questions about their future."[1949]

The Browns were blown out in their next two games, 10-37 and 3-20. After winning four of eight games in the first half of 1995 (that might have been six wins with a bit of luck), the Browns won only one of eight in the second half. Modell's decision to uproot the team precipitated players' complete mental meltdown, and the rest of the season was a total loss. Only Belichick himself remained focused: "Bill Belichick came into the office every day, and it was the same as I imagine it is with the Patriots: He was only interested in talking about whatever the thing was that he thought would give his team the best chance to win the game."[1950] Belichick remained so focused, in fact, that he failed to address his players' inability to cope. His players were not concentrating on football because, for example, Cleveland's infamous "Dawg Pound" was so incensed by the team's impending move that rowdy fans who formerly hurled dog bones onto the field instead began chucking batteries.[1951]

To this day, virtually every coach and executive from Belichick's Browns insists Belichick put Cleveland on the road to a Super Bowl. Owner Art Modell uprooted the 1995 Cleveland Browns and turned into the 1996 Baltimore Ravens. The 2000 Ravens won the Super Bowl. Ravens general manager and executive VP Ozzie Newsome, who credits Belichick for his transition from player to executive, says flatly: "If we would have remained in Cleveland, we would have won a Super Bowl. We were headed in the right direction... A lot of what we did in Baltimore, the foundation was built in Cleveland."[1952] Nick Saban, who coached LSU to college football's 2003 national championship after serving as the Browns' defensive coordinator under Belichick, says: "Bill built a good Browns team from 1991 to 1994. There's no doubt he would've had the same success there that he's had everywhere else."[1953]

Belichick's offensive line coach in Cleveland, Kirk Ferentz (who won college football's Coach of the Year award in 2002), agrees with Saban:

"After things didn't work out in Cleveland for Bill, I told my wife, 'I predict he's going to hit a home run if he gets another chance.' He's so meticulous, so reflective, that there was no doubt in my mind he'd succeed. We all make mistakes, and I'm sure he feels he made his share. But I'm not surprised to see how well he's done now. He's just so... detail oriented, and he's willing to have the courage of his convictions to try things that he feels will work."[1954]

Bill's long-time close friend and special assistant in both Cleveland and New England, Ernie Adams, noted back in 1994 that building a winning organization takes time:

"People around here didn't understand this whole building process. They acted like they thought Bill could come in here, wave the magic wand, sprinkle some stardust and everything was going to get better instantly. In his first couple of years here, he didn't have a snowball's chance in hell of making the playoffs with the talent he was left with. The reason Bill has turned it around, is because he had a clear and consistent vision of this team from Day One, and he never deviated from it. That's Bill, make a plan and stick to it."[1955]

Indeed, in his first news conference as head coach of the Cleveland Browns in 1991, Belichick stressed some key attributes that later characterized his Patriots championship teams: "Everybody is going to work together and we are going to get it done. I want an aggressive, hustling team with a good work ethic."[1956] And Bill had already developed one of his most famous defensive strategies when the Browns took on the Warren Moon-led pass-crazy Houston Oilers in 1991. Before that game, he told Ernie Accorsi, "you better warn the owner, it could get ugly. I don't know how we're going to stop them. ...There's only one thing we can do. They're going to catch a thousand passes. They're going to get the crap knocked out of them every time they catch one."[1957]

Current Oakland Raiders player personnel director Mike Lombardi, who worked with Belichick in Cleveland before helping Oakland reach Super Bowl XXXVII, agrees with Adams that Belichick's vision and coaching is largely unchanged:

"the perception of Bill has changed. But I'm telling you he's the same guy. ...I thought then, and I think now, that he was everything you could want in a head coach."[1958] Legendary Cleveland Browns running back Jim Brown similarly swears that "he's exactly the same man I knew 10 years ago."[1959]

The man who hired Belichick as Cleveland's head coach, Ernie Accorsi, left Cleveland a year after the hiring but agrees Belichick turned the Browns around: "I chuckle when people say Bill failed in Cleveland. I give him a free pass for 1995."[1960] "[Bill] didn't fail, he was coaching in an impossible situation."[1961]

Meddling owner

Belichick's Browns were also hampered by owner Art Modell's interference in personnel decisions. When the league instituted a salary cap, Browns executives smartly traveled to meet Jerry West for three hours of advice on how he maintained the Los Angeles Lakers as a perpetual NBA power. The Browns could not follow West's advice because Modell insisted on overpaying for players Belichick didn't even want, most notably $27 million for Bernie Kosar whom Belichick believed, largely correctly, was washed up. Just five weeks after Modell handed that mega-contract to Kosar (whom Modell said was "like a son to me"[1962] ...as Patriots owner Bob Kraft would later say about Drew Bledsoe), Belichick released Kosar, officially for diminishing performance but also (unofficially) for insubordination and to save some money. Belichick's entire staff (plus legendary Browns running back Jim Brown,[1963] whom Belichick brought along to bolster his case in Modell's eyes) confirmed to Modell that Kosar was washed up and was harming the team by sowing discord in the locker room and defiantly ignoring the coaches' plays and calling his own.[1964] Kosar later joined the Cowboys as a backup (for just $1 million) and stepped in and won the January 2004 NFC Championship Game after Troy Aikman suffered a concussion. But Kosar was never again a #1 quarterback deserving of a multi-million dollar contract. His completion percentage and yards-per-attempt had dipped markedly in 1993 and never really bounced back. (Belichick was apparently to blame, however, for deciding to pay troubled wide receiver Andre "Bad Moon" Rison $17.5 million.[1965])

Ironically, after Belichick saved Modell over $20 million by releasing Kosar, Modell argued he had to move the team to Baltimore because he was "financially strapped." Modell fired Belichick during a phone call but found time to interview Belichick's replacement in person later that same day.[1966]

(Getting burned by lack of personnel control in Cleveland and then ignominiously fired by the Browns played a major role in Belichick's decision five years later to walk away from the New York Jets' head coaching job. Belichick feared coaching a team while someone else, Bill Parcells, controlled team personnel. A *New York Post* headline screamed "Belichicken," but Belichick didn't want to repeat his Cleveland experience. On January 21, 2000, Belichick's attorney informed the new

New York Jets owner that Belichick was willing to return as Jets head coach but only if he were given full control.[1967])

Learning curve

Belichick was a 39-year-old rookie head coach in 1991 and admits that being a first-time head coach is "a big learning experience."[1968] It's unrealistic to expect instant success from any coach who takes over a team in shambles, especially a coach with no prior head coaching experience at either the college or NFL level. NFL owners realize this and frequently hire retread former NFL coaches with poor-to-average track records or even former college head coaches over otherwise stellar candidates lacking head coaching experience. Dallas Cowboys owner Jerry Jones, for example, insisted on an experienced NFL head coach in his search that ended with Bill Parcells because "We couldn't afford to go with someone who hadn't had [head coaching] experience in the NFL."[1969]

Former Browns quarterback Bernie Kosar believes one of Belichick's rookie mistakes was stretching himself too thin by trying to do too much of the stuff assistant coaches and executives should do: "He tried to do everything–offense and defense, contract negotiations, personnel negotiations. At any age, that's a difficult job. I think bluntly he wasn't ready."[1970] Belichick actually agrees: "I've learned from the previous coaching experience… to delegate more. Previously, I think I maybe tried to do too many little things; too many things that maybe took me away from bigger-picture things that I should've been doing."[1971] In Cleveland, Belichick once naively attempted to serve simultaneously as head coach, offensive coordinator and defensive coordinator.[1972]

Belichick's shift to head coach was even more painful because he tried to become Bill Parcells. Belichick should have been himself. Instead, players responded badly when Belichick successfully mimicked Parcells' tough guy routine but none of Parcells' endearing qualities. Mike Baab, who played for the Cleveland Browns in Belichick's first season (1991), recalls the misery: "He was the most profane coach I've ever heard. I don't think he was interested in becoming your friend in any way, shape, or form. He didn't endear himself to anyone at all. There was nothing to love there, except the hope we would win. …That first year, he was completely lacking in people skills."[1973] Belichick worked players mercilessly: "It was almost horrifying. We ran gassers until we vomited. He never had a good thing to say to anybody. He didn't care."[1974] The media had no love for him either. *Cleveland Plain Dealer* journalist Tony Grossi compared a Belichick press conference to "putting a sharp pencil into your eye."[1975] The *Hartford Courant*'s Alan Greenberg compared it with "a root canal."[1976] Belichick confesses "I had an adversarial relationship with the team and the media. I made winning football games the No. 1 priority, and everything else was a distant second."[1977] He also admits "I might have been a little too rough on [the players] at times" but not because he's sadistic: "In the end, my intent isn't to try to have conflict, or try to be iron-fisted, or tyrannical, or anything like that–but to just try to get it done, get through a message."[1978]

Belichick eventually figured out that his system is so demanding that players will work that hard only if they are motivated and self-disciplined. Threats and punishments cannot extract such intensity. So, when Belichick tried to impose his grueling system on the Cleveland Browns before jettisoning players who would never accept his intensity and before earning the players' respect and trust, the unsurprising result was chaos and rebellion. Some Browns players reacted to Belichick's imperious discipline by calling him "Little Hitler."[1979] Looking back, Anthony Pleasant, who played on both Belichick's Browns and Patriots, says:

> "Bill's changed a lot. He was tough and hard-nosed [in Cleveland]. It was always his way or no way. He's more lenient now. It's good. It's not anything negative towards Bill, but I wish he did this when he was in Cleveland. It was always pound, pound, pound. We never wore shorts. It was always in pads and going full tilt. Now, he's cut back and he don't beat up his players like he did. He's learned from his mistakes. I think he's learned that there has to be a balance."[1980]

In Cleveland, Belichick was initially obsessively focused on football and too little concerned about his football *players*:

> "I'm more aware of [off-field events like news that the Browns would relocate to Baltimore] and their importance to the team now and will be more responsive to them than I was in Cleveland. Somebody's moving. Somebody's wife is having a baby. Things like that can affect the way a player performs. In Cleveland I dealt with things like the depth of pass routes and tackling angles. That's it. By the end of the time in Cleveland I had a better understanding of the overall picture."[1981]

Belichick has also admitted trying too hard to copy his former boss, Bill "The Tuna" Parcells, whose gruff, no-nonsense style worked well for him. (Belichick, dubbed by some "Tuna Helper," cringes at the suggestion Parcells was his "mentor," pointing out with great validity that his coaching philosophy is a pastiche of ideas he has acquired during a lifetime hanging out with football coaches and thoughtful players: "I have learned a lot of football from a lot of people. Some of them I learned from, I was the boss."[1982]) But where Giants players and New York sportswriters viewed Parcells' tough-guy routine as endearing, Belichick's acting lacked Parcells' sly, playful "wink, wink, nudge, nudge" style that implicitly said, "I'm not *really* a jerk but just giving you tough love for your own good and entertainment":

> "I watched what Bill [Parcells] did with the New York media when I was there, and maybe I tried to do some of those things. And he was in a position where, honestly, he could get away with some things that other people can't get away with. And I don't think I really realized that."[1983]

The logic underlying Belichick's aversion to share information with the media was impeccable. As sports radio personality Steve DeOssie, who played for both "Big Bill" (Parcells) and "Little Bill" (Belichick), explains: "They realize that the media is the enemy. Let's face it, the media cannot do anything positive for a team, but they can put stuff out there that could lose a game. The bottom line with both guys is whether it helps his team win."[1984] Belichick's PR problem, in his first years as head coach, was style, not substance. Belichick hadn't yet figured out how to be engaging and charming and talk a lot without saying anything of substantive importance. Belichick's humorless drill sergeant act alienated most everyone in the city by appearing contemptuous, arrogant, profane, and tyrannical. *Cleveland Plain Dealer* sportswriter Bill Livingston gave an example:

> "I'm driving around one day. listening to Belichick's radio show. They take a call, and this guy says, 'First of all, Bill, I want to wish you and your family a Merry Christmas.' And there was, like, 20 seconds of dead air. I remember looking at the radio and screaming, 'Well, wish him a Merry Christmas back, you little schmuck.'"[1985]

But Belichick improved his people skills as he matured in Cleveland. Says Baab: "I heard from [my former Browns teammates] three or four years later that he let the guys out of camp early [and] threw them a beer party. I said, 'Belichick?'"[1986] Another former Brown, Brian Kinchen, was stunned by the new Bill Belichick he met in late 2003 when he joined the Patriots after they lost two long snappers to injuries: "I told Bill when I saw him that I noticed a vast difference in him as far as his presence. He was always just so tense."[1987] The new and improved Bill Belichick is no accident: "It took me time to learn that some of the things I could have handled better. I could have granted more access for the media and more freedom for the players. I'm not as tough as I used to be. You could say I've mellowed."[1988]

Some of Belichick's problems in Cleveland stemmed from uncoachable players, another problem Belichick and Pioli have eliminated in New England:

> "Another former Browns player who despised Belichick has also come around. Defensive tackle Michael Dean Perry used to feud with Belichick over a two-gap role Perry hated. Perry was talking with ex-Browns defensive end Anthony Pleasant, now playing for the Patriots, when Perry said, 'Put Bill on the phone.' Perry conceded that he had been immature and the two made up."[1989]

The right stuff

Other than needing to traverse the steep learning curve that confronts all new NFL head coaches and needing to stop acting like Bill Parcells and start being himself, Belichick was primed to be a winning NFL head coach back in the early 1990s. The same Bill Belichick vision and stick-to-it-iveness that Adams described back in 1994 proved the blueprint for two Patriots Super Bowls a decade later. The following chart of Belichick's Browns' cumulative winning margin (points scored less points surrendered) shows clearly that the Browns were an average NFL team from 1991 through 1993 but played great throughout 1994 and early 1995 before floundering, presumably due to relocation-related distractions:

In 1991, Bill Belichick was new to head coaching and required a few years to implement his winning system, but he probably had most of the formula figured out before that unfortunate 1995 season, as the 1994 season suggests. And 1995 might have turned out very differently if not for Art Modell. Belichick basically had no starting-caliber quarterback that season but had, in May 1995, convinced brainy former Giants quarterback (and Super Bowl winner) Phil Simms to un-retire… until owner Art Modell flummoxed things up by surprising Simms (who had not yet agreed to sign) with a press conference during what Simms understood was only a fact-finding visit: "When I got on the plane to go out there, I thought it was almost 100 percent that I'd sign with Cleveland."[1990] Afterwards, Simms told his agent, "I feel like I just got my pants pulled down."[1991]

Despite it all, Belichick made something out of nothing in Cleveland and deserves some credit for the Baltimore Ravens' 2000 Super Bowl victory for setting the Browns (who became the Ravens in 1996) on course for the Super Bowl. Not only did Belichick turn the 3-13 Browns into a playoff winner, but he also cultivated management talent that helped the Ravens succeed after his departure. For example, Belichick gave former Browns player Ozzie Newsome his start in the executive suite: "When I retired as a player, [Belichick] didn't just stick me in a corner and say, 'You're an ex-player.' He trusted me and exposed me to every aspect of the business."[1992] Newsome blossomed after the Browns/Ravens moved to Baltimore, helping draft the talented players who won the 2000 Super Bowl, including linebacker Ray Lewis and offensive lineman Jonathan Ogden two months after Belichick's firing. Belichick would likely have worked coaching magic with such talented players. As Ted Marchibroda said days before he replaced Belichick as head coach, "You're getting a football team now that is a veteran football team. You're not getting an expansion team or a team that you'd have to build."[1993]

WAITING FOR A SECOND CHANCE

Belichick's consistent post-Cleveland success has proven that the Browns' 1994 season was no fluke. After Belichick took over as the Patriots' defensive coordinator and assistant head coach in 1996, the team immediately made the playoffs with an 11-5 record and went all the way to the Super Bowl. When head coach Bill Parcells fled New England for the Jets, Belichick followed. Belichick helped instantly transform a Jets team that had surrendered 454 points while going 1-15 in 1996 into a 9-7 team with just 287 points allowed in 1997. In 1998, the Jets went 12-4 with only 266 points allowed and did not lose in the playoffs until the AFC Championship Game even though:

> "He lost his top linebacker, Marvin Jones, before the season, and the Jets traded away their best pass rusher, Hugh Douglas, who now has 12.5 sacks in Philadelphia. Belichick has questionable personnel at cornerback, safety and defensive tackle."[1994]

In 1999, the Jets finished a disappointing 8-8 but played in an extremely competitive AFC East that finished, collectively, an astonishing eighteen games above .500.

PATRIOTS HIRE BELICHICK

Belichick's outstanding performance with the Browns in 1994 and early 1995, the Patriots in 1996, and the Jets from 1997 through 1999 proved that he was absolutely primed for success. Parcells knew this, which is why Parcells' Jets paid Belichick $1 million to serve as defensive coordinator in 1999... more money than any other coordinator in the NFL.[1995] Multiple Super Bowl-winner Jimmy Johnson, then coach of the Dolphins and a close friend and admirer of Belichick, knew this and would have loved to hire Belichick as his defensive coordinator. Bob Kraft also knew this, precipitating his fight with the Jets for Belichick. The deep skepticism of many in the media when Belichick took over reflects poorly on their understanding of Belichick's many successes, his abandonment of behaviors that caused his early troubles in Cleveland, and the irrelevance of the Browns' disastrous 1995 season.

Throughout January 2000, the New York Jets and New England Patriots played tug-of-war over Bill Belichick's rights. As the two battled for Belichick, *Boston Globe* reporter Michael Holley (who in October 2004 published the superb behind-the-scenes book *Patriot Reign*, which once had as its working subtitle "The Genius of Bill Belichick") was savaging Belichick, saying his hiring would leave the Patriots "looking like the ruins of Rome":

> "the Patriots are in trouble. ...Robert Kraft and his team... have actually flirted with becoming worse without [recently fired head coach Pete] Carroll. I say flirted because Kraft might have completed the disaster if Bill Parcells hadn't done him a huge favor by [making] Belichick... the No. 1 football man for the New York Jets, an organization he will destroy if Parcells doesn't hold his hand—especially when it's time to draft players. Kraft... had intentions of giving Belichick coaching and personnel power; it would have left his organization looking like the ruins of Rome... The fact that [Kraft] was even thinking about it shows that he has already gotten off to a bad start with his job search for a new coach/general manager. The first thing Kraft should do this morning is find the list with Belichick's name atop it and torch it. I'd hate to see the second name on the list. ... Kraft was going to give the keys to [Belichick] rather than stick with Grier/Carroll? That's like

telling your 16-year-old daughter that she is not responsible enough to drive the family car, but that your 12-year-old son is."[1996]

In Holley's mind, Belichick would never amount to more than "Little Bill," understudy to "Big Bill," Belichick's former boss, the great Bill Parcells.

Holley's position was not only quite understandable but probably even the majority opinion on Belichick in media circles. Many sports journalists were slamming Belichick. One reporter asked, rhetorically, "what do you expect from an owner who doesn't have a clue" and criticized Kraft for hiring a defensive-minded coach (when, the reporter claimed, the Patriots' problems in 1999 were on offense) and for naïveté: "Kraft gave up his No. 1 draft pick to the Jets to land Belichick after he said he wouldn't. But he got a friendly call from Parcells who wanted to kiss and make up, and Kraft, like Mickey The Dunce, fell for it—once again."[1997]

A few reporters supported Belichick. The late Bill Parrillo wrote, "I think he's worth… a first- and second-round selection."[1998] But even some reporters who initially supported Belichick's hiring jumped off the bandwagon as losses mounted. Bill Burt, for example, initially said "Other than Parcells, there isn't a sure thing [but] Belichick is the next best thing"[1999] and predicted a successful 2000 season. By mid-November, Burt was close to calling for Belichick's head: "It's time for Belichick to quiet his own critics. And that means winning, now and often. Belichick has something to prove. Some people think Belichick… doesn't have the persona to become a successful head coach."[2000]

In contrast to much of the media in 2000, Patriots players who knew Belichick during his one-year term as defensive coordinator and assistant head coach in the Patriots' 1996 Super Bowl season were very excited about the possibility of Belichick coming to New England. Veterans knew how successfully Belichick had transformed their lousy defense in just one season into a great one (which forced four turnovers in the AFC Championship Game, including a 47-yard Otis Smith touchdown return) and then built a horrid Jets defense into a stout one. So many openly lobbied owner Bob Kraft to hire Belichick. For example, Patriots cornerback Ty Law told the media, "Now that coach Carroll is gone, I can say it. I'm putting my bid in for Belichick. The season's over, so I'm allowed to talk about Belichick now. I'm going to call him, tell him to come over."[2001] Quarterback Drew Bledsoe also urged Kraft to hire Belichick. After Belichick's signing, Bledsoe said, "to get a coach of the caliber of Bill Belichick, [surrendering a #1 draft pick is] probably a worthwhile thing to do."[2002] Patriot players were smart enough to ask for Bill Belichick. They wanted tough love. As Patriots safety Lawyer Milloy admitted, following Belichick's signing, "We just needed a kick in the pants—all of us."[2003] Departing wide receiver Shawn Jefferson was perhaps most effusive in his praise:

"[With Belichick] the Patriots win the division. Mark it down right now. If Mr. Kraft hires that man, it's all over for everybody else. The guys on this team will go all out for him. He's the smartest defensive coach in the league and the offensive guys respect him. There'd be no bull around here if Bill was the coach."[2004]

Jefferson, who signed a free agent contract with the Atlanta Falcons soon after Belichick became Patriots head coach, expressed disappointment he was leaving because "Belichick will definitely get this team back to the Super Bowl eventually. I just know it."[2005]

Patriots players expressed to Robert and Jonathan Kraft, in both 1996 (when Belichick served as Patriots assistant head coach and defensive coordinator) and 2000, their admiration for Belichick and their belief that he helped them win. Would Bob Kraft have hired Belichick if players had not begged him to? I suspect yes. Kraft says "It got my attention"[2006] when Belichick's Cleveland Browns won their 1994 playoff game over a Patriots team coached by Belichick's former boss, Bill Parcells. And Kraft and Belichick grew to respect and like each other during long talks in 1996 when Belichick coordinated the Patriots defense for head coach Bill Parcells. Belichick, who majored in economics at Wesleyan, admired Krafts' smarts and guts in founding a successful corporation (International Forest Products), acquiring another (Rand-Whitney), and slyly maneuvering to purchase the Patriots by grabbing the land first and then leasing the stadium in a deal that later made it impossible for the team's owner to move the Patriots to St. Louis (because the team was locked into its stadium lease). Belichick also thought Kraft, a Patriots season ticket holder since 1971, had impressive football knowledge and intuition for a non-professional. Likewise, Kraft was impressed in 1996 that Belichick was not only a brilliant football tactician but also had innovative ideas about managing rosters in the NFL's post-1994 salary cap and free agency era: "He knew the players. He would say, 'We should sign this guy,' players who are maybe in that mid range. It was clear to me that he had a system, an outlook that was different."[2007] Jonathan Kraft also believed by 1996 that Belichick's ideas for building an NFL team in the salary cap era were "on another plane, another dimension."[2008]

The real question is why, after Patriots coach Bill Parcells fled the January 1997 Super Bowl to join the Jets without even saying "good bye" to his Patriots players (despite preaching "team, team, team"), Kraft didn't promote Belichick from defensive coordinator to head coach. Before the Super Bowl, *New York Times* reporter Gerald Eskenazi raised that possibility.[2009] Kraft instead hired Pete Carroll. It was a mistake, but not one he would repeat three years later. The players' strong desire for Belichick in 2000 made easier for Bob Kraft what was, among fans and reporters, an unpopular decision:

> "When I brought him in a lot of people criticized me, saying he hadn't done a good job in Cleveland when he was head coach there, but I had gotten to know him in 1996 when he was assistant head coach here and I liked him a lot. I started to see his magic then. So when we went 5-11 in 2000 then had a 1-3 record a month into [the 2001 season], they were calling for my head

and his head. But I told him I believed in him, that I supported him … and then it started to come together. …[H]e's the same great coach I met six years ago… That's why I had no doubt about trading a No. 1 draft choice to the Jets to get him as our coach in early 2000. He has matured as a person, and that's what I was counting on."[2010]

THE PRIVATE BILL BELICHICK

Contrary to media reports, Belichick has a life. He remains married to his high school sweetheart, the former Debbie Clark, with whom he has raised three children (Amanda, Stephen, and Brian). After falling in love with Nantucket in junior high school, Belichick now owns (and helped design and build) several homes on the island, where he vacations and goes sailing every summer. Rock star Bon Jovi and basketball star Charles Barkley are close personal friends. Bon Jovi, who watched a ZZ Top concert with Bill in 1990, claims Bill is a "closet drummer,"[2011] but Bill seems to have used the drum set Bon Jovi bought him primarily for anger management while coaching some poor Cleveland Browns teams: "It was a good way to take out your frustrations. Just bang away; it didn't hit back."[2012] In early 2002, Barkley thought highly enough of Belichick to bet $600,000 ($550,000 with the point spread and another $50,000 straight up) on the Patriots to beat the Rams in Super Bowl XXXVI, bets Barkley won to the tune of $787,000.[2013]

Belichick enjoys talking defense with NBA coach Mike Fratello. He has long loved rock music, and he and Scott Pioli have attended concerts by Bon Jovi, Bruce Springsteen, the Eagles, and Pink Floyd.[2014] Phil Simms wrote, "I once told Bill I had a video of him dancing at one of those [Bon Jovi] concerts. He had this frightened look in his eyes, so there must be some tape of him out there."[2015] When Belichick first met Snoop Dogg, a friend of Patriots linebacker Willie McGinest, he needed no introduction to the rapper: "Gin and juice, right?"[2016] After meeting Snoop Dogg, Belichick displayed his characteristic self-deprecating sense of humor: "Snoop's got me beat on fashion. I can't keep up with him."[2017] (*The Washington Post* said of Belichick's attire: "The guy shows up on national television wearing wrinkled khakis and a lumpy hooded sweatshirt, looking like a recent divorcé who has never learned to do his own laundry. …[He] stalk[s] the sidelines looking like a complete slob. Throw the flag for a lack of dignity."[2018])

Though Belichick happens to have famous friends, he's not star-struck. Despite loving rock music and knowing the lyrics of every Beatles song by heart, he turned down an opportunity to golf with Ringo Starr.[2019] Belichick even collects football cards… and buys them on eBay!

> "[In 1999] I was cleaning out my bedroom closet, found a stack of 1958 Topps football cards–including a Ted Marchibroda, Chicago Cardinals card– and put them on eBay. A week later, when the winning bidder contacted me and asked where to send his $28 check, it was Belichick, then an assistant

with the New York Jets. We exchanged several e-mails, including one in which he wrote that he wanted to 'corner the market' on the cards of former coaches. By the way, all this happened smack in the middle of NFL training camp, a period in which Belichick is supposed to be some monomaniacal defensive-minded huddle-monger."[2020]

Belichick has deep admiration for former coaching greats and has collected at least 300 books on football,[2021] including "instructional football books from the 1930s"[2022] and books by "immortals" such as Amos Alonzo Stagg (an innovator and perfectionist who coached college football till age 98, four years before his death in 1965) and Dave Meggyesy (a politically-active NFL player from 1963-69).[2023] Another report claims Belichick owns over 500 football books.[2024] Belichick says of his collection: "Most of those books are technical football books. They are about the single wing. They are about the double-team block. They are the 5-4 defense and option football and that kind of thing. Really, that is what the books are about. That stuff interests me."[2025] One of Belichick's highlights from his first Super Bowl victory was receiving congratulations from legendary defensive coaching genius Buddy Ryan (whose son was the Patriots' outside linebackers coach until the Raiders stole him away after the 2003 season to be their defensive coordinator): "Belichick never smiled so big."[2026]

Belichick once answered a letter from a Giants fan by visiting him and fifty other violent prisoners for two hours at Sing Sing prison. He observed an arthroscopic surgery operation. He worked at a homeless shelter. He rode around Newark, NJ with Drug Enforcement Agency officers till 4:00 a.m. to understand drug dealers and see how police buy-and-bust drug dealers. That night, "He saw young, unattended children playing in the halls at 3 a.m. He saw people passed out on the stairs. He passed through areas that smelled of urine and had piles of feces on the floor."[2027] When friend Joe Bellino asked him to help feed the homeless, "He dug right in."[2028] Such experiences help Belichick better relate to players, especially players raised in tough environments or going through medical procedures, and they also make Belichick a better human being. That he seeks out such experiences demonstrates his depth of character and curiosity. And these experiences have clearly affected his perspective on life. After listening to a group of Amer-I-Can participants describe their fears and problems, Belichick became better able to confront his own challenges:

> "I was thinking, 'What are my problems?' I'd like to do a little better on third down. My kid got a C in spelling. These guys weren't sure they would be alive in the next hour. The fact that they were able to talk about it and deal with it reasonably was remarkable. I'm ready to accept any challenge."[2029]

NFL legend Jim Brown (who created and runs Ameri-I-Can and many consider "the greatest [running back] ever"[2030]) says he bonded with Belichick instantly:

"He's been an unbelievable force. After five minutes with Bill, we became friends. We have the same desire to win, the same work ethic. We think the same. He is a special person and a lot of people don't understand how special he is."[2031]

Belichick no doubt admires Brown's group because, as Brown explains, it preaches self-reliance and self-discipline, traits Belichick values deeply:

"There are many programs out there that treat the symptoms. We believe that change begins when you affect the way a person thinks. If we can help the thinking change so that these young men take responsibility for their actions, then we can help change things. There's a lot of 'I' in this. We make our students speak in the first person and take responsibility for their actions. Then a person can be helped. Self-esteem is a key to training. A lot of our students react negatively because of their low self-esteem. With our program, they can learn the fundamentals of life-management skills."[2032]

Belichick's close friendship with Bon Jovi reflects their shared passion for rock music, football, and fundamentals-driven achievement: "He's a football fan and I'm a Bon Jovi fan–perfect match."[2033] Bon Jovi dedicated his 2002 song "Bounce" to Belichick, something Belichick considers "really awesome,"[2034] and brings Belichick pre-release copies of his new songs.

Bon Jovi is not just a rock star who has sold 100 million albums. Like Belichick, he's also a great listener, a very grounded and authentic guy, a shrewd financial manager, and a devoted husband. He's also a successful Arena League football owner who impressed the heck out of entrepreneur magazine *Inc.*:

"the Philadelphia Soul is leading the AFL in ticket sales, advertising sales, and merchandising revenue. Bon Jovi also had a personal hand in selling advertising to national sponsors such as Samsung. And he works the local media, too, bringing players to local radio stations, guaranteeing airtime. Much of the team's commitment to the community and charity work springs directly from his vision. ...When I finished the interview, I was convinced that he is a genuine *Inc.*-style entrepreneur."[2035]

After Bon Jovi heard his players complaining about mismatched duffle bags and eating by themselves, he lined up a bus, team meals, *etc.*: "[T]he team was so grateful because now when they walk into an airport they're all in jacket and tie, carrying those bags, having a lot of pride."[2036]

Bon Jovi's vision for the Philadelphia Soul sounds deeply Belichickian, partly because Bon Jovi follows Belichick's advice ("It's like going to Muhammad"[2037]), and partly because Bon Jovi is a blend of Belichick and Bob Kraft:

"my vision of this was hard work, dedication, and commitment to each other makes for a successful organization. I told our coach, Mike Trigg, when I hired him that we had a 'no thug' rule. I want our guys going out into the community. Once, we found a guy was selling his T-shirt on eBay. He complained about his living quarters, said, 'I don't room with nobody.' So we said, you're right, you're not rooming with anybody. Get out."[2038]

Belichick cares deeply for his family, just as his parents cared deeply for him. Belichick has always had a powerful personal bond with his father, Steve, who took 4-year-old Bill golfing, introduced young Bill to Navy players, and turned down multiple NFL assistant coaching positions to spend more time with his family. So it's natural that Bill Belichick values not only his New England Patriots family but also his real family. Explains Steve: "[Bill]'s a great person and a great family man. That's what I'm most proud of. He cares deeply about his family. Sure, he's had a lot of success as a coach, but that's not everything."[2039] Steve cites as an example "When we [his parents] come up to visit him, we may have not seen him in a long time, but the first thing he does when he walks in is spend time with his children, helping them with homework and things."[2040] Steve cares more about Bill's character than his professional success: "if he was the coach in the Super Bowl and he was an ass, he'd still be an ass. He's not. I'm proud of Bill because he's a good, thoughtful person and a wonderful son. He has no ego. He never did."[2041] Steve Belichick would be disappointed if his son weren't humble because "you're talking about somebody who walks up and down a football field."[2042] The strong bond between Steve and Bill Belichick was on rare public display when they hugged following the Patriots' gutsy, gritty, come-from-behind victory over the Miami Dolphins in the final game of the 2002 season, which pulled the Patriots into a tie for first place and gave them a momentary shot at a playoff berth (that never materialized after the Jets won their game and the Patriots lost the third tie-breaker). Said Steve, "I ALMOST had tears in my eyes when we hugged. He didn't want to let go. I didn't want to let go. But we had to. People would talk."[2043]

The number of people who have known Bill Belichick for decades and speak spontaneously of his "loyalty" and of the deepness of their friendship speaks volumes for Belichick the person and for his focus on friendship, not just coaching a football team. Many Belichick friends spontaneously offer comments similar to the following from Belichick's lacrosse and football teammate, David Campbell: "He was a very loyal friend to a lot of people."[2044] Belichick's loyalty is also on display through his frequent speaking engagements at and fund-raising activities for his alma maters, Phillips Andover and Wesleyan.

Belichick's friends gladly reciprocate his loyalty. Scott Pioli, for example, followed Belichick to the Giants, the Browns, the Jets, and the Patriots, where he has ensconced himself despite potential promotion opportunities (to become general manager) from teams like the Miami Dolphins. Scott jokes that following Belichick to the Jets required the greatest personal sacrifice:

"My whole home town [Washingtonville, NY], you're either a Giants fan or a Jets fan. If you're one, you're obviously not the other. It was a tough day in my family, actually, in 1997 when I took a job with the Jets. ...I remember telling [my dad], 'Dad, I'm going to the Jets.' There was a long pause and in his typical Bronx way, he said, 'How could you do this to the family?' I'm like, 'Dad, I have to pay bills.'"[2045]

Sense of humor

"People don't realize how funny Belichick is, but he's also a great teacher and a great coach."[2046]
    – Patriots fullback Fred McCrary

Finally, the private Bill Belichick is not the humorless Mr. Spock the media has long painted him as. Those who know only the public Belichick suggest he needs a personality transplant. Belichick's public persona is indeed boring, but Peter King correctly says "Bill Belichick *chooses* to be Joe Schmo."[2047] Long-time Belichick friend and former Patriots assistant coach Steve Szabo says "Bill has a human side to him... He's not an outward-going guy the media likes to talk to because ...He doesn't choose to exert his energy in that direction. He chooses to exert his energy in managing a football team."[2048] Another friend, basketball star Charles Barkley, who calls Belichick every few weeks, says, "Everybody thinks he's stiff and boring. But the guy I've come to know has a great sense of humor and can really relate to all sorts of different individuals."[2049] Here's a sampling of Belichick's self-deprecating sense of humor and deadpan delivery:

- Against Buffalo, 305-pound Patriots defensive lineman Richard Seymour scooped up a fumble and lumbered 68 yards for a touchdown. Seymour looked like a guy who had never run 68 yards in his life and confessed to "a lot of sucking air."[2050] Afterwards, Belichick joked: "Once Richard is in the open field, he's 'Swivel Hips Seymour.'"[2051]

- Asked to sign a football before a talk at his alma mater, Phillips Andover Academy, Belichick joked, "I hope we don't see this on eBay on Monday."[2052]

- Asked whether he had set any rules for his players the week before Super Bowl XXXVIII, Belichick replied, "Try not to get arrested."[2053]

- Describing the team's victory parade in 2004: "I was riding on the cart with [Tom Brady] in the parade the other day and the fans were cheering... I know they weren't cheering for me, but it was fun to be there and take some of his throwaway."[2054]

- After pointing to fatigue as the reason why Super Bowl XXXVIII opened with two shutdown defenses but finished with almost non-existent defenses, Belichick added, "As dumb as I am, I could figure that out after the game."[2055]

- What kind of reception did Belichick anticipate when the Patriots arrived in Charlotte, NC to play a preseason game against the Carolina Panthers, the team they edged in the Super Bowl? "Probably a parade when we land. A lot of cheering when they introduce us. Maybe some fireworks. They're going to be happy to see us."[2056]

- Following the team's 31-3 trouncing by the Bengals in the 2004 preseason, Belichick asked reporters, "You want to list the highlights from last week?" After a momentary pause, he answered himself: "Well, that didn't take long."

- On 36-year-old linebacker Roman Phifer, who played on both Super Bowl teams and has played 200 NFL games: "When we signed him, I talked to Roman about how I envisoned him as more of a role player. It turned out his role is to play every down."[2057]

- Asked why he insists that songs played to simulate crowd noise during practice sessions include a few Springsteen and Bon Jovi selections, Belichick claimed: "It's one of the few things I have control over."[2058]

- Asked before the famous "Snow Bowl" playoff game in Foxboro whether Patriots kicker Adam Vinatieri held an advantage over Oakland Raiders kicker Sebastian Janikowski because Vinatieri grew up in snowy South Dakota, knew how the wind swirls in Foxboro, and had played many more NFL games in the cold and snow than the Oakland kicker, Belichick said, "I'd have to give the edge to the guy who kicked in Poland."[2059]

- Angered by another frustrating defeat while Cleveland Browns head coach, Belichick was sardonic in his statements to the media: "We don't have any defenses designed to give up 26-yard receptions."[2060]

- He says Super Bowl winners should be prepared to "wonder how you could have forgotten the names of so many others who claim to be old friends."[2061]

- Asked how his wife Debbie felt about him riding around one night with Drug Enforcement agents in Newark, NJ to see the drug culture, Belichick admitted "She wasn't too fired up about it."[2062]

- In his first press conference as Patriots head coach, roughly three weeks following his bizarre first and final press conference as Jets head coach (during which he resigned), Belichick joked, "Hopefully, this press conference will go a little bit better than the last one I had. Hopefully, my tenure here will be a little bit longer."[2063]

- Asked whether NFL coaching is "as all time-consuming as it appears to be," Belichick explained (I hope in jest) that "I have some free time between two and four in the morning."[2064]

- On the team's trip to Houston for Super Bowl XXXVIII: "It's a business trip; we have a lot of work to do... We're not here to go sightseeing."[2065]

- On rookie tight end Benjamin Watson's 2004 holdout: "It's certainly not helping him any. And it's not helping us any. So I don't know who it's helping."[2066]

- With his team preparing for what would be an NFL-record 19th consecutive victory, Belichick made light of the larger-than-normal media presence and baseball's prominence in the hearts of Bostonians: "Full house here. Red Sox are on the road."[2067]

- When the Patriots returned to the White House two years following their first Super Bowl victory, President Bush teased Belichick for his brevity two years earlier: "You said you were going to say a few words and you said like four words." Without missing a beat, Belichick replied, "I got carried away."[2068]

- Asked by Dave Letterman whether the Patriots were aware of the halftime scandal involving Janet Jackson's bare boob, Belichick remarked, with a twinkle in his eye, "We were in the locker room so we missed that. Nobody kept us *abreast* of that."

- On how training camp has changed over the years: "We never had the beer vendors."[2069]

- On the ubiquitous trucks and non-stop construction of four stages Elton John, Lenny Kravitz, and others will perform from before the 2004 season opener: "The circus is in town."[2070] Also: "If the players want to watch Mary Blige sing then I'll get 'em a good seat in the stands and they can watch it to their hearts' content. What we need are people to go out there and... perform better than the Colts."[2071]

- Asked about injuries to Tennessee Titans stars Eddie George and Steve "Air" McNair, Belichick said they were irrelevant: "You can take that injury report and put whatever you want on it, probable, doubtful, questionable, maybe, definitely in, definitely out. They're going to be there."[2072]

- After instructing longsnapper Lonie Paxton to intentionally snap the ball over the punter's head to surrender a safety (in a clever maneuver that enabled the Patriots to come from behind to defeat the Denver Broncos), Belichick (a longsnapper in high school and college) quipped, "I used to do that when I snapped on regular punts."[2073]

- Asked whether he was worried Troy Brown's injury might cause him to miss substantial time, Belichick answered, "No. Not at this point. Are you?"[2074]

- Growing frustrated with repeated questions about his relationship with former colleague Bill Parcells before a game between their teams, Belichick said, "people are making this like it's 'VH-1 Behind the Music' or something."[2075]

- Informed in 2000 that former Jets receiver Keyshawn Johnson would be cheering for Belichick's Patriots to beat his former team, Belichick said, "If that translates into any points on the board, I'll take it. I doubt that it does."[2076]

- After startling everyone who knows him by celebrating on the sidelines following a string of narrow victories in 2003, Belichick said, "Even as unemotional as I am, I react to those."[2077]

- When a reporter good-naturedly gave Belichick a hard time for making it harder for reporters to intercept players heading to or from the parking lot (by installing an opaque window and, initially, also posting a guard), Belichick said, "I'll get you a ball and chain if you want."[2078]

- After the Patriots acquired mammoth and talented nose tackle Ted Washington, who would help the Patriots earn their second Super Bowl championship, from the Chicago Bears for just a 4th round draft pick, Patriots players were jumping for joy. Star offensive lineman Damien Woody, for example, said "He's an immovable object. It's like hitting a brick wall. ...Try running into that steel beam for a couple of hours. That's about the equivalent of it."[2079] Belichick refrained from admitting his excitement, instead saying, with obvious ironic understatement, just "We're comfortable with the deal."[2080]

- When *60 Minutes* suggested "more people know your name than know your quarterback's name," a grinning Belichick said, "There's no way."[2081]

- Asked by reporters worried by the absence of the Patriots' top three punt returners (Troy Brown, Kevin Faulk, and Terrell Buckley) who would return punts in the 2004 season opener against the Indianapolis Colts, Belichick sounded unsure his defense could even slow down the Colts: "If we can make them punt, we'll put somebody back there. They went through the first two playoff games [and] nobody made them punt. We didn't make 'em punt too many times, either. So hopefully, we can just make 'em punt."[2082] This joke, however, was on Belichick. As he feared, the Patriots forced the Colts to punt only twice. But, almost disastrously, the Patriots' returner (Deion Branch) failed to catch the ball and the Colts recovered it, a mistake that nearly gifted the game to the Colts.

ACKNOWLEDGMENTS

Without the encouragement of David Welch,[2] I might never have begun this book. I knew I had this book inside me, and I knew others would be interested. But David's timely encouragement spurred me to go for it. David was a wonderful teacher while I was at Harvard, and he has continued helping me ever since, for reasons I cannot fathom.

I wish to thank everyone who read portions of my manuscript, offered support and encouragement, and provided constructive criticism. Special thanks to Brodie Hefner, Keith Hefner, Mark Kupper, Alison Lavin, Eric Lavin, Robert Lavin, John Mann, Brenda Rosenbaum, Paul Rosenbaum, Jonathan Sari, and Annie Segan.

Thanks, of course, to the entire New England Patriots organization, top to bottom, for inspiring millions with your incredible guts and for serving as such a brilliant case study in how to run an organization! You are professional, classy people. We New Englanders are lucky and proud to cheer for you. I hope my admiration for your dedication and character shines through in this book. Your story is truly inspiring.

I wish to thank the outstanding teachers I was blessed to learn from in the Wayland Public Schools from 1976 through 1987. Even the Patriots could learn from your dedication, sacrifice, selflessness, intelligence, and passion. Your kindness and concern taught me to analyze and write. I could name fifty teachers, but the following had an especially profound impact on me: Virginia Buckley, Steve Feinberg, Shirley Lowe (and "Rana"!), Helene Mensh Lerner, Joe Porrell, Frank Smith, and every teacher who ever volunteered an afternoon to help Wayland High School's Academic Decathlon team become state champions.

Finally, I never could have finished this book without my incredible wife, Yingmei. She believed in me and my crazy project. She has tolerated my Patriots addiction since we met ten years ago. And she waited patiently for many, many months, trusting that I would finish this book, even as it grew to well over 600 8.5" x 11" pages (including Vol 2). Working full-time on this project has been a joy. Focusing completely on this project would have been an impossible luxury without my wife's indulgence and support.

---

[2] The University of Toronto political science professor, not the U.S. Ambassador to Egypt or the molecular biologist. There sure are many "David Welch"es!

ENDNOTES

[1] Hall of Fame head coach Bill Walsh (formerly of the San Francisco 49ers), quoted in: Tom Pedulla, "Patriots: How Perfect Are They?" *USA Today*, 7 October 2004, www.usatoday.com/sports/football/nfl/patriots/2004-10-06-perfect_x.htm.

[2] Len Pasquarelli, "Franchise takes it 'one game at a time,'" *ESPN*, 6 October 2004, http://sports.espn.go.com/nfl/columns/story?columnist=pasquarelli_len&page=/trend/2004week4.

[3] Hall of Fame head coach Don Shula (formerly of the Miami Dolphins), quoted in: Michael Felger, "Shula backs Belichick: Downplaying streak is perfect approach," *Boston Herald*, 22 September 2004, http://patriots.bostonherald.com/patriots/view.bg?articleid=45372.

[4] Paul Zimmerman, "Mix Master," *Sports Illustrated*, 6 October 2004, http://sportsillustrated.cnn.com/2004/writers/dr_z/10/06/drz.patriots/.

[5] New York Giants general manager Ernie Accorsi, quoted in: Ira Miller, "On verge of a record, Patriots play it down," *San Francisco Chronicle*, 3 October 2004, http://sfgate.com/cgi-bin/article.cgi?f=/chronicle/archive/2004/10/03/SPGAE92ROS1.DTL.

[6] St. Louis Rams head coach Mike Martz, quoted in: Roger Mills, "New England simply the model franchise," *St. Petersburg Times*, 15 October 2004, www.sptimes.com/2004/10/15/Sports/New_England_simply_th.shtml and in: Jeff Gordon, "No hard feelings: Martz raves about Belichick, and vice versa," *St. Louis Post-Dispatch*, 4 November 2004, www.stltoday.com/stltoday/emaf.nsf/Popup?ReadForm&db=stltoday%5Csports%5Ccolumnists.nsf&docid=98079A77DFCE09B586256F420062D68C.

[7] Official statement of NFL Commissioner Paul Tagliabue, on the Patriots' NFL-record 19-game winning streak, quoted in: NFL.com wire reports, "Pats top Miami for record 19th straight win," 10 October 2004, www.nfl.com/gamecenter/recap/NFL_20041010_MIA@NE.

[8] Jay Mariotti, "Patriots build modern sports dynasty," *Chicago Sun-Times*, 11 October 2004, www.suntimes.com/output/mariotti/cst-spt-jay111.html.

[9] Philadelphia Eagles owner Jeff Lurie, on the 2001 Patriots' Super Bowl victory, quoted in: Will McDonough, "A few musings on a miracle in the Big Easy," *Patriots United*, Canada: Team Power Publishing, 2002, p. 12.

[10] New York Jets receiver Wayne Chrebet, quoted in: Vic Carucci, "Patriots have knockout punch for Jets," *NFL.com*, 24 October 2004, www.nfl.com/news/story/7825494.

[11] Kansas City Chiefs general manager Carl Peterson, quoted in: Randy Covitz, "Patriots' formula for success makes it envy of NFL," *Kansas City Star*, 8 September 2004, www.kansascity.com/mld/kansascity/sports/football/nfl/kansas_city_chiefs/9603764.htm?1c.

[12] NFL Commissioner Paul Tagliabue, quoted in: Tom E. Curran, "Pats owner has created a masterpiece," *Providence Journal*, 13 June 2004, www.projo.com/patriots/content/projo_20040613_13kraft.1b891c.html.

[13] Dallas Cowboys owner Jerry Jones, quoted in: Tom E. Curran, "Pats owner has created a masterpiece," *Providence Journal*, 13 June 2004, www.projo.com/patriots/content/projo_20040613_13kraft.1b891c.html.

[14] Bill Polian, president of the Indianapolis Colts and 5-time NFL Executive of the Year, quoted in: Ira Miller, "New England quite simply knows how to win," *San Francisco Chronicle*, 15 October 2004, http://sfgate.com/cgi-bin/article.cgi?f=/chronicle/archive/2004/10/15/SPG0R99R9K1.DTL.

[15] Dave Bolling, "Lack of Maturity Dooms Seahawks," *Tacoma News Tribune*, 18 October 2004, www.wtev.com/sports/commentary/story.aspx?content_id=83661BB5-0FAB-4E17-8A5F-FE8B36B96ECA.

[16] Vic Carucci, "Pats choose to leave nothing to chance," *NFL.com*, 17 October 2004, www.nfl.com/news/story/7802996.

[17] Bill Parcells, on the 2001 Patriots' Super Bowl victory, quoted in: Will McDonough, "A few musings on a miracle in the Big Easy," *Patriots United*, Canada: Team Power Publishing, 2002, p. 12.

[18] Ron Jaworski, ESPN analyst and former NFL quarterback, "A Coaching Job for the Ages," in: *Patriots United*, Canada: Team Power Publishing, 2002, p. 186.

[19] Doug Farrar, "MMQB - The House of Blue Leaves, Vol. 1," *Seahawks.net*, 18 October 2004, http://story.theinsiders.com/a.z?s=65&p=2&c=307556.

[20] Bob Dicesare, "Few kings have ruled like the Pats," *The Buffalo News*, 19 October 2004, www.buffalonews.com/editorial/20041019/1016331.asp.

[21] New York Jets head coach Herman Edwards, quoted in: Michael Smith, "Jets trying to follow Pats' mold," *ESPN.com*, 21 October 2004, http://sports.espn.go.com/nfl/columns/story?id=1906485.

[22] Pete Prisco, "This victory what Patriots 'team' is all about," *SportsLine.com*, 7 November 2004, www.sportsline.com/nfl/story/7865974.

[23] Kimberly Jones, "NFL Tuesday Morning QB," *The Star-Ledger*, 26 October 2004, www.nj.com/sports/ledger/index.ssf?/base/sports-4/10987662193630.xml.

[24] Mark Starr (*Newsweek*), "The Amazing, Enigmatic Belichick," MSNBC.com, 13 November 2004.

[25] Frank Deford, "The Patriots act," *Sports Illustrated*, 20 October 2004, http://sportsillustrated.cnn.com/2004/writers/frank_deford/10/20/deford.patriots/.

[26] Len Pasquarelli, "Hard to compare teams from different eras," *ESPN*, 6 October 2004, http://sports.espn.go.com/espn/print?id=1896257story.

[27] Seattle Seahawks head coach Mike Holmgren, quoted in: Roger Mills, "New England simply the model franchise," *St. Petersburg Times*, 15 October 2004, www.sptimes.com/2004/10/15/Sports/New_England_simply_th.shtml.

[28] Peter King, "Blame Wayne," *Sports Illustrated*, 9 November 2004, http://sportsillustrated.cnn.com/2004/writers/peter_king/11/09/mmqbte.dolphins/.

[29] Al Michaels and John Madden, "Monday Night Football," late 3rd quarter, 22 November 2004.

[30] *ESPN* "Sports Center," televised 6 December 2004.

[31] Patriots head coach Bill Belichick, quoted in: Nolan Nawrocki, "There's no 'I' in 'team,'" *Pro Football Weekly*, 3 February 2002, http://archive.profootballweekly.com/content/archives2001/features_2001/sb_0203023.asp.

[32] Running back Corey Dillon, quoted with 5:45 left in the first quarter of the Patriots-Cardinals Week 2 2004 matchup by the CBS announcers who interviewed him before the game, 19 September 2004.

[33] Bill Belichick, "A Special Championship Contribution," in: Bryan Morry, *Patriots United*, Canada: Team Power Publishing, 2002, p. 64.

[34] John Clayton, "Patriots shopping spree pays off," *ESPN*, 20 December 2001, http://espn.go.com/nfl/columns/clayton_john/1298726.html.

[35] *Pro Football Weekly* poll of NFL personnel directors, cited in: Bill Burt, "Pats buy in or say bye, bye," *Eagle Tribune*, 9 October 2000, www.eagletribune.com/news/stories/20001009/SP_008.htm.

[36] Bill Belichick, quoted in: Mike Freeman, "Belichick Has Patriots' Ears; Now the Hard Part," *New York Times*, 26 July 2000, p. D1, ProQuest Historical Newspapers.

[37] Pete Prisco, "Ranking the NFL's coaches," *CBS Sportsline*, 8 June 2001, http://groups.google.com/groups?selm=Pine.OSF.4.21.0106081349260.50-100000@gonzo.wolfenet.com.

[38] Bill Burt, "One believer in Belichick is now in hiding," *Eagle Tribune*, 15 November 2000, www.eagletribune.com/news/stories/20001115/SP_002.htm.

[39] Early season 2001 prediction of *Pro Football Weekly*, quoted in: Jeff Reynolds, "Patriots becoming accustomed to dominance," 15 December 2003, www.profootballweekly.com/PFW/NFL/AFC/AFC+East/New+England/Features/2003/reynolds121503.htm.

[40] Athlon, quoted in: Bryan Morry, *Patriots United*, Canada: Team Power Publishing, 2002, p. 70.

[41] *Street & Smith's*, quoted in: Bryan Morry, *Patriots United*, Canada: Team Power Publishing, 2002, p. 70.

[42] Bill Belichick, quoted in: "Miami 30, New England 10," Sports Illustrated, 7 October 2001, http://sportsillustrated.cnn.com/football/nfl/recaps/2001/10/07/dolphins_patriots/.

[43] Peter King, "The sincerest form of flattery," *Sports Illustrated*, 4 February 2002, http://sportsillustrated.cnn.com/inside_game/peter_king/news/2002/02/04/mmqb/.

[44] Vic Carucci, "Destiny's darlings now America's team," *NFL Insider*, 3 February 2002, ww2.nfl.com/xxxvi/ce/feature/0,3892,4948910,00.html.

[45] Pete Prisco, "Upstart Pats assume role of aggressors to snatch victory," *CBS Sportsline*, 4 February 2002, http://cbs.sportsline.com/b/page/pressbox/0,1328,4948860,00.html.

[46] "Readers: Worst championship teams," *ESPN*, http://espn.go.com/page2/s/list/readers/champions/worst.html, no date given.

[47] Dan O'Neill, "Belichick's gruff football facade gives way to a serious softy," *St. Louis Post-Dispatch*, 1 February 2002, www.ramsfan.us/oldnews/2002/020102-9.htm.

[48] Patriots VP of player personnel, Scott Pioli, quoted in: Michael Silver, "Pat Answer," *Sports Illustrated*, 11 February 2002, http://sportsillustrated.cnn.com/si_online/news/2002/02/11/pat_answer/.

[49] Patriots VP of player personnel, Scott Pioli, quoted in: "Central Connecticut State University Athletics," 13 November 2002, http://ccsubluedevils.collegesports.com/administration/ccon-ninequestionsscottpioli.html.

[50] Patriots linebacker Mike Vrabel, quoted in: Peter King, "The sincerest form of flattery," *Sports Illustrated*, 4 February 2002, http://sportsillustrated.cnn.com/inside_game/peter_king/news/2002/02/04/mmqb/.

[51] New York Giants quarterback-crushing defensive end Michael Strahan, quoted in: Peter King, "The sincerest form of flattery," *Sports Illustrated*, 4 February 2002, http://sportsillustrated.cnn.com/inside_game/peter_king/news/2002/02/04/mmqb/.

[52] Patriots safety Lawyer Milloy, quoted in: Alan Greenberg, "THESE AREN'T DREW'S PATRIOTS ; TURNAROUND GOES TO TEAM'S CORE," *Hartford Courant*, 22 December 2001, p. C1, ProQuest database.

[53] Miami (twice), Indianapolis (twice), Tennessee (twice), Denver, Dallas, Philadelphia, and Carolina.

[54] Jimmy Johnson, on Fox Sports' pre-game show, 17 October 2004.

[55] Patriots linebacker Mike Vrabel, quoted in: Paul Attner, "Super Bowl 38: Red, white and two," *The Sporting News*, 9 February 2004, www.sportingnews.com/archives/superbowl/.

[56] Peter King, "What more could you want?" *Sports Illustrated*, 2 February 2004, http://sportsillustrated.cnn.com/2004/writers/peter_king/02/02/mmqb/index.html.

[57] Gary Myers, "He gets top Bill-ing," *New York Daily News*, 24 July 2004, www.nydailynews.com/sports/story/215433p-185477c.html.

[58] "Best of the Best," *The Sporting News Pro Football Fantasy Rankings and Tips*, p. 9.

[59] *Sports Illustrated*, "SI Players Poll," survey of 354 current and former NFL players, http://sportsillustrated.cnn.com/2004/players/09/14/players.poll/index.html.

[60] $(.5)^{21} = .000000477 = 0.0000477\%$.

[61] Patriots linebacker Willie McGinest, quoted in: Larry Weisman, "Brady and Vinatieri shine again as Pats beat Panthers 32-29," *USA Today*, 1 February 2004 (updated 3 February), www.usatoday.com/sports/football/super/2004-02-01-game-story_x.htm.

[62] Patriots safety Rodney Harrison, quoted in: Michael Felger, "Pats sing same ol' tune, cool off Jets: Win battle of unbeatens for 21st straight," *Boston Herald*, 25 October 2004, http://patriots.bostonherald.com/patriots/view.bg?articleid=50698.

[63] Peter King, "Born to win," *Sports Illustrated*, 23 August 2004, http://sportsillustrated.cnn.com/2004/writers/peter_king/08/20/king.mmqb/.

[64] Frank Fleming, "Arizona Cardinals," www.sportsecyclopedia.com/nfl/az/cardsarizona.html.

[65] New Arizona Cardinals head coach Dennis Green, quoted in: Jerry Magee, "The Heat is On," *San Diego Union-Tribune*, 18 July 2004, www.signonsandiego.com/sports/nfl/20040718-9999-lz1s18sunspcl.html.

[66] Patriots rookie Cedric Cobbs, quoted in: *Patriots.com*, "Rookie Spotlight: RB Cedric Cobbs," 11 August 2004, www.patriots.com/Common/PrintThis.sps?id=30048&keytype=NEWS&type=training.

[67] Three-time Pro Bowl running back Corey Dillon, who joined the Patriots in 2004, quoted in: Michael Smith, "In a different arena, Cleeland did his best," *Boston Globe*, 30 May 2004, www.boston.com/sports/football/patriots/articles/2004/05/30/in_a_different_arena_cleeland_did_his_best.

[68] Phil Simms, quarterback of the New York Giants and MVP of Super Bowl XXI while Belichick was the Giant's defensive coordinator, quoted in: Jeff Goodman, "Once Unwanted, Belichick Is the Savior of New England," *Washington Post*, 28 November 2003, D9, ProQuest database.

[69] Patriots tight end Christian Fauria, quoted in: Bob Glauber, "Genius at work," *Newsday*, 24 October 2004, www.newsday.com/sports/football/jets/ny-spsunspec2440179437oct24.0.3329835.story.

[70] Former Patriots quarterback Drew Bledsoe, quoted in: Ernest Hooper, "N.E.'s Belichick now flexible," *St. Petersburg Times*, 1 September 2000, www.sptimes.com/News/090100/Sports/NE_s_Belichick_now_fl.shtml.

[71] Patriots wide receiver Deion Branch, quoted in: Kevin Paul Dupont, "Mr. Cool," *Again!*, Chicago: Triumph Books, 2004, p. 18.

[72] *Sports Illustrated*, "SI Players Poll," survey of 354 current and former NFL players, http://sportsillustrated.cnn.com/2004/players/09/14/players.poll/index.html.

[73] Boston Red Sox 2nd baseman Pokey Reese, who grew up with David Patten, quoted in: Nick Cafardo, "Pats' Patten must prove himself again," *Berkshire Eagle*, 11 August 2004, www.berkshireeagle.com/Stories/0,1413,101~6295~2326911,00.html.

[74] Bill Belichick, quoted in: Peter King, "The sincerest form of flattery," *Sports Illustrated*, 4 February 2002, http://sportsillustrated.cnn.com/inside_game/peter_king/news/2002/02/04/mmqb/.

[75] Bob McGinn, "A priceless collection," *Milwaukee Journal-Sentinel*, 31 January 2002, www.jsonline.com/packer/prev/jan02/16658.asp.

[76] Bob McGinn, "A priceless collection," *Milwaukee Journal-Sentinel*, 31 January 2002, www.jsonline.com/packer/prev/jan02/16658.asp.

[77] 39-year NFL veteran and ten-year general manager of the Green Bay Packers Ron Wolf, "Ron Wolf's Scouting Report," *CNN-Sports Illustrated*, 18 January 2002, http://sportsillustrated.cnn.com/football/2002/playoffs/news/2002/01/18/wolf_scouting_report/.

[78] Len Pasquarelli, "Belichick and Pioli have winning formula," *ESPN.com*, 27 July 2002, http://espn.go.com/nfl/trainingcamp02/columns/patriots/1410739.html.

[79] Vrabel friend and former Ohio State teammate/housemate Luke Fickell, quoted in: Charles P. Pierce, "The Patriot," *Boston Globe*, 5 September 2004, www.boston.com/news/globe/magazine/articles/2004/09/05/the_patriot/.

[80] Former Ohio State Buckeyes strength coach Dave Kennedy, quoted in: Charles P. Pierce, "The Patriot," *Boston Globe*, 5 September 2004, www.boston.com/news/globe/magazine/articles/2004/09/05/the_patriot/.

[81] Patriots kicker Adam Vinatieri, quoted in: Jon Saraceno, "Patriots prove to be no patsies," *USA Today*, 4 February 2002, www.usatoday.com/sports/comment/saraceno/2002-02-04-saraceno.htm.

[82] Patriots linebacker Roman Phifer, quoted in: Jon Saraceno, "Patriots prove to be no patsies," *USA Today*, 4 February 2002, www.usatoday.com/sports/comment/saraceno/2002-02-04-saraceno.htm.

[83] Patriots cornerback Ty Law, quoted in: Jon Saraceno, "Patriots prove to be no patsies," *USA Today*, 4 February 2002, www.usatoday.com/sports/comment/saraceno/2002-02-04-saraceno.htm.

[84] *Pro Football Weekly* staff, "Previewing the NFC West," 8 August 2002, www.footballproject.com/story.php?storyid=81.

[85] Patriots quarterback Tom Brady, quoted in: Michael Felger, "Age not acting his age," *Boston Herald*, 12 June 2004, http://patriots.bostonherald.com/patriots/view.bg?articleid=31608.

[86] Bill Belichick, quoted in: Tom E. Curran, "For Pats, it'll be hard work defending title," *Providence Journal*, 28 July 2004, www.projo.com/patriots/content/projo_20040728_28pats.5df0.html.

[87] Eric Edholm, "'Three Games To Glory II' reveals Patriots' marketing smarts – and much more," *Pro Football Weekly*, 29 April 2004, www.profootballweekly.com/PFW/NFL/AFC/AFC+East/New+England/Features/2004/edholm042904.htm.

[88] Paul Katcher, "Super Bowl XXXVI Q&A," *Time*, 29 January 2002, www.time.com/time/sampler/article/0,8599,198160,00.html.

[89] Patriots cornerback Ty Law, quoted in: "St. Louis at New England," *Sports Illustrated*, 3 February 2002, http://sportsillustrated.cnn.com/football/nfl/previews/2002/02/03/patriots_rams/.

[90] Michael Eisen, "Pats' Patten knew Warner was special," *NFL Insider*, 30 January 2002, www.superbowl.com/xxxvi/ce/feature/0,3892,4919846,00.html.

[91] Patriots quarterback Tom Brady, quoted in: Len Pasquarelli, "Brady's MVP legacy? Pats 20, Rams 17," *ESPN.com*, 4 February 2002 (?), http://espn.go.com/nfl/playoffs01/columns/pasquarelli_len/1322334.html.

[92] Patriots running back Antowain Smith, quoted in: Hector Longo, "Smith's fumble starts Pats' tumble," *Eagle-Tribune*, 19 November 2001, www.eagletribune.com/news/stories/20011119/SP_006.htm.

[93] St. Louis Rams head coach Mike Martz, quoted in: *Sports Illustrated*, "St. Louis 24, New England 17," 19 November 2001, http://sportsillustrated.cnn.com/football/nfl/recaps/2001/11/18/patriots_rams/.

[94] St. Louis Rams head coach Mike Martz, quoted in: "St. Louis at New England," *Sports Illustrated*, 3 February 2002, http://sportsillustrated.cnn.com/football/nfl/previews/2002/02/03/patriots_rams/.

[95] St. Louis Rams wide receiver Ricky Proehl, quoted in: Greg Garber, "Only consistent theme is disbelief," *ESPN*, 4 February 2002 (?), http://espn.go.com/nfl/playoffs01/columns/garber_greg/1322321.html.

[96] Rams head coach Mike Martz, quoted in: Greg Garber, "Only consistent theme is disbelief," *ESPN*, 4 February 2002 (?), http://espn.go.com/nfl/playoffs01/columns/garber_greg/1322321.html.

[97] Patriots linebacker Tedy Bruschi, quoted in: (Arizona Wildcats) Cat Tracks staff, "It's good to be Tedy Bruschi," 17 February 2004, http://arizona.theinsiders.com/2/235079.html.

[98] New Patriot wide receiver Kevin Kasper, quoted in: Mike Reiss, "Patriots beat: Team Desirable," *Daily News Tribune*, 10 October 2004, www.dailynewstribune.com/sportsNews/view.bg?articleid=42486.

[99] Bill Belichick, quoted in: Andrew Mason, "Pats bring new meaning to 'team,'" *NFL.com*, 3 February 2002, ww2.nfl.com/xxxvi/ce/feature/0,3892,4948702,00.html.

[100] Defensive lineman Richard Seymour, quoted in: Jay Glazer, "Pats notes: New England defense lays down the Law," *CBS Sportsline*, 4 February 2002, http://cbs.sportsline.com/b/page/pressbox/0,1328,4948780,00.html.

[101] Bill Belichick, quoted in: Andrew Mason, "Pats bring new meaning to 'team,'" *NFL.com*, 3 February 2002, ww2.nfl.com/xxxvi/ce/feature/0,3892,4948702,00.html.

[102] Patriots VP of player personnel, Scott Pioli, quoted in: Len Pasquarelli, "Belichick and Pioli have winning formula," *ESPN.com*, 27 July 2002, http://espn.go.com/nfl/trainingcamp02/columns/patriots/1410739.html.

[103] Bill Belichick, "Bill Belichick Press Conference," 22 January 2002, www.patriots.com/news/FullArticle.sps?id=16686&type=general.

[104] Buffalo Bills head coach Mike Mularkey, quoted in: Rick Westhead, "Patriots Make the Bills Pay and Win Their 18th Game in a Row," *New York Times*, 4 October 2004, www.nytimes.com/2004/10/04/sports/football/04patriots.html.

[105] Super Bowl XXI MVP quarterback Phil Simms, "Patriots show value of team," *NFL.com*, 24 January 2002, www.nfl.com/xxxvi/ce/feature/0,3892,4885490,00.html.

[106] Patriots owner Robert Kraft, quoted in: Judy Battista, "Patriots Adhere to Bottom Line to Stay on Top," *New York Times*, 8 August 2004, www.nytimes.com/2004/08/08/sports/football/08patriots.html.

[107] Patriots director of football research Ernie Adams, quoted in: Michael Holley, *Patriot Reign*, William Morrow, 2004, p. 170.

[108] Carolina Panthers owner Jerry Richardson, quoted in: Jimmy Golen (AP), "Kraft, Richardson know when to get out of the way," *San Francisco Chronicle*, 28 January 2004, www.sfgate.com/cgi-bin/article.cgi?file=/news/archive/2004/01/28/sports1617EST0369.DTL.

[109] Judy Battista, "Kraft Changes a Heavy Hand Into a Guiding Hand," *New York Times*, 17 January 2004, p. D5, ProQuest database.

[110] Patriots owner Robert Kraft, quoted in: Tom E. Curran, "Pats owner has created a masterpiece," *Providence Journal*, 13 June 2004, www.projo.com/patriots/content/projo_20040613_13kraft.1b891c.html.

[111] Patriots VP of player personnel Scott Pioli, quoted in: Michael Felger, "Pioli helps put it together," *Boston Herald*, 26 January 2004, http://patriots.bostonherald.com/patriots/view.bg?articleid=510.

[112] Bill Belichick, quoted in: Harvey Mackay, *We Got Fired!*, New York: Ballantine Books, 2004, p. 62.

[113] Patriots owner Robert Kraft, quoted in: Jeff Goodman, "Once Unwanted, Belichick Is the Savior of New England," *Washington Post*, 28 November 2003, D9, ProQuest database.

[114] Patriots owner Robert Kraft, quoted in: John Powers, "Mr. Fix-It," *Boston Globe*, 25 January 2004, http://redsoxnation.net/forum/lofiversion/index.php/t1298.html.

[115] Carolina Panthers safety Mike Minter, quoted in: Charles Chandler, "Brady gets a bunch of yards," *Charlotte Observer*, 29 August 2004, www.charlotte.com/mld/charlotte/sports/football/nfl/carolina_panthers/9527119.htm.

[116] Patriots running back Antowain Smith, quoted in: Paul Attner, "'Whatever 'It' is, Brady has 'It,'" *Sports Illustrated*, 6 October 2004, http://msn.foxsports.com/story/3059636.

[117] Troy Aikman, "Brady has something the others don't," The Sporting News, 7 October 2004, http://msn.foxsports.com/story/3026030.

[118] Patriots tight end Christian Fauria, quoted in: Mark Emmons (*San Jose Mercury News*), "Patriots' Brady the talk of the town," *Star-Telegram*, 25 January 2004, www.dfw.com/mld/dfw/sports/columnists/troy_phillips/7789659.htm?1c.

[119] Patriots offensive coordinator Charlie Weis, quoted in: Frank Tadych, "Patriots Notebook: Weis high on Brady," *Patriots.com*, 23 September 2004, www.patriots.com/news/FullArticle.sps?id=31308.

[120] Tom Brady, quoted in: AP, "Quarterback spotlight is on Brady vs. Manning ," *Daily News*, 18 January 2004, www.tdn.com/articles/2004/01/18/sports/news02.txt.

[121] Patriots receiver David Patten, quoted in: Jeffri Chadiha, "The Brady Hunch," *Sports Illustrated*, special commemorative issue, 13 February 2002, p. 47.

[122] Dave Anderson, "Unknown Three Years Ago, Brady Is Now Patriots' Difference," *New York Times*, 25 October 2004, www.nytimes.com/2004/10/25/sports/football/25anderson.html.

[123] Gayle Fee and Laura Raposa, "No. 12 Trumps all for Ivanka," *Boston Herald*, 8 January 2004, http://thetrack.bostonherald.com/moreTrack/view.bg?articleid=297.

[124] Bill Belichick, quoted in: AP, "Quarterback spotlight is on Brady vs. Manning ," *Daily News*, 18 January 2004, www.tdn.com/articles/2004/01/18/sports/news02.txt.

[125] Bill Belichick on *The David Letterman Show*, 4 February 2004, www.patriots.com/mediaworld/mediadetail.sps?id=27974.

[126] Bill Belichick, quoted in: Jeff Reynolds, "Patriots becoming accustomed to dominance," 15 December 2003, www.profootballweekly.com/PFW/NFL/AFC/AFC+East/New+England/Features/2003/reynolds121503.htm.

[127] Bill Belichick, quoted in: Alan Greenberg, "A Working Relationship," *Hartford Courant*, 9 September 2004, www.ctnow.com/sports/hc-nflpatsmain0908.artsep09,1,2684889.story.

[128] Bill Belichick, quoted in: Jarrett Bell, "Patriots defy odds in face of salary cap, free agency," *USA Today*, 10 September 2004, www.usatoday.com/sports/football/nfl/patriots/2004-09-09-building-champ_x.htm.

[129] Michigan head coach Lloyd Carr, quoted in: "Quotes," http://bostonbrat.net/brady/quotes.html.

[130] Hall of Fame quarterback Joe Montana, quoted in: Greg Garber, "Brady following in steps of his idol," *ESPN*, 27 January 2004, http://sports.espn.go.com/espn/print?id=1719979&type=story.

[131] Patriots quarterback Tom Brady, quoted in: Joe Greenlight, "If I Were at Super Bowl Media Day," 27 January 2004, http://joegreenlight.typepad.com/blog/2004/01/if_i_were_at_su.html.

[132] Patriots quarterback Tom Brady, quoted in: Associated Press, "Bledsoe: 'I look forward to my future,'" *ESPN*, 4 February 2002, http://espn.go.com/nfl/playoffs01/news/2002/0204/1322906.html.

[133] Patriots quarterback Tom Brady, quoted in: Associated Press, "Bledsoe: 'I look forward to my future,'" *ESPN*, 4 February 2002, http://espn.go.com/nfl/playoffs01/news/2002/0204/1322906.html.

[134] Tom Brady, quoted in: Len Pasquarelli, "Brady's MVP legacy? Pats 20, Rams 17," *ESPN.com*, 4 February 2002 (?), http://espn.go.com/nfl/playoffs01/columns/pasquarelli_len/1322334.html.

[135] Patriots quarterback Tom Brady, quoted in: Tim Polzer, "Super Bowl XXXVI: New England 20, St. Louis 17," 3 February 2002, www.superbowl.com/history/mvps/game/sbxxxvi.

[136] Tom Brady, quoted in: Sam Farmer (*Los Angeles Times*), "Pats' Brady continues to amaze," 24 August 2004, www.nashuatelegraph.com/apps/pbcs.dll/article?AID=/20040824/SPORTS/208240338/-1/sports.

[137] Tom Brady, quoted in: Tom E. Curran, "Tom Brady: The man behind the growing legend," *Providence Journal*, 25 July 2004, www.projo.com/patriots/content/projo_20040725_brad25.eb8fb.html.

[138] Tom Brady, quoted in: Michael Felger, "Patriots notebook: Brady feels he can be better," *MetroWest Sports*, 9 August 2004, www.metrowestdailynews.com/sportsNews/view.bg?articleid=75106.

[139] Tom Brady, quoted in: Howard Ulman, "Patriots get scare, then 20th consecutive win," Fox Sports, 17 October 2004, http://msn.foxsports.com/story/3088516.

[140] Jeff Capotosto, "Saturday Night Fever," www2.bc.edu/~capotost/homework/finalproject/patriots.html.

[141] Hall of Fame 49ers coach Bill Walsh, quoted in: George Kimball, "Architects: Hard to build on success," *Boston Herald*, 1 February 2004.

[142] Boomer Esiason, "Making reads on traded wide receivers," *NFL.com*, 20 October 2004, www.nfl.com/news/story/7812716.

[143] ESPN analyst and former NFL quarterback Ron Jaworski, quoted in: Mark Maske, "Selfless Patriots show how it's done," *Washington Post*, 4 February 2004, www.msnbc.msn.com/id/4144383/.

[144] Patriots quarterback Tom Brady, "Tom Brady Press Conference Transcript," *Patriots.com*, 6 January 2004, www.patriots.com/games/GamesDetails.sps?matchid=27174&matchreportid=27208.

[145] Patriots quarterback Tom Brady, quoted in: John Tomase, "Built To Win," *Eagle Tribune*, 27 January 2004, www.eagletribune.com/news/stories/20040127/SP_001.htm.

[146] Tom Brady, interview with Jim Nantz, CBS halftime show of Patriots-Panthers game, 28 August 2004.

[147] Tom Brady, quoted in: Tom E. Curran, "Tom Brady: The man behind the growing legend," *Providence Journal*, 25 July 2004, www.projo.com/patriots/content/projo_20040725_brad25.eb8fb.html.

[148] Patriots cornerback Ty Law, quoted in: Greg Beacham (AP), "Patriots are guests of honour in Hawaii for Pro Bowl all-star game," 4 February 2004, http://ca.sports.yahoo.com/040204/6/wmn9.html.

[149] Patriots inside linebackers coach Pepper Johnson, *Won For All*, Chicago: Contemporary Books, 2003, p. 103.

[150] Michael Felger, "Pioli: Scout's Honor," *Boston Herald*, 19 December 2001, www.allthingsbillbelichick.com/articles/piolihonor.htm.

[151] Peter King, "Master And Commander," *Sports Illustrated*, 9 August 2004, www.allthingsbillbelichick.com/articles/master.htm..

[152] Jay Glazer, "Divisional draft preview: AFC East needs," *SportsLine.com*, 6 April 2004, http://cbs.sportsline.com/nfl/story/7236258.

[153] Patriots VP of player personnel, Scott Pioli, quoted in: "Central Connecticut State University Athletics," 13 November 2002, http://ccsubluedevils.collegesports.com/administration/ccon-ninequestionsscottpioli.html.

[154] Scott Pioli, Patriots VP of player personnel, quoted in: Hector Longo, "All the right moves," *Eagle-Tribune*, 30 January 2004, www.eagletribune.com/news/stories/20040130/SP_001.htm.

[155] Scott Pioli, Patriots VP of player personnel, quoted in: Hector Longo, "All the right moves," *Eagle-Tribune*, 30 January 2004, www.eagletribune.com/news/stories/20040130/SP_001.htm.

[156] Bill Belichick, quoted in: Jimmy Golen (AP), "Belichick might not be slick, but he makes Pats tick," *Arizona Daily Star*, 20 January 2004, www.dailystar.com/dailystar/relatedarticles/6555.php.

[157] Bill Belichick, quoted in: Don Banks, "Five Questions with … Bill Belichick," *Sports Illustrated*, 17 August 2004, http://sportsillustrated.cnn.com/2004/football/nfl/specials/preview/2004/08/17/fivequestion.belichick/.

[158] Bill Belichick, quoted in: Bob Duffy, "Whiz Kid To Defensive Genius," *Boston Globe*, 28 January 2000, www.allthingsbillbelichick.com/articles/whizkid.htm.

[159] Bill Belichick, quoted in: Dan O'Neill, "Belichick's gruff football facade gives way to a serious softy," *St. Louis Post-Dispatch*, 1 February 2002, www.ramsfan.us/oldnews/2002/020102-9.htm.

[160] New York Giants general manager Ernie Accorsi, quoted in: Judy Battista, "Patriots Adhere to Bottom Line to Stay on Top," *New York Times*, 8 August 2004, www.nytimes.com/2004/08/08/sports/football/08patriots.html.

[161] Dom Amore, "BELICHICK, BROWNS GETTING SOMEWHERE FORMER GIANTS HELP TEAM TO 9 3 START," *Hartford Courant*, 3 December 1994, p. C3, ProQuest database.

[162] Gerald Eskenazi, "Who Are These Guys? Jets' Defense Sparkles," *New York Times*, 3 November 1998, p. D3, ProQuest database.

[163] Patriots inside linebackers coach Pepper Johnson, *Won For All*, Chicago: Contemporary Books, 2003, p. 7.

[164] Tom Brady, quoted in: Tom E. Curran, "Tom Curran: Brady, Belichick seem perfect for each other," *Providence Journal*, 12 August 2004, www.projo.com/patriots/content/projo_20040812_12currcol.dcb5f.html.

[165] Defensive coordinator Romeo Crennel, quoted in: Gordon Edes, "Patriots coach has well-earned reputation for stopping whatever's thrown his way," *Boston Globe*, 2 February 2002, www.boston.com/sports/football/patriots/superbowl/globe_stories/020202/patriots_coach_has_well_earned_reputation_for_stopping_whatever_s_thrown_his_way+.shtml.

[166] Defensive coordinator Romeo Crennel, quoted in: Thomas George, "After Years of Waiting, Crennel Moves to Head of Line," *New York Times*, 23 December 2003, p. D1, ProQuest database.

[167] Patriots backup quarterback Rohan Davey, quoted in: Dan Pires, "Is Dillon too good to be true?" *Standard-Times*, 13 August 2004, www.southcoasttoday.com/daily/08-04/08-13-04/c01sp051.htm.

[168] Patriots owner Robert Kraft, quoted in: Jarrett Bell, "Patriots defy odds in face of salary cap, free agency," *USA Today*, 10 September 2004, www.usatoday.com/sports/football/nfl/patriots/2004-09-09-building-champ_x.htm.

[169] Patriots owner Robert Kraft, quoted in: Jimmy Golen (AP), "Kraft, Richardson know when to get out of the way," *San Francisco Chronicle*, 28 January 2004, www.sfgate.com/cgi-bin/article.cgi?file=/news/archive/2004/01/28/sports1617EST0369.DTL.

[170] Laurie Jerome, 40-year old Patriots fan from Westwood, MA, quoted in: Associated Press, "Estimated 1.2 million fans pack Boston streets," *ESPN*, 5 February 2002, http://espn.go.com/nfl/playoffs01/news/2002/0205/1323015.html.

[171] Patriots safety Rodney Harrison, quoted in: Michael Smith, "Jets trying to follow Pats' mold," *ESPN.com*, 21 October 2004, http://sports.espn.go.com/nfl/columns/story?id=1906485.

[172] Patriots safety Rodney Harrison, quoted in: Anthony Cotton, "Patriots take simple route to superiority," *Denver Post*, 20 October 2004, www.denverpost.com/Stories/0,1413,36~86~2479163,00.html.

[173] Patriots safety Lawyer Milloy, quoted in: *Patriots United*, Canada: Team Power Publishing, 2002, p. 168.

[174] For example: Bob Kraft, quoted in: The White House, "President Welcomes New England Patriots to White House," 2 April 2004, www.whitehouse.gov/news/releases/2002/04/20020402-3.html.

[175] Michael Holley, *Patriot Reign*, William Morrow, 2004, p. 109.

[176] Patriots offensive guard, quoted in: Alan Greenberg, "Finding words a year later," *Hartford Courant*, 12 September 2002, p. C7, ProQuest database.

[177] Patriots running back Kevin Faulk, quoted in: Frank Tadych, "Patriots Notebook: Faulk speaks about return," *Patriots.com*, 22 September 2004, www.patriots.com/news/fullarticle.sps?id=31306.

[178] Patriots special teams ace Don Davis, quoted in: Mike Reiss, "Patriots beat: Team Desirable," *Daily News Tribune*, 10 October 2004, www.dailynewstribune.com/sportsNews/view.bg?articleid=42486.

[179] Jim Moore, "Go 2 Guy: Tale of a dogged newshound," *Seattle Post-Intelligencer*, 14 October 2004, http://seattlepi.nwsource.com/football/195099_moore14.html.

[180] Patriots linebacker Tedy Bruschi, quoted in: Michael Felger, "Bruschi's just happy to be here," *Boston Herald*, 5 August 2004, http://patriots.bostonherald.com/patriots/view.bg?articleid=38585.

[181] Patriots linebacker Tedy Bruschi, quoted in: Michael Smith, "Solid backing," *Boston Globe*, 9 September 2004, www.boston.com/sports/football/patriots/articles/2004/09/09/solid_backing.

[182] Patriots linebacker Tedy Bruschi, quoted in: Michael Smith, "Solid backing," *Boston Globe*, 9 September 2004, www.boston.com/sports/football/patriots/articles/2004/09/09/solid_backing.

[183] *NFL.com*, "Jones released by team after arrest" 26 October 2003, www.nfl.com/teams/story/NE/6782344.

[184] NFL Films president Steve Sabol, www.bostonsportsmedia.com/archives/001032.php.

[185] Christopher Young, "The Patriots pass the torch," *The Phoenix*, 13 January 2003, www.bostonphoenix.com/boston/news_features/sportingeye/documents/02649783.htm.

[186] Patriots linebacker Roman Phifer, quoted in: David J. Neal, "Patriots' path to greatness," *San Jose Mercury News*, 4 September 2004, www.mercurynews.com/mld/mercurynews/sports/9583523.htm?1c.

[187] VP of Player Personnel Scott Pioli, quoted in: Vic Carucci, "Being a true Patriot has its rewards," *NFL.com*, 30 March 2004, www.nfl.com/news/story/7219076.

[188] Marv Levy, who coached the Buffalo Bills to four straight Super Bowl appearances, quoted in: Howard Ulman (AP), "Two-time NFL champs focus on next game, not making history," *Canada.com*, 3 September 2004, www.canada.com/sports/football/story.html?id=5F09B45F-C14D-417C-96B5-36A7704F010B.

[189] Patriots offensive coordinator Charlie Weis, quoted in: Frank Tadych, "Weis facing future unknown," *Patriots.com*, 17 November 2004, http://cachewww.patriots.com/news/index.cfm?ac=latestnewsdetail&pid=9760&pcid=41.

[190] Coach Bill Belichick, quoted in: Tom E. Curran, "Savoring victory is alien to Belichick," *Providence Journal*, 7 February 2004, www.projo.com/patriots/content/projo_20040207_07pats.1902d4.html.

[191] Patriots linebacker Roman Phifer, quoted in: Alan Greenberg, "Pat-ended process; Belichick can find those keepers," 1 February 2004, p. E1, ProQuest database.

[192] Patriots special teams captain Larry Izzo, quoted in: Tom E. Curran, "For Pats, it'll be hard work defending title," *Providence Journal*, 28 July 2004, www.projo.com/patriots/content/projo_20040728_28pats.5df0.html.

[193] Patriots tight end Christian Fauria, quoted in: Michael Smith, "Dream Team," *Boston Globe*, 9 September 2004, www.boston.com/sports/football/patriots/articles/2004/09/09/dream_team.

[194] Defensive lineman Richard Seymour, quoted in: Mark Singelais, "Patriots get record-tying win," *Times Union*, 4 October 2004, www.timesunion.com/AspStories/story.asp?storyID=291514&category=SPORTS&BCCode=SPORTS&newsdate=10/4/2004.

[195] Patriots inside linebackers coach Pepper Johnson, *Won For All*, Chicago: Contemporary Books, 2003, p. 114.

[196] Legendary NFL running back Jim Brown, "Interview with Jim Brown, Part V," *ClevelandBrowns.com*, 10 September 2004, www.clevelandbrowns.com/news_room/news/arts/3038.0.html.

[197] Bill Belichick, quoted in: Michael Holley, "Winners are one of a kind," *Boston Globe*, 2 February 2004, www.boston.com/sports/football/patriots/articles/2004/02/02/winners_are_one_of_a_kind.

[198] Bill Belichick, quoted in: Jarrett Bell, "Patriots defy odds in face of salary cap, free agency," *USA Today*, 10 September 2004, www.usatoday.com/sports/football/nfl/patriots/2004-09-09-building-champ_x.htm.

[199] Patriots safety Rodney Harrison, quoted in: Thomas George, "Still Bill: Patriots' Belichick Adapts and Thrives," *New York Times*, 16 November 2003, section 8, p. 1, ProQuest database.

[200] Michael Holley, *Patriot Reign*, William Morrow, 2004, p. 201.

[201] Bill Belichick, quoted in: Alex Timiraos, "Pats coach talks leadership at BC," *The Heights*, 9 April 2004, www.bcheights.com/news/2004/04/09/News/Pats-Coach.Talks.Leadership.At.Bc-656659.shtml.

[202] Patriots defensive lineman Richard Seymour, quoted in: Ethan J. Skolnick, "Patriots are best because they're the smartest," *South Florida Sun-Sentinel*, 7 October 2004, www.sun-sentinel.com/sports/columnists/sfl-skolnick06oct07,0,7494511.column.

[203] Patriots safety Rodney Harrison, quoted in: Michael Smith, "Extra conditioning works for defense," *Boston Globe*, 12 August 2004, www.boston.com/sports/football/patriots/articles/2004/08/12/extra_conditioning_works_for_defense.

[204] Patriots safety Rodney Harrison, quoted in: Michael Smith, "Extra conditioning works for defense," *Boston Globe*, 12 August 2004, www.boston.com/sports/football/patriots/articles/2004/08/12/extra_conditioning_works_for_defense.

[205] Patriots safety Rodney Harrison, quoted in: Adam Kilgore, "Samuel turning corner," *Boston Globe*, 19 August 2004, www.boston.com/sports/football/patriots/articles/2004/08/19/samuel_turning_corner.

[206] Patriots offensive lineman Kenyatta Jones, quoted in: Alan Greenberg, "No Average Jones; Starting Job Comes With Maturity," *Hartford Courant*, 19 September 2002, p. C4, ProQuest database.

[207] Patriots defensive lineman Anthony Pleasant, quoted in: Alan Greenberg, "No Average Jones; Starting Job Comes With Maturity," *Hartford Courant*, 19 September 2002, p. C4, ProQuest database.

[208] Patriots veteran defensive lineman Anthony Pleasant, quoted in: Nick Cafardo, "It doesn't weigh on Light," *Boston Globe*, 11 July 2004, www.boston.com/sports/football/patriots/articles/2004/07/11/it_doesnt_weigh_on_light.

[209] Dick Anderson, who played on the undefeated 1972 Dolphins' "no name" defense, quoted in: Karen Guregian, "Playing with a porpoise: In streaking toward greatness, Pats have makeup similar to famed 1972 Dolphins," *Boston Herald*, 3 October 2004, http://patriots.bostonherald.com/patriots/view.bg?articleid=47143.

[210] Bob Ryan, "Trying to recapture glory days," *Boston Globe*, 9 September 2004, www.boston.com/sports/football/patriots/articles/2004/09/09/trying_to_recapture_glory_days.

[211] Detroit Pistons general manager, Joe Dumars, quoted in: Chris Perkins, "Pistons remind some of Patriots," *Palm Beach Post*, 15 June 2004, www.palmbeachpost.com/sports/content/auto/epaper/editions/tuesday/sports_04ec3623209180d70012.html.

[212] Tom Brady, quoted in: Mark Maske, "Selfless Patriots show how it's done," *Washington Post*, 4 February 2004, www.msnbc.msn.com/id/4144383/.

[213] Tom Brady, quoted in: Larry Weisman, "Brady and Vinatieri shine again as Pats beat Panthers 32-29," *USA Today*, 1 February 2004 (updated 3 February), www.usatoday.com/sports/football/super/2004-02-01-game-story_x.htm.

[214] Panthers players quoted in: Kevin Mannix, "Panthers real serious about rematch," *Boston Herald*, 26 August 2004, http://patriots.bostonherald.com/patriots/view.bg?articleid=41461.

[215] Analysis by Pat Kirwan, "Games inside the game," *Superbowl.com*, 30 January 2004, www.superbowl.com/news/story/7049412.

[216] Analysis by Pat Kirwan, "Games inside the game," *Superbowl.com*, 30 January 2004, www.superbowl.com/news/story/7049412.

[217] Panthers linebacker Dan Morgan, quoted in: John Clayton, "Belichick and Fox will match wits Sunday," *ESPN*, 28 January 2004, http://sports.espn.go.com/nfl/playoffs03/columns/story?columnist=clayton_john&id=1720970.

[218] Super Bowl XXI MVP quarterback Phil Simms, "Call it the Retro Bowl," *NFL.com*, 21 January 2002, www.superbowl.com/news/story/7024331.

[219] Carolina Panthers GM Marty Hurney, quoted in: Paul Attner, "Super Bowl 38: Red, white and two," *The Sporting News*, 9 February 2004, www.sportingnews.com/archives/superbowl/.

[220] Carolina Panthers head coach John Fox, "From the Foxhole: Media blitz," *Panthers.com*, 21 January 2004, www.panthers.com/news/newsroomNewsDetail.jsp?id=11198.

[221] Carolina Panthers offensive coordinator Dan Henning, quoted in: Dave Anderson, "The Super Bowl's Offensive Minds," *New York Times*, 28 January 2004, p. D5, ProQuest database.

[222] Carolina Panthers head coach John Fox, quoted in: Bob LaMonte with Robert L. Shook, *Winning the NFL Way*, USA: HarperBusiness, 2004, p. 43.

[223] Patriots safety Rodney Harrison, quoted in: Michael Felger, "Pats lose 'rematch' vs. Panthers, 20-17: Real progress made on both sides of ball," *Boston Herald*, 29 August 2004, http://patriots.bostonherald.com/patriots/view.bg?articleid=41873.

[224] Smith and Muhammad, quoted in: Nick Cafardo, "Track record earns Patriots knowing look," *Boston Globe*, 30 August 2004, www.boston.com/sports/football/patriots/articles/2004/08/30/track_record_earns_patriots_knowing_look.

[225] Charles Stein, "Bill Belichick, CEO," *Boston Globe*, 28 January 2004, www.boston.com/sports/football/patriots/articles/2004/01/28/bill_belichick_ceo/.

[226] Adam Vinatieri, quoted in: "San Diego Chargers down to New England Patriots 26-29," 14 October 2001, http://stats.staugustine.com/football/pro/nfl/2001/recap/153681.shtml.

[227] New Patriots running back Corey Dillon, quoted in: Frank Tadych, "The Think Tank: Patriots balanced offense nearly at full throttle," *Patriots.com*, 18 October 2004, http://cachewww.patriots.com/news/index.cfm?ac=latestnewsdetail&PID=9370&PCID=41.

[228] Patriots running back Rabih Abdullah, quoted in: Tim Weisberg and Jonathan Darling, "Breaking down the streak," *Standard-Times*, 11 October 2004, www.southcoasttoday.com/daily/10-04/10-11-04/c12sp693.htm.

[229] Bill Belichick, "Bill Belichick Press Conf. Transcript - 9/14/2004," *Patriots.com*, 14 September 2004, www.patriots.com/Common/PrintThis.sps?id=30535.

[230] Patriots safety Rodney Harrison, quoted in: Rich Thompson, "Harrison keeps his focus on new year," *Boston Herald*, 30 July 2004, http://patriots.bostonherald.com/patriots/view.bg?articleid=37861.

[231] Bill Belichick, quoted in: Judy Battista, "An Exhibition of Total Football, New England Style," *New York Times*, 12 January 2004, p. D6, ProQuest database.

[232] Patriots defensive lineman Richard Seymour, quoted in: Andy Hart, "On the offensive; Monday's notes," *Patriots Football Weekly*, 13 September 2004, www.patriots.com/news/fullarticle.sps?id=30518.

[233] Patriots offensive coordinator Charlie Weis, quoted in: Jay Glazer, "Brady leads way as Patriots drive to shocking upset," *CBS Sportsline*, 4 February 2002, http://cbs.sportsline.com/b/page/pressbox/0,1328,4948886,00.html.

[234] New York Jets running back Curtis Martin, quoted in: Alan Greenberg, "Unique Gathering of Old Friends; Martin Has Patriot Ties," *Hartford Courant*, 13 September 2002, p. C4.

[235] Ron Borges, "There's a Risk Factor At Work For Belichick," *Boston Globe*, 22 November 2001, www.allthingsbillbelichick.com/articles/riskfactor.htm.

[236] Len Pasquarelli, "Belichick Becomes Life of Patriots' Party," *ESPN.com*, 22 December 2001, www.allthingsbillbelichick.com/articles/lifeofparty.htm.

[237] Bill Belichick, quoted in: *Patriots United*, Canada: Team Power Publishing, 2002, p. 38.

[238] Bill Belichick, quoted in: Steve Conroy, "Bruschi comes up big again," *Boston Herald*, 5 October 2004, http://patriots.bostonherald.com/patriots/view.bg?articleid=47464.

[239] Former Patriots assistant coach Al Groh, quoted in: Jackie MacMullen, "Tedy Bruschi," in: *Again!*, Chicago: Triumph Books, 2004, pp. 120 & 122.

[240] Pat Kirwan, "Belichick setting the standard in the NFL," *NFL.com*, 16 September 2002, www.nfl.com/teams/story/NE/5721265.

[241] Bill Belichick, quoted in: Michael Felger, "Standing tall: Patriots determined to defend their title," *Boston Herald*, 9 September 2004, http://patriots.bostonherald.com/patriots/view.bg?articleid=43430.

[242] NFL.com wire reports, "Vinatieri, Patriots ice Titans 17-14," *NFL.com*, 10 January 2004, www.nfl.com/gamecenter/recap/NFL_20040110_TEN@NE.

[243] NFL years are confusing. The 2003 Patriots won the February 2004 Super Bowl. They sent players to the February 2004 Pro Bowl. Because the Pro Bowl played in February 2004 involved the stars of the 2003 season, I refer to it as the "2003 Pro Bowl."

[244] Bill Belichick, quoted in: Jim Donaldson, "No past or future for Pats -- only the here and now," *Providence Journal*, 1 October 2004, www.projo.com/patriots/content/projo_20041001_01jdcol.1bae68.html.

[245] Bill Belichick, 2004 pre-Super Bowl speech, quoted in: Eric Edholm, "'Three Games To Glory II' reveals Patriots' marketing smarts – and much more," *Pro Football Weekly*, 29 April 2004, www.profootballweekly.com/PFW/NFL/AFC/AFC+East/New+England/Features/2004/edholm042904.htm.

[246] Patriots linebacker Mike Vrabel, quoted in: Michael Silver, "Pat Answer," *Sports Illustrated*, 11 February 2002, http://sportsillustrated.cnn.com/si_online/news/2002/02/11/pat_answer/.

[247] Bill Belichick, quoted in: Tom E. Curran, "To Patriots, Pro Bowl secondary right now," *Providence Journal*, 18 December 2003, www.projo.com/patriots/content/projo_20031218_18pats.309836.html.

[248] Patriots middle linebacker Tedy Bruschi, quoted in: Tom E. Curran, "To Patriots, Pro Bowl secondary right now," *Providence Journal*, 18 December 2003, www.projo.com/patriots/content/projo_20031218_18pats.309836.html.

[249] Patriots fullback Larry Centers, quoted in: Tom E. Curran, "To Patriots, Pro Bowl secondary right now," *Providence Journal*, 18 December 2003, www.projo.com/patriots/content/projo_20031218_18pats.309836.html.

[250] Ron Borges, "Don't marginalize the players," *Boston Globe*, 21 September 2004, www.boston.com/sports/football/patriots/articles/2004/09/21/dont_marginalize_the_players.

[251] Patriots offensive coordinator Charlie Weis, quoted in: Mike Reiss, "Patriots beat: What a difference," *MetroWest Sports*, 26 September 2004, www.metrowestdailynews.com/sportsNews/view.bg?articleid=78944.

[252] Former New Orleans Saints GM Randy Mueller, quoted in: Paul Attner, "Super Bowl 38: Red, white and two," *The Sporting News*, 9 February 2004, www.sportingnews.com/archives/superbowl/.

[253] Joel Buchsbaum, "Maximum overdrive," *Pro Football Weekly*, October 5, 1998, http://archive.profootballweekly.com/content/archives/features_1998/joel_100598.asp.

[254] Joel Buchsbaum, "Maximum overdrive," *Pro Football Weekly*, October 5, 1998, http://archive.profootballweekly.com/content/archives/features_1998/joel_100598.asp.

[255] Tom Brady, quoted in: Mark Maske, "Selfless Patriots show how it's done," *Washington Post*, 4 February 2004, www.msnbc.msn.com/id/4144383/.

[256] Scott Pioli, Patriots VP of player personnel, quoted in: Hector Longo, "All the right moves," *Eagle-Tribune*, 30 January 2004, www.eagletribune.com/news/stories/20040130/SP_001.htm.

[257] Tom E. Curran, "To Patriots, Pro Bowl secondary right now," *Providence Journal*, 18 December 2003, www.projo.com/patriots/content/projo_20031218_18pats.309836.html.

[258] May 12-26 poll of 22 NFL personnel directors by *USA Today Sports Weekly*, cited in: Michael Smith, "Whipping them into shape," *Boston Globe*, 27 June 2004, www.boston.com/sports/football/patriots/articles/2004/06/27/whipping_them_into_shape.

[259] Patriots safety Rodney Harrison, quoted in: Tom E. Curran, "To Patriots, Pro Bowl secondary right now," *Providence Journal*, 18 December 2003, www.projo.com/patriots/content/projo_20031218_18pats.309836.html.

[260] Unnamed NFL team's pro scout, cited in: Peter King, "A League of Their Own," *Sports Illustrated*, 18 October 2004, p. 69.

[261] Former General Electric CEO Jack Welch, quoted in: Charles Stein, "Bill Belichick, CEO," *Boston Globe*, 28 January 2004.

[262] Peter King, "The sincerest form of flattery," *Sports Illustrated*, 4 February 2002, http://sportsillustrated.cnn.com/inside_game/peter_king/news/2002/02/04/mmqb/.

[263] Patriots defensive lineman Richard Seymour, quoted in: Michael Smith, "Dream Team," *Boston Globe*, 9 September 2004, www.boston.com/sports/football/patriots/articles/2004/09/09/dream_team.

[264] *Pro Football Weekly NFL Preview 2004*, "The Top 50 Regardless of Position," pp. 28-29.

[265] 39-year NFL veteran and ten-year general manager of the Green Bay Packers Ron Wolf. Original quotation from the *Hartford Courant*, republished in: Tom E. Curran, "Patriots Notebook: 3 rookies unsigned as camp dawns," *Providence Journal*, 28 July 2004, www.projo.com/patriots/content/projo_20040728_28patsjo.5524.html.

[266] *Sports Illustrated*, "SI Players Poll," survey of 354 current and former NFL players, http://sportsillustrated.cnn.com/2004/players/09/21/poll.qbs/index.html.

[267] Bob Oates, "Patriots Can Be Best Again," *Los Angeles Times*, 26 August 2002, http://new.blackvoices.com/sports/nationworld/la-082702oates,0,6136320.story?coll=sns-sports-headlines.

[268] Tennessee Titans offensive coordinator Mike Heimerdinger, quoted in: Mike Reiss, "Complications arise: Pats defense tough to read," *Boston Herald*, 22 January 2004, http://patriots.bostonherald.com/patriots/view.bg?articleid=14162.

[269] *NFL.com*, "NFL Stats: 2003 Regular Season," www.nfl.com/stats/2003/regular.

[270] Michael Felger, "Pats subject of cheap talk," *Boston Herald*, 4 April 2004, http://patriots.bostonherald.com/patriots/view.bg?articleid=13945.

[271] Former Patriots safety Tebucky Jones, quoted in: Alan Greenberg, "Jones Saw It Coming; Pats Didn't Make Him Feel Special," *Hartford Courant*, 16 April 2003, p. C2, ProQuest database.

[272] These ratings are obviously subjective, and I am no expert. Also note that Willie McGinest started in Super Bowl XXXVIII where Anthony Pleasant (not even activated for Super Bowl XXXVIII) had started two years earlier.

[273] These are: Chris Akins, Wilbert Brown, Damon Huard, Shawn Mayer, Brandon Gorin, Dedric Ward, David Givens, Ty Warren, Bethel Johnson, Jarvis Green, Brian Kinchen, Tully Banta-Cain, Christian Fauria, Don Davis, and Asante Samuel.

[274] These are: Rohan Davey, Mike Cloud, Fred Baxter, J.J. Stokes, Dan Klecko, and Rick Lyle.

[275] These are: Rosevelt Colvin, Kliff Kingsbury, Adrian Klemm, Fred McCrary, Sean McDermott, Gene Mruczkowski, Stephen Neal, Dan Stricker, Bill Conaty, Chas Gessner, and Kenyatta Jones.

[276] These are: Troy Brown, Matt Light, Joe Andruzzi, Tom Brady, Antowain Smith, Bobby Hamilton, Richard Seymour, Willie McGinest, Mike Vrabel, Tedy Bruschi, Roman Phifer, Ty Law, Matt Chatham, Je'Rod Cherry, Kevin Faulk, Larry Izzo, Ted Johnson, Patrick Pass, Adam Vinatieri, and Ken Walter.

[277] Cherry was re-signed in mid-2003 to strengthen the special teams and help reinforce the injured secondary. Chatham was injured and rejoined the team in mid-2003.

[278] Bill Belichick, quoted in: Glen Farley, "It's a wonderful life," *The Enterprise*, 5 September 2004, http://enterprise.southofboston.com/articles/2004/09/05/news/sports/sports03.txt.

[279] Michael Roberto, professor of strategy and management at Harvard Business School, quoted in: Charles Stein, "Bill Belichick, CEO," *Boston Globe*, 28 January 2004.

[280] Bill Belichick, "Bill Belichick Press Conf. Transcript - 9/14/2004," *Patriots.com*, 14 September 2004, www.patriots.com/Common/PrintThis.sps?id=30535.

[281] Patriots offensive coordinator Charlie Weis, quoted in: Jay Glazer, "Brady leads way as Patriots drive to shocking upset," *CBS Sportsline*, 4 February 2002, http://cbs.sportsline.com/b/page/pressbox/0,1328,4948886,00.html.

[282] Bill Belichick, quoted in: Jeff Reynolds, "Patriots becoming accustomed to dominance," 15 December 2003, www.profootballweekly.com/PFW/NFL/AFC/AFC+East/New+England/Features/2003/reynolds121503.htm.

[283] Bill Belichick, "Belichick, Patriots ready to defend title," NFL.com, 29 July 2004, www.nfl.com/nflnetwork/story/7536560.

[284] Former Patriots quarterback Steve Grogan, quoted in: Steve Grogan and R.R. Marshall, "Grogan's Grade: Week 2," *PatsFans.com*, 20 September 2004, www.patsfans.com/grogan/grogan_04.php?story_id=2511.

[285] Bill Belichick, quoted in: Pete Thamel, "A Cloud Over Belichick Lifts After the Patriots Win 7 of 8," *New York Times*, 6 November 2003, p. D3, ProQuest database.

[286] Patriots safety Rodney Harrison, quoted in: Thomas George, "Still Bill: Patriots' Belichick Adapts and Thrives," *New York Times*, 16 November 2003, section 8, p. 1, ProQuest database.

[287] Patriots safety Rodney Harrison, quoted in: Mark Curnutte, "Patriots epitomize meaning of team," *Cincinnati Enquirer*, 28 January 2004, http://bengals.enquirer.com/2004/01/28/ben1mc.html.

[288] Len Pasquarelli, "Brady's MVP legacy? Pats 20, Rams 17," *ESPN.com*, 4 February 2002 (?), http://espn.go.com/nfl/playoffs01/columns/pasquarelli_len/1322334.html.

[289] Len Pasquarelli, "Coach, QB rewarded for Super Bowl heroics," *ESPN.com*, 4 February 2002, http://espn.go.com/nfl/playoffs01/columns/pasquarelli_len/1322633.html.

[290] Peter King, "What more could you want?" *Sports Illustrated*, 2 February 2004, http://sportsillustrated.cnn.com/2004/writers/peter_king/02/02/mmqb/index.html.

[291] Pro Football Hall of Fame, "Top 20 Passers At the Start of the 2004 NFL Season," www.profootballhof.com/index.cfm?section=history&cont_id=230255.

[292] Michael Felger, "Wilson punches clock: Pats safety turns out to be big steal," *Milford Daily News*, 29 September 2004, www.milforddailynews.com/sportsNews/view.bg?articleid=56720.

[293] Scott Pioli, VP of player personnel, quoted in: Rick Braun, "Patriots built with free agents, draft," *Milwaukee Journal Sentinel*, 4 February 2004, www.jsonline.com/packer/rev/feb04/204957.asp.

[294] Former NFL quarterback Jim Harbaugh, quoted in: Jeff D'Alessio, "Picking a star quarterback can be a tossup," *Florida Today*, 10 January 2004, http://bengals.enquirer.com/2004/01/10/ben2qb.html.

[295] Tom Brady, quoted in: Clare Farnsworth, "Hawks, Pats QBs stand on common ground," *Seattle Post-Intelligencer*, 14 October 2004, http://seattlepi.nwsource.com/football/195156_hawk14.html.

[296] Tom Brady, quoted in: Peter King, "Cool Comparison," *ESPN*, 9 February 2004, http://sportsillustrated.cnn.com/2004/writers/peter_king/02/09/mmqb/.

[297] Patriots coach Bill Belichick, quoted in: Nick Cafardo, "For coach, it's hard to relate," *Boston Globe*, 2 February 2004, www.boston.com/sports/football/patriots/articles/2004/02/02/for_coach_its_hard_to_relate/.

[298] Chris Mortensen, "In Glenn case, who do you trust?" ESPN, 8 August 2001, http://espn.go.com/chrismortensen/s/2001/0808/1236769.html.

[299] Patriots inside linebackers coach Pepper Johnson, *Won For All*, Chicago: Contemporary Books, 2003, pp. 139-140.

[300] Patriots linebacker Roman Phifer, quoted in: Len Pasquarelli, "Super Bowl champs… now what?" ESPN, 3 February 2002 (?), http://espn.go.com/nfl/playoffs01/columns/pasquarelli_len/1322587.html.

[301] Patriots inside linebackers coach Pepper Johnson, *Won For All*, Chicago: Contemporary Books, 2003, p. 5.

[302] Executive professor Leonard J. Glick, Northeastern University College of Business Administration, "Patriots tap top management practices," *Boston Business Journal*, 2 February 2004, www.bizjournals.com/boston/stories/2004/02/02/editorial2.html.

[303] Pat McQuillan, professor in Boston College's Lynch School of Education, quoted in: Alex Timiraos, "Pats coach talks leadership at BC," *The Heights*, 9 April 2004, www.bcheights.com/news/2004/04/09/News/Pats-Coach.Talks.Leadership.At.Bc-656659.shtml.

[304] Bill Belichick, as remembered by former Cleveland Browns player Mike Baab, quoted in: Bob Duffy, "Whiz Kid To Defensive Genius," *Boston Globe*, 28 January 2000, www.allthingsbillbelichick.com/articles/whizkid.html.

[305] Buffalo Bills general manager Tom Donahoe, quoted in: "Copying Patriots won't be easy," 19 February 2004.

[306] New York Giants general manager Ernie Accorsi, quoted in: "Copying Patriots won't be easy," 19 February 2004.

[307] Patriots quarterback Tom Brady, quoted in: "New England 20, St. Louis 17," *Sports Illustrated*, 4 February 2002, http://sportsillustrated.cnn.com/football/nfl/recaps/2002/02/03/patriots_rams/.

[308] Paul Attner, "Super Bowl 36: Standing Pat," *The Sporting News*, 4 February 2002, www.a1-sports-odds.com/292.htm.

[309] "Current Odds As of Monday, July 16, 2001: SUPER BOWL XXXVI," 16 July 2001, www.angelfire.com/sports/ravensnest13/game_schedule.html. (It lists the game as January 27, 2002, but it was later postponed a week due to 9/11.)

[310] Paul Attner, "Super Bowl 36: Standing Pat," *The Sporting News*, 4 February 2002, www.a1-sports-odds.com/292.htm.

[311] Ron Borges, "Belichick Has a Gifted Touch," *Boston Globe*, 24 December 2001, www.allthingsbillbelichick.com/articles/giftedtouch.htm.

[312] Buffalo Bills general manager Tom Donohoe, quoted in: Len Pasquarelli, "Belichick Becomes Life of Patriots' Party," *ESPN.com*, 22 December 2001, www.allthingsbillbelichick.com/articles/lifeofparty.htm.

[313] NFL Players Association statistics, cited in: John Clayton, "Patriots shopping spree pays off," *ESPN.com*, 20 December 2001, http://espn.go.com/nfl/columns/clayton_john/1298726.html.

[314] Patriots Vice President of Player Personnel Scott Pioli, quoted in: Michael Felger, "Pioli: Scout's Honor," *Boston Herald*, 19 December 2001, www.allthingsbillbelichick.com/articles/piolihonor.htm.

[315] Patriots safety Lawyer Milloy, quoted in: Bryan Morry, *Patriots United*, Canada: Team Power Publishing, 2002, p. 153.

[316] Cleveland Browns kicker Phil Dawson, quoted in: George Kimball, "Former Vinatieri understudy has proven to be …More than a Phil-in," *Boston Herald*, 5 December 2004, http://patriots.bostonherald.com/patriots/view.bg?articleid=57264.

[317] Patriots kicker Adam Vinatieri, quoted in: Shane Donaldson, "Patriots earn spot in AFC Championship game," *Patriots.com*, 20 January 2002, www.patriots.com/games/GamesDetails.sps?matchid=16435.

[318] Patriots running back Antowain Smith, quoted in: Jay Glazer, "Brady leads way as Patriots drive to shocking upset," *CBS Sportsline*, 4 February 2002, http://cbs.sportsline.com/b/page/pressbox/0,1328,4948886,00.html.

[319] Walt Coleman, quoted in: *NFL.com*, "Patriots win with late flurry of points," 19 January 2002, www.nfl.com/xxxvi/ce/recap/0,3895,NFL_20020119_OAK@NE.00.htm.

[320] Walt Coleman, quoted in: *Pro Football Weekly*, "Random quotes from around the NFL," 2 July 2003, www.profootballweekly.com/PFW/Features/They+Said+It/2003/said43.htm.

[321] Walt Coleman, quoted in: Henry C. Apple, "NFL referee reveals his human side to sports editors," *The Courier* (Russellville, Arkansas), 23 July 2004, www.couriernews.com/story.asp?ID=6231.

[322] John Clayton, "'Tuck rule' not among rule changes," *ESPN.com*, 20 March 2002 (?), http://espn.go.com/nfl/columns/clayton_john/1354105.html.

[323] Joel Buchsbaum, "Buchsbaum's impressions of the divisional playoff games," *Pro Football Weekly*, 21 January 2002, http://archive.profootballweekly.com/content/archives2001/features_2001/spin_012102.asp.

[324] Oakland cornerback Charles Woodson, quoted in: Peter Lawrence-Riddell, "Controversy thrives in Patriots-Raiders encounters," *ESPN*, http://espn.go.com/nfl/playoffs01/s/2002/0119/1314426.html.

[325] Oakland Raiders receiver Jerry Rice, quoted in: AP, "Ice man cometh," *Sports Illustrated*, 20 January 2002, http://sportsillustrated.cnn.com/football/2002/playoffs/news/2002/01/19/raiders_patriots_ap/.

[326] Tom Brady, quoted in: *NFL.com*, "Patriots win with late flurry of points," 19 January 2002, www.nfl.com/xxxvi/ce/recap/0,3895,NFL_20020119_OAK@NE.00.htm.

[327] Oakland Raiders owner Al Davis, quoted in: Henry C. Apple, "NFL referee reveals his human side to sports editors," *The Courier* (Russellville, Arkansas), 23 July 2004, www.couriernews.com/story.asp?ID=6231.

[328] Former Patriots defensive back Terrance Shaw, quoted in: John Ryan, "Raiders protest referees, walk out on them Tuesday," *Standard-Times*, 4 August 2002, www.southcoasttoday.com/daily/08-02/08-04-02/e04sp133.htm.

[329] Joel Buchsbaum, "Buchsbaum's impressions of the divisional playoff games," *Pro Football Weekly*, 21 January 2002, http://archive.profootballweekly.com/content/archives2001/features_2001/spin_012102.asp.

[330] Jim Donaldson, "Raider fans still whining? Hey, we've all 'Ben' there," *Providence Journal*, 17 November 2002, www.projo.com/sports/jimdonaldson/projo_20021117_17jdcol.50335.html.

[331] Pittsburgh Steelers receiver Hines Ward, quoted in: Ed Bouchette, "Steelers figure they owe Patriots a payback for 2002 AFC championship loss," *Pittsburgh Post-Gazette*, 31 October 2004, www.post-gazette.com/pg/04305/404012.stm.

[332] Defensive lineman Anthony Pleasant, quoted in: Hector Longo, "Patriots again bayou bound after Belichick baffles Kordell," *Eagle Tribune*, 28 January 2002, www.eagletribune.com/news/stories/20020128/SP_001.htm.

[333] Bill Belichick quoted in: Associated Press, "Drew story," *CNNSI.com*, 28 January 2002, http://sportsillustrated.cnn.com/football/2002/playoffs/news/2002/01/27/patriots_steelers_ap/.

[334] Bill Belichick, as quoted by his father Steve Belichick, in: Hank Gola, "Patriots find their destiny," *South Coast Today*, 8 February 2002, www.s-t.com/daily/02-02/02-08-02/d06ae114.htm. The same story with slightly different wording is presented in: Ken Denlinger, "Coaching Out of the Blocks," *Washington Post*, 2002 (no date cited), www.allthingsbillbelichick.com/articles/outoftheblocks.htm and Michael Gee, "Belichicks Follow Paternal Instinct," *Boston Herald*, no date mentioned, www.allthingsbillbelichick.com/articles/followpaternal.htm.

[335] Steelers receiver Hines Ward, cited in: Ed Bouchette, "Steelers figure they owe Patriots a payback for 2002 AFC championship loss," *Pittsburgh Post-Gazette*, 31 October 2004, www.post-gazette.com/pg/04305/404012.stm.

[336] Vic Carucci, "Face it, Pats: Luck is on your side," *NFL Insider*, 27 January 2002, www.nfl.com/xxxvi/ce/feature/0,3892,4904282,00.html.

[337] Bob Ryan, "Rams invincible? Hardly," *Boston Globe*, 3 February 2002, www.boston.com/sports/football/patriots/superbowl/globe_stories/020302/rams_invincible_hardly+.shtml.

[338] Bill Belichick, as quoted by his father Steve Belichick, in: Hank Gola, "Patriots find their destiny," *South Coast Today*, 8 February 2002, www.s-t.com/daily/02-02/02-08-02/d06ae114.htm.

[339] Ron Wolf, "What they say about Belichick," www.patriots.com/team/Personal.sps?biotextid=4320&playerid=506&playertype=2.

[340] Ron Jaworski, ESPN commentator and former NFL great, quoted in: "What they say about Belichick," www.patriots.com/team/Personal.sps?biotextid=4320&playerid=506&playertype=2.

[341] Rams coach Mike Martz, quoted in: "What they say about Belichick," www.patriots.com/team/Personal.sps?biotextid=4320&playerid=506&playertype=2.

[342] Hall of Fame coach Don Shula, quoted in: Michael Holley, "Shula impressed by streak," Boston Globe, 21 January 2004, www.boston.com/sports/football/patriots/articles/2004/01/21/shula_impressed_by_streak/.

[343] Former Patriots safety Lawyer Milloy, quoted in: "What they say about Belichick," www.patriots.com/team/Personal.sps?biotextid=4320&playerid=506&playertype=2.

[344] Patriots linebacker Tedy Bruschi, quoted in: Bill Burt, "Bruschi a true blue Patriot," *Eagle Tribune*, 31 January 2002, www.eagletribune.com/news/stories/20020131/SP_004.htm.

[345] Patriots quarterback Tom Brady, quoted in: AP, "Third time's a charm," *CNNSI.com*, 3 February 2002, http://sportsillustrated.cnn.com/football/2002/playoffs/news/2002/02/03/rams_patriots_ap/.

[346] Patriots quarterback Tom Brady, quoted in: AP, "Bunch of success," *CNNSI.com*, 4 February 2002, http://sportsillustrated.cnn.com/football/2002/playoffs/news/2002/02/03/brady_mvp_ap/.

[347] Patriots quarterback Tom Brady, quoted in: *BBC*, "Pats' Brady hunch pays off," 4 February 2002, http://news.bbc.co.uk/sport1/hi/other_sports/sun/1799953.stm.

[348] Patriots offensive lineman Damien Woody, quoted in: Nick Cafardo, *The Impossible Team*, Triumph Books, 2002, p. 4.

[349] Patriots safety Lawyer Milloy, quoted in: Jon Saraceno, "Patriots prove to be no patsies," *USA Today*, 4 February 2002, www.usatoday.com/sports/comment/saraceno/2002-02-04-saraceno.htm.

[350] "Jeff Sagarin NFL ratings," www.usatoday.com/sports/sagarin/nfl01.htm.

[351] Bill Belichick, quoted in: Bryan McGovern, "Patriot Day," *The Sports Network*, 3 February 2002, www.sportsnetwork.com/default.asp?c=sportsnetwork&page=nfl/misc/mcgovern/nfl-weekly-020302.htm.

[352] Bill Belichick, quoted in: Peter King, "The sincerest form of flattery," *Sports Illustrated*, 4 February 2002, http://sportsillustrated.cnn.com/inside_game/peter_king/news/2002/02/04/mmqb/.

[353] Michael Holbrook, "Super Bowl musings," *Pro Football Weekly*, 3 February 2002, http://archive.profootballweekly.com/content/archives2001/features_2001/sb_0203022.asp.

[354] Patriots linebacker Willie McGinest, quoted in: *Patriots United*, Canada: Team Power Publishing, 2002, p. 197.

[355] Rams linebacker London Fletcher, quoted in: NFL, "Official Super Bowl XXXVI game summary," www.absolutebrady.com/SB36.html.

[356] Michael Holbrook, "Super Bowl musings," *Pro Football Weekly*, 3 February 2002, http://archive.profootballweekly.com/content/archives2001/features_2001/sb_0203022.asp.

[357] Pete Thamel, "Patriots' Super Bowl Seems Like Long Ago," *New York Times*, 11 September 2003, p. D3, ProQuest database.

[358] Patriots wide receiver Troy Brown, foreword to: Nick Cafardo, *The Impossible Team*, Triumph Books, 2002, p. *ix*.

[359] Bill Belichick, quoted in: Alan Greenberg, "RING TRILOGY ; PATS BEGIN QUEST FOR TITLE NO. 3," *Hartford Courant*, 27 July 2004, p. C3, ProQuest database.

[360] Bill Belichick, quoted in: Tom E. Curran, "For Pats, it'll be hard work defending title," *Providence Journal*, 28 July 2004, www.projo.com/patriots/content/projo_20040728_28pats.5df0.html.

[361] Kevin Gleason, "We love NFL because 'on any given Sunday…'" *Times Herald-Record*, 24 November 2002, www.recordonline.com/archive/2002/11/24/kkgsunda.htm.

[362] Bill Belichick, quoted in: Don Banks, "Five Questions with … Bill Belichick," *Sports Illustrated*, 17 August 2004, http://sportsillustrated.cnn.com/2004/football/nfl/specials/preview/2004/08/17/fivequestion.belichick/.

[363] Michael Holley, *Patriot Reign*, William Morrow, 2004, p. 142.

[364] Bill Belichick, quoted in: Rodney McKissic, "Bills hope to derail Patriots' express," *Buffalo News*, 28 September 2004, www.buffalonews.com/editorial/20040928/1027154.asp.

[365] Denver Broncos head coach Mike Shanahan, quoted in: Peter King, "Most NFL teams have a Super chance," *Sports Illustrated*, 24 January 2001, http://sportsillustrated.cnn.com/football/nfl/2001/playoffs/news/2001/01/24/king_fivethings/.

[366] Oakland Raiders owner Al Davis, quoted in: Bill Williamson, "Broncos fined money, pick," *Denver Post*, 17 September 2004, www.denverpost.com/Stories/0,1413,36~86~2407549,00.html.

[367] Mark Kiszla, "Shame part of Broncos' shine," *Denver Post*, 17 September 2004, www.denverpost.com/Stories/0,1413,36%257E86%257E2407550,00.html.

[368] Phil Simms, quoted in: Mark Maske, "Patriots, Looking to Buck Trend, Appear Stronger," *Washington Post*, 9 September 2004, www.washingtonpost.com/wp-dyn/articles/A8704-2004Sep9.html.

[369] Troy Aikman, "Consistent, resilient Eagles can't be forgotten," *NFL.com*, 27 October 2004, www.nfl.com/news/story/7833901.

[370] Super Bowl-winning former Dallas Cowboys quarterback Troy Aikman, quoted in: Tom Pedulla, "Patriots feel Super with 'extra ingredient' Dillon," *USA Today*, 22 July 2004, www.usatoday.com/sports/football/nfl/patriots/2004-07-22-camp_x.htm.

[371] Bill Belichick, "O.K. Champ, Now Comes the Hard Part," *New York Times*, 26 January 2003, www.allthingsbillbelichick.com/articles/okchamp.html.

[372] Patriots kicker Adam Vinatieri, quoted in: Glen Farley, "Patriots ready to defend," *The Enterprise*, 25 July 2004, http://enterprise.southofboston.com/articles/2004/07/25/news/sports/sports02.txt.

[373] Patriots offensive guard Joe Andruzzi, quoted in: Michael Felger, "Pats gear for trip back to the top," *Boston Herald*, 29 July 2004, http://patriots.bostonherald.com/patriots/view.bg?articleid=37690.

[374] Patriots safety Rodney Harrison, quoted in: Michael Felger, "Loss leaves bad taste: Patriots can't respond to Bengals' best shot," *Boston Herald*, 24 August 2004, http://patriots.bostonherald.com/patriots/view.bg?articleid=41138.

[375] Bill Belichick, "O.K. Champ, Now Comes the Hard Part," *New York Times*, 26 January 2003, www.allthingsbillbelichick.com/articles/okchamp.html.

[376] Tim O'Sullivan, " All eyes on the big prize: Top pick Wilfork adjusts to life with the champions," *Concord Monitor*, 11 August 2004, www.concordmonitor.com/apps/pbcs.dll/article?Date=20040811&Category=REPOSITORY&ArtNo=408110355&SectionCat=SPORTS&Template=printart.

[377] Len Pasquarelli, "Patriots suddenly struggling to address woes," *ESPN*, 31 October 2002, http://espn.go.com/nfl/columns/pasquarelli_len/1453171.html.

[378] Unnamed Patriot player, quoted in: Len Pasquarelli, "Patriots suddenly struggling to address woes," *ESPN*, 31 October 2002, http://espn.go.com/nfl/columns/pasquarelli_len/1453171.html.

[379] Patriots defensive lineman Richard Seymour, quoted in: Alan Greenberg, "Belichick's Chief Concern Is Only What Lies Ahead," *Hartford Courant*, 17 September 2002, p. C3, ProQuest database.

[380] Patriots center Damien Woody, quoted in: Alan Greenberg, "Belichick's Chief Concern Is Only What Lies Ahead," *Hartford Courant*, 17 September 2002, p. C3, ProQuest database.

[381] Michael Holley, *Patriot Reign*, William Morrow, 2004, p. 114.

[382] Former Patriots backup quarterback Damon Huard, quoted in: Randy Covitz, "Patriots' formula for success makes it envy of NFL," *Kansas City Star*, 8 September 2004, www.kansascity.com/mld/kansascity/sports/football/nfl/kansas_city_chiefs/9603764.htm?1c.

[383] Tom Brady, quoted in: Tom Pedulla, "Patriots feel Super with 'extra ingredient' Dillon," *USA Today*, 22 July 2004, www.usatoday.com/sports/football/nfl/patriots/2004-07-22-camp_x.htm.

[384] Miami Dolphins, "Historical Highlights," www.miamidolphins.com/history/historicalhighlights/historicalhighlights17.asp.

[385] Patriots safety Rodney Harrison, quoted in: Associated Press, "Pats' Harrison gets back to winning ways," 14 January 2004, http://msnbc.msn.com/id/3960632/.

[386] Len Pasquarelli, "Picks give Patriots flexibility in draft," *ESPN.com*, 20 April 2004, http://espn.go.com/nfldraft/draft04/columns/story?columnist=pasquarelli_len&id=1786175.

[387] Dan Pires, "Inside the Patriots: An interesting effort," *Standard-Times*, 30 August 2004, www.southcoasttoday.com/daily/08-04/08-30-04/c07sp277.htm.

[388] Rick Gosselin, "Patriots' organization stacks up with Cowboys of early '90s," *Dallas Morning News*, 30 January 2004, www.cowboysplus.com/columnists/rgosselin/stories/013004cpgosselin.41d23.html.

[389] Patriots coach Bill Belichick, quoted in: Jim Donaldson, "Dictionary helps in describing the Pats," *Providence Journal*, 13 October 2003, www.projo.com/patriots/content/projo_20031013_13jdcol.1e250.html.

[390] Patriots coach Bill Belichick, quoted in: Michael Murphy, "Pats positioned to keep winning," *Houston Chronicle*, 3 February 2004, www.chron.com/cs/CDA/ssistory.mpl/special/04/sb/2384506.

[391] Many of these stats can be found at http://sports.espn.go.com/nfl/statistics?stat=teampass&pos=def&league=nfl&season=2&year=2003.

[392] www.vegas.com/gaming/futures/superbowl.html, 5 August 2003.

[393] Patriots coach Bill Belichick, quoted in: Nick Cafardo, "For coach, it's hard to relate," *Boston Globe*, 2 February 2004, www.boston.com/sports/football/articles/2004/02/02/for_coach_its_hard_to_relate/.

[394] Patriots coach Bill Belichick, quoted in: Mark Maske, "Selfless Patriots show how it's done," *Washington Post*, 4 February 2004, www.msnbc.msn.com/id/4144383/.

[395] 1972 Dolphins head coach Don Shula, quoted in: Armando Salguero, "No equal to '72 team," *Miami Herald*, 15 September 2004, www.miami.com/mld/miamiherald/sports/football/9665703.htm?1c.

[396] Hall of Fame head coach Bill Walsh (formerly of the San Francisco 49ers), quoted in: Kevin Paul Dupont, "Winner's Circle," *Boston Globe*, 23 January 2004, www.boston.com/sports/football/patriots/articles/2004/01/23/winners_circle/.

[397] 1972 Dolphins linebacker Nick Buoniconti, quoted in: Armando Salguero, "No equal to '72 team," *Miami Herald*, 15 September 2004, www.miami.com/mld/miamiherald/sports/football/9665703.htm?1c.

[398] Dolphins running back Jim Kiick, quoted in: Greg A. Bedard, "The Patriots can't lose," *Palm Beach Post*, 8 October 2004, www.palmbeachpost.com/sports/content/sports/epaper/2004/10/08/a1b_patriots_100804.html.

[399] 1972 Dolphins running back Eugene "Mercury" Morris, quoted in: Joe Burris, "Not a perfect match," *Boston Globe*, 10 October 2004, www.boston.com/sports/articles/2004/10/10/not_a_perfect_match.

[400] 1972 Dolphins offensive lineman Bob Kuechenberg, quoted in: Joe Burris, "Not a perfect match," *Boston Globe*, 10 October 2004, www.boston.com/sports/articles/2004/10/10/not_a_perfect_match.

[401] 1972 Dolphins tight end Jim Mandich, quoted in: Karen Guregian, "Playing with a porpoise: In streaking toward greatness, Pats have makeup similar to famed 1972 Dolphins," *Boston Herald*, 3 October 2004, http://patriots.bostonherald.com/patriots/view.bg?articleid=47143.

[402] 1972 Dolphins tight end Jim Mandich, quoted in: Leonard Shapiro, "On Record, Patriots Just Don't Care," *Washington Post*, 9 October 2004, p. D1, www.washingtonpost.com/wp-dyn/articles/A18426-2004Oct8.html.

[403] 1972 Dolphins tight end Jim Mandich, "Perfect Argument," *Sports Illustrated*, 18 October 2004, p. 71.

[404] 1972 Dolphins tight end Jim Mandich, "Perfect Argument," *Sports Illustrated*, 18 October 2004, p. 71.

[405] Tom E. Curran, "Patriots Notebook: '72 Dolphins stubbornly refuse to acknowledge Pats' streak," *Providence Journal*, 17 September 2004, www.projo.com/patriots/content/projo_20040917_17patsjo.1377c6.html.

[406] 1972 Dolphins defender Dick Anderson, quoted in: Karen Guregian, "Playing with a porpoise: In streaking toward greatness, Pats have makeup similar to famed 1972 Dolphins," *Boston Herald*, 3 October 2004, http://patriots.bostonherald.com/patriots/view.bg?articleid=47143.

[407] Defensive tackle Manny Fernandez, quoted in: Greg A. Bedard, "The Patriots can't lose," *Palm Beach Post*, 8 October 2004, www.palmbeachpost.com/sports/content/sports/epaper/2004/10/08/a1b_patriots_100804.html.

[408] Defensive tackle Manny Fernandez, quoted in: Greg A. Bedard, "The Patriots can't lose," *Palm Beach Post*, 8 October 2004, www.palmbeachpost.com/sports/content/sports/epaper/2004/10/08/a1b_patriots_100804.html.

[409] 1972 Dolphins offensive lineman Bob Kuechenberg, quoted in: Karen Guregian, "Playing with a porpoise: In streaking toward greatness, Pats have makeup similar to famed 1972 Dolphins," *Boston Herald*, 3 October 2004, http://patriots.bostonherald.com/patriots/view.bg?articleid=47143.

[410] 1972 Dolphins head coach Don Shula, quoted in: Steven Wine (AP), "Shula says Patriots could go 19-0," *San Francisco Chronicle*, 5 October 2004, http://sfgate.com/cgi-bin/article.cgi?f=/news/archive/2004/10/05/sports1646EDT0199.DTL.

[411] 1972 Dolphins linebacker Nick Buoniconti, quoted in: Karen Guregian, "Playing with a porpoise: In streaking toward greatness, Pats have makeup similar to famed 1972 Dolphins," *Boston Herald*, 3 October 2004, http://patriots.bostonherald.com/patriots/view.bg?articleid=47143.

[412] www.hickoksports.com/history/nfldraft1970.shtml; www.hickoksports.com/history/nfldraft1971.shtml; www.hickoksports.com/history/nfldraft1972.shtml.

[413] Peter King, "The Patriots' streak rules," *Sports Illustrated*, 30 September 2004, http://sportsillustrated.cnn.com/2004/football/nfl/09/30/h2h.patriots/.

[414] Jay Mariotti, "Patriots build modern sports dynasty," *Chicago Sun-Times*, 11 October 2004, www.suntimes.com/output/mariotti/cst-spt-jay111.html.

[415] Clark Judge, "Week 5 Judgements: Time to use the D-word?" *CBS Sportsline*, 11 October 2004, www.sportsline.com/nfl/story/7782957.

[416] David Whitley (*Orlando Sentinel*), "Patriots follow genius to best NFL streak ever," *Centre Daily Times*, 15 October 2004, www.centredaily.com/mld/centredaily/9922616.htm.

[417] 1972 Dolphins head coach Don Shula, quoted in: Jim Donaldson, "Shula: Pats the best, but not perfect yet," *Providence Journal*, 6 October 2004, www.projo.com/sports/jimdonaldson/projo_20041006_06jdcol.1629bd.html.

[418] 1972 Dolphins tight end Jim Mandich, quoted in: Karen Guregian, "Playing with a porpoise: In streaking toward greatness, Pats have makeup similar to famed 1972 Dolphins," *Boston Herald*, 3 October 2004, http://patriots.bostonherald.com/patriots/view.bg?articleid=47143.

[419] 1972 Dolphins running back Eugene "Mercury" Morris, quoted in: Joe Burris, "Not a perfect match," *Boston Globe*, 10 October 2004, www.boston.com/sports/articles/2004/10/10/not_a_perfect_match.

[420] 1972 Dolphins head coach Don Shula, quoted by running back Eugene "Mercury" Morris, in: Joe Burris, "Not a perfect match," *Boston Globe*, 10 October 2004, www.boston.com/sports/articles/2004/10/10/not_a_perfect_match.

[421] Patriots cornerback Ty Law, quoted in: Rich Thompson, "Streak on back burner," *Boston Herald*, 5 October 2004, http://patriots.bostonherald.com/patriots/view.bg?articleid=47463.

[422] Don Shula, quoted in: Alan Greenberg, "Patriots: Streak? What Streak?" *Hartford Courant*, 26 September 2004, www.ctnow.com/sports/hc-patsstreak0926.artsep26,1,3170251,print.story.

[423] 1972 Dolphins head coach Don Shula, quoted in: Jim Donaldson, "Shula: Pats the best, but not perfect yet," *Providence Journal*, 6 October 2004, www.projo.com/sports/jimdonaldson/projo_20041006_06jdcol.1629bd.html.

[424] Patriots kicker Adam Vinatieri, quoted in: Bryan McGovern, "Patriot Day," *The Sports Network*, 3 February 2002, www.sportsnetwork.com/default.asp?c=sportsnetwork&page=nfl/misc/mcgovern/nfl-weekly-020302.htm.

[425] Bill Belichick, quoted in: Ed Duckworth, "Belichick crafts new image," *New England Sports Service*, 6 June 2000, www.standardtimes.com/daily/06-00/06-06-00/c02sp105.htm.

[426] Patriots owner Bob Kraft, quoted in: Dave Goldberg (AP), "New England and Washington: NFL free agency contrasts," *Yahoo! Canada Sports*, 27 February 2004, http://ca.sports.yahoo.com/040227/6/wxki.html.

[427] Patriots director of football research Ernie Adams, quoted in: Pete Thamel, "Low-Key Adams Makes High Impact on Patriots," *New York Times*, 16 January 2004, p. D7, ProQuest database.

[428] Former Patriot Terrell Buckley, quoted in: Mark Cannizzaro, "Showdown hype can't be ignored," *New York Post*, 18 October 2004, www.nypost.com/sports/jets/30587.htm.

[429] *ESPN* commentator Trey Wingo, "Wingo: Team introduction is way cool," *ESPN*, 5 January 2002, http://espn.go.com/espnradio/extrapointindex020201_020215.html.

[430] Patriots cornerback Ty Law, quoted in: Michael Smith, "Look for a team effort," *Boston Globe*, 30 January 2004, www.boston.com/sports/football/patriots/articles/2004/01/30/look_for_a_team_effort/.

[431] Michael Felger, "Belichick method comes full circle," *Boston Herald*, 3 May 2004, http://patriots.bostonherald.com/patriots/view.bg?articleid=18878.

[432] Tom Brady, quoted in: *Patriots United*, Canada: Team Power Publishing, 2002, p. 208.

[433] Tom Brady, quoted in: Bryan McGovern, "Patriot Day," *The Sports Network*, 3 February 2002, www.sportsnetwork.com/default.asp?c=sportsnetwork&page=nfl/misc/mcgovern/nfl-weekly-020302.htm.

[434] Patriots defensive lineman Richard Seymour, quoted in: Michael Smith, "Look for a team effort," *Boston Globe*, 30 January 2004, www.boston.com/sports/football/patriots/articles/2004/01/30/look_for_a_team_effort/.

[435] Patriots offensive coordinator Charlie Weis, quoted in: Jeff Reynolds, "Brady, coordinator share special bond," *Pro Football Weekly*, 31 January 2004, www.profootballweekly.com/PFW/NFL/AFC/AFC+East/New+England/Features/2004/reynolds013104.htm.

[436] Patriots offensive coordinator Charlie Weis, quoted in: Jeff Reynolds, "Brady, coordinator share special bond," *Pro Football Weekly*, 31 January 2004, www.profootballweekly.com/PFW/NFL/AFC/AFC+East/New+England/Features/2004/reynolds013104.htm.

[437] Jeff Reynolds, "Brady, coordinator share special bond," *Pro Football Weekly*, 31 January 2004, www.profootballweekly.com/PFW/NFL/AFC/AFC+East/New+England/Features/2004/reynolds013104.htm.

[438] Bill Belichick, quoted in: Tom E. Curran, "Patriots Notebook: Belichick points finger at himself for loss to Bills," *Providence Journal*, 11 September 2003, www.projo.com/patriots/content/projo_20030911_11patsjo.24d37.html.

[439] Patriots owner Bob Kraft, quoted in: Jimmy Golen (AP), "Baying the Bill," *SouthCoast Today*, 28 January 2000, www.s-t.com/daily/01-00/01-28-00/d01sp116.htm.

[440] Peter Drucker, *The Practice of Management*, 1954, p. 157.

[441] Patriots linebacker Tedy Bruschi, quoted in: *Patriots United*, Canada: Team Power Publishing, 2002, p. 212.

[442] Safety Rodney Harrison, quoted in: Peter May, "Master of the plan," *Boston Globe*, 3 February 2004, www.boston.com/sports/football/patriots/articles/2004/02/03/master_of_the_plan/.

[443] Michael Holley, *Patriot Reign*, William Morrow, 2004, p. 124-5.

[444] Tom Brady, quoted in: Tom E. Curran, "Patriots Notebook: Team is fast out of the gate," *Providence Journal*, 11 June 2004, www.projo.com/patriots/content/projo_20040611_11patsjo.fcc1f.html.

[445] New Patriots linebackers coach Dean Pees, quoted in: Michael Smith, "Dream Team," *Boston Globe*, 9 September 2004, www.boston.com/sports/football/patriots/articles/2004/09/09/dream_team.

[446] New Patriots linebackers coach Dean Pees, quoted in: Michael Smith, "Dream Team," *Boston Globe*, 9 September 2004, www.boston.com/sports/football/patriots/articles/2004/09/09/dream_team.

[447] Patriots defensive lineman Richard Seymour, quoted in: Michael Smith, "Dream Team," *Boston Globe*, 9 September 2004, www.boston.com/sports/football/patriots/articles/2004/09/09/dream_team.

[448] Patriots linebacker Mike Vrabel, quoted in: Jackie MacMullen, "Willie McGinest," in: *Again!*, Chicago: Triumph Books, 2004, p. 117.

[449] Patriot offensive lineman Tom Ashworth, quoted in: Nick Cafardo, "Brady braces for rush jobs," *Boston Globe*, 12 October 2004, www.boston.com/sports/football/patriots/articles/2004/10/12/brady_braces_for_rush_jobs.

[450] Tom Brady, quoted in: Peter King, "Cool Comparison," *ESPN*, 9 February 2004, http://sportsillustrated.cnn.com/2004/writers/peter_king/02/09/mmqb/.

[451] Linebacker Tedy Bruschi, quoted in: Nick Cafardo, "A Battle of QBs," *Boston Globe*, 12 September 2003, www.boston.com/sports/football/patriots/extras/asknick/09_12_03.

[452] Patriot Dan Klecko, quoted in: Chris Kennedy, "Klecko OK with roles," *MassLive.com*, 6 August 2004, www.masslive.com/printer/printer.ssf?/base/sports-2/10917819456431.xml.

[453] Pro Bowl offensive tackle James "Big Cat" Williams, quoted in: Rich Thompson, "'Big Cat's focus: right tackle," *Boston Herald*, www.metrowestdailynews.com/sportsNews/view.bg?articleid=74347.

[454] Patriots offensive lineman Tom Ashworth, quoted in: Judy Battista, "A Season-Long Victory Shuffle," *New York Times*, 10 January 2004, D1, ProQuest database.

[455] Doug Farrar, "MMQB – 'Patriot Games,'" *Seahawks.net*, 13 September 2004, http://seahawks.theinsiders.com/2/293907.html.

[456] Patriots center Dan Koppen, quoted in: Rich Thompson, "Dillon gives Pats a decisive leg up," *Boston Herald*, 28 September 2004, http://patriots.bostonherald.com/patriots/view.bg?articleid=46336.

[457] Patriots owner Bob Kraft, quoted in: Nick Cafardo, "For coach, it's hard to relate," *Boston Globe*, 2 February 2004, www.boston.com/sports/football/patriots/articles/2004/02/02/for_coach_its_hard_to_relate/.

[458] 36-year-old Patriots linebacker Roman Phifer, quoted in: Nick Cafardo, "Phifer still has that old touch," *Boston Globe*, 28 September 2004, www.boston.com/sports/football/patriots/articles/2004/09/28/phifer_still_has_that_old_touch.

[459] Running back Corey Dillon, quoted in: Ron Indrisano, "Dillon's determination not questionable," *Boston Globe*, 18 October 2004, www.boston.com/sports/football/patriots/articles/2004/10/18/dillons_determination_not_questionable/.

[460] Tory Holt, St. Louis Rams wide receiver, 2 March 2002, in: "What they say about Belichick," www.patriots.com/team/Personal.sps?biotextid=4320&playerid=506&playertype=2.

[461] Patriots cornerback Ty Law, quoted in: AP, "Third time's a charm," *CNNSI.com*, 3 February 2002, http://sportsillustrated.cnn.com/football/2002/playoffs/news/2002/02/03/rams_patriots_ap/.

[462] Patriots linebacker Mike Vrabel, quoted in: John Hassan, "Inside Belichick's Brain," *ESPN The Magazine*, 9 September 2002, www.allthingsbillbelichick.com/articles/insidebrain.htm.

[463] Miami (twice), Indianapolis (twice), Tennessee (twice), Denver, Dallas, Philadelphia, and Carolina.

[464] According to the final 2003 Sagarin's Eatings.

[465] Michael Silver, "What a Finish!" *Sports Illustrated*, Championship Edition, 11 February 2004, p. 58.

[466] Hector Longo, "Injuries force Patriots to mix it up offensively," *Eagle Tribune*, 23 November 2003, www.eagletribune.com/news/stories/20031123/SP_013.htm.

[467] Phil Simms, quoted in: Jeff Goodman, "Once Unwanted, Belichick Is the Savior of New England," *Washington Post*, 28 November 2003, D9, ProQuest database.

[468] Tom Brady, quoted in: Sam Farmer, "Turning Up the Heat; Snow is in the forecast, but Pollard's comments light a fire under Patriots," *Los Angeles Times*, 18 January 2004, p. D12, ProQuest database.

[469] Patriots safety Rodney Harrison, quoted in: Vic Carucci, "Pats' defense already in championship form," 18 January 2004, www.superbowl.com/playoffs/story/7017737.

[470] Patriots linebacker Tedy Bruschi, quoted in: Kevin Mannix, "'Backer to the basics: Johnson goes old school," *Boston Herald*, 25 October 2004, http://patriots.bostonherald.com/patriots/view.bg?articleid=50697.

[471] Karen Price, "Business of sport is no game," *Tribune-Review*, 12 September 20004, http://pittsburghlive.com/x/tribune-review/sports/s_250331.html.

[472] Patriots offensive coordinator Charlie Weis, quoted in: Frank Tadych, "Patriots Notebook: Weis high on Brady," *Patriots.com*, 23 September 2004, www.patriots.com/news/FullArticle.sps?id=31308.

[473] Patriots Vice President of Player Personnel Scott Pioli, quoted in: Jimmy Golen, *Associated Press*, "Patriots get their players, their way," *Boston Globe*, 2/7/2004.

[474] Multiple Super Bowl-winning coach Jimmy Johnson, quoted in: "WEEK 6: Pregame show hits the road for Seattle-New England," 15 October 2004 (approximately), http://msn.foxsports.com/story/3082476.

[475] Fox NFL analyst Howie Long, quoted in: "WEEK 6: Pregame show hits the road for Seattle-New England," 15 October 2004 (approximately), http://msn.foxsports.com/story/3082476.

[476] Bill Belichick, quoted in: Jim McCabe, "It was nothing to kick about," *Boston Globe*, 19 October 2004, www.boston.com/sports/football/patriots/articles/2004/10/19/it_was_nothing_to_kick_about.

[477] Bill Belichick, "Bill Belichick Press Conf. Transcript - 4/30," *Patriots.com*, 30 April 2004, www.patriots.com/news/FullArticle.sps?id=28597&type=general.

[478] Kansas City Chiefs general manager Carl Peterson, quoted in: Randy Covitz, "Patriots' formula for success makes it envy of NFL," *Kansas City Star*, 8 September 2004, www.kansascity.com/mld/kansascity/sports/football/nfl/kansas_city_chiefs/9603764.htm?1c.

[479] Multiple Super Bowl-winning coach Jimmy Johnson, quoted in: "WEEK 6: Pregame show hits the road for Seattle-New England," 15 October 2004 (approximately), http://msn.foxsports.com/story/3082476.

[480] Patriots cornerback Ty Law, quoted in: Peter King, "A League of Their Own," *Sports Illustrated*, 18 October 2004, p. 70.

[481] Patriots Vice President of Player Personnel Scott Pioli, quoted in: Dan Pompei, "Scott Pioli, Patriots (TSN NFL Executive Of The Year)," *The Sporting News*, www.findarticles.com/cf_dls/m1208/14_228/114985732/p1/article.jhtml.

[482] Bill Belichick, after defeating the Rams in Super Bowl XXXVI, quoted in: Len Pasquarelli, "Coach, QB rewarded for Super Bowl heroics," *ESPN.com*, 4 February 2002, http://espn.go.com/nfl/playoffs01/columns/pasquarelli_len/1322633.html.

[483] Dr. Peter F. Drucker, *Management: Tasks, Responsibilities, Practices*, USA: HarperCollins, 1973, pp. 187-8.

[484] Patriots linebacker Mike Vrabel, quoted in: Jackie MacMullen, "Tedy Bruschi," in: *Again!*, Chicago: Triumph Books, 2004, p. 121.

[485] Quotations from: Michael Silver, "All Systems Go," *Sports Illustrated*, Championship Edition, 11 February 2004, p. 49.

[486] Patriots special teams captain Larry Izzo, quoted in: Jerome Solomon, "Hometown heroes save the day," *Houston Chronicle*, 2 February 2004, www.chron.com/cs/CDA/printstory.mpl/special/04/sb/2383088.

[487] Patriots linebacker Matt Chatham, quoted in: Dan Pires, "Postgame talk ranges from Sapp to streaker," *Standard-Times*, 4 February 2004, www.southcoasttoday.com/daily/02-04/02-04-04/c01sp273.htm.

[488] Patriots special teams captain Larry Izzo, quoted in: NFL, "Official Super Bowl XXXVI game summary," www.absolutebrady.com/SB36.html.

[489] Patriots left tackle Matt Light, quoted in: Ken Berger, "Pats' offensive line has last laugh," *Newsday*, 1 February 2004, www.southcoasttoday.com/daily/02-04/02-01-04/e03sp876.htm.

[490] Charles P. Pierce, "The Patriot," *Boston Globe*, 5 September 2004, www.boston.com/news/globe/magazine/articles/2004/09/05/the_patriot/.

[491] Matt Light and Dan Klecko, quoted in: Hector Longo, "Light makes might," *Eagle Tribune*, 28 January 2004, www.eagletribune.com/news/stories/20040128/SP_001.htm.

[492] Patriots left tackle Matt Light, quoted in: Chris Kennedy, "Brady's offensive line worries tackled," *MassLive.com*, www.masslive.com/printer/printer.ssf?/base/sports-0/1092734127304750.xml.

[493] Patriots left tackle Matt Light, "Patriots Video News," *Patriots.com*, 18 August 2004.

[494] Patriots left tackle Matt Light, "Patriots Video News," *Patriots.com*, 18 August 2004.

[495] Adam Kilgore, "Smiles, on further review," *Boston Globe*, 27 August 2004, www.boston.com/sports/football/patriots/articles/2004/08/27/smiles_on_further_review.

[496] Offensive lineman Russ Hochstein, quoted in: Tom E. Curran, "Massive Hochstein won't joust with smart alecks," *Providence Journal*, 29 August 2004, www.projo.com/patriots/content/projo_20040829_29quest.163aa7.html.

[497] Tom Brady, quoted in: Nick Cafardo, "Light decides to stay awhile," *Boston Globe*, 7 October 2004, www.boston.com/sports/football/patriots/articles/2004/10/07/light_decides_to_stay_awhile.

[498] "The Makeover of Matt Light: Team Survey," www.boston.com/yourlife/fashion/makeover/matt_light/his_friends/.

[499] "The Makeover of Matt Light: Team Survey," www.boston.com/yourlife/fashion/makeover/matt_light/his_friends/.

[500] "The Makeover of Matt Light: Team Survey," www.boston.com/yourlife/fashion/makeover/matt_light/his_friends/.

[501] "The Makeover of Matt Light: Team Survey," www.boston.com/yourlife/fashion/makeover/matt_light/his_friends/.

[502] Patriots defensive lineman Richard Seymour, "Camp Daze," in: Bryan Morry, *Patriots United*, Canada: Team Power Publishing, 2002, p. 58.

[503] Patriots defensive back Victor Green, quoted in: AP, "Patriots dominant again in rout of Jets," *NFL.com*, 15 September 2002, www.nfl.com/gamecenter/recap/NFL_20020915_NE@NYJ.

[504] Jeff Jacobs, "Dumped By Jets, Green Picks Up Game Ball," *Hartford Courant*, 16 September 2002, p. C1, ProQuest database.

[505] Patriots defensive lineman Richard Seymour, quoted in: Jim McCabe, "Dillon has a gang of admirers," *Boston Globe*, 19 October 2004, www.boston.com/sports/football/patriots/articles/2004/10/19/dillon_has_a_gang_of_admirers.

[506] Linebacker Mike Vrabel, quoted in: Michael Smith, "Ruling on field: complete," *Boston Globe*, 13 June 2004, www.boston.com/sports/football/patriots/articles/2004/06/13/ruling_on_field_complete/.

[507] Patriots punter Josh Miller, quoted in: Tom King, "Miller gets his kicks," *The Nashua Telegraph*, 28 October 2004, www.nashuatelegraph.com/apps/pbcs.dll/article?AID=/20041028/SPORTS/41028027/-1/sports.

[508] Patriots punter Josh Miller, quoted in: Joe Burris, "Punter Miller a return man this week," *Boston Globe*, 28 October 2004, www.boston.com/sports/football/patriots/articles/2004/10/28/punter_miller_a_return_man_this_week.

[509] Patriots punter Josh Miller, quoted in: Rich Thompson, "Miller steps right in: Win-win situation for Pats' new punter," *Boston Herald*, 9 September 2004, http://patriots.bostonherald.com/patriots/view.bg?articleid=43420.

[510] Patriots punter Josh Miller, "Patriots Video News," 12 October 2004, http://originwww.patriots.com/mediacenter/index.cfm?ac=VideoNewsDetail&pid=9282&pcid=78.

[511] Patriots punter Josh Miller, "Patriots Video News," 12 October 2004, http://originwww.patriots.com/mediacenter/index.cfm?ac=VideoNewsDetail&pid=9282&pcid=78.

[512] Patriots punter Josh Miller, "Patriots Video News," 27 October 2004,
http://cachewww.patriots.com/mediacenter/index.cfm?ac=videonewsdetail&pid=9484&pcid=78.
[513] Patriots linebacker Roman Phifer, quoted in: Chris Kennedy, "Phifer enjoys jokes, respect," *MassLive.com*, 9 August 2004,
www.masslive.com/sports/republican/index.ssf?/base/sports-0/1092041272304.xml.
[514] Patriots linebacker Rosevelt Colvin, quoted in: Michael Smith, "Two ring circus," *Boston Globe*, 14 August 2004,
www.boston.com/sports/football/patriots/articles/2004/08/14/two_ring_circus.
[515] Patriots linebacker Rosevelt Colvin, quoted in: Frank Tadych, "The Think Tank: I'm already bored with this," *Patriots.com*, 17 August 2004,
www.patriots.com/news/fullarticle.sps?id=30156&type=general.
[516] Patriots linebacker Willie McGinest, quoted in: Damon Hack, "Hard Contact Is Music to Bruschi's Ears," *New York Times*, 29 January 2004, D1, ProQuest
database.
[517] Patriots tight end Christian Fauria, quoted in: Greg Bishop, "Hasselbeck, Brady in the draft: Better late than early?" *Seattle Post-Intelligencer*, 14 October 2004,
http://seattletimes.nwsource.com/html/sports/2002062745_hawk14.html.
[518] Patriots tight end Christian Fauria, quoted in: Bob Ryan, "No disguise, Fauria is just one of the guys," *Boston Globe*, 2 February 2004,
www.boston.com/sports/football/patriots/articles/2004/02/02/no_disguise_fauria_is_just_one_of_the_guys.
[519] Patriots wide receiver Troy Brown, quoted in: Chris Kennedy, "Brown expands skills, works on defense," *MassLive.com*, 11 August 2004,
www.masslive.com/printer/printer.ssf?/base/sports-0/1092271500205820.xml.
[520] Patriots center Dan Koppen, quoted in: Kevin Mannix, "Model QB an easy target: Teammates love to needle Brady," *Boston Herald*, 7 September 2004,
http://patriots.bostonherald.com/patriots/view.bg?articleid=43099.
[521] Tight end Christian Fauria, quoted in: Kevin Mannix, "Model QB an easy target: Teammates love to needle Brady," *Boston Herald*, 7 September 2004,
http://patriots.bostonherald.com/patriots/view.bg?articleid=43099.
[522] Tom Brady, Sr., paraphrased in: Mark Emmons (*San Jose Mercury News*), "Patriots' Brady the talk of the town," *Star-Telegram*, 25 January 2004,
www.dfw.com/mld/dfw/sports/columnists/troy_phillips/7789659.htm?1c.
[523] Patriots guard Joe Andruzzi, quoted in: Nick Cafardo, "Robertson emerges with time," *Boston Globe*, 22 October 2004,
www.boston.com/sports/football/patriots/articles/2004/10/22/robertson_emerges_with_time/.
[524] Patriots kicker Adam Vinatieri, quoted in: Glen Farley, "Patriots jump on Red Sox wagon," *The Enterprise*, 22 October 2004,
http://enterprise.southofboston.com/articles/2004/10/22/news/sports/sports03.txt.
[525] Patriots rookie running back Cedric Cobbs, "Cedric Cobbs Player Journal," *NFLPlayers.com*, 23 June 2004,
www.patriots.com/news/FullArticle.sps?id=29002&type=nfl.
[526] Bill Belichick, quoted in: Tom Pedulla, "Patriots feel Super with 'extra ingredient' Dillon," *USA Today*, 22 July 2004,
www.usatoday.com/sports/football/nfl/patriots/2004-07-22-camp_x.htm.
[527] Bill Belichick, quoted in: Harvey Mackay, *We Got Fired!*, New York: Ballantine Books, 2004, p. 63.
[528] 2nd-year linebacker Tully Banta-Cain, quoted in: Charles P. Pierce, "The Patriot," *Boston Globe*, 5 September 2004,
www.boston.com/news/globe/magazine/articles/2004/09/05/the_patriot/.
[529] David Newton, "Watson close to fulfilling his dream," *TheState.com* (South Carolina), 19 April 2004, www.thestate.com/mld/thestate/sports/8464509.htm.
[530] David Newton, "Watson close to fulfilling his dream," *TheState.com* (South Carolina), 19 April 2004, www.thestate.com/mld/thestate/sports/8464509.htm.
[531] Patriots defensive lineman Richard Seymour, quoted in: Tom E. Curran, "Pats' Seymour presses on," *Providence Journal*, 6 July 2004,
www.projo.com/patriots/content/projo_20040706_06seymour.3bb42.html.
[532] Patriots cornerback Tyrone Poole, quoted in: Mike Reiss, "Poole dives in for more: Pats cornerback not looking back after pondering retirement," *MetroWest
Daily News*, 4 July 2004, www.metrowestdailynews.com/sportsColumnists/view.bg?articleid=72348.
[533] Patriots linebacker Roman Phifer, quoted in: Paul Kenyon, "Understated Phifer is Pats' leading tackler," *Providence Journal*, 10 August 2004,
www.projo.com/cgi-bin/bi/gold_print.cgi.
[534] Fullback Fred McCrary, quoted in: Shalise Manza Young, "McCrary confident he's cut out for his versatile role," *Providence Journal*, 11 August 2004,
www.projo.com/patriots/content/projo_20040811_11pats.b06e2.html.
[535] Patriots wide receiver Deion Branch, interviewed near end of ABC's "Monday Night Football," 22 November 2004.
[536] Patriots wide receiver David Patten, quoted in: Nick Cafardo, "Pats' Patten must prove himself again," *Berkshire Eagle*, 11 August 2004,
www.berkshireeagle.com/Stories/0,1413,101~6295~2326911,00.html.
[537] Patriots linebacker Rosevelt Colvin, quoted in: Dave D'Onofrio, "Road to recovery," *Concord Monitor*, 13 August 2004,
www.concordmonitor.com/apps/pbcs.dll/article?AID=/20040813/REPOSITORY/408130325/1007.
[538] Jim Moore, "Dillon's 'questionable' status a misnomer," *Seattle Post-Intelligencer*, 18 October 2004,
http://seattlepi.nwsource.com/football/195710_hside18.html.
[539] Wide receiver Bethel Johnson, quoted in: Don Banks, "From doghouse to penthouse," *Sports Illustrated*, 17 October 2004,
http://sportsillustrated.cnn.com/2004/writers/don_banks/10/17/patshawks.sider/.
[540] Wide receiver Bethel Johnson, quoted in: Clark Judge, "Pats' hero du jour just some guy named Johnson," *CBS Sportsline*, 17 October 2004,
www.sportsline.com/nfl/story/7802819.
[541] New Patriots running back Corey Dillon, quoted in: Michael Smith, "Distance runner," *Boston Globe*, 16 May 2004,
www.boston.com/sports/football/patriots/articles/2004/05/16/distance_runner?mode=PF.
[542] New Patriots running back Corey Dillon, quoted in: Michael Smith, "Distance runner," *Boston Globe*, 16 May 2004,
www.boston.com/sports/football/patriots/articles/2004/05/16/distance_runner?mode=PF.
[543] New Patriots running back Corey Dillon, quoted in: Michael Smith, "Dillon adds weapon to Patriots' offense," *ESPN.com*, 17 October 2004,
http://sports.espn.go.com/nfl/columns/story?id=1903876.
[544] Patriots safety Rodney Harrison, quoted in: Michael Smith, "Dream Team," *Boston Globe*, 9 September 2004,
www.boston.com/sports/football/patriots/articles/2004/09/09/dream_team.
[545] Patriots running back Corey Dillon, quoted in: Anthony Cotton, "Patriots take simple route to superiority," *Denver Post*, 20 October 2004,
www.denverpost.com/Stories/0,1413,36~86~2479163,00.html.
[546] Wide receiver Deion Branch, quoted in: Michael Smith, "Small role may produce star," *Boston Globe*, 4 July 2004,
www.boston.com/sports/football/patriots/articles/2004/07/04/small_role_may_produce_star.
[547] Patriots rookie wide receiver Michael Jennings, quoted in: Paul Perillo and Andy Hart, "Saturday mini-camp notebook," *Patriots Football Weekly*,
www.patriots.com/news/FullArticle.sps?id=28924.
[548] Patriots wide receiver Deion Branch, quoted in: David Pevear, "Wideouts receiving plenty of praise," *Lowell Sun*, 5 August 2004,
www.lowellsun.com/Stories/0,1413,105~4767~2316378,00.html.
[549] Dr. Peter F. Drucker, *Management: Tasks, Responsibilities, Practices*, USA: HarperCollins, 1973, pp. 187-8.
[550] Scott Pioli, quoted in: Bill Burt, "More than a coach," *Eagle Tribune*, 25 January 2004, www.eagletribune.com/news/stories/20040125/SP_001.htm.
[551] Patriots guard Joe Andruzzi, quoted in: Kevin Mannix, "Model QB an easy target: Teammates love to needle Brady," *Boston Herald*, 7 September 2004,
http://patriots.bostonherald.com/patriots/view.bg?articleid=43099.
[552] Tight end Christian Fauria, quoted in: David Pevear, "Tom Cool: Brady has a way to go," January 2004, http://bostonbrat.net/brady/arcjan04.html.
[553] Patriots backup quarterback Rohan Davey, "Davey NFL Europe diary - Week 7," *Patriots.com*, 14 May 2004,
www.patriots.com/news/FullArticle.sps?id=28761&type=general.
[554] Bill Belichick, quoted in: Alan Greenberg (*Hartford Courant*), "Pats' defense thrives with pack mentality," *Philadelphia Inquirer*, 17 January 2004,
www.philly.com/mld/inquirer/7731121.htm?1c.
[555] Patriots linebacker Mike Vrabel, quoted in: Michael Felger, "They like Mike: Award shows teammates' respect for Vrabel," 18 March 2004,
http://patriots.bostonherald.com/patriots/view.bg?articleid=13964.
[556] Patriots linebacker Mike Vrabel, quoted in: Jim McCabe, "They were playing for pride," *Boston Globe*, 18 October 2004,
www.boston.com/sports/football/patriots/articles/2004/10/18/they_were_playing_for_pride/.
[557] Patriots safety Rodney Harrison, quoted in: Jim McCabe, "They were playing for pride," *Boston Globe*, 18 October 2004,
www.boston.com/sports/football/patriots/articles/2004/10/18/they_were_playing_for_pride/.
[558] Patriots fullback Malaefou Mackenzie, quoted in: Adam Kilgore, "Rookie Scott to miss season," *Boston Globe*, 25 August 2004,
www.boston.com/sports/football/patriots/articles/2004/08/25/rookie_scott_to_miss_season.
[559] Richard Seymour's mother Deborah, quoted in: Charles P. Pierce, "Three Days, One Life," *Sports Illustrated*, 18 October 2004, p. 78.

[560] Richard Seymour, quoted in: Charles P. Pierce, "Three Days, One Life," *Sports Illustrated*, 18 October 2004, p. 78.
[561] Patriots defensive lineman Richard Seymour, "Camp Daze," in: Bryan Morry, *Patriots United*, Canada: Team Power Publishing, 2002, p. 58.
[562] Patriots VP of player personnel Scott Pioli, quoted in: Jackie MacMullan, "Pioli and Belichick a nice team," *Boston Globe*, 26 January 2004, www.bostonsports/football/patriots/articles/2004/01/26/pioli_and_belichick_a_nice_team/.
[563] Bill Belichick, "Bill Belichick Press Conf.Transcript 8/11/04," *Patriots.com*, 11 August 2004, www.patriots.com/Common/PrintThis.sps?id=30054&keytype=NEWS&type=training.
[564] Patriots defensive coordinator Romeo Crennel, quoted in: Mike Holbrook, "'Black Cloud' has lifted," *Pro Football Weekly*, 30 January 2004, www.profootballweekly.com/PFW/NFL/AFC/AFC+East/New+England/Features/2004/phifer013004.htm.
[565] Patriots safety Victor Green, who played for the Jets in 2001, quoted in: Len Pasquarelli, "Belichick and Pioli have winning formula," *ESPN.com*, 27 July 2002, http://espn.go.com/nfl/trainingcamp02/columns/patriots/1410739.html.
[566] Patriots safety Rodney Harrison, quoted in: "Having the final say," *Boston Globe*, 18 October 2004, www.boston.com/sports/football/patriots/articles/2004/10/18/having_the_final_say/.
[567] Patriots inside linebackers coach Pepper Johnson, *Won For All*, Chicago: Contemporary Books, 2003, p. 238.
[568] Patriots inside linebackers coach Pepper Johnson, *Won For All*, Chicago: Contemporary Books, 2003, p. 19.
[569] Andy Hanacek, "What were the Patriots thinking when they cut Milloy loose?" *Pro Football Weekly*, 3 September 2003, www.profootballweekly.com/PFW/NFL/AFC/AFC+East/New+England/Features/2003/hanacek090303.htm.
[570] ESPN analyst and famous former 49ers quarterback Steve Young, quoted in: Michael Parente, "Next up for Pats: winless defending AFC East champs," *Woonsocket Call*, 16 September 2003, www.woonsocketcall.com/site/news.cfm?newsid=10170361&BRD=1712&PAG=461&dept_id=106787&rfi=6.
[571] Patriots safety Rodney Harrison, quoted in: Associated Press, "League looks into Denver coach's fib," *St. Petersburg Times*, 16 September 2003, www.sptimes.com/2003/09/16/Sports/League_looks_into_Den.shtml.
[572] Bill Belichick, quoted in: Thomas George, "Still Bill: Patriots' Belichick Adapts and Thrives," *New York Times*, 16 November 2003, section 8, p. 1, ProQuest database.
[573] Patriots cornerback Ty Law, quoted in: Associated Press, "Pats' Harrison gets back to winning ways," 14 January 2004, http://msnbc.msn.com/id/3960632/.
[574] Patriots coach Bill Belichick, "Bill Belichick Press Conference," 14 April 2004, www.allthingsbillbelichick.com/0414transcript.htm.
[575] Bill Belichick, quoted in: Dan Pompei, "Patriots succeed because of their balance," *The Sporting News*, 11 January 2004, http://msnbc.msn.com/id/3606530/.
[576] Bill Belichick, quoted in: Dan Pompei, "Patriots succeed because of their balance," *The Sporting News*, 11 January 2004, http://msnbc.msn.com/id/3606530/.
[577] Patriots cornerback Tyrone Poole, quoted in: Tom King, "Pats' ailing secondary becoming primary concern ," *Nashua Telegraph*, 4 November 2004, www.nashuatelegraph.com/apps/pbcs.dll/article?AID=/20041104/SPORTS/41104018/-1/sports.
[578] Patriots linebacker Tedy Bruschi, quoted in: *Patriots United*, Canada: Team Power Publishing, 2002, p. 212.
[579] Bill Belichick, quoted in: Thomas George, "Belichick Was Pushed To the End," *New York Times*, 3 February 2004, p. D4, ProQuest database.
[580] Patriots linebacker Tedy Bruschi, quoted in: Pete Prisco, "This victory what Patriots 'team' is all about," *SportsLine.com*, 7 November 2004, www.sportsline.com/nfl/story/7865974.
[581] Bill Belichick, quoted in: Glen Farley, "Lawless frontier looms ahead for Patriots," *The Enterprise*, 3 November 2004, http://enterprise.southofboston.com/articles/2004/11/03/news/sports/sports04.txt.
[582] Patriots linebacker Tedy Bruschi, quoted in: Mike Lowe, "Hobbled Pats may be playing catch-up against speedy Rams," *Portland Press-Herald*, 4 November 2004, http://sports.mainetoday.com/pro/patriots/041104lowecolumn.shtml.
[583] Adrian Marcewicz, "Dallas Cowboys Preseason Preview," www.sportsdialogue.com/NFL.html.
[584] Jerry Fontenot, a 15-year NFL veteran and New Orleans Saints center, quoted in: Michael Silver, "No Pain, No Gain," *Sports Illustrated*, 2 December 2003, www.cnnsi.com/pr/subs/siexclusive/2003/12/02/linemen1208/.
[585] Minnesota Vikings tight end Hunter Goodwin, quoted in: Michael Silver, "No Pain, No Gain," *Sports Illustrated*, 2 December 2003, www.cnnsi.com/pr/subs/siexclusive/2003/12/02/linemen1208/.
[586] http://sports.espn.go.com/nfl/statistics?stat=team&sort=ypg&pos=off&league=nfl&order=true&season=2&year=2003.
[587] Michael Silver, "No Pain, No Gain," *Sports Illustrated*, 2 December 2003, www.cnnsi.com/pr/subs/siexclusive/2003/12/02/linemen1208/.
[588] Kansas City Chiefs offensive line coach Mike Solari, quoted in: *Pro Football Weekly* staff, "Packers have best OL in NFL," 23 September 2004, *ESPN.com*, http://sports.espn.go.com/nfl/news/story?id=1887354.
[589] Michael Silver, "Little Big Men," *Sports Illustrated*, 21 January 1998, http://sportsillustrated.cnn.com/features/1998/weekly/980126/littlebigmen.html.
[590] San Diego Chargers GM Bobby Beathard, quoted in: Michael Silver, "Little Big Men," *Sports Illustrated*, 21 January 1998, http://sportsillustrated.cnn.com/features/1998/weekly/980126/littlebigmen.html.
[591] Bill Williamson, "Patriots, Eagles look like Super favorites," *NBCSports.com*, 28 July 2004, http://msnbc.msn.com/id/5538111/.
[592] Patriots offensive tackle Kenyatta Jones, quoted in: Hector Longo, "Belichick may have been a Branch manager," *Eagle Tribune*, 10 September 2002, www.eagletribune.com/news/stories/20020910/SP_004.htm.
[593] Patriots left tackle Matt Light, quoted in: Ken Berger, "Pats' offensive line has last laugh," *Newsday*, 1 February 2004, www.southcoasttoday.com/daily/02-04/02-01-04/e03sp876.htm.
[594] Patriots offensive guard Russ Hochstein, quoted in: Michael Smith, "A chip on block," *Boston Globe*, 29 July 2004, www.boston.com/sports/football/patriots/articles/2004/07/29/a_chip_on_block.
[595] Bill Belichick, quoted in: Joe Burris, "Rhythm not thrown off by their line dance," *Boston Globe*, 2 October 2004, www.boston.com/sports/football/patriots/articles/2004/10/02/rhythm_not_thrown_off_by_their_line_dance.
[596] Bill Belichick, quoted in: Kevin Mannix: "Brown on defensive: Receiver given secondary role," *Boston Globe*, 12 August 2004, http://patriots.bostonherald.com/patriots/view.bg?articleid=39462.
[597] Bill Belichick, quoted in: Bryan Morry, "Belichick's three F's help Patriots earn A's," *NFL.com*, 21 October 2003, www.nfl.com/news/story/6739641.
[598] Bill Belichick, quoted in: Michael Smith, "They'll develop down the line," *Boston Globe*, 2 May 2004, www.boston.com/sports/football/patriots/articles/2004/05/02/theyll_develop_down_the_line/.
[599] Bill Belichick, quoted in: "Meet the Patriots picks," *Eagle Tribune*, 26 April 2004, www.eagletribune.com/news/stories/20040426/SP_008.htm.
[600] Bill Belichick, "Bill Belichick Press Conf. Transcript," *Patriots.com*, 22 September 2004, www.patriots.com/Common/PrintThis.sps?id=31304.
[601] Terry Bradshaw, quoted in: "WEEK 6: Pregame show hits the road for Seattle-New England," 15 October 2004 (approximately), http://msn.foxsports.com/story/3082476.
[602] Jim Moore, "Go 2 Guy: Tale of a dogged newshound," *Seattle Post-Intelligencer*, 14 October 2004, http://seattlepi.nwsource.com/football/195099_moore14.html.
[603] David Whitley (Orlando Sentinel), "Patriots follow genius to best NFL streak ever," *San Jose Mercury News*, 14 October 2004, www.mercurynews.com/mld/mercurynews/sports/9916698.htm.
[604] Jim Collins, *Good to Great*, USA: HarperBusiness, 2001, p. 39.
[605] Jim Collins, *Good to Great*, USA: HarperBusiness, 2001, p. 22.
[606] Bill Belichick, quoted in: Scott Pitoniak, "Belichick's NFL success is anything but boring," *Democrat and Chronicle*, 1 October 2004, www.democratandchronicle.com/apps/pbcs.dll/article?AID=/20041001/SPORTS0102/410010321/1007/SPORTS.
[607] Bill Belichick, quoted in: Jeff Goldberg, "Coaching Fraternity," *Hartford Courant*, 1 October 2004, www.ctnow.com/sports/hc-sidecover1001.artoct01,1,4313054.print.story?coll=hc-headlines-sports.
[608] Bill Belichick, quoted in: Pete Thamel, "Building Programs Using Belichick's Blueprint," 18 September 2004, www.nytimes.com/2004/09/18/sports/ncaafootball/18college.html.
[609] Bill Belichick, quoted in: Mike Reiss, "Patriots beat: Team Desirable," *Daily News Tribune*, 10 October 2004, www.dailynewstribune.com/sportsNews/view.bg?articleid=42486.
[610] Jim Collins, *Good to Great*, USA: HarperBusiness, 2001, p. 27.
[611] Dan Daly, "Patriots look like all-time winners," *Washington Times*, 7 October 2004.
[612] CBS announcer Jim Nantz, with 8:50 remaining in 4th quarter during CBS broadcast of the Patriots-Jets game, 24 October 2004.
[613] Patriots Vice President of Player Personnel Scott Pioli, quoted in: TSX / The Insiders, "Team Report: Patriots," 14 April 2003, http://patriots.theinsiders.com/2/105082.html.
[614] Bill Belichick, quoted in: Michael Holley, "Winners are one of a kind," *Boston Globe*, 2 February 2004, www.boston.com/sports/football/patriots/articles/2004/02/02/winners_are_one_of_a_kind.
[615] "Miguel's VERY UNOFFICIAL Patriots Salary Cap Information Page," www.patscap.com.

[616] Unnamed contract analyst at the NFL Players Association, quoted in: Nick Cafardo, "The Patriots are equipped for camping," *Boston Globe*, 25 July 2004, www.boston.com/sports/football/patriots/articles/2004/07/25/the_patriots_are_equipped_for_camping.

[617] Colts quarterback Peyton Manning, quoted in: Michael Gee, "The dynamic duo: Manning, Brady in mutual admiration society," *Boston Herald*, 9 September 2004, http://patriots.bostonherald.com/patriots/view.bg?articleid=43433.

[618] "Miguel's VERY UNOFFICIAL Patriots Salary Cap Information Page," www.patscap.com.

[619] Fox football announcer Cris Collinsworth, quoted in: Bill Griffith, "Earning double coverage," *Boston Globe*, 19 October 2004, www.boston.com/sports/football/patriots/articles/2004/10/19/earning_double_coverage/.

[620] Kevin Mannix, "Pats a study in excellence," *Boston Herald*, 8 February 2004, http://patriots.bostonherald.com/patriots/view.bg?articleid=14008.

[621] Patriots defensive coordinator Romeo Crennel, quoted in: Mike Reiss, "Patriots beat: More NFL teams spread the wealth," *MetroWest Daily News*, 16 May 2004, www.metrowestdailynews.com/sportsColumnists/view.bg?articleid=68425.

[622] Alex Marvez, "Not business as usual for owners; it's `sticker shock,'" *San Jose Mercury News*, 28 March 2004, www.mercurynews.com/mld/mercurynews/sports/8299794.htm?1c.

[623] Mike Reiss, "Decision on Patten due soon," *Boston Herald*, 14 March 2004, http://patriots.bostonherald.com/patriots/view.bg?articleid=13969.

[624] Steve Politi, "Is Belichick A Genius?" *Star-Ledger*, 30 January 2004, www.allthingsbillbelichick.com/articles/agenius.htm.

[625] Patriots offensive lineman Stephen Neal, quoted in: Michael Vega, "No longer wrestling with job," *Boston Globe*, 8 October 2004, www.boston.com/sports/football/patriots/articles/2004/10/08/no_longer_wrestling_with_job.

[626] Patriots running back Kevin Faulk, quoted in: Arthur Staple, "Everybody contributes," *Newsday*, 25 October 2004, www.newsday.com/sports/football/jets/ny-sppats254019000oct25,0,3546069,print.story.

[627] Bill Belichick, quoted in: Michael Parente, " No time to rest for New England," *New Britain Herald*, 3 November 2004, www.zwire.com/site/news.cfm?newsid=13280454&BRD=1641&PAG=461&dept_id=17739&rfi=6.

[628] Dan Pompei, "Patriots succeed because of their balance," *The Sporting News*, 11 January 2004, http://msnbc.msn.com/id/3606530/.

[629] Bill Belichick, quoted in: Gerald Eskenazi (*New York Times*), "Pats defense built in reverse," *SouthCoast Today*, 22 January 1997, www.s-t.com/daily/01-97/01-22-97/d04sp157.htm.

[630] Rick Gosselin, "Team theme drives Patriots," 2 February 2004, www.cowboysplus.com/columnists/rgosselin/stories/020304cpgosselin.2dc3d.html.

[631] Patriots linebacker Mike Vrabel, quoted in: John Clayton, "Belichick and Fox will match wits Sunday," *ESPN*, 28 January 2004, http://sports.espn.go.com/nfl/playoffs03/columns/story?columnist=clayton_john&id=1720970.

[632] Former New York Giants and Cleveland Browns linebacker Carl Banks, quoted in: Bob Glauber, "Billy Ball," *Newsday*, 25 January 2004, www.allthingsbillbelichick.com/articles/billyball.htm.

[633] Tom Brady, quoted in: Peter May, "Master of the plan," *Boston Globe*, 3 February 2004, www.boston.com/sports/football/patriots/articles/2004/02/03/master_of_the_plan/.

[634] Veteran Patriots wide receiver Troy Brown, quoted in: Tom E. Curran, "Trying Brown at DB a matter of depth," *Providence Journal*, 15 August 2004, www.projo.com/patriots/content/projo_20040815_15beat.136343.html.

[635] Patriots VP of player personnel Scott Pioli, quoted in: Michael Felger, "Pioli helps put it together," *Boston Herald*, 26 January 2004, http://patriots.bostonherald.com/patriots/_view.bg?articleid=510.

[636] Patriots wide receiver Troy Brown, quoted in: Alex Marvez, "Pats' Brown samples life on defense," *South Florida Sun-Sentinel*, 14 August 2004, www.mercurynews.com/mld/mercurynews/sports/9403239.htm?1c.

[637] Patriots wide receiver/punt returner/defensive back Troy Brown, quoted in: George Kimball, "Brown helps out as a real 2-way threat," *Boston Herald*, 8 November 2004, http://patriots.bostonherald.com/patriots/view.bg?articleid=53015.

[638] Patriots wide receiver/punt returner/defensive back Troy Brown, quoted in: Mike Reiss, "New twist to Beli-flex system aids Patriots' charge," *Milford Daily News*, 9 November 2004.

[639] Patriots linebacker Rosevelt Colvin, quoted in: Peter King, "Backup plan," *Sports Illustrated*, 18 August 2004, http://sportsillustrated.cnn.com/inside_game/peter_king/news/2003/08/18/mmqb/.

[640] Offensive lineman Stephen Neal, quoted in: Michael Felger, "Pats are running low on tackles," *Boston Herald*, 12 November 2004.

[641] Patriots linebacker Mike Vrabel, quoted in: Alan Greenberg, "A String Of Successful Conversions," *Hartford Courant*, 14 November 2004.

[642] Bill Belichick, quoted in: Frank Tadych, "Patriots Notebook: Injuries raising doubts," 5 November 2004, http://cachewww.patriots.com/news/index.cfm?ac=latestnewsdetail&pid=9607&pcid=41.

[643] Patriots longsnapper Lonie Paxon, quoted in: Steve Buckley, "Offense powers Patriots," *Boston Herald*, 14 November 2004.

[644] Patriots owner Bob Kraft, quoted in: Michael Felger, "Kraft OK with deal: Has faith in Belichick's judgment," *Boston Globe*, 21 April 2004, http://patriots.bostonherald.com/patriots/view.bg?articleid=13916.

[645] Former Patriots offensive lineman Damien Woody, quoted in: Nick Cafardo, "It doesn't pay for Weis to stay," *Boston Globe*, 16 May 2004, www.boston.com/sports/football/patriots/articles/2004/05/16/it_doesnt_pay_for_weis_to_stay/.

[646] New Patriot and former Cincinnati Bengals star running back Corey Dillon, quoted in: Associated Press, "Dillon Changes Patriots' Draft Plan," *NBC Sports*, 24 April 2004, http://msnbc.msn.com/id/4790265/.

[647] New Patriots running back Corey Dillon, quoted in: Mike Lowe, "He's Dillon, he's here and he's happy," *Portland Press Herald*, 9 September 2004, http://pressherald.mainetoday.com/sports/pro/patriots/040909patriots.shtml.

[648] Unnamed NFL general manager, quoted in: Michael Felger, "Training camp preview: A fresh start," *The Sporting News*, http://msn.foxsports.com/story/2572440.

[649] New Patriots running back Corey Dillon, quoted in: "A conversation with Corey Dillon," *NFL.com*, 20 April 2004, www.nfl.com/nflnetwork/story/7271974.

[650] New Patriots running back Corey Dillon, quoted in: Michael Felger, "Training camp preview: A fresh start," *The Sporting News*, http://msn.foxsports.com/story/2572440.

[651] New Patriots running back Corey Dillon, quoted in: "A conversation with Corey Dillon," *NFL.com*, 20 April 2004, www.nfl.com/nflnetwork/story/7271974.

[652] Brian Murphy, "Prime Time live," *ESPN*, 27 October 2004, http://sports.espn.go.com/espn/page2/story?page=murphy/041025.

[653] New Patriots running back Corey Dillon, quoted in: Michael Felger, "Training camp preview: A fresh start," *The Sporting News*, http://msn.foxsports.com/story/2572440.

[654] New Patriots running back Corey Dillon, quoted in: Ken Lechtanski, "A bunch of happy campers report," *The Enterprise*, 30 July 2004, http://enterprise.southofboston.com/articles/2004/07/30/news/sports/sports02.txt.

[655] Patriots fullback Fred McCrary, quoted in: Marc Carig, "Fullback McCrary at full speed," *Boston Globe*, 6 August 2004, www.boston.com/sports/football/patriots/articles/2004/08/06/fullback_mccrary_at_full_speed.

[656] Cincinnati Bengals assistant defensive coach Chuck Bresnahan, quoted in: "An officer and a coach," *Bengals.com*, 13 May 2004, www.bengals.com/press/news.asp?iCurPage=0&news_id=2218.

[657] Patriots quarterback Tom Brady, quoted in: AP, "Bunch of success," *CNNSI.com*, 4 February 2002, http://sportsillustrated.cnn.com/football/2002/playoffs/news/2002/02/03/brady_mvp_ap/.

[658] See: Michael Holley, *Patriot Reign*, William Morrow, 2004, pp. 171-2.

[659] Peter King, "Brains over brawn," *Sports Illustrated*, 12 October 2004, http://sportsillustrated.cnn.com/2004/writers/peter_king/10/12/mmqb.te/.

[660] Rohan Davey, "Davey NFL Europe diary – Week 5," *Patriots.com*, 29 April 2004, www.patriots.com/news/FullArticle.sps?id=28559&type=general.

[661] Michael Felger, "Peers honor Pioli: Pats' personnel guru named exec of year," *Boston Herald*, 30 March 2004, http://patriots.bostonherald.com/patriots/view.bg?articleid=13955.

[662] Patriots Vice President of Player Personnel Scott Pioli, quoted in: Dan Pompei, "Scott Pioli, Patriots (TSN NFL Executive Of The Year)," *The Sporting News*, www.findarticles.com/cf_dls/m1208/14_228/114985732/p1/article.jhtml.

[663] Patriots Vice President of Player Personnel Scott Pioli, quoted in: "CCSU Alum Scott Pioli Named NFL Executive of the Year," 30 March 2004, http://ccsubluedevils.collegesports.com/sports/m-footbl/spec-rel/033004aaa.html.

[664] VP of Player Personnel Scott Pioli, quoted in: Vic Carucci, "Being a true Patriot has its rewards," *NFL.com*, 30 March 2004, www.nfl.com/news/story/7219076.

[665] Patriots VP of player personnel Scott Pioli, quoted in: Harvey Araton, "Pioli Prefers the Back Seat In the Patriots' Front Office," *New York Times*, 29 January 2004, www.nytimes.com/2004/01/29/sports/football/29ARAT.html.

[666] Bill Belichick, "Bill Belichick Press Transcript - 1/5," *Patriots.com*, 5 January 2004, www.patriots.com/news/fullarticle.sps?id=27192&type=general.

[667] Bill Belichick, "Bill Belichick Press Transcript - 1/5," *Patriots.com*, 5 January 2004, www.patriots.com/news/fullarticle.sps?id=27192&type=general.

[668] Coach Bill Belichick, quoted in: Tom E. Curran, "Savoring victory is alien to Belichick," *Providence Journal*, 7 February 2004, www.projo.com/patriots/content/projo_20040207_07pats.1902d4.html.

[669] Bill Belichick, quoted in: Rick Gosselin, "Team theme drives Patriots," 2 February 2004, www.cowboysplus.com/columnists/rgosselin/stories/020304cpgosselin.2dc3d.html.

[670] Nolan Nawrocki, "There's no 'I' in 'team,'" *Pro Football Weekly*, 3 February 2002, http://archive.profootballweekly.com/content/archives2001/features_2001/sb_0203023.asp.

[671] Bill Belichick, quoted in: Tom E. Curran, "Patriots Notebook: Signing will add depth," *Providence Journal*, 1 October 2004, www.projo.com/patriots/content/projo_20041001_01patsjo.1baca9.html.

[672] Gregg Easterbrook, "Why football is intellectual, plus weather forecasts for inside domed stadia," *NFL.com*, 26 October 2004, www.nfl.com/features/tmq/102604.

[673] Patriots linebacker Ted Johnson, quoted in: Michael Smith, "Camp fires burning," *Boston Globe*, 30 July 2004, www.boston.com/sports/football/patriots/articles/2004/07/30/camp_fires_burning/.

[674] Patriots linebacker Tedy Bruschi, quoted in: Jody Foldesy, "Patriots win piece of history," *Washington Times*, 2 February 2004, www.washingtontimes.com/functions/print.php?StoryID=20040202-012334-6654r.

[675] Rookie defensive tackle Vince Wilfork, quoted in: Michael Felger, "Pats' Wilfork will weight and see," *Boston Herald*, 30 April 2004, http://patriots.bostonherald.com/patriots/view.bg?articleid=13894.

[676] Rookie tight end Benjamin Watson, quoted in: Alan Greenberg, "Draftees Are Family Friendly," *Hartford Courant*, 30 April 2004, www.ctnow.com/sports/hc-patriots0430.artapr30,1,1721503,print.story?coll=hc-headlines-sports.

[677] Bill Belichick, "Bill Belichick Press Conf. Transcript 8/3/04," *Patriots.com*, 3 August 2004, www.patriots.com/news/fullarticle.sps?id=29867&special_section=TrainingCamp2004&type=training.

[678] Bill Belichick, "Bill Belichick Press Conf. Transcript 8/3/04," *Patriots.com*, 3 August 2004, www.patriots.com/news/fullarticle.sps?id=29867&special_section=TrainingCamp2004&type=training.

[679] Bill Belichick, speaking on: Yes Network, *This Week in Football*, 20 October 2004, http://boss.streamos.com/real/yesnet/real/twif_belichick102004.ram.

[680] Three-time Pro Bowl running back Corey Dillon, quoted in: Bob Glauber, "Improved Pats primed to repeat," *Newsday*, 6 August 2004, www.newsday.com/sports/football/ny-spglaub063920634aug06,0,7182695,print.column?coll=ny-sports-columnists.

[681] Patriots cornerback Ty Law, quoted in: Jody Foldesy, "Patriots win piece of history," *Washington Times*, 2 February 2004, www.washingtontimes.com/functions/print.php?StoryID=20040202-012334-6654r.

[682] Bill Belichick, "Bill Belichick Press Conf. Transcript - 9/14/2004," *Patriots.com*, 14 September 2004, www.patriots.com/Common/PrintThis.sps?id=30535.

[683] Patriots veteran backup linebacker Don Davis, quoted in: Alan Greenberg, "Pat-ended process; Belichick can find those keepers," 1 February 2004, p. E1, ProQuest database.

[684] Bill Belichick, quoted in: Hector Longo, "Living on the Edge," *Eagle Tribune*, 26 December 2003, www.eagletribune.com/news/stories/20031226/SP_001.htm.

[685] Bill Belichick, quoted in: Alan Greenberg, "Belichick Game Plan For Life," *Hartford Courant*, 3 May 2004, www.ctnow.com/sports/hc-belichick0503.artmay03,1,707205.story.

[686] Patriots linebacker Mike Vrabel, quoted in: Len Pasquarelli, "Patriots suddenly struggling to address woes," *ESPN*, 31 October 2002, http://espn.go.com/nfl/columns/pasquarelli_len/1453171.html.

[687] Patriots linebacker Ted Johnson, quoted in: Kevin Mannix, "Rundown feeling? No. Pats insist defense will remain active, effective," *Boston Herald*, 7 November 2004, http://patriots.bostonherald.com/patriots/view.bg?articleid=52893.

[688] Patriots safety Rodney Harrison, quoted in: Kevin Mannix, "Rundown feeling? No. Pats insist defense will remain active, effective," *Boston Herald*, 7 November 2004, http://patriots.bostonherald.com/patriots/view.bg?articleid=52893.

[689] Patriots rookie nose tackle Vince Wilfork, quoted in: Tony Chamberlain, "Developing nose for ball," *Boston Globe*, 11 October 2004, www.boston.com/sports/football/patriots/articles/2004/10/11/developing_nose_for_ball.

[690] Patriots rookie nose tackle Vince Wilfork, quoted in: Alan Greenberg, "Dolphins Find Out This Was Personal," *Hartford Courant*, 11 October 2004, www.ctnow.com/sports/football/patriots/hc-patriotsside1011.artoct11,1,6687215.story.

[691] Bill Belichick, "Bill Belichick Press Conference," 3 November 2004, http://cachewww.patriots.com/mediacenter/index.cfm?ac=audionewsdetail&pid=9555&pcid=85.

[692] Bill Belichick, quoted in: Alex Timiraos, "Pats coach talks leadership at BC," *The Heights*, 9 April 2004, www.bcheights.com/news/2004/04/09/News/Pats-Coach.Talks.Leadership.At.Bc-656659.shtml.

[693] Bill Belichick, quoted in: Alan Greenberg, "Belichick Game Plan For Life," *Hartford Courant*, 3 May 2004, www.ctnow.com/sports/hc-belichick0503.artmay03,1,707205.story.

[694] Tom E. Curran, "Patriots Notebook: Fix sought for broken pass plays," *Providence Journal*, 19 August 2004, www.projo.com/patriots/content/projo_20040819_19patsjo.fab8d.html.

[695] Patriots left tackle Matt Light, quoted in: Michael Parente, " Light saves 'mates anguish," *Middletown Press*, 19 August 2004, www.zwire.com/site/news.cfm?newsid=12729188&BRD=1645&PAG=461&dept_id=17758&rfi=6.

[696] Linebacker Rosevelt Colvin, quoted in: George Kimball, "Klemm takes hold of role," *Boston Herald*, 22 September 2004, http://patriots.bostonherald.com/patriots/view.bg?articleid=45375.

[697] Offensive lineman Tom Ashworth, quoted in: Len Pasquarelli, "Pats primed for second title," *ESPN.com*, 1 February 2004, http://sports.espn.go.com/nfl/playoffs03/columns/story?columnist=pasquarelli_len&id=1725040.

[698] Tom Brady, quoted in: George Kimball, "The art of the game: On the field or in the studio, David Givens has designs on greatness," *Boston Herald*, 10 October 2004, http://patriots.bostonherald.com/patriots/view.bg?articleid=48342.

[699] Tom Brady, quoted in: Ashley McGeachy Fox, "Patriots-Steelers an intriguing matchup, and other notes," San Jose Mercury News, 30 October 2004, www.mercurynews.com/mld/mercurynews/sports/10051288.htm?1c.

[700] Patriots safety Rodney Harrison, quoted in: Rob Longley, "A winning Pat-tern," *Toronto Sun*, 18 October 2004, http://slam.canoe.ca/Slam/Football/NFL/2004/10/18/674389.html.

[701] Running back Corey Dillon, quoted in: Ron Indrisano, "Dillon's determination not questionable," *Boston Globe*, 18 October 2004, www.boston.com/sports/football/patriots/articles/2004/10/18/dillons_determination_not_questionable/.

[702] Tom Brady, quoted in: Mark Maske, "Selfless Patriots show how it's done," *Washington Post*, 4 February 2004, www.msnbc.msn.com/id/4144383/.

[703] Patriots linebacker Mike Vrabel, quoted in: Charles P. Pierce, "The Patriot," *Boston Globe*, 5 September 2004, www.boston.com/news/globe/magazine/articles/2004/09/05/the_patriot/.

[704] Arizona Cardinals head coach Dennis Green, quoted in: Bob Baum (AP), "McCown anxious to get close look at Brady," *Tuscaloosa News*, 15 September 2004, www.tuscaloosanews.com/apps/pbcs.dll/article?AID=/20040915/APS/409151124.

[705] Patriots' star defensive lineman Richard Seymour, quoted in: Eric McHugh, "Seymour says he's doing all he can," *Patriot Ledger*, 23 September 2004, http://ledger.southofboston.com/articles/2004/09/23/sports/sports02.txt.

[706] Bill Belichick, live video news conference, streamed online from Patriots.com, 20 October 2004.

[707] Patriots quarterback Tom Brady, "Tom Brady Press Conference 7/23/03," bostonbrat.net/brady/arcjuly.html.

[708] Bill Belichick, quoted in: Frank Tadych, "Cobbs, Scott expected to sign soon," *Patriots.com*, 30 July 2004, www.patriots.com/news/FullArticle.sps?id=29709&type=training.

[709] Bill Belichick, quoted in: Paul Perillo, "Belichick rolls with preseason punches; Monday's notes," *Patriots.com*, 9 August 2004, www.patriots.com/news/FullArticle.sps?id=30020&type=general.

[710] Patriots wide receiver Deion Branch, quoted in: Howard Bryant, "Receivers earn respect: New blood revives Pats," *Boston Herald*, 28 January 2004, http://patriots.bostonherald.com/patriots/view.bg?articleid=14108.

[711] Patriots linebacker Tedy Bruschi, quoted in: Peter King, "A League of Their Own," *Sports Illustrated*, 18 October 2004, p. 69.

[712] Patriots linebacker Mike Vrabel, quoted in: Michael Felger, "They like Mike: Award shows teammates' respect for Vrabel," 18 March 2004, http://patriots.bostonherald.com/patriots/view.bg?articleid=13964.

[713] Patriots linebacker Mike Vrabel, quoted in: Damon Hack, "Hard Contact Is Music to Bruschi's Ears," *New York Times*, 29 January 2004, D1, ProQuest database.

[714] Patriots linebacker Tedy Bruschi, quoted in: Mark Maske, "Ailing Bruschi Participates in Patriots' Practice," *Washington Post*, 29 January 2004, p. D4, ProQuest database.

[715] Patriots cornerback Terrell Buckley, quoted in: Chris Kennedy, "Buckley still knows," *MassLive.com*, 8 August 2004, www.masslive.com/printer/printer.ssf?/base/sports-2/1091954772194311.xml.

[716] Patriots cornerback Ty Law, quoted in: Bryan McGovern, "Patriot Day," *The Sports Network*, 3 February 2002, www.sportsnetwork.com/default.asp?c=sportsnetwork&page=nfl/misc/mcgovern/nfl-weekly-020302.htm.

[717] Patriots linebacker Mike Vrabel, quoted in: Michael Felger, "Patriots Super win over Rams changed all," *Milford Daily News*, 5 November 2004, www.milforddailynews.com/sportsNews/view.bg?articleid=59185.

[718] Patriots wide receiver David Patten, quoted in: Bryan McGovern, "Patriot Day," *The Sports Network*, 3 February 2002, www.sportsnetwork.com/default.asp?c=sportsnetwork&page=nfl/misc/mcgovern/nfl-weekly-020302.htm.

[719] Dan Pires, "Postgame talk ranges from Sapp to streaker," *Standard-Times*, 4 February 2004, www.southcoasttoday.com/daily/02-04/02-04-04/c01sp273.htm.

[720] Tom Brady, quoted in: Michael Gee, "Brady blows off blitz: QB handles pressure," *Boston Herald*, 4 October 2004, http://patriots.bostonherald.com/patriots/view.bg?articleid=47278.

[721] Berlin Thunder coach Rick Lantz, quoted in: Michael Preston, "The man with the golden arm," *NFL.com*, 26 April 2004, www.nfl.com/international/story/7286329.

[722] Patriots backup quarterback Rohan Davey, quoted in: Michael Preston, "The man with the golden arm," *NFL.com*, 26 April 2004, www.nfl.com/international/story/7286329.

[723] Patriots backup quarterback Rohan Davey, as told to *Patriots Football Weekly*'s Paul Perillo, "Davey NFL Europe diary – Week 6," *Patriots.com*, 6 May 2004, www.patriots.com/news/FullArticle.sps?id=28670&type=general.

[724] Jon Bon Jovi, quoted in: Michael Holley, "More than Xs and Os," in: *Again!*, Chicago: Triumph Books, 2004, p. 101.

[725] *The David Letterman Show*, 4 February 2004, www.patriots.com/mediaworld/mediadetail.sps?id=27974.

[726] Steve Belichick, father of Bill Belichick, quoted in: Michael Holley, "More than Xs and Os," in: *Again!*, Chicago: Triumph Books, 2004, pp. 98 & 100.

[727] Patriots quarterback Tom Brady, quoted in: AP, "Patriots dominant again in rout of Jets," *NFL.com*, 15 September 2002, www.nfl.com/gamecenter/recap/NFL_20020915_NE@NYJ.

[728] Bill Belichick, quoted in: Kent Somers, "Always a step ahead," *Arizona Republic*, 16 September 2004, www.azcentral.com/arizonarepublic/sports/articles/0916cards0916.html.

[729] Peter F. Drucker, *The Effective Executive*, HarperBusiness, 1967 [1996], 32-33.

[730] Rick Gosselin, "Redrafting the class of 2003," *Dallas Morning News*, 15 November 2003, www.cowboysplus.com/columnists/rgosselin/stories/111603cpgosselinchart.75f80.html.

[731] Michael Holley, "Best-case scenarios," *Boston Globe*, 5 November 2003, www.boston.com/sports/football/patriots/articles/2003/11/05/best_case_scenarios.

[732] Patriots VP of Player Personnel Scott Pioli, quoted in: Kevin Paul Dupont, "Pioli Finding Success With Patriots," *Boston Globe*, 13 January 2002, www.allthingsbillbelichick.com/articles/piolisuccess.htm.

[733] Scott Pioli, Patriots VP of player personnel, quoted in: Hector Longo, "All the right moves," *Eagle-Tribune*, 30 January 2004, www.eagletribune.com/news/stories/20040130/SP_001.htm.

[734] Mark Curnutte, "Patriots epitomize meaning of team," *Cincinnati Enquirer*, 28 January 2004, http://bengals.enquirer.com/2004/01/28/ben1mc.html.

[735] Michael Smith, "In a different arena, Cleeland did his best," *Boston Globe*, 30 May 2004, www.boston.com/sports/football/patriots/articles/2004/05/30/in_a_different_arena_cleeland_did_his_best.

[736] Patriots VP of Player Personnel Scott Pioli, quoted in: Leonard Shapiro, "Different routes, same path in mind," *Washington Post*, 24 March 2004, p. D3, www.washingtonpost.com/wp-dyn/articles/A18695-2004Mar23.html.

[737] VP of player personnel Scott Pioli, quoted in: Vic Carucci, "Being a true Patriot has its rewards," *NFL.com*, 30 March 2004, www.nfl.com/news/story/7219076.

[738] VP of player personnel Scott Pioli, quoted in: Bob Ryan, "Mike Vrabel," in: *Again!*, Chicago: Triumph Books, 2004, p. 126.

[739] Steve Belichick, Bill's father, quoted in: Hank Gola, "Patriots find their destiny," *South Coast Today*, 8 February 2002, www.s-t.com/daily/02-02/02-08-02/d06ae114.htm.

[740] Michael Felger, "Pioli: Scout's Honor," *Boston Herald*, 19 December 2001, www.allthingsbillbelichick.com/articles/piolihonor.htm.

[741] Michael Holley, *Patriot Reign*, William Morrow, 2004, p. 158.

[742] Bill Belichick, quoted in: Ethan J. Skolnick, "Patriots are best because they're the smartest," *South Florida Sun-Sentinel*, 7 October 2004, www.sun-sentinel.com/sports/columnists/sfl-skolnick06oct07,0,7494511.column.

[743] Scott Pioli, VP of player personnel, quoted in: Rick Braun, "Patriots built with free agents, draft," *Milwaukee Journal Sentinel*, 4 February 2004, www.jsonline.com/packer/rev/feb04/204957.asp.

[744] Patriots linebacker Roman Phifer, quoted in: John Tomase, "Built To Win," *Eagle Tribune*, 27 January 2004, www.eagletribune.com/news/stories/20040127/SP_001.htm.

[745] Former Cowboys personnel director Gil Brandt, quoted in: Rick Braun, "Patriots built with free agents, draft," *Milwaukee Journal Sentinel*, 4 February 2004, www.jsonline.com/packer/rev/feb04/204957.asp.

[746] Patriots safety Victor Green, who played for the Jets in 2001, quoted in: Len Pasquarelli, "Belichick and Pioli have winning formula," *ESPN.com*, 27 July 2002, http://espn.go.com/nfl/trainingcamp02/columns/patriots/1410739.html.

[747] Rick Spielman, head of player personnel for the Miami Dolphins, quoted in: Jay Glazer, "Patriots proving to be model franchise," *CBS Sportsline*, 3 December 2003, http://cbs.sportsline.com/nfl/story/6889325.

[748] Patriots cornerback Ty Law, quoted in: Dan Pires "Defense first job for Law," *Standard-Times*, 20 August 2000, www.southcoasttoday.com/daily/08-00/08-20-00/b01sp052.htm.

[749] Miami fullback Rob Konrad, quoted in: Hector Longo, "Living on the Edge," *Eagle Tribune*, 26 December 2003, www.eagletribune.com/news/stories/20031226/SP_001.htm.

[750] Charles P. Pierce, "The Patriot," *Boston Globe*, 5 September 2004, www.boston.com/news/globe/magazine/articles/2004/09/05/the_patriot/.

[751] Bill Belichick, quoted in: Michael Parente, " Klecko a younger Bruschi?" *The Herald News*, 18 August 2004, www.zwire.com/site/news.cfm?newsid=12717675&BRD=1710&PAG=740&dept_id=353135&rfi=6.

[752] Steve Jones, "Voice of Penn State Football: Steve Jones," 9 April 2000, www.happyvalley.com/PSUSports/sj040901.cfm.

[753] Patriots linebacker Tedy Bruschi, quoted in: Kevin Mannix, "Klecko shifts gears: Leans on Bruschi for move to linebacker," *Boston Herald*, 18 August 2004, http://patriots.bostonherald.com/patriots/view.bg?articleid=40316.

[754] Patriots linebacker Tedy Bruschi, quoted in: Howard Ulman (AP), "Lineman progressing in switch to linebacker," *SFGate.com*, 25 August 2004, http://sfgate.com/cgi-bin/article.cgi?f=/news/archive/2004/08/25/sports1644EDT0463.DTL.

[755] Patriots linebacker Tedy Bruschi, quoted in: Bill Burt, "Bruschi a true blue Patriot," *Eagle Tribune*, 31 January 2002, www.eagletribune.com/news/stories/20020131/SP_004.htm.

[756] Patriots linebacker Tedy Bruschi, quoted in: Kevin Mannix, "Klecko shifts gears: Leans on Bruschi for move to linebacker," *Boston Herald*, 18 August 2004, http://patriots.bostonherald.com/patriots/view.bg?articleid=40316.

[757] Patriots linebacker Willie McGinest, quoted in: Associated Press, "Patriots are on top of their game," *The Desert Sun* (Palm Springs, CA), 30 January 2004, www.thedesertsun.com/news/stories2004/football/20040130022302.shtml.

[758] Patriots linebacker Willie McGinest, quoted in: Luke Sacks, "A Championship Season For McGinest," *NFLPlayers.com*, 7 July 2004, www.patriots.com/news/FullArticle.sps?id=29558&type=nfl.

[759] New York Jets quarterback Chad Pennington, quoted in: Kit Stier, "Jets, Patriots stay focused," *The Journal News*, 21 October 2004, www.thejournalnews.com/newsroom/102104/c0721jetsweb.html.

[760] Former Miami Dolphins quarterback Dan Marino, quoted in: *Patriots United*, Canada: Team Power Publishing, 2002, p. 41.

[761] Pittsburgh Steelers quarterback Ben Roethlisberger, quoted in: Skip Wood, "Steelers set to give Patriots a challenge," *USA Today*, 29 October 2004, www.usatoday.com/sports/football/nfl/2004-10-29-steelers-patriots_x.htm.

[762] Phil Simms, "Parcells-Belichick will be exciting," *NFL.com*, 11 November 2003, www.nfl.com/news/story/6823639.

[763] Bill Belichick, "Bill Belichick Press Conference," *Patriots.com*, 15 October 2004, http://originwww.patriots.com/search/index.cfm?ac=SearchDetail&PID=9337&PCID=85.

[764] New York Jets running back Curtis Martin, quoted in: Judy Battista, "The Patriots' Tougher Defense Will Test the Jets' Delicate State," *New York Times*, 15 October 2000, p. SP8.

[765] Patriots tight end Daniel Graham, quoted in: Glen Farley, "Graham trying to grasp his opportunity," *The Enterprise*, 16 August 2004, http://enterprise.southofboston.com/articles/2004/08/16/news/sports/sports02.txt.

[766] Patriots quarterback Tom Brady, "Tom Brady Press Conference 7/23/03," bostonbrat.net/brady/arcjuly.html.

[767] Bill Belichick, "Bill Belichick Press Conf. Transcript 8/30/04," *Patriots.com*, www.patriots.com/Common/PrintThis.sps?id=30322&keytype=NEWS&type=general.

[768] Rams president Jay Zygmunt, quoted in: Bob McGinn, "A priceless collection," *Milwaukee Journal-Sentinel*, 31 January 2002, www.jsonline.com/packer/prev/jan02/16658.asp.

[769] Patriots Vice President of Player Personnel Scott Pioli, quoted in: Charles Stein, "Bill Belichick, CEO," *Boston Globe*, 28 January 2004.

[770] Patriots VP of player personnel, Scott Pioli, quoted in: Bob McGinn, "A priceless collection," *Milwaukee Journal-Sentinel*, 31 January 2002, www.jsonline.com/packer/prev/jan02/16658.asp.

[771] Patriots VP of player personnel, Scott Pioli, quoted in: Bob McGinn, "A priceless collection," *Milwaukee Journal-Sentinel*, 31 January 2002, www.jsonline.com/packer/prev/jan02/16658.asp.

[772] Patriots scout Jason Licht, quoted in: Michael Holley, *Patriot Reign*, William Morrow, 2004, p. 154.

[773] Jay Glazer, "Divisional draft preview: AFC East needs," *SportsLine.com*, 6 April 2004, http://cbs.sportsline.com/nfl/story/7236258.

[774] CBS analyst and former 49er Randy Cross, quoted in: Randy Covitz, "Patriots' formula for success makes it envy of NFL," *Kansas City Star*, 8 September 2004, www.kansascity.com/mld/kansascity/sports/football/nfl/kansas_city_chiefs/9603764.htm?1c.

[775] Michael Smith, "Whipping them into shape," *Boston Globe*, 27 June 2004, www.boston.com/sports/football/patriots/articles/2004/06/27/whipping_them_into_shape.

[776] Bill Burt, "Don't believe what you've read about Belichick," *Eagle Tribune*, 24 November 2001, www.eagletribune.com/news/stories/20011124/SP_001.htm.

[777] Michael Felger, "Pats ease into camp: Coach rewards offseason work," *Boston Herald*, 30 July 2004, http://patriots.bostonherald.com/patriots/view.bg?articleid=37864.

[778] Unnamed Patriot player, quoted in: Michael Felger, "Belichick goes on the offensive," *Boston Herald*, 25 July 2004, http://patriots.bostonherald.com/patriots/view.bg?articleid=37051.

[779] Patriots cornerback Ty Law, quoted in: Charean Williams, "Streak does matter to Patriots," *Fort Worth Star-Telegram*, 14 October 2004, www.mercurynews.com/mld/mercurynews/sports/9916663.htm?1c.

[780] Bill Belichick, "Bill Belichick Press Conf. Transcript 8/3/04," 3 August 2004, www.patriots.com/news/fullarticle.sps?id=29867&special_section=TrainingCamp2004&type=training.

[781] Bill Belichick, "Bill Belichick Conf. Call Transcript 8/17/04," *Patriots.com*, 17 August 2004, www.patriots.com/news/FullArticle.sps?id=30167&type=general.

[782] Patriots safety Rodney Harrison, quoted in: Paul Attner, "Super Bowl 36: Standing Pat," *The Sporting News*, 4 February 2002, www.a1-sports-odds.com/292.htm.

[783] 36-year-old Patriots linebacker Roman Phifer, quoted in: Nick Cafardo, "Phifer still has that old touch," *Boston Globe*, 28 September 2004, www.boston.com/sports/football/patriots/articles/2004/09/28/phifer_still_has_that_old_touch.

[784] Second-year Patriots linebacker Tully Banta-Cain, quoted in: Alan Greenberg, "Perfectly Fit To Handle An Inside Job," *Hartford Courant*, 7 October 2004, www.ctnow.com/sports/football/hc-patriots1007.artoct07,1,5367297.story.

[785] Patriots linebacker Willie McGinest, quoted in: Tom E. Curran, "Patriots of 2004 find their identity," *Providence Journal*, 9 November 2004, www.projo.com/patriots/content/projo_20041109_09patanal.94368.html.

[786] Patriots rookie defensive lineman Marquise Hill, quoted in: "Patriots Video News," 24 June 2004, www.patriots.com/mediaworld/MediaDetail.sps?ID=29494&keywords=VIDEONEWS&media=video.

[787] Jets tight end Anthony Becht, quoted in: Bill Burt, "Smilin' in the rain," *Eagle Tribune*, 16 September 2002, www.eagletribune.com/news/stories/20020916/SP_002.htm.

[788] Veteran punter and former Pittsburgh Steeler Josh Miller, quoted in: Tom E. Curran, "Patriots Notebook: Team is fast out of the gate," *Providence Journal*, 11 June 2004, www.projo.com/patriots/content/projo_20040611_11patsjo.fcc1f.html.

[789] Scott Pioli, Patriots VP of player personnel, quoted in: Bob Brookover, "Star wideout may not be a prize catch," *Philadelphia Inquirer*, 31 January 2004, www.philly.com/mld/inquirer/sports/7839686.htm?1c.

[790] Bill Belichick, quoted in: Jarrett Bell, "Patriots defy odds in face of salary cap, free agency," *USA Today*, 10 September 2004, www.usatoday.com/sports/football/nfl/patriots/2004-09-09-building-champ_x.htm.

[791] Scott Pioli, Patriots VP of player personnel, quoted in: Charles P. Pierce, "The Patriot," *Boston Globe*, 5 September 2004, www.boston.com/news/globe/magazine/articles/2004/09/05/the_patriot/.

[792] Bill Belichick, quoted in: Alan Greenberg, "Buckley accepts his role," *Hartford Courant*, 15 September 2002, p. E4, ProQuest database.

[793] XXX

[794] Joel Buchsbaum, "There's more to draft busts, steals than meets the eye," *Pro Football Weekly*, June 1, 1999, http://archive.profootballweekly.com/content/archives/features_1998/buchsbaum_060199.asp.

[795] Coach Bill Belichick, quoted in: Alan Greenberg, "Belichick Game Plan For Life," *Hartford Courant*, 3 May 2004, www.ctnow.com/sports/hc-belichick0503.artmay03,1,707205.story.

[796] Patriots wide receiver Troy Brown, quoted in: Michael Felger, "Brown in the flow: Timing may be right for action," *Boston Herald*, 1 October 2004, http://patriots.bostonherald.com/patriots/view.bg?articleid=46906.

[797] Safety Rodney Harrison, quoted in: Rich Thompson, "Group's character a primary asset," *Boston Herald*, 9 September 2004, http://patriots.bostonherald.com/patriots/view.bg?articleid=43431.

[798] Joel Buchsbaum, "There's more to draft busts, steals than meets the eye," *Pro Football Weekly*, June 1, 1999, http://archive.profootballweekly.com/content/archives/features_1998/buchsbaum_060199.asp.

[799] Patriots owner Bob Kraft, quoted in: Felice J. Freyer, "'Don't be afraid to dream big,'" *Providence Journal*, 23 May 2004, www.projo.com/extra/graduation/college/content/projo_20040523_jw23.21e45b.html.

[800] Bill Belichick, quoted in: Harvey Mackay, *We Got Fired!*, New York: Ballantine Books, 2004, p. 68.

[801] Patriots linebacker Mike Vrabel, quoted in: Charles P. Pierce, "The Patriot," *Boston Globe*, 5 September 2004, www.boston.com/news/globe/magazine/articles/2004/09/05/the_patriot/.

[802] Patriots VP of player personnel, Scott Pioli, quoted in: Bob McGinn, "A priceless collection," *Milwaukee Journal-Sentinel*, 31 January 2002, www.jsonline.com/packer/prev/jan02/16658.asp.

[803] You can hear Lehrer himself sing his song at fightmusic.com/ivy.html under "Crimson."

[804] Steve Belichick, quoted in: Dennis Dodd, "Insider: Johnson rights Navy's ship," *CBS Sportsline*, 14 October 2004, www.sportsline.com/collegefootball/story/7793172.

[805] Bill Belichick, quoted in: Alex Timiraos, "Pats coach talks leadership at BC," *The Heights*, 9 April 2004, www.bcheights.com/news/2004/04/09/News/Pats-Coach.Talks.Leadership.At.Bc-656659.shtml.

[806] Patriots offensive lineman Stephen Neal, quoted in: Paul Kenyon, "Pats' Neal is no longer grappling with his role," *Providence Journal*, 12 November 2004.

[807] Tom Brady, quoted in: Tom E. Curran, "Tom Brady: The man behind the growing legend," *Providence Journal*, 25 July 2004, www.projo.com/patriots/content/projo_20040725_brad25.e8f8fb.html.

[808] Tennessee Titans defensive coordinator Jim Schwartz, quoted in: Nick Cafardo, "Schwartz's way is stat of the art," *Boston Globe*, 8 January 2004, www.boston.com/sports/football/patriots/articles/2004/01/08/schwartzs_way_is_stat_of_the_art.

[809] New York Giants general manager Ernie Accorsi, quoted in: Bob Glauber, "Billy Ball," *Newsday*, 25 January 2004, www.allthingsbillbelichick.com/articles/billyball.htm.

[810] Bill Belichick, quoted in: Alex Timiraos, "Pats coach talks leadership at BC," *The Heights*, 9 April 2004, www.bcheights.com/news/2004/04/09/News/Pats-Coach.Talks.Leadership.At.Bc-656659.shtml.

[811] Patriots fullback Fred McCrary, quoted in: Andy Kent, "NFL: McCrary eyes Pats starting role," *Naples Daily News*, 20 July 2004, www.naplesnews.com/npdn/sports/article/0,2071,NPDN_15000_3049089,00.html.

[812] Patriots offensive lineman Damien Woody, quoted in: Jackie MacMullan, "Some of these boys have been here before," *Boston Globe*, 2 February 2004, www.boston.com/sports/football/patriots/articles/2004/02/02/some_of_these_boys_have_been_here_before/.

[813] Patriots cornerback Ty Law, quoted in: Jackie MacMullan, "Some of these boys have been here before," *Boston Globe*, 2 February 2004, www.boston.com/sports/football/patriots/articles/2004/02/02/some_of_these_boys_have_been_here_before/.

[814] Patriots wide receiver Troy Brown, quoted in: AP, "Brown is Brady's guy," *WFSB Channel 3*, www.wfsb.com/Global/story.asp?S=1618650.

[815] Troy Brown, quoted in: Anthony Hanshew, "Humble hero," *Herald-Dispatch*, 27 June 2004, www.herald-dispatch.com/2004/June/27/MUspot.htm.

[816] Patriots wide receiver David Patten, quoted in: Glen Farley, "Patten raring to answer age-old questions," *The Enterprise*, 18 August 2004, http://enterprise.southofboston.com/articles/2004/08/18/news/sports/sports01.txt.

[817] Patriots special teams captain and standout Larry Izzo, quoted in: Mike Holbrook, "Welcome to 'The Izzone South,'" *Pro Football Weekly*, 28 January 2004, www.profootballweekly.com/PFW/NFL/AFC/AFC+East/New+England/Features/2004/izzo012804.htm.

[818] Patriots rookie defensive tackle Vince Wilfork, quoted in: Ian M. Clark, "Patriots Notebook: Win doesn't impress Belichick," *Union Leader*, 15 August 2004, www.theunionleader.com/articles_showfast.html?article=42308.

[819] Patriots rookie Vince Wilfork, quoted in: Michael Felger, "Pats' Wilfork will weight and see," *Boston Herald*, 30 April 2004, http://patriots.bostonherald.com/patriots/view.bg?articleid=13894.

[820] Tom Brady, quoted in: Mark Maske, "Selfless Patriots show how it's done," *Washington Post*, 4 February 2004, www.msnbc.msn.com/id/4144383/.

[821] Bill Belichick, quoted in: Mark Maske, "Selfless Patriots show how it's done," *Washington Post*, 4 February 2004, www.msnbc.msn.com/id/4144383/.

[822] Michael Felger, "Belichick goes on the offensive," *Boston Herald*, 25 July 2004, http://patriots.bostonherald.com/patriots/view.bg?articleid=37051.

[823] Unnamed Patriot, quoted in: Nick Cafardo, "The Patriots are equipped for camping," *Boston Globe*, 25 July 2004, www.boston.com/sports/football/patriots/articles/2004/07/25/the_patriots_are_equipped_for_camping.

[824] Patriots offensive guard Joe Andruzzi, quoted in: Michael Felger, "Pats gear for trip back to the top," *Boston Herald*, 29 July 2004, http://patriots.bostonherald.com/patriots/view.bg?articleid=37690.

[825] Patriots safety Rodney Harrison, quoted in: Rich Eisen, "A conversation with Rodney Harrison," *NFL.com*, 19 July 2004, www.nfl.com/nflnetwork/story/7513397.

[826] Bill Belichick, quoted in: Michael Felger, "Watson sits out practice," *Boston Herald*, 17 September 2004, http://patriots.bostonherald.com/patriots/view.bg?articleid=44676.

[827] Bill Belichick, quoted in: Michael Felger, "Watson sits out practice," *Boston Herald*, 17 September 2004, http://patriots.bostonherald.com/patriots/view.bg?articleid=44676.

[828] Bill Belichick, quoted in: Tom E. Curran, "Patriots Notebook: '72 Dolphins stubbornly refuse to acknowledge Pats' streak," *Providence Journal*, 17 September 2004, www.projo.com/patriots/content/projo_20040917_17patsjo.1377c6.html.

[829] Coach Bill Belichick, cited in: Associated Press, "Belichick tells grads to find their passion," *HeraldNews.com*, 3 May 2004, www.zwire.com/site/news.cfm?newsid=11427445&BRD=1710&PAG=740&dept_id=353135&rfi=6.

[830] Patriots linebacker Mike Vrabel, quoted in: Patrick McManamon, "The Mastermind," *Akron Beacon Journal*, 1 February 2004, www.fortwayne.com/mld/ohio/sports/columnists/patrick_mcmanamon/7848542.htm.

[831] Ray Mickens, who played safety on Belichick's New York Jets defense from 1997 through 1999, quoted in: Bill Burt, "Smilin' in the rain," *Eagle Tribune*, 16 September 2002, www.eagletribune.com/news/stories/20020916/SP_002.htm.

[832] Patriots linebacker Mike Vrabel, quoted in: Hector Longo, "Walter attempting to redeem himself," *Eagle Tribune*, 18 December 2003, eagletribune.com/news/stories/20031218/SP_005.htm.

[833] Bill Belichick, "Bill Belichick Press Conf.Transcript 7/31/04," 31 July 2004, www.patriots.com/news/fullarticle.sps?id=29754&type=general.

[834] Fresno State head coach Pat Hill, quoted in: Bill Reynolds, "Belichick paving way for students' success," *Pro Football Weekly*, 1 December 2003, www.profootballweekly.com/PFW/NFL/AFC/AFC+East/New+England/Features/2003/reynolds120103.htm.

[835] Dave Jennings, New York Giants punter in 1978, quoted in: Terry Pluto, "The Man Behind the Mask," *Akron Beacon Journal*, 18 December 1994, www.allthingsbillbelichick.com/articles/behindthemask.htm.

[836] Ernie Accorsi, quoted in: George Vecsey, "Super Bowl Coaches With a Giants Connection," *New York Times*, 21 January 2004, p. D4, ProQuest database.

[837] Ernie Accorsi, quoted in: Michael Eisen, "Belichick, Fox Earn Praise From Accorsi," *Giants.com*, 28 January 2004, www.giants.com/news/index.cfm?cont_id=226897&right_include=/includes/eisens_archive_module.cfm.

[838] Patriots linebacker Roman Phifer, quoted in: Ron Borges, "What Makes Belichick Tick," *Boston Globe Magazine*, 10 September 2000, www.allthingsbillbelichick.com/articles/makestick.html.

[839] Michael Holley, "Best seat in the house," *Boston Globe*, 7 December 2000, www.allthingsbillbelichick.com/articles/bestseat.htm.

[840] Michael Holley, "'It's Just Another Sideline,'" *Boston Globe*, 28 April 2000, www.allthingsbillbelichick.com/articles/sideline.html.

[841] Former Navy and Detroit Lions head coach Rick Forzano, quoted in: Jerry Green, "Belichick was raised to be a coach," *Detroit News*, 29 January 2004, www.detnews.com/2004/lions/0401/29/g01-49608.htm.

[842] Matt Straub, " Role model honors those who helped form him," *Middletown Press*, 30 April 2004, www.zwire.com/site/news.cfm?newsid=11416332&BRD=1645&PAG=461&dept_id=17758&rfi=6.

[843] Coach Bill Belichick, quoted in: Alan Greenberg, "Belichick Game Plan For Life," *Hartford Courant*, 3 May 2004, www.ctnow.com/sports/hc-belichick0503.artmay03,1,707205.story.

[844] Coach Bill Belichick, cited in: Associated Press, "Belichick tells grads to find their passion," *HeraldNews.com*, 3 May 2004, www.zwire.com/site/news.cfm?newsid=11427445&BRD=1710&PAG=740&dept_id=353135&rfi=6.

[845] Bill Belichick, quoted in: Alan Greenberg, "Getting Along Well Belichick Still A Little Grim, But With A Grin," *Hartford Courant*, 3 September 2000, p. E1, ProQuest database.

[846] Patriots VP of player personnel, Scott Pioli, quoted in: "Central Connecticut State University Athletics," 13 November 2002, http://ccsubluedevils.collegesports.com/administration/con-ninequestionsscottpioli.html.

[847] Patriots linebacker Roman Phifer, quoted in: Chris Kennedy, "Phifer enjoys jokes, respect," *MassLive.com*, 9 August 2004, www.masslive.com/sports/republican/index.ssf?/base/sports-0/1092041272304150.xml.

[848] Ricky Williams, quoted in: Skip Bayless, "Ricky Williams was always fool's gold," *San Jose Mercury News*, 27 July 2004, www.mercurynews.com/mld/mercurynews/sports/9258270.htm?1c.

[849] Ricky Williams' agent, Leigh Steinberg, quoted in: "Need genius to crack 'The Williams Code,'" *San Diego Union-Tribune*, 27 July 2004, www.signonsandiego.com/sports/20040727-9999-lz1s27galry.html.

[850] Ricky Williams, quoted in: AP, "Report: Williams Said He Failed Drug Test," *Patriot Ledger*, 29 July 2004, http://hosted.ap.org/dynamic/stories/F/FBN_DOLPHINS_WILLIAMS?SITE=MAQUI&SECTION=HOME&TEMPLATE=DEFAULT.

[851] NFL Hall of Fame running back Barry Sanders, quoted in: Associated Press, "Sanders Surprised by Williams's Decision," *New York Times*, 27 July 2004, www.nytimes.com/aponline/sports/AP-FBN-Sanders-Williams.html.

[852] Skip Bayless, "Ricky Williams was always fool's gold," *San Jose Mercury News*, 27 July 2004, www.mercurynews.com/mld/mercurynews/sports/9258270.htm?1c.

[853] Patriots special teams standout and 9-year veteran Je'Rod Cherry, quoted in: Mike Reiss, "Football's end game: The challenge of post-career planning," *Metrowest Daily News*, 30 May 2004, www.metrowestdailynews.com/sportsNews/view.bg?articleid=69553.

[854] Baltimore Ravens assistant coach Dennis Thurman, who recruited Russell to USC and mentored him at USC, quoted in: Skip Bayless, "Ricky Williams was always fool's gold," *San Jose Mercury News*, 27 July 2004, www.mercurynews.com/mld/mercurynews/sports/9258270.htm?1c.

[855] Patriot Dan Klecko, quoted in: Chris Kennedy, "Klecko OK with roles," *MassLive.com*, 6 August 2004, www.masslive.com/printer/printer.ssf?/base/sports-2/10917819456431.xml.

[856] Patriot Dan Klecko, quoted in: Chris Kennedy, "Klecko OK with roles," *MassLive.com*, 6 August 2004, www.masslive.com/printer/printer.ssf?/base/sports-2/10917819456431.xml.

[857] St. Louis Rams defensive end Chidi Ahanotu, quoted in: Michael Silver, "Pat Answer," *Sports Illustrated*, 11 February 2002, http://sportsillustrated.cnn.com/si_online/news/2002/02/11/pat_answer/.

[858] St. Louis Rams head coach Mike Martz, on the 2001 Patriots' Super Bowl victory, quoted in: Will McDonough, "A few musings on a miracle in the Big Easy," *Patriots United*, Canada: Team Power Publishing, 2002, p. 13.

[859] Patriots linebacker Mike Vrabel, quoted in: Bill Burt, "What a kick!" *Eagle Tribune*, 4 February 2004, www.eagletribune.com/news/stories/20020204/FP_001.htm.

[860] Patriots offensive lineman Joe Andruzzi, quoted in: "Patriots are just ... well ... different," David Pevear, *Lowell Sun*, 18 October 2004, www.lowellsun.com/Stories/0,1413,105~4767~2476150,00.html.

[861] Patriots quarterback Tom Brady, quoted in: Len Pasquarelli, "MVP poised, poignant on morning after," *ESPN.com*, 2 February 2004, http://sports.espn.go.com/nfl/playoffs03/columns/story?columnist=pasquarelli_len&id=1725363.

[862] Patriots quarterback Tom Brady, quoted in: Len Pasquarelli, "MVP poised, poignant on morning after," *ESPN.com*, 2 February 2004, http://sports.espn.go.com/nfl/playoffs03/columns/story?columnist=pasquarelli_len&id=1725363.

[863] Tom Brady, quoted in: Glen Farley, "It's a wonderful life," *The Enterprise*, 5 September 2004, http://enterprise.southofboston.com/articles/2004/09/05/sports/sports03.txt.

[864] Tom Brady, quoted in: Mike O'Hara, "Patriots have plan to win," *Detroit News*, 9 September 2004, www.detnews.com/2004/lions/0409/09/d03-267659.htm.

[865] Patriots inside linebackers coach Pepper Johnson, *Won For All*, Chicago: Contemporary Books, 2003, p. 1-2.

[866] Patriots wide receiver David Patten, quoted in: Joe Burris, "Deep route," *Boston Globe*, 29 October 2004, www.boston.com/sports/football/patriots/articles/2004/10/29/deep_route.

[867] Patriots wide receiver David Patten, quoted in: Paul Kenyon, "Patriots' Patten refuses to let himself fade away," *Providence Journal*, 29 October 2004, www.projo.com/patriots/content/projo_20041029_29pats.77d77.html.

[868] Patriots cornerback Ty Law, quoted in: Glen Farley, "They have the Law on their side," November 9, 1998, http://archive.profootballweekly.com/content/archives/features_1998/defense_newengland_110998.asp.

[869] Former Patriots coach Pete Carroll, quoted in: Glen Farley, "They have the Law on their side," November 9, 1998, http://archive.profootballweekly.com/content/archives/features_1998/defense_newengland_110998.asp.

[870] Bill Belichick, quoted in: John Tomase, "Belichick has a few surprises ready," *Eagle Tribune*, 2 February 2000, www.eagletribune.com/news/stories/20000202/SP_011.htm.

[871] Patriots cornerback Ty Law, quoted in: Glen Farley, "They have the Law on their side," November 9, 1998, http://archive.profootballweekly.com/content/archives/features_1998/defense_newengland_110998.asp.

[872] Patriots wide receiver Troy Brown, quoted in: Tom Silverstein, "Brown's style: never give up," *Milwaukee Journal-Sentinel*, 30 January 2004, www.jsonline.com/packer/prev/jan02/16409.asp.

[873] Patriots wide receiver Troy Brown, quoted in: Tom Silverstein, "Brown's style: never give up," *Milwaukee Journal-Sentinel*, 30 January 2004, www.jsonline.com/packer/prev/jan02/16409.asp.

[874] *The Sporting News*, quoted in: Jeff D'Alessio, "Picking a star quarterback can be a tossup," *Florida Today*, 10 January 2004, http://bengals.enquirer.com/2004/01/10/ben2qb.html.

[875] Draftnik Mel Kiper Jr., quoted in: Clare Farnsworth, "Hawks, Pats QBs stand on common ground," *Seattle Post-Intelligencer*, 14 October 2004, http://seattlepi.nwsource.com/football/195156_hawk14.html.

[876] Former New Orleans Saints general manager Randy Mueller, quoted in: Paul Attner, " Whatever 'It' is, Brady has 'It,'" *Sports Illustrated*, 6 October 2004, http://msn.foxsports.com/story/3059636.

[877] Patriots VP of player personnel, Scott Pioli, quoted in: Jeff D'Alessio, "Picking a star quarterback can be a tossup," *Florida Today*, 10 January 2004, http://bengals.enquirer.com/2004/01/10/ben2qb.html.

[878] Super Bowl-winning quarterback Phil Simms, quoted in: Greg Bishop, "Hasselbeck, Brady in the draft: Better late than early?" *Seattle Post-Intelligencer*, 14 October 2004, http://seattletimes.nwsource.com/html/sports/2002062745_hawk14.html.

[879] "In control under fire," *New York Times*, 1 February 2004, http://extras.journalnow.com/superbowl/panthers/preview/brady.html.

[880] Patriots VP of player personnel Scott Pioli, quoted in: Jody Foldesy, "Patriots win piece of history," *Washington Times*, 2 February 2004, www.washingtontimes.com/functions/print.php?StoryID=20040202-012334-6654r.

[881] Wide receiver Donald Hayes, quoted in: Tom Barnidge, "Cinderella deja vu: Brady seeks encore," *NFL Insider*, 9 September 2002, www.nfl.com/insider/story/5688388.

[882] Patriots quarterback Tom Brady, quoted in: Tom Barnidge, "Cinderella deja vu: Brady seeks encore," NFL Insider, 9 September 2002, www.nfl.com/insider/story/5688388.

[883] Tom Brady, quoted in: Joe Burris, "No flash in the plan," *Boston Globe*, 9 September 2004, www.boston.com/sports/football/patriots/articles/2004/09/09/no_flash_in_the_plan.

[884] Seth Wickersham, "The Brady Hunch," *ESPN The Magazine*, 14 December 2001, www.absolutebrady.com/Articles/ESPN121401.html.

[885] Dan Pompei, "Inside Pats' Super Bowl Preparations," *Sporting News*, 2 February 2004, www.allthingsbillbelichick.com/articles/insidesbprep.htm.

[886] Tom Brady, quoted in: Kevin McNamara, "Notebook: First roster cuts, heading toward 65," *Providence Journal*, 31 August 2004, www.projo.com/patriots/content/projo_20040831_31patsjo.2f3eb.html.

[887] Bob Glauber, "Hoist white flag for defenders," *Newsday*, 29 August 2004, www.nynewsday.com/sports/football/ny-spglaub293946790aug29,0,79452.column?coll=ny-sports-columnists.

[888] Patriots rookie tight end Benjamin Watson, quoted in: Glen Farley, "Even growing up, rookie Watson had Patriots covered," *The Enterprise*, 26 August 2004, http://enterprise.southofboston.com/articles/2004/08/26/news/sports/sports02.txt.

[889] Patriots defensive lineman Richard Seymour, quoted in: Associated Press, "Patriots say they've hit jackpot with former Bulldog defensive line star," *Athens Banner-Herald*, 30 January 2004, www.onlineathens.com/stories/013104/spo_20040131022.shtml.

[890] Patriots tight end Christian Fauria, quoted in: Bob Ryan, "No disguise, Fauria is just one of the guys," *Boston Globe*, 2 February 2004, www.boston.com/sports/football/patriots/articles/2004/02/02/no_disguise_fauria_is_just_one_of_the_guys.

[891] Offensive guard Russ Hochstein, quoted in: Terry Hersom, "Hartington's Hochstein making his mark in NFL," *Sioux City Journal*, 29 September 2004, www.siouxcityjournal.com/articles/2004/09/29/sports/sports/1010b9bbc8168b7386256f1e00177779.txt.

[892] Wide receiver David Givens, quoted in: George Kimball, "The art of the game: On the field or in the studio, David Givens has designs on greatness," *Boston Herald*, 10 October 2004, http://patriots.bostonherald.com/patriots/view.bg?articleid=48342.

[893] Patriots rookie Marquise Hill, quoted in: Michael Felger, "Hill truly digs the down under," *Boston Herald*, 2 May 2004, http://patriots.bostonherald.com/patriots/view.bg?articleid=17351.

[894] Patriot special teamer Je'Rod Cherry, quoted in: Mike Reiss, "Football's end game: The challenge of post-career planning," *Metrowest Daily News*, 30 May 2004, www.metrowestdailynews.com/sportsNews/view.bg?articleid=69553.

[895] Patriots Vice President of Player Personnel Scott Pioli, quoted in: Michael Felger, "Pioli: Scout's Honor," *Boston Herald*, 19 December 2001, www.allthingsbillbelichick.com/articles/piolihonor.htm.

[896] Patriots special teamer Shawn Mayer, quoted in: Michael Smith, "These rookies class acts," *Boston Globe*, 29 January 2004, www.boston.com/sports/football/patriots/articles/2004/01/29/these_rookies_class_acts/.

[897] Patriots linebacker Mike Vrabel, quoted in: David Pevear, "Vrabel: Poster child for Patriot football," *Lowell Sun*, 10 August 2004, www.lowellsun.com/Stories/0,1413,105~4767~2325627,00.html.

[898] Patriots rookie tight end Benjamin Watson, quoted in: Howard Ullman (AP), "Pats get first pick in fold," *Union Leader*, 17 August 2004, www.theunionleader.com/articles_showa.html?article=42432.

[899] Alan Greenberg, "Draftees Are Family Friendly," *Hartford Courant*, 30 April 2004, www.ctnow.com/sports/hc-patriots0430.artapr30,1,1721503.print.story?coll=hc-headlines-sports.

[900] Buffalo Bills running back Willis McGahee, quoted in: Karen Guregian, "McGahee won't trash talk opponent," *Boston Herald*, 14 November 2004, http://patriots.bostonherald.com/patriots/view.bg?articleid=53962.

[901] Michael Felger, "Pats' Wilfork will weight and see," *Boston Herald*, 30 April 2004, http://patriots.bostonherald.com/patriots/view.bg?articleid=13894.

[902] Tom E. Curran, "Patriots Notebook: Stronger Brady greets rookies at Gillette Stadium," *Providence Journal*, 1 May 2004, http://www.projo.com/patriots/content/projo_20040501_01patsjo.fbbc0.html.

[903] Patriots rookie Vince Wilfork, quoted in: Michael Felger, "Pats' Wilfork will weight and see," *Boston Herald*, 30 April 2004, http://patriots.bostonherald.com/patriots/view.bg?articleid=13894.

[904] Patriots rookie Vince Wilfork, "Vince Wilfork Conf. Call Transcript - 4/24," *Patriots.com*, 24 April 2004, www.patriots.com/news/FullArticle.sps?id=28458&type=general.

[905] Patriots rookie Vince Wilfork, "Vince Wilfork Conf. Call Transcript - 4/24," *Patriots.com*, 24 April 2004, www.patriots.com/news/FullArticle.sps?id=28458&type=general.

[906] Bill Burt, "'Baby Sapp' arrives," *Eagle Tribune*, 25 April 2004, www.eagletribune.com/news/stories/20040425/SP_002.htm.

[907] Patriots defensive tackle Vince Wilfork, quoted in: George Kimball, "Wilfork's no homer," *Boston Herald*, 11 October 2004, http://patriots.bostonherald.com/patriots/view.bg?articleid=48461.

[908] Patriots rookie running back Cedric Cobbs, quoted in: Nick Cafardo, "Cobbs gets fresh start," *Boston Globe*, 26 April 2004, www.boston.com/sports/football/patriots/articles/2004/04/26/cobbs_gets_fresh_start/.

[909] Alan Grant, "Running man," *ESPN The Magazine*, May 14, 2001, http://espn.go.com/magazine/vol4no10dillon.html.

[910] Mark Curnutte, "Dillon investigated for assault on wife," *Cincinnati Enquirer*, 29 August 2000, http://bengals.enquirer.com/2000/08/29/ben_dillon_investigated.html.

[911] Coach Bill Belichick: "Bill Belichick Press Conf. Transcript 4/25/04," *Patriots.com*, 25 April 2004, www.patriots.com/news/FullArticle.sps?id=28531&type=draft.

[912] Len Pasquarelli, "Belichick and Pioli have winning formula," *ESPN.com*, 27 July 2002, http://espn.go.com/nfl/trainingcamp02/columns/patriots/1410739.html.

[913] Patriots safety Rodney Harrison, quoted in: Howard Balzer, "New England rings out the old year," *USA Today*, 24 June 2004, www.usatoday.com/sports/football/columnist/balzer/2004-06-24-super-rings_x.htm.

[914] Patriots defensive lineman Richard Seymour, quoted in: Michael Felger, "Tackling adversity: Seymour grapples with his father's death," *Boston Herald*, 9 June 2004, http://patriots.bostonherald.com/patriots/view.bg?articleid=31193.

[915] Patriots defensive lineman Richard Seymour, quoted in: Michael Parente, " Pats' DL Seymour continues to rise," *New Britain Herald*, 11 August 2004, www.zwire.com/site/news.cfm?newsid=12664369&BRD=1641&PAG=461&dept_id=17739&rfi=6.

[916] Jamil Soriano, quoted in: Andy Hart, "Soriano seeking experience, NFL Europe ring," *Patriots Football Weekly*, 5 May 2004, www.patriots.com/news/FullArticle.sps?id=28665&type=general.

[917] Bill Belichick, quoted in: Bill Burt, "Belichick: It was one tough Patriot draft," *Eagle Tribune*, 17 April 2000, www.eagletribune.com/news/stories/20000417/SP_004.htm.

[918] Patriots fullback Jermaine Wiggins, after the Patriots beat the Oakland Raiders in the January 2002 "Snow Bowl," quoted in: AP, "Ice man cometh," *Sports Illustrated*, 20 January 2002, http://sportsillustrated.cnn.com/football/2002/playoffs/news/2002/01/19/raiders_patriots_ap/.

[919] Patriots wide reciever David Patten, quoted in: David Pevear, "Wideouts receiving plenty of praise," *Lowell Sun*, 5 August 2004, www.lowellsun.com/Stories/0,1413,105~4767~2316378,00.html.

[920] Patriots wide receiver David Givens, quoted in: Joe Burris, "Givens grabs the spotlight," *Boston Globe*, 20 September 2004, www.boston.com/sports/football/patriots/articles/2004/09/20/givens_grabs_the_spotlight.

[921] Patriots safety Rodney Harrison, quoted in: Joe Burris, "Hitting back," *Boston Globe*, 19 September 2004, www.boston.com/sports/football/patriots/articles/2004/09/19/hitting_back.

[922] Patriots safety Rodney Harrison, quoted in: Michael Parente, "Pats' Wilson a big hit," *Woonsocket Call*, 22 September 2004, www.woonsocketcall.com/site/news.cfm?newsid=12976112&BRD=1712&PAG=461&dept_id=106787&rfi=6.

[923] Patriots linebacker Tedy Bruschi, quoted in: "Notes from Redskins game 9/28/03," *Boston Herald*, www.patriotworld.com/TotallyTedyMedia/2003articles.htm.

[924] Patriots rookie safety Dexter Reid, quoted in: Hector Longo, "Patriots' hopes set on fifth-round pick Sam," *Eagle Tribune*, 26 April 2004, www.eagletribune.com/news/stories/20040426/SP_007.htm.

[925] Patriots Vice President of Player Personnel Scott Pioli, quoted in: Jay Glazer, "Patriots proving to be model franchise," *CBS Sportsline*, 3 December 2003, http://cbs.sportsline.com/nfl/story/6889325.

[926] Patriot linebacker Willie McGinest, quoted in: Steve DeCosta, "Both sides agree, it'll be violent," *Standard-Times*, www.southcoasttoday.com/daily/02-04/02-01-04/e04sp875.htm.

[927] Carolina Panthers defensive lineman Kris Jenkins, quoted in: Associated Press, "Brains Against Brawn / Patriots smart and savvy while Panthers play the power game," *Los Angeles Times*, 1 February 2004, p. D1, ProQuest database.

[928] Carolina Panthers safety Mike Minter, quoted in: Mark Maske, "Secrets of Their Success; Wisdom of Defensive Gurus Belichick, Fox Is Reflected on Field," *Washington Post*, 1 February 2004, p. E1, ProQuest database.

[929] Dan Pires, "Postgame talk ranges from Sapp to streaker," *Standard-Times*, 4 February 2004, www.southcoasttoday.com/daily/02-04/02-04-04/c01sp273.htm.

[930] Patriots linebacker Tedy Bruschi, quoted in: Jay Glazer, "For Belichick vs. Manning, it's check and checkmate," *CBS Sportsline*, 18 January 2004, cbs.sportsline.com/nfl/story/7017545.

[931] Patriots linebacker Tedy Bruschi, quoted in: Nolan Nawrocki, "There's no 'I' in 'team,'" *Pro Football Weekly*, 3 February 2002, http://archive.profootballweekly.com/content/archives2001/features_2001/sb_0203023.asp.

[932] Bill Belichick, quoted in: Bill Burt, "Bruschi a true blue Patriot," *Eagle Tribune*, 31 January 2002, www.eagletribune.com/news/stories/20020131/SP_004.htm.

[933] Patriots cornerback Ty Law, quoted in: Tom E. Curran, "Matchup with undefeated Jets has touch of history attached," *Providence Journal*, 21 October 2004, www.projo.com/patriots/content/projo_20041021_21patsjo.30b349.html.

[934] Patriots cornerback Tyrone Poole, quoted in: Adam Kilgore, "Patriots secondary may face tough task," *Boston Globe*, 6 September 2004, www.boston.com/sports/football/patriots/articles/2004/09/06/patriots_secondary_may_face_tough_task.

[935] Patriots safety Rodney Harrison, quoted in: Mike Lowe, "It's a super way to start the season," *Portland Press Herald*, 8 September 2004, http://pressherald.mainetoday.com/sports/pro/patriots/040908lowecolumn.shtml.

[936] Patriots inside linebackers coach Pepper Johnson, quoted in: Paul Attner, "Super Bowl 36: Standing Pat," *The Sporting News*, 4 February 2002, www.a1-sports-odds.com/292.htm.

[937] Patriots rookie nose tackle Vince Wilfork, quoted in: Tony Chamberlain, "Developing nose for ball," *Boston Globe*, 11 October 2004, www.boston.com/sports/football/patriots/articles/2004/10/11/developing_nose_for_ball.

[938] Tom Brady, quoted in interview with Matthew McConaughey, "Tom Brady," *Interview Magazine*, October 2004, www.interviewmagazine.com/images/TomBrady.pdf.

[939] Patriots linebacker Tedy Bruschi, quoted in: Damon Hack, "Hard Contact Is Music to Bruschi's Ears," *New York Times*, 29 January 2004, D1, ProQuest database.

[940] Patriots offensive lineman Damien Woody, quoted in: Hector Longo, "Pats' Belichick passes all tests," *Eagle Tribune*, 13 January 2002, www.eagletribune.com/news/stories/20020113/SP_001.htm.

[941] Phil Simms, "Parcells-Belichick will be exciting," *NFL.com*, 11 November 2003, www.nfl.com/news/story/6823639.

[942] Bill Belichick, quoted in: Jim McCabe, "Dillon has a gang of admirers," *Boston Globe*, 19 October 2004, www.boston.com/sports/football/patriots/articles/2004/10/19/dillon_has_a_gang_of_admirers.

[943] Bill Belichick, quoted in: Jim McCabe, "Dillon has a gang of admirers," *Boston Globe*, 19 October 2004, www.boston.com/sports/football/patriots/articles/2004/10/19/dillon_has_a_gang_of_admirers.

[944] Kurt Kittner's coach at Schaumburg (Ill.) High, Tom Cerasani, quoted in: Bill Burt, "Kittner's high school coach: Pats will love backup QB," *Eagle Tribune*, 25 July 2004, www.eagletribune.com/news/stories/20040725/SP_005.htm.

[945] LSU cornerback and current Patriot Randall Gay, quoted in: Gannett News Service, "Daniels, Landry fitting in on Tigers' defense," *The Advertiser* (Lafayette, LA), 10 October 2004, www.theadvertiser.com/news/html/752BEA5B-4E8C-4C31-808E-1A652DFF58C4.shtml.

[946] Tom Brady, quoted in: Bryan Morry, "Managing the Moment," *Lindy's 2004 Pro Football*, p. 9.

[947] Tom Brady, quoted in: Glen Farley, "It's a wonderful life," *The Enterprise*, 5 September 2004, http://enterprise.southofboston.com/articles/2004/09/05/news/sports/sports03.txt.

[948] Patriots offensive guard Russ Hochstein, quoted in: Michael Smith, "A chip on block," *Boston Globe*, 29 July 2004, www.boston.com/sports/football/patriots/articles/2004/07/29/a_chip_on_block.

[949] Patriots linebacker Ted Johnson, quoted in: Michael Smith, "Camp fires burning," *Boston Globe*, 30 July 2004, www.boston.com/sports/football/patriots/articles/2004/07/30/camp_fires_burning/.

[950] Bill Belichick, quoted in: Bryan Morry, *Patriots United*, Canada: Team Power Publishing, 2002, p. 89.

[951] Bill Belichick, on Rosevelt Colvin before he suffered a season-ending injury the second week of the 2003 season, quoted in: Hector Longo, "All Colvin has to do is produce," *Eagle Tribune*, 27 July 2004, www.eagletribune.com/news/stories/20030727/SP_005.htm.

[952] Dan Pompei, "Inside Pats' Super Bowl Preparations," *Sporting News*, 2 February 2004, www.allthingsbillbelichick.com/articles/insidesbprep.htm.

[953] Patriots tight ends coach Christian Fauria, quoted in: Dan Pires, "Postgame talk ranges from Sapp to streaker," *Standard-Times*, 4 February 2004, www.southcoasttoday.com/daily/02-04/02-04-04/c01sp273.htm.

[954] Willie McGinest, quoted in: Jarrett Bell, "Patriots defy odds in face of salary cap, free agency," *USA Today*, 10 September 2004, www.usatoday.com/sports/football/nfl/patriots/2004-09-09-building-champ_x.htm.

[955] Patriots offensive lineman Damien Woody, quoted in: Hector Longo, "Pats' Belichick passes all tests," *Eagle Tribune*, 13 January 2002, www.eagletribune.com/news/stories/20020113/SP_001.htm.

[956] Patriots linebacker Rosevelt Colvin, quoted in: Michael Smith, "Colvin really gets into it," *Boston Globe*, 10 August 2004, www.boston.com/sports/football/patriots/articles/2004/08/10/colvin_really_gets_into_it.

[957] Patriots wide receiver David Patten, quoted in: Vic Carucci, "Patriots could be team of destiny," *NFL Insider*, 20 January 2002, www.nfl.com/xxxvi/ce/feature/0,3892,4870900,00.html.

[958] Patriots wide receiver David Patten, quoted in: Jay Glazer, "Brady leads way as Patriots drive to shocking upset," *CBS Sportsline*, 4 February 2002, http://cbs.sportsline.com/b/page/pressbox/0,1328,4948886,00.html.

[959] Patriots wide receiver David Patten, quoted in: Don Banks, "Move over Paul Revere," *Sports Illustrated*, 4 February 2002, http://sportsillustrated.cnn.com/inside_game/don_banks/news/2002/02/03/banks_insider/.

[960] Tom Brady, quoted in: Paul Attner, "Super Bowl 38: Red, white and two," *The Sporting News*, 9 February 2004, www.sportingnews.com/archives/superbowl/.

[961] Patriots tight end Christian Fauria, quoted in: Glen Farley, "It's a wonderful life," *The Enterprise*, 5 September 2004, http://enterprise.southofboston.com/articles/2004/09/05/news/sports/sports03.txt.

[962] Patriots center/guard Damien Woody, quoted in: Michael Holley, *Patriot Reign*, William Morrow, 2004, p. 220.

[963] Former Patriot defensive end and Tom Brady housemate Dave Nugent, quoted in: Bill Beuttler, "Tom Brady Avoids the Blitz," *Boston Magazine*, August 2002, www.absolutebrady.com/Articles/BIOBM080102.html.

[964] Joe Theismann, "Patriots had the look of winners," *ESPN.com*, 31 January 2002, http://espn.go.com/nfl/playoffs01/columns/theismann_joe/1320654.html.

[965] Patriots wide receiver Troy Brown, quoted in: Seth Wickersham, "The Brady Hunch," *ESPN The Magazine*, 14 December 2001, www.absolutebrady.com/Articles/ESPN121401.html.

[966] Seth Wickersham, "The Brady Hunch," *ESPN The Magazine*, 14 December 2001, www.absolutebrady.com/Articles/ESPN121401.html.

[967] Jeremy Hus, in: Paul Perillo, "Ask PFW: Offseason concern," *Patriots.com*, 16 November 2004, http://cachewww.patriots.com/news/index.cfm?ac=latestnewsdetail&pid=9748&pcid=41.

[968] Bill Belichick, quoted in: Harvey Mackay, *We Got Fired!*, New York: Ballantine Books, 2004, p. 65.

[969] Patriots safety Rodney Harrison, quoted in: Len Pasquarelli, "Defensive game plan overwhelms Colts," *ESPN.com*, 4 January 2004, http://sports.espn.go.com/nfl/playoffs03/columns/story?columnist=pasquarelli_len&id=1700338.

[970] Patriots linebacker Mike Vrabel, quoted in: Charles P. Pierce, "The Patriot," *Boston Globe*, 5 September 2004, www.boston.com/news/globe/magazine/articles/2004/09/05/the_patriot/.

[971] Patriots rookie tight end Benjamin Watson, "Ben Watson Player Journal," *Patriots.com*, 17 June 2004, www.patriots.com/news/fullarticle.sps?id=28971.

[972] Patriots rookie wide receiver P.K. Sam, "PK Sam Player Journal," *Patriots.com*, 17 June 2004, www.patriots.com/news/fullarticle.sps?id=28972.

[973] *PatriotsInsider.com*, "News and notes from Foxboro," 4 August 2004, http://patriots.theinsiders.com/2/280243.html.

[974] Ethan J. Skolnick, "Patriots are best because they're the smartest," *South Florida Sun-Sentinel*, 7 October 2004, www.sun-sentinel.com/sports/columnists/sfl-skolnick06oct07,0,7494511.column.

[975] Philadelphia Eagles head coach Andy Reid, quoted in: Damon Hack, "Final Review: Victory Is a Videotape Away," *New York Times*, 1 February 2004, section 8, p. 1, ProQuest database.

[976] Cris Collinsworth, "Part 1: Answering the burning questions," *NFL.com*, 16 August 2004, www.nfl.com/news/story/7582518.

[977] Andy Hart, "Media members walk in players' shoes," *Patriots Football Weekly*, 17 July 2003, www.patriots.com/news/fullarticle.sps?id=24287&type=general&special_section=TrainingCamp2003&bhcp=1.

[978] Dan Pompei, "Pass protection evolves into a complex job," *The Sporting News*, 13 May 2003, http://i.tsn.com/voices/dan_pompei/20030513.html.

[979] St. Louis Rams coach Mike Martz, quoted in: Dan Pompei, "Pass protection evolves into a complex job," *The Sporting News*, 13 May 2003, http://i.tsn.com/voices/dan_pompei/20030513.html.

[980] Patriots linebacker Ted Johnson, quoted in: Alan Greenberg (*Hartford Courant*), "Pats' defense thrives with pack mentality," *Philadelphia Inquirer*, 17 January 2004, www.philly.com/mld/inquirer/7731121.htm?1c.

[981] St. Louis Rams coach Mike Martz, quoted in: Dan Pompei, "Pass protection evolves into a complex job," *The Sporting News*, 13 May 2003, http://i.tsn.com/voices/dan_pompei/20030513.html.

[982] Bill Belichick, quoted in: Michael Parente, " Backups provide worthy role for Pats," *New Britain Herald*, 7 September 2004, www.zwire.com/site/news.cfm?newsid=12864399&BRD=1641&PAG=461&dept_id=17739&rfi=6.

[983] Patriots linebacker Willie McGinest, quoted in: Associated Press, "Patriots are on top of their game," *The Desert Sun* (Palm Springs, CA), 30 January 2004, www.thedesertsun.com/news/stories2004/football/20040130022302.shtml.

[984] Patriots rookie wide receiver P.K. Sam, quoted in: Michael Smith, "Out of college, Patriots rookies in work-study," *Boston Globe*, 3 May 2004, www.boston.com/sports/football/patriots/articles/2004/05/03/out_of_college_patriots_rookies_in_work_study/.

[985] Tom Brady, quoted in: Tom E. Curran, "Pats' Branch working his way into the elite fleet of receivers," *Providence Journal*, 17 September 2004, www.projo.com/patriots/content/projo_20040917_17pats.137948.html.

[986] Patriots rookie running back Cedric Cobbs, quoted in: Paul Perillo, "Cobbs looking to land supporting role," *Patriots.com*, 13 May 2004, www.patriots.com/news/FullArticle.sps?id=28760&type=general.

[987] Patriots rookie running back Cedric Cobbs, quoted in: Michael Felger, "Cobbs a project: Pats want RB to be complete," *Boston Herald*, 2 May 2004, http://patriots.bostonherald.com/patriots/view.bg?articleid=17352.

[988] Former Patriot wide receiver Donald Hayes, quoted in: Steve Reed, "Hayes hoping to reignite his career with Panthers," *Freedom News Service*, 10 June 2004, www.newbernsj.com/SiteProcessor.cfm?Template=/GlobalTemplates/Details.cfm&StoryID=15796&Section=Sports.

[989] Patriots cornerback/safety Eugene Wilson, quoted in: Kevin Mannix, "Safety first in key moves: Decision to play rookie turned tide," *Boston Herald*, 27 January 2004, http://patriots.bostonherald.com/patriots/view.bg?articleid=517&format=.

[990] Patriots cornerback/safety Eugene Wilson, quoted in: Associated Press, "Patriots are on top of their game," *The Desert Sun* (Palm Springs, CA), 30 January 2004, www.thedesertsun.com/news/stories2004/football/20040130022302.shtml.

[991] Patriots cornerback/safety Eugene Wilson, quoted in: Hector Longo, "Grade A for Coach B," *Eagle Tribune*, 27 April 2003, www.eagletribune.com/news/stories/20030427/SP_004.htm.

[992] Patriots linebacker Tedy Bruschi, quoted in: Hector Longo, "Belichick may have been a Branch manager," *Eagle Tribune*, 10 September 2002, www.eagletribune.com/news/stories/20020910/SP_004.htm.

[993] Michael Smith, "Small role may produce star," *Boston Globe*, 4 July 2004, www.boston.com/sports/football/patriots/articles/2004/07/04/small_role_may_produce_star.

[994] Bill Belichick, quoted in: Seth Wickersham, "The Brady Hunch," *ESPN The Magazine*, 14 December 2001, www.absolutebrady.com/Articles/ESPN121401.html.

[995] Tom Brady, quoted in: Seth Wickersham, "The Brady Hunch," *ESPN The Magazine*, 14 December 2001, www.absolutebrady.com/Articles/ESPN121401.html.

[996] Hector Longo, "Are you ready for some football?" *Eagle Tribune*, 25 July 2004, www.eagletribune.com/news/stories/20040725/SP_004.htm.

[997] Ron Pollack, "Will Katzenmoyer boom or bust?" *Pro Football Weekly*, 26 March 1999, http://archive.profootballweekly.com/content/archives/draft_1998/ddaily_032699.asp.

[998] Ron Pollack, "Will Katzenmoyer boom or bust?" *Pro Football Weekly*, 26 March 1999, http://archive.profootballweekly.com/content/archives/draft_1998/ddaily_032699.asp.

[999] Hector Longo, "Take Patriots' defections as positive, not negative," *Eagle Tribune*, 28 July 2001, www.eagletribune.com/news/stories/20010728/SP_001.htm.

[1000] Tennessee Titans offensive coordinator Mike Heimerdinger, quoted in: Mike Reiss, "Complications arise: Pats defense tough to read," *Boston Herald*, 22 January 2004, http://patriots.bostonherald.com/patriots/view.bg?articleid=14162.

[1001] Patriots cornerback Terrell Buckley, quoted in: Gordon Edes, "Patriots coach has well-earned reputation for stopping whatever's thrown his way," *Boston Globe*, 2 February 2002, www.boston.com/sports/football/patriots/superbowl/globe_stories/020202/patriots_coach_has_well_earned_reputation_for_stopping_whatever_s_thrown_his_way+.shtml.

[1002] Patriots cornerback Ty Law, quoted in: Bob Glauber, "Billy Ball," *Newsday*, 25 January 2004, www.allthingsbillbelichick.com/articles/billyball.htm.

[1003] Patriots cornerback Ty Law, quoted in: Dan Pires, "Belichick on the verge of history," *Standard-Times*, 1 February 2004, www.southcoasttoday.com/daily/02-04/02-01-04/e01sp874.htm.

[1004] Patriots safety Rodney Harrison, quoted in: Jeff Reynolds, "Harrison, Pats patch wounds, march forward," *Pro Football Weekly*, 27 October 2003, www.profootballweekly.com/PFW/NFL/AFC/AFC+East/New+England/Features/2003/reynolds102703.htm.

[1005] Patriots free agent defensive lineman Dana Stubblefield, quoted in: Chris Kennedy, "Stubblefield has book work to do," *MassLive.com*, www.masslive.com/printer/printer.ssf?/base/sports-0/1092095101201590.xml.

[1006] 49ers offensive lineman Ron Stone, quoted in: Michael Silver, "No Pain, No Gain," *Sports Illustrated*, 2 December 2003, www.cnnsi.com/pr/subs/siexclusive/2003/12/02/linemen1208/.

[1007] New Orleans Saints head coach Jim Haslett, quoted in: Dan Pompei, "Draft rush shows the value of DTs," *The Sporting News*, 6 May 2003, http://i.tsn.com/voices/dan_pompei/20030506.html.

[1008] Second-year Patriot Tully Banta-Cain, quoted in: Adam Kilgore, "LBs are built from ground up," *Boston Globe*, 18 August 2004, www.boston.com/sports/football/patriots/articles/2004/08/18/lbs_are_built_from_ground_up.

[1009] Patriots rookie defensive tackle Vince Wilfork, quoted in: Tim O'Sullivan, " All eyes on the big prize: Top pick Wilfork adjusts to life with the champions," *Concord Monitor*, 11 August 2004, http://www.concordmonitor.com/apps/pbcs.dll/article?Date=20040811&Category=REPOSITORY&ArtNo=408110355&SectionCat=SPORTS&Template=printart.

[1010] Patriots defensive lineman Ty Warren, quoted in: Mike Reiss, "Patriots notebook: Patriots focus on 3 picks," *MetroWest Daily News*, 28 July 2004, www.dailynewstranscript.com/sportsNews/view.bg?articleid=38054.

[1011] Bill Belichick, "Bill Belichick Press Conf. Transcript 8/3/04," 3 August 2004, www.patriots.com/news/fullarticle.sps?id=29867&special_section=TrainingCamp2004&type=training.

[1012] Bill Belichick, quoted in: Todd Archer, "Patriots pick their way to Super Bowl, 24-14," *Dallas Morning News*, 19 January 2004, www.cowboysplus.com/nfl/stories/011904cpafclede.2b7f5ea5.html.

[1013] Rookie running back Cedric Cobbs, quoted in: Paul Kenyon, "Patriots Notebook: Cobbs returns to drills wiser and healthier," *Providence Journal*, 29 October 2004, www.projo.com/patriots/content/projo_20041029_29patsjo.77c1f.html.

[1014] Patriots rookie cornerback Randall Gay, quoted in: Chris Kennedy, "LSU rookie makes team," *The Republican*, 7 September 2004, www.masslive.com/sports/republican/index.ssf?/base/sports-0/1094543587209320.xml.

[1015] Patriot Dan Klecko, quoted in: Sun wire reports, "Klecko on move for Patriots," *Las Vegas Sun*, 6 August 2004, www.lasvegassun.com/sunbin/stories/text/2004/aug/06/517297968.html.

[1016] Patriots left tackle Matt Light, quoted in: Chris Kennedy, "Pats putting season on line," *MassLive.com*, 26 August 2004, www.masslive.com/printer/printer.ssf?/base/sports-2/1093506641191050.xml.

[1017] Patriots left tackle Matt Light, quoted in: Chris Kennedy, "Pats putting season on line," *MassLive.com*, 26 August 2004, www.masslive.com/printer/printer.ssf?/base/sports-2/1093506641191050.xml.

[1018] Seattle Seahawks quarterback Matt Hasselbeck, quoted in: Chris Kennedy, "Hasselbeck finally all grown up," *The Republican*, 14 October 2004, www.masslive.com/sports/republican/index.ssf?/base/sports-0/109771650117930.xml.

[1019] Dr. Peter F. Drucker, *Management: Tasks, Responsibilities, Practices*, USA: HarperCollins, 1973, p. 70.

[1020] Rick Stroud, "Cat defense," *St. Petersburg Times*, 31 January 2004, www.sptimes.com/2004/01/31/Sports/Cat_defense.shtml.

[1021] Bill Belichick, quoted in: Hector Longo, "Grade A for Coach B," *Eagle Tribune*, 27 April 2003, www.eagletribune.com/news/stories/20030427/SP_004.htm.

[1022] Bill Belichick, quoted in: Michael Felger, "QB quandary: Davey, Palmer in the spotlight tonight," *Boston Herald*, 21 August 2004, http://patriots.bostonherald.com/patriots/view.bg?articleid=40794.

[1023] Scott Pioli, quoted in: Jeff D'Alessio, "Picking a star quarterback can be a tossup," *Florida Today*, 10 January 2004, http://bengals.enquirer.com/2004/01/10/ben2qb.html.

[1024] Super Bowl XXXV-winning quarterback Trent Dilfer, quoted in: Greg Bishop, "Hasselbeck, Brady in the draft: Better late than early?" *Seattle Post-Intelligencer*, 14 October 2004, http://seattletimes.nwsource.com/html/sports/2002062745_hawk14.html.

[1025] FOX Sports and Sporting News analyst Brian Baldinger, quoted in: Paul Attner, " Whatever 'It' is, Brady has 'It,'" *Sports Illustrated*, 6 October 2004, http://msn.foxsports.com/story/3059636.

[1026] Steve Szabo, coach of the Buffalo Bills' cornerbacks and safeties, quoted in: Peter King, "A League of Their Own," *Sports Illustrated*, 18 October 2004, p. 70.

[1027] Bill Belichick, quoted in: Alan Greenberg, "Warm Feeling Toward Pats," *Hartford Courant*, 26 April 2004, www.ctnow.com/sports/hc-patriots0426.artapr26,1,1879973.story.

[1028] Bill Belichick, quoted in: Michael Parente, " Patriots won't pass up opportunity to improve offensive line," *Woonsocket Call*, 2 May 2004, www.zwire.com/site/news.cfm?newsid=11425425&BRD=1712&PAG=461&dept_id=106787&rfi=6.

[1029] Tom Brady, quoted in: Dan Pires, "The changing face of Bill Belichick," *SouthCoast Today*, 22 December 2001, www.s-t.com/daily/12-01/12-22-01/c01sp071.htm.

[1030] Gary Shelton, "Story, as usual, is Sapp," *St. Petersburg Times*, 28 January 2004, www.sptimes.com/2004/01/28/Columns/Story_as_usual_is_S.shtml.

[1031] Kevin Mannix, "Pats a study in excellence," *Boston Herald*, 8 February 2004, http://patriots.bostonherald.com/patriots/view.bg?articleid=14008.

[1032] Star defensive lineman Warren Sapp, quoted in: Rick Stroud, "Cat defense," *St. Petersburg Times*, 31 January 2004, www.sptimes.com/2004/01/31/Sports/Cat_defense.shtml.

[1033] Star defensive lineman Warren Sapp, quoted in: Gary Shelton, "Story, as usual, is Sapp," *St. Petersburg Times*, 28 January 2004, www.sptimes.com/2004/01/28/Columns/Story_as_usual_is_S.shtml.

[1034] Russ Charpentier, "Pressure heavily on Hochstein," *Cape Cod Times*, January 2003, www.capecodonline.com/cctimes/sports/russ131.htm.

[1035] Patriots wide receiver Troy Brown, quoted in: Dan Pires, "Postgame talk ranges from Sapp to streaker," *Standard-Times*, 4 February 2004, www.southcoasttoday.com/daily/02-04/02-04-04/c01sp273.htm.

[1036] Patriots offensive guard Russ Hochstein, quoted in: Michael Smith, "A chip on block," *Boston Globe*, 29 July 2004, www.boston.com/sports/football/patriots/articles/2004/07/29/a_chip_on_block.

[1037] Patriots offensive lineman Damien Woody, quoted in: Dan Pires, "Postgame talk ranges from Sapp to streaker," *Standard-Times*, 4 February 2004, www.southcoasttoday.com/daily/02-04/02-04-04/c01sp273.htm.

[1038] Patriots offensive lineman Damien Woody, quoted in: Michael Smith, "After blocking it all out, offensive line is secure," *Boston Globe*, 2 February 2004, www.boston.com/sports/football/patriots/articles/2004/02/02/after_blocking_it_all_out_offensive_line_is_secure.

[1039] Patriots VP of Player Personnel Scott Pioli, quoted in: Kevin Paul Dupont, "Pioli Finding Success With Patriots," *Boston Globe*, 13 January 2002, www.allthingsbillbelichick.com/articles/piolisuccess.htm.

[1040] Bill Belichick, "Bill Belichick Press Conf. Transcript 6/11/04," *Patriots.com*, 11 June 2004, www.patriots.com/news/FullArticle.sps?id=28920.

[1041] Hall of Fame guard Joe DeLamielleure, quoted in: Ron Borges, "Making a case for Tippett," *Boston Globe*, 24 October 2004, www.boston.com/sports/football/articles/2004/10/24/making_a_case_for_tippett.

[1042] Bill Belichick, "Bill Belichick Press Conf. Transcript," *Patriots.com*, 22 September 2004, www.patriots.com/Common/PrintThis.sps?id=31304.

[1043] Patriots offensive coordinator Charlie Weis, quoted in: Alan Greenberg, "Weis Looking For A Super Sendoff," *Hartford Courant*, 27 September 2004, www.ctnow.com/sports/hc-patriots0927.artsep27,1,1154488.story.

[1044] Paul Zimmerman, "Mix Master," *Sports Illustrated*, 6 October 2004, http://sportsillustrated.cnn.com/2004/writers/dr_z/10/06/drz.patriots/.

[1045] Michael Felger, "Pioli: Scout's Honor," *Boston Herald*, 19 December 2001, www.allthingsbillbelichick.com/articles/piolihonor.htm.

[1046] Patriots scouting manual, quoted in: Michael Holley, *Patriot Reign*, William Morrow, 2004, p. 158.

[1047] Patriots scouting manual, quoted in: Michael Holley, *Patriot Reign*, William Morrow, 2004, p. 158.

[1048] Joe Theismann, "Patriots had the look of winners," *ESPN.com*, 31 January 2002, http://espn.go.com/nfl/playoffs01/columns/theismann_joe/1320654.html.

[1049] Bill Belichick, quoted in: Bill Burt, "Belichick: It was one tough Patriot draft," *Eagle Tribune*, 17 April 2000, www.eagletribune.com/news/stories/20000417/SP_004.htm.

[1050] NFL quarterback Jim Harbaugh, quoted in: Rich Thompson, "Brady: Pride of Michigan: Harbaugh high on Patriots QB," *Boston Herald*, 13 September 2004, http://patriots.bostonherald.com/patriots/view.bg?articleid=43943.

[1051] Bill Belichick, quoted in: Hector Longo, "Pats pick players like champs they are," *Eagle Tribune*, 22 April 2002, www.eagletribune.com/news/stories/20020422/SP_008.htm.

[1052] Patriots VP of Player Personnel Scott Pioli, quoted in: Kevin Paul Dupont, "Pioli Finding Success With Patriots," *Boston Globe*, 13 January 2002, www.allthingsbillbelichick.com/articles/piolisuccess.htm.

[1053] Patriots VP of Player Personnel Scott Pioli, quoted in: Charles P. Pierce, "The Patriot," *Boston Globe*, 5 September 2004, www.boston.com/news/globe/magazine/articles/2004/09/05/the_patriot/.

[1054] Bill Belichick, quoted in: Tom E. Curran, "Notebook: Watson signs deal in time for practice," *Providence Journal*, 17 August 2004, www.projo.com/patriots/content/projo_20040817_17patsjo.2d6a6.html.

[1055] Patriots linebacker Ted Johnson, quoted in: Tom E. Curran, "Mental waters run deep for surfing linebacker," *Providence Journal*, 26 September 2004, www.projo.com/patriots/content/projo_20040926_quest26.2d2e0c.html.

[1056] Patriots linebacker Tedy Bruschi, quoted in: Peter King, "Brains over brawn," *Sports Illustrated*, 12 October 2004, http://sportsillustrated.cnn.com/2004/writers/peter_king/10/12/mmqb.te/.

[1057] Patriots wide receiver prospect Michael Jennings, quoted in: Chris Kennedy, "Speedster hopes to run to job with Pats," *The Republican*, 18 August 2004, www.masslive.com/sports/republican/index.ssf?/base/sports-2/1092821009310300.xml.

[1058] Bill Belichick, quoted in: Tom E. Curran, "Patriots Notebook: Belichick likes Klecko's knack for fitting in," *Providence Journal*, 26 August 2004, www.projo.com/patriots/content/projo_20040826_26patsjo.946cb.html.

[1059] Coach Bill Belichick, quoted in: Ron Hobson, "NFL DRAFT 2004: Belichick: Defensive mission complete," *Patriot Ledger* (Quincy, MA), 26 April 2004, http://ledger.southofboston.com/articles/2004/04/26/sports/sports03.txt.

[1060] Bill Belichick, quoted in: Mark Curnutte, "Patriots epitomize meaning of team," *Cincinnati Enquirer*, 28 January 2004, http://bengals.enquirer.com/2004/01/28/ben1mc.html.

[1061] Patriots scouting manual, quoted in: Michael Holley, *Patriot Reign*, William Morrow, 2004, p. 53.

[1062] Scott Pioli, Patriots VP of player personnel, quoted in: Hector Longo, "All the right moves," *Eagle-Tribune*, 30 January 2004, www.eagletribune.com/news/stories/20040130/SP_001.htm.

[1063] Bill Belichick, quoted in: Michael Felger, "With Scott done, Reid must step up," *Boston Herald*, 25 August 2004, http://patriots.bostonherald.com/patriots/view.bg?articleid=41280.

[1064] Bill Belichick, quoted in: Ian M. Clark, "Patriots Notebook: Tough calls at receiver," *The Union Leader*, 12 August 2004, www.theunionleader.com/articles_showfast.html?article=42150.

[1065] Patriots VP of Player Personnel Scott Pioli, quoted in: Kevin Paul Dupont, "Pioli Finding Success With Patriots," *Boston Globe*, 13 January 2002, www.allthingsbillbelichick.com/articles/piolisuccess.htm.

[1066] Patriots VP of Player Personnel Scott Pioli, quoted in: Barry Wilner (AP), "More Big Names to Hit the NFL Market," 31 May 2004, hosted.ap.org/dynamic/stories/F/FBN_FREE_AGENCY_PART_II.

[1067] Patriots linebacker Mike Vrabel, quoted in: Steve Campbell, "Brady, Pats outlast Panthers," *Houston Chronicle*, 2 February 2004, www.chron.com/cs/CDA/ssistory.mpl/special/04/sb/2382379.

[1068] Patriots linebacker Mike Vrabel, quoted in: Peter King, "Master And Commander," *Sports Illustrated*, 9 August 2004, www.allthingsbillbelichick.com/articles/master.htm.

[1069] Bill Belichick, "Bill Belichick Press Conf. Transcript - 9/14/2004," *Patriots.com*, 14 September 2004, www.patriots.com/Common/PrintThis.sps?id=30535.

[1070] Bill Belichick, quoted in: Alan Greenberg, "Pat-ended process; Belichick can find those keepers," 1 February 2004, p. E1, ProQuest database.

[1071] Bill Belichick, "Bill Belichick Press Conf. Transcript," *Patriots.com*, 22 September 2004, www.patriots.com/Common/PrintThis.sps?id=31304.

[1072] Michael Vega, "No longer wrestling with job," *Boston Globe*, 8 October 2004, www.boston.com/sports/football/patriots/articles/2004/10/08/no_longer_wrestling_with_job.

[1073] Offensive lineman Joe Andruzzi, quoted in: Michael Vega, "No longer wrestling with job," *Boston Globe*, 8 October 2004, www.boston.com/sports/football/patriots/articles/2004/10/08/no_longer_wrestling_with_job.

[1074] Bill Belichick, quoted in: Kevin McNamara, "Patriots Notebook: Jennings proves a quick study," *Providence Journal*, 18 August 2004, www.projo.com/patriots/content/projo_20040818_18patsjo.116b44.html.

[1075] Patriots free agent wide receiver Michael Jennings, quoted in: Joe Burris, "Stops and starts in the fast lane," *Boston Globe*, 18 August 2004, www.boston.com/sports/football/patriots/articles/2004/08/18/stops_and_starts_in_the_fast_lane.

[1076] Patriots receiver Bethel Johnson, quoted in: Hector Longo, "Grade A for Coach B," *Eagle-Tribune*, www.eagletribune.com/news/stories/20030427/SP_004.htm.

[1077] Mel Kiper Jr., paraphrased by Hector Longo, "Upgraded arsenal at Brady's disposal," *Eagle-Tribune*, 6 September 2004, www.eagletribune.com/news/stories/20040906/SP_004.htm.

[1078] Michael Felger, "Wilson punches clock: Pats safety turns out to be big steal," *Milford Daily News*, 29 September 2004, www.milforddailynews.com/sportsNews/view.bg?articleid=56720.

[1079] Patriots safety/cornerback Eugene Wilson, quoted in: Michael Parente, "Pats' Wilson a big hit," Woonsocket Call, 22 September 2004, www.woonsocketcall.com/site/news.cfm?newsid=12976112&BRD=1712&PAG=461&dept_id=106787&rfi=6.

[1080] Bill Belichick, quoted in: Hector Longo, "Light makes might," *Eagle Tribune*, 28 January 2004, www.eagletribune.com/news/stories/20040128/SP_001.htm.

[1081] Patriots left tackle Matt Light, quoted in: Hector Longo, "Londonderry's Ball catches Pats' attention," *Eagle Tribune*, 26 September 2002, www.eagletribune.com/news/stories/20020926/SP_003.htm.

[1082] Defensive line star Richard Seymour, quoted in: Hector Longo, "Light makes might," *Eagle Tribune*, 28 January 2004, www.eagletribune.com/news/stories/20040128/SP_001.htm.

[1083] Bill Belichick, quoted in: Alan Greenberg, "Pats Have Plenty Of Work For Bye Week," *Hartford Courant*, 21 September 2004, www.ctnow.com/sports/football/patriots/hc-patriots0921.artsep21,1,4724649.print.story.

[1084] Pro Football Hall of Fame, "Top 20 Passers At the Start of the 2004 NFL Season," www.profootballhof.com/index.cfm?section=history&cont_id=230255.

[1085] Patriots VP of player personnel Scott Pioli, quoted in: Michael Felger, "Pioli helps put it together," *Boston Herald*, 26 January 2004, http://patriots.bostonherald.com/patriots/view.bg?articleid=510.

[1086] Patriots offensive coordinator Charlie Weis, quoted in: Mike Reiss, "Patriots beat: What a difference," *MetroWest Sports*, 26 September 2004, www.metrowestdailynews.com/sportsNews/view.bg?articleid=78944.

[1087] Patriots running back Corey Dillon, quoted in: Steve Conway, "Dillon takes toll on Bills," *Boston Herald*, 15 November 2004, http://patriots.bostonherald.com/patriots/view.bg?articleid=54119.

[1088] Bill Belichick, quoted in: Thomas George, "Belichick Was Pushed To the End," *New York Times*, 3 February 2004, p. D4, ProQuest database.

[1089] Patriots VP of player personnel Scott Pioli, quoted in: Paul Zimmerman, "While the offense stands pat, a rebuilt defense looks to regain that Super Bowl swagger," *CNNSI.com*, 1 September 2003, http://sportsillustrated.cnn.com/2003/magazine/08/25/patriots/.

[1090] Patriots VP of player personnel Scott Pioli, quoted in: Michael Felger, "Pioli: Scout's Honor," *Boston Herald*, 19 December 2001, www.allthingsbillbelichick.com/articles/piolihonor.htm.

[1091] Michael Holley, *Patriot Reign*, William Morrow, 2004, p. 147.

[1092] Patriots safety Rodney Harrison, quoted in: Jackie MacMullan, "Pioli and Belichick a nice team," *Boston Globe*, 26 January 2004, www.boston.com/sports/football/patriots/articles/2004/01/26/pioli_and_belichick_a_nice_team/.

[1093] Patriots safety Rodney Harrison, quoted in: Paul Zimmerman, "While the offense stands pat, a rebuilt defense looks to regain that Super Bowl swagger," *CNNSI.com*, 1 September 2003, http://sportsillustrated.cnn.com/2003/magazine/08/25/patriots/.

[1094] Patriots safety Rodney Harrison, quoted in: Paul Zimmerman, "While the offense stands pat, a rebuilt defense looks to regain that Super Bowl swagger," *CNNSI.com*, 1 September 2003, http://sportsillustrated.cnn.com/2003/magazine/08/25/patriots/.

[1095] Patriots safety Rodney Harrison, quoted in: Jeff Reynolds, "Harrison, Pats patch wounds, march forward," *Pro Football Weekly*, 27 October 2003, www.profootballweekly.com/PFW/NFL/AFC/AFC+East/New+England/Features/2003/reynolds102703.htm.

[1096] Patriots safety Rodney Harrison, quoted in: Paul Zimmerman, "While the offense stands pat, a rebuilt defense looks to regain that Super Bowl swagger," *CNNSI.com*, 1 September 2003, http://sportsillustrated.cnn.com/2003/magazine/08/25/patriots/.

[1097] Patriots safety Rodney Harrison, quoted in: Charles Stein, "Bill Belichick, CEO," *Boston Globe*, 28 January 2004.

[1098] Patriots safety Rodney Harrison, quoted in: Jeff Reynolds, "Harrison, Pats patch wounds, march forward," *Pro Football Weekly*, 27 October 2003, www.profootballweekly.com/PFW/NFL/AFC/AFC+East/New+England/Features/2003/reynolds102703.htm.

[1099] Patriots linebacker Rosevelt Colvin, quoted in: Jackie MacMullan, "Pioli and Belichick a nice team," *Boston Globe*, 26 January 2004, www.boston.com/sports/football/patriots/articles/2004/01/26/pioli_and_belichick_a_nice_team/.

[1100] Patriots linebacker Rosevelt Colvin, quoted in: Paul Zimmerman, "While the offense stands pat, a rebuilt defense looks to regain that Super Bowl swagger," *CNNSI.com*, 1 September 2003, http://sportsillustrated.cnn.com/2003/magazine/08/25/patriots/.

[1101] Patriots linebacker Rosevelt Colvin, quoted in: Jackie MacMullan, "Pioli and Belichick a nice team," *Boston Globe*, 26 January 2004, www.boston.com/sports/football/patriots/articles/2004/01/26/pioli_and_belichick_a_nice_team/.

[1102] Bill Belichick, quoted in: Don Banks, "Holding their ground," *Sports Illustrated*, 26 July 2003, http://sportsillustrated.cnn.com/football/2003/preview/2003/07/26/patriots_postcard/.

[1103] Special teams captain Larry Izzo, quoted in: Hector Longo, "All the right moves," *Eagle-Tribune*, 30 January 2004, www.eagletribune.com/news/stories/20040130/SP_001.htm.

[1104] Coach Bill Belichick, quoted in: Ron Borges, "What Makes Belichick Tick," *Boston Globe Magazine*, 10 September 2000, www.allthingsbillbelichick.com/articles/makestick.html.

[1105] Coach Bill Belichick, quoted in: Steve Politi, "Is Belichick A Genius?" *Star-Ledger*, 30 January 2004, www.allthingsbillbelichick.com/articles/agenius.htm.

[1106] Coach Bill Belichick, quoted in: Alan Greenberg, "Belichick: Call Him the Bred Winner," *Hartford Courant*, 27 January 2004, p. C1, ProQuest database.

[1107] Bill Belichick, quoted in: Alan Greenberg, "Belichick: Call Him the Bred Winner," *Hartford Courant*, 27 January 2004, p. C1, ProQuest database.

[1108] Patriots offensive coordinator Charlie Weis, quoted in: Gordon Edes, "Patriots coach has well-earned reputation for stopping whatever's thrown his way," *Boston Globe*, 2 February 2002, www.boston.com/sports/football/patriots/superbowl/globe_stories/020202/patriots_coach_has_well_earned_reputation_for_stopping_whatever_s_thrown_his_way+.shtml.

[1109] Patriots VP of Player Personnel Scott Pioli, quoted in: Kevin Paul Dupont, "Pioli Finding Success With Patriots," *Boston Globe*, 13 January 2002, www.allthingsbillbelichick.com/articles/piolisuccess.htm.

[1110] Patriots VP of player personnel, Scott Pioli, quoted in: "Central Connecticut State University Athletics," 13 November 2002, http://ccsubluedevils.collegesports.com/administration/ccon-ninequestionsscottpioli.html.

[1111] Bill Belichick, as related by Patriots VP of player personnel, Scott Pioli, quoted in: "Central Connecticut State University Athletics," 13 November 2002, http://ccsubluedevils.collegesports.com/administration/ccon-ninequestionsscottpioli.html.

[1112] Patriots VP of Player Personnel Scott Pioli, quoted in: Kevin Paul Dupont, "Pioli Finding Success With Patriots," Boston Globe, 13 January 2002, www.allthingsbillbelichick.com/articles/piolisuccess.htm.

[1113] Patriots linebacker Willie McGinest, quoted in: Greg Reed, "Like true patriots, these guys endure," Holland Sentinel, 4 February 2002, www.thehollandsentinel.net/stories/020402/loc_020402043.shtml.

[1114] Help wanted advertisement run by British explorer Sir Ernest Shackleton, quoted in: Bob Glauber, "Inspired By History Lesson," Greenwich Time, 30 November 2001, www.allthingsbillbelichick.com/articles/historylesson.htm.

[1115] Bill Belichick, quoted in: Jackie MacMullan, "Pioli and Belichick a nice team," Boston Globe, 26 January 2004, www.boston.com/sports/football/patriots/articles/2004/01/26/pioli_and_belichick_a_nice_team/.

[1116] Patriots safety Rodney Harrison, quoted in: Michael Smith, "Dream Team," Boston Globe, 9 September 2004, www.boston.com/sports/football/patriots/articles/2004/09/09/dream_team.

[1117] Dr. Peter F. Drucker, Management: Tasks, Responsibilities, Practices, USA: HarperCollins, 1973, p. 177.

[1118] Patriots safety Rodney Harrison, quoted in: Joe Burris, "Hitting back," Boston Globe, 19 September 2004, www.boston.com/sports/football/patriots/articles/2004/09/19/hitting_back.

[1119] Jimmy Golen, Associated Press, "Patriots get their players, their way," Boston Globe, 2/7/2004.

[1120] Former Patriots wide receiver Donald Hayes, quoted in: Len Pasquarelli, "Belichick and Pioli have winning formula," ESPN.com, 27 July 2002, http://espn.go.com/nfl/trainingcamp02/columns/patriots/1410739.html.

[1121] Patriots linebacker Tedy Bruschi, quoted in: Mike Reiss (MetroWest Daily News), "Bruschi just having a ball,", Boston Herald, 6 January 2004, http://patriots.bostonherald.com/patriots/view.bg?articleid=14258.

[1122] Patriots linebacker Tedy Bruschi, quoted in: Mike Reiss (MetroWest Daily News), "Bruschi just having a ball,", Boston Herald, 6 January 2004, http://patriots.bostonherald.com/patriots/view.bg?articleid=14258.

[1123] Tony Bruschi, older brother of Patriots linebacker Tedy Bruschi, quoted in: Mike Reiss (MetroWest Daily News), "Bruschi just having a ball,", Boston Herald, 6 January 2004, http://patriots.bostonherald.com/patriots/view.bg?articleid=14258.

[1124] Patriots linebacker Tedy Bruschi, quoted in: Mike Reiss (MetroWest Daily News), "Bruschi just having a ball,", Boston Herald, 6 January 2004, http://patriots.bostonherald.com/patriots/view.bg?articleid=14258.

[1125] Michael Felger, "Grant an aid in Colvin comeback," Boston Herald, 20 June 2004, http://patriots.bostonherald.com/patriots/view.bg?articleid=32598.

[1126] Patriots linebacker Tedy Bruschi, quoted in: Michael Felger, "Bruschi's just happy to be here," Boston Herald, 5 August 2004, http://patriots.bostonherald.com/patriots/view.bg?articleid=38585.

[1127] Patriots linebacker Tedy Bruschi, quoted in: Michael Felger, "Bruschi's just happy to be here," Boston Herald, 5 August 2004, http://patriots.bostonherald.com/patriots/view.bg?articleid=38585.

[1128] Patriots linebacker Tedy Bruschi, quoted in: Paul Kenyon, "Bruschi adds another twist to Patriots' victory," Providence Journal, 15 November 2004, www.projo.com/patriots/content/projo_20041115_pside2.49754.html.

[1129] Patriots linebacker Tedy Bruschi, quoted in: Michael Smith, "Snowballin'," Boston Globe, 8 December 2003, www.boston.com/sports/football/patriots/articles/2003/12/08/snowballin/.

[1130] Patriots linebacker Tedy Bruschi, quoted in: Michael Felger, "Bruschi's just happy to be here," Boston Herald, 5 August 2004, http://patriots.bostonherald.com/patriots/view.bg?articleid=38585.

[1131] Dr. Peter F. Drucker, Management: Tasks, Responsibilities, Practices, USA: HarperCollins, 1973, p. 125.

[1132] Patriots owner Bob Kraft, quoted in: Associated Press, "Dillon Changes Patriots' Draft Plan," NBC Sports, 24 April 2004, http://msnbc.msn.com/id/4790265/.

[1133] Bill Belichick, quoted in: Kevin Mannix, "Belichick builds a sage secondary," Boston Herald, 12 June 2004, http://patriots.bostonherald.com/patriots/view.bg?articleid=31609.

[1134] Bill Belichick, quoted in: Harvey Mackay, We Got Fired!, New York: Ballantine Books, 2004, p. 64.

[1135] Nick Cafardo, "Cobbs gets fresh start," Boston Globe, 26 April 2004, www.boston.com/sports/football/patriots/articles/2004/04/26/cobbs_gets_fresh_start/.

[1136] Unnamed AFC general manager, quoted in: Nick Cafardo, "It doesn't weigh on Light," Boston Globe, 11 July 2004, www.boston.com/sports/football/patriots/articles/2004/07/11/it_doesnt_weigh_on_light.

[1137] Dan Pires, "Draft brings smile to Belichick," Standard-Times, 17 April 2000, www.s-t.com/daily/04-00/04-17-00/c03sp093.htm.

[1138] Bill Belichick, quoted in: Hector Longo, "Confident Patriots coach stacks up talent," Eagle Tribune, 25 April 2004, www.eagletribune.com/news/stories/20040425/SP_003.htm.

[1139] Bill Belichick, quoted in: Hector Longo, "If you can't beat Kleckos then start drafting them," Eagle Tribune, 28 April 2003, www.eagletribune.com/news/stories/20030428/SP_008.htm.

[1140] Bill Belichick, quoted in: Tom E. Curran, "Patriots Notebook: Team is fast out of the gate," Providence Journal, 11 June 2004, www.projo.com/patriots/content/projo_20040611_11patsjo.fcc1f.html.

[1141] Dan Pires, "Armstrong a happy camper," South Coast Today, 17 July 2000, www.s-t.com/daily/07-00/07-17-00/c04sp096.htm.

[1142] John Clayton, "Patriots shopping spree pays off," ESPN, 20 December 2001, http://espn.go.com/nfl/columns/clayton_john/1298726.html.

[1143] John Clayton, "Patriots shopping spree pays off," ESPN, 20 December 2001, http://espn.go.com/nfl/columns/clayton_john/1298726.html.

[1144] Bill Belichick, quoted in: Peter King, "The sincerest form of flattery," Sports Illustrated, 4 February 2002, http://sportsillustrated.cnn.com/inside_game/king/news/2002/02/04/mmqb/.

[1145] John Clayton, "Patriots shopping spree pays off," ESPN, 20 December 2001, http://espn.go.com/nfl/columns/clayton_john/1298726.html.

[1146] Patriots VP of Player Personnel Scott Pioli, quoted in: Paul Solman, "Goal Line Economics," 23 September 2002, www.pbs.org/newshour/bb/economy/july-dec02/football_9-23.html.

[1147] Peter King, "Value proposition," Sports Illustrated, 1 March 2004, http://sportsillustrated.cnn.com/2004/writers/peter_king/03/01/mmqb/.

[1148] Former NFL quarterback Joe Theismann, quoted in: Kevin Paul Dupont, "Winner's Circle," Boston Globe, 23 January 2004, www.boston.com/sports/football/patriots/articles/2004/01/23/winners_circle/.

[1149] Patriots Vice President of Player Personnel Scott Pioli, quoted in: Michael Felger, "Pioli: Scout's Honor," Boston Herald, 19 December 2001, www.allthingsbillbelichick.com/articles/piolihonor.htm.

[1150] Patriots Vice President of Player Personnel Scott Pioli, quoted in: Kevin Paul Dupont, "Pioli Finding Success With Patriots," Boston Globe, 13 January 2002, www.allthingsbillbelichick.com/articles/piolisuccess.htm.

[1151] TSX / The Insiders, "Team Report: Patriots," 14 April 2003, http://patriots.theinsiders.com/2/105082.html.

[1152] May 12-26 poll of 22 NFL personnel directors by USA Today Sports Weekly, cited in: Michael Smith, "Whipping them into shape," Boston Globe, 27 June 2004, www.boston.com/sports/football/patriots/articles/2004/06/27/whipping_them_into_shape.

[1153] Don Shula, winningest coach in NFL history who coached the Miami Dolphins to their miraculous undefeated season in 1972, quoted in: Vic Carucci, "Shula sees more Super wins for Belichick," NFL.com, 4 February 2004, www.nfl.com/news/story/7063350.

[1154] Len Pasquarelli, "Kearse's record deal includes $16M bonus," ESPN, 3 March 2004, http://sports.espn.go.com/nfl/columns/story?columnist=pasquarelli_len&id=1750089&partnersite=espn.

[1155] Shawn Culcasi, "2004 Offseason Player Movement - Defensive Linemen," 26 April 2004, www.footballguys.com/04offseason_dl.htm.

[1156] Patriots Vice President of Player Personnel Scott Pioli, quoted in: Dan Pompei, "Draft picks are worth more to builders than to winners – NFL," The Sporting News, 12 April 2004, http://articles.findarticles.com/p/articles/mi_m1208/is_15_228/ai_115345174/print.

[1157] Glen Farley, "Patriots get younger and faster," The Enterprise (Brockton, MA), 14 May 2004, http://enterprise.southofboston.com/articles/2004/05/14/news/sports/sports03.txt.

[1158] Patriots coach Bill Belichick, quoted in: Ron Hobson, "Pats in a good spot to deal," Patriot Ledger (Quincy, MA), 23 April 2004, http://ledger.southofboston.com/articles/2004/04/23/sports/sports03.txt.

[1159] Bill Belichick: "Bill Belichick Press Conf. Transcript 4/25/04," Patriots.com, 25 April 2004, www.patriots.com/news/FullArticle.sps?id=28531&type=draft.

[1160] Light's salary numbers from "Miguel's VERY UNOFFICIAL Patriots Salary Cap Information Page," www.patsfans.com/miguel/.

[1161] Steve Feldman, agent to Patriots safety Rodney Harrison, quoted in: Jackie MacMullan, "Pioli and Belichick a nice team," Boston Globe, 26 January 2004, www.boston.com/sports/football/patriots/articles/2004/01/26/pioli_and_belichick_a_nice_team/.

[1162] Michael Felger, "Bush praises Pats: President hosts champs in D.C.," *Boston Herald*, 11 May 2004, http://patriots.bostonherald.com/patriots/view.bg?articleid=27409.

[1163] Michael Felger, "Needful things up first: Linebacker, big receiver likely to be top priorities," *Boston Herald*, 22 April 2004, http://patriots.bostonherald.com/patriots/view.bg?articleid=13912.

[1164] Patriots inside linebackers coach Pepper Johnson, *Won For All*, Chicago: Contemporary Books, 2003, p. 145.

[1165] According to: Michael Holley, "Milloy move showed Patriots who was boss," *Boston Globe*, 26 September 2004, www.boston.com/sports/football/patriots/articles/2004/09/26/milloy_move_showed_patriots_who_was_boss.

[1166] Patriots coaches' post-2001 self-scouting report on Milloy, in: Michael Holley, "Milloy move showed Patriots who was boss," *Boston Globe*, 26 September 2004, www.boston.com/sports/football/patriots/articles/2004/09/26/milloy_move_showed_patriots_who_was_boss.

[1167] Patriots quarterback Tom Brady, quoted in: Tom Barnidge, "Cinderella deja vu: Brady seeks encore," *NFL Insider*, 9 September 2002, www.nfl.com/insider/story/5688388.

[1168] Pat Kirwan, "Defense does it in AFC East," *Bengals.com*, www.bengals.com/press/news.asp?iCurPage=0&news_id=2254.

[1169] Allen Wilson, "Pats pick on Bledsoe again," *Buffalo News*, 15 November 2004, www.buffalonews.com/editorial/20041115/1065927.asp.

[1170] Former Patriots quarterback Drew Bledsoe, quoted in: Damon Hack, "In Homecoming, Bledsoe Has a Forgettable Day," *New York Times*, 9 December 2002, D4, ProQuest database.

[1171] Buffalo Bills quarterback Drew Bledsoe, quoted in: Chris Kennedy, "No longer in the same league?" *The Republican*, 16 November 2004, www.masslive.com/sports/republican/index.ssf?/base/sports-0/110057490196270.xml.

[1172] Dr. Peter F. Drucker, *Management: Tasks, Responsibilities, Practices*, USA: HarperCollins, 1973, p. 179.

[1173] Patriots linebacker Willie McGinest, quoted in: Luke Sacks, "A Championship Season For McGinest," *NFLPlayers.com*, 7 July 2004, www.patriots.com/news/FullArticle.sps?id=29558&type=nfl.

[1174] Cornerback Terrell Buckley, quoted in: Andy Hart, "Report: Buckley to rejoin Pats for third tour," *Patriots.com*, 4 June 2004, www.patriots.com/news/FullArticle.sps?id=28814.

[1175] Patriots owner Robert Kraft, quoted in: Michael Felger, "Pats subject of cheap talk," *Boston Herald*, 4 April 2004, http://patriots.bostonherald.com/patriots/view.bg?articleid=13945.

[1176] New Patriots running back Corey Dillon, quoted in: Peter King, "A League of Their Own," *Sports Illustrated*, 18 October 2004, p. 70.

[1177] Michael Felger, "Training camp preview: A fresh start," *The Sporting News*, http://msn.foxsports.com/story/2572440.

[1178] "Miguel's VERY UNOFFICIAL Patriots Salary Cap Information Page," www.patscap.com/capfootnotes.html#dillon; It has been incorrectly reported that Dillon would receive "$500,000 for 1,600 yards" (Tom Pedulla, "Patriots feel Super with 'extra ingredient' Dillon," *USA Today*, 22 July 2004, www.usatoday.com/sports/football/nfl/patriots/2004-07-22-camp_x.htm.)

[1179] "Miguel's VERY UNOFFICIAL Patriots Salary Cap Information Page," www.patscap.com/capfootnotes.html#dillon.

[1180] Cornerback Terrell Buckley, quoted in: Michael Smith, "Buckley set to rejoin Patriots," *Boston Globe*, 3 June 2004, www.boston.com/sports/football/patriots/articles/2004/06/03/buckley_set_to_rejoin_patriots.

[1181] VP of player personnel Scott Pioli, quoted in: Judy Battista, "Patriots Adhere to Bottom Line to Stay on Top," *New York Times*, 8 August 2004, www.nytimes.com/2004/08/08/sports/football/08patriots.html.

[1182] ESPN.com news services, "Johnson unhappy with role on Patriots," 5 September 2002, http://msn.espn.go.com/nfl/news/2002/0905/1427509.html.

[1183] Patriots inside linebacker Ted Johnson, quoted in: Michael Smith, "Dream Team," *Boston Globe*, 9 September 2004, www.boston.com/sports/football/patriots/articles/2004/09/09/dream_team.

[1184] Then-rookie defensive lineman Richard Seymour, quoted in: Skip Wood, "Wins loosen Belichick's reserve," *USA Today*, 3 December 2001, www.usatoday.com/sports/nfl/patriots/2001-12-04-belichick-giddy.htm.

[1185] Patriots inside linebacker Ted Johnson, quoted in: Mike Reiss, "A powerful visit: Seven Patriots amazed by tour of Medical Center," *Boston Herald*, 17 May 2004, www.dailynewstranscript.com/sportsNews/view.bg?articleid=33377.

[1186] Patriots linebacker Ted Johnson, quoted in: Nick Cafardo, "For coach, it's hard to relate," *Boston Globe*, 2 February 2004, www.boston.com/sports/football/patriots/articles/2004/02/for_coach_its_hard_to_relate/.

[1187] Bill Belichick, quoted in: Michael Silver, "All Systems Go," *Sports Illustrated*, Championship Edition, 11 February 2004, p. 50.

[1188] Patriots inside linebackers coach Pepper Johnson, *Won For All*, Chicago: Contemporary Books, 2003, p. 208.

[1189] Patriots cornerback Tyrone Poole, quoted in: Mike Reiss, "Poole dives in for more: Pats cornerback not looking back after pondering retirement," *MetroWest Daily News*, 4 July 2004, www.metrowestdailynews.com/sportsColumnists/view.bg?articleid=72348.

[1190] Patriots defensive end Jarvis Green, "Patriots Video News," 9 July 2004, www.patriots.com/mediaworld/MediaDetail.sps?ID=29567&keywords=VIDEONEWS&media=video.

[1191] Michael H., "John Elway," www.teenink.com/Past/1999/10667.html.

[1192] St. Louis Rams defensive tackle Tyoka Jackson, quoted in: AP, "Held in check," 4 February 2002, http://sportsillustrated.cnn.com/football/2002/playoffs/news/2002/02/03/rams_sidebar1_ap/.

[1193] St. Louis Rams defensive tackle Tyoka Jackson, quoted in: Chris Kennedy, "There but for fortune," *The Republican*, 5 November 2004, www.masslive.com/sports/republican/index.ssf?/base/sports-0/1099622700264241.xml.

[1194] St. Louis Rams defensive tackle Ryan Pickett, quoted in: Jim Thomas, "Pain of facing the Patriots is less now for the Rams," *St. Louis Post-Dispatch*, 3 November 2004, www.stltoday.com/stltoday/emaf.nsf/Popup?ReadForm&db=stltoday%5Csports%5Cstories.nsf&docid=45E388ACAF0B7EA286256F420020CA78.

[1195] Carolina Panthers defensive tackle Brentson Buckner, quoted in: Brian McTaggart, "Second place more like last for Panthers," *Houston Chronicle*, 2 February 2004, www.chron.com/cs/CDA/ssistory.mpl/special/04/sb/2384616.

[1196] Rams (2001) and Panthers (2003) wide receiver Ricky Proehl, quoted in: John Powers, "Glory Days," *Boston Globe*, 8 February 2004, www.boston.com/sports/football/patriots/articles/2004/02/08/glory_days/.

[1197] Rams (2001) and Panthers (2003) wide receiver Ricky Proehl, quoted in: Bob Ryan, "Perhaps best Super Bowl ever played," *Boston Globe*, 2 February 2004, www.boston.com/sports/football/patriots/articles/2004/02/perhaps_best_super_bowl_ever_played/.

[1198] Patriots linebacker Roman Phifer, quoted in: Mike Holbrook, "'Black Cloud' has lifted," *Pro Football Weekly*, 30 January 2004, www.profootballweekly.com/PFW/NFL/AFC/AFC+East/New+England/Features/2004/phifer013004.htm.

[1199] Patriots safety Rodney Harrison, quoted in: Rich Eisen, "A conversation with Rodney Harrison," *NFL.com*, 19 July 2004, www.nfl.com/nflnetwork/story/7513397.

[1200] Bill Belichick, "O.K. Champ, Now Comes the Hard Part," *New York Times*, 26 January 2003, www.allthingsbillbelichick.com/articles/okchamp.html.

[1201] Bill Belichick, quoted in: Jackie MacMullan, "Pioli and Belichick a nice team," *Boston Globe*, 26 January 2004, www.boston.com/sports/football/patriots/articles/2004/01/26/pioli_and_belichick_a_nice_team/.

[1202] Patriots special teams captain Larry Izzo, quoted in: Mike Reiss, "Patriots beat: Team Desirable," *Daily News Tribune*, 10 October 2004, www.dailynewstribune.com/sportsNews/view.bg?articleid=42486.

[1203] Dr. Peter F. Drucker, *Management: Tasks, Responsibilities, Practices*, USA: HarperCollins, 1973, pp. 41.

[1204] Patriots tight end Christian Fauria, quoted in: Paul Perillo, "Free agents know Patriots way," *Patriots Football Weekly*, 25 January 2004, www.patriots.com/news/fullarticle.sps?id=27673&type=general&special_section=SuperBowlXXXVIII.

[1205] Patriots tight end Christian Fauria, quoted in: Paul Perillo, "Free agents know Patriots way," *Patriots Football Weekly*, 25 January 2004, www.patriots.com/news/fullarticle.sps?id=27673&type=general&special_section=SuperBowlXXXVIII.

[1206] Patriots linebacker Roman Phifer, quoted in: Mike Holbrook, "'Black Cloud' has lifted," *Pro Football Weekly*, 30 January 2004, www.profootballweekly.com/PFW/NFL/AFC/AFC+East/New+England/Features/2004/phifer013004.htm.

[1207] New Patriots running back Corey Dillon, quoted in: Peter King "No rush to judgment," *Sports Illustrated*, 11 October 2004, http://sportsillustrated.cnn.com/2004/writers/peter_king/10/11/mmqb.pats/.

[1208] Art Thiel, "Patriots, Dillon curious study in NFL risk taking," *Seattle Post-Intelligencer*, 15 October 2004, http://seattlepi.nwsource.com/football/195351_thiel15.html.

[1209] Patriots special teams captain and standout Larry Izzo, quoted in: Mike Holbrook, "Welcome to 'The Izzone South,'" *Pro Football Weekly*, 28 January 2004, www.profootballweekly.com/PFW/NFL/AFC/AFC+East/New+England/Features/2004/izzo012804.htm.

[1210] Patriots punter Josh Miller, quoted in: Joe Burris, "Punter Miller a return man this week," *Boston Globe*, 28 October 2004, www.boston.com/sports/football/patriots/articles/2004/10/28/punter_miller_a_return_man_this_week.

[1211] Patriots linebacker Don Davis, quoted in: Alan Greenberg, "Pat-ended process; Belichick can find those keepers," 1 February 2004, p. E1, ProQuest database.

[1212] Patriots defensive lineman Bobby Hamilton, quoted in: Michael Felger, "Hamilton a tough loss for Pats," *Boston Herald*, 23 May 2004, http://patriots.bostonherald.com/patriots/view.bg?articleid=28994.

[1213] Defensive lineman Bobby Hamilton, quoted in: Bill Burt, "Man with the plan Belichick's sure hand guides Patriots back to Super Bowl," *Eagle Tribune*, 19 January 2004, www.eagletribune.com/news/stories/20040119/FP_003.htm.

[1214] Patriots left tackle Matt Light, quoted in: Nick Cafardo, "It doesn't weigh on Light," *Boston Globe*, 11 July 2004, www.boston.com/sports/football/patriots/articles/2004/07/11/it_doesnt_weigh_on_light.

[1215] Matt Light's agent Ben Dogra, quoted in: Len Pasquarelli, "Franchise takes it 'one game at a time,'" *Sports Illustrated*, 6 October 2004, http://sports.espn.go.com/nfl/columns/story?columnist=pasquarelli_len&page=/trend/2004week4.

[1216] Patriots kicker Adam Vinatieri, quoted in: Mike Reiss, "Patriots beat: Team Desirable," *Daily News Tribune*, 10 October 2004, www.dailynewstribune.com/sportsNews/view.bg?articleid=42486.

[1217] Patriots defensive lineman Bobby Hamilton, quoted in: Michael Felger, "Hamilton a tough loss for Pats," *Boston Herald*, 23 May 2004, http://patriots.bostonherald.com/patriots/view.bg?articleid=28994.

[1218] Patriots backup quarterback Damon Huard, quoted in: Nick Cafardo, "It doesn't weigh on Light," *Boston Globe*, 11 July 2004, www.boston.com/sports/football/patriots/articles/2004/07/11/it_doesnt_weigh_on_light.

[1219] Former Patriots center Damien Woody, quoted in: Peter King, "Born to win," *Sports Illustrated*, 23 August 2004, http://sportsillustrated.cnn.com/2004/writers/peter_king/08/20/king.mmqb/.

[1220] New Patriots punter Josh Miller, quoted in: Michael Smith, "No Snap Judgment," *Boston Globe*, 12 August 2004, www.boston.com/sports/football/patriots/articles/2004/08/12/no_snap_judgment.

[1221] Indianapolis Colts quarterback Peyton Manning, quoted in: Tom E. Curran, "Is this Belichick's version of I've Got A Secret?" *Providence Journal*, 7 September 2004, www.projo.com/patriots/content/projo_20040907_07pats.2e05d.html.

[1222] Patriots running back Corey Dillon, quoted in: Michael Smith, "Pats capitalize on others' mistakes," *ESPN*, 3 October 2004, http://sports.espn.go.com/nfl/columns/story?id=1894443.

[1223] Bill Belichick on *The David Letterman Show*, 4 February 2004, www.patriots.com/mediaworld/mediadetail.sps?id=27974.

[1224] Tom E. Curran, "Nobody better than the Pats when it comes to closing act," *Providence Journal*, 8 August 2004, www.projo.com/cgi-bin/bi/gold_print.cgi; Tom E. Curran, "Patriots Notebook: So far, seven-day weeks aren't on team's calendar," *Providence Journal*, 23 September 2004, www.projo.com/patriots/content/projo_20040923_23patsjo.defde.html.

[1225] Alan J. Burge, "Voice of the Fan: Keeping it close," *HoustonTexans.com*, www.houstontexans.com/news/news_detail.php?PRKey=932.

[1226] Former Giants quarterback and CBS analyst Phil Simms, quoted in: Kevin Paul Dupont, "Winner's Circle," *Boston Globe*, 23 January 2004, www.boston.com/sports/football/patriots/articles/2004/01/23/winners_circle/.

[1227] Patriots tight end Christian Fauria, quoted in: Michael Smith, "Pats capitalize on others' mistakes," *ESPN*, 3 October 2004, http://sports.espn.go.com/nfl/columns/story?id=1894443.

[1228] Bill Belichick, quoted in: Andrew Mason, "Pats bring new meaning to 'team,'" *NFL.com*, 3 February 2002, ww2.nfl.com/xxxvi/ce/feature/0,3892,4948702,00.html.

[1229] Bill Belichick, quoted in: Bob Baum (AP), "Patriots' streak reaches 17 after beating Cardinals," *Seattle Times*, 20 September 2004, http://seattletimes.nwsource.com/html/sports/2002040730_arizona20.html.

[1230] Patriots tight end Christian Fauria, quoted in: Mark Craig, "Patriots play it cool," *Minneapolis Star Tribune*, 3 October 2004, www.startribune.com/stories/503/5011269.html.

[1231] Coach Bill Belichick, quoted in: Alan Greenberg, "Belichick Game Plan For Life," *Hartford Courant*, 3 May 2004, www.ctnow.com/sports/hc-belichick0503.artmay03,1,707205.story.

[1232] Bill Belichick, quoted in: Peter King, "The ultimate betrayal?" *Sports Illustrated*, 23 September 2004, http://sportsillustrated.cnn.com/2004/writers/peter_king/09/20/mmqb/.

[1233] Patriots quarterback Tedy Bruschi, quoted in: Howard Ulman (AP), "Two-time NFL champs focus on next game, not making history," *Canada.com*, 3 September 2004, www.canada.com/sports/football/story.html?id=5F09B45F-C14D-417C-96B5-36A7704F010B.

[1234] Tom Brady, quoted in: Rob Longley, "Belichick and crew are playing down streak," *Toronto Sun*, 25 October 2004, http://slam.canoe.ca/Slam/Football/NFL/2004/10/25/684629.html.

[1235] Bill Belichick, quoted in: Jim Donaldson, "No past or future for Pats -- only the here and now," *Providence Journal*, 1 October 2004, www.projo.com/patriots/content/projo_20041001_01jdcol.1bae68.html.

[1236] Patriots linebacker Tedy Bruschi, quoted in: Bob Ryan, "Carolina on their mind," *Boston Globe*, 20 January 2004, www.boston.com/sports/football/patriots/articles/2004/01/20/carolina_on_their_mind.

[1237] Patriots linebacker Tedy Bruschi, quoted in: (Arizona Wildcats) Cat Tracks staff, "It's good to be Tedy Bruschi," 17 February 2004, http://arizona.theinsiders.com/2/235079.html.

[1238] Tom Brady, quoted in: Associated Press, "NFL opener: Patriots 27, Colts 24," *ABC Action News*, 10 September 2004, www.tampabaylive.com/stories/2004/09/040910pats.shtml.

[1239] Patriots kicker Adam Vinatieri, quoted in: Tom Pedulla, "Patriots not keeping tabs on streak," *USA Today*, 16 September 2004, www.usatoday.com/sports/football/nfl/patriots/2004-09-16-pats-streak_x.htm.

[1240] Patriots safety Rodney Harrison, quoted in: Michael Parente, "Back from a day off, Pats ready to roll," *Middletown Press*, 28 September 2004, www.zwire.com/site/news.cfm?newsid=13019680&BRD=1645&PAG=461&dept_id=177588&rfi=6.

[1241] Patriots linebacker Willie McGinest, quoted in: Tom E. Curran, "Dillon helps Pats run down Cards," *Providence Journal*, 20 September 2004, www.projo.com/patriots/content/projo_20040920_20pats.df995.html.

[1242] Bill Belichick, quoted in: Ira Miller, "On verge of a record, Patriots play it down," *San Francisco Chronicle*, 3 October 2004, http://sfgate.com/cgi-bin/article.cgi?f=/chronicle/archive/2004/10/03/SPGAE92ROS1.DTL.

[1243] Bill Belichick, quoted in: Chris Ruddick, " Even Belichick revels in Patriots' winning streak," *Sports Network*, 12 October 2004, www.sportsnetwork.com/default.asp?c=sportsnetwork&page=nfl/news/abn3546911.htm.

[1244] Tom Brady, quoted in: Tom King, "NFL's longest win streak fits the Bill," *Nashua Telegraph*, 11 October 2004, www.nashuatelegraph.com/apps/pbcs.dll/article?AID=/20041011/COLUMNISTS11/110110034/-1/columnists.

[1245] Linebacker Mike Vrabel, quoted in: Dave Curtis, "19th Win Fits Bill For Pats," *New York Post*, 11 October 2004, www.nypost.com/sports/30086.htm.

[1246] Bill Belichick, quoted in: Howard Ulman (AP), "Two-time NFL champs focus on next game, not making history," *Canada.com*, 3 September 2004, www.canada.com/sports/football/story.html?id=5F09B45F-C14D-417C-96B5-36A7704F010B.

[1247] Bill Belichick, "Bill Belichick Press Conf. Transcript - 9/14/2004," *Patriots.com*, 14 September 2004, www.patriots.com/Common/PrintThis.sps?id=30535.

[1248] Unnamed Patriots player, paraphrased by Phil Simms, "Relentless Patriots don't wilt under pressure," *NFL.com*, 28 September 2004, www.nfl.com/news/story/7731266.

[1249] Patriots quarterback Tom Brady, quoted in: Todd Archer, "Patriots pick their way to Super Bowl, 24-14," *Dallas Morning News*, 19 January 2004, www.cowboysplus.com/nfl/stories/011904cpafclede.2b7f5ea5.html.

[1250] Patriots linebacker Tedy Bruschi, quoted in: Frank Tadych, "The Think Tank: Patriots face high expectations," Patriots.com, 24 September 2004, www.patriots.com/news/fullarticle.sps?id=31312.

[1251] Patriots linebacker Tedy Bruschi, quoted in: Howard Ulman (AP), "Tight end talks about another streak," *San Francisco Chronicle*, 11 October 2004, http://sfgate.com/cgi-bin/article.cgi?f=/news/archive/2004/10/11/sports1904EDT0348.DTL.

[1252] Bill Belichick, quoted in: Howard Ulman (AP), "Two-time NFL champs focus on next game, not making history," *Canada.com*, 3 September 2004, www.canada.com/sports/football/story.html?id=5F09B45F-C14D-417C-96B5-36A7704F010B.

[1253] Tom Brady, quoted in: Michael Gee, "Brady blows off blitz: QB handles pressure," *Boston Herald*, 4 October 2004, http://patriots.bostonherald.com/patriots/view.bg?articleid=47278.

[1254] Patriots safety Rodney Harrison, quoted in: Rich Thompson, "Harrison keeps his focus on new year," *Boston Herald*, 30 July 2004, http://patriots.bostonherald.com/patriots/view.bg?articleid=37861.

[1255] Patriots defensive lineman Richard Seymour, quoted in: Glen Farley, "Patriots prepare for unfamiliar opponent," *The Enterprise*, 17 September 2004, http://enterprise.southofboston.com/articles/2004/09/17/news/sports/sports03.txt.

[1256] Tom Brady, quoted in: Mark Singelais, " Patriots' focus solely on this year," *Times-Union*, 10 October 2004, www.timesunion.com/AspStories/storyprint.asp?StoryID=293582.

[1257] Bill Belichick, quoted in: Chris Kennedy, "Patriots still have right idea," *The Republican*, 5 September 2004, www.masslive.com/sports/republican/index.ssf?/base/sports-2/1094386522323061.xml.

[1258] Patriots wide receiver David Patten, quoted in: Nick Cafardo, "Pats' Patten must prove himself again," *Berkshire Eagle*, 11 August 2004, www.berkshireeagle.com/Stories/0,1413,101~6295~2326911,00.html.

[1259] Rohan Davey, quoted in: Ron Borges, "Backup plan for Davey working perfectly," *Boston Globe*, 9 May 2004, www.boston.com/sports/football/patriots/articles/2004/05/09/backup_plan_for_davey_working_perfectly?pg=full.

[1260] Bill Belichick, quoted in: Bill Burt, "Super Bowl success won't change Belichick," *Eagle Tribune*, 28 February 2002, www.eagletribune.com/news/stories/20020228/SP_004.htm.

[1261] Bill Belichick, quoted in: Dave Hutchinson, " Jets: Belichick remains the answer man," *Star-Ledger*, 21 October 2004, www.nj.com/sports/ledger/index.ssf?/base/sports-1/109834152157120.xml.

[1262] Patriots players quoted in: Tom E. Curran, "Most Pats prefer not to look back," *Providence Journal*, 27 August 2004, www.projo.com/patriots/content/projo_20040827_27pats.c013f.html.

[1263] Patriots center Dan Koppen, quoted in: Mike Lowe, "It's a super way to start the season," *Portland Press Herald*, 8 September 2004, http://pressherald.mainetoday.com/sports/pro/patriots/040908lowecolumn.shtml.

[1264] Patriots linebacker Mike Vrabel, quoted in: Len Pasquarelli, "Patriots put Super Bowl championship in past," *ESPN.com*, 30 July 2004, http://sports.espn.go.com/nfl/trainingCamp04/columns/story?columnist=pasquarelli_len&id=1849143.

[1265] Former Bengal and new Patriots running back Corey Dillon, quoted in: Mark Curnutte, "Bengals focus on Bengals," *Cincinnati Enquirer*, 21 August 2004, http://bengals.enquirer.com/2004/08/21/ben1a.html.

[1266] Geoff Hobson, "Dillon on call," *Bengals.com*, 18 August 2004, www.bengals.com/press/news.asp?iCurPage=0&news_id=2325.

[1267] Cincinnati Bengals offensive lineman Willie Anderson, quoted in: Kevin Goheen, "Dillon makes return in new uniform," *Cincinnati Post*, 21 August 2004, www.cincypost.com/2004/08/21/beng08-21-2004.html.

[1268] Mrs. Deb Belichick, Bill Belichick's husband, quoted in: Peter King, "The sincerest form of flattery," *Sports Illustrated*, 4 February 2002, http://sportsillustrated.cnn.com/inside_game/peter_king/news/2002/02/04/mmqb/.

[1269] Dr. Peter F. Drucker, *Management: Tasks, Responsibilities, Practices*, USA: HarperCollins, 1973, p. 125 & 127.

[1270] Bill Belichick, live video news conference, streamed online from Patriots.com, 20 October 2004.

[1271] Patriots linebacker/special teamer Tully Banta-Cain, quoted in: Marc Carig, "Banta-Cain positive he can play," *Boston Globe*, 10 August 2004, www.boston.com/sports/football/patriots/articles/2004/08/10/banta_cain_positive_he_can_play.

[1272] Patriots center Dan Koppen, quoted in: Nick Cafardo, "It doesn't weigh on Light," *Boston Globe*, 11 July 2004, www.boston.com/sports/football/patriots/articles/2004/07/11/it_doesnt_weigh_on_light.

[1273] Patriots wide receiver David Givens, quoted in: Howard Ulman (AP), "QB not satisfied despite strong start," *San Francisco Chronicle*, 15 September 2004, http://sfgate.com/cgi-bin/article.cgi?f=/news/archive/2004/09/15/sports1800EDT0419.DTL.

[1274] Hall of Fame coach Joe Gibbs (of the Washington Redskins), quoted in: Chris Harry, "Holley's book shows Belichick in a different light," *Orlando Sentinel*, 24 September 2004, www.mercurynews.com/mld/mercurynews/sports/9753171.htm?1c.

[1275] Bill Belichick, quoted in: Alan Greenberg, "A Working Relationship," *Hartford Courant*, 9 September 2004, www.ctnow.com/sports/hc-nflpatsmain0908.artsep09,1,2684889.story.

[1276] Former Patriots quarterback Drew Bledsoe, quoted in: David Pevear, "Drew who? Brady's the main man now," *Lowell Sun*, 30 September 2004, www.lowellsun.com/Stories/0,1413,105~4767~2437335,00.html.

[1277] Patriots left tackle Matt Light, quoted in: Dan Pires, "An unbelievable opener," *Standard-Times*, 11 September 2002, www.s-t.com/daily/09-02/09-11-02/c01sp130.htm.

[1278] Former New Orleans Saints general manager Randy Mueller, quoted in: Paul Attner, " Whatever 'It' is, Brady has 'It,'" *Sports Illustrated*, 6 October 2004, http://msn.foxsports.com/story/3059636.

[1279] Tom Brady, quoted in: Howard Ulman (AP), "QB not satisfied despite strong start," *San Francisco Chronicle*, 15 September 2004, http://sfgate.com/cgi-bin/article.cgi?f=/news/archive/2004/09/15/sports1800EDT0419.DTL.

[1280] Tom Brady, quoted in: Mike Lowe, "Can it get better? Patriots say yes," *Portland Press Herald*, 26 September 2004, http://pressherald.mainetoday.com/sports/pro/patriots/040926patsbye.shtml.

[1281] Bill Belichick, quoted in: Don Banks, "From doghouse to penthouse," *Sports Illustrated*, 17 October 2004, http://sportsillustrated.cnn.com/2004/writers/don_banks/10/17/patshawks.sider/.

[1282] Tom Brady, quoted in: Ron Borges, "He's a fast learner," *Boston Globe*, 18 October 2004, www.boston.com/sports/football/patriots/articles/2004/10/18/hes_a_fast_learner.

[1283] Safety Rodney Harrison, quoted in: Paul Attner, " Whatever 'It' is, Brady has 'It,'" *Sports Illustrated*, 6 October 2004, http://msn.foxsports.com/story/3059636.

[1284] Scott M. Johnson, "Dillon is wicked awesome," *Daily Herald*, 18 October 2004, www.heraldnet.com/stories/04/10/18/spo_dillon002.cfm.

[1285] Patriots defensive lineman Jarvis Green, quoted in: Michael Parente, " Patriots' line did the job," *MiddletownPress.com*, 12 November 2004.

[1286] Bill Belichick, "Bill Belichick Press Conf. Transcript - 4/30," *Patriots.com*, 30 April 2004, www.patriots.com/news/FullArticle.sps?id=28597&type=general.

[1287] Patriots wide receiver David Patten, quoted in: Paul Kenyon, "Patriots' Patten refuses to let himself fade away," *Providence Journal*, 29 October 2004, www.projo.com/patriots/content/projo_20041029_29pats.77d77.html.

[1288] Patriots left tackle Matt Light, quoted in: Hector Longo, "Light makes might,", *Eagle Tribune*, 28 January 2004, www.eagletribune.com/news/stories/20040128/SP_001.htm.

[1289] Patriots linebacker Tedy Bruschi, quoted in: Mike Reiss (*MetroWest Daily News*), "Bruschi just having a ball," *Boston Herald*, 6 January 2004, http://patriots.bostonherald.com/patriots/view.bg?articleid=14258.

[1290] Undrafted Patriots rookie cornerback Randall Gay, quoted in: Alan Greenberg, "Pats' Gay Out To Prove He Belongs," *Hartford Courant*, 14 September 2004, www.ctnow.com/sports/hc-patriots0914.artsep14,1,6042292.print.story.

[1291] Bill Belichick, quoted in: Michael Parente, " Rookie CB Gay making an impression on Pats," *Woonsocket Call*, 21 October 2004, www.zwire.com/site/news.cfm?newsid=13190161&BRD=1712&PAG=461&dept_id=106787&rfi=6.

[1292] Patriots cornerback Ty Law, quoted in: Michael Parente, " Rookie CB Gay making an impression on Pats," *Woonsocket Call*, 21 October 2004, www.zwire.com/site/news.cfm?newsid=13190161&BRD=1712&PAG=461&dept_id=106787&rfi=6.

[1293] Patriots cornerback Ty Law, quoted in: Ron Borges, "Time has been on Gay's side," *Boston Globe*, 21 October 2004, www.boston.com/sports/football/patriots/articles/2004/10/21/time_has_been_on_gays_side/.

[1294] Patriots cornerback Ty Law, quoted in: Ron Borges, "Time has been on Gay's side," *Boston Globe*, 21 October 2004, www.boston.com/sports/football/patriots/articles/2004/10/21/time_has_been_on_gays_side/.

[1295] Recently acquired free agent defensive lineman Rodney Bailey, quoted in: Tom E. Curran, "Patriots Notebook: Klecko could add linebacker to crowded résumé," *Providence Journal*, 22 May 2004, www.projo.com/patriots/content/projo_20040522_22patsjo.dc264.html.

[1296] Bill Belichick, quoted in: Tom E. Curran, "Patriots Notebook: Belichick points finger at himself for loss to Bills," *Providence Journal*, 11 September 2003, www.projo.com/patriots/content/projo_20030911_11patsjo.24d37.html.

[1297] Bill Belichick, quoted in: Dan Pires, "The changing face of Bill Belichick," *SouthCoast Today*, 22 December 2001, www.s-t.com/daily/12-01/12-22-01/c01sp071.htm.

[1298] Bill Belichick, quoted in: Mike Freeman, "Belichick Has Patriots' Ears; Now the Hard Part," *New York Times*, 26 July 2000, p. D1, ProQuest Historical Newspapers.

[1299] Former Navy coach Rick Forzano, quoted in: Gordon Edes, "Patriots coach has well-earned reputation for stopping whatever's thrown his way," *Boston Globe*, 2 February 2002, www.boston.com/sports/football/patriots/superbowl/globe_stories/020202/patriots_coach_has_well_earned_reputation_for_stopping_whatever_s_thrown_his_way+.shtml.

[1300] Coach Bill Belichick, quoted in: Tom E. Curran, "Savoring victory is alien to Belichick," *Providence Journal*, 7 February 2004, www.projo.com/patriots/content/projo_20040207_07pats.1902d4.html.

[1301] Bill Belichick, quoted in: Steve Cohen, "Belichick keeping Pats focused," *NFL.com*, 9 September 2002, www.nfl.com/teams/story/NE/5697584.

[1302] Bill Belichick, quoted in: Steve Cohen, "Belichick keeping Pats focused," *NFL.com*, 9 September 2002, www.nfl.com/teams/story/NE/5697584.

[1303] Patriots fullback/linebacker/defensive lineman Dan Klecko, quoted in: Stephen Edelson, "Klecko, Patriots streaking," *Asbury Park Press*, 3 October 2004, www.app.com/app/story/0,21625,1068629,00.html.

[1304] Hector Longo, "Upgraded arsenal at Brady's disposal," *Eagle-Tribune*, 6 September 2004, www.eagletribune.com/news/stories/20040906/SP_004.htm.

[1305] Bill Belichick, quoted in: Michael Felger, "Watson, Pats cut deal: Holdout ends, work begins," *Boston Herald*, 17 August 2004, http://patriots.bostonherald.com/patriots/view.bg?articleid=40154.

[1306] Patriots tight end Daniel Graham, quoted in: Mike Lowe, "Graham takes advantage as New England's new option," *Portland Press Herald*, 14 October 2004, http://sports.mainetoday.com/pro/patriots/041014lowecolumn.shtml.

[1307] Tom Brady, quoted in: Mike Lowe, "Graham takes advantage as New England's new option," *Portland Press Herald*, 14 October 2004, http://sports.mainetoday.com/pro/patriots/041014lowecolumn.shtml.

[1308] Patriots tight end Daniel Graham, quoted in: Mike Lowe, "Graham takes advantage as New England's new option," *Portland Press Herald*, 14 October 2004, http://sports.mainetoday.com/pro/patriots/041014lowecolumn.shtml.

[1309] Patriots linebacker Tedy Bruschi, quoted in: (Arizona Wildcats) Cat Tracks staff, "It's good to be Tedy Bruschi," 17 February 2004, http://arizona.theinsiders.com/2/235079.html.

[1310] Patriots quarterback Tom Brady, "Tom Brady Press Conference 7/23/03," bostonbrat.net/brady/arcjuly.html.

[1311] Special teams captain Larry Izzo, quoted in: "Tom's Posse, New England Patriots," www.tombradyfan.com/quotes.html.

[1312] Bill Belichick, quoted in: John Tomase, "Belichick has a few surprises ready," *Eagle Tribune*, 2 February 2000, www.eagletribune.com/news/stories/20000202/SP_011.htm.

[1313] TSX / The Insiders, "Team Report: Patriots," March 2003, bostonbrat.net/brady/arcmar.html.

[1314] Patriots inside linebacker Tedy Bruschi, quoted in: TSX / The Insiders, "Team Report: Patriots," March 2003, bostonbrat.net/brady/arcmar.html.

[1315] Tom Brady, "New England Patriots Quarterback Tom Brady Press Conference March 27, 2003," www.absolutebrady.com/Transcripts/032703.html.

[1316] Patriots linebacker Roman Phifer, quoted in: Glen Farley, "Patriots ready to defend," *The Enterprise*, 25 July 2004, http://enterprise.southofboston.com/articles/2004/07/25/news/sports/sports02.txt.

[1317] Patriots inside linebacker Tedy Bruschi, quoted in: TSX / The Insiders, "Team Report: Patriots," March 2003, bostonbrat.net/brady/arcmar.html.

[1318] Patriots fullback Fred McCrary, quoted in: Marc Carig, "Fullback McCrary at full speed," *Boston Globe*, 6 August 2004, www.boston.com/sports/football/patriots/articles/2004/08/06/fullback_mccrary_at_full_speed.

[1319] Patriots rookie running back Cedric Cobbs, "Cedric Cobbs Player Journal," *NFLPlayers.com*, 23 June 2004, www.patriots.com/news/FullArticle.sps?id=29002&type=nfl.

[1320] Patriots defensive lineman Richard Seymour, quoted in: Len Pasquarelli, "Patriots put Super Bowl championship in past," *ESPN.com*, 30 July 2004, http://sports.espn.go.com/nfl/trainingCamp04/columns/story?columnist=pasquarelli_len&id=1849143.

[1321] Patriots safety Rodney Harrison, quoted in: Ed Bouchette, "Is Adams a genius' genius?" *Pittsburgh Post-Gazette*, 29 January 2004, www.post-gazette.com/pg/04029/266893.stm.

[1322] Patriots safety Rodney Harrison, quoted in: Frank Tadych, "Patriots Notebook: Brady not into comparisons," *Patriots.com*, 6 September 2004, www.patriots.com/news/fullarticle.sps?id=30449.

[1323] Bill Belichick Press Conf. Transcript - 4/30," *Patriots.com*, 30 April 2004, www.patriots.com/news/FullArticle.sps?id=28597&type=general.

[1324] Hall of Fame coach Don Shula, quoted in: Michael Holley, "Shula impressed by streak," *Boston Globe*, 21 January 2004, www.boston.com/sports/football/patriots/articles/2004/01/21/shula_impressed_by_streak/.

[1325] Bill Belichick, quoted in: Peter May, "Master of the plan," *Boston Globe*, 3 February 2004, www.boston.com/sports/football/patriots/articles/2004/02/03/master_of_the_plan/.

[1326] Wide receiver Troy Brown, quoted in: Kevin Mannix, "Pats lose memory: `Forget 2003' is camp theme," *Boston Herald*, 30 July 2004, http://patriots.bostonherald.com/patriots/view.bg?articleid=37863.

[1327] Don Shula, quoted in: Alan Greenberg, "Patriots: Streak? What Streak?" *Hartford Courant*, 26 September 2004, www.ctnow.com/sports/hc-patsstreak0926.artsep26,1,3170251.print.story.

[1328] Patriots linebacker Willie McGinest, quoted in: *Patriots United*, Canada: Team Power Publishing, 2002, p. 197.

[1329] Patriots cornerback Ty Law, quoted in: Don Banks, "Move over Paul Revere," *Sports Illustrated*, 4 February 2002, http://sportsillustrated.cnn.com/inside_game/don_banks/news/2002/02/03/banks_insider/.

[1330] Tom Brady, quoted in: Tim Polzer, "Super Bowl XXXVI: New England 20, St. Louis 17," 3 February 2002, www.superbowl.com/history/mvps/game/sbxxxvi.

[1331] Patriots wide receiver David Patten, quoted in: Joe Burris, "Deep route," *Boston Globe*, 29 October 2004, www.boston.com/sports/football/patriots/articles/2004/10/29/deep_route.

[1332] Patriots cornerback Ty Law, quoted in: Dan Pires, "An unbelievable opener," *Standard-Times*, 11 September 2002, www.s-t.com/daily/09-02/09-11-02/c01sp130.htm.

[1333] Tom Brady, quoted in: Paul Attner, "Super Bowl 36: Standing Pat," *The Sporting News*, 4 February 2002, www.a1-sports-odds.com/292.htm.

[1334] Patriots inside linebackers coach Pepper Johnson, *Won For All*, Chicago: Contemporary Books, 2003, p. 2-3.

[1335] Bill Belichick, "Bill Belichick Press Conference," 22 January 2002, www.patriots.com/news/FullArticle.sps?id=16686&type=general.

[1336] Patriots safety Tebucky Jones, quoted in: Jim Donaldson, "It's about time to pick the Patriots for a change," *Providence Journal*, 16 September 2002, www.southcoasttoday.com/daily/09-02/09-16-02/c10sp115.htm.

[1337] Bill Belichick, quoted in: Glen Farley, "Pats not playing favorites," *The Enterprise*, 7 January 2004, http://enterprise.southofboston.com/articles/2004/01/07/news/sports/sports02.txt.

[1338] Bill Belichick, quoted in: Glen Farley, "Pats not playing favorites," *The Enterprise*, 7 January 2004, http://enterprise.southofboston.com/articles/2004/01/07/news/sports/sports02.txt.

[1339] Tom Brady, quoted in: Glen Farley, "Pats not playing favorites," *The Enterprise*, 7 January 2004, http://enterprise.southofboston.com/articles/2004/01/07/news/sports/sports02.txt.

[1340] Former Patriots linebacker Chris Slade, quoted in: Michael Silver, "Once and again," *Sports Illustrated*, 4 September 2002, http://sportsillustrated.cnn.com/inside_game/michael_silver/news/2002/09/04/open_mike/.

[1341] Michael Silver, "Once and again," *Sports Illustrated*, 4 September 2002, http://sportsillustrated.cnn.com/inside_game/michael_silver/news/2002/09/04/open_mike/.

[1342] Former Ram and current Patriot special teamer Don Davis, quoted in: Michael Felger, "Patriots Super win over Rams changed all," *Milford Daily News*, 5 November 2004, www.milforddailynews.com/sportsNews/view.bg?articleid=59185.

[1343] Patriots defensive lineman Richard Seymour, quoted in: Kevin Mannix, "Seymour was right pick for Patriots," *NFL Insider*, 23 January 2002, www.nfl.com/xxxvi/ce/feature/0,3892,4880669,00.html.

[1344] Patriots linebacker Tedy Bruschi, quoted in: (Arizona Wildcats) Cat Tracks staff, "It's good to be Tedy Bruschi," 17 February 2004, http://arizona.theinsiders.com/2/235079.html.

[1345] Patriots backup quarterback Jim Miller, quoted in: Frank Tadych, "The Think Tank: Patriots face high expectations," Patriots.com, 24 September 2004, www.patriots.com/news/fullarticle.sps?id=31312.

[1346] Patriots safety Rodney Harrison, quoted in: Frank Tadych, "The Think Tank: Patriots face high expectations," Patriots.com, 24 September 2004, www.patriots.com/news/fullarticle.sps?id=31312.

[1347] Patriots outside linebackers coach Rob Ryan, quoted in: Michael Holley, *Patriot Reign*, William Morrow, 2004, p. 97.

[1348] Patriots safety Rodney Harrison, quoted in: Jackie MacMullan, "As promised, party was quite subdued," *Boston Globe*, 11 October 2004, www.boston.com/sports/football/patriots/articles/2004/10/11/as_promised_party_was_quite_subdued/.

[1349] Patriots quarterback Tom Brady, "Tom Brady Press Conference 7/23/03," bostonbrat.net/brady/arcjuly.html.

[1350] Coach Bill Belichick, quoted in: Tom King, "Belichick establishes a no-nonsense policy," *Nashua Telegraph*, 6 June 2000, archive.nashuatelegraph.com/Daily_Sections/Sports/_Archives/2000/June/stories/0606w-beli.htm.

[1351] Coach Bill Belichick, quoted in: Tom King, "Belichick establishes a no-nonsense policy," *Nashua Telegraph*, 6 June 2000, archive.nashuatelegraph.com/Daily_Sections/Sports/_Archives/2000/June/stories/0606w-beli.htm.

[1352] Glen Farley, "NFL team previews — AFC East: Patriots," *Pro Football Weekly*, 21 August 2000, http://archive.profootballweekly.com/content/archives/features_2000/teampreview_nwe_082100.asp.

[1353] Buffalo Bills cornerback Terrence McGee, quoted in: Sal Maiorana, "McGee may move into a starting job," *Democrat and Chronicle*, 5 October 2004, www.democratandchronicle.com/apps/pbcs.dll/article?AID=/20041005/SPORTS03/410050314/1007/SPORTS.

[1354] Patriots Vice President of Player Personnel Scott Pioli, quoted in: Michael Felger, "Pioli: Scout's Honor," *Boston Herald*, 19 December 2001, www.allthingsbillbelichick.com/articles/piolihonor.htm.

[1355] Bill Belichick, quoted in: Tom King, " Glass is always half-empty for New England, Belichick," *Nashua Telegraph*, 21 September 2004, http://nsnlb.us.publicus.com/apps/pbcs.dll/article?AID=/20040921/SPORTS/40921025/-1/sports.

[1356] Dr. Peter F. Drucker, *Management: Tasks, Responsibilities, Practices*, USA: HarperCollins, 1973, pp. 76-77.

[1357] Patriots center/guard Damien Woody, quoted in: Michael Holley, *Patriot Reign*, William Morrow, 2004, p. 234.

[1358] Buffalo Bills head coach Mike Mularkey, quoted in: Chuck Pollock, "POLLOCK: Pats' streak among most impressive," *Times Herald* (Olean, NY), 30 September 2004, www.zwire.com/site/news.cfm?BRD=386&dept_id=444921&newsid=13040313&PAG=461&rfi=9.

[1359] Patriots offensive coordinator Charlie Weis, quoted in: Dave Anderson, "The Super Bowl's Offensive Minds," *New York Times*, 28 January 2004, p. D5, ProQuest database.

[1360] VP of player personnel Scott Pioli, quoted in: Michael Felger, "Pioli helps put it together," *Boston Herald*, 26 January 2004, http://patriots.bostonherald.com/patriots/ view.bg?articleid=510.

[1361] Patriots quarterback Tom Brady, "Tom Brady Press Conference 7/23/03," bostonbrat.net/brady/arcjuly.html.

[1362] Peter King, "The sincerest form of flattery," *Sports Illustrated*, 4 February 2002, http://sportsillustrated.cnn.com/inside_game/peter_king/news/2002/02/04/mmqb/.

[1363] Patriots wide receiver Charles Johnson, quoted in: Dan O'Neill, "Belichick's gruff football facade gives way to a serious softy," *St. Louis Post-Dispatch*, 1 February 2002, www.ramsfan.us/oldnews/2002/020102-9.htm.

[1364] John Lynch, quoted in: Michael Smith, "Lynch has high praise for Patriots," *Boston Globe*, 3/19/2004.

[1365] New Patriots running back Corey Dillon, quoted in: Ken Lechtanski, "A bunch of happy campers report," *The Enterprise*, 30 July 2004, http://enterprise.southofboston.com/articles/2004/07/30/news/sports/sports02.txt.

[1366] Scott Pioli, Patriots VP of player personnel, quoted in: Hector Longo, "All the right moves," *Eagle-Tribune*, 30 January 2004, www.eagletribune.com/news/stories/20040130/SP_001.htm.

[1367] Former New Orleans Saints general manager Randy Mueller, quoted in: Clare Farnsworth, "Hawks, Pats QBs stand on common ground," *Seattle Post-Intelligencer*, 14 October 2004, http://seattlepi.nwsource.com/football/195156_hawk14.html.

[1368] Coach Bill Belichick, quoted in: Alan Greenberg, "Belichick Game Plan For Life," *Hartford Courant*, 3 May 2004, www.ctnow.com/sports/hc-belichick0503.artmay03,1,707205.story.

[1369] Patriots running back Rabih Abdullah, quoted in: Michael Vega, "Fantastic Four: Reserves had a common bond," *Boston Globe*, 11 October 2004, www.boston.com/sports/football/patriots/articles/2004/10/11/fantastic_four_reserves_had_a_common_bond.

[1370] Michael Felger, "Where's the beef? So far, league 'iron' not so hot," *Boston Herald*, 27 October 2004, http://patriots.bostonherald.com/patriots/view.bg?articleid=51095.

[1371] Patriots linebacker Willie McGinest, quoted in: Chris Ruddick, "Still Perfect: Win streak reaches 21 for Patriots," *Sports Network*, 25 October 2004, www.sportsnetwork.com/default.asp?c=sportsnetwork&page=nfl/news/abn3567151.htm.

[1372] Ken Berger, "Pennington 'disgusted,'" *Newsday*, 26 October 2004, www.newsday.com/sports/football/jets/ny-spjets264019799oct26,0,5945564.story.

[1373] Patriots safety Rodney Harrison, quoted in: Nick Cafardo, "Patriots' timing is perfect," *Boston Globe*, 25 October 2004, www.boston.com/sports/football/patriots/articles/2004/10/25/patriots_timing_is_perfect.

[1374] Bill Belichick, quoted in: *Washington Post*, "Pats make big plays, down Jets," *Charleston Daily Mail*, 25 October 2004, www.dailymail.com/news/Sports/2004102519/.

[1375] Ken Berger, "Chad tipping his passes?" *Newsday*, 27 October 2004, www.newsday.com/sports/football/jets/ny-spjets1027,0,4043869.story.

[1376] Tight end Christian Fauria, quoted in: Sam Farmer (*L.A. Times*), " The beat goes on in New England," *San Francisco Chronicle*, 18 October 2004, http://sfgate.com/cgi-bin/article.cgi?f=/chronicle/archive/2004/10/18/SPGGR9BKKB1.DTL.

[1377] Patriots center/guard Damien Woody, quoted in: Jimmy Golen (AP), "Belichick might not be slick, but he makes Pats tick," *Arizona Daily Star*, 20 January 2004, www.dailystar.com/dailystar/relatedarticles/6555.php.

[1378] Bill Belichick, quoted in: Alan Greenberg, "A Working Relationship," *Hartford Courant*, 9 September 2004, www.ctnow.com/sports/hc-nflpatsmain0908.artsep09,1,2684889.story.

[1379] Bill Belichick, quoted in: Bill Reynolds, "Bill Reynolds: Pats' Belichick the model teams now want to copy," *Providence Journal*, 30 September 2004, www.projo.com/patriots/content/projo_20040930_30rencol.18ef7f.html.

[1380] Bill Belichick interview, "The Coach," *60 Minutes*, aired on CBS 19 September 2004.

[1381] Alan Greenberg, "Getting Along Well Belichick Still A Little Grim, But With A Grin," *Hartford Courant*, 3 September 2000, p. E1, ProQuest database.

[1382] Patriots tight end Christian Fauria, quoted in: Frank Tadych, "Patriots Notebook: Miller nearing return," *Patriots.com*, 25 August 2004, www.patriots.com/news/FullArticle.sps?id=30274&type=general.

[1383] Patriots quarterback Tom Brady, quoted in: Michael Parente, "Trend of fumbles causing grumbles," *Woonsocket Call*, 26 August 2004, www.zwire.com/site/news.cfm?newsid=12783330&BRD=1712&PAG=461&dept_id=106787&rfi=6.

[1384] Michael Holley, *Patriot Reign*, William Morrow, 2004, p. 90.

[1385] Patriots defensive coordinator Romeo Crennel, quoted in: Thomas George, "After Years of Waiting, Crennel Moves to Head of Line," *New York Times*, 23 December 2003, p. D1, ProQuest database.

[1386] Tom Brady, quoted in: Tom King, " NFL's longest win streak fits the Bill," *Nashua Telegraph*, 11 October 2004, www.nashuatelegraph.com/apps/pbcs.dll/article?AID=/20041011/COLUMNISTS11/110110034/-1/columnists.

[1387] Jamil Soriano, quoted in: Andy Hart, "Soriano seeking experience, NFL Europe ring," *Patriots Football Weekly*, 5 May 2004, www.patriots.com/news/FullArticle.sps?id=28665&type=general.

[1388] Bill Belichick, quoted in: Mike Reiss, "Patriots notebook: Seymour sees a challenge," *Daily News Transcript*, 14 October 2004, www.dailynewstranscript.com/sportsNews/view.bg?articleid=43092.

[1389] Barry Scanlon, "'Never a dull moment' in arena football," *Lowell Sun*, 11 July 2004, www.lowellsun.com/Stories/0,1413,105~4767~2265817,00.html.

[1390] Michael Holley, *Patriot Reign*, William Morrow, 2004, p. 151.

[1391] Tom Brady, quoted in: Tom E. Curran, "Patriots Notebook: Team is fast out of the gate," *Providence Journal*, 11 June 2004, www.projo.com/patriots/content/projo_20040611_11patsjo.fcc1f.html.

[1392] Patriots running back Antowain Smith, quoted in: Paul Attner, " Whatever 'It' is, Brady has 'It,'" *Sports Illustrated*, 6 October 2004, http://msn.foxsports.com/story/3059636.

[1393] Patriots tight end Daniel Graham, quoted in: Mike Lowe, "Graham takes advantage as New England's new option," *Portland Press Herald*, 14 October 2004, http://sports.mainetoday.com/pro/patriots/041014lowecolumn.shtml.

[1394] Bill Belichick, "Bill Belichick Press Conference," 22 January 2002, www.patriots.com/news/FullArticle.sps?id=16686&type=general.

[1395] Bill Belichick, quoted in: Alan Greenberg, "Rams Unlikely To Pass This Up," *Hartford Courant*, 4 November 2004, www.ctnow.com/sports/football/hc-patriots1104.artnov04,1,7202313.story?coll=hc-headlines-football.

[1396] Bill Belichick, "Bill Belichick Press Conf. Transcript - 9/14/2004," *Patriots.com*, 14 September 2004, www.patriots.com/Common/PrintThis.sps?id=30535.

[1397] Bill Belichick, "Bill Belichick Press Conf. Transcript - 4/30," *Patriots.com*, 30 April 2004, www.patriots.com/news/FullArticle.sps?id=28597&type=general.

[1398] Bill Belichick, quoted in: Joe Burris, "Deep route," *Boston Globe*, 29 October 2004, www.boston.com/sports/football/patriots/articles/2004/10/29/deep_route.

[1399] Don Shula, winningest coach in NFL history who coached the Miami Dolphins to their miraculous undefeated season in 1972, quoted in: Vic Carucci, "Shula sees more Super wins for Belichick," *NFL.com*, 4 February 2004, www.nfl.com/news/story/7063350.

[1400] Patriots safety Rodney Harrison, quoted in: Sam Donnellon, "Pats emerge from scrum with record victory," *Philadelphia Daily News*, 10 October 2004, www.mercurynews.com/mld/mercurynews/sports/9887249.htm?1c.

[1401] Bill Belichick, quoted in: Kevin McNamara, "A chink in the Pats' armor," *Providence Journal*, 2 November 2004, www.projo.com/patriots/content/projo_20041102_02pats.5aaec.html.

[1402] Patriots linebacker Tedy Bruschi, quoted in: Michael Smith, "Brown baggers," in: *Again!*, Chicago: Triumph Books, 2004, p. 64.

[1403] Patriots safety Rodney Harrison, quoted in: Nick Cafardo, "Losing Tys leaves Patriots in a bind," *Boston Globe*, 4 November 2004, www.boston.com/sports/football/patriots/articles/2004/11/04/losing_tys_leaves_patriots_in_a_bind/.

[1404] Patriots linebacker Tedy Bruschi, quoted in: Hector Longo, "It's time to sort out the walking wounded," *Eagle Tribune*, 22 September 2003, www.eagletribune.com/news/stories/20030922/SP_011.htm.

[1405] Patriots linebacker Tedy Bruschi, quoted in: Jim Donaldson, "Dictionary helps in describing the Pats," *Providence Journal*, 13 October 2003, www.projo.com/patriots/content/projo_20031013_13jdcol.1e250.html.

[1406] Patriots safety Rodney Harrison, quoted in: Jeff Reynolds, "Harrison, Pats patch wounds, march forward," *Pro Football Weekly*, 27 October 2003, www.profootballweekly.com/PFW/NFL/AFC/AFC+East/New+England/Features/2003/reynolds102703.htm.

[1407] Patriots receiver David Givens, quoted in: George Kimball, "Givens takes opportunity: Receiver enjoys career day," *Boston Herald*, 20 September 2004, http://patriots.bostonherald.com/patriots/view.bg?articleid=45104.

[1408] Patriots linebacker Willie McGinest, quoted in: Tom E. Curran, "Patriots of 2004 find their identity," *Providence Journal*, 9 November 2004, www.projo.com/patriots/content/projo_20041109_09patanal.94368.html.

[1409] Bill Belichick, quoted in: George Kimball, "Brown helps out as a real 2-way threat," *Boston Herald*, 8 November 2004, http://patriots.bostonherald.com/patriots/view.bg?articleid=53015.

[1410] Mark Starr (*Newsweek*), "The Amazing, Enigmatic Belichick," MSNBC.com, 13 November 2004.

[1411] Patriots kicker Adam Vinatieri, quoted in: Steve Buckley, "Offense powers Patriots," *Boston Herald*, 14 November 2004.

[1412] Scene from *Monty Python and the Holy Grail*, www.mwscomp.com/movies/grail/grail-04.htm.

[1413] Patriots cornerback Ty Law, quoted in: Michael Felger, "Pats confront Law decision: Should team play ailing veteran?" *MetroWest Daily News*, 15 September 2004, www.dailynewstranscript.com/sportsNews/view.bg?articleid=41142.

[1414] Offensive line coach Dante Scarnecchia, quoted in: Ken Berger, "Pats' offensive line has last laugh," *Newsday*, 1 February 2004, www.southcoasttoday.com/daily/02-04/02-01-04/e03sp876.htm.

[1415] Patriots wide receiver Deion Branch, quoted in: Kevin Paul Dupont, "Mr. Cool," *Again!*, Chicago: Triumph Books, 2004, p. 18.

[1416] Patriots safety Lawyer Milloy, quoted in: Pepper Johnson, *Won For All*, Chicago: Contemporary Books, 2003, p. 137.

[1417] Patriots linebacker Bryan Cox, quoted in: Hector Longo, "Pats' Belichick passes all tests," *Eagle Tribune*, 13 January 2002, www.eagletribune.com/news/stories/20020113/SP_001.htm.

[1418] Bill Belichick, "Bill Belichick Press Conf. - 09/05/2002," Patriots.com, www.patriots.com/mediaworld/MediaDetail.sps?ID=20143&keywords=Press+Conference&media=audio&team=0&player=0&game=0&currpgno=27&pageid=2.

[1419] Patriots linebacker Ted Johnson, quoted in: Tom E. Curran, "Johnson takes long view on longevity," *Providence Journal*, 20 August 2004, www.projo.com/patriots/content/projo_20040820_20pats.24d4af.html.

[1420] Bill Belichick, "Bill Belichick Press Conference," 22 January 2002, www.patriots.com/news/FullArticle.sps?id=16686&type=general.

[1421] Bill Belichick, "Bill Belichick Press Conf. Transcript 8/3/04," *Patriots.com*, 3 August 2004, www.patriots.com/news/fullarticle.sps?id=29867&special_section=TrainingCamp2004&type=training.

[1422] Tom Brady, quoted in: Associated Press, "NFL opener: Patriots 27, Colts 24," *ABC Action News*, 10 September 2004, www.tampabaylive.com/stories/2004/09/040910pats.shtml.

[1423] Oakland cornerback Charles Woodson, quoted in: AP, "Ice man cometh," *Sports Illustrated*, 20 January 2002, http://sportsillustrated.cnn.com/football/2002/playoffs/news/2002/01/19/raiders_patriots_ap/.

[1424] Raiders linebacker William Thomas, quoted in: Jeffri Chadiha, "Chilling!" *Sports Illustrated*, special commemorative issue, 13 February 2002, p. 54.

[1425] Patriots inside linebackers coach Pepper Johnson, *Won For All*, Chicago: Contemporary Books, 2003, p. 185.

[1426] *NFL Films* president Steve Sabol, in: *Patriots United*, Canada: Team Power Publishing, 2002, p. 158.

[1427] Patriots cornerback Ty Law, quoted in: Larry Weisman, "Receivers catch break with contact crackdown," *USA Today*, 9 August 2004, www.usatoday.com/sports/football/nfl/2004-08-08-rule-cover_x.htm.

[1428] Patriots cornerback Ty Law, quoted in: Larry Weisman, "Receivers catch break with contact crackdown," *USA Today*, 9 August 2004, www.usatoday.com/sports/football/nfl/2004-08-08-rule-cover_x.htm.

[1429] Bill Belichick, quoted in: " Pats' Law thankful there's time to heal," *The Herald News*, 12 September 2004, www.zwire.com/site/news.cfm?BRD=1710&dept_id=353135&newsid=12909714&PAG=740&rfi=9.

[1430] Unnamed Patriot player after ESPN analyst Tom Jackson reported Patriots players "hate their coach" after the Patriots released star safety Lawyer Milloy, quoted in: Nick Cafardo, "Patriots won't fan any flames," *Boston Globe*, 16 September 2003, www.boston.com/sports/football/patriots/articles/2003/09/16/patriots_wont_fan_any_flames/.

[1431] Patriots offensive lineman Russ Hochstein, quoted in: Ken Berger, "Pats' offensive line has last laugh," *Newsday*, 1 February 2004, www.southcoasttoday.com/daily/02-04/02-01-04/e03sp876.htm.

[1432] Pats offensive lineman Damien Woody, quoted in: Eric Wilbur, "Sapp's comments don't faze Patriots," *Boston Globe*, 22 January 2004, www.boston.com/sports/football/patriots/articles/2004/01/22/sapps_comments_dont_faze_patriots/.

[1433] Tom Brady, quoted in: Eric Wilbur, "Sapp's comments don't faze Patriots," *Boston Globe*, 22 January 2004, www.boston.com/sports/football/patriots/articles/2004/01/22/sapps_comments_dont_faze_patriots/.

[1434] Pats offensive lineman Russ Hochstein, quoted in: Eric Wilbur, "Sapp's comments don't faze Patriots," *Boston Globe*, 22 January 2004, www.boston.com/sports/football/patriots/articles/2004/01/22/sapps_comments_dont_faze_patriots/.

[1435] Tom Brady, quoted in: Gary Shelton, "Story, as usual, is Sapp," *St. Petersburg Times*, 28 January 2004, www.sptimes.com/2004/01/28/Columns/Story_as_usual_is_S.shtml.

[1436] Bill Belichick, quoted in: Dan Pires "Defense first job for Law," *Standard-Times*, 20 August 2000, www.southcoasttoday.com/daily/08-00/08-20-00/b01sp052.htm.

[1437] Former Patriots coach Pete Carroll, quoted in: Alan Greenberg, "Belichick caught in Grier's draft," *Hartford Courant*, 26 November 2000, p. E3, ProQuest database.

[1438] Bill Belichick, quoted in: Alan Greenberg, "Belichick caught in Grier's draft," *Hartford Courant*, 26 November 2000, p. E3, ProQuest database.

[1439] LSU Tigers head coach Nick Saban, quoted in: Josh Dubow (AP), "LSU's Nick Saban Wins AP Coach of Year," 11 December 2003, www.tallahassee.com/mld/tallahassee/sports/special_packages/orange/7464888.htm.

[1440] Bill Belichick, quoted in: Michael Silver, "Pat Answer," *Sports Illustrated*, 11 February 2002, http://sportsillustrated.cnn.com/si_online/news/2002/02/11/pat_answer/.

[1441] Bill Belichick, "Bill Belichick Press Conf. Transcript 8/3/04," *Patriots.com*, 3 August 2004, www.patriots.com/news/fullarticle.sps?id=29867&special_section=TrainingCamp2004&type=training.

[1442] Bill Belichick, "Bill Belichick Press Conf.Transcript 7/31/04," 31 July 2004, www.patriots.com/news/fullarticle.sps?id=29754&type=general.

[1443] Patriots linebacker Tedy Bruschi, quoted in: Michael Smith, "Solid backing," *Boston Globe*, 9 September 2004, www.boston.com/sports/football/patriots/articles/2004/09/09/solid_backing.

[1444] Patriots wide receiver Troy Brown after beating the Rams in Super Bowl XXXVI, quoted in: Associated Press, "Estimated 1.2 million fans pack Boston streets," *ESPN*, 5 February 2002, http://espn.go.com/nfl/playoffs01/news/2002/0205/1323015.html.

[1445] Patriots safety Rodney Harrison, quoted in: Frank Tadych, "Patriots Notebook: Harrison makes point of emphasis," *Patriots.com*, 29 October 2004, http://cachewww.patriots.com/news/index.cfm?ac=latestnewsdetail&pid=9504&pcid=41.

[1446] Tom Brady, quoted in: Don Banks, "Move over Paul Revere," *Sports Illustrated*, 4 February 2002, http://sportsillustrated.cnn.com/inside_game/don_banks/news/2002/02/03/banks_insider/.

[1447] Patriots defensive lineman Bobby Hamilton, quoted in: Michael Felger, "Hamilton a tough loss for Pats," *Boston Herald*, 23 May 2004, http://patriots.bostonherald.com/patriots/view.bg?articleid=28994.

[1448] Patriots cornerback Ty Law, quoted in: Mark Singelais, "Secondary delivers lessons," *Times Union*, 18 October 2004, www.timesunion.com/AspStories/story.asp?storyID=295947&category=SPORTS&BCCode=&newsdate=10/18/2004.

[1449] Patriots defensive lineman Richard Seymour, quoted in: Jon Japha, "Patriots beat: Clear class distinctions," *MetroWest Daily News*, 18 October 2004, www.metrowestdailynews.com/sportsNews/view.bg?articleid=80807.

[1450] Jay Glazer, "Pats notes: New England defense lays down the Law," *CBS Sportsline*, 4 February 2002, http://cbs.sportsline.com/b/page/pressbox/0,1328,4948780,00.html.

[1451] Patriots safety Lawyer Milloy, quoted in: *Patriots United*, Canada: Team Power Publishing, 2002, p. 168.

[1452] IHOP restaurant manager, quoted in: *Patriots United*, Canada: Team Power Publishing, 2002, p. 168.

[1453] Pittsburgh Steelers receiver Plaxico Burress, quoted in: *AP*, "Brady, new-look Patriots shut down Steelers," *ESPN*, 9 September 2004, http://sports.espn.go.com/nfl/recap?gameId=220909017.

[1454] Tom Brady, quoted in: Dan Pires, "An unbelievable opener," *Standard-Times*, 11 September 2002, www.s-t.com/daily/09-02/09-11-02/c01sp130.htm.

[1455] Tom Brady, quoted in: "Quotes," http://bostonbrat.net/brady/quotes.html.

[1456] Steelers defensive end Kimo von Oelhoffen, quoted in: Ed Bouchette, "Steelers figure they owe Patriots a payback for 2002 AFC championship loss," *Pittsburgh Post-Gazette*, 31 October 2004, www.post-gazette.com/pg/04305/404012.stm.

[1457] Steelers receiver Hines Ward, quoted in: Alan Robinson, "Still on a roll, Patriots return to the place their mini-dynasty began – Pittsburgh," www.canada.com/sports/football/story.html?id=efdc2a7f-542e-4ba5-94d0-bd99d4648301.

[1458] Joe Wells, "A Day of Dynasties and Destiny," 31 October 2004, http://steelers.scout.com/2/312953.html.

[1459] Bill Belichick, quoted in: Frank Tadych, "Patriots Notebook: Injuries a major concern," *Patriots.com*, 31 October 2004, http://cachewww.patriots.com/news/index.cfm?ac=latestnewsdetail&pid=9517&pcid=41.

[1460] Bill Belichick, quoted in: Brian Gillespie, "Steelers sack Patriots' streak," *Sports Network*, 1 November 2004, www.sportsnetwork.com/default.asp?c=sportsnetwork&page=nfl/news/abn3577519.htm.

[1461] Steelers defender Deshea Townsend, quoted in: Mark Kaboly, "Steelers stop streak by stunning New England," *The Daily News*, 1 November 2004, www.zwire.com/site/news.cfm?BRD=1282&dept_id=182120&newsid=13265666&PAG=461&rfi=9.

[1462] Gerry Dulac, "After two more TDs, Burress credits receivers coach for improved play," *Pittsburgh Post-Gazette*, 1 November 2004, www.post-gazette.com/pg/04306/404972.stm.

[1463] Patriots safety Rodney Harrison, quoted in: "Game 7: Steelers 34, Patriots 20," *The Republican*, 1 November 2004, www.masslive.com/sports/republican/index.ssf?/base/sports-0/1099298875142440.xml.

[1464] Patriots linebacker Willie McGinest, quoted in: Chris Ruddick, " Pats suffer first loss in more than a year," *Sports Network*, 1 November 2004, www.sportsnetwork.com/default.asp?c=sportsnetwork&page=nfl/news/ABN3577698.htm.

[1465] Defensive lineman Richard Seymour, quoted in: Michael Felger, "Pats hit Steel wall, streak ends: Turnovers too costly as run halts at 21 games," *Boston Herald*, 1 November 2004, http://patriots.bostonherald.com/patriots/view.bg?articleid=51912.

[1466] Bill Belichick, quoted in: AP, "Steelers snap Patriots' 21-game win streak," *SI.com*, 31 October 2004, http://sportsillustrated.cnn.com/2004/football/nfl/10/31/bc.fbn.patriots.steelers.ap/.

[1467] Tom Brady, quoted in: Joe Burris, "Struggling Brady lives to fight another day," *Boston Globe*, 1 November 2004, www.boston.com/sports/football/patriots/articles/2004/11/01/struggling_brady_lives_to_fight_another_day.

[1468] Patriots receiver Troy Brown, quoted in: Chris Ruddick, "Pats suffer first loss in more than a year," *Sports Network*, 1 November 2004, www.sportsnetwork.com/default.asp?c=sportsnetwork&page=nfl/news/ABN3577698.htm.

[1469] "Game 7: Steelers 34, Patriots 20," *The Republican*, 1 November 2004, www.masslive.com/sports/republican/index.ssf?/base/sports-0/1099298875142440.xml.

[1470] Steelers running back Duce Staley, quoted in: Len Pasquarelli, "Steelers capitalize on Dillon's absence," *ESPN.com*, 31 October 2004, http://sports.espn.go.com/nfl/columns/story?columnist=pasquarelli_len&id=1913583.

[1471] Unnamed Patriot, quoted in: Michael Felger, "The best — and worst — of 2004 Patriots at midway point," *Boston Herald*, 10 November 2004, http://patriots.bostonherald.com/patriots/view.bg?articleid=53418.

[1472] Indianapolis Colts kicker Mike Vanderjagt, quoted in: Michael Smith, "Another Indy effort bites the dust," *ESPN.com*, 10 September 2004, http://sports.espn.go.com/nfl/news/story?id=1878509.

[1473] St. Louis Rams linebacker London Fletcher, quoted in: AP, "Picking up the pieces," 4 February 2002, http://sportsillustrated.cnn.com/football/2002/playoffs/news/2002/02/04/rams_wrap_ap/.

[1474] Titans guard Zach Piller, quoted in: "Titans Post-Game Quotes," *Patriots.com*, 10 January 2004, www.patriots.com/games/GamesDetails.sps?matchid=27174&matchreportid=27284.

[1475] Tennessee Titans guard Zach Piller, quoted in: Michael Holley, "Bitter Piller sure to have company," *Boston Globe*, 11 January 2004, www.boston.com/sports/articles/2004/01/11/bitter_piller_sure_to_have_company/.

[1476] Seattle Seahawks safety Terreal Bierria, quoted in: Jose Miguel Romero, "Hawks drop the ball against Patriots," *Seattle Times*, 18 October 2004, http://seattletimes.nwsource.com/html/sports/2002065959_hawk18.html.

[1477] Steelers quarterback Kordell Stewart, quoted in: Jerry DiPaola, "Steelers spotlight," (Pittsburgh) *Tribune-Review*, www.pittsburghlive.com/x/tribune-review/sports/s_14540.html.

[1478] Ian Logue, "Steelers Can't Say Much Now, Lose 30-14," *PatsFans.com*, 9 September 2002, www.patsfans.com/stories/display_story.php?story_id=2064.

[1479] Patriots rookie defensive lineman Vince Wilfork, quoted in: Michael Smith, "Patriots take tackle Wilfork," *Boston Globe*, 25 April 2004, www.boston.com/sports/articles/2004/04/25/patriots_take_tackle_wilfork/.

[1480] Patriots cornerback Ty Law, quoted in: Michael Parente, "Trend of fumbles causing grumbles," *Woonsocket Call*, 26 August 2004, www.zwire.com/site/news.cfm?newsid=12783330&BRD=1712&PAG=461&dept_id=106787&rfi=6.

[1481] Patriots receiver Troy Brown, quoted in: Michael Felger, "Brown in the flow: Timing may be right for action," *Boston Herald*, 1 October 2004, http://patriots.bostonherald.com/patriots/view.bg?articleid=46906.

[1482] Patriots cornerback Ty Law, quoted in: Associated Press, "Patriots still stinging from last game at Buffalo," *MSNBC*, 2 October 2004, http://msnbc.msn.com/id/6145520/.

[1483] Bill Belichick, quoted in: Associated Press, "Patriots still stinging from last game at Buffalo," *MSNBC*, 2 October 2004, http://msnbc.msn.com/id/6145520/.

[1484] Tom E. Curran, "Is this Belichick's version of I've Got A Secret?" *Providence Journal*, 7 September 2004, www.projo.com/patriots/content/projo_20040907_07pats.2e05d.html.

[1485] Patriots inside linebackers coach Pepper Johnson, *Won For All*, Chicago: Contemporary Books, 2003, p. 155.

[1486] Carolina Panthers defensive tackle Brentson Buckner, quoted in: Rick Stroud, "Cat defense," *St. Petersburg Times*, 31 January 2004, www.sptimes.com/2004/01/31/Sports/Cat_defense.shtml.

[1487] Patriots offensive lineman Joe Andruzzi, quoted in: Tom E. Curran, "Pats' Andruzzi keeps leading by example," *Providence Journal*, 15 September 2004, www.projo.com/patriots/content/projo_20040915_15pats.a329f.html.

[1488] Panthers safety Deon Grant, quoted in: Dan Pires, "Are Patriots in the Dogg house?" *Standard-Times*, 1 February 2004, www.southcoasttoday.com/daily/02-04/02-01-04/e06sp882.htm.

[1489] Panthers defensive lineman Julius Peppers, quoted in: Dan Pires, "Are Patriots in the Dogg house?" *Standard-Times*, 1 February 2004, www.southcoasttoday.com/daily/02-04/02-01-04/e06sp882.htm.

[1490] Former Seahawk and current Patriot tight end Christian Fauria, quoted in: Clare Farnsworth, "Up Next: New England Patriots," *Seattle Post-Intelligencer*, 13 October 2004, http://seattlepi.nwsource.com/football/194887_hnext13.html.

[1491] http://sportsillustrated.cnn.com/football/nfl/boxscores/2001/12/22/patriots_dolphins/.

[1492] Dolphins cornerback Sam Madison, quoted in: Alex Marvez, "Dolphins' rally comes up short in the New England chill," *South Florida Sun-Sentinel*, 30 June 2001, www.staugustine.com/stories/122301/spo_380892.shtml.

[1493] www.nfl.com/ce/recap/0,3762,NFL_20011007_NE@MIA,00.html.

[1494] Patriots inside linebackers coach Pepper Johnson, *Won For All*, Chicago: Contemporary Books, 2003, p. 158.

[1495] Bill Belichick, quoted in: Alan Greenberg, "Belichick's Chief Concern is Only What Lies Ahead," *Hartford Courant*, 17 September 2002, p. C3, ProQuest database.

[1496] Shane Donaldson, "Update: Fauria deal made official," *Patriots.com*, 22 March 2002, www.patriots.com/news/FullArticle.sps?id=17640&type=general&bhcp=1.

[1497] Michael Holley, *Patriot Reign*, William Morrow, 2004, p. 80.

[1498] Former Patriots defensive lineman Steve Martin, quoted in: Rich Cimini, "A wild & crazy situation," *New York Daily News*, 20 December 2002, www.nydailynews.com/sports/football/v-pfriendly/story/45021p-42366c.html.

[1499] "SI Players Poll: 'Who is the dirtiest player in the NFL?'" *Sports Illustrated*, 12 October 2004, http://sportsillustrated.cnn.com/2004/players/10/12/poll.dirtiest/index.html.

[1500] Jay Glazer, "Game-day notebook: Williams' future in Buffalo uncertain," *CBS Sportsline.com*, 21 December 2003, http://cbs.sportsline.com/nfl/story/6943613; and Michael Felger, "Mawae fires at Washington: Battle of midway resumes," *Boston Herald*, 18 December 2004, http://patriots.bostonherald.com/patriots/patriots.bg?articleid=321.

[1501] New York Jets center Kevin Mawae, quoted in: Jay Glazer, "Game-day notebook: Williams' future in Buffalo uncertain," *CBS Sportsline.com*, 21 December 2003, http://cbs.sportsline.com/nfl/story/6943613.

[1502] Erik Boland and Ken Berger, "Extra bad: Too early for two," *Newsday*, 18 October 2004, www.newsday.com/sports/football/jets/ny-spjqa184010893oct18,0,319771.story.

[1503] Rich Cimini, "Can't stand Pat," *New York Daily News*, 19 October 2004, www.nydailynews.com/sports/story/244048p-209137c.html.

[1504] New York Jets center Kevin Mawae, quoted in: Kit Stier, "Mawae: Stop complaining," *The Journal News*, 21 October 2004, www.thejournalnews.com/newsroom/102104/c0721jetsnotesweb.html.

[1505] Patriots safety Rodney Harrison, quoted in: Nick Cafardo, "The real dirt on Mawae," *Boston Globe*, 22 October 2004, www.boston.com/sports/football/patriots/articles/2004/10/22/the_real_dirt_on_mawae/.

[1506] Defensive end Ty Warren, quoted in: Michael Parente, " Rookie CB Gay making an impression on Pats," *Woonsocket Call*, 21 October 2004, www.zwire.com/site/news.cfm?newsid=13190161&BRD=1712&PAG=461&dept_id=106787&rfi=6.

[1507] Patriots defensive tackle Keith Traylor, quoted in: Nick Cafardo, "The real dirt on Mawae," *Boston Globe*, 22 October 2004, www.boston.com/sports/football/patriots/articles/2004/10/22/the_real_dirt_on_mawae/.

[1508] Patriots linebacker Mike Vrabel, quoted in: Nick Cafardo, "The real dirt on Mawae," *Boston Globe*, 22 October 2004, www.boston.com/sports/football/patriots/articles/2004/10/22/the_real_dirt_on_mawae/.

[1509] Bill Belichick, quoted in: Frank Tadych, "Patriots Notebook: Home field advantage is definite," *Patriots.com*, 21 October 2004, http://cachewww.patriots.com/news/index.cfm?ac=latestnewsdetail&PID=9416&PCID=41.

[1510] Patriots offensive coordinator Charlie Weis, quoted in: John Clayton, "Pats among greatest-ever clutch teams," ESPN.com, 1 February 2004, http://sports.espn.go.com/nfl/playoffs03/columns/story?columnist=clayton_john&id=1725043.

[1511] Patriots offensive coordinator Charlie Weis, quoted in: Dan Pompei, "Inside Pats' Super Bowl Preparations," *Sporting News*, 2 February 2004, www.allthingsbillbelichick.com/articles/insidesbprep.htm.

[1512] Bill Belichick, quoted in: Mike Freeman, "Belichick shows his relaxed side," *New York Times*, 4 April 2000, www.allthingsbillbelichick.com/articles/relaxedside.htm.

[1513] Patriots quarterback Tom Brady, after beating the Rams in Super Bowl XXXVI, quoted in: BBC, "Pats' Brady hunch pays off," 4 February 2002, http://news.bbc.co.uk/sport1/hi/other_sports/us_sport/1799953.stm.

[1514] Patriots safety Rodney Harrison, quoted in: Sam Farmer (*LA. Times*), " The beat goes on in New England," *San Francisco Chronicle*, 18 October 2004, http://sfgate.com/cgi-bin/article.cgi?f=/chronicle/archive/2004/10/18/SPGGR9BKKB1.DTL.

[1515] Sean Smith, "Reign fall was in forecast," *Boston Globe*, 18 October 2004, www.boston.com/sports/football/articles/2004/10/18/reign_fall_was_in_forecast.

[1516] Patriots offensive coordinator Charlie Weis, quoted in: John Clayton, "Pats among greatest-ever clutch teams," ESPN.com, 1 February 2004, http://sports.espn.go.com/nfl/playoffs03/columns/story?columnist=clayton_john&id=1725043.

[1517] Jerry Sullivan, "Bills nothing but a joke to Belichick," *Buffalo News*, 30 September 2004, www.buffalonews.com/editorial/20040930/1000893.asp.

[1518] Buffalo Bills running back Travis Henry, quoted in: Chris Kennedy, "Bills use book as motivation," *The Republican*, 1 October 2004, www.masslive.com/sports/republican/index.ssf?/base/sports-0/109667610047650.xml.

[1519] Patriots offensive lineman Russ Hochstein, quoted in: Russ Charpentier, "Pressure heavily on Hochstein," *Cape Cod Times*, January 2003, www.capecodonline.com/cctimes/sports/russ131.htm.

[1520] Bill Belichick, quoted in: Michael Holley, *Patriot Reign*, William Morrow, 2004, p. 5.

[1521] Patriots VP of player personnel Scott Pioli, quoted in: Bill Burt, "What a kick!" *Eagle Tribune*, 4 February 2004, www.eagletribune.com/news/stories/20020204/FP_001.htm.

[1522] Patriots tight end Christian Fauria, quoted in: Scott M. Johnson, "No time for small talk," *Daily Herald*, 16 October 2004, www.heraldnet.com/stories/04/10/16/spo_hawks%20notes001.cfm.

[1523] Bill Belichick, after his Patriots won Super Bowl XXXVI, quoted in: Bryan Morry, *Patriots United*, Canada: Team Power Publishing, 2002, p. 159.

[1524] Tom Brady, quoted in: Associated Press, "Tom Brady doubles up on MVP trophies," *Houston Chronicle*, 2 February 2004, www.chron.com/cs/CDA/ssistory.mpl/special/04/sb/2383714.

[1525] Statistics on knock downs, sacks, hurries, and batted balls displayed in a graphic by CBS during their broadcast with 2:38 remaining in game.

[1526] Arizona Cardinals quarterback Jake McCown, quoted in: Jerry Brown, "Crunch time came early, often for McCown," *Boston Globe*, 20 September 2004, www.boston.com/sports/football/patriots/articles/2004/09/20/crunch_time_came_early_often_for_mccown.

[1527] Patriots linebacker Willie McGinest, *3 Games to Glory II* (DVD), NFL Productions, 2004.

[1528] John Madden, quoted in: Bob George, "Super Team, Super Drive, Super Kick Makes Super Patriots," *BosSports.net*, 4 February 2002, www.bossports.net/patriots/020402.shtml.

[1529] Tom Brady's recollection of what Bill Belichick said to him, quoted in: Don Banks, "Move over Paul Revere," *Sports Illustrated*, 4 February 2002, http://sportsillustrated.cnn.com/inside_game/don_banks/news/2002/02/03/banks_insider/.

[1530] Tom Brady's recollection of what Patriots quarterback Drew Bledsoe said to him, quoted in: Don Banks, "Move over Paul Revere," *Sports Illustrated*, 4 February 2002, http://sportsillustrated.cnn.com/inside_game/don_banks/news/2002/02/03/banks_insider/.

[1531] Nick Cafardo, "Super cramming," *Boston Globe*, 5 February 2004, www.boston.com/sports/football/patriots/extras/asknick/02_05_04.

[1532] John Powers, "Drive to game-winner went like clockwork," *Boston Globe*, 2 February 2004, www.boston.com/sports/football/patriots/articles/2004/02/02/drive_to_game_winner_went_like_clockwork/.

[1533] Tom Brady, quoted in: Bryan Morry, "Managing the Moment," *Lindy's 2004 Pro Football*, p. 9.

[1534] Mark Curnutte, "Patriots epitomize meaning of team," *Cincinnati Enquirer*, 28 January 2004, http://bengals.enquirer.com/2004/01/28/ben1mc.html.

[1535] Mark Curnutte, "Patriots epitomize meaning of team," *Cincinnati Enquirer*, 28 January 2004, http://bengals.enquirer.com/2004/01/28/ben1mc.html.

[1536] Coach Bill Belichick, quoted in: Patriots inside linebackers coach Pepper Johnson, *Won For All*, Chicago: Contemporary Books, 2003, p. 84.

[1537] Cornerback Ty Law, quoted in: Michael Felger, "Pats wobble, but don't fall: Tie record wire streak by holding off Bills," *Boston Herald*, 4 October 2004, http://patriots.bostonherald.com/patriots/view.bg?articleid=47280.

[1538] Coach Bill Belichick, Nick Cafardo, "For coach, it's hard to relate," *Boston Globe*, 2 February 2004, www.boston.com/sports/football/patriots/articles/2004/02/02/for_coach_its_hard_to_relate/.

[1539] Patriots defensive tackle Richard Seymour, quoted in: Tom E. Curran, "For Pats, it'll be hard work defending title," *Providence Journal*, 28 July 2004, www.projo.com/patriots/content/projo_20040728_28pats.5df0.html.

[1540] Vic Carucci, "How the mighty have fallen," *NFL.com*, 19 October 2003, www.nfl.com/news/story/6734100.

[1541] Patriots linebacker prospect Justin Kurpeikis, quoted in: Tom E. Curran, "Patriots on a losing Jag," *Providence Journal*, 3 September 2004, www.projo.com/patriots/content/projo_20040903_03pats.287e20.html.

[1542] Patriots safety Rodney Harrison, quoted in: Ron Borges, "Rodney Harrison," in: *Again!*, Chicago: Triumph Books, 2004, p. 122.

[1543] Hector Longo, "Injury report proves to be a Belichick ruse," *Eagle Tribune*, 12 November 2001, www.eagletribune.com/news/stories/20011112/SP_003.htm.

[1544] Patriots linebacker Tedy Bruschi, quoted in: Hector Longo, "Living on the Edge," *Eagle Tribune*, 26 December 2003, www.eagletribune.com/news/stories/20031226/SP_001.htm.

[1545] Patriots cornerback Ty Law, quoted in: Shira Springer, "Hot topic loses a little steam," *Boston Globe*, 15 September 2004, www.boston.com/sports/football/patriots/articles/2004/09/15/hot_topic_loses_a_little_steam.

[1546] Patriots offensive lineman Joe Andruzzi, quoted in: "NFL's Andruzzi knows who the real heroes are," *Savannah Morning News*, 27 June 2004, www.savannahnow.com/stories/062704/2265614.shtml.

[1547] Patriots offensive lineman Stephen Neal, quoted in: Tom E. Curran, "Pats' Andruzzi keeps leading by example," *Providence Journal*, 15 September 2004, www.projo.com/patriots/content/projo_20040915_15pats.a329f.html.

[1548] Bill Belichick, quoted in: Hector Longo, "Belichick keeping high Pats grounded," *Eagle Tribune*, 1 August 2002, www.eagletribune.com/news/stories/20020801/SP_001.htm.

[1549] Tom Brady, quoted in: *NFL.com*, "Patriots win with late flurry of points," 19 January 2002, www.nfl.com/xxxvi/ce/recap/0,3895,NFL_20020119_OAK@NE,00.html.

[1550] Patriots kicker Adam Vinatieri, quoted in: Bill Burt, "Pats hopeful sure-footed kicker's struggles are over," *Eagle Tribune*, 8 January 2004, www.eagletribune.com/news/stories/20040108/SP_001.htm.

[1551] Patriots wide receiver Troy Brown, quoted in: Steve Cohen, "Brown's basics make Pats exceptional," *NFL.com*, 22 January 2002, www.nfl.com/xxxvi/ce/feature/0,3892,4879913,00.html.

[1552] Patriots defensive lineman Richard Seymour, quoted in: Nick Cafardo, "Patriots won't fan any flames," *Boston Globe*, 16 September 2003, www.boston.com/sports/football/patriots/articles/2003/09/16/patriots_wont_fan_any_flames/.

[1553] Patriots special teams captain Larry Izzo, quoted in: AP, "Twice as nice," *Sports Illustrated*, 2 February 2004, http://premium.si.cnn.com/2004/football/nfl/specials/playoffs/2003/02/01/belichick.twotitles.ap/.

[1554] Unnamed player, quoted in: Dan Pires, "The changing face of Bill Belichick," *SouthCoast Today*, 22 December 2001, www.s-t.com/daily/12-01/12-22-01/c01sp071.htm.

[1555] Bill Belichick, quoted in: Pete Prisco, "What streak? Pats keep winning, streaking with shrug," *CBS Sportsline*, 24 October 2004, www.sportsline.com/nfl/story/7825601.

[1556] Bill Belichick, "Sports Center," *ESPN*, 8 September 2004.

[1557] Vic Carucci, "Being a true Patriot has its rewards," *NFL.com*, 30 March 2004, www.nfl.com/news/story/7219076.

[1558] Patriots owner Robert Kraft, quoted in: Tom E. Curran, "Pats owner has created a masterpiece," *Providence Journal*, 13 June 2004, www.projo.com/patriots/content/projo_20040613_13kraft.1b891c.html.

[1559] Patriots safety Rodney Harrison, quoted in: Kevin Mannix, "No blues for streak: Patriots just don't like to lose, period," *Boston Herald*, 1 November 2004, http://patriots.bostonherald.com/patriots/view.bg?articleid=51911.

[1560] Boston Globe reporter Nick Cafardo, "A Battle of QBs," *Boston Globe*, 12 September 2003, www.boston.com/sports/football/patriots/extras/asknick/09_12_03.

[1561] Patriots cornerback Ty Law, quoted in: Bill Burt, "Pats buy in or say bye, bye," *Eagle-Tribune*, 9 October 2000, www.eagletribune.com/news/stories/20001009/SP_008.htm.

[1562] Bill Belichick, quoted in: Austin Murphy, "End Of An Epic," *Sports Illustrated*, December 4, 1995, www.allthingsbillbelichick.com/articles/endofepic.htm.

[1563] Bill Belichick, quoted in: Alan Greenberg, "Belichick caught in Grier's draft," *Hartford Courant*, 26 November 2000, p. E3, ProQuest database.

[1564] Bill Belichick, quoted in: Pete Thamel, "Patriots' Super Bowl Seems Like Long Ago," *New York Times*, 11 September 2003, p. D3, ProQuest database.

[1565] Tom Brady, quoted in: Pete Thamel, "Patriots' Super Bowl Seems Like Long Ago," *New York Times*, 11 September 2003, p. D3, ProQuest database.

[1566] Patriots inside linebackers coach Pepper Johnson, *Won For All*, Chicago: Contemporary Books, 2003, p. 52.

[1567] Patriots inside linebackers coach Pepper Johnson, *Won For All*, Chicago: Contemporary Books, 2003, p. 74.

[1568] Bill Belichick, quoted in: Alan Greenberg, "Pats Have Plenty Of Work For Bye Week," *Hartford Courant*, 21 September 2004, www.ctnow.com/sports/football/patriots/hc-patriots0921.artsep21,1,4724649.print.story.

[1569] Patriots safety Rodney Harrison, quoted in: David Pevear, "Eighteen going on 19? Pats aren't impressed," *Lowell Sun*, 7 October 2004, www.lowellsun.com/Stories/0,1413,105~4767~2452415,00.html.

[1570] Bill Belichick, quoted by Patriots safety Rodney Harrison, in: Howard Ullman (AP), "Patriots make history," *Chicago Sun-Times*, 11 October 2004, www.suntimes.com/output/football/cst-spt-pats111.html.

[1571] David Pevear, "Streak? They'd rather not talk about it," *Lowell Sun*, 21 September 2004, www.lowellsun.com/Stories/0,1413,105~4767~2416855,00.html.

[1572] www.tmsdancer.com/patsday.html; http://sportsillustrated.cnn.com/football/2002/playoffs/news/2002/02/05/patriots_parade_ap/.

[1573] Patriots inside linebackers coach Pepper Johnson, *Won For All*, Chicago: Contemporary Books, 2003, p. 230.

[1574] LSU Tigers head coach Nick Saban, quoted in: Peter King, "Master And Commander," *Sports Illustrated*, 9 August 2004, www.allthingsbillbelichick.com/articles/master.htm..

[1575] Bill Belichick, quoted in: Peter King, "Master And Commander," *Sports Illustrated*, 9 August 2004, www.allthingsbillbelichick.com/articles/master.htm..

[1576] Patriots running back Kevin Faulk, quoted in: "Carencro's Faulk has busy offseason," *DailyWorld.com*, 9 July 2004, www.dailyworld.com/html/5E2CD1A6-2313-4EC1-98C2-1FAF76EB6048.shtml.

[1577] Tom E. Curran, "Belichick: team gets mixed reviews," *Providence Journal*, 15 August 2004, www.projo.com/patriots/content/projo_20040815_15pats.1365b0.html.

[1578] Bill Belichick, quoted in: Tom E. Curran, "Patriots Notebook: Fix sought for broken pass plays," *Providence Journal*, 19 August 2004, www.projo.com/patriots/content/projo_20040819_19patsjo.fab8d.html.

[1579] Patriots center Dan Koppen, quoted in: Michael Parente, "Pass Game Sloppy," *Herald News*, 19 August 2004, www.zwire.com/site/news.cfm?newsid=12728523&BRD=1710&PAG=740&dept_id=353135&rfi=6.

[1580] Patriots wide receiver David Patten, quoted in: Michael Parente, "Pass Game Sloppy," *Herald News*, 19 August 2004, www.zwire.com/site/news.cfm?newsid=12728523&BRD=1710&PAG=740&dept_id=353135&rfi=6.

[1581] Bill Belichick, quoted in: David Pevear, "Streak? They'd rather not talk about it," *Lowell Sun*, 21 September 2004, www.lowellsun.com/Stories/0,1413,105~4767~2416855,00.html.

[1582] Bill Belichick, quoted in: Shalise Manza Young, "Pats' penalties unacceptable to Belichick," *Providence Journal*, 21 September 2004, www.projo.com/patriots/content/projo_20040921_21pats.67bf2.html.

[1583] Tom Brady, quoted in: Tony Chamberlain, "Big statistics? He'll pass," *Boston Globe*, 11 October 2004, www.boston.com/sports/football/patriots/articles/2004/10/11/big_statistics_hell_pass/.

[1584] Patriots safety Rodney Harrison, quoted in: Pete Prisco, "This victory what Patriots 'team' is all about," *SportsLine.com*, 7 November 2004, www.sportsline.com/nfl/story/7865974.

[1585] Patriots linebacker Bryan Cox, quoted in: *Patriots United*, Canada: Team Power Publishing, 2002, p. 93.

[1586] Patriots defensive lineman Richard Seymour, quoted in: Phil Richardson, "Opening lines," *Indianapolis Star*, 9 September 2004, www.indystar.com/articles/2/177203-5062-036.html.

[1587] Quarterback Tom Brady, quoted in: Len Pasquarelli, "Pats primed for second title," *ESPN.com*, 1 February 2004, http://sports.espn.go.com/nfl/playoffs03/columns/story?columnist=pasquarelli_len&id=1725040.

[1588] Patriots owner Bob Kraft, in commencement address to graduates at Johnson & Wales, quoted in: Frank Belsky, "'Dare to dream and follow your passions,'" *Pawtucket Times*, 24 May 2004, www.zwire.com/site/news.cfm?newsid=11778018&BRD=1713&PAG=461&dept_id=24491&rfi=6.

[1589] Patriots cornerback Rodney Harrison, quoted in: Tom King, "Pats' ailing secondary becoming primary concern'," *Nashua Telegraph*, 4 November 2004, www.nashuatelegraph.com/apps/pbcs.dll/article?AID=/20041104/SPORTS/41104018/-1/sports.

[1590] Coach Bill Belichick, "Belichick: Concentrating on Carolina," *NFL.com*, 27 December 2001, www.nfl.com/news/2001/NE/belichickchat_122701.htm.

[1591] Rohan Davey, "Davey NFL Europe diary – Week 5," *Patriots.com*, 29 April 2004, www.patriots.com/news/FullArticle.sps?id=28559&type=general.

[1592] Patriots defensive lineman Richard Seymour, quoted in: Michael Felger, "Tackling adversity: Seymour grapples with his father's death," *Boston Herald*, 9 June 2004, http://patriots.bostonherald.com/patriots/view.bg?articleid=31193.

[1593] Richard Seymour Sr., father of Patriot Richard Seymour, quoted in: Thomas George, "Seymour Sheds Potential Grudge," *New York Times*, 31 January 2004, p. D1, ProQuest database.

[1594] Patriots defensive lineman Richard Seymour, quoted in: Michael Felger, "Tackling adversity: Seymour grapples with his father's death," *Boston Herald*, 9 June 2004, http://patriots.bostonherald.com/patriots/view.bg?articleid=31193.

[1595] www.kcchiefs.com/news_article.asp?ID=X2TPNHFNFPE55Q9UC2I4QUE7P6.

[1596] Patriots punter Ken Walter, quoted in: Hector Longo, "Walter attempting to redeem himself," *Eagle Tribune*, 18 December 2003, eagletribune.com/news/stories/20031218/SP_005.htm.

[1597] St. Louis Rams linebacker London Fletcher, quoted in: Pete Prisco, "Upstart Pats assume role of aggressors to snatch victory," *CBS Sportsline*, 4 February 2002, http://cbs.sportsline.com/b/page/pressbox/0,1328,4948860,00.html.

[1598] Patriots center Damien Woody, quoted in: Len Pasquarelli, "Belichick Becomes Life of Patriots' Party," *ESPN.com*, 22 December 2001, www.allthingsbillbelichick.com/articles/lifeofparty.htm.

[1599] Defensive lineman Richard Seymour, quoted in: Hector Longo, "Patriots again bayou bound after Belichick baffles Kordell," *Eagle Tribune*, 28 January 2002, www.eagletribune.com/news/stories/20020128/SP_001.htm.

[1600] This exchange reported by: Malcolm Moran, "Boston throws a party for its Patriots," *USA Today*, 6 February 2002, www.usatoday.com/sports/nfl/super/2002-02-05-parade.htm.

[1601] Patriots wide receiver David Patten, quoted in: Nick Cafardo, "Pats' Patten must prove himself again," *Berkshire Eagle*, 11 August 2004, www.berkshireeagle.com/Stories/0,1413,101~6295~2326911,00.html.

[1602] Bill Belichick, quoted in: *Sports Network*, "Patriots Super Bowl Report: Belichick's biggest moment," 27 January 2004, http://sportsnetwork.com/default.asp?c=sportsnetwork&page=nfl/news/ABN3025008.htm.

[1603] New Patriots running back Corey Dillon, quoted in: Clark Judge, "Lackluster Dillon doesn't leave much for Bengals to regret," *CBS Sportsline*, 22 August 2004, www.sportsline.com/nfl/story/7601936.

[1604] Bill Belichick, *3 Games to Glory II* (DVD), NFL Productions, 2004.

[1605] Bill Belichick, quoted in: Alex Timiraos, "Pats coach talks leadership at BC," *The Heights*, 9 April 2004, www.bcheights.com/news/2004/04/09/News/Pats-Coach.Talks.Leadership.At.Bc-656659.shtml.

[1606] Tom Brady, quoted in: Hector Longo, "Walter attempting to redeem himself," *Eagle Tribune*, 18 December 2003, eagletribune.com/news/stories/20031218/SP_005.htm.

[1607] Tom Brady, quoted in: Kevin Mannix, "Cracks emerge in Arizona desert," *Boston Herald*, 20 September 2004, http://patriots.bostonherald.com/patriots/view.bg?articleid=45105.

[1609] Tom Brady, quoted in: Nick Cafardo, "Patriots' ducks all in a row," *Boston Globe*, 20 September 2004, www.boston.com/sports/articles/2004/09/20/patriots_ducks_all_in_a_row.

[1610] Patriots running back Antowain Smith, quoted in: "St. Louis at New England," *Sports Illustrated*, 3 February 2002, http://sportsillustrated.cnn.com/football/nfl/previews/2002/02/03/patriots_rams/.

[1611] Patriots running back Corey Dillon, quoted in: Chris Kennedy, "Dillon bears the burden," *MassLive.com*, 20 September 2004, www.masslive.com/printer/printer.ssf?/base/sports-0/1095666469251662.xml.

[1612] Patriots quarterback Tom Brady, "Tom Brady Press Conference 7/23/03," bostonbrat.net/brady/arcjuly.html.

[1613] Patriots inside linebackers coach Pepper Johnson, *Won For All*, Chicago: Contemporary Books, 2003, pp. 61-62.

[1614] 1960 Heisman winner Joe Bellino, quoted in: Bob Socci, "A Friendship Formed By Fate," *Navy Sports*, 28 January 2004, www.navysports.com/football/release.asp?RELEASE_ID=15595.

[1615] Tom Brady, quoted in: Dan Pires, "Belichick on the verge of history," *Standard-Times*, 1 February 2004, www.southcoasttoday.com/daily/02-04/02-01-04/e01sp874.htm.

[1616] Patriots inside linebackers coach Pepper Johnson, *Won For All*, Chicago: Contemporary Books, 2003, p. 32.

[1617] Patriots owner Bob Kraft, quoted in: Michael Felger, "Kraft OK with deal: Has faith in Belichick's judgment," *Boston Globe*, 21 April 2004, http://patriots.bostonherald.com/patriots/view.bg?articleid=13916.

[1618] D. Orlando Ledbetter, "Hard times: Glenn overcomes much in life, career," *Milwaukee Journal Sentinel*, 21 January 1997, www.jsonline.com/packer/arc/13097/opp/glenn121.html.

[1619] Bobby Grier "as legend has it," in: John Tomase, "The Patriots' roster has soured under Bobby Grier," *Eagle-Tribune*, 5 December 1999, www.eagletribune.com/news/stories/19991205/SP_001.htm.

[1620] Former Patriots coach Bill Parcells, quoted in: Michael Felger, *Tales From the Patriots Sideline*, Sports Publishing, 2004, p. 175.

[1621] Former Patriots coach Bill Parcells, quoted in: Jim Reineking, "THE A-LIST: Ranking Super Bowl XXXVIII," *Fox Sports*, 2 February 2004, www.foxsports.com/content/view?contentId=325626.

[1622] Bill Belichick, quoted in: Glen Farley, "New chapter to coaches' feud," *The Enterprise*, 21 September 2004, www.enterprisenews.com/articles/2004/09/21/news/sports/sports02.txt.

[1623] Michael Felger, *Tales From the Patriots Sideline*, Sports Publishing, 2004, p. 179. Other sources say "dozens" of calls were made. For example: *Hartford Courant*, "Closer Look At Parcells' Departure From Patriots," 26 September 2004, www.ctnow.com/sports/hc-nflsun0926.artsep26,1,7847127.story.

[1624] Patriots linebacker Tedy Bruschi, quoted in: Bill Burt, "Bruschi a true blue Patriot," *Eagle Tribune*, 31 January 2002, www.eagletribune.com/news/stories/20020131/SP_004.htm.

[1625] Former starting quarterback Drew Bledsoe, quoted in: Michael Felger, *Tales From the Patriots Sideline*, Sports Publishing, 2004, p. 180.

[1626] Patriots quarterback Drew Bledsoe, quoted in: Tim Polzer, "Bledsoe Q&A: Hey, it's football," *NFL Insider*, 27 January 2002, www.nfl.com/xxxvi/ce/feature/0,3892,4903665,00.html.

[1627] Bill Belichick, quoted in: Hector Longo, "Now hard part begins for rebuilding Patriots," *Eagle-Tribune*, 8 March 2001, www.eagletribune.com/news/stories/20010308/SP_002.htm.

[1628] Bob Kraft interview, "The Coach," *60 Minutes*, aired on CBS 19 September 2004.

[1629] NFL commentator and former NFL quarterback Joe Theismann, "In title games, no place like home," *ESPN.com*, 25 January 2002, http://espn.go.com/nfl/playoffs01/columns/theismann_joe/1317361.html.

[1630] Ray "Sugar Bear" Hamilton, assistant coach under former Patriots head coach Pete Carroll, quoted in: Michael Felger, *Tales From the Patriots Sideline*, Sports Publishing, 2004, p. 183.

[1631] Patriots inside linebackers coach Pepper Johnson, *Won For All*, Chicago: Contemporary Books, 2003, p. 87.

[1632] Defensive coordinator Romeo Crennel, quoted in: Michael Holley, *Patriot Reign*, William Morrow, 2004, p. 96.

[1633] Bill Belichick, quoted in: Tom E. Curran, "Patriots are torn apart by Bengals," *Providence Journal*, 22 August 2004, www.projo.com/patriots/content/projo_20040822_22pats.10e94e.html.

[1634] Bill Belichick, quoted in: Judy Battista, "The Patriots Become 20-Game Winners," *New York Times*, 18 October 2004, www.nytimes.com/2004/10/18/sports/football/18patriots.html.

[1635] Bill Belichick, quoted in: Nick Cafardo, "The top banana, Belichick, slips up," *Boston Globe*, 18 October 2004, www.boston.com/sports/football/patriots/articles/2004/10/18/the_top_banana_belichick_slips_up/.

[1636] Bill Belichick, quoted in: Ian M. Clark, "Johnson bursts out of doghouse," *Union Leader*, 17 October 2004, www.theunionleader.com/articles_showfast.html?article=45766.

[1637] Patriots cornerback Ty Law, quoted in: Nick Cafardo, "The top banana, Belichick, slips up," *Boston Globe*, 18 October 2004, www.boston.com/sports/football/patriots/articles/2004/10/18/the_top_banana_belichick_slips_up/.

[1638] Patriots safety Rodney Harrison, quoted in: Michael Felger, "Belichick can take a hit: Accepts blame on blown coverage," *Boston Herald*, 18 October 2004, http://patriots.bostonherald.com/patriots/view.bg?articleid=49586.

[1639] Patriots offensive coordinator Charlie Weis, quoted in: Nick Cafardo, "Aiming to call his own shots," *Boston Globe*, 24 September 2004, www.boston.com/sports/football/patriots/articles/2004/09/24/aiming_to_call_his_own_shots.

[1640] Patriots quarterback Tom Brady, "Tom Brady Press Conference 7/23/03," bostonbrat.net/brady/arcjuly.html.

[1641] Patriots defensive lineman Rick Lyle, quoted in: Tom E. Curran, "Patriots Notebook: Belichick points finger at himself for loss to Bills," *Providence Journal*, 11 September 2003, www.projo.com/patriots/content/projo_20030911_11patsjo.24d37.html.

[1642] Unnamed Patriot, quoted in: Tom E. Curran, "Patriots Notebook: Belichick points finger at himself for loss to Bills," *Providence Journal*, 11 September 2003, www.projo.com/patriots/content/projo_20030911_11patsjo.24d37.html.

[1643] Patriots defender Antwan Harris, quoted in: Nick Cafardo, "Sunday worst," *Boston Globe*, 8 September 2003, www.boston.com/sports/articles/2003/09/08/sunday_worst/.

[1644] Patriots safety Rodney Harrison, quoted in: Nick Cafardo, "Losing Tys leaves Patriots in a bind,"*Boston Globe*, 4 November 2004, www.boston.com/sports/football/patriots/articles/2004/11/04/losing_tys_leaves_patriots_in_a_bind/.

[1645] Bill Belichick, "Bill Belichick Press Conf. Transcript 8/3/04," *Patriots.com*, 3 August 2004, www.patriots.com/news/fullarticle.sps?id=29867&special_section=TrainingCamp2004&type=training.

[1646] Patriots kicker Adam Vinatieri, quoted in: Jackie MacMullan, "Mr. Clutch, no doubt about it," *Boston Globe*, 2 February 2004, www.boston.com/sports/football/patriots/articles/2004/02/02/mr_clutch_no_doubt_about_it/.

[1647] Patriots safety Rodney Harrison, quoted in: Mike Lowe, "Hobbled Pats may be playing catch-up against speedy Rams," *Portland Press-Herald*, 4 November 2004, http://sports.mainetoday.com/pro/patriots/041104lowecolumn.shtml.

[1648] Bill Belichick, quoted in: *Sports Network*, "Patriots Super Bowl Report: Belichick's biggest moment," 27 January 2004, http://sportsnetwork.com/default.asp?c=sportsnetwork&page=nfl/news/ABN3025008.htm.

[1649] Patriots linebacker Mike Vrabel, quoted in: Peter King, "What more could you want?" *Sports Illustrated*, 2 February 2004, http://sportsillustrated.cnn.com/2004/writers/peter_king/02/02/mmqb/index.html.

[1650] Patriots kicker Adam Vinatieri, quoted in: Hank Gola, "Patriots find their destiny," *South Coast Today*, 8 February 2002, www.s-t.com/daily/02-02/02-08-02/d06ae114.htm.

[1651] Peter King, "What more could you want?" *Sports Illustrated*, 2 February 2004, http://sportsillustrated.cnn.com/2004/writers/peter_king/02/02/mmqb/index.html.

[1652] Jackie MacMullan, "Mr. Clutch, no doubt about it," *Boston Globe*, 2 February 2004, www.boston.com/sports/football/patriots/articles/2004/02/02/mr_clutch_no_doubt_about_it/.

[1653] Unnamed source, quoted in: Michael Felger, "Pats play through pain: Woody, Vinatieri, Brady carry on," *Boston Herald*, 12 January 2004, http://patriots.bostonherald.com/patriots/view.bg?articleid=14228.

[1654] Howard Balzer, "Kinchen Back Where He Belongs," *Lindy's 2004 Pro Football*, p. 217.

[1655] Patriots kicker Adam Vinatieri, quoted in: Len Pasquarelli, "Vinatieri does it again for Patriots," *Boston Globe*, 1 February 2004, http://sports.espn.go.com/nfl/playoffs03/columns/story?columnist=pasquarelli_len&id=1725062.

[1656] Patriots kicker Adam Vinatieri, quoted in: Len Pasquarelli, "Vinatieri does it again for Patriots," *Boston Globe*, 1 February 2004, http://sports.espn.go.com/nfl/playoffs03/columns/story?columnist=pasquarelli_len&id=1725062.

[1657] Patriots linebacker Mike Vrabel, quoted in: Jackie MacMullan, "Mr. Clutch, no doubt about it," *Boston Globe*, 2 February 2004, www.boston.com/sports/football/patriots/articles/2004/02/02/mr_clutch_no_doubt_about_it/.

[1658] Patriots linebacker Mike Vrabel, quoted in: Joe Kay, "Tom Brady, Adam Vinatieri fail, then deliver for Patriots in Super Bowl," *Yahoo! Sports Canada*, 2 February 2004, http://ca.sports.yahoo.com/040202/6/wl1v.html.

[1659] Patriots running back Corey Dillon, quoted in: Michael Smith, "Pats capitalize on others' mistakes," *ESPN*, 3 October 2004, http://sports.espn.go.com/nfl/columns/story?id=1894443.

[1660] Patriots linebacker Tedy Bruschi, quoted in: Mark Cannizzaro, "Patriots Put Pete in Pinch," *New York Post*, 21 October 2004, www.nypost.com/sports/jets/30775.htm.

[1661] Tom Brady, quoted in: "Tom Brady Post-Game Interview," *Patriots.com*, 17 October 2004, http://originwww.patriots.com/news/index.cfm?ac=LatestNewsDetail&PID=9364&PCID=41.

[1662] Dr. Peter F. Drucker, *Management: Tasks, Responsibilities, Practices*, USA: HarperCollins, 1973, p. 159.

[1663] Bill Belichick, quoted in: Michael Felger, "Vrabel hurt in practice," *Boston Herald*, 13 November 2004.

[1664] Ozzie Newsome, Baltimore Ravens VP of player personnel, who worked with Belichick in Cleveland, quoted in: Paul Attner, "Doom's Day," *The Sporting News*, 18 January 1999, www.allthingsbillbelichick.com/articles/doomsday.htm.

[1665] Patriots defensive tackle Vince Wilfork, quoted in: Dave Goldberg (AP), "Patriots finally acknowledge the streak _ sort of," *San Francisco Chronicle*, 10 October 2004, http://sfgate.com/cgi-bin/article.cgi?f=/news/archive/2004/10/10/sports1838EDT0309.DTL.

[1666] Patriots left tackle Matt Light, quoted in: Michael Smith, "Brown baggers," in: *Again!*, Chicago: Triumph Books, 2004, p. 66.

[1667] Bill Belichick, quoted in: Bob Labriola, "Steelers-Patriots Matchup," *Steelers.com*, 29 October 2004, www.steelers.com/article/46630/.

[1668] Patriots cornerback Ty Law, quoted in: Jackie MacMullan, "As promised, party was quite subdued," *Boston Globe*, 11 October 2004, www.boston.com/sports/football/patriots/articles/2004/10/11/as_promised_party_was_quite_subdued/.

[1669] Tom Brady, quoted in: Jay Mariotti, "Patriots build modern sports dynasty," *Chicago Sun-Times*, 11 October 2004, www.suntimes.com/output/mariotti/cst-spt-jay111.html.

[1670] Tom Brady, quoted in: Nick Cafardo, "Vrabel knows tricks of the trade," *Boston Globe*, 20 September 2004, www.boston.com/sports/football/patriots/articles/2004/09/20/vrabel_knows_tricks_of_the_trade.

[1671] Patriots safety Rodney Harrison, quoted in: Michael Parente, "Back from a day off, Pats ready to roll," *Middletown Press*, 28 September 2004, www.zwire.com/site/news.cfm?newsid=13019680&BRD=1645&PAG=461&dept_id=17758&rfi=6.

[1672] Patriots safety Rodney Harrison, quoted in: Howard Ulman (AP), "One year after last loss, Patriots focus on next game," *San Francisco Chronicle*, 27 September 2004, http://sfgate.com/cgi-bin/article.cgi?file=/news/archive/2004/09/27/sports1844EDT0394.DTL.

[1673] Patriots defensive lineman Richard Seymour, quoted in: Michael Parente, "Back from a day off, Pats ready to roll," *Middletown Press*, 28 September 2004, www.zwire.com/site/news.cfm?newsid=13019680&BRD=1645&PAG=461&dept_id=17758&rfi=6.

[1674] Don Steinberg, "Top NFL coaches give leadership tips in book," *Philadelphia Inquirer*, 20 July 2004, www.philly.com/mld/inquirer/9193903.htm?1c.

[1675] Home Depot CEO Robert Nardelli, quoted in: Brian Grow, "Thinking Outside the Big Box," *BusinessWeek*, 25 October 2004, p. 72.

[1676] Rohan Davey, "Davey NFL Europe diary – Week 5," *Patriots.com*, 29 April 2004, www.patriots.com/news/FullArticle.sps?id=28559&type=general.

[1677] Patriots defensive lineman Richard Seymour , quoted in: Shira Springer, "Hot topic loses a little steam," *Boston Globe*, 15 September 2004, www.boston.com/sports/football/patriots/articles/2004/09/15/hot_topic_loses_a_little_steam.

[1678] Patriots wide receiver Troy Brown, quoted in: Steve Cohen, "Brown's basics make Pats exceptional," *NFL.com*, 22 January 2002, www.nfl.com/xxxvi/ce/feature/0,3892,4879913,00.html.

[1679] Patriots cornerback Tyrone Poole, quoted in: Hector Longo, "Simply the Best," *Eagle Tribune*, 16 January 2004, www.eagletribune.com/news/stories/20040116/SP_001.htm.

[1680] Patriots linebacker Tedy Bruschi, quoted in: Bill Burt, "Bruschi a true blue Patriot," *Eagle Tribune*, 31 January 2002, www.eagletribune.com/news/stories/20020131/SP_004.htm.

[1681] Patriots offensive coordinator Charlie Weis, quoted in: Damon Hack, "Final Review: Victory Is a Videotape Away," *New York Times*, 1 February 2004, section 8, p. 1, ProQuest database.

[1682] Patriots safety Rodney Harrison, quoted in: Pete Thamel, "Jets Face Patriots' Resurgent Defense," *New York Times*, 18 September 2003, p. D3, ProQuest database.

[1683] Bill Belichick, "Bill Belichick Press Conference," 22 January 2002, www.patriots.com/news/FullArticle.sps?id=16686&type=general.

[1684] Panthers defensive tackle Brentson Buckner, quoted in: Steve DeCosta, "Both sides agree, it'll be violent," *Standard-Times*, www.southcoasttoday.com/daily/02-04/02-01-04/e04sp875.htm.

[1685] Patriots wide receiver David Givens, quoted in: Steve DeCosta, "Both sides agree, it'll be violent," *Standard-Times*, www.southcoasttoday.com/daily/02-04/02-01-04/e04sp875.htm.

[1686] Patriots left tackle Matt Light, quoted in: Ken Berger, "Pats' offensive line has last laugh," *Newsday*, 1 February 2004, www.southcoasttoday.com/daily/02-04/02-01-04/e03sp876.htm.

[1687] Patriots coach Bill Belichick, quoted in: Len Pasquarelli, "Dynasty? Pats have pieces in place," *ESPN.com*, 2 February 2004, http://sports.espn.go.com/nfl/playoffs03/columns/story?columnist=pasquarelli_len&id=1725473

[1688] New England Patriots running back Corey Dillon, quoted in: Nick Cafardo and Jim McCabe, "Dillon fights through pain," *Boston Globe*, 15 November 2004, www.boston.com/sports/football/patriots/articles/2004/11/15/dillon_fights_through_pain/.

[1689] Bill Belichick, quoted in: Michael Felger, "Loss leaves bad taste: Patriots can't respond to Bengals' best shot," *Boston Herald*, 24 August 2004, http://patriots.bostonherald.com/patriots/view.bg?articleid=41138.

[1690] Patriots defensive lineman Richard Seymour, quoted in: Tom E. Curran, "Pats' Seymour presses on," *Providence Journal*, 6 July 2004, www.projo.com/patriots/content/projo_20040706_06seymour.3bb42.html.

[1691] NFL analyst and Super Bowl-winning coach John Madden, quoted in: Bill Griffith, "Showtime for ABC," *Boston Globe*, 9 September 2004, www.boston.com/sports/football/patriots/articles/2004/09/09/showtime_for_abc.

[1692] Bill Belichick, quoted in: Rob Longley, "Belichick and crew are playing down streak," *Toronto Sun*, 25 October 2004, http://slam.canoe.ca/Slam/Football/NFL/2004/10/25/684629.html.

[1693] Bill Belichick, quoted in: Steve Buckley, " Meet Bill Belichick, Mr. Popular," *Boston Herald*, 17 January 2002, www.allthingsbillbelichick.com/articles/meetbb.htm.

[1694] Coach Bill Belichick, quoted in: Steve Politi, "Is Belichick A Genius?" *Star-Ledger*, 30 January 2004, www.allthingsbillbelichick.com/articles/agenius.htm.

[1695] New Patriot tight end Jed Weaver, quoted in: Howard Ullman, "New tight end checks in: Weaver happy to join Pats," *Milford Daily News*, 1 October 2004, www.milforddailynews.com/sportsNews/view.bg?articleid=56876.

[1696] Patriots safety Rodney Harrison, quoted in: Bob Glauber, "Improved Pats primed to repeat," *Newsday*, 6 August 2004, www.newsday.com/sports/football/ny-spglaub063920634aug06,0,7182695.print.column?coll=ny-sports-columnists.

[1697] Bill Belichick, quoted in: Peter May, "Master of the plan," *Boston Globe*, 3 February 2004, www.boston.com/sports/football/patriots/articles/2004/02/03/master_of_the_plan/.

[1698] Hall of Fame former 49ers head coach Bill Walsh, quoted in: Kevin Paul Dupont, "Winner's Circle," *Boston Globe*, 23 January 2004, www.boston.com/sports/football/patriots/articles/2004/01/23/winners_circle/.

[1699] Patriots safety Lawyer Milloy, quoted in: Hector Longo, "Londonderry's Ball catches Pats' attention," *Eagle Tribune*, 26 September 2002, www.eagletribune.com/news/stories/20020926/SP_003.htm.

[1700] Tom Brady, quoted in: Michael Felger, "Tom not acting his age," *Boston Herald*, 12 June 2004, http://patriots.bostonherald.com/patriots/view.bg?articleid=31608.

[1701] Tom Brady, quoted in: Steve Conroy, "Buffalo debacle still fresh: Ugly defeat haunts Brady," *Boston Herald*, 30 September 2004, http://patriots.bostonherald.com/patriots/view.bg?articleid=46704.

[1702] Special teams captain Larry Izzo, quoted in: Tom E. Curran, "For Pats, it'll be hard work defending title," *Providence Journal*, 28 July 2004, www.projo.com/patriots/content/projo_20040728_28pats.5df0.html.

[1703] Tom Brady, quoted in: Michael Felger, "Close calls no problem: Brady's heroics become routine," *Boston Herald*, 16 September 2004, http://patriots.bostonherald.com/patriots/view.bg?articleid=44493.

[1704] Patriots linebacker Tedy Bruschi, quoted in: Jackie MacMullen, "Tedy Bruschi," in: *Again!*, Chicago: Triumph Books, 2004, p. 118.

[1705] Patriots left tackle Matt Light, quoted in: Mike Reiss, "Patriots beat: It's a win, but..." *MetroWest Daily News*, 11 September 2004, www.metrowestdailynews.com/sportsNews/view.bg?articleid=77570.

[1706] Bill Belichick, quoted in: Jimmy Golen (AP), "New England Patriots hope to extend streak one more game in Super Bowl," 30 January 2004, http://ca.sports.yahoo.com/040130/6/wkdt.html.

[1707] Bill Belichick, quoted in: Hector Longo, "Belichick not going to reinvent Patriots," *Eagle Tribune*, 27 February 2002, www.eagletribune.com/news/stories/20020227/SP_004.htm.

[1708] Bill Belichick, quoted in: Hector Longo, "Belichick keeping high Pats grounded," *Eagle Tribune*, 1 August 2002, www.eagletribune.com/news/stories/20020801/SP_001.htm.

[1709] Bill Belichick, quoted in: Jeff Goodman, "Once Unwanted, Belichick Is the Savior of New England," *Washington Post*, 28 November 2003, D9, ProQuest database.

[1710] Patriots linebacker Tedy Bruschi, quoted in: Jeff Goodman, "Pats as Good as Billed; Belichick Gets Best of Parcells In Game Dominated by Defense," *Washington Post*, 17 November 2003, D9, ProQuest database.

[1711] Patriots defensive lineman Richard Seymour, quoted in: Joe Burris, "Running afoul of Law, Manning handcuffed," *Boston Globe*, 8 February 2004, www.boston.com/sports/football/patriots/articles/2004/02/08/running_afoul_of_law_manning_handcuffed/.

[1712] Joe Burris, "Running afoul of Law, Manning handcuffed," *Boston Globe*, 8 February 2004, www.boston.com/sports/football/patriots/articles/2004/02/08/running_afoul_of_law_manning_handcuffed/.

[1713] Patriots safety Rodney Harrison, quoted in: Associated Press, "Manning's best receiver – Pats' Law," *MSNBC.com*, 19 January 2004, http://msnbc.msn.com/id/3995294/.

[1714] Patriots safety Rodney Harrison, quoted in: Vic Carucci, "Pats' defense already in championship form," 18 January 2004, www.superbowl.com/playoffs/story/7017737.

[1715] Patriots safety Rodney Harrison, quoted in: Nick Canepa, "Patriots only failure: Trying to play the no-respect card," *San Diego Union-Tribune*, www.signonsandiego.com/sports/canepa/20040119-9999_1s19canepa.html.

[1716] Bill Belichick, quoted in: Michael Holley, *Patriot Reign*, William Morrow, 2004, p. 222.

[1717] Patriots center/guard Damien Woody, quoted in: Michael Holley, "A Texas steel-cage match to the finish," *Boston Globe*, 27 September 2004, www.boston.com/sports/football/patriots/articles/2004/09/27/a_texas_steel_cage_match_to_the_finish.

[1718] Patriots linebacker Mike Vrabel, quoted in: Paul Attner, "Super Bowl 38: Red, white and two," *The Sporting News*, 9 February 2004, www.sportingnews.com/archives/superbowl/.

[1719] Patriots wide receiver Troy Brown, quoted in: Dan Pires, "Postgame talk ranges from Sapp to streaker," *Standard-Times*, 4 February 2004, www.southcoasttoday.com/daily/02-04/02-04-04/c01sp273.htm.

[1720] Patriots safety Rodney Harrison, quoted in: Dan Ventura, "Harrison noise: Silences Seahawks on field," *Boston Herald*, 18 October 2004, http://patriots.bostonherald.com/patriots/view.bg?articleid=49585.

[1721] Seattle Seahawks receiver Darrell Jackson, quoted in: Michael Felger, "Johnson in the dark on demotion," *Boston Herald*, 14 October 2004, http://patriots.bostonherald.com/patriots/view.bg?articleid=48959.

[1722] Patriots safety Rodney Harrison, quoted in: "Having the final say," *Boston Globe*, 18 October 2004, www.boston.com/sports/football/patriots/articles/2004/10/18/having_the_final_say/.

[1723] Patriots safety Rodney Harrison, quoted in: Michael Felger, "Pats punch 'Hawks in mouth: Actions speak louder in 20th straight win," *Boston Herald*, 18 October 2004, http://patriots.bostonherald.com/patriots/view.bg?articleid=49588.

[1724] Patriots safety Rodney Harrison, quoted in: "Having the final say," *Boston Globe*, 18 October 2004, www.boston.com/sports/football/patriots/articles/2004/10/18/having_the_final_say/.

[1725] Patriots cornerback Ty Law, quoted in: Michael Felger, "Pats punch 'Hawks in mouth: Actions speak louder in 20th straight win," *Boston Herald*, 18 October 2004, http://patriots.bostonherald.com/patriots/view.bg?articleid=49588.

[1726] Seattle Seahawks receiver Darrell Jackson, quoted in: Mark Singelais, "Secondary delivers lessons," *Times Union*, 18 October 2004, www.timesunion.com/AspStories/story.asp?storyID=295947&category=SPORTS&BCCode=&newsdate=10/18/2004.

[1727] Seattle Seahawks receiver Darrell Jackson, quoted in: Michael Felger, "Belichick can take a hit: Accepts blame on blown coverage," *Boston Herald*, 18 October 2004, http://patriots.bostonherald.com/patriots/view.bg?articleid=49586.

[1728] Marv Levy, who coached the Buffalo Bills to four straight Super Bowls, "Those amazin' Pats," *NFL.com*, 10 October 2004, www.nfl.com/news/story/7782461.

[1729] Former Patriots assistant coach Steve Szabo, quoted in: Leo Roth, "Can Szabo's secrets help the Bills?" *Democrat and Chronicle*, 28 September 2004, www.democratandchronicle.com/apps/pbcs.dll/article?AID=/20040928/SPORTS03/409280310/1007/SPORTS.

[1730] Tom Brady, quoted in: Carmine Frongillo, "Any questions?" *Lowell Sun*, 11 October 2004, www.lowellsun.com/Stories/0,1413,105~4746~2459958,00.html.

[1731] Patriots cornerback Ty Law, quoted in: Sam Donnellon, "Pats emerge from scrum with record victory," *Philadelphia Daily News*, 10 October 2004, www.mercurynews.com/mld/mercurynews/sports/9887249.htm?1c.

[1732] Patriots safety Rodney Harrison, quoted in: Carmine Frongillo, "Any questions?" *Lowell Sun*, 11 October 2004, www.lowellsun.com/Stories/0,1413,105~4746~2459958,00.html.

[1733] Bill Belichick, quoted in: Paul Solman, "Goal Line Economics," 23 September 2002, www.pbs.org/newshour/bb/economy/july-dec02/football_9-23.html.

[1734] Bill Belichick conference call, *Steelers.com*, late October 2004, www.steelers.com/article/46622/.

[1735] Bill Belichick, quoted in: Scott Pitoniak, "Belichick's NFL success is anything but boring," *Democrat and Chronicle*, 1 October 2004, www.democratandchronicle.com/apps/pbcs.dll/article?AID=/20041001/SPORTS0102/410010321/1007/SPORTS.

[1736] Bill Belichick, quoted in: Jerry Sullivan, "Bills nothing but a joke to Belichick," *Buffalo News*, 30 September 2004, www.buffalonews.com/editorial/20040930/1000893.asp.

[1737] Jim Moore, "Go 2 Guy: Tale of a dogged newshound," *Seattle Post-Intelligencer*, 14 October 2004, http://seattlepi.nwsource.com/football/195099_moore14.html.

[1738] Patriots running back Antowain Smith, quoted in: Michael Smith, "Snowballing into the playoffs," in: *Again!*, Chicago: Triumph Books, 2004, p. 84.

[1739] St. Louis Rams head coach Mike Martz, quoted in: Dennis Dillon, "Coach-O-Meter gives slight edge to Rams' Martz," *The Sporting News*, 1 February 2002, http://lists.rollanet.org/pipermail/rampage/Week-of-Mon-20020128/022989.html.

[1740] Rams head coach Mike Martz, quoted in: AP, "Picking up the pieces," 4 February 2002, http://sportsillustrated.cnn.com/football/2002/playoffs/news/2002/02/04/rams_wrap_ap/.

[1741] Rams receiver Tory Holt, quoted in: AP, "Picking up the pieces," 4 February 2002, http://sportsillustrated.cnn.com/football/2002/playoffs/news/2002/02/04/rams_wrap_ap/.

[1742] Patriots running back Antowain Smith, quoted in: Michael Smith, "Snowballin'," *Boston Globe*, 8 December 2003, www.boston.com/sports/football/patriots/articles/2003/12/08/snowballin/.

[1743] Panthers quarterback Jake Delhomme, quoted in: Michael Felger, "Pats must be tougher team: Look to continue mastery of Colts," *Boston Herald*, 13 January 2004.

[1744] Tom Brady, quoted in: "Quotes," 22 January 2004, http://bostonbrat.net/brady/quotes.html.

[1745] Tom Brady, quoted in: Phil Sheridan, "Terrific Tom playing perfect role," *Standard-Times*, 1 February 2004, www.southcoasttoday.com/daily/02-04/02-01-04/e03sp873.htm.

[1746] Tom Brady, quoted in: Phil Sheridan, "Terrific Tom playing perfect role," *Standard-Times*, 1 February 2004, www.southcoasttoday.com/daily/02-04/02-01-04/e03sp873.htm.

[1747] Michael Felger, "Pioli: Scout's Honor," *Boston Herald*, 19 December 2001, www.allthingsbillbelichick.com/articles/piolihonor.htm.

[1748] Bill Belichick, quoted in: Charles P. Pierce, "Three Days, One Life," *Sports Illustrated*, 18 October 2004, p. 76.

[1749] Bill Beuttler, "Tom Brady Avoids the Blitz," *Boston Magazine*, August 2002, www.absolutebrady.com/Articles/BIOBM080102.html.

[1750] Tom Brady, quoted in: Dan Shaughnessy, "Champs again," *Boston Globe*, 2 February 2004, www.boston.com/sports/football/patriots/articles/2004/02/02/champs_again/.

[1751] Tom Brady, quoted in: Dan Shaughnessy, "Champs again," *Boston Globe*, 2 February 2004, www.boston.com/sports/football/patriots/articles/2004/02/02/champs_again/.

[1752] Tom Brady, quoted in: Mike Reiss, "Camping season: Plenty to digest as defending champion Patriots hit field," *Milford Daily News*, 30 July 2004, www.milforddailynews.com/sportsNews/view.bg?articleid=52825.

[1753] Tom Brady's father, quoted in: Bryan Morry, "Managing the Moment," *Lindy's 2004 Pro Football*, p. 9.

[1754] Mark Emmons (*San Jose Mercury News*), "Patriots' Brady the talk of the town," *Star-Telegram*, 25 January 2004, www.dfw.com/mld/dfw/sports/columnists/troy_phillips/7789659.htm?1c.

[1755] Tom Brady, quoted in: Tom E. Curran, "Tom Brady: The man behind the growing legend," *Providence Journal*, 25 July 2004, www.projo.com/patriots/content/projo_20040725_brad25.eb8fb.html.

[1756] Tom Brady, quoted in: Bryan Morry, "Managing the Moment," *Lindy's 2004 Pro Football*, p. 9.

[1757] Tom Brady, quoted in: Bryan Morry, "Managing the Moment," *Lindy's 2004 Pro Football*, p. 10.

[1758] Patriots quarterback Tom Brady, "Tom Brady Press Conference 7/23/03," bostonbrat.net/brady/arcjuly.html.

[1759] Patriots linebacker Mike Vrabel, quoted in: Peter King, "A League of Their Own," *Sports Illustrated*, 18 October 2004, p. 69.

[1760] Patriots VP of player personnel, Scott Pioli, quoted in: Len Pasquarelli, "Belichick and Pioli have winning formula," *ESPN.com*, 27 July 2002, http://espn.go.com/nfl/trainingcamp02/columns/patriots/1410739.html.

[1761] Bill Belichick, quoted in: Frank Tadych, "Patriots Notebook: No Faulk in Arizona," *Patriots.com*, 15 September 2004, www.patriots.com/news/FullArticle.sps?id=30562.

[1762] Patriots rookie P.K. Sam, quoted in: Mike Lowe, "They go from past to the Pats," *Portland Press Herald* (Maine), 2 May 2004, www.pressherald.com/sports/pro/patriots/040502patsrookies.shtml.

[1763] Bill Belichick, quoted in: Ian M. Clark, "Patriots Notebook: Positions of strength," *The Union Leader*, 28 July 2004, www.theunionleader.com/articles_showfast.html?article=41453.

[1764] Bill Belichick, quoted in: Frank Tadych, "Camp competition is life as usual," *Patriots.com*, 23 August 2004, www.patriots.com/news/fullarticle.sps?id=30243&type=general.

[1765] Robert Fachet, "With the Belichicks, the Apple Hasn't Fallen Far From the Tree," *Washington Post*, 7 February 1991, p. C7, ProQuest database.

[1766] Bill Belichick, quoted in: Ron Borges, "What Makes Belichick Tick," *Boston Globe Magazine*, 10 September 2000, www.allthingsbillbelichick.com/articles/makestick.html.

[1767] Bill Belichick, quoted in: Bill Burt, "More than a coach," *Eagle Tribune*, 25 January 2004, www.eagletribune.com/news/stories/20040125/SP_001.htm.

[1768] Patriots VP of player personnel, Scott Pioli, quoted in: John Clayton, "Patriots' run gives AFC East teams hope," *ESPN.com*, 27 June 2001, http://espn.go.com/nfl/columns/clayton_john/1399601.html.

[1769] Starting left tackle Matt Light, quoted in: Michael Parente, " Light nearing return to play," *Woonsocket Call*, 10 August 2004, www.woonsocketcall.com/site/news.cfm?newsid=12655661&BRD=1712&PAG=461&dept_id=106787&rfi=6.

[1770] Starting left tackle Matt Light, quoted in: Mike Reiss, "Light back on: Left tackle nearly ready to return after surgery," *MetroWest News*, 10 August 2004, www.metrowestdailynews.com/sportsNews/view.bg?articleid=75154.

[1771] Bill Belichick, quoted in: Mike Reiss, "New twist to Beli-flex system aids Patriots' charge," *Milford Daily News*, 9 November 2004.

[1772] Bill Belichick, quoted in: Tom E. Curran, "Patriots slowly coming together," *Providence Journal*, 30 August 2004, www.projo.com/patriots/content/projo_20040830_30pats.a155b.html.

[1773] Patriots running back Kevin Faulk, quoted in: Len Pasquarelli, "Faulk rejoins Pats after mother's death," *ESPN*, 23 September 2004, http://sports.espn.go.com/nfl/columns/story?columnist=pasquarelli_len&id=1887320.

[1774] New Patriots right tackle James "Big Cat" Williams, quoted in: Tom E. Curran, "Patriots Notebook: Defense breathing a little easier," *Providence Journal*, 30 July 2004, www.projo.com/patriots/content/projo_20040730_30patsjo.94354.html.

[1775] Bill Belichick, "Bill Belichick Press Conf. Transcript 6/11/04," *Patriots.com*, 11 June 2004, www.patriots.com/news/FullArticle.sps?id=28920.

[1776] Joe Linta, agent for new Patriots backup quarterback Jim Miller, quoted in: Michael Smith, "Patriots send signal with Kittner, Miller," *Boston Globe*, 16 July 2004, www.boston.com/sports/football/patriots/articles/2004/07/16/patriots_send_signal_with_kittner_miller.

[1777] Patriots cornerback Terrell Buckley, quoted in: Michael Smith, "Buckley set to rejoin Patriots," *Boston Globe*, 3 June 2004, www.boston.com/sports/football/patriots/articles/2004/06/03/buckley_set_to_rejoin_patriots.

[1778] Terrell Buckley, quoted in: Greg Hardwig, "NFL: For Buckley, if not Miami, the obvious choice was New England," *Naples News*, 6 June 2004, www.naplesnews.com/npdn/sports/article/0,2071,NPDN_15000_2942239,00.html.

[1779] Patriots running back Mike Cloud, quoted in: "Patriots Notebook: With clean start, Cloud not settling for backup role," *Providence Journal*, 27 August 2004, www.projo.com/patriots/content/projo_20040827_27patsjo.bfeea.html.

[1780] Patriots safety Shawn Mayer, quoted in: Michael Parente, " Backup battles at fore," *Woonsocket Call*, 20 August 2004, www.woonsocketcall.com/site/news.cfm?newsid=12739136&BRD=1712&PAG=461&dept_id=106787&rfi=6.

[1781] Patriots backup quarterback Damon Huard, quoted in: Ivan Carter, "Huard ready to make up for lost time," *San Jose Mercury News*, 26 August 2004, www.mercurynews.com/mld/mercurynews/sports/9506875.htm.

[1782] Joe Linta, agent for new Patriots backup quarterback Jim Miller, quoted in: Michael Smith, "Patriots send signal with Kittner, Miller," *Boston Globe*, 16 July 2004, www.boston.com/sports/football/patriots/articles/2004/07/16/patriots_send_signal_with_kittner_miller.

[1783] Patriots running back Kevin Faulk, quoted in: "Carencro's Faulk has busy offseason," *DailyWorld.com*, 9 July 2004, www.dailyworld.com/html/5E2CD1A6-2313-4EC1-98C2-1FAF76EB6048.shtml.

[1784] Bill Belichick, quoted in: Michael Felger, "Youth serves on Pats," *Boston Herald*, 1 May 2004, http://patriots.bostonherald.com/patriots/view.bg?articleid=17274.

[1785] Bill Belichick, quoted in: Tom E. Curran, "Davey may be ready to be Pats' backup QB," *Providence Journal*, 4 May 2004, www.projo.com/patriots/content/projo_20040503_03pats.a2eaa.html.

[1786] Bill Belichick, quoted in: Glen Farley, "Patriots get younger and faster," *The Enterprise* (Brockton, MA), 14 May 2004, http://enterprise.southofboston.com/articles/2004/04/26/news/sports/sports03.txt.

[1787] Coach Bill Belichick, "Bill Belichick Press Conf. Transcript - 4/30," *Patriots.com*, 30 April 2004, www.patriots.com/news/FullArticle.sps?id=28597&type=general.

[1788] Patriots inside linebackers coach Pepper Johnson, *Won For All*, Chicago: Contemporary Books, 2003, p. 18.

[1789] Bill Belichick, quoted in: Judy Battista, "In Foxboro, Starting at the Bottom for the Team at the Top," *New York Times*, 5 September 2004, www.nytimes.com/2004/09/05/sports/football/05patism.html.

[1790] Rookie defensive tackle Vince Wilfork, quoted in: Michael Felger, "Youth serves on Pats," *Boston Herald*, 1 May 2004, http://patriots.bostonherald.com/patriots/view.bg?articleid=17274.

[1791] Rookie tight end Benjamin Watson, quoted in: Michael Felger, "Youth serves on Pats," *Boston Herald*, 1 May 2004, http://patriots.bostonherald.com/patriots/view.bg?articleid=17274.

[1792] Rookie running back Cedric Cobbs, quoted in: Michael Felger, "Youth serves on Pats," *Boston Herald*, 1 May 2004, http://patriots.bostonherald.com/patriots/view.bg?articleid=17274.

[1793] Jamil Soriano, quoted in: Andy Hart, "Soriano seeking experience, NFL Europe ring," *Patriots Football Weekly*, 5 May 2004, www.patriots.com/news/FullArticle.sps?id=28665&type=general.

[1794] Patriots offensive lineman Stephen Neal, quoted in: Kevin Mannix, "Neal shoulders load," *Boston Herald*, 3 May 2004, http://patriots.bostonherald.com/patriots/view.bg?articleid=18877.

[1795] Patriots running back Kevin Faulk, quoted in: "Carencro's Faulk has busy offseason," *DailyWorld.com*, 9 July 2004, www.dailyworld.com/html/5E2CD1A6-2313-4EC1-98C2-1FAF76EB6048.shtml.

[1796] New undrafted Patriots cornerback Randall Gay, quoted in: Michael Parente, "For Gay, these are happy times in New England," *The Herald News*, 7 September 2004, www.zwire.com/site/news.cfm?newsid=12864509&BRD=1710&PAG=740&dept_id=353135&rfi=6.

[1797] New Patriot free agent defensive lineman Keith Traylor, quoted in: Mark Farinella, "Traylor mans the line," *Sun Chronicle*, 8 August 2004, www.thesunchronicle.com/articles/2004/08/08/sports/sports1.txt.

[1798] Patriots rookie wide receiver P.K. Sam, "PK Sam Player Journal," *Patriots.com*, 17 June 2004, www.patriots.com/news/fullarticle.sps?id=28972.

[1799] Bill Belichick, quoted in: Frank Tadych, "Camp competition is life as usual," *Patriots.com*, 23 August 2004, www.patriots.com/news/fullarticle.sps?id=30243&type=general.

[1800] Patriots VP of player personnel Scott Pioli, quoted in: Jeff Jacobs, "Class Clown Gets Serious With Patriots," *Hartford Courant*, 3 February 2002, p. A1.

[1801] Patriots inside linebackers coach Pepper Johnson, *Won For All*, Chicago: Contemporary Books, 2003, p. 103.

[1802] Tom Brady, quoted in: Mark Maske, "Selfless Patriots show how it's done," *Washington Post*, 4 February 2004, www.msnbc.msn.com/id/4144383/.

[1803] Joe Theismann, "Patriots had the look of winners," *ESPN.com*, 31 January 2002, http://espn.go.com/nfl/playoffs01/columns/theismann_joe/1320654.html.

[1804] That the team plays dominos is common knowledge. The quotation comes from Michael Holley, *Patriot Reign*, William Morrow, 2004, p. 124.

[1805] Wide receiver Troy Brown, quoted in: Kim Dunbar, "Troy Brown Event: Brown's 'Celebrity Bingo' a Success," *TroyBrown80.com*, 14 May 2004, www.troybrown80.com/modules.php?op=modload&name=News&file=article&sid=28&mode=thread&order=0&thold=0.

[1806] Patriots offensive lineman Matt Light, quoted in: Kim Dunbar, "Troy Brown Event: Brown's 'Celebrity Bingo' a Success," *TroyBrown80.com*, 14 May 2004, www.troybrown80.com/modules.php?op=modload&name=News&file=article&sid=28&mode=thread&order=0&thold=0.

[1807] Wide receiver Troy Brown, quoted in: Kim Dunbar, "Troy Brown Event: Brown's 'Celebrity Bingo' a Success," *TroyBrown80.com*, 14 May 2004, www.troybrown80.com/modules.php?op=modload&name=News&file=article&sid=28&mode=thread&order=0&thold=0.

[1808] Cornerback Antonio Langham, quoted in: Alan Greenberg, "Getting Along Well Belichick Still A Little Grim, But With A Grin," *Hartford Courant*, 3 September 2000, p. E1, ProQuest database.

[1809] Patriots rookie safety Dexter Reid, quoted in: Ed Miller, "Granby grad vies for job with the champs," *HamptonRoads.com*, 12 May 2004, http://home.hamptonroads.com/stories/story.cfm?story=70227&ran=29846.

[1810] Patriots inside linebackers coach Pepper Johnson, *Won For All*, Chicago: Contemporary Books, 2003, p. 93-94

[1811] Baltimore Ravens VP Kevin Byrne, who worked for Belichick in Cleveland, quoted in: Ron Borges, "What Makes Belichick Tick," *Boston Globe Magazine*, 10 September 2000, www.allthingsbillbelichick.com/articles/makestick.html.

[1812] Coach Bill Belichick, "Bill Belichick Press Conf. Transcript - 4/30," *Patriots.com*, 30 April 2004, www.patriots.com/news/FullArticle.sps?id=28597&type=general.

[1813] Roger Mooney, "Lee just wants another shot at pro ball," *Bradenton Herald* (Florida), 27 April 2004, www.bradenton.com/mld/bradenton/sports/8527599.htm.

[1814] Patriots quarterback Tom Brady, "Tom Brady Press Conference 7/23/03," bostonbrat.net/brady/arcjuly.html.

[1815] Shawn Mayer, quoted in: Frank Tadych, "Camp competition is life as usual," *Patriots.com*, 23 August 2004, www.patriots.com/fullarticle.sps?id=30243&type=general.

[1816] Bill Belichick, "Bill Belichick Press Conf. Transcript 6/11/04," *Patriots.com*, 11 June 2004, www.patriots.com/news/FullArticle.sps?id=28920.

[1817] Bill Belichick, "Bill Belichick Press Conf. Transcript 6/11/04," *Patriots.com*, 11 June 2004, www.patriots.com/news/FullArticle.sps?id=28920.

[1818] Bill Belichick, quoted in: Jim McCabe, "Dillon has a gang of admirers," *Boston Globe*, 19 October 2004, www.boston.com/sports/football/patriots/articles/2004/10/19/dillon_has_a_gang_of_admirers.

[1819] Patriots inside linebackers coach Pepper Johnson, *Won For All*, Chicago: Contemporary Books, 2003, p. 236.

[1820] Patriots offensive lineman Kenyatta Jones, quoted in: Alan Greenberg, "No Average Jones; Starting Job Comes With Maturity," *Hartford Courant*, 19 September 2002, p. C4, ProQuest database.

[1821] Michael Holley, *Patriot Reign*, William Morrow, 2004, p. 140.

[1822] Patriots offensive line coach Dante Scarnecchia, quoted in: Michael Holley, *Patriot Reign*, William Morrow, 2004, p. 140.

[1823] Washington Redskins assistant head coach-offense, Joe Bugel, quoted in; Nunyo Demasio, "K. Jones Is Released; Ex-Charger Is Signed," *Washington Post*, 25 October 2004, www.washingtonpost.com/wp-dyn/articles/A61674-2004Oct25.html.

[1824] Judy Battista, "Kraft Changes a Heavy Hand Into a Guiding Hand," *New York Times*, 17 January 2004, p. D5, ProQuest database.

[1825] Patriots owner Bob Kraft, quoted in: Judy Battista, "Kraft Changes a Heavy Hand Into a Guiding Hand," *New York Times*, 17 January 2004, p. D5, ProQuest database.

[1826] Bob George, "Secondary Really Put It On 'Em," *BosSports.net*, 2 March 2002, www.bossports.net/patriots/030202.shtml.

[1827] Associated Press, "Colts hit with jaw, knee injuries to Manning, James," *Kenai Peninsula Online*, 13 November 2001, http://peninsulaclarion.com/stories/111301/spo_1113010007.shtml. "Speeding" and "driving without a license" come from Patriots inside linebackers coach Pepper Johnson, *Won For All*, Chicago: Contemporary Books, 2003, p. 142.

[1828] Patriots inside linebackers coach Pepper Johnson, *Won For All*, Chicago: Contemporary Books, 2003, p. 142.

[1829] Greg Auman, "Ex-Buc WR Walker charged with DUI after crash in Tampa," *St. Petersburg Times*, 20 July 2004, www.sptimes.com/2004/07/20/Sports/Ex_Buc_WR_Walker_char.shtml.

[1830] Patriots quarterback Drew Bledsoe, quoted in: Bill Burt, "NFL Preview: Patriots will make the playoffs," *Eagle Tribune*, 27 August 2000, www.eagletribune.com/news/stories/20000827/SP_002.htm.

[1831] Patriots receiver Bethel Johnson, quoted in: Michael Felger, "Proceed with caution: Fast start may hit speed bumps," Boston Herald, 13 October 2004, http://patriots.bostonherald.com/patriots/view.bg?articleid=48814.

[1832] Michael Felger, "Proceed with caution: Fast start may hit speed bumps," Boston Herald, 13 October 2004, http://patriots.bostonherald.com/patriots/view.bg?articleid=48814.

[1833] Tom E. Curran, "Pats gasping when it comes to air," *Providence Journal*, 12 October 2004, www.projo.com/patriots/content/projo_20041012_12pats.ddbd6.html.

[1834] Nick Cafardo, "Johnson receives a message with benching," *Boston Globe*, 14 October 2004, www.boston.com/sports/football/patriots/articles/2004/10/14/johnson_receives_a_message_with_benching.

[1835] Patriots wide receiver Bethel Johnson, quoted in: Tom E. Curran, "Patriots Notebook: Johnson is miffed about his benching," *Providence Journal*, 14 October 2004, www.projo.com/patriots/content/projo_20041014_14patsjo.319b47.html.

[1836] Bill Belichick, quoted in: Frank Tadych, "Patriots Notebook: Johnson at a loss over benching," *Patriots.com*, 13 October 2004, http://cachewww.patriots.com/news/index.cfm?ac=LatestNewsDetail&PID=9313&PCID=41.

[1837] Bill Belichick, quoted in: Nick Cafardo, "Dillon still hobbled by sore foot," *Boston Globe*, 15 October 2004, www.boston.com/sports/football/patriots/articles/2004/10/15/dillon_still_hobbled_by_sore_foot/.

[1838] Unnamed Patriots veteran, quoted in: Michael Felger, "Shaw may catch on," Boston Herald, 15 October 2004, http://patriots.bostonherald.com/patriots/view.bg?articleid=49170.

[1839] Veteran linebacker Willie McGinest, quoted in: Michael Felger, "Shaw may catch on," Boston Herald, 15 October 2004, http://patriots.bostonherald.com/patriots/view.bg?articleid=49170.

[1840] Bill Belichick, quoted in: Ed Duckworth, "Belichick crafts new image," *New England Sports Service*, 6 June 2000, www.standardtimes.com/daily/06-00/06-06-00/c02sp105.htm.

[1841] Baltimore Ravens VP Kevin Byrne, who worked with Belichick in Cleveland, quoted in: Ron Borges, "What Makes Belichick Tick," *Boston Globe Magazine*, 10 September 2000, www.allthingsbillbelichick.com/articles/makestick.html.

[1842] Former New York Giant linebacker Pepper Johnson, quoted in: Ron Borges, "What Makes Belichick Tick," *Boston Globe Magazine*, 10 September 2000, www.allthingsbillbelichick.com/articles/makestick.html.

[1843] Bill Belichick, quoted in: Ed Duckworth, "Belichick crafts new image," *New England Sports Service*, 6 June 2000, www.standardtimes.com/daily/06-00/06-06-00/c02sp105.htm.

[1844] Ernest Hooper, "N.E.'s Belichick now flexible," *St. Petersburg Times*, 1 September 2000, www.sptimes.com/News/090100/Sports/NE_s_Belichick_now_fl.shtml.

[1845] Wide receiver Troy Brown, quoted in: Greg Garber, "Belichick Gets Second Chance In New England," *ESPN.com*, 20 June 2000, www.allthingsbillbelichick.com/articles/secondchance.htm.

[1846] Former New York Jets wide receiver Keyshawn Johnson, quoted in: Ernest Hooper, "N.E.'s Belichick now flexible," *St. Petersburg Times*, 1 September 2000, www.sptimes.com/News/090100/Sports/NE_s_Belichick_now_fl.shtml.

[1847] Patriots tryout player Ryan Ferguson, quoted in: Mike Reiss, "Reiss: Ferguson gets chance with Patriots," *Metro West Daily News*, 3 May 2004, www.metrowestdailynews.com/sportsColumnists/view.bg?articleid=67348.

[1848] Patriots defensive lineman Richard Seymour, quoted in: Thomas George, "Seymour Sheds Potential Grudge," *New York Times*, 31 January 2004, p. D1, ProQuest database.

[1849] Thomas George, "Seymour Sheds Potential Grudge," *New York Times*, 31 January 2004, p. D1, ProQuest database.

[1850] Mary Kay Cabot, "Belichick's influence reaches far in football," *Plain Dealer*, 31 January 2004, www.cleveland.com/sports/plaindealer/index.ssf?/base/sports/1075545297213372.xml.

[1851] Coach Bill Belichick, quoted in: Ron Borges, "What Makes Belichick Tick," *Boston Globe Magazine*, 10 September 2000, www.allthingsbillbelichick.com/articles/makestick.html.

[1852] Patriots coach Bill Belichick, quoted in: Marla Ridenourhen, " Human Interests," *Akron Beacon Journal*, 9 December 2001, www.allthingsbillbelichick.com/articles/humaninterests.htm.

[1853] Patriots owner Robert Kraft, quoted in: AP, "Pats fire Pete Carroll," *Sports Illustrated*, 3 January 2000, http://sportsillustrated.cnn.com/football/nfl/news/2000/01/03/patriots_carroll_ap/.

[1854] Former Patriots head coach Pete Carroll, quoted in: Michael Felger, *Tales From the Patriots Sideline*, Sports Publishing, 2004, p. 185.

[1855] Hector Longo, "Upgraded arsenal at Brady's disposal," *Eagle-Tribune*, 6 September 2004, www.eagletribune.com/news/stories/20040906/SP_004.htm.

[1856] Bill Belichick press release, quoted in: Ed Duckworth (*Scripps Howard*), "Belichick fires Kraft favorite Grier," *Eagle Tribune*, 2 May 2000, www.eagletribune.com/news/stories/20000502/SP_001.htm.

[1857] Bill Belichick, quoted in: Thomas George, "A Changed Dr. Doom Returns," *New York Times*, 15 September 2002, p. 8.1, ProQuest database.

[1858] Bill Belichick, quoted in: Harvey Mackay, *We Got Fired!*, New York: Ballantine Books, 2004, pp. 66-67.

[1859] Bob Oates, "Patriots Great Because…" *L.A. Times*, 6 October 2004, www.latimes.com/sports/la-100504oates,0,1651798.story.

[1860] Former Navy football team coach Rick Forzano, quoted in: Bob Duffy, "Whiz Kid To Defensive Genius," *Boston Globe*, 28 January 2000, www.allthingsbillbelichick.com/articles/whizkid.htm.

[1861] Bill Belichick, "O.K. Champ, Now Comes the Hard Part," *New York Times*, 26 January 2003, www.allthingsbillbelichick.com/articles/okchamp.html.

[1862] Michael Holley, "Script casts coach in new light," *Boston Globe*, 4 February 2004, www.boston.com/sports/football/patriots/superbowl/globe_stories/020402/script_casts_coach_in_new_light+.shtml.

[1863] See: www.bostonsportsmedia.com/herald.php, www.patsfans.com/xtreme/story/print_story.php?story_id=5115 and http://profootballnews.net/Draft/article.asp?ArtNum=3760.

[1864] Steve Buckley, " Meet Bill Belichick, Mr. Popular," *Boston Herald*, 17 January 2002, www.allthingsbillbelichick.com/articles/meetbb.htm.

[1865] Dan Pompeii, "There's no sane reason for all the fuss over Belichick," *The Sporting News*, 17 January 2000, www.findarticles.com/p/articles/mi_m1208/is_3_224/ai_59021115.

[1866] Patriots owner Bob Kraft, quoted in: Peter May, "Master of the plan," *Boston Globe*, 3 February 2004, www.boston.com/sports/football/patriots/articles/2004/02/03/master_of_the_plan/.

[1867] Patriots owner Bob Kraft, quoted in: Thomas George, "Still Bill: Patriots' Belichick Adapts and Thrives," *New York Times*, 16 November 2003, section 8, p. 1, ProQuest database.

[1868] Len Pasquarelli, "Coach, QB rewarded for Super Bowl heroics," *ESPN.com*, 4 February 2002, http://espn.go.com/nfl/playoffs01/columns/pasquarelli_len/1322633.html.

[1869] Bill Murphy, "POINT/COUNTERPOINT," *Eagle-Tribune*, 9 January 2000, www.eagletribune.com/news/stories/20000109/SP_004.htm.

[1870] Larry Felser, "Patriots no longer dark horse in Bay State," *The Buffalo News*, 3 October 2004, www.buffalonews.com/editorial/20041003/1056969.asp.

[1871] Father of Bill Belichick, quoted in: Ian O'Connor, "Invincibility of Belichick enhanced by his invisibility," *USA Today*, 19 January 2004, www.usatoday.com/sports/columnist/oconnor/2004-01-20-oconnor_x.htm.

[1872] Peter King, "It's official: Rams 24, Titans 20," *Sports Illustrated*, 28 January 2000, http://sportsillustrated.cnn.com/inside_game/peter_king/news/2000/01/28/ten_things/.

[1873] Scott Pioli, Patriots VP of player personnel, quoted in: Bob Brookover, "Star wideout may not be a prize catch," *Philadelphia Inquirer*, 31 January 2004, www.philly.com/mld/inquirer/sports/7839686.htm?1c.

[1874] Nakia Hogan, "Coaches are mirror image," *The Times*, 26 January 2004, www.nwlouisiana.com/html/61AB98A9-6CBE-464D-90BA-EAB997A6289E.shtml.

[1875] Roger Staubach, Super Bowl-winning quarterback who knew the Belichicks during his college days at Navy, quoted in: Paul Doyle, "A Navy Education Goes a Long Way, Belichick Got an Early Start," *Hartford Courant*, 18 January 2004, p. E3, ProQuest database.

[1876] Robert Fachet, "With the Belichicks, the Apple Hasn't Fallen Far From the Tree," *Washington Post*, 7 February 1991, p. C7, ProQuest database.

[1877] Steve Belichick, father of Bill Belichick, quoted in: Robert Fachet, "With the Belichicks, the Apple Hasn't Fallen Far From the Tree," *Washington Post*, 7 February 1991, p. C7, ProQuest database.

[1878] *Pro Football Hall of Fame*, "A salute to veterans," 15 November 2003, www.profootballhof.com/hall/release.jsp?release_id=25.

[1879] Ian O'Connor, "Invincibility of Belichick enhanced by his invisibility," *USA Today*, 19 January 2004, www.usatoday.com/sports/columnist/oconnor/2004-01-20-oconnor_x.htm.

[1880] Bill Belichick, quoted in: Michael Gee, "Belichicks Follow Paternal Instinct," *Boston Herald*, no date mentioned, www.allthingsbillbelichick.com/articles/followpaternal.htm.

[1881] Steve Belichick, father of Bill Belichick, quoted in: Kevin Paul Dupont, "Father knows (Belichick) best," *Boston Globe*, 1 February 2002, www.boston.com/sports/football/patriots/superbowl/globe_stories/020102/father_knows_belichick_best+.shtml.

[1882] Steve Belichick, father of Bill Belichick, quoted in: Robert Fachet, "With the Belichicks, the Apple Hasn't Fallen Far From the Tree," *Washington Post*, 7 February 1991, p. C7, ProQuest database.

[1883] Bill Belichick, quoted in: Ken Denlinger, "Coaching Out of the Blocks," *Washington Post*, 2002 (no date cited), www.allthingsbillbelichick.com/articles/outoftheblocks.htm.

[1884] Bill Belichick, quoted in: Michael Gee, "Belichicks Follow Paternal Instinct," *Boston Herald*, no date mentioned, www.allthingsbillbelichick.com/articles/followpaternal.htm.

[1885] Bill Belichick, quoted in: Gordon Edes, "Patriots coach has well-earned reputation for stopping whatever's thrown his way," *Boston Globe*, 2 February 2002, www.boston.com/sports/football/patriots/superbowl/globe_stories/020202/patriots_coach_has_well_earned_reputation_for_stopping_whatever_s_thrown_his_way+.shtml.

[1886] Bill Belichick, quoted in: Jerry Green, "Belichick was raised to be a coach," *Detroit News*, 29 January 2004, www.detnews.com/2004/lions/0401/29/g01-49608.htm.

[1887] Steve Belichick, father of Bill Belichick, quoted in: Bill Burt, "More than a coach," *Eagle Tribune*, 25 January 2004, www.eagletribune.com/news/stories/20040125/SP_001.htm.

[1888] Steve Belichick, Bill's father, quoted in: Peter King, "Master And Commander," *Sports Illustrated*, 9 August 2004, www.allthingsbillbelichick.com/articles/master.htm.

[1889] Jeannette Belichick, Bill's mother, quoted in: Pete Thamel, "For Belichick, An Economy Of Thought," *New York Times*, 16 January 2004, p. D1, ProQuest database.

[1890] Bill Belichick, quoted in: "In Young Belichick, Browns See Old Shula; Giants' Defensive Boss a Head Coach at 38," *Washington Post*, 6 February 1991, p. F3, ProQuest database.

[1891] Unnamed kid, quoted by Bill Belichick's mother, Jeannette, in: Edwin Pope, "Surly? Arrogant? These coaches might have good reasons," *South Coast Today*, 3 February 2002, www.s-t.com/daily/02-02/02-03-02/c07sp101.htm.

[1892] Former Navy football team coach Rick Forzano, quoted in: Ron Borges, "What Makes Belichick Tick," *Boston Globe Magazine*, 10 September 2000, www.allthingsbillbelichick.com/articles/makestick.htm.

[1893] Former Navy and Detroit Lions head coach Rick Forzano, quoted in: Jerry Green, "Belichick was raised to be a coach," *Detroit News*, 29 January 2004, www.detnews.com/2004/lions/0401/29/g01-49608.htm.

[1894] Peter King, "Born to win," *Sports Illustrated*, 23 August 2004, http://sportsillustrated.cnn.com/2004/writers/peter_king/08/20/king.mmqb/.

[1895] Robert Fachet, "With the Belichicks, the Apple Hasn't Fallen Far From the Tree," *Washington Post*, 7 February 1991, p. C7, ProQuest database.

[1896] 1960 Heisman winner Joe Bellino, quoted in: Bob Socci, "A Friendship Formed By Fate," *Navy Sports*, 28 January 2004, www.navysports.com/sports/football/release.asp?RELEASE_ID=15595.

[1897] Steve Belichick, Bill's father, quoted in: Thomas George, "A Changed Dr. Doom Returns," *New York Times*, 15 September 2002, p. 8.1, ProQuest database.

[1898] Bill Belichick, quoted in: Eric McHugh, "STEEL-TRAP MIND: Belichick's first NFL boss recalls his dedication to the job," *The Patriot Ledger*, 22 January 2004, http://ledger.southofboston.com/articles/2004/01/22/sports/sports01.txt.

[1899] Steve Belichick, father of Bill Belichick, quoted in: Robert Fachet, "With the Belichicks, the Apple Hasn't Fallen Far From the Tree," *Washington Post*, 7 February 1991, p. C7, ProQuest database.

[1900] Bill Belichick, quoted in: Harvey Mackay, *We Got Fired!*, New York: Ballantine Books, 2004, p. 67.

[1901] Steve Belichick, Bill's father, quoted in: Terry Pluto, "The Man Behind the Mask," *Akron Beacon Journal*, 18 December 1994, www.allthingsbillbelichick.com/articles/behindthemask.htm.

[1902] Bill Belichick, quoted in: Peter King, "Master And Commander," *Sports Illustrated*, 9 August 2004, www.allthingsbillbelichick.com/articles/master.htm.

[1903] Pete Thamel, "For Belichick, An Economy Of Thought," *New York Times*, 16 January 2004, p. D1, ProQuest database.

[1904] Dana Seero, who played on the offensive line with Belichick at Phillips Andover, quoted in: Bill Burt, "'One of the best years of my life,'" *Eagle Tribune*, 30 January 2000, www.allthingsbillbelichick.com/articles/oneofthebest.htm.

[1905] Phillips Andover lacrosse coach Paul Kalkstein, quoted in: Steve Politi, "Is Belichick A Genius?" *Star-Ledger*, 30 January 2004, www.allthingsbillbelichick.com/articles/agenius.htm.

[1906] Coach Bill Belichick, quoted in: Ron Borges, "What Makes Belichick Tick," *Boston Globe Magazine*, 10 September 2000, www.allthingsbillbelichick.com/articles/makestick.htm.

[1907] Michael Holley, *Patriot Reign*, William Morrow, 2004, p. 61.

[1908] Former Phillips Andover trainer Al Coulthard, quoted in: Richard A. Johnson, "Returning To Patriots Country," *Phillips Academy Andover 2000 Spring Bulletin*, www.andover.edu/publications/2000spring_bulletin/belichick/belichick.htm.

[1909] Longtime Wesleyan assistant football coach Peter Kostacopolous, quoted in: Richard A. Johnson, "Returning To Patriots Country," *Phillips Academy Andover 2000 Spring Bulletin*, www.andover.edu/publications/2000spring_bulletin/belichick/belichick.htm.

[1910] Pete Thamel, "For Belichick, An Economy Of Thought," *New York Times*, 16 January 2004, p. D1, ProQuest database.

[1911] Peter Kostacopolous, Wesleyan football defensive coordinator Belichick's senior season, quoted in: Bob Duffy, "Whiz Kid To Defensive Genius," *Boston Globe*, 28 January 2000, www.allthingsbillbelichick.com/articles/whizkid.htm.

[1912] Michael Holley, "Best-case scenarios," *Boston Globe*, 5 November 2003, www.boston.com/sports/football/patriots/articles/2003/11/05/best_case_scenarios.

[1913] John Biddiscombe, Belichick's football position coach at Wesleyan and now the school's athletic director, quoted in: Brad Parks, "Belichick: He Has The Edge, Just Needs To Soften It," *Star-Ledger*, 4 January 2000, www.allthingsbillbelichick.com/articles/theedge.htm.

[1914] Former Green Bay Packers general manager Ron Wolf, quoted in: Ira Miller, "Patriots have staying power," *San Francisco Chronicle*, 15 August 2004, http://sfgate.com/cgi-bin/article.cgi?file=/chronicle/archive/2004/08/15/SPGNJ88GV11.DTL&type=printable.

[1915] Steve Belichick, quoted in: Terry Pluto, "The Man Behind the Mask," *Akron Beacon Journal*, 18 December 1994, www.allthingsbillbelichick.com/articles/behindthemask.htm.

[1916] Mark Purdy, "This Super Bowl won't be a pretty sight," *Knight Ridder Newspapers*, 31 January 2004, www.miami.com/mld/charlotte/sports/football/nfl/carolina_panthers/7846216.htm?1c.

[1917] Steve Belichick, quoted in: Ken Denlinger, "Coaching Out of the Blocks," *Washington Post*, 2002 (no date cited), www.allthingsbillbelichick.com/articles/outoftheblocks.htm.

[1918] Ernie Adams, quoted in: Terry Pluto, "The Man Behind the Mask," *Akron Beacon Journal*, 18 December 1994, www.allthingsbillbelichick.com/articles/behindthemask.htm.

[1919] Bill Belichick, quoted in: Eric McHugh, "STEEL-TRAP MIND: Belichick's first NFL boss recalls his dedication to the job," *The Patriot Ledger*, 22 January 2004, http://ledger.southofboston.com/articles/2004/01/22/sports/sports01.txt.

[1920] Rick Forzano said, "I tried to get him to come with me in 1975. He was doing gofer work for Ted Marchibroda in Baltimore." Source: Jerry Green, "Belichick was raised to be a coach," *Detroit News*, 29 January 2004, www.detnews.com/2004/lions/0401/29/g01-49608.htm.

[1921] Ernie Adams, quoted in: Pete Thamel, "Low-Key Adams Makes High Impact on Patriots," *New York Times*, 16 January 2004, p. D7, ProQuest database.

[1922] Peter King, "Master And Commander," *Sports Illustrated*, 9 August 2004, www.allthingsbillbelichick.com/articles/master.htm.

[1923] Steve Belichick, father of Bill Belichick, quoted in: Robert Fachet, "With the Belichicks, the Apple Hasn't Fallen Far From the Tree," *Washington Post*, 7 February 1991, p. C7, ProQuest database.

[1924] Coach Bill Belichick, quoted in: Ron Borges, "What Makes Belichick Tick," *Boston Globe Magazine*, 10 September 2000, www.allthingsbillbelichick.com/articles/makestick.html.

[1925] Steve Belichick, quoted in: Terry Pluto, "The Man Behind the Mask," *Akron Beacon Journal*, 18 December 1994, www.allthingsbillbelichick.com/articles/behindthemask.htm.

[1926] Bill Belichick, quoted in: Eric McHugh, "STEEL-TRAP MIND: Belichick's first NFL boss recalls his dedication to the job," *The Patriot Ledger*, 22 January 2004, http://ledger.southofboston.com/articles/2004/01/22/sports/sports01.txt.

[1927] Former NFL head coach Ted Marchibroda, quoted in: Bob McGinn, "Secretary of Defense," *Milwaukee Journal-Sentinel*, 25 January 1997, www.allthingsbillbelichick.com/articles/secretaryofd.htm.

[1928] Former NFL head coach Ted Marchibroda, who gave 23-year-old Bill Belichick his first NFL job in 1975, quoted in: Bob Glauber, "Billy Ball," *Newsday*, 25 January 2004, www.allthingsbillbelichick.com/articles/billyball.htm.

[1929] Bill Belichick, quoted in: Andrew Mason, "Pats bring new meaning to 'team,'" *NFL.com*, 3 February 2002, ww2.nfl.com/xxxvi/ce/feature/0,3892,4948702,00.html.

[1930] Former NFL head coach Ted Marchibroda, who gave 23-year-old Bill Belichick his first NFL job in 1975, quoted in: Bob Glauber, "Billy Ball," *Newsday*, 25 January 2004, www.allthingsbillbelichick.com/articles/billyball.htm.

[1931] Patriots coach Bill Belichick, quoted in: Bob Glauber, "Billy Ball," *Newsday*, 25 January 2004, www.allthingsbillbelichick.com/articles/billyball.htm.

[1932] According to Ernie Accorsi, in: Michael Eisen, "Belichick, Fox Earn Praise From Accorsi," *Giants.com*, 28 January 2004, www.giants.com/news/index.cfm?cont_id=226897&right_include=/includes/eisens_archive_module.cfm.

[1933] Bill Belichick, quoted in: Alan Greenberg, "Belichick: Call Him the Bred Winner," *Hartford Courant*, 27 January 2004, p. C1, ProQuest database.

[1934] Bill Belichick, quoted in: Bob Glauber, "Genius at work," *Newsday*, 24 October 2004, www.newsday.com/sports/football/jets/ny-spsunspec244017937oct24,0,3329835.story.

[1935] Bill Macdermott, head coach of Belichick's Wesleyan football team, quoted in: Bob Duffy, "Whiz Kid To Defensive Genius," *Boston Globe*, 28 January 2000, www.allthingsbillbelichick.com/articles/whizkid.htm.

[1936] Brad Parks, "Belichick: He Has The Edge, Just Needs To Soften It," *Star-Ledger*, 4 January 2000, www.allthingsbillbelichick.com/articles/theedge.htm.

[1937] Ernie Accorsi, quoted in: Michael Eisen, "Belichick, Fox Earn Praise From Accorsi," *Giants.com*, 28 January 2004, www.giants.com/news/index.cfm?cont_id=226897&right_include=/includes/eisens_archive_module.cfm.

[1938] Eric McHugh, "STEEL-TRAP MIND: Belichick's first NFL boss recalls his dedication to the job," *The Patriot Ledger*, 22 January 2004, http://ledger.southofboston.com/articles/2004/01/22/sports/sports01.txt.

[1939] Rick Forzano, who was Detroit Lions head coach when Belichick was a 24-year-old assistant coach, quoted in: Bob Duffy, "Whiz Kid To Defensive Genius," *Boston Globe*, 28 January 2000, www.allthingsbillbelichick.com/articles/whizkid.htm. Page 12 of Michael Holley's *Patriot Reign* reports a $10,000 salary.

[1940] Bill Burt, "Chicago writer: Belichick has always been worth watching," *Eagle Tribune*, 29 January 2004, www.eagletribune.com/news/stories/20040129/SP_007.htm.

[1941] Steve Belichick, father of Bill Belichick, quoted in: Michael Gee, "Belichicks Follow Paternal Instinct," *Boston Herald*, no date mentioned, www.allthingsbillbelichick.com/articles/followpaternal.htm.

[1942] "Battles in Black and Blue," www.geocities.com/Colosseum/Loge/4705/part2.html.

[1943] Bill Belichick, quoted in: Harvey Mackay, *We Got Fired!*, New York: Ballantine Books, 2004, p. 67.

[1944] Ernie Accorsi, quoted in: George Vecsey, "Super Bowl Coaches With a Giants Connection," *New York Times*, 21 January 2004, p. D4, ProQuest database.

[1945] Brad Parks, "Belichick: He Has The Edge, Just Needs To Soften It," *Star-Ledger*, 4 January 2000, www.allthingsbillbelichick.com/articles/theedge.htm.

[1946] Bill Belichick, quoted in: Peter King, "Master And Commander," *Sports Illustrated*, 9 August 2004, www.allthingsbillbelichick.com/articles/master.htm.

[1947] Bill Belichick, quoted in: "In Young Belichick, Browns See Old Shula; Giants' Defensive Boss a Head Coach at 38," *Washington Post*, 6 February 1991, p. F3, ProQuest database.

[1948] Harvey Mackay, *We Got Fired!*, New York: Ballantine Books, 2004, p. 60.

[1949] Bill Belichick, quoted in: Harvey Mackay, *We Got Fired!*, New York: Ballantine Books, 2004, p. 61.

[1950] Oakland Raiders player personnel director Mike Lombardi, who worked with Belichick in Cleveland, quoted in: *New York Daily News*, "For Bill, difference is then ... and now," 29 January 2004, www.nydailynews.com/sports/story/159631p-140099c.html.

[1951] Austin Murphy, "End Of An Epic," *Sports Illustrated*, December 4, 1995, www.allthingsbillbelichick.com/articles/endofepic.htm.

[1952] Ravens general manager and executive VP Ozzie Newsome, quoted in: Susan Vinella, "Thirsting for a crown," *The Plain Dealer* (Cleveland), 29 August 2004, www.cleveland.com/sports/plaindealer/index.ssf?/base/sports/109377690472430.xml.

[1953] Nick Saban, 2003 Coach of the Year, head coach of the 2003 national champion LSU Tigers, and assistant coach on Bill Belichick's Cleveland Browns, quoted in: Mary Kay Cabot, "Belichick's influence reaches far in football," *The Plain Dealer* (Cleveland), 31 January 2004, www.cleveland.com/sports/plaindealer/index.ssf?/base/sports/1075544529721372.xml.

[1954] Belichick's offensive line coach in Cleveland, Kirk Ferentz, quoted in: Bob Glauber, "Billy Ball," *Newsday*, 25 January 2004, www.allthingsbillbelichick.com/articles/billyball.htm.

[1955] Ernie Adams, quoted in: Terry Pluto, "The Man Behind the Mask," *Akron Beacon Journal*, 18 December 1994, www.allthingsbillbelichick.com/articles/behindthemask.htm.

[1956] Bill Belichick, quoted in: "In Young Belichick, Browns See Old Shula; Giants' Defensive Boss a Head Coach at 38," *Washington Post*, 6 February 1991, p. F3, ProQuest database.

[1957] Bill Belichick, as remembered by Ernie Accorsi, quoted in: Michael Eisen, "Belichick, Fox Earn Praise From Accorsi," *Giants.com*, 28 January 2004, www.giants.com/news/index.cfm?cont_id=226897&right_include=/includes/eisens_archive_module.cfm.

[1958] Oakland Raiders player personnel director Mike Lombardi, who worked with Belichick in Cleveland, quoted in: *New York Daily News*, "For Bill, difference is then ... and now," 29 January 2004, www.nydailynews.com/sports/story/159631p-140099c.html.

[1959] Legendary Cleveland Browns running back Jim Brown, quoted in: Peter King, "Master And Commander," *Sports Illustrated*, 9 August 2004, www.allthingsbillbelichick.com/articles/master.htm.

[1960] Ernie Accorsi, quoted in: George Vecsey, "Super Bowl Coaches With a Giants Connection," *New York Times*, 21 January 2004, p. D4, ProQuest database.

[1961] Ernie Accorsi, quoted in: Michael Eisen, "Belichick, Fox Earn Praise From Accorsi," *Giants.com*, 28 January 2004, www.giants.com/news/index.cfm?cont_id=226897&right_include=/includes/eisens_archive_module.cfm.

[1962] Former Cleveland Browns owner Art Modell, quoted in: Leonard Shapiro, "Browns Cut Kosar After Much Feuding; Quarterback Signed 7-Year Deal Recently," *New York Times*, 9 November 1993, p. E4, ProQuest database.

[1963] Leonard Shapiro, "Changing Horses in Midstream Once Again," *New York Times*, 27 September 2001, p. D9, ProQuest database.

[1964] Leonard Shapiro, "Browns Cut Kosar After Much Feuding; Quarterback Signed 7-Year Deal Recently," *New York Times*, 9 November 1993, p. E4, ProQuest database; and, Bill Plaschke, "Stubborn Kosar Cut by Browns," *Los Angeles Times*, 9 November 1993, sports section, p. 1, ProQuest database.

[1965] Peter King, "Master And Commander," *Sports Illustrated*, 9 August 2004, www.allthingsbillbelichick.com/articles/master.htm.

[1966] Leonard Shapiro, "Belichick Fired in Baltimore; Marchibroda Might Coach NFL Team," *New York Times*, 15 February 1996, p. D1, ProQuest database.

[1967] Judy Battista, "A Setback for Bellichick In His Bid to Move On," *New York Times*, p. D4, ProQuest Historical Newspapers.

[1968] Bill Belichick, quoted in: Dan Pompei, "Many second-chance coaches deliver first-rate results," *The Sporting News*, 14 January 2003, http://i.tsn.com/voices/dan_pompei/20030114.html.

[1969] Dallas Cowboys owner Jerry Jones, quoted in: Dan Pompei, "Many second-chance coaches deliver first-rate results," *The Sporting News*, 14 January 2003, http://i.tsn.com/voices/dan_pompei/20030114.html.

[1970] Former Browns quarterback Bernie Kosar, quoted in: Bob Duffy, "Whiz Kid To Defensive Genius," *Boston Globe*, 28 January 2000, www.allthingsbillbelichick.com/articles/whizkid.htm.

[1971] Bill Belichick, quoted in: Bob Duffy, "Whiz Kid To Defensive Genius," *Boston Globe*, 28 January 2000, www.allthingsbillbelichick.com/articles/whizkid.htm.

[1972] David DeGregorio, "Belichick Gets it Right This Time," *ProFootballNews.net*, 28 January 2002, http://profootballnews.net/Draft/article.asp?ArtNum=3760.

[1973] Former Cleveland Browns player Mike Baab, quoted in: Bob Duffy, "Whiz Kid To Defensive Genius," *Boston Globe*, 28 January 2000, www.allthingsbillbelichick.com/articles/whizkid.htm.

[1974] Former Cleveland Browns player Mike Baab, quoted in: Bob Duffy, "Whiz Kid To Defensive Genius," *Boston Globe*, 28 January 2000, www.allthingsbillbelichick.com/articles/whizkid.htm.

[1975] *Cleveland Plain Dealer* journalist Tony Grossi, quoted in: Peter King, "Master And Commander," *Sports Illustrated*, 9 August 2004, www.allthingsbillbelichick.com/articles/master.htm.

[1976] Alan Greenberg, "Getting Along Well Belichick Still A Little Grim, But With A Grin," *Hartford Courant*, 3 September 2000, p. E1, ProQuest database.

[1977] Bill Belichick, quoted in: Thomas George, "A Changed Dr. Doom Returns," *New York Times*, 15 September 2002, p. 8.1, ProQuest database.

[1978] Bill Belichick, quoted in: Kevin Paul Dupont, "Father knows (Belichick) best," *Boston Globe*, 1 February 2002, www.boston.com/sports/football/patriots/superbowl/globe_stories/020102/father_knows_belichick_best+.shtml.

[1979] Ron Borges, "Belichick Has a Gifted Touch," *Boston Globe*, 24 December 2001, www.allthingsbillbelichick.com/articles/giftedtouch.htm.

[1980] Former Cleveland Brown and New England Patriot Anthony Pleasant, quoted in: Dan Pires, "The changing face of Bill Belichick," *SouthCoast Today*, 22 December 2001, www.s-t.com/daily/12-01/12-22-01/c01sp071.htm.

[1981] Coach Bill Belichick, quoted in: Kevin Mannix, "Top Billing," *Boston Herald*, 31 August 2000, www.allthingsbillbelichick.com/articles/topbilling.htm.

[1982] Bill Belichick, quoted in: Thomas George, "Still Bill: Patriots' Belichick Adapts and Thrives," *New York Times*, 16 November 2003, section 8, p. 1, ProQuest database.

[1983] Coach Bill Belichick, quoted in: Steve Buckley, " Meet Bill Belichick, Mr. Popular," *Boston Herald*, 17 January 2002, www.allthingsbillbelichick.com/articles/meetbb.htm.

[1984] Steve DeOssie of Sportsradio 850 WEEI and WBZ-TV 4, quoted in: John Molori, "DeOssie knows score between Belichick, Parcells," *Eagle Tribune*, 12 January 2004, www.eagletribune.com/news/stories/20040112/SP_010.htm.

[1985] Bill Livingston, sports columnist for the *Cleveland Plain Dealer*, quoted in: Steve Buckley, "The Metamorphosis Of Bill Belichick," *Boston Herald*, 9 December 2001, www.allthingsbillbelichick.com/articles/metofbb.htm.

[1986] Former Cleveland Browns player Mike Baab, quoted in: Bob Duffy, "Whiz Kid To Defensive Genius," *Boston Globe*, 28 January 2000, www.allthingsbillbelichick.com/articles/whizkid.htm.

[1987] Former Cleveland Brown (1993-95) and 2003 Patriot Brian Kinchen, quoted in: Bud Shaw, "Follow the Belichick highway," *Plain Dealer* (Cleveland), 28 January 2004, www.cleveland.com/sports/plaindealer/index.ssf?/base/sports/1075285922190293.xml.

[1988] Bill Belichick, quoted in: Thomas George, "A Changed Dr. Doom Returns," *New York Times*, 15 September 2002, p. 8.1, ProQuest database.

[1989] Marla Ridenourhen, " Human Interests," *Akron Beacon Journal*, 9 December 2001, www.allthingsbillbelichick.com/articles/humaninterests.htm.

[1990] Former Giants quarterback (and Super Bowl-winner) Phil Simms, quoted in: Peter King, "Born to win," *Sports Illustrated*, 23 August 2004, http://sportsillustrated.cnn.com/2004/writers/peter_king/08/20/king.mmqb/.

[1991] Former Giants quarterback (and Super Bowl-winner) Phil Simms, quoted in: Peter King, "Born to win," *Sports Illustrated*, 23 August 2004, http://sportsillustrated.cnn.com/2004/writers/peter_king/08/20/king.mmqb/.

[1992] Former Cleveland Browns player and Baltimore Ravens executive Ozzie Newsome, quoted in: Mary Kay Cabot, "Belichick's influence reaches far in football," *Plain Dealer*, 31 January 2004, www.cleveland.com/sports/plaindealer/index.ssf?/base/sports/1075545297213372.xml.

[1993] Ted Marchibroda, days before he replaced Bill Belichick as Cleveland Browns head coach, quoted in: Dave Sell, "Out as Colts Coach, Marchibroda Looking; If Baltimore Calls, He Would Listen," *Washington Post*, 10 February 1996, p. H5, ProQuest database.

[1994] Pat Kirwan, "Belichick making most of Jets defense," *Sports Illustrated*, 24 November 1998, http://sportsillustrated.cnn.com/football/nfl/news/1998/11/24/kirwan_unsung/index.html.

[1995] Bill Burt, "Time to see if Belichick can lead," *Eagle Tribune*, 2 February 2001, www.eagletribune.com/news/stories/20010202/SP_001.htm.

[1996] Michael Holley, "Doubts About Jets' Choice Aren't Just Nitpicks," *Boston Globe*, 4 January 2000, www.allthingsbillbelichick.com/articles/jetschoice.htm.

[1997] Joe Murphy, "Patriots remain a puzzle," *Eagle Tribune*, 12 February 2000, www.eagletribune.com/news/stories/20000212/SP_008.htm.

[1998] Bill Parrillo, "Patriots need to go back to school," *South Coast Today*, 11 January 2000, www.southcoasttoday.com/daily/01-00/01-11-00/d03sp146.htm.

[1999] Bill Burt, "POINT/COUNTERPOINT," *Eagle Tribune*, 9 January 2000, www.eagletribune.com/news/stories/20000109/SP_005.htm.

[2000] Bill Burt, "One believer in Belichick is now in hiding," *Eagle Tribune*, 15 November 2000, www.eagletribune.com/news/stories/20001115/SP_002.htm.

[2001] Patriots cornerback Ty Law, quoted in: John Tomase, "Landing Belichick will not be easy job," *Eagle-Tribune*, 4 January 2000, www.eagletribune.com/news/stories/20000104/SP_002.htm.

[2002] Patriots quarterback Drew Bledsoe, quoted in: Jimmy Golen (AP), "Baying the Bill," *SouthCoast Today*, 28 January 2000, www.s-t.com/daily/01-00/01-28-00/d01sp116.htm.

[2003] Patriots safety Lawyer Milloy, quoted in: Bill Burt, "NFL Preview: Patriots will make the playoffs," *Eagle Tribune*, 27 August 2000, www.eagletribune.com/news/stories/20000827/SP_002.htm.

[2004] Former Patriots wide receiver Shawn Jefferson, quoted in: Richard Oliver, "Drew's pick? Belichick." *Newsday*, 23 January 2000, www.allthingsbillbelichick.com/articles/drewspick.htm.

[2005] Former Patriots wide receiver Shawn Jefferson, quoted in: Bill Burt, "NFL Preview: Patriots will make the playoffs," *Eagle Tribune*, 27 August 2000, www.eagletribune.com/news/stories/20000827/SP_002.htm.

[2006] Patriots owner Robert Kraft, quoted in: Bud Shaw, "Follow the Belichick highway," *Plain Dealer* (Cleveland), 28 January 2004, www.cleveland.com/sports/plaindealer/index.ssf?/base/sports/1075285922190293.xml.

[2007] Patriots owner Robert Kraft, quoted in: Damon Hack, "Hard Contact Is Music to Bruschi's Ears," *New York Times*, 29 January 2004, D1, ProQuest database.

[2008] Patriots vice chairman Jonathan Kraft, quoted in: Michael Holley, *Patriot Reign*, William Morrow, 2004, p. 31.

[2009] Gerald Eskenazi (*New York Times*), "Pats defense built in reverse," *SouthCoast Today*, 22 January 1997, www.s-t.com/daily/01-97/01-22-97/d04sp157.htm.

[2010] Patriots owner Robert Kraft, quoted in: John Wiebusch, "Pats' Kraft has had a year to remember," *NFL Insider*, 9 September 2002, www.nfl.com/insider/story/5688930.

[2011] John Bon Jovi, quoted in: Rich Cimini, "Who knows the real Bill Belichick?" *New York Daily News*, 24 January 2004, www.kansas.com/mld/kansas/2004/01/20/sports/7789572.htm?template=contentModules/printstory.jsp.

[2012] Bill Belichick, quoted in: Rich Cimini, "Who knows the real Bill Belichick?" *New York Daily News*, 24 January 2004, www.kansas.com/mld/kansas/2004/01/20/sports/7789572.htm?template=contentModules/printstory.jsp.

[2013] Kevin Iole, "Barkley says Super Bowl bet was not against rules," *Las Vegas Review-Journal*, 16 March 2002, www.reviewjournal.com/lvrj_home/2002/Mar-16-Sat-2002/sports/18320838.html.

[2014] Jeff Jacobs, "Class Clown Gets Serious With Patriots," *Hartford Courant*, 3 February 2002, p. A1.

[2015] Phil Simms, "Bill Belichick: Not as dull as he seems," *Time*, vol. 163, no. 17, 26 April 2004, www.allthingsbillbelichick.com/TIME.htm.

[2016] Bill Belichick, quoted in: Michael Holley, "Winners are one of a kind," *Boston Globe*, 2 February 2004, www.boston.com/sports/football/patriots/articles/2004/02/02/winners_are_one_of_a_kind.

[2017] Bill Belichick, quoted in: Dan Pompei, "Inside Pats' Super Bowl Preparations," *Sporting News*, 2 February 2004, www.allthingsbillbelichick.com/articles/insidesbprep.htm.

[2018] David Larimer, "Throw the Flag; The league didn't penalize it, but someone should," *Washington Post*, 30 November 2003, E6, ProQuest database.

[2019] Paul Attner, "Super Bowl 38: Red, white and two," *The Sporting News*, 9 February 2004, www.sportingnews.com/archives/superbowl/.

[2020] John Canzano, "Belichick does just fine by himself," *The Oregonian*, 30 January 2004, www.oregonlive.com/sports/oregonian/john_canzano/index.ssf?/base/exclude/1075468056315520.xml.

[2021] Thomas George, "A Changed Dr. Doom Returns," *New York Times*, 15 September 2002, p. 8.1, ProQuest database.

[2022] Jim Moore, "Go 2 Guy: Tale of a dogged newshound," *Seattle Post-Intelligencer*, 14 October 2004, http://seattlepi.nwsource.com/football/195099_moore14.html.

[2023] Peter King, "A League of Their Own," *Sports Illustrated*, 18 October 2004, p. 70.

[2024] Glen Farley, "Belichick has the magic touch," *The Enterprise*, 14 August 2004, http://enterprise.southofboston.com/articles/2004/08/14/news/sports/sports01.txt.

[2025] Bill Belichick, quoted in: Kit Stier (*Journal News*), "Two undefeated teams, two coaches with contrasting styles," *Cincinnati Enquirer*, 20 October 2004, http://bengals.enquirer.com/2004/10/20/ben2a.html.

[2026] Michael Smith, "Taking the city by storm," *Boston Globe*, 5 February 2002, www.boston.com/sports/football/patriots/superbowl/globe_stories/020502/taking_the_city_by_storm+.shtml.

[2027] Michael Holley, "'It's Just Another Sideline,'" *Boston Globe*, 28 April 2000, www.allthingsbillbelichick.com/articles/sideline.html.

[2028] 1960 Heisman winner Joe Bellino, quoted in: Bob Socci, "A Friendship Formed By Fate," *Navy Sports*, 28 January 2004, www.navysports.com/sports/football/release.asp?RELEASE_ID=15595.

[2029] Bill Belichick, quoted in: Michael Holley, "'It's Just Another Sideline,'" *Boston Globe*, 28 April 2000, www.allthingsbillbelichick.com/articles/sideline.html.

[2030] Don Pierson, "Dolphins to flounder without Williams," *NBCSports.com*, 28 July 2004, http://msnbc.msn.com/id/5537952/.

[2031] Legendary NFL running back and Amer-I-Can founder Jim Brown, quoted in: Tom E. Curran, "Jim Brown still building his powerful legacy," *Providence Journal*, 5 June 2004, www.projo.com/patriots/content/projo_20040605_05jbrown.326f22.html.

[2032] Legendary NFL running back and Amer-I-Can founder Jim Brown, quoted in: Tom E. Curran, "Jim Brown still building his powerful legacy," *Providence Journal*, 5 June 2004, www.projo.com/patriots/content/projo_20040605_05jbrown.326f22.html.

[2033] Bill Belichick, quoted in: Rich Cimini, "Who knows the real Bill Belichick?" *New York Daily News*, 24 January 2004, www.kansas.com/mld/kansas/2004/01/20/sports/7789572.htm?template=contentModules/printstory.jsp.

[2034] Bill Belichick, quoted in: Rich Cimini, "Who knows the real Bill Belichick?" *New York Daily News*, 24 January 2004, www.kansas.com/mld/kansas/2004/01/20/sports/7789572.htm?template=contentModules/printstory.jsp.

[2035] Adam Hanft, "Soul Proprietor: Jon Bon Jovi," *Inc.*, June 2004, www.inc.com/magazine/20040701/bonjovi_1.html.

[2036] Jon Bon Jovi, quoted in: Adam Hanft, "Soul Proprietor: Jon Bon Jovi," *Inc.*, June 2004, www.inc.com/magazine/20040701/bonjovi_1.html.

[2037] Jon Bon Jovi, quoted in: Rich Cimini, "Who knows the real Bill Belichick?" *New York Daily News*, 24 January 2004, www.kansas.com/mld/kansas/2004/01/20/sports/7789572.htm?template=contentModules/printstory.jsp.

[2038] Jon Bon Jovi, quoted in: Adam Hanft, "Soul Proprietor: Jon Bon Jovi," *Inc.*, June 2004, www.inc.com/magazine/20040701/bonjovi_1.html.

[2039] Steve Belichick, father of Bill Belichick, quoted in: Bill Burt, "More than a coach," *Eagle Tribune*, 25 January 2004, www.eagletribune.com/news/stories/20040125/SP_001.htm.

[2040] Steve Belichick, father of Bill Belichick, quoted in: Dan O'Neill, "Belichick's gruff football facade gives way to a serious softy," *St. Louis Post-Dispatch*, 1 February 2002, www.ramsfan.us/oldnews/2002/020102-9.htm.

[2041] Steve Belichick, father of Bill Belichick, quoted in: Michael Gee, "Belichicks Follow Paternal Instinct," *Boston Herald*, no date mentioned, www.allthingsbillbelichick.com/articles/followpaternal.htm.

[2042] Steve Belichick, father of Bill Belichick, quoted in: Gordon Edes, "Patriots coach has well-earned reputation for stopping whatever's thrown his way," *Boston Globe*, 2 February 2002, www.boston.com/sports/football/patriots/superbowl/globe_stories/020202/patriots_coach_has_well_earned_reputation_for_stopping_whatever_s_thrown_his_way+.shtml.

[2043] Steve Belichick, father of Bill Belichick, quoted in: Lenny Megliola, "Moment in the sun," *Boston Herald*, 23 December 2001, www.allthingsbillbelichick.com/articles/inthesun.htm.

[2044] Belichick's lacrosse and football teammate, David Campbell, quoted in: Bob Duffy, "Whiz Kid To Defensive Genius," *Boston Globe*, 28 January 2000, www.allthingsbillbelichick.com/articles/whizkid.htm.

[2045] Patriots VP of player personnel Scott Pioli, quoted in: Mark Maske and Leonard Shapiro, "With Patriots' Pioli, It's All in the Family, but There's No Feud," *Washington Post*, 29 January 2004, ProQuest database.

[2046] Patriots fullback Fred McCrary, quoted in: Andy Kent, "NFL: McCrary eyes Pats starting role," *Naples Daily News*, 20 July 2004, www.naplesnews.com/npdn/sports/article/0,2071,NPDN_15000_3049089,00.html.

[2047] Peter King of *Sports Illustrated*, quoted in: "NFL Films Presents: Perfect Patriots," 12 September 2004, on *ESPN*.

[2048] Long-time Belichick friend and former Patriots assistant coach Steve Szabo, quoted in: Paul Kenyon, "Are Belichick's secrets safe with Szabo?" *Providence Journal*, 2 October 2004, www.projo.com/patriots/content/projo_20041002_02pats.1545e0.html.

[2049] Basketball star and Bill Belichick friend Charles Barkley, quoted in: Fran Blinebury, "Belichick, Barkley proof that opposites attract," *Houston Chronicle*, 31 January 2004, www.chron.com/cs/CDA/ssistory.mpl/sports/2379958.

[2050] Patriots defensive lineman Richard Seymour, quoted in: Associated Press, "Patriots tie NFL mark with 18th win in row," *Indianapolis Star*, 4 October 2004, www.indystar.com/articles/4/183702-6414-196.html.

[2051] Bill Belichick, quoted in: Jim Donaldson, "New England defense keeps Bills bumbling," *Providence Journal*, 4 October 2004, www.projo.com/patriots/content/projo_20041004_04defense.93dcb.html.

[2052] Bill Belichick, quoted in: Bill Burt, "Patriots coach scores big at Phillips," *Eagle Tribune*, 28 February 2002, www.eagletribune.com/news/stories/20020228/FP_001.htm.

[2053] Bill Belichick, quoted in: Bill Burt, "Secretive Bruschi day-to-day," *Eagle Tribune*, 23 January 2004, www.eagletribune.com/news/stories/20040123/SP_005.htm.

[2054] Bill Belichick on *The David Letterman Show*, 4 February 2004, www.patriots.com/mediaworld/mediadetail.sps?id=27974.

[2055] Bill Belichick, quoted in: Michael Felger, "Patriots notebook: Who's No. 2?" *Boston Herald*, 29 August 2004, www.metrowestdailynews.com/sportsColumnists/view.bg?articleid=76657.

[2056] Bill Belichick, quoted in: Ian M. Clark, "Patriots Notebook: Super Bowl 'rematch' in unfriendly confines," *The Union Leader*, 27 August 2004, www.theunionleader.com/articles_showfast.html?article=42942.

[2057] Bill Belichick, quoted in: Paul Kenyon, "Understated Phifer is Pats' leading tackler," *Providence Journal*, 10 August 2004, www.projo.com/cgi-bin/bi/gold_print.cgi.

[2058] Bill Belichick, quoted in: Dan Pompei, "Inside Pats' Super Bowl Preparations," *Sporting News*, 2 February 2004, www.allthingsbillbelichick.com/articles/insidesbprep.htm.

[2059] Bill Belichick, quoted in: Hector Longo, "Belichick not offering any bulletin-board material for Raiders," *Eagle-Tribune*, 17 January 2002, www.eagletribune.com/news/stories/20020117/SP_012.htm.

[2060] Bill Belichick, quoted in: Austin Murphy, "End Of An Epic," *Sports Illustrated*, December 4, 1995, www.allthingsbillbelichick.com/articles/endofepic.htm.

[2061] Bill Belichick, "O.K. Champ, Now Comes the Hard Part," *New York Times*, 26 January 2003, www.allthingsbillbelichick.com/articles/okchamp.html.

[2062] Bill Belichick, quoted in: Michael Holley, "'It's Just Another Sideline,'" *Boston Globe*, 28 April 2000, www.allthingsbillbelichick.com/articles/sideline.html.

[2063] Bill Belichick, quoted in: Jimmy Golen (AP), "Baying the Bill," *SouthCoast Today*, 28 January 2000, www.s-t.com/daily/01-00/01-28-00/d01sp116.htm.

[2064] Coach Bill Belichick, quoted in: Ethan Butterfield, "Familiar Face In Foxboro," *Inquirer and Mirror*, 17 August 2000, www.allthingsbillbelichick.com/articles/familiarface.htm.

[2065] Bill Belichick, quoted in: Judy Battista, "Back at the Super Bowl, As a Player Once Again," *New York Times*, 26 January 2004, p. D4, ProQuest database.

[2066] Bill Belichick, quoted in: Michael Felger, "Watson, Pats cut deal: Holdout ends, work begins," *Boston Herald*, 17 August 2004, http://patriots.bostonherald.com/patriots/view.bg?articleid=40154.

[2067] Bill Belichick, quoted in: Howard Ullman, "Reluctant players discuss record win streak," *San Francisco Chronicle*, 6 October 2004, http://sfgate.com/cgi-bin/article.cgi?f=/news/archive/2004/10/06/sports1750EDT0223.DTL.

[2068] Quotations from: John E. Mulligan, "President Bush honors Super Bowl champions," *Providence Journal*, 11 May 2004, www.projo.com/patriots/content/projo_20040511_11pats.96273.html.

[2069] Bill Belichick, "Bill Belichick Press Conf. Transcript 8/3/04," *Patriots.com*, 3 August 2004, www.patriots.com/news/fullarticle.sps?id=29867&special_section=TrainingCamp2004&type=training.

[2070] Bill Belichick, quoted in: Kevin Mannix, "All signs point to start of a new season," *Boston Herald*, 7 September 2004, http://patriots.bostonherald.com/patriots/view.bg?articleid=43098.

[2071] BillBelichick, quoted in: "Patriots Video News," Patriots.com, 7 September 2004, www.patriots.com/mediaworld/MediaDetail.sps?ID=30472.

[2072] Bill Belichick, quoted in: Pete Thamel, "Belichick Expects Changes In Rematch With the Titans," *New York Times*, 6 January 2004, p. D3, ProQuest database.

[2073] Coach Bill Belichick, quoted in: Pete Thamel, "A Cloud Over Belichick Lifts After the Patriots Win 7 of 8," *New York Times*, 6 November 2003, p. D3, ProQuest database.

[2074] Bill Belichick, quoted in: Alan Greenberg, "Pats Tiptoe As Brown Limps," *Hartford Courant*, 31 August 2004, www.ctnow.com/sports/football/hc-patriots0831.artaug31,1,184327.print.story.

[2075] Bill Belichick, quoted in: Thomas George, "Still Bill: Patriots' Belichick Adapts and Thrives," *New York Times*, 16 November 2003, section 8, p. 1, ProQuest database.

[2076] Bill Belichick, quoted in: Alan Greenberg, "CAN'T GO HOME AGAIN, WHEREVER HOME MAY BE BELICHICK, GROH SAY THEY DON'T CARE ABOUT THE PAST," *Hartford Courant*, 7 September 2000, p. C3, ProQuest database.

[2077] Bill Belichick, quoted in: Pete Thamel, "A Cloud Over Belichick Lifts After the Patriots Win 7 of 8," *New York Times*, 6 November 2003, p. D3, ProQuest database.

[2078] Bill Belichick, quoted in: Alan Greenberg, "Getting Along Well Belichick Still A Little Grim, But With A Grin," *Hartford Courant*, 3 September 2000, p. E1, ProQuest database.

[2079] Patriots offensive lineman Damien Woody, quoted in: Hector Longo, "Two-nosed monster," *Eagle Tribune*, 24 August 2003, www.eagletribune.com/news/stories/20030824/SP_004.htm.

[2080] Bill Belichick, quoted in: Hector Longo, "Two-nosed monster," *Eagle Tribune*, 24 August 2003, www.eagletribune.com/news/stories/20030824/SP_004.htm.

[2081] Bill Belichick interview, "The Coach," *60 Minutes*, aired on CBS 19 September 2004.

[2082] Bill Belichick, quoted in: Alan Greenberg, "For Pats, Past Is Past," *Hartford Courant*, 9 September 2004, www.ctnow.com/sports/hc-patriots0909.artsep09,1,3416259,print.story.

INDEX

We hope you have enjoyed Volume 1 of this two-volume set, *Management Secrets of the New England Patriots*.

James Lavin has already completed a first draft of *Volume 2*. He expects to complete revisions and make it available for purchase in June 2005. Please visit PointerPress.com or PatriotsBook.com for updates.

Pointer Press

www.PointerPress.com
sales@pointerpress.com
41 Minivale Rd, Stamford, CT 06907
203.355.0677

Management Secrets of the New England Patriots, Vol 1 is available for purchase online at PatriotsBook.com, Amazon.com, and BN.com and at select bookstores.

To exchange a defective book, please contact Pointer Press.

Books are not returnable. We urge you, before buying, to read the more than fifty book pages posted on PatriotsBook.com.

Single copies cost $19.95 + actual mailing cost. We charge no additional packaging or handling fee. All shipments to Connecticut addresses are subject to a 6% sales tax (*i.e.*, $1.20 for single-copy purchases).

To order five or more copies at a 40% discount, click on the "Bulk Sales" link on the PatriotsBook.com website. We expect to offer the following discounts on bulk orders shipped to a single address (all prices subject to change and subject to availability):

# of copies in order shipped together to single address	Discount	Price per copy (excluding mailing cost and tax)	Shipping & handling (via UPS Ground)
1	0%	$19.95	$6
2 to 4	10%	$17.95	$6
5 to 99	40%	$11.97	FREE
100 or more	50%	$9.98	FREE

You may mail a check payable to "Pointer Press" to our Stamford, CT office. Personal check orders will ship only to the address printed (not written) on the check and are subject to delays. Institutions can indicate a shipping address different from the address on their check.

We thank you for your interest in *Management Secrets of the New England Patriots*!